Humongous Zits®

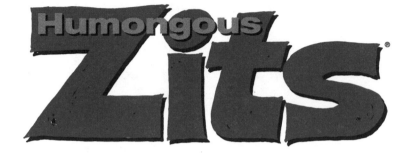

Also by Jerry Scott and Jim Borgman

Zits: Sketchbook 1
Growth Spurt: Zits Sketchbook 2

Humongous Zits

A Zits Treasury

by JERRY SCOTT and JIM BORGMAN

**Andrews McMeel
Publishing**

Kansas City

Zits is syndicated internationally by King Features Syndicate, Inc. For information, write King Features Syndicate, Inc., 216 East 45th Street, New York, New York 10017.

 For information, write Andrews McMeel Publishing, an Andrews McMeel Universal company, 4520 Main Street, Kansas City, Missouri 64111.

01 02 03 04 BAM 10 9 8 7 6 5 4 3 2

ISBN: 0-7407-0013-8

Library of Congress Catalog Card Number: 99-68663

For Dylan, Chelsea and Abbey.
No more fish for breakfast—
we promise.

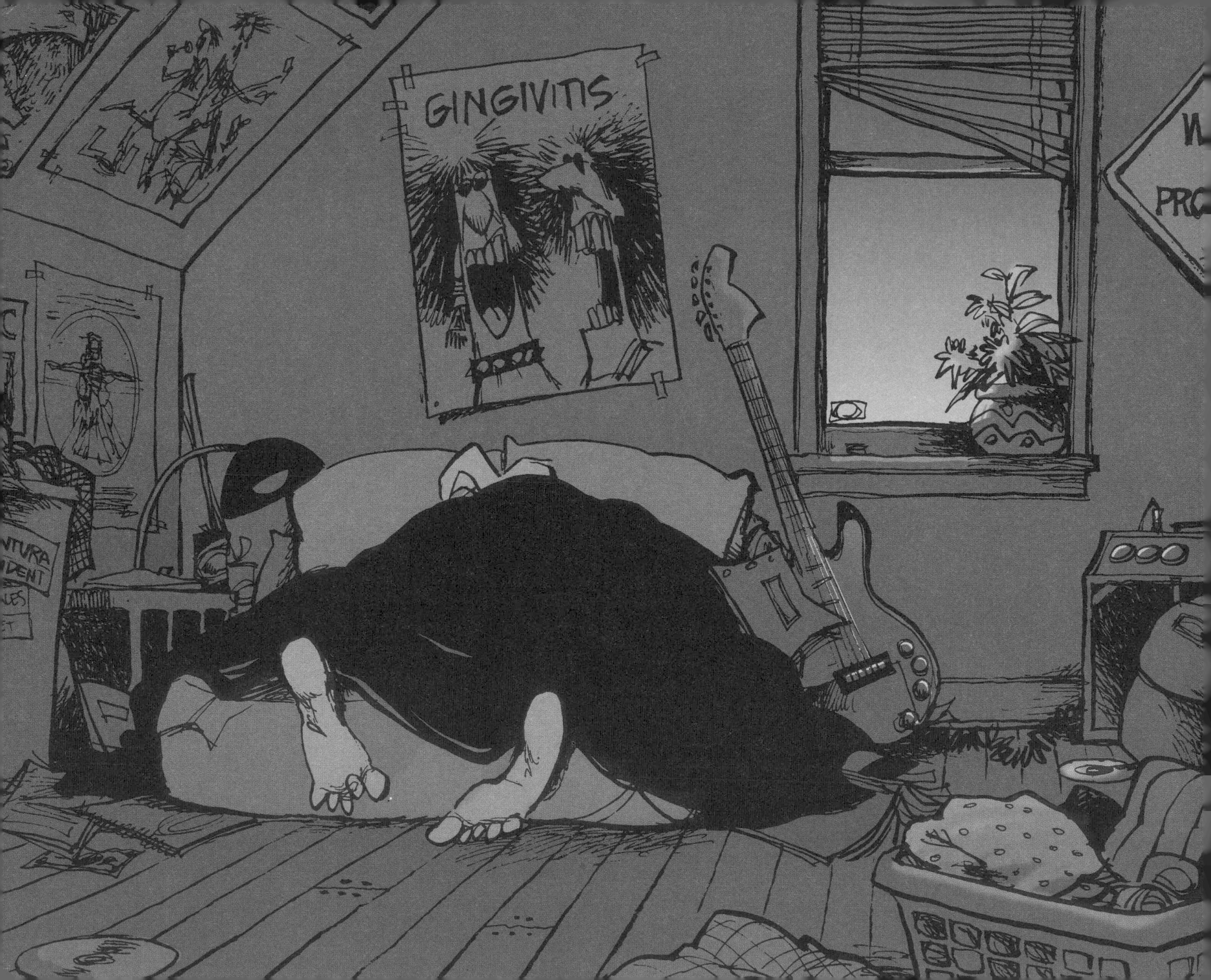
GINGIVITIS

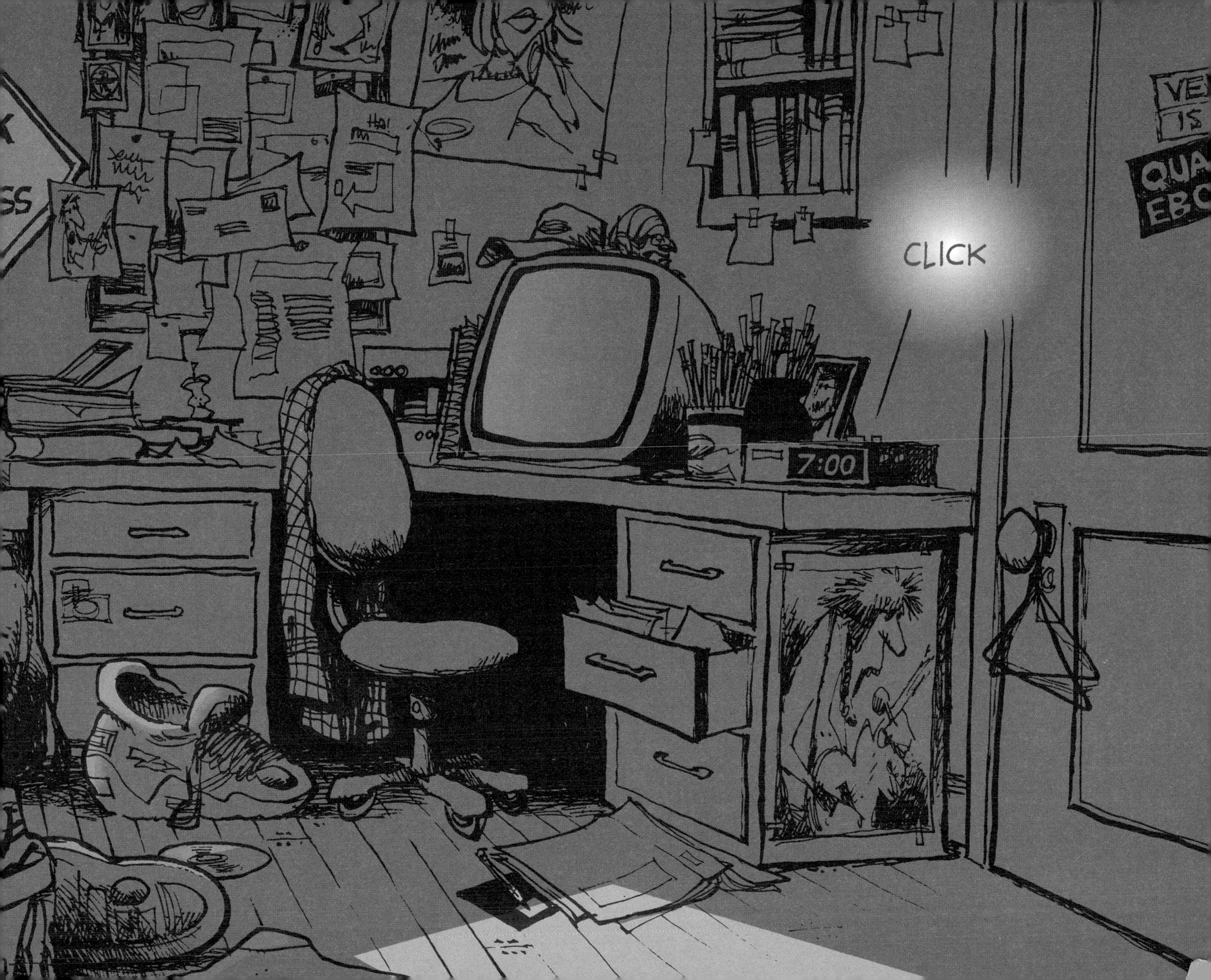
CLICK
7:00

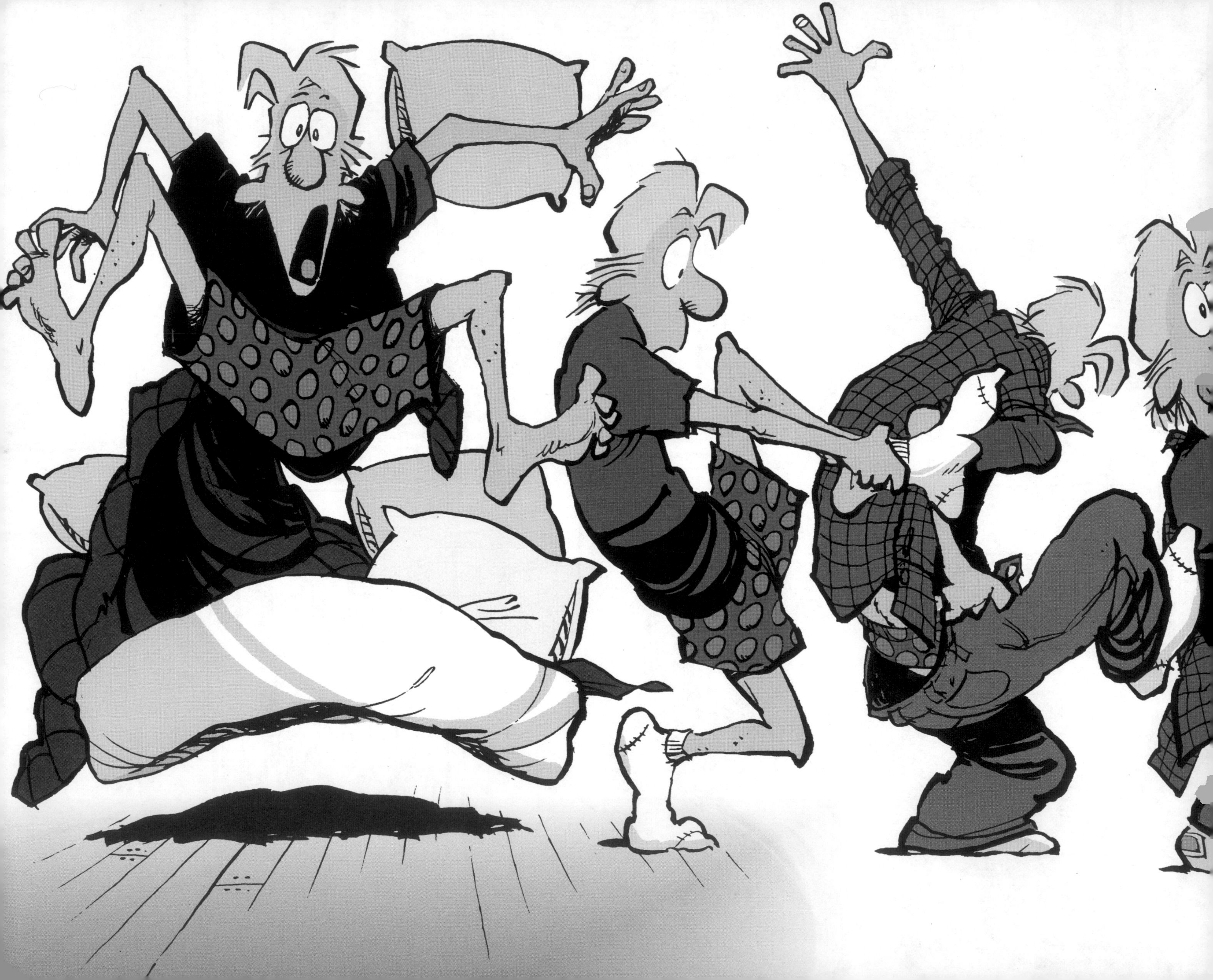

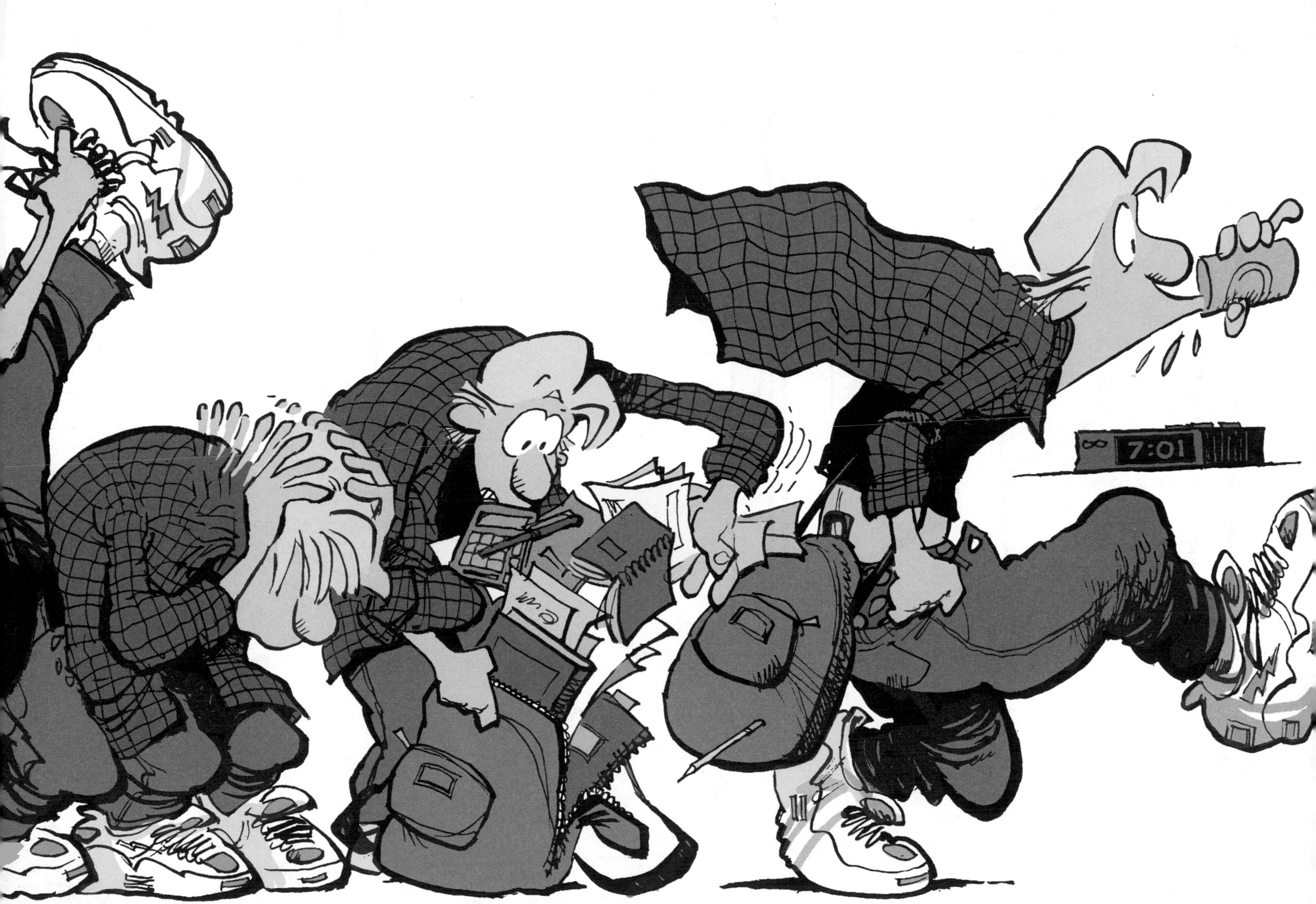
7:01

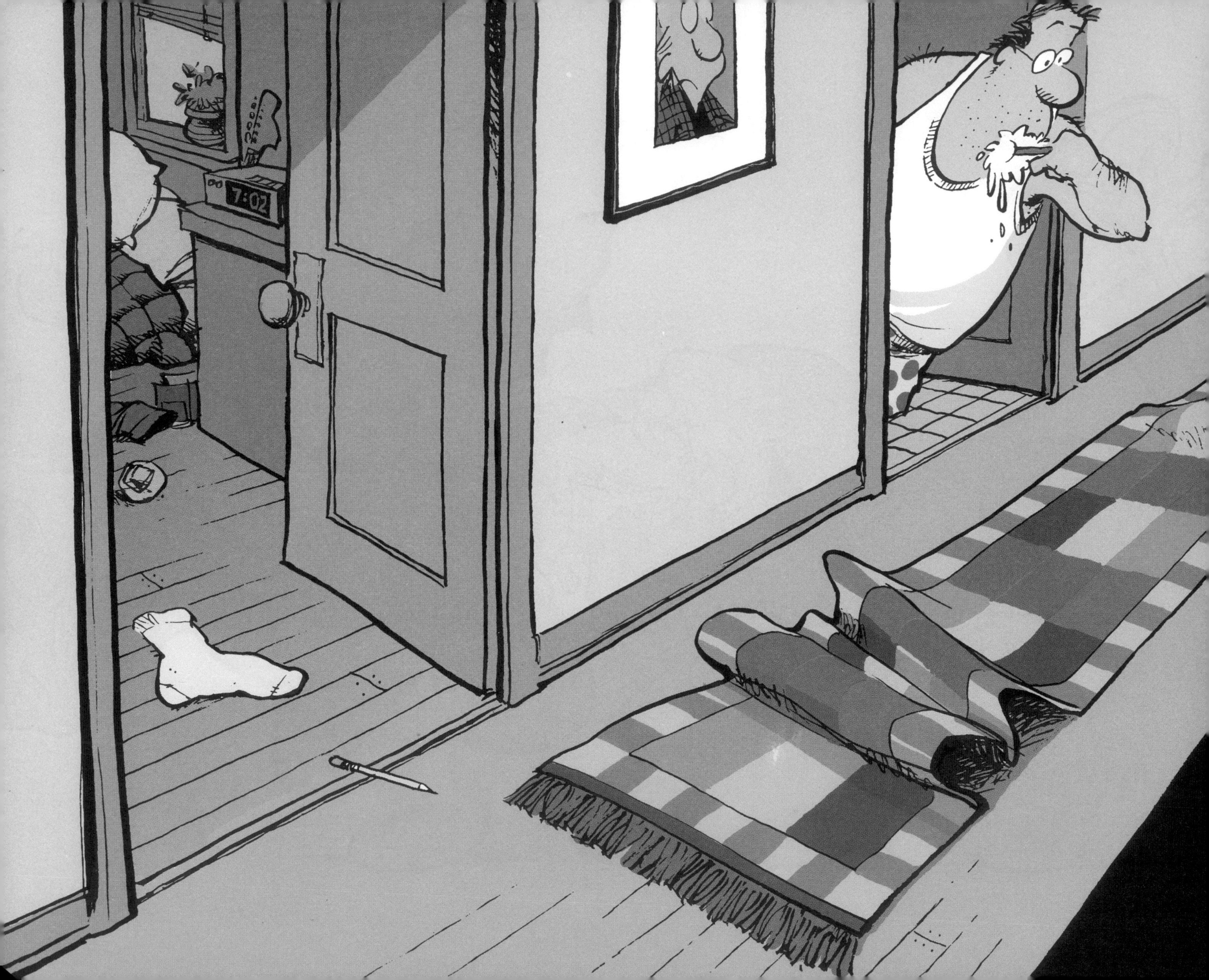
7:02

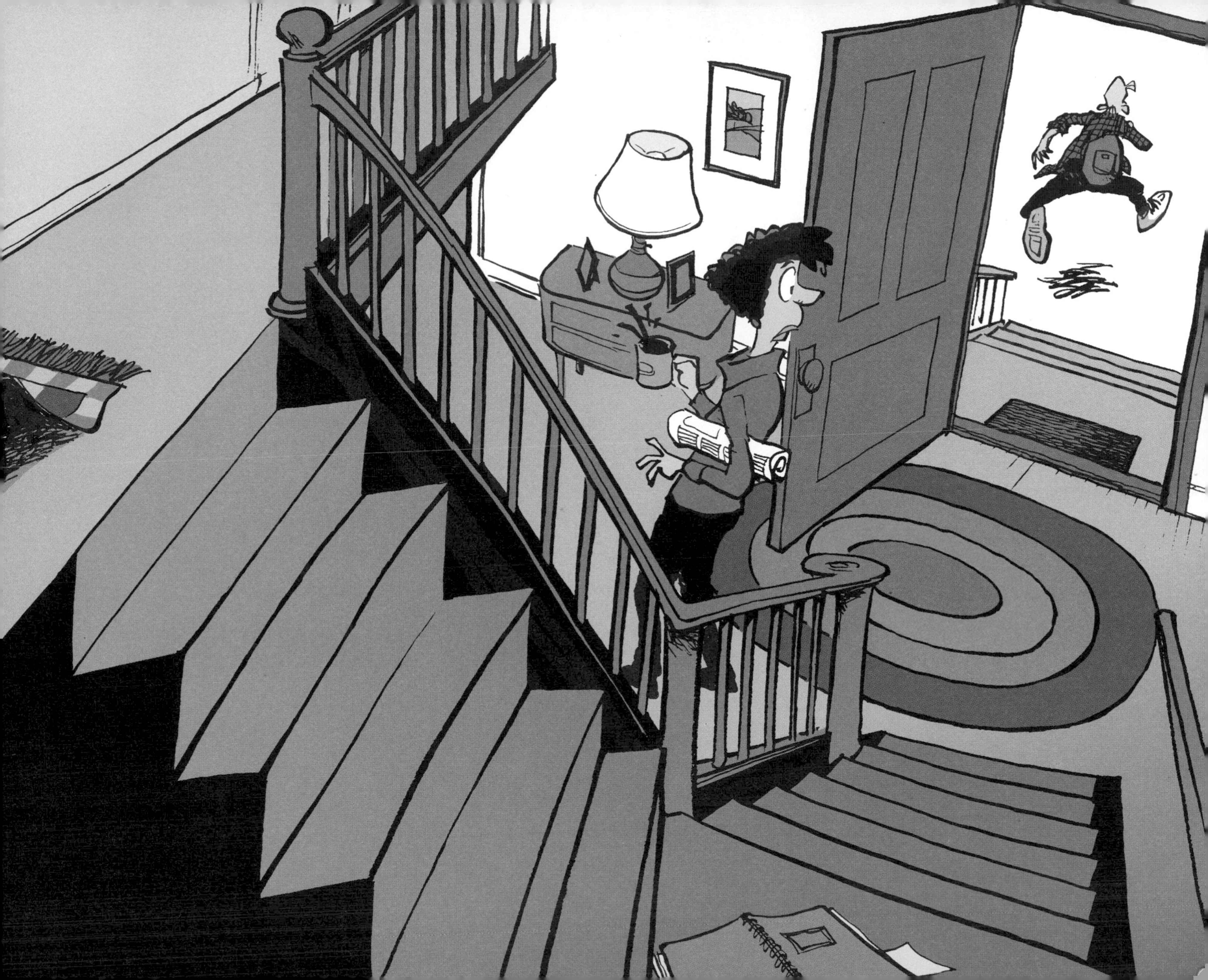

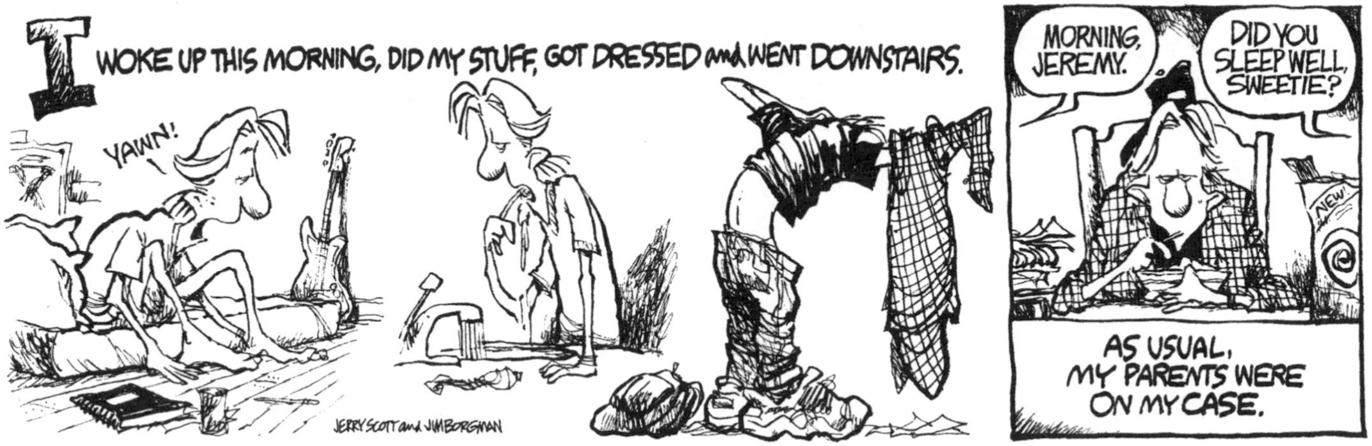
I WOKE UP THIS MORNING, DID MY STUFF, GOT DRESSED and WENT DOWNSTAIRS.
YAWN!
JERRY SCOTT and JIM BORGMAN
MORNING, JEREMY.
DID YOU SLEEP WELL, SWEETIE?
NEW!
AS USUAL, MY PARENTS WERE ON MY CASE.

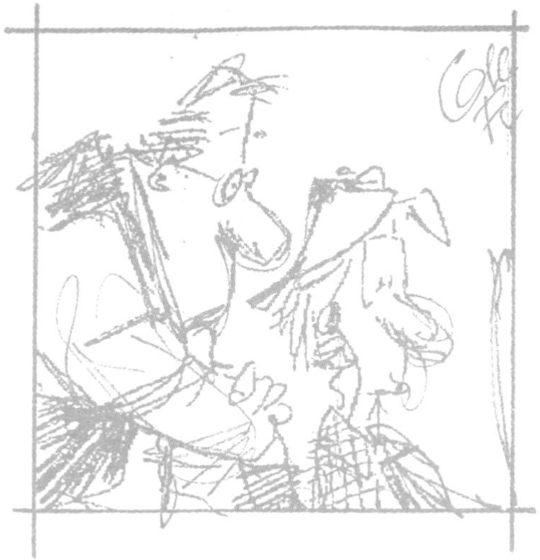

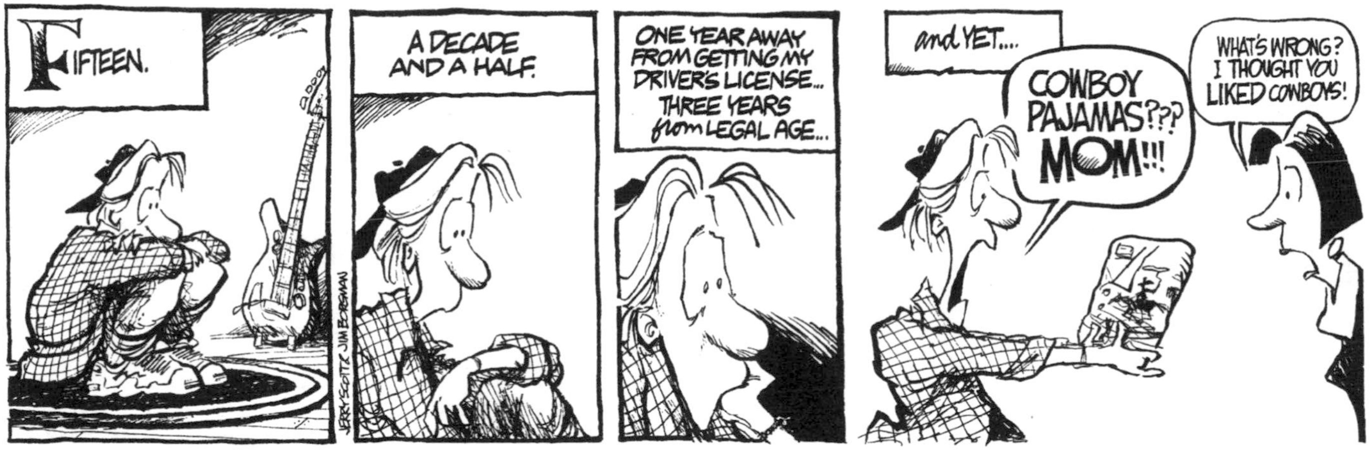
FIFTEEN.
A DECADE AND A HALF.
ONE YEAR AWAY FROM GETTING MY DRIVER'S LICENSE... THREE YEARS from LEGAL AGE...
and YET....
COWBOY PAJAMAS??? MOM!!!
WHAT'S WRONG? I THOUGHT YOU LIKED COWBOYS!

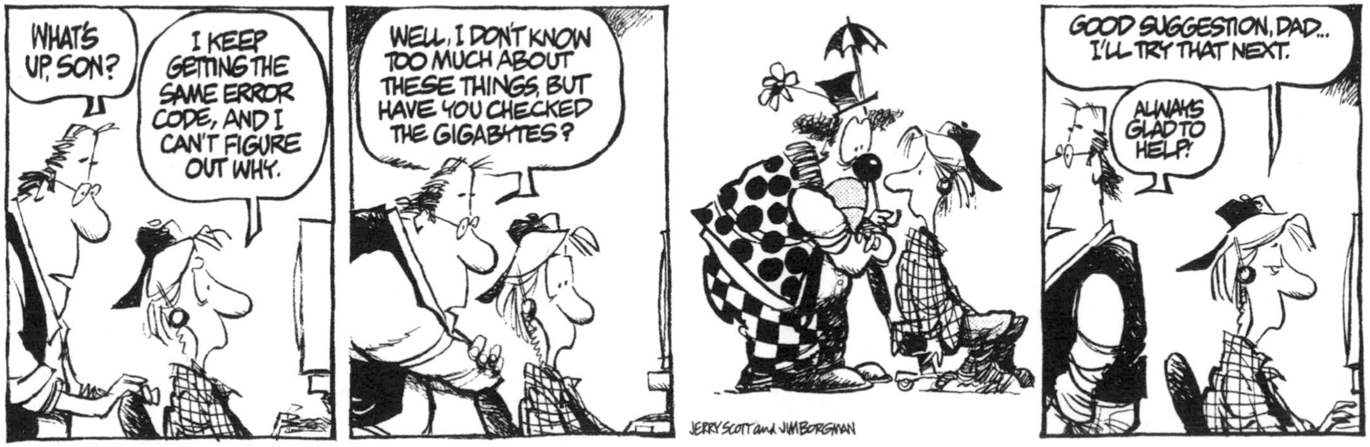
WHAT'S UP, SON?
I KEEP GETTING THE SAME ERROR CODE, AND I CAN'T FIGURE OUT WHY.
WELL, I DON'T KNOW TOO MUCH ABOUT THESE THINGS, BUT HAVE YOU CHECKED THE GIGABYTES?
JERRY SCOTT and JIM BORGMAN
GOOD SUGGESTION, DAD... I'LL TRY THAT NEXT.
ALWAYS GLAD TO HELP!

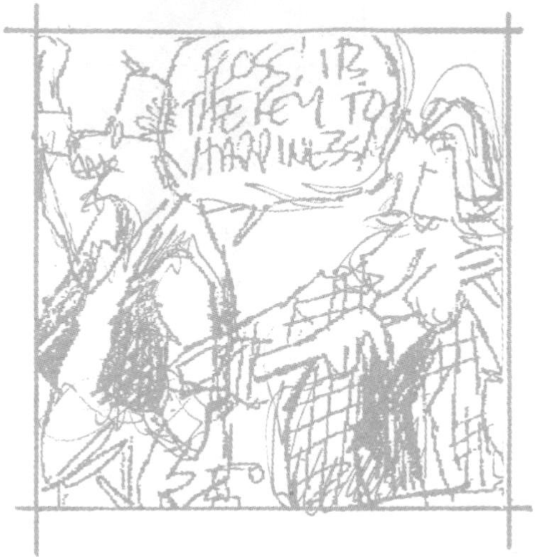

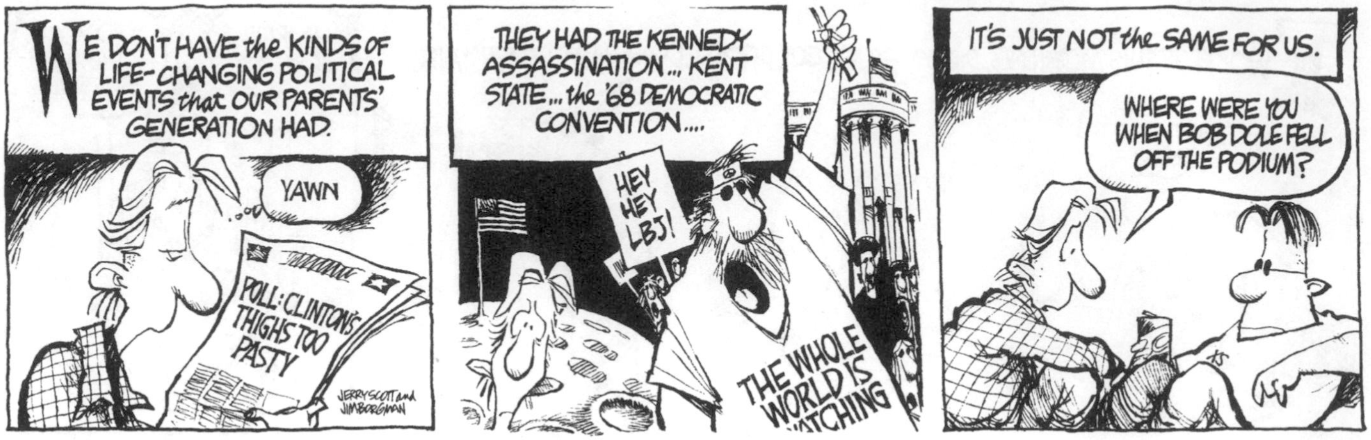
WE DON'T HAVE the KINDS OF LIFE-CHANGING POLITICAL EVENTS that OUR PARENTS' GENERATION HAD.
YAWN
POLL: CLINTON'S THIGHS TOO PASTY
JERRY SCOTT and JIM BORGMAN
THEY HAD THE KENNEDY ASSASSINATION... KENT STATE... the '68 DEMOCRATIC CONVENTION....
HEY HEY LBJ!
THE WHOLE WORLD IS
IT'S JUST NOT the SAME FOR US.
WHERE WERE YOU WHEN BOB DOLE FELL OFF THE PODIUM?

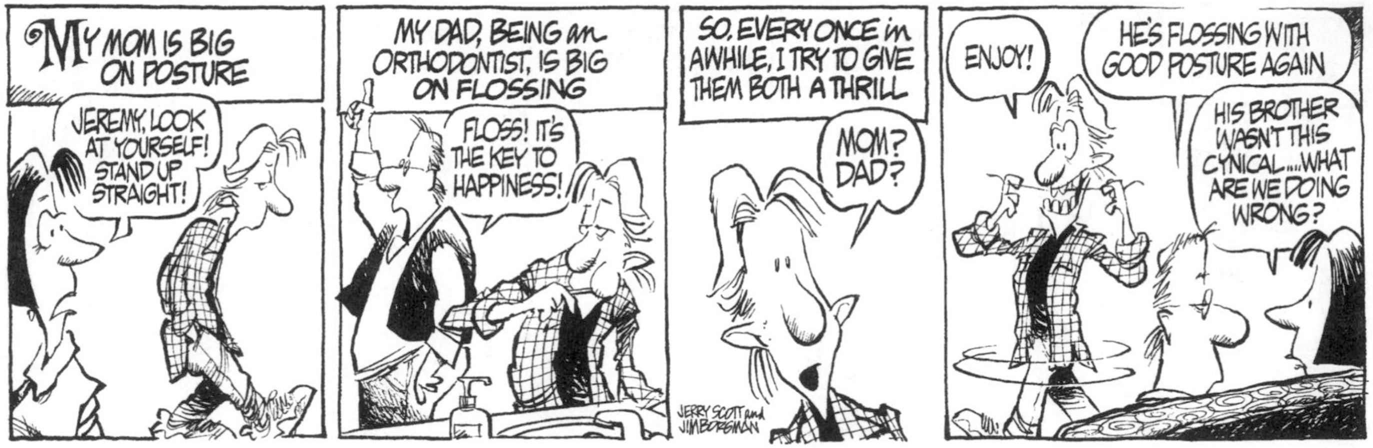
MY MOM IS BIG ON POSTURE
JEREMY, LOOK AT YOURSELF! STAND UP STRAIGHT!
MY DAD, BEING an ORTHODONTIST, IS BIG ON FLOSSING
FLOSS! IT'S THE KEY TO HAPPINESS!
SO, EVERY ONCE in AWHILE, I TRY TO GIVE THEM BOTH A THRILL
MOM? DAD?
JERRY SCOTT and JIM BORGMAN
ENJOY!
HE'S FLOSSING WITH GOOD POSTURE AGAIN
HIS BROTHER WASN'T THIS CYNICAL... WHAT ARE WE DOING WRONG?

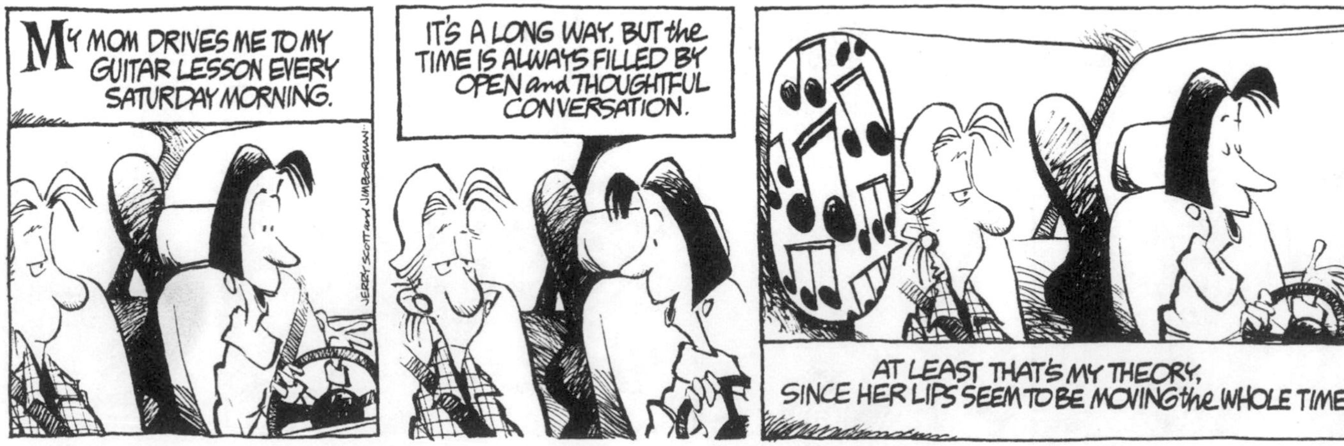
MY MOM DRIVES ME TO MY GUITAR LESSON EVERY SATURDAY MORNING.
JERRY SCOTT and JIM BORGMAN
IT'S A LONG WAY, BUT the TIME IS ALWAYS FILLED BY OPEN and THOUGHTFUL CONVERSATION.
AT LEAST THAT'S MY THEORY, SINCE HER LIPS SEEM TO BE MOVING the WHOLE TIME.

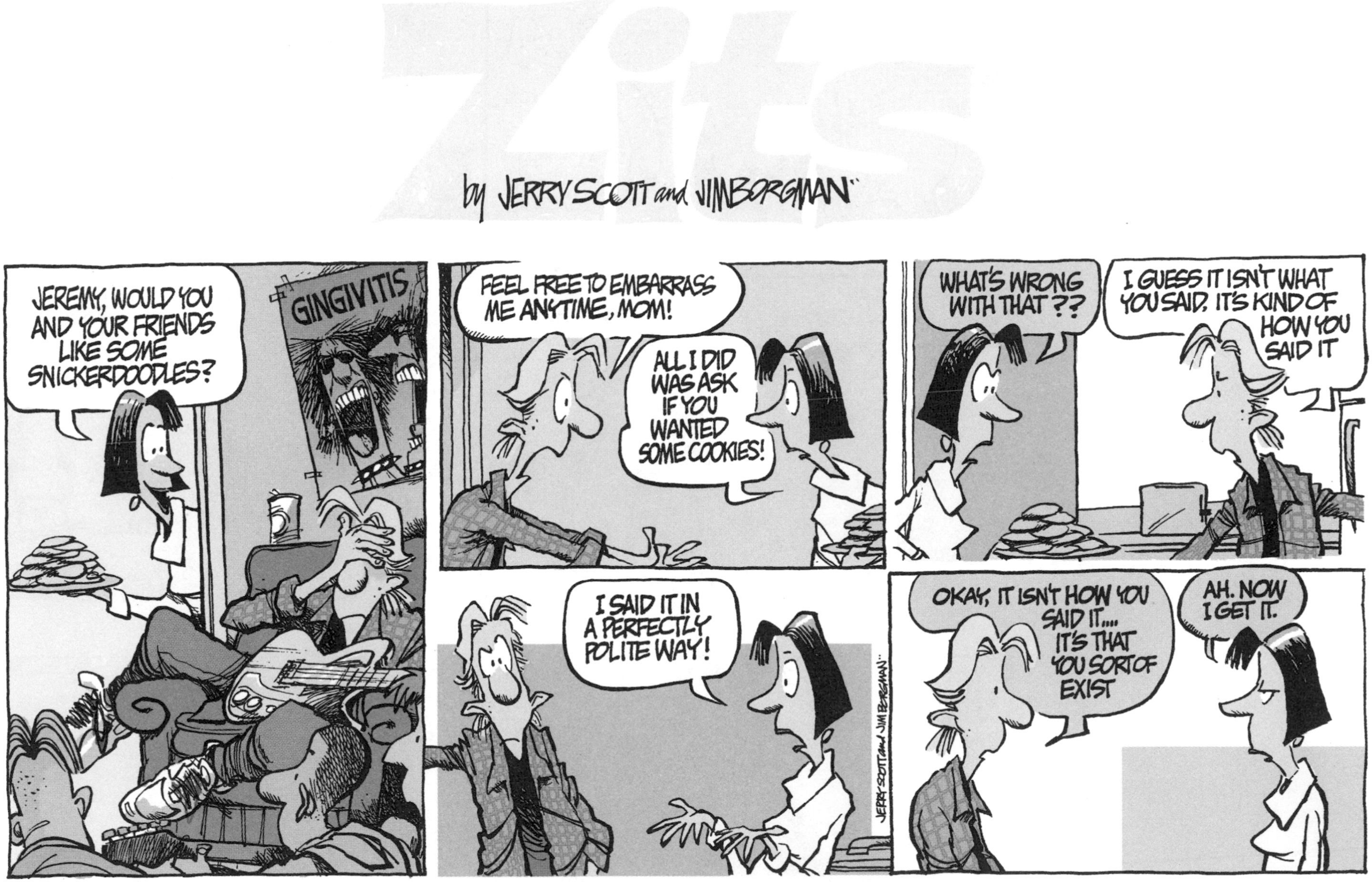
Zits
by JERRY SCOTT and JIM BORGMAN
JEREMY, WOULD YOU AND YOUR FRIENDS LIKE SOME SNICKERDOODLES?
GINGIVITIS
FEEL FREE TO EMBARRASS ME ANYTIME, MOM!
ALL I DID WAS ASK IF YOU WANTED SOME COOKIES!
WHAT'S WRONG WITH THAT ??
I GUESS IT ISN'T WHAT YOU SAID. IT'S KIND OF HOW YOU SAID IT
I SAID IT IN A PERFECTLY POLITE WAY!
JERRY SCOTT and JIM BORGMAN
OKAY, IT ISN'T HOW YOU SAID IT.... IT'S THAT YOU SORT OF EXIST
AH. NOW I GET IT.

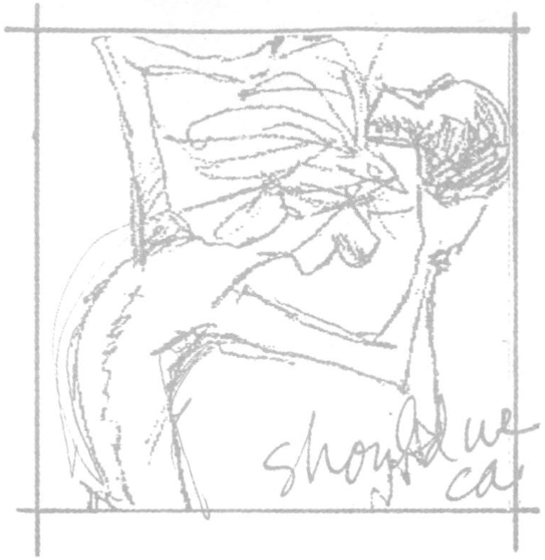
should we

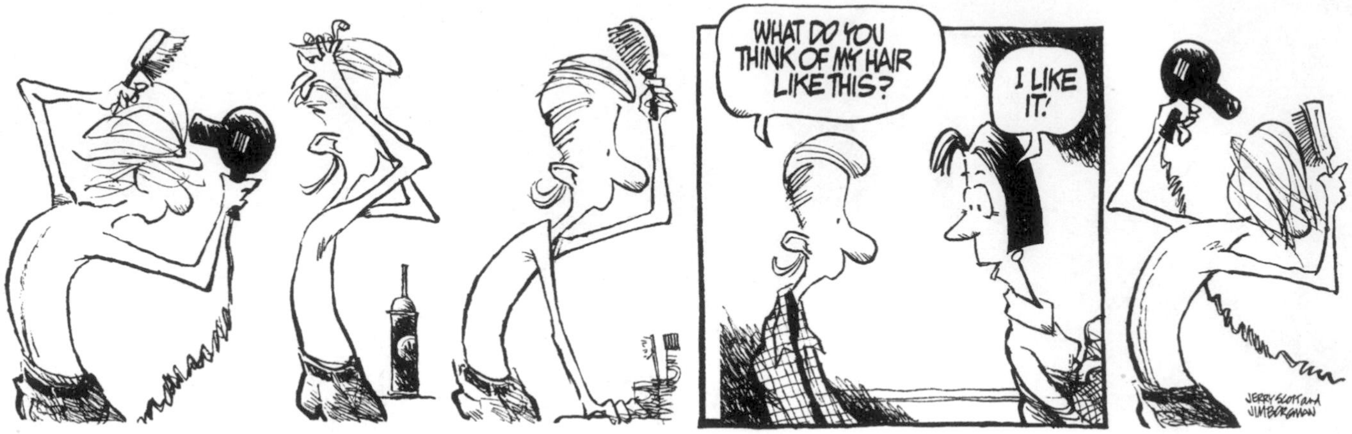
WHAT DO YOU THINK OF MY HAIR LIKE THIS?
I LIKE IT!
JERRY SCOTT and JIM BORGMAN

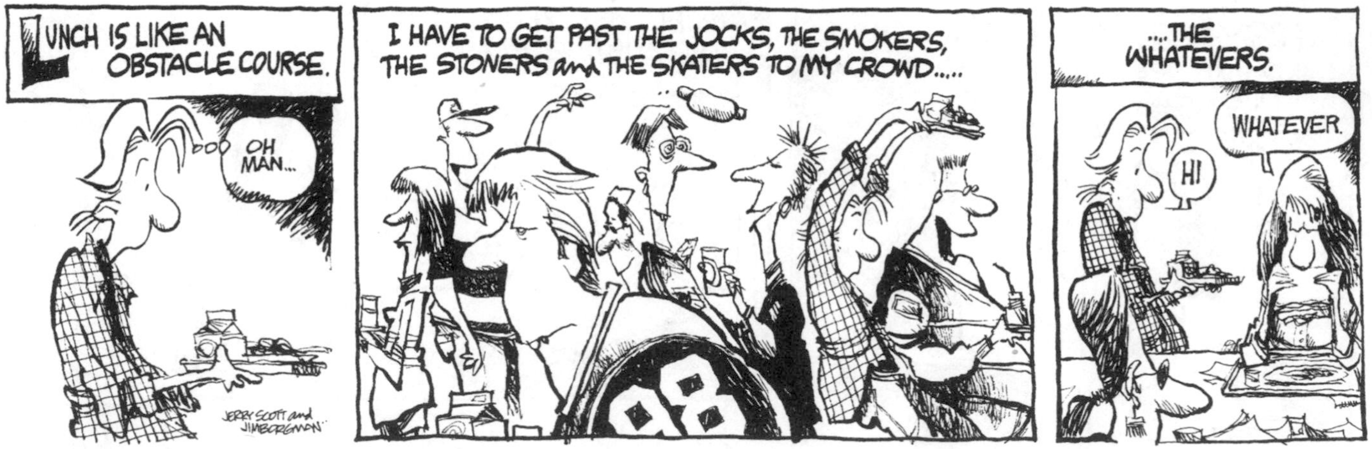
LUNCH IS LIKE AN OBSTACLE COURSE.
OH MAN...
JERRY SCOTT and JIM BORGMAN
I HAVE TO GET PAST THE JOCKS, THE SMOKERS, THE STONERS and THE SKATERS TO MY CROWD.....
88
....THE WHATEVERS.
HI
WHATEVER.

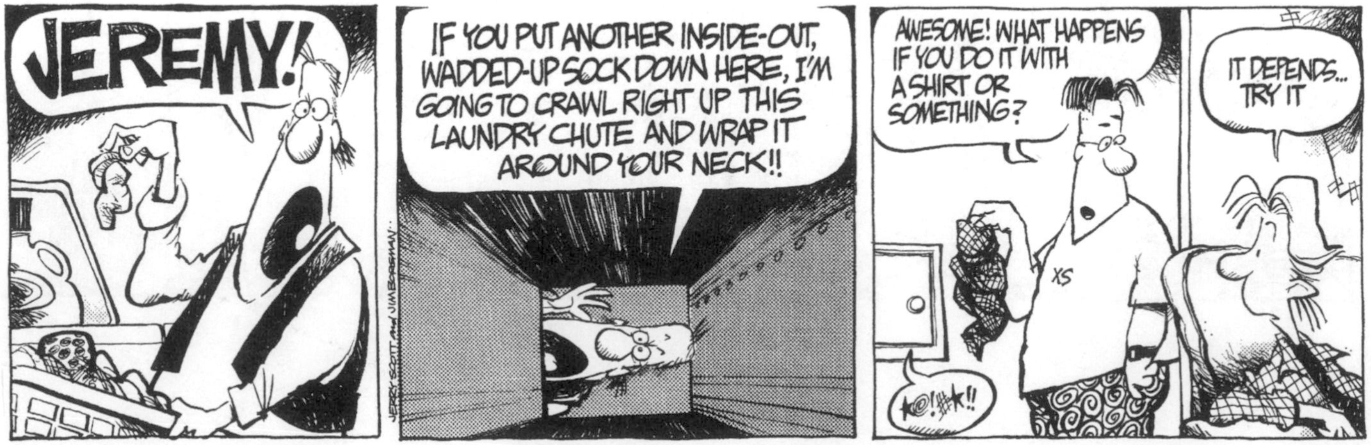
JEREMY!
JERRY SCOTT and JIM BORGMAN
IF YOU PUT ANOTHER INSIDE-OUT, WADDED-UP SOCK DOWN HERE, I'M GOING TO CRAWL RIGHT UP THIS LAUNDRY CHUTE AND WRAP IT AROUND YOUR NECK!!
AWESOME! WHAT HAPPENS IF YOU DO IT WITH A SHIRT OR SOMETHING?
IT DEPENDS... TRY IT
XS
@!#!!

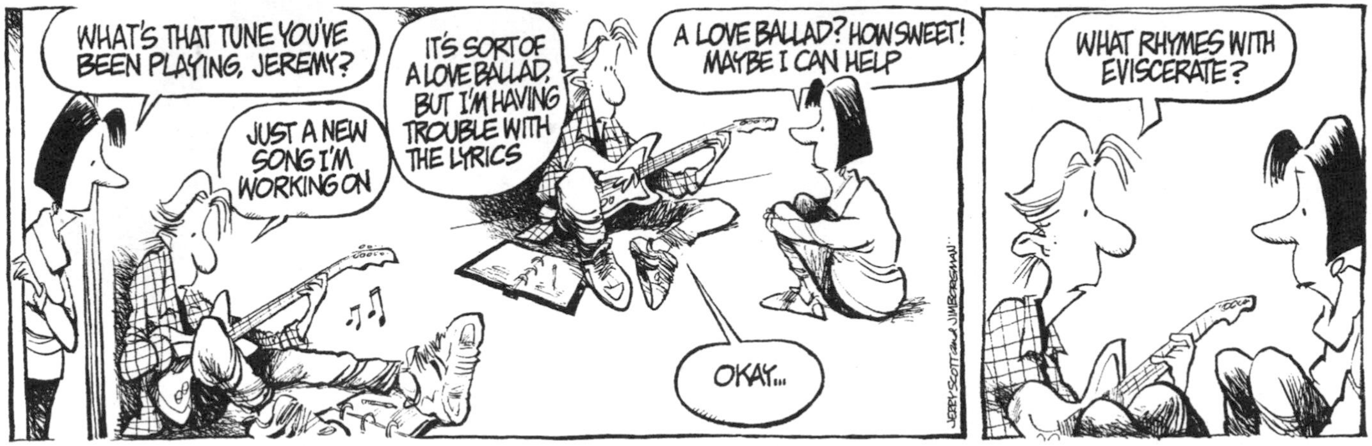
WHAT'S THAT TUNE YOU'VE BEEN PLAYING, JEREMY?
JUST A NEW SONG I'M WORKING ON
IT'S SORT OF A LOVE BALLAD, BUT I'M HAVING TROUBLE WITH THE LYRICS
A LOVE BALLAD? HOW SWEET! MAYBE I CAN HELP
OKAY...
WHAT RHYMES WITH EVISCERATE?

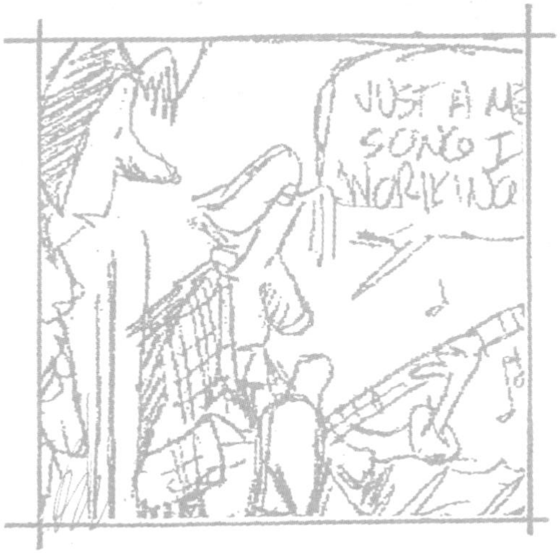

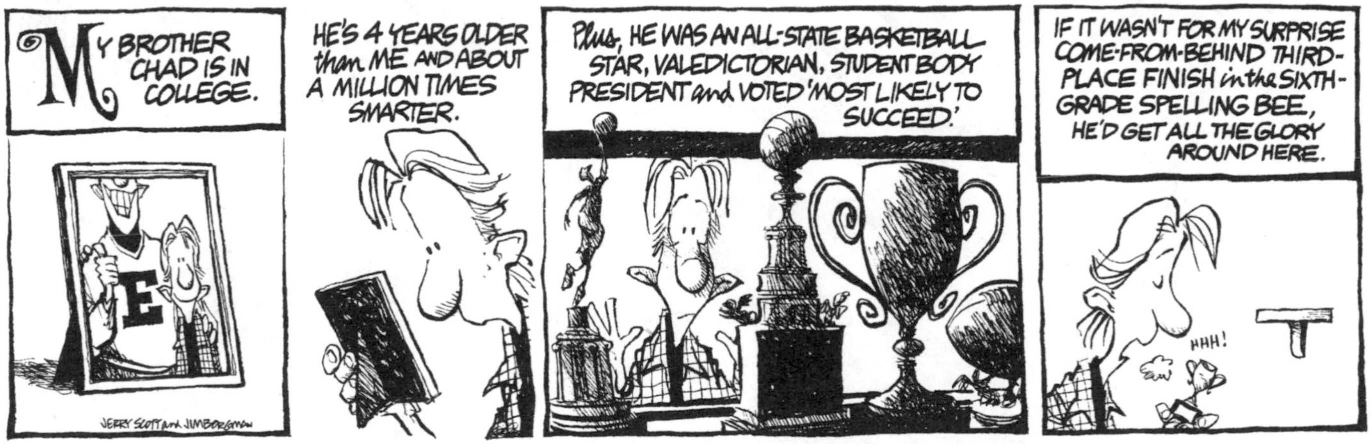
MY BROTHER CHAD IS IN COLLEGE.
E
HE'S 4 YEARS OLDER than ME AND ABOUT A MILLION TIMES SMARTER.
Plus, HE WAS AN ALL-STATE BASKETBALL STAR, VALEDICTORIAN, STUDENT BODY PRESIDENT and VOTED 'MOST LIKELY TO SUCCEED.'
IF IT WASN'T FOR MY SURPRISE COME-FROM-BEHIND THIRD-PLACE FINISH in the SIXTH-GRADE SPELLING BEE, HE'D GET ALL THE GLORY AROUND HERE.
HHH!

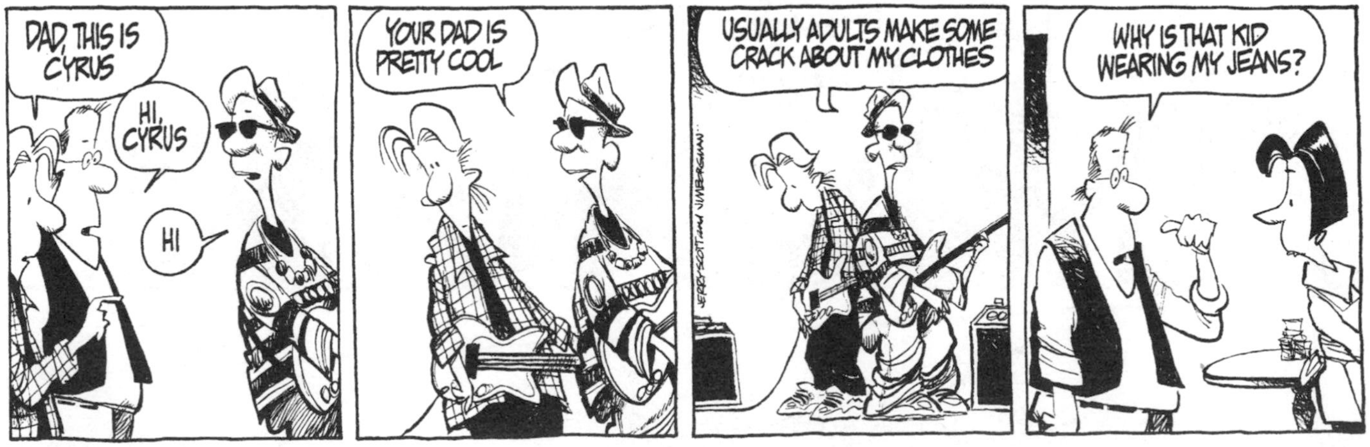
DAD, THIS IS CYRUS
HI, CYRUS
HI
YOUR DAD IS PRETTY COOL
USUALLY ADULTS MAKE SOME CRACK ABOUT MY CLOTHES
WHY IS THAT KID WEARING MY JEANS?

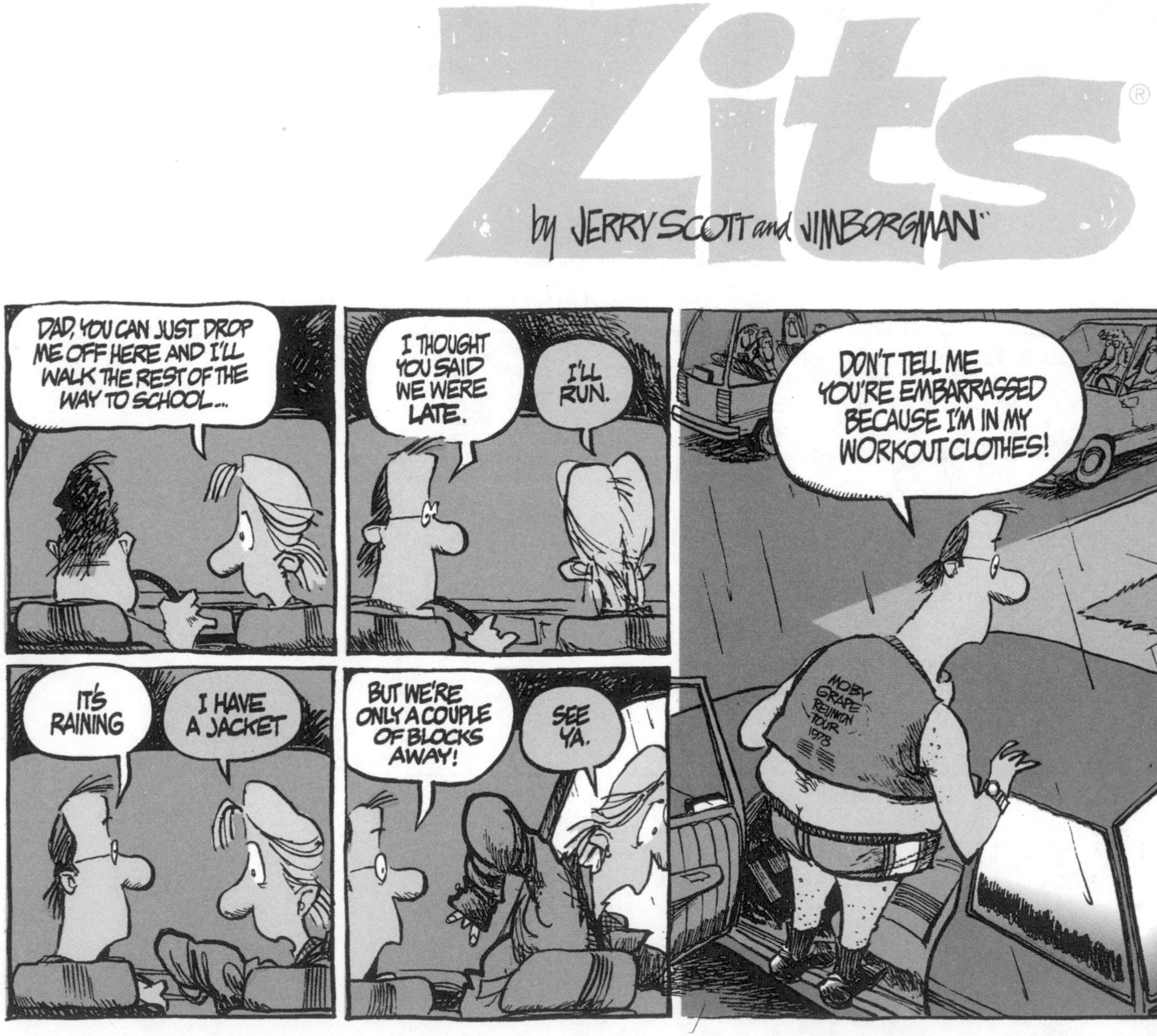
Zits®
by JERRY SCOTT and JIMBORGMAN
DAD, YOU CAN JUST DROP ME OFF HERE AND I'LL WALK THE REST OF THE WAY TO SCHOOL...
I THOUGHT YOU SAID WE WERE LATE.
I'LL RUN.
IT'S RAINING
I HAVE A JACKET
BUT WE'RE ONLY A COUPLE OF BLOCKS AWAY!
SEE YA.
DON'T TELL ME YOU'RE EMBARRASSED BECAUSE I'M IN MY WORKOUT CLOTHES!
MOBY GRAPE REUNION TOUR 1978
PLEEZE! JUST GET BACK IN THE CAR, DAD.... I MEAN, MISTER!
JERRY SCOTT and JIMBORGMAN

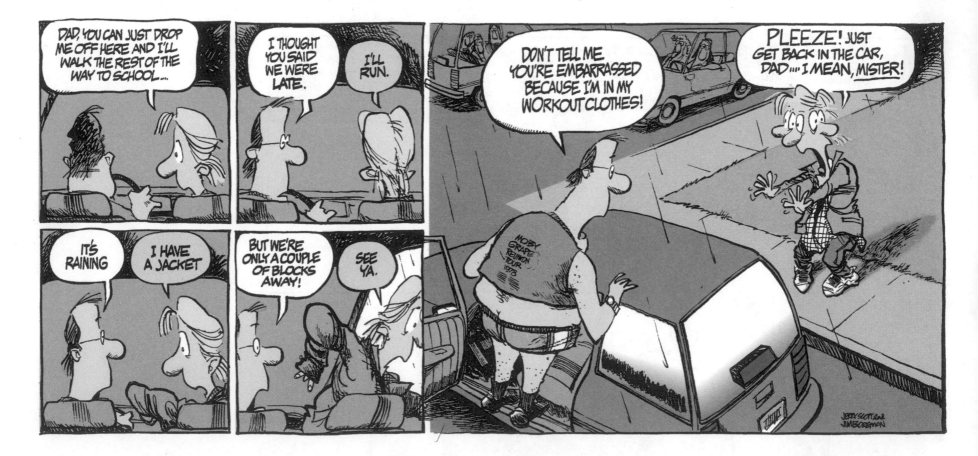

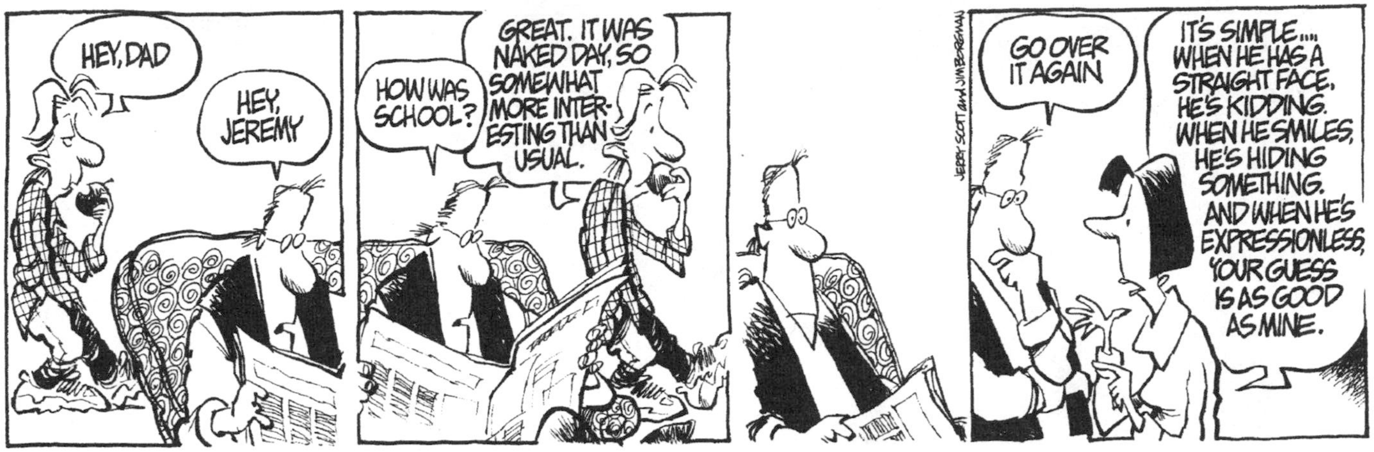
HEY, DAD
HEY, JEREMY
HOW WAS SCHOOL?
GREAT. IT WAS NAKED DAY, SO SOMEWHAT MORE INTERESTING THAN USUAL.
JERRY SCOTT and JIM BORGMAN
GO OVER IT AGAIN
IT'S SIMPLE.... WHEN HE HAS A STRAIGHT FACE, HE'S KIDDING. WHEN HE SMILES, HE'S HIDING SOMETHING. AND WHEN HE'S EXPRESSIONLESS, YOUR GUESS IS AS GOOD AS MINE.

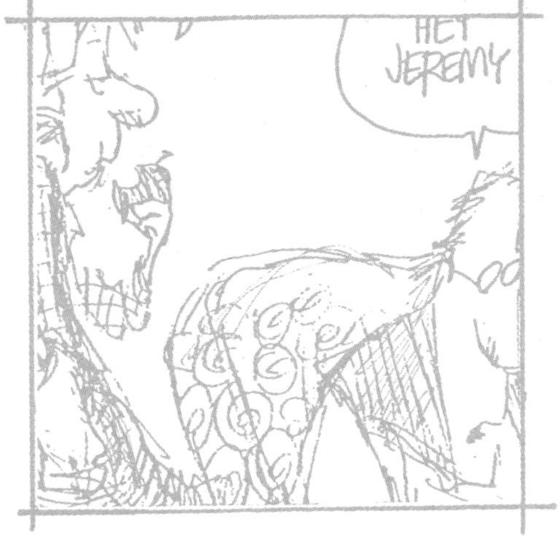
HEY JEREMY

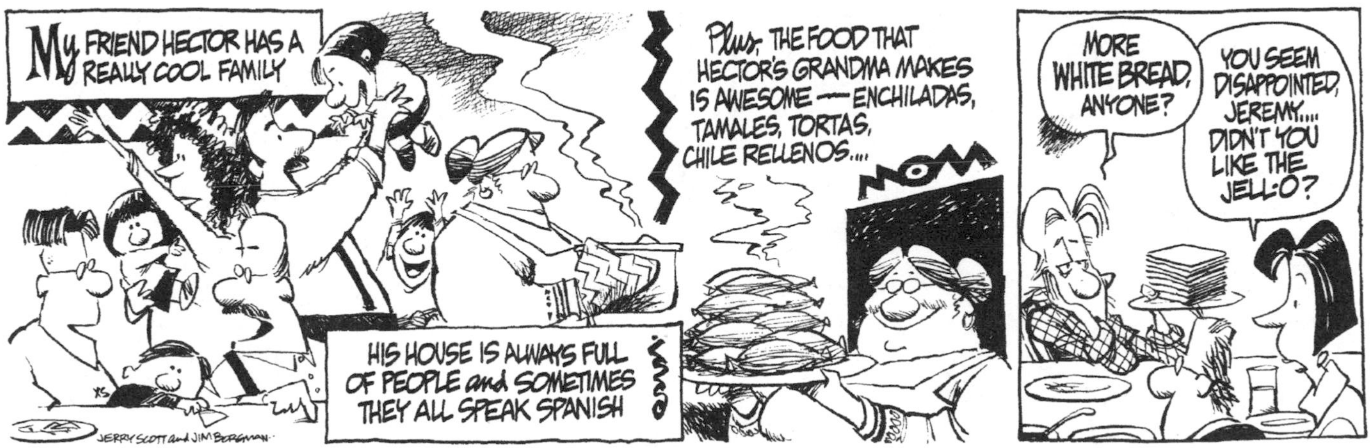
My FRIEND HECTOR HAS A REALLY COOL FAMILY
HIS HOUSE IS ALWAYS FULL OF PEOPLE and SOMETIMES THEY ALL SPEAK SPANISH
JERRY SCOTT and JIM BORGMAN
Plus, THE FOOD THAT HECTOR'S GRANDMA MAKES IS AWESOME — ENCHILADAS, TAMALES, TORTAS, CHILE RELLENOS....
MOM
MORE WHITE BREAD, ANYONE?
YOU SEEM DISAPPOINTED, JEREMY.... DIDN'T YOU LIKE THE JELL-O?

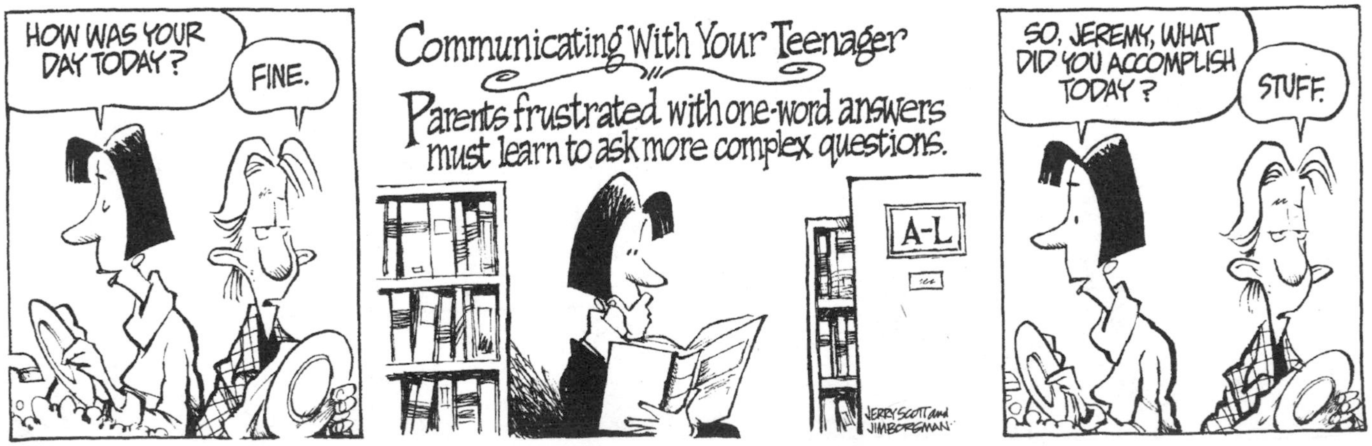
HOW WAS YOUR DAY TODAY?
FINE.
Communicating With Your Teenager
Parents frustrated with one-word answers must learn to ask more complex questions.
A-L
JERRY SCOTT and JIM BORGMAN
SO, JEREMY, WHAT DID YOU ACCOMPLISH TODAY?
STUFF.

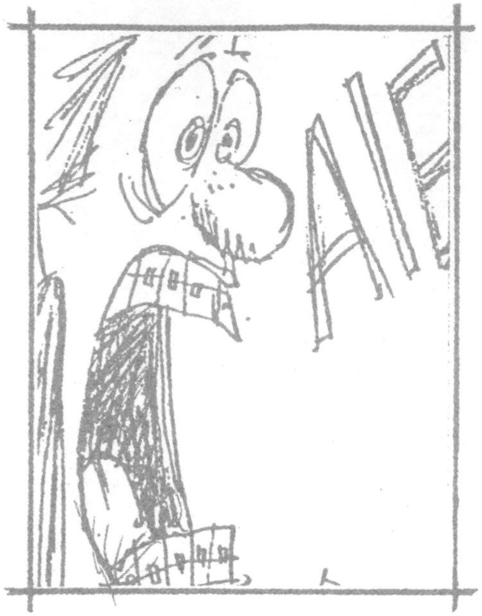
AIE

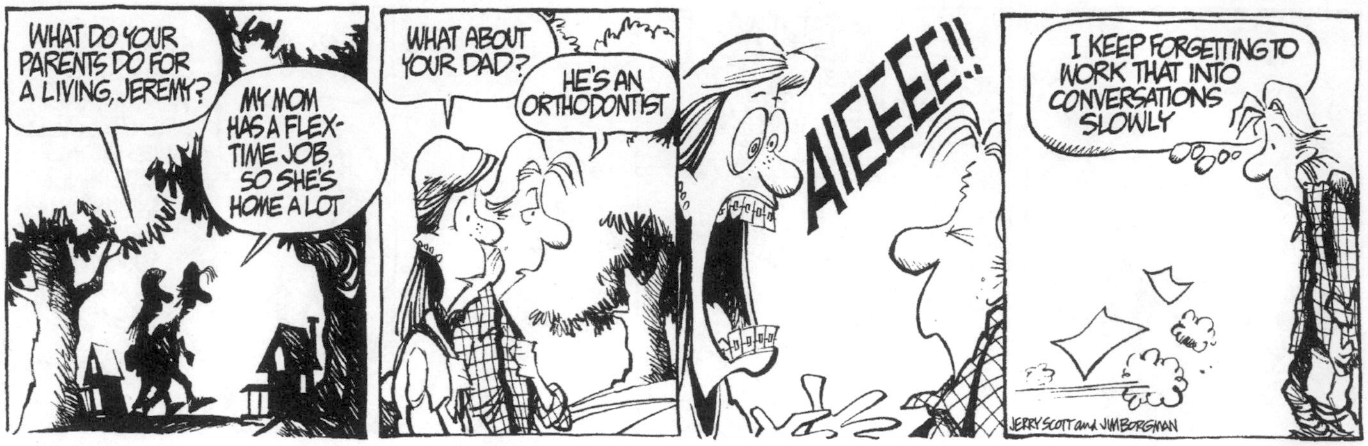
WHAT DO YOUR PARENTS DO FOR A LIVING, JEREMY?
MY MOM HAS A FLEX-TIME JOB, SO SHE'S HOME A LOT
WHAT ABOUT YOUR DAD?
HE'S AN ORTHODONTIST
AIEEEE!!
I KEEP FORGETTING TO WORK THAT INTO CONVERSATIONS SLOWLY
JERRY SCOTT and JIM BORGMAN

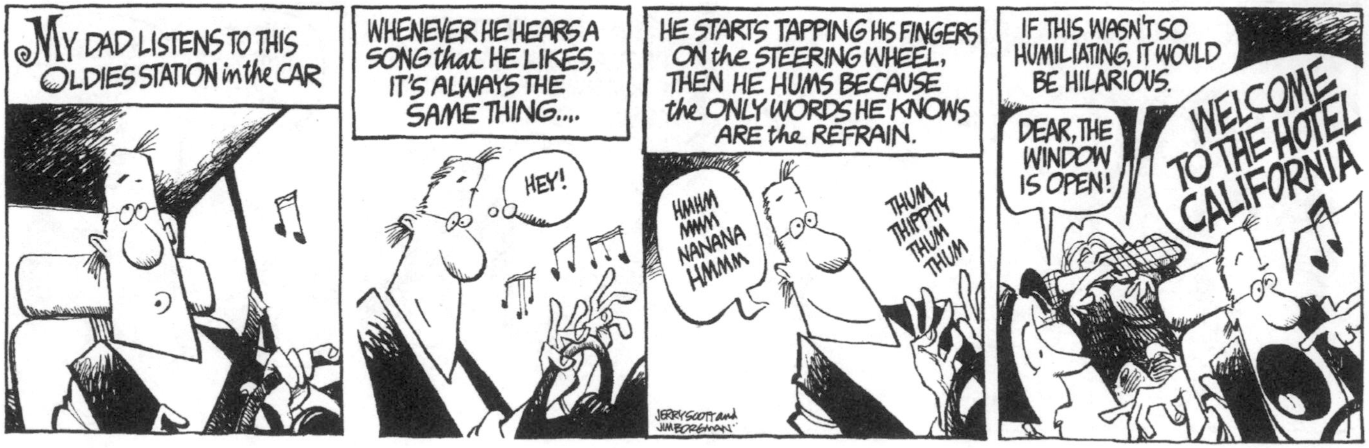
MY DAD LISTENS TO THIS OLDIES STATION in the CAR
WHENEVER HE HEARS A SONG that HE LIKES, IT'S ALWAYS THE SAME THING....
HEY!
HE STARTS TAPPING HIS FINGERS ON the STEERING WHEEL, THEN HE HUMS BECAUSE the ONLY WORDS HE KNOWS ARE the REFRAIN.
HMHM MMM NANANA HMMM
THUM THIPPITY THUM THUM
JERRY SCOTT and JIM BORGMAN
IF THIS WASN'T SO HUMILIATING, IT WOULD BE HILARIOUS.
DEAR, THE WINDOW IS OPEN!
WELCOME TO THE HOTEL CALIFORNIA

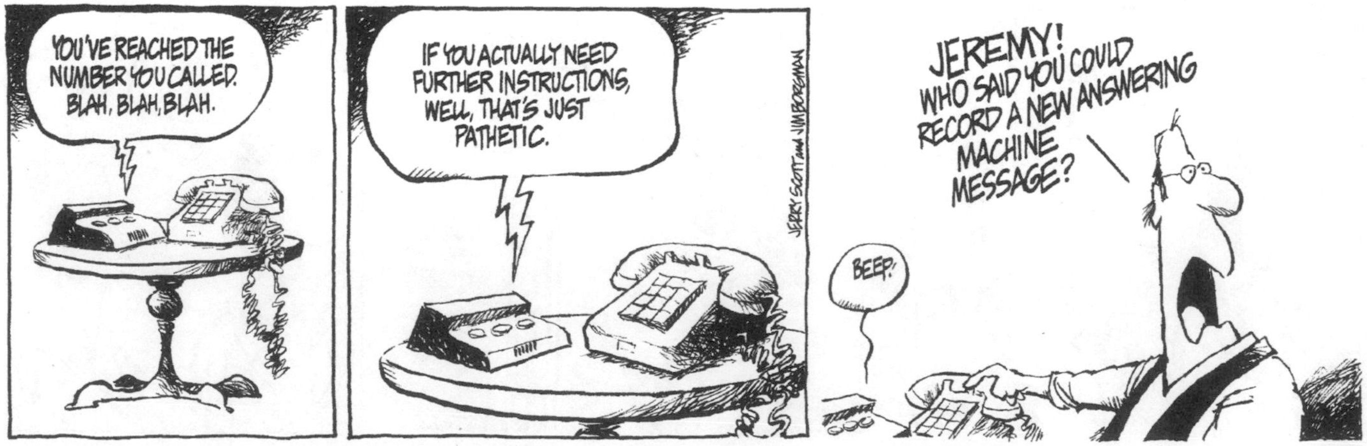
YOU'VE REACHED THE NUMBER YOU CALLED. BLAH, BLAH, BLAH.
IF YOU ACTUALLY NEED FURTHER INSTRUCTIONS, WELL, THAT'S JUST PATHETIC.
JERRY SCOTT and JIM BORGMAN
BEEP.
JEREMY! WHO SAID YOU COULD RECORD A NEW ANSWERING MACHINE MESSAGE?

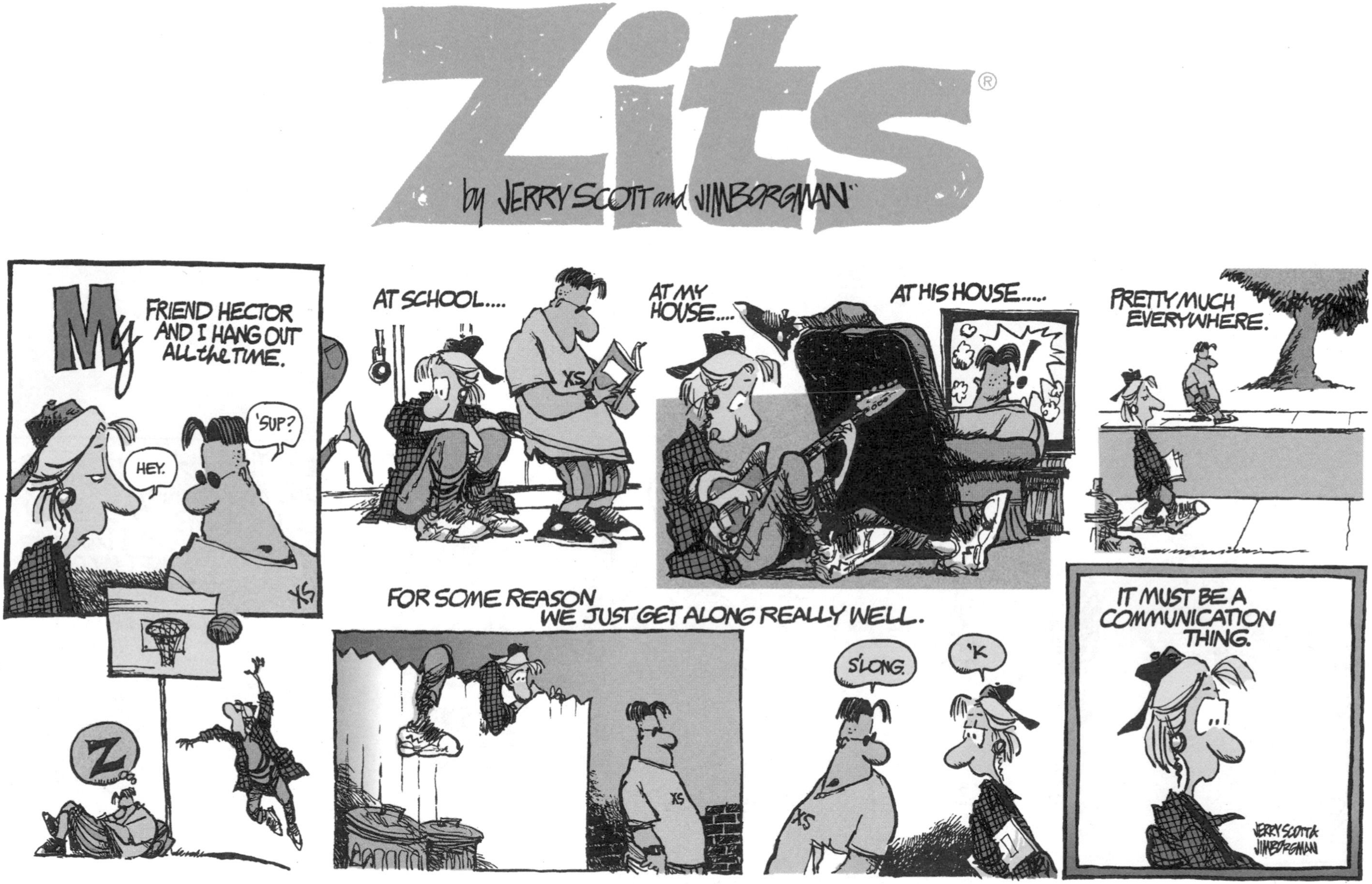
Zits®
by JERRY SCOTT and JIM BORGMAN
My FRIEND HECTOR AND I HANG OUT ALL the TIME.
HEY.
'SUP?
AT SCHOOL....
AT MY HOUSE....
AT HIS HOUSE.....
PRETTY MUCH EVERYWHERE.
FOR SOME REASON WE JUST GET ALONG REALLY WELL.
Z
S'LONG.
'K
IT MUST BE A COMMUNICATION THING.
JERRY SCOTT & JIM BORGMAN

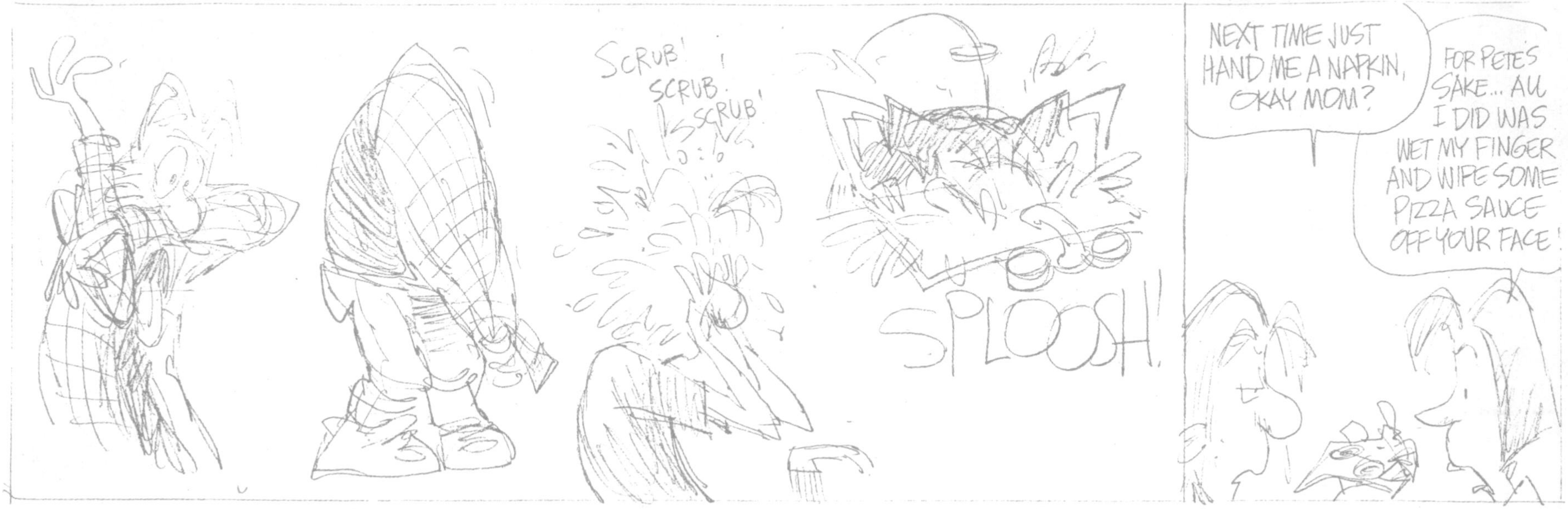
SCRUB!
SCRUB!
SCRUB!
SPLOOSH!
NEXT TIME JUST HAND ME A NAPKIN, OKAY MOM?
FOR PETE'S SAKE... ALL I DID WAS WET MY FINGER AND WIPE SOME PIZZA SAUCE OFF YOUR FACE!

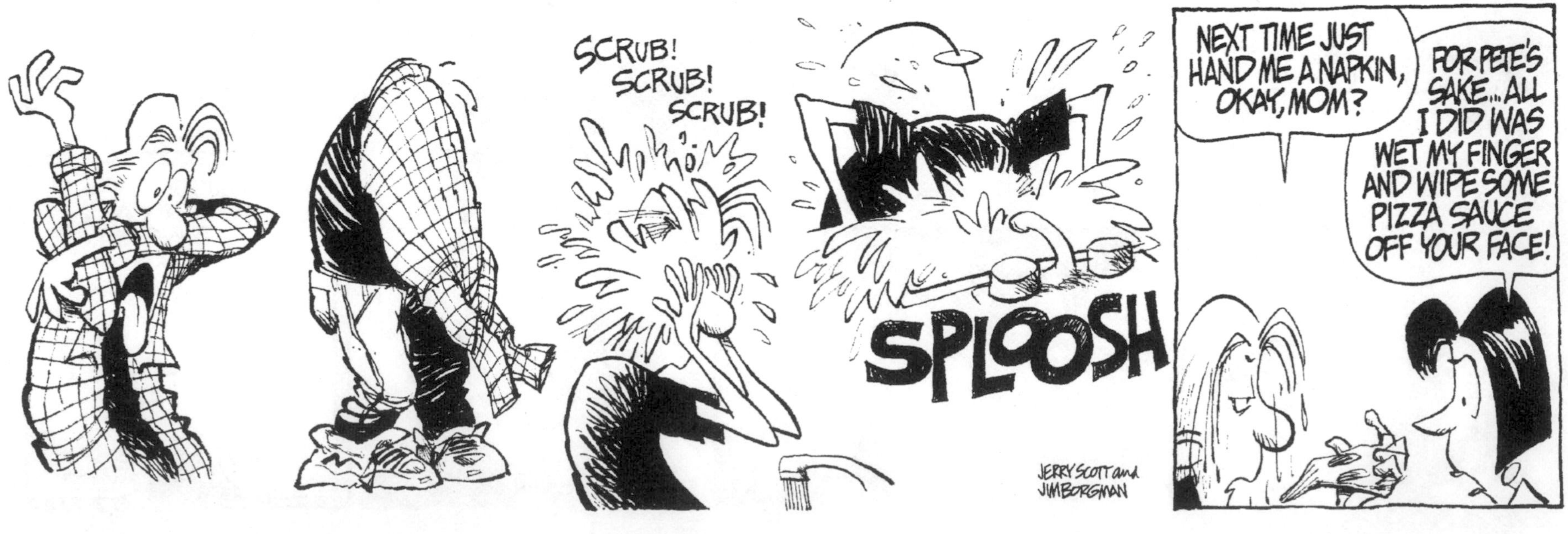
SCRUB!
SCRUB!
SCRUB!
SPLOOSH
JERRY SCOTT and JIM BORGMAN
NEXT TIME JUST HAND ME A NAPKIN, OKAY, MOM?
FOR PETE'S SAKE... ALL I DID WAS WET MY FINGER AND WIPE SOME PIZZA SAUCE OFF YOUR FACE!

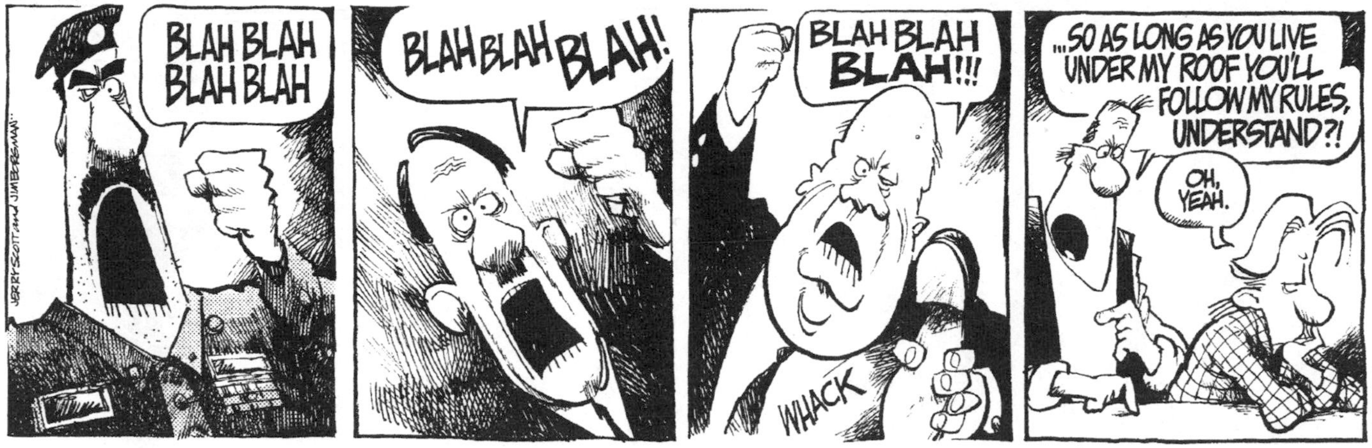
BLAH BLAH BLAH BLAH
BLAH BLAH BLAH!
BLAH BLAH BLAH!!!
WHACK
...SO AS LONG AS YOU LIVE UNDER MY ROOF YOU'LL FOLLOW MY RULES, UNDERSTAND?!
OH, YEAH.

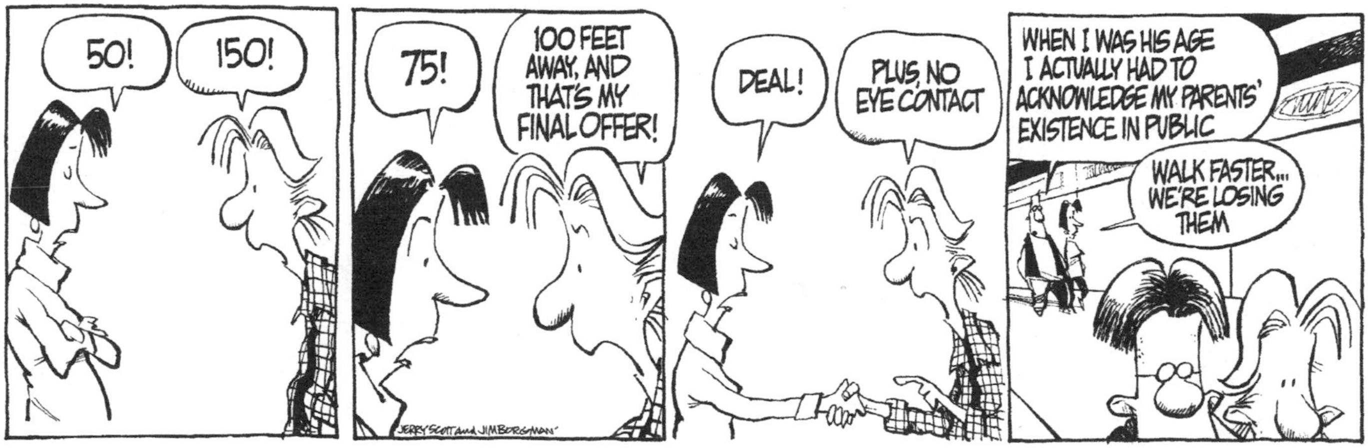
50!
150!
75!
100 FEET AWAY, AND THAT'S MY FINAL OFFER!
DEAL!
PLUS, NO EYE CONTACT
WHEN I WAS HIS AGE I ACTUALLY HAD TO ACKNOWLEDGE MY PARENTS' EXISTENCE IN PUBLIC
WALK FASTER... WE'RE LOSING THEM

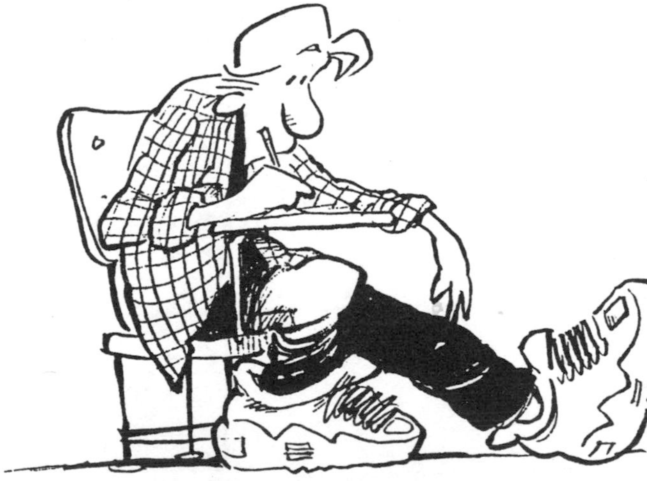

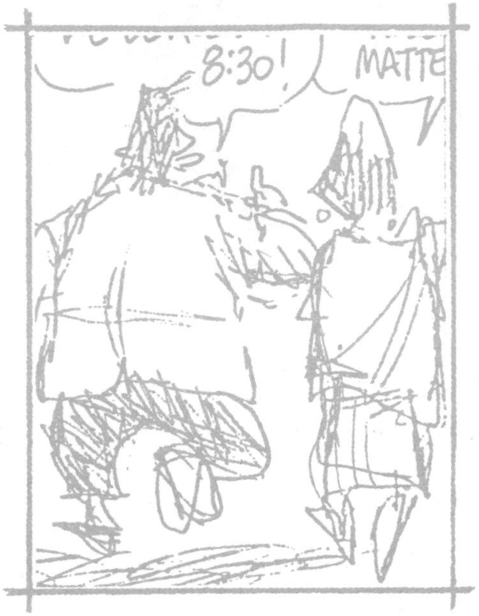

8:30!

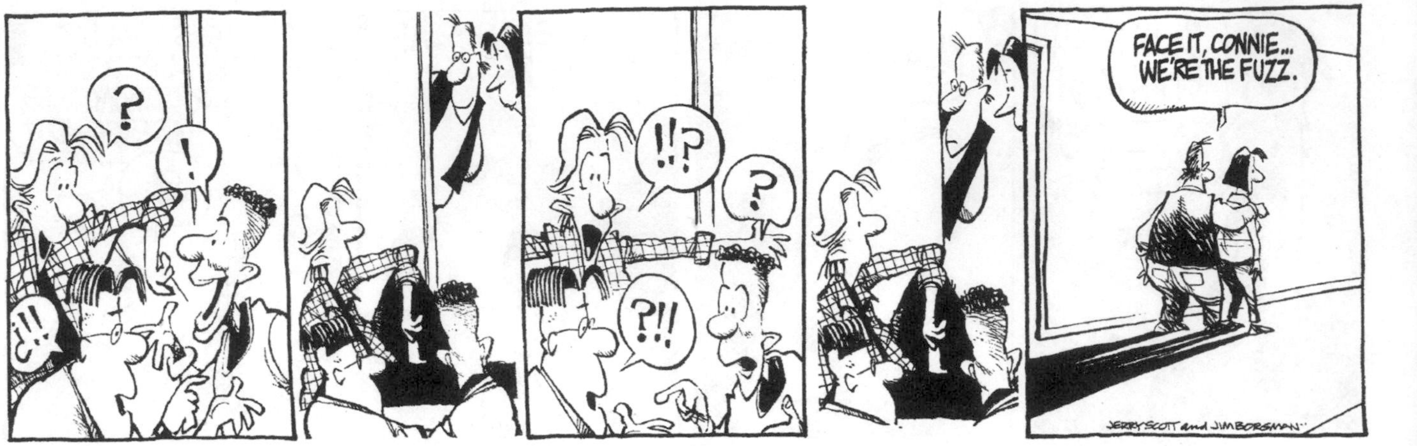

?
!
¡!!
!!?
?
?!!
FACE IT, CONNIE... WE'RE THE FUZZ.
JERRY SCOTT and JIM BORGMAN

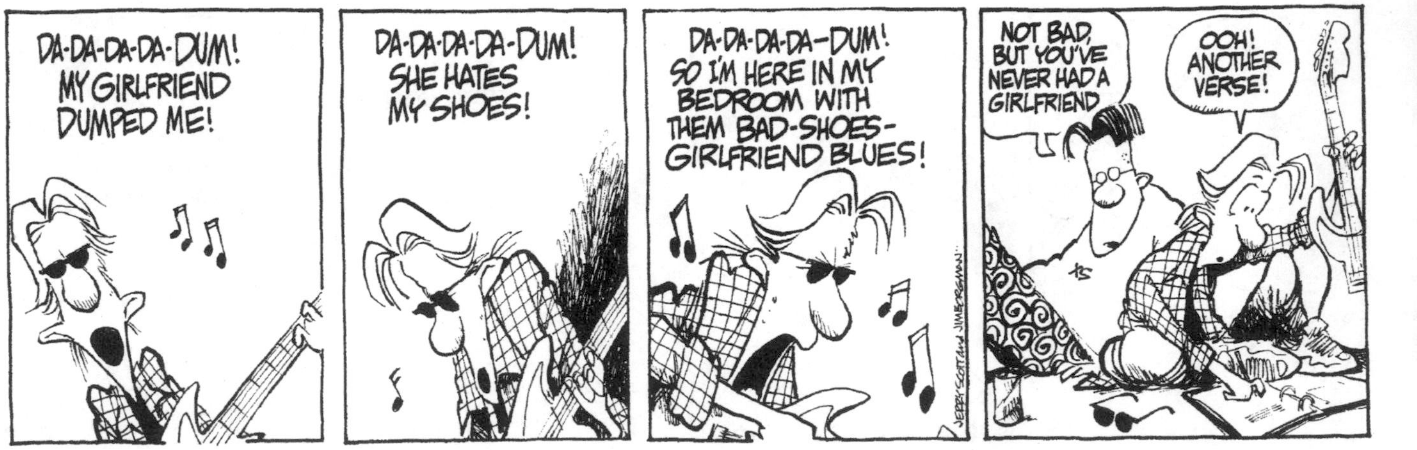

DA-DA-DA-DA-DUM! MY GIRLFRIEND DUMPED ME!
DA-DA-DA-DA-DUM! SHE HATES MY SHOES!
DA-DA-DA-DA-DUM! SO I'M HERE IN MY BEDROOM WITH THEM BAD-SHOES-GIRLFRIEND BLUES!
JERRY SCOTT and JIM BORGMAN
NOT BAD, BUT YOU'VE NEVER HAD A GIRLFRIEND
OOH! ANOTHER VERSE!

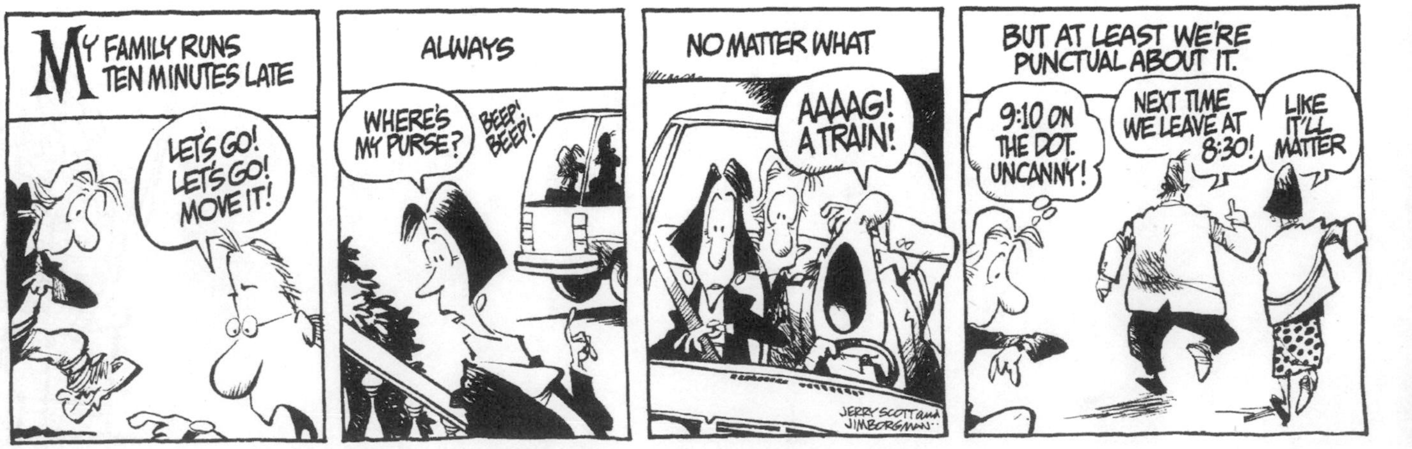

MY FAMILY RUNS TEN MINUTES LATE
LET'S GO! LET'S GO! MOVE IT!
ALWAYS
WHERE'S MY PURSE?
BEEP! BEEP!
NO MATTER WHAT
AAAAG! A TRAIN!
JERRY SCOTT and JIM BORGMAN
BUT AT LEAST WE'RE PUNCTUAL ABOUT IT.
9:10 ON THE DOT. UNCANNY!
NEXT TIME WE LEAVE AT 8:30!
LIKE IT'LL MATTER

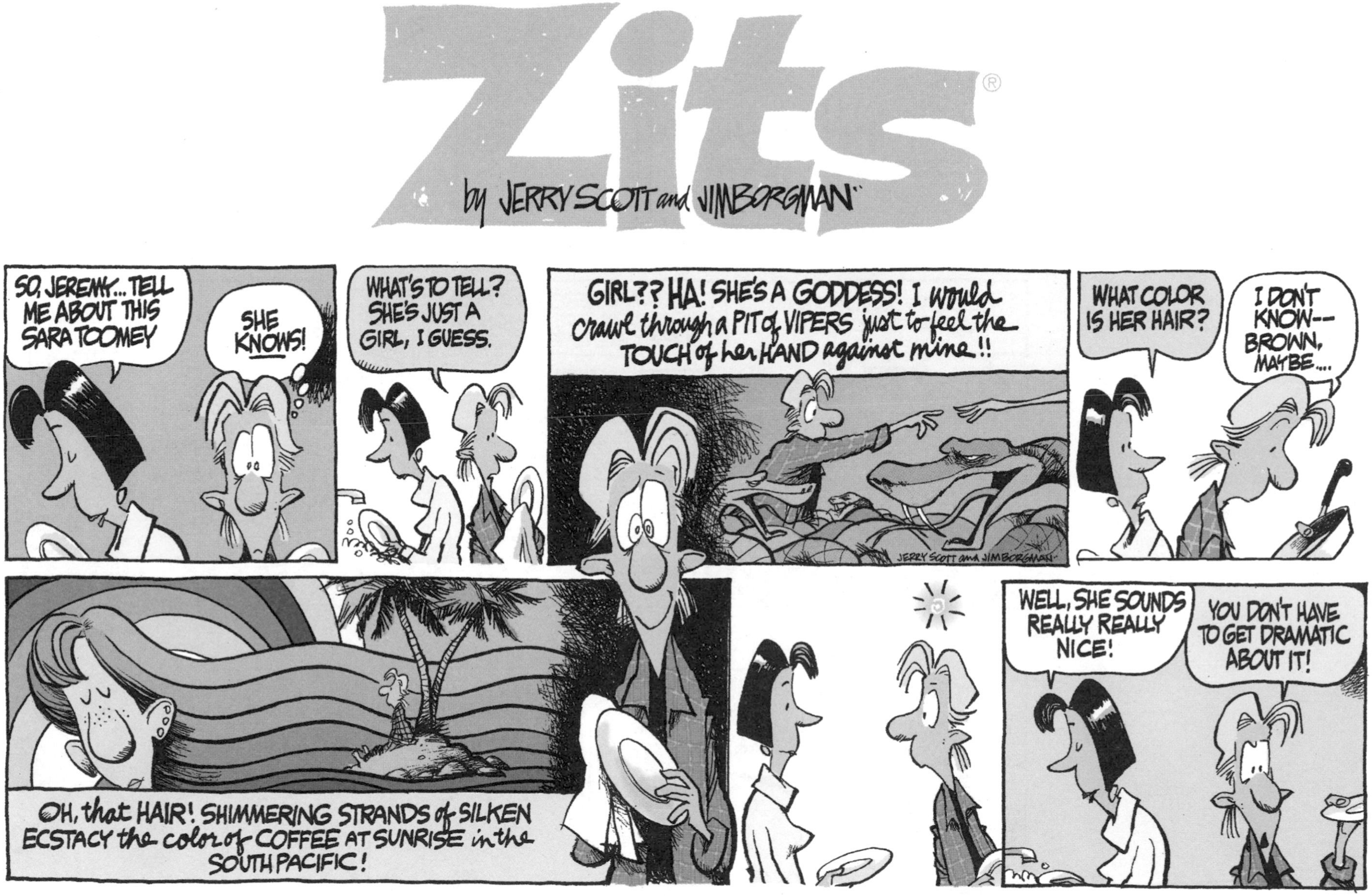
Zits®
by JERRY SCOTT and JIM BORGMAN
SO, JEREMY... TELL ME ABOUT THIS SARA TOOMEY
SHE KNOWS!
WHAT'S TO TELL? SHE'S JUST A GIRL, I GUESS.
GIRL?? HA! SHE'S A GODDESS! I would crawl through a PIT of VIPERS just to feel the TOUCH of her HAND against mine!!
JERRY SCOTT and JIMBORGMAN
WHAT COLOR IS HER HAIR?
I DON'T KNOW-- BROWN, MAYBE....
OH, that HAIR! SHIMMERING STRANDS of SILKEN ECSTACY the color of COFFEE AT SUNRISE in the SOUTH PACIFIC!
WELL, SHE SOUNDS REALLY REALLY NICE!
YOU DON'T HAVE TO GET DRAMATIC ABOUT IT!

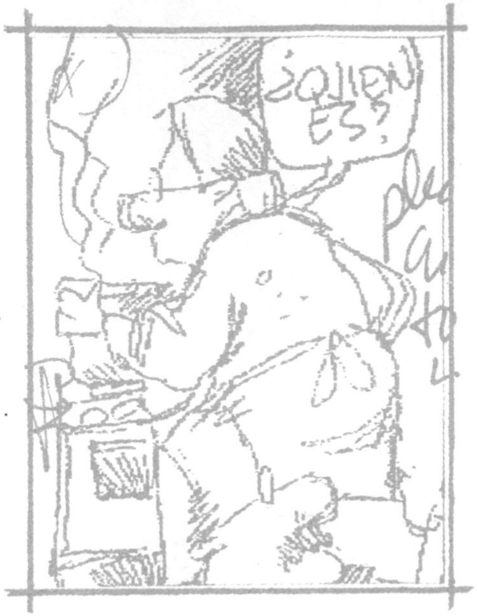
¿QUIEN ES?

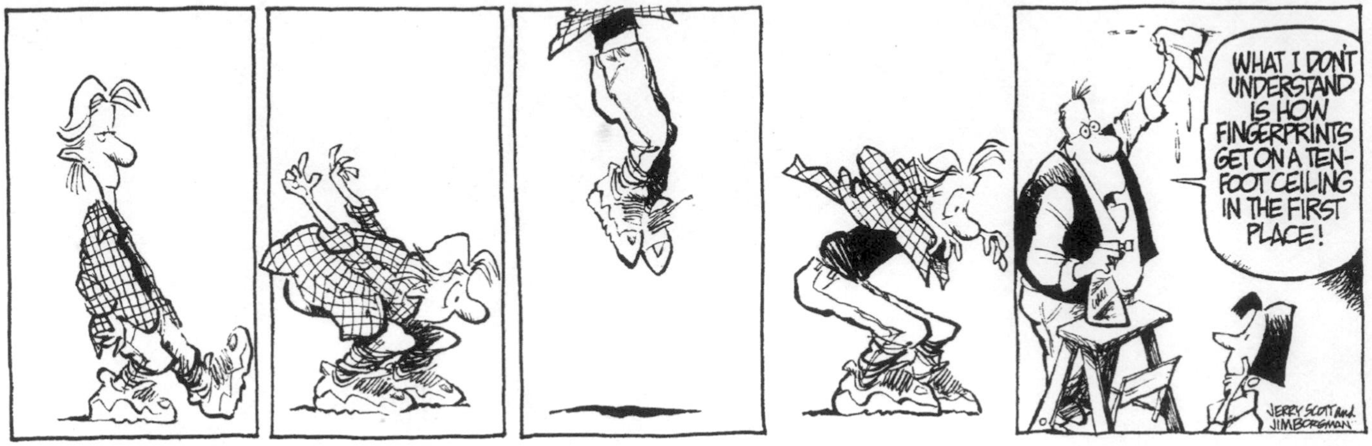
WHAT I DON'T UNDERSTAND IS HOW FINGERPRINTS GET ON A TEN-FOOT CEILING IN THE FIRST PLACE!
JERRY SCOTT and JIM BORGMAN

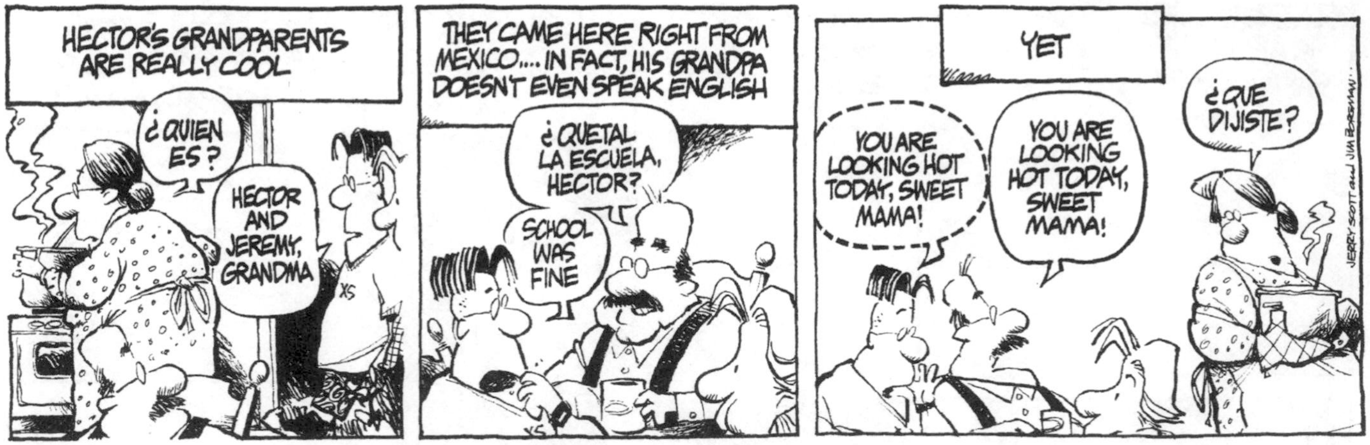
HECTOR'S GRANDPARENTS ARE REALLY COOL
¿QUIEN ES?
HECTOR AND JEREMY, GRANDMA
THEY CAME HERE RIGHT FROM MEXICO.... IN FACT, HIS GRANDPA DOESN'T EVEN SPEAK ENGLISH
¿QUE TAL LA ESCUELA, HECTOR?
SCHOOL WAS FINE
YET
YOU ARE LOOKING HOT TODAY, SWEET MAMA!
YOU ARE LOOKING HOT TODAY, SWEET MAMA!
¿QUE DIJISTE?
JERRY SCOTT and JIM BORGMAN

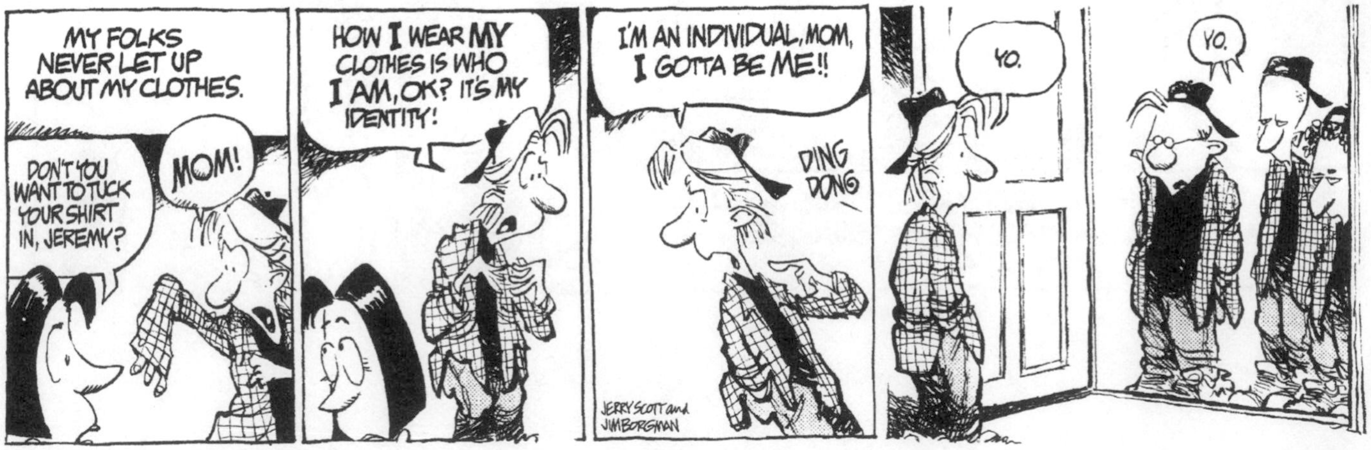
MY FOLKS NEVER LET UP ABOUT MY CLOTHES.
DON'T YOU WANT TO TUCK YOUR SHIRT IN, JEREMY?
MOM!
HOW I WEAR MY CLOTHES IS WHO I AM, OK? IT'S MY IDENTITY!
I'M AN INDIVIDUAL, MOM, I GOTTA BE ME!!
DING DONG
JERRY SCOTT and JIM BORGMAN
YO.
YO.

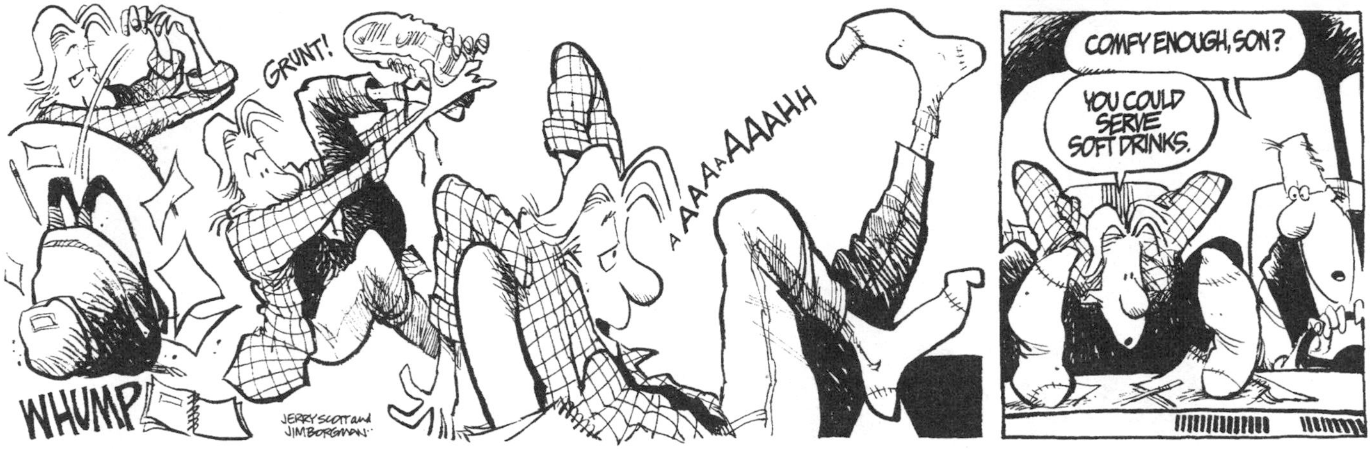
GRUNT!
WHUMP
AAAAAAAHH
JERRY SCOTT and JIM BORGMAN
COMFY ENOUGH, SON?
YOU COULD SERVE SOFT DRINKS.

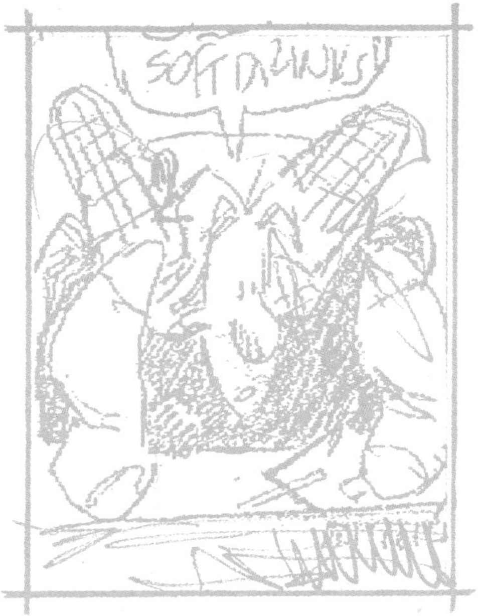

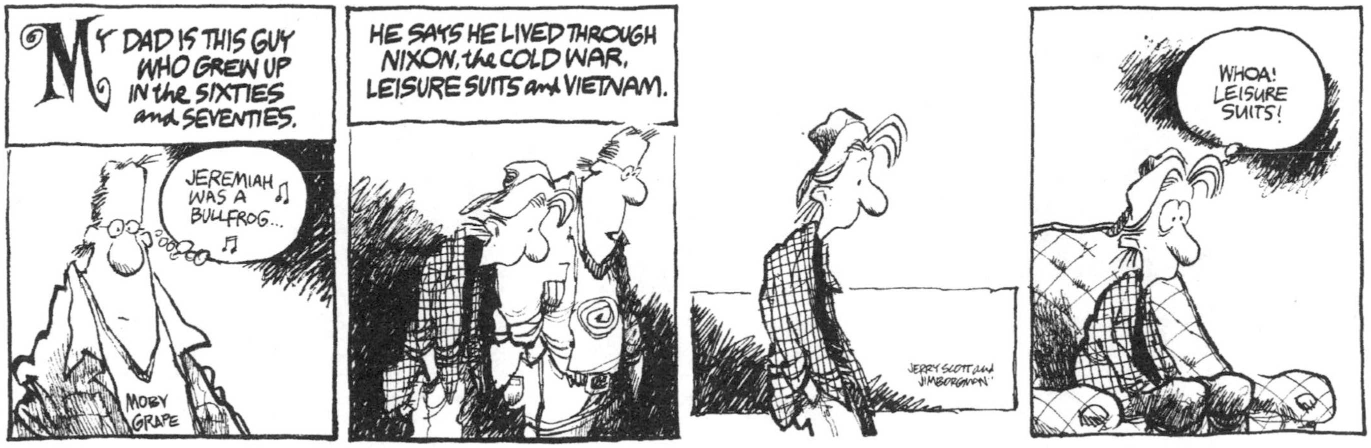
MY DAD IS THIS GUY WHO GREW UP IN the SIXTIES and SEVENTIES.
JEREMIAH WAS A BULLFROG...
MOBY GRAPE
HE SAYS HE LIVED THROUGH NIXON, the COLD WAR, LEISURE SUITS and VIETNAM.
JERRY SCOTT and JIM BORGMAN
WHOA! LEISURE SUITS!

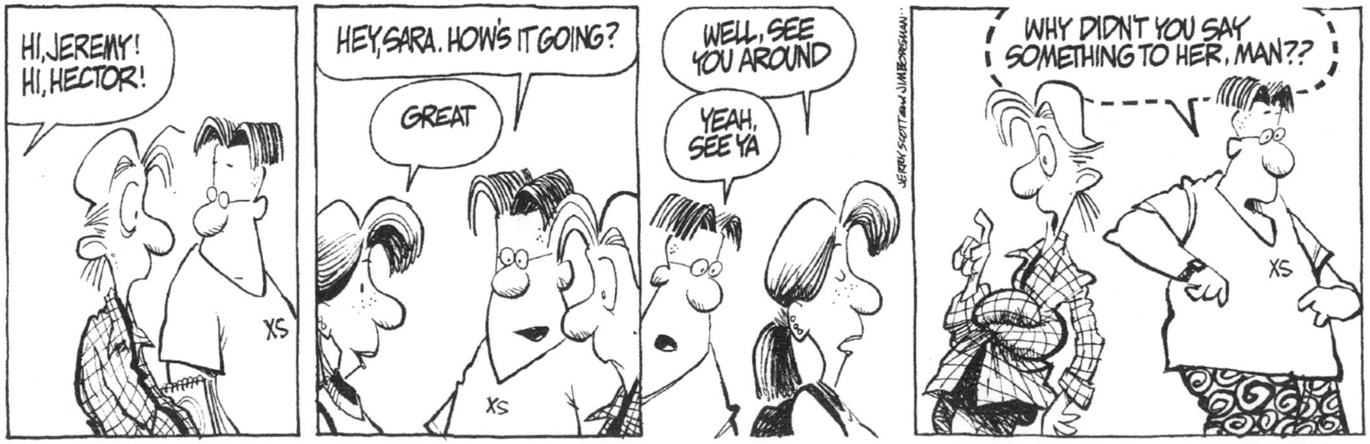
HI, JEREMY! HI, HECTOR!
XS
HEY, SARA. HOW'S IT GOING?
GREAT
XS
WELL, SEE YOU AROUND
YEAH, SEE YA
JERRY SCOTT and JIM BORGMAN
WHY DIDN'T YOU SAY SOMETHING TO HER, MAN??
XS

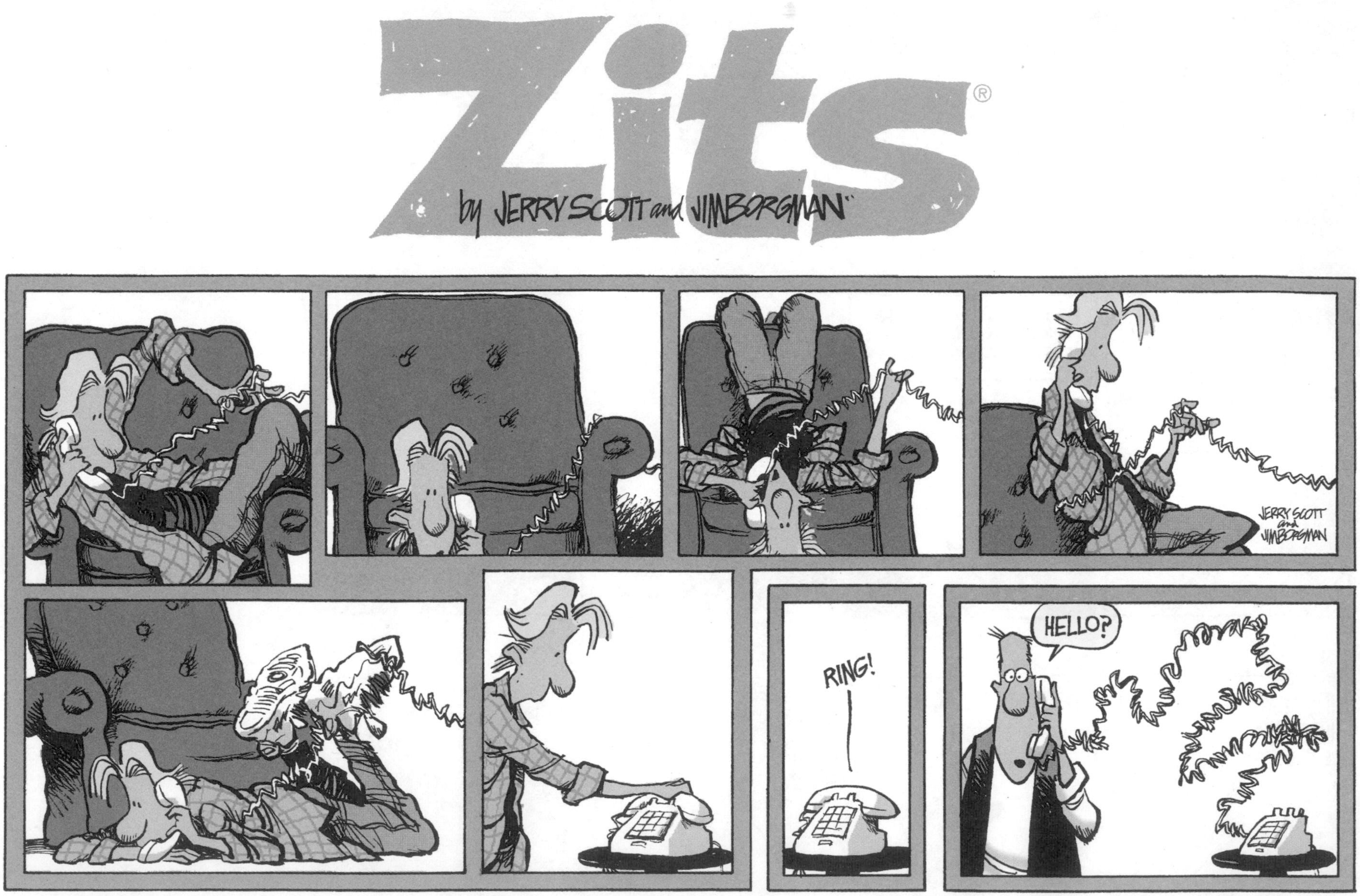
Zits
by JERRY SCOTT and JIM BORGMAN
JERRY SCOTT and JIM BORGMAN
RING!
HELLO?

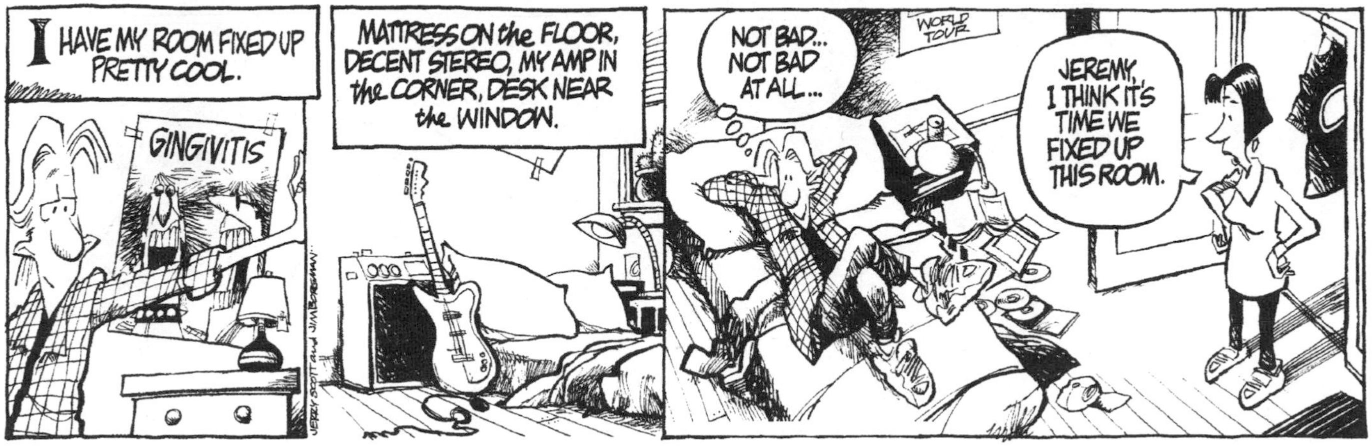
I HAVE MY ROOM FIXED UP PRETTY COOL.
GINGIVITIS
JERRY SCOTT and JIM BORGMAN
MATTRESS ON the FLOOR, DECENT STEREO, MY AMP IN the CORNER, DESK NEAR the WINDOW.
WORLD TOUR
NOT BAD... NOT BAD AT ALL...
JEREMY, I THINK IT'S TIME WE FIXED UP THIS ROOM.

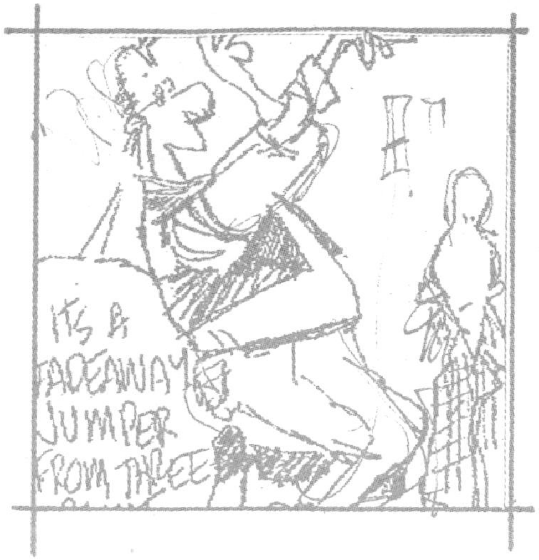
IT'S A FADEAWAY JUMPER FROM THREE

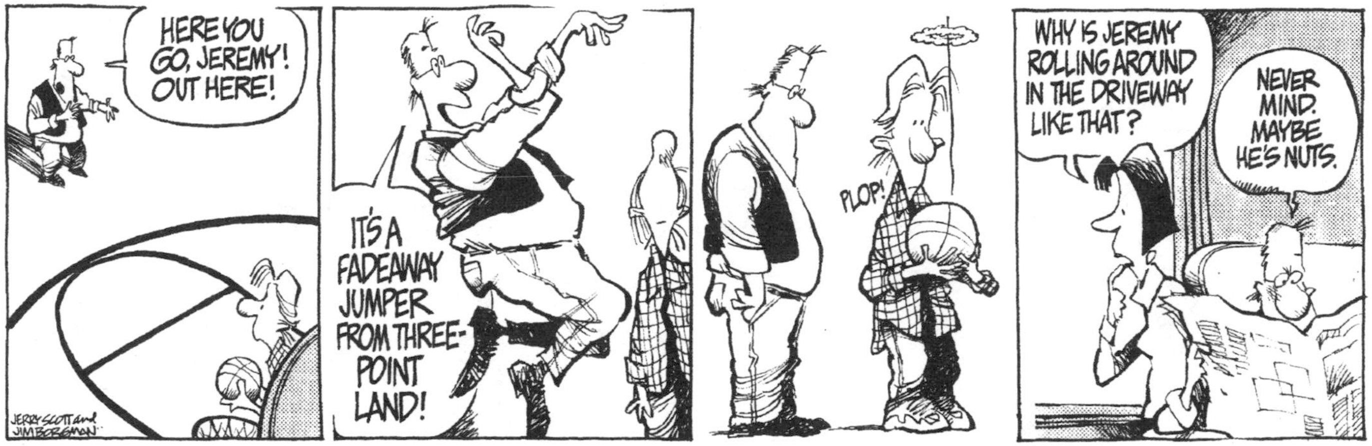
HERE YOU GO, JEREMY! OUT HERE!
JERRY SCOTT and JIM BORGMAN
IT'S A FADEAWAY JUMPER FROM THREE-POINT LAND!
PLOP!
WHY IS JEREMY ROLLING AROUND IN THE DRIVEWAY LIKE THAT?
NEVER MIND. MAYBE HE'S NUTS.

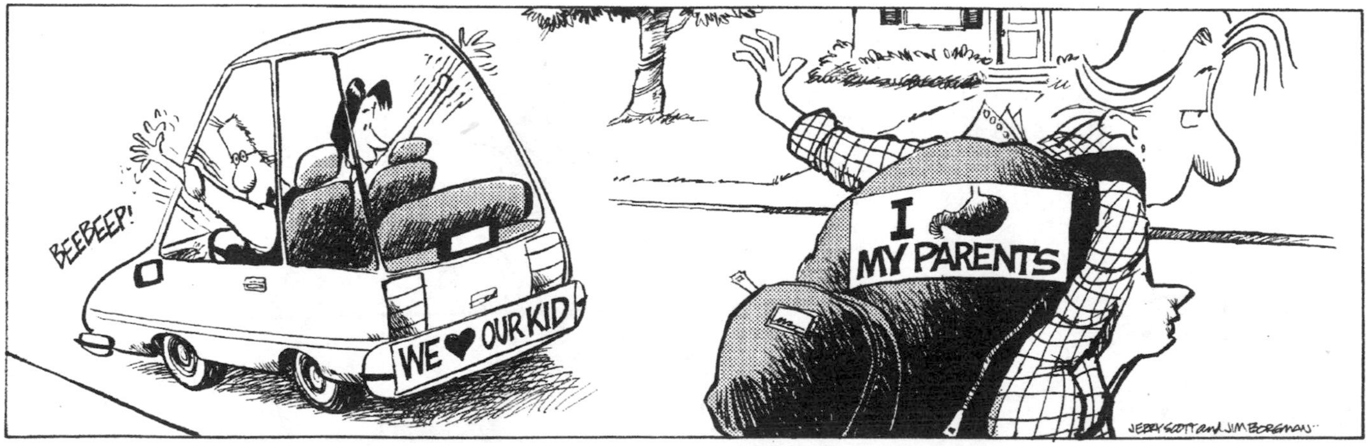
BEEBEEP!
WE ♥ OUR KID
I MY PARENTS
JERRY SCOTT and JIM BORGMAN

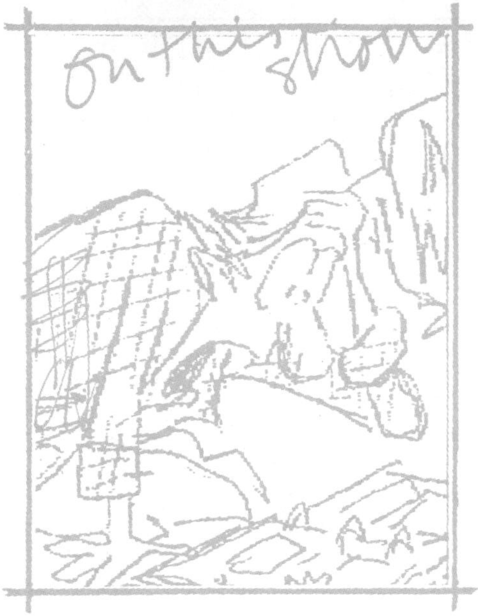

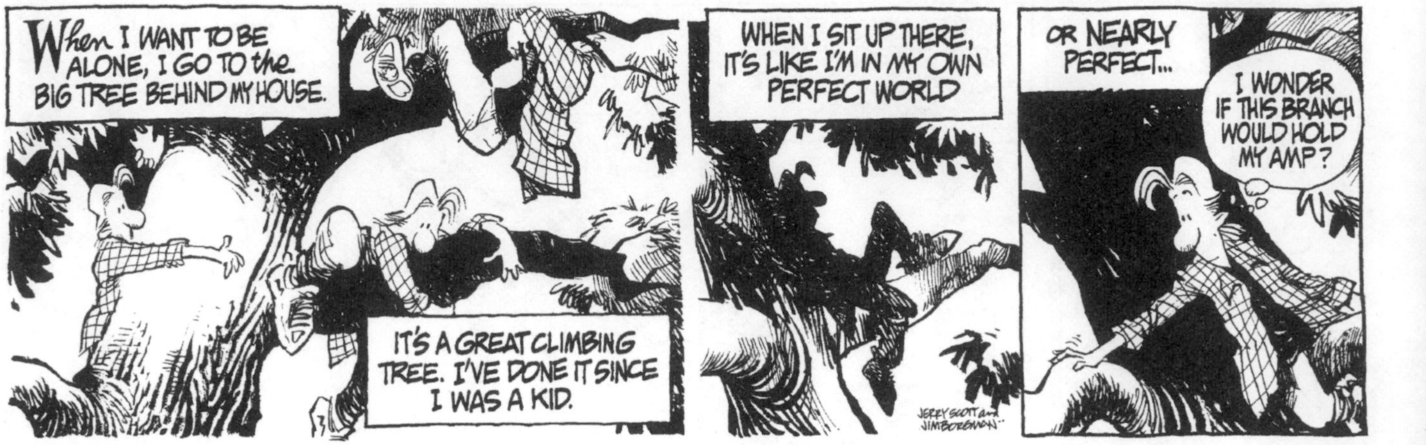

WHEN I WANT TO BE ALONE, I GO TO THE BIG TREE BEHIND MY HOUSE.
IT'S A GREAT CLIMBING TREE. I'VE DONE IT SINCE I WAS A KID.
WHEN I SIT UP THERE, IT'S LIKE I'M IN MY OWN PERFECT WORLD
OR NEARLY PERFECT...
I WONDER IF THIS BRANCH WOULD HOLD MY AMP?

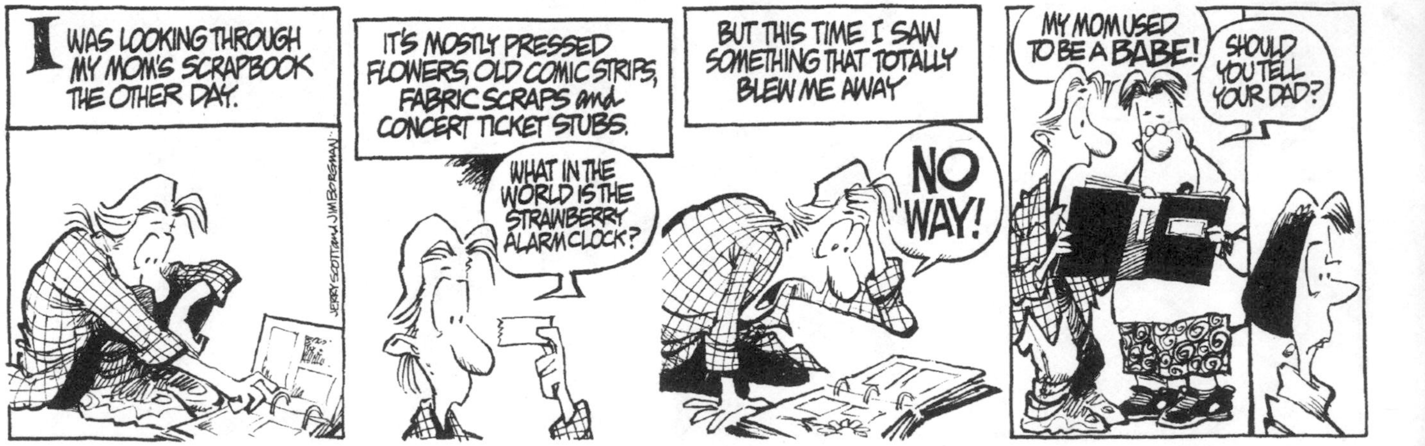

I WAS LOOKING THROUGH MY MOM'S SCRAPBOOK THE OTHER DAY.
IT'S MOSTLY PRESSED FLOWERS, OLD COMIC STRIPS, FABRIC SCRAPS AND CONCERT TICKET STUBS.
WHAT IN THE WORLD IS THE STRAWBERRY ALARM CLOCK?
BUT THIS TIME I SAW SOMETHING THAT TOTALLY BLEW ME AWAY
NO WAY!
MY MOM USED TO BE A BABE!
SHOULD YOU TELL YOUR DAD?

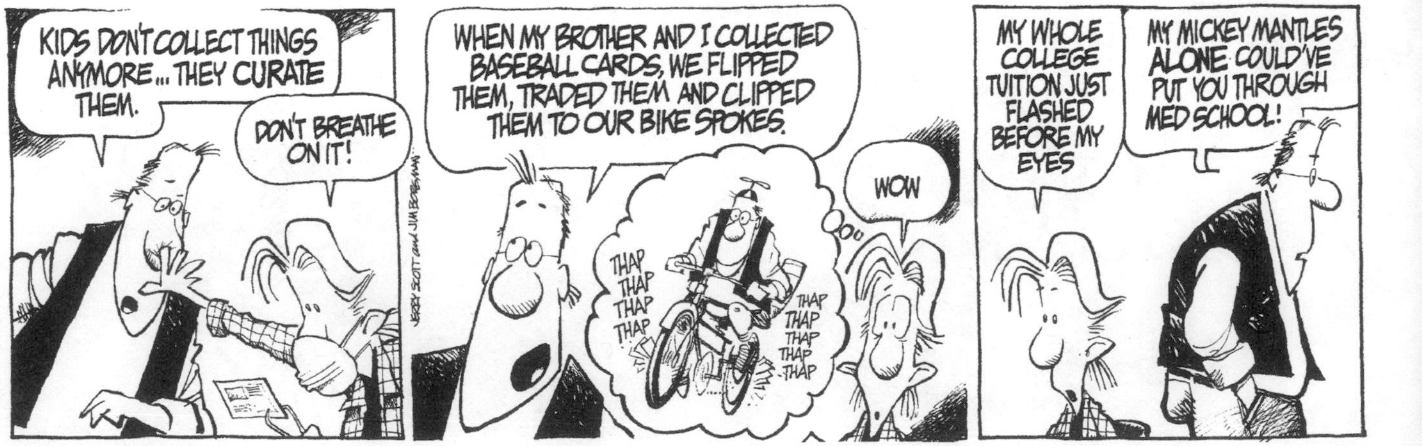

KIDS DON'T COLLECT THINGS ANYMORE... THEY CURATE THEM.
DON'T BREATHE ON IT!
WHEN MY BROTHER AND I COLLECTED BASEBALL CARDS, WE FLIPPED THEM, TRADED THEM AND CLIPPED THEM TO OUR BIKE SPOKES.
THAP THAP THAP THAP
THAP THAP THAP THAP THAP
WOW
MY WHOLE COLLEGE TUITION JUST FLASHED BEFORE MY EYES
MY MICKEY MANTLES ALONE COULD'VE PUT YOU THROUGH MED SCHOOL!

Zits®

by JERRY SCOTT and JIM BORGMAN

JERRY SCOTT and JIM BORGMAN
SO IT'S AGREED.... WE TELL JEREMY HE CAN HAVE HIS FRIENDS OVER, BUT FROM NOW ON THEY HAVE TO PARK THEIR SHOES IN THE GARAGE.

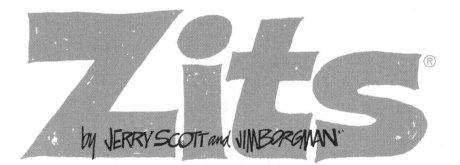

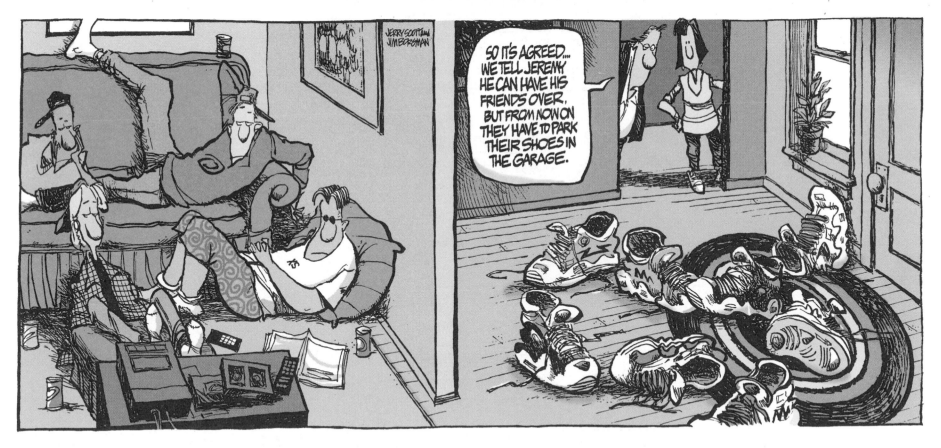

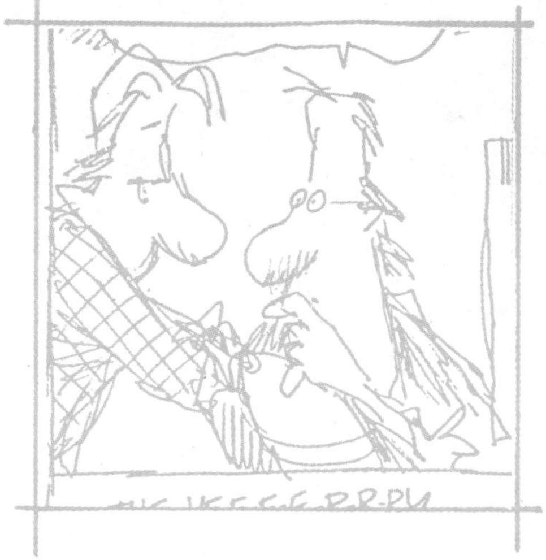

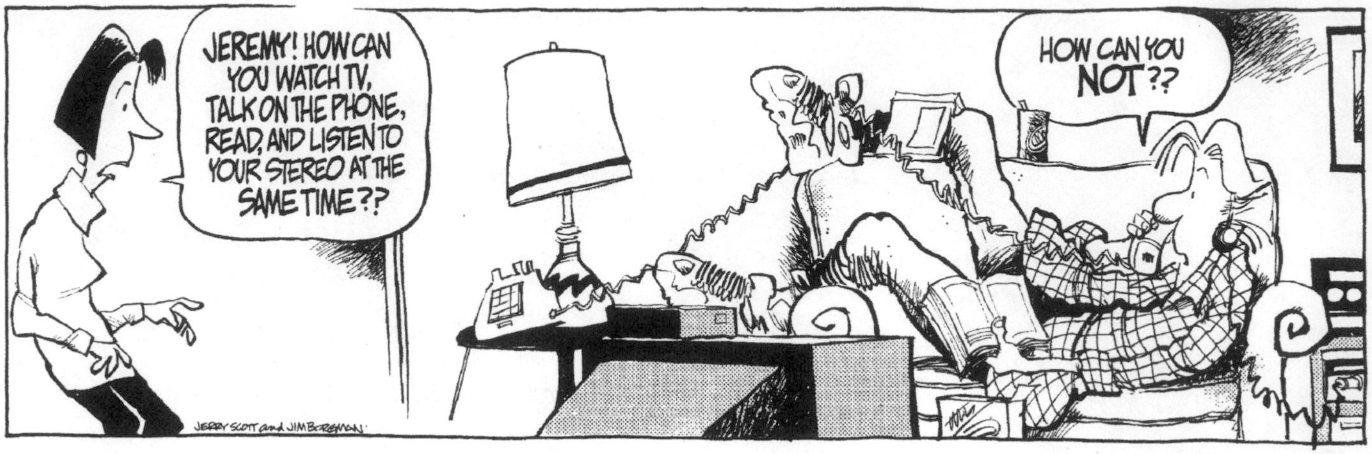
JEREMY! HOW CAN YOU WATCH TV, TALK ON THE PHONE, READ, AND LISTEN TO YOUR STEREO AT THE SAME TIME??
HOW CAN YOU NOT??
JERRY SCOTT and JIM BORGMAN

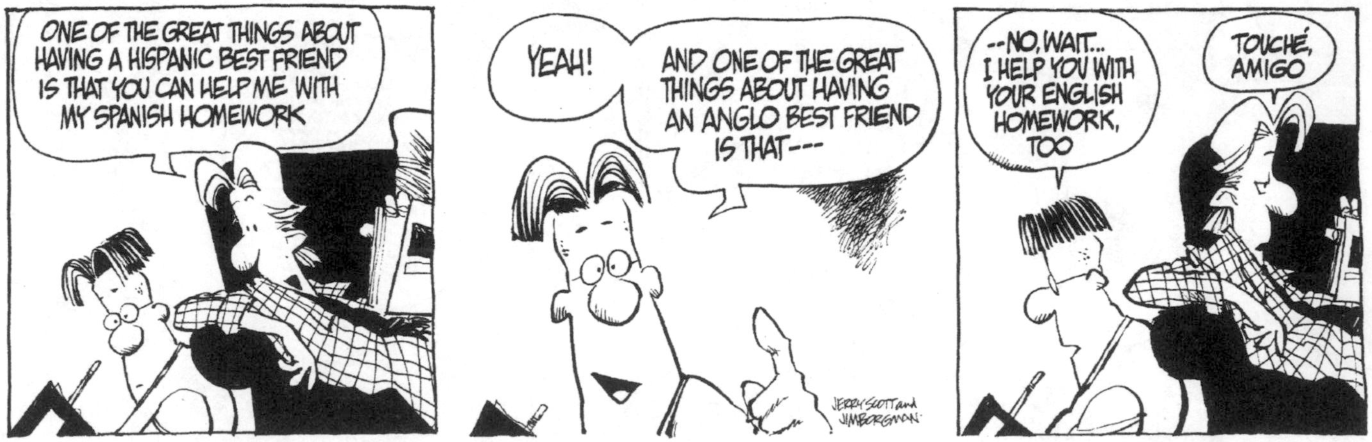
ONE OF THE GREAT THINGS ABOUT HAVING A HISPANIC BEST FRIEND IS THAT YOU CAN HELP ME WITH MY SPANISH HOMEWORK
YEAH!
AND ONE OF THE GREAT THINGS ABOUT HAVING AN ANGLO BEST FRIEND IS THAT---
JERRY SCOTT and JIM BORGMAN
--NO, WAIT... I HELP YOU WITH YOUR ENGLISH HOMEWORK, TOO
TOUCHÉ, AMIGO

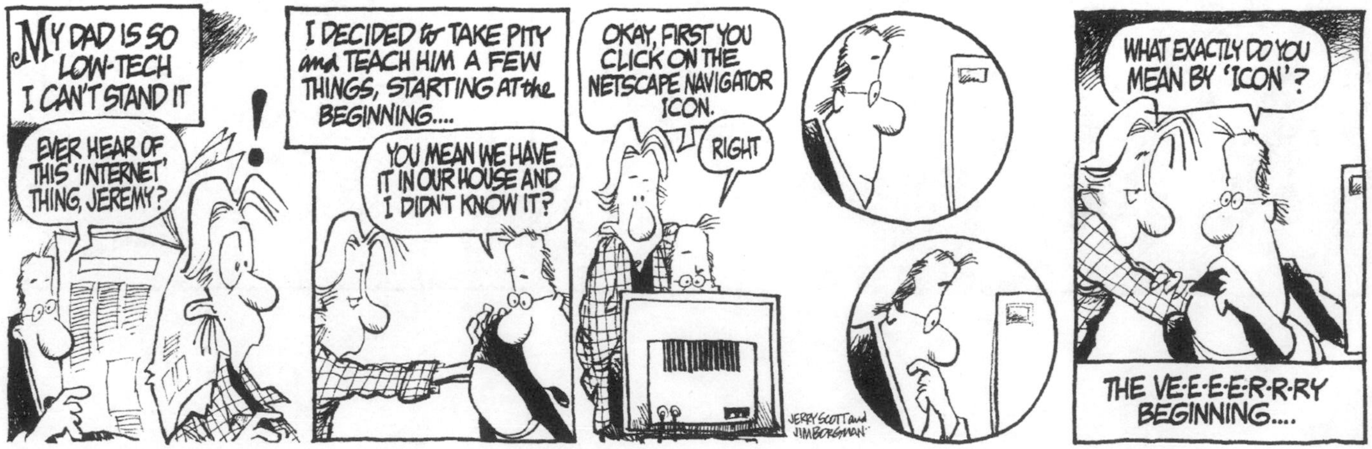
MY DAD IS SO LOW-TECH I CAN'T STAND IT
EVER HEAR OF THIS 'INTERNET' THING, JEREMY?
!
I DECIDED to TAKE PITY and TEACH HIM A FEW THINGS, STARTING AT the BEGINNING....
YOU MEAN WE HAVE IT IN OUR HOUSE AND I DIDN'T KNOW IT?
OKAY, FIRST YOU CLICK ON THE NETSCAPE NAVIGATOR ICON.
RIGHT
JERRY SCOTT and JIM BORGMAN
WHAT EXACTLY DO YOU MEAN BY 'ICON'?
THE VE-E-E-E-R-R-RY BEGINNING....

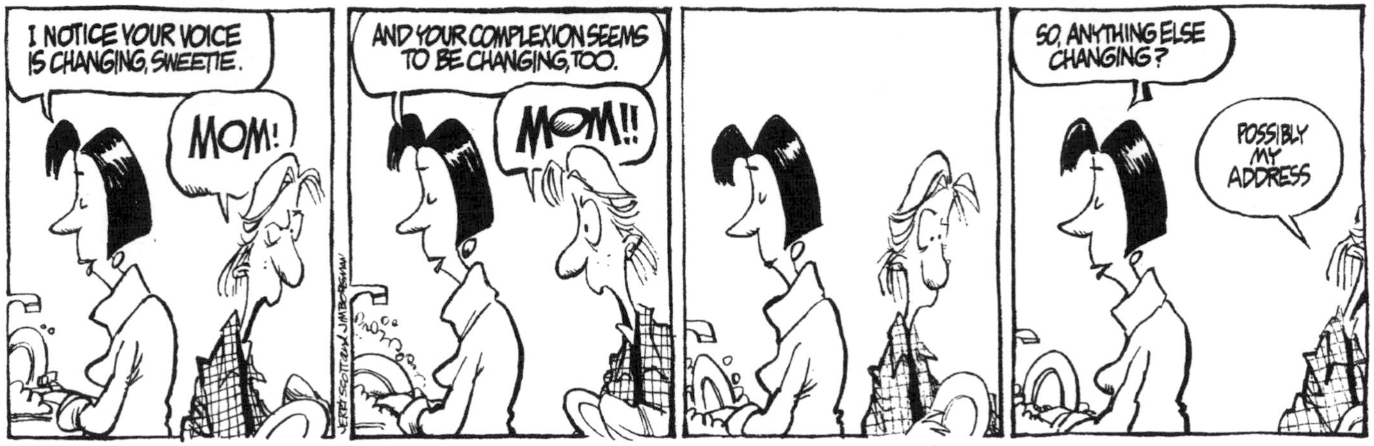
I NOTICE YOUR VOICE IS CHANGING, SWEETIE.
MOM!
AND YOUR COMPLEXION SEEMS TO BE CHANGING, TOO.
MOM!!
SO, ANYTHING ELSE CHANGING?
POSSIBLY MY ADDRESS

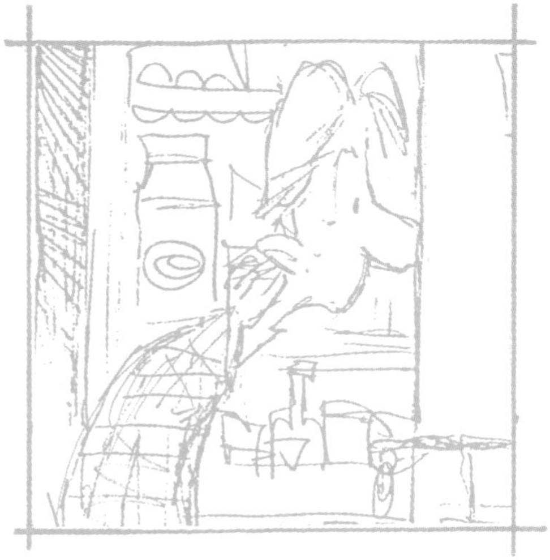

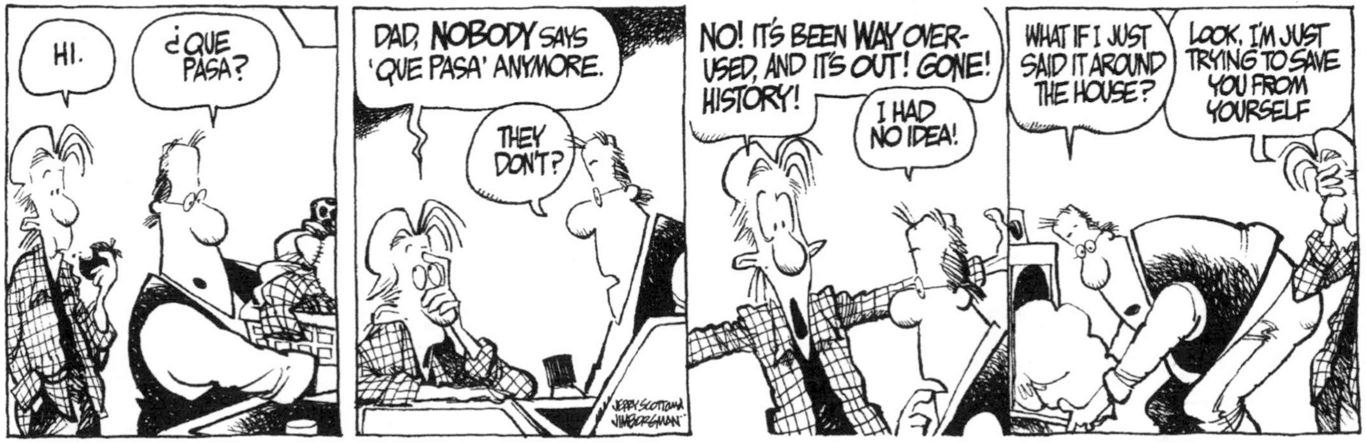
HI.
¿QUE PASA?
DAD, NOBODY SAYS 'QUE PASA' ANYMORE.
THEY DON'T?
NO! IT'S BEEN WAY OVER-USED, AND IT'S OUT! GONE! HISTORY!
I HAD NO IDEA!
WHAT IF I JUST SAID IT AROUND THE HOUSE?
LOOK, I'M JUST TRYING TO SAVE YOU FROM YOURSELF

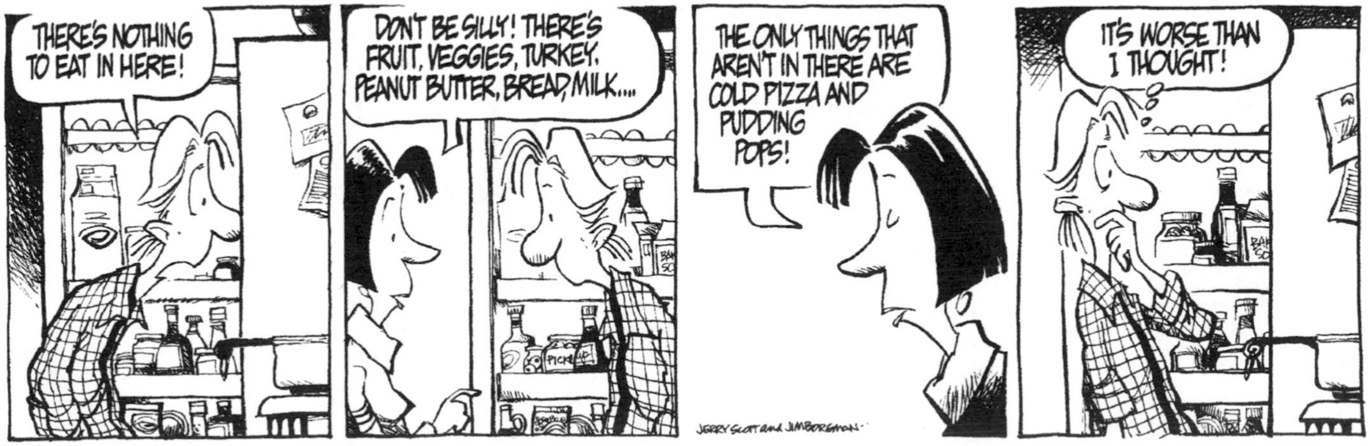
THERE'S NOTHING TO EAT IN HERE!
DON'T BE SILLY! THERE'S FRUIT, VEGGIES, TURKEY, PEANUT BUTTER, BREAD, MILK....
THE ONLY THINGS THAT AREN'T IN THERE ARE COLD PIZZA AND PUDDING POPS!
IT'S WORSE THAN I THOUGHT!

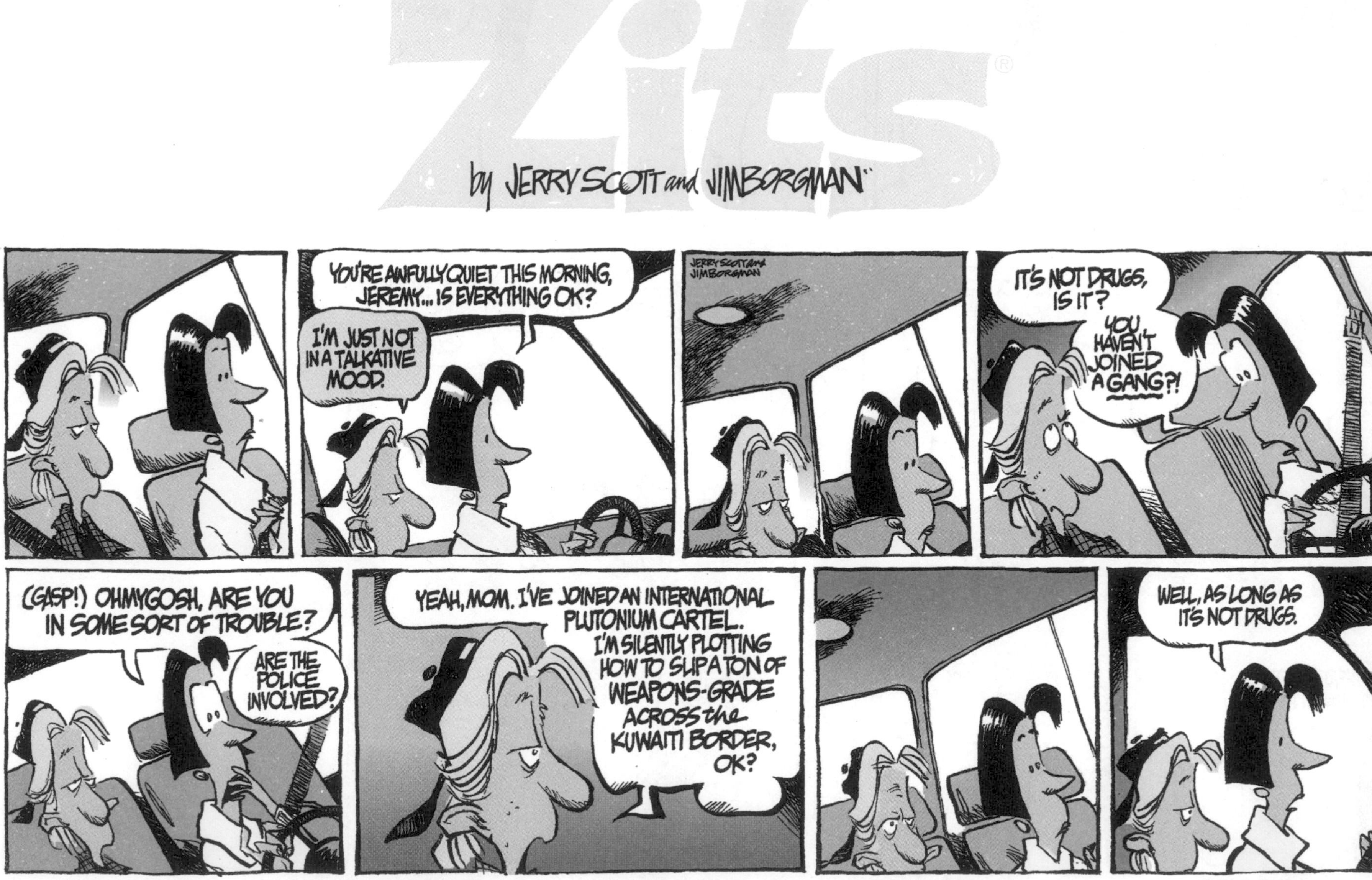
Zits®
by JERRY SCOTT and JIM BORGMAN
YOU'RE AWFULLY QUIET THIS MORNING, JEREMY... IS EVERYTHING OK?
I'M JUST NOT IN A TALKATIVE MOOD.
JERRY SCOTT and JIM BORGMAN
IT'S NOT DRUGS, IS IT?
YOU HAVEN'T JOINED A GANG?!
(GASP!) OHMYGOSH, ARE YOU IN SOME SORT OF TROUBLE?
ARE THE POLICE INVOLVED?
YEAH, MOM. I'VE JOINED AN INTERNATIONAL PLUTONIUM CARTEL. I'M SILENTLY PLOTTING HOW TO SLIP A TON OF WEAPONS-GRADE ACROSS the KUWAITI BORDER, OK?
WELL, AS LONG AS IT'S NOT DRUGS.

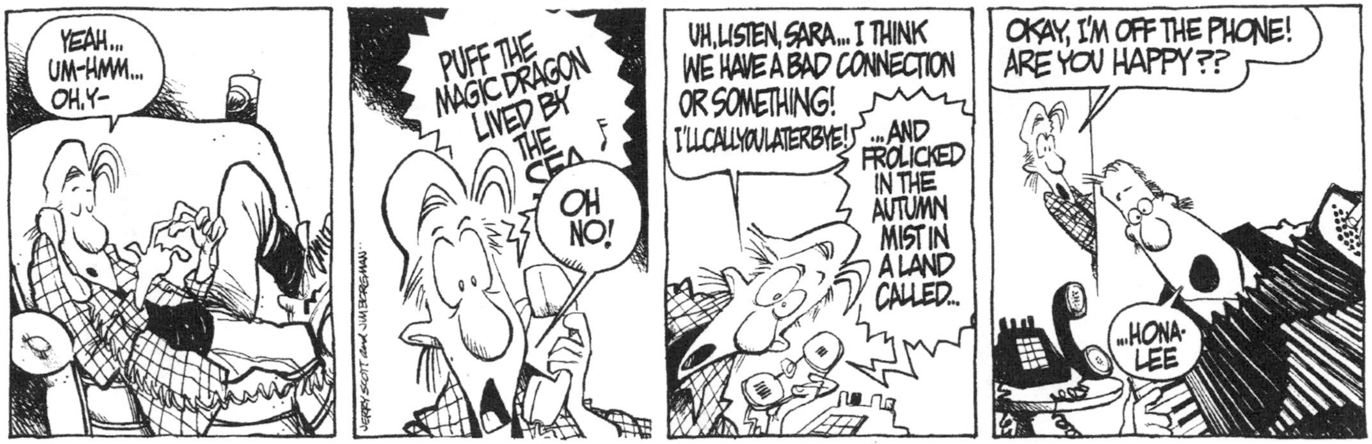
YEAH... UM-HMM... OH, Y-
PUFF THE MAGIC DRAGON LIVED BY THE SEA
OH NO!
JERRY SCOTT and JIM BORGMAN
UH, LISTEN, SARA... I THINK WE HAVE A BAD CONNECTION OR SOMETHING! I'LLCALLYOULATERBYE!
...AND FROLICKED IN THE AUTUMN MIST IN A LAND CALLED...
OKAY, I'M OFF THE PHONE! ARE YOU HAPPY??
...HONA-LEE

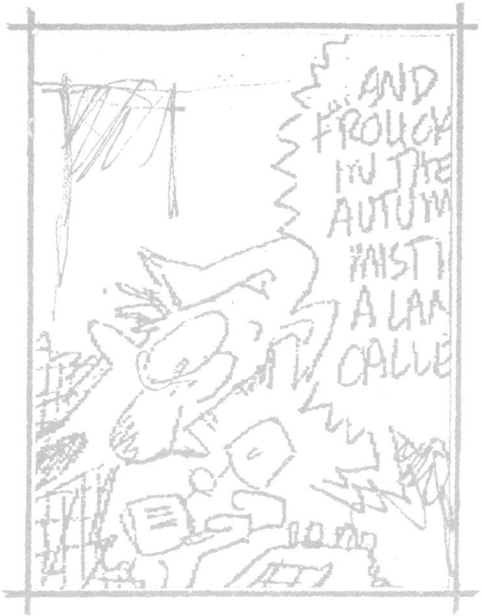
...AND FROLICK IN THE AUTUM MIST I A LAN CALLE

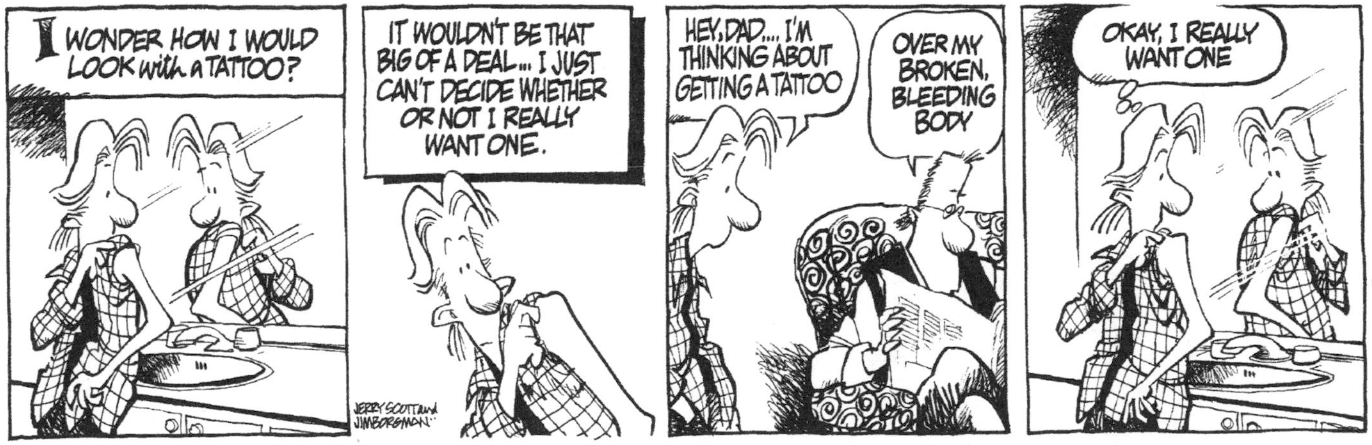
I WONDER HOW I WOULD LOOK with a TATTOO?
IT WOULDN'T BE THAT BIG OF A DEAL... I JUST CAN'T DECIDE WHETHER OR NOT I REALLY WANT ONE.
JERRY SCOTT and JIM BORGMAN
HEY, DAD.... I'M THINKING ABOUT GETTING A TATTOO
OVER MY BROKEN, BLEEDING BODY
OKAY, I REALLY WANT ONE

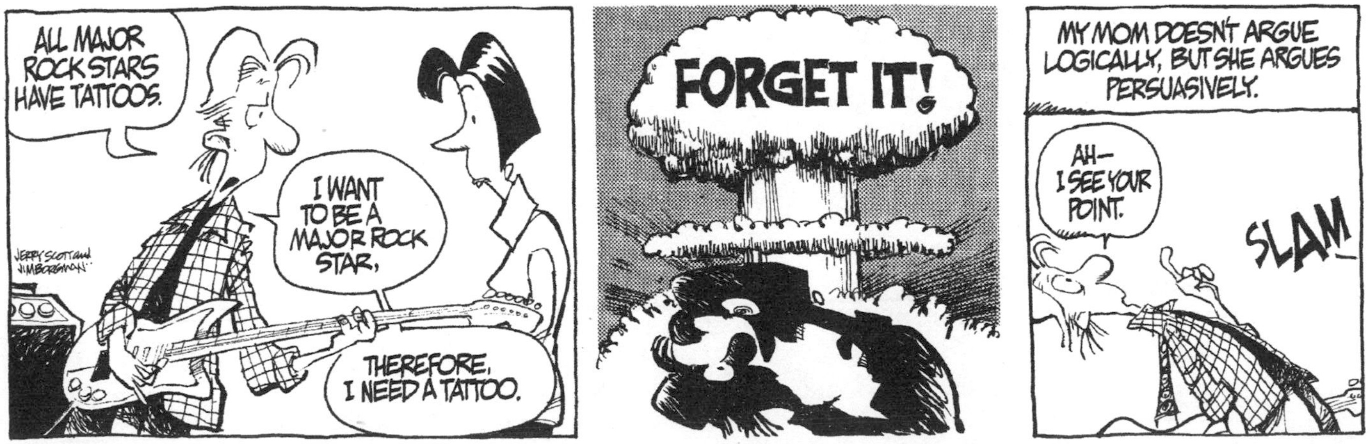
ALL MAJOR ROCK STARS HAVE TATTOOS.
I WANT TO BE A MAJOR ROCK STAR,
THEREFORE, I NEED A TATTOO.
JERRY SCOTT and JIM BORGMAN
FORGET IT!
MY MOM DOESN'T ARGUE LOGICALLY, BUT SHE ARGUES PERSUASIVELY.
AH— I SEE YOUR POINT.
SLAM

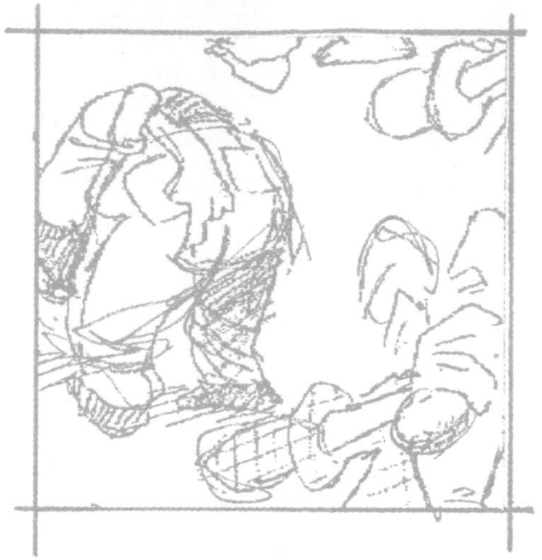

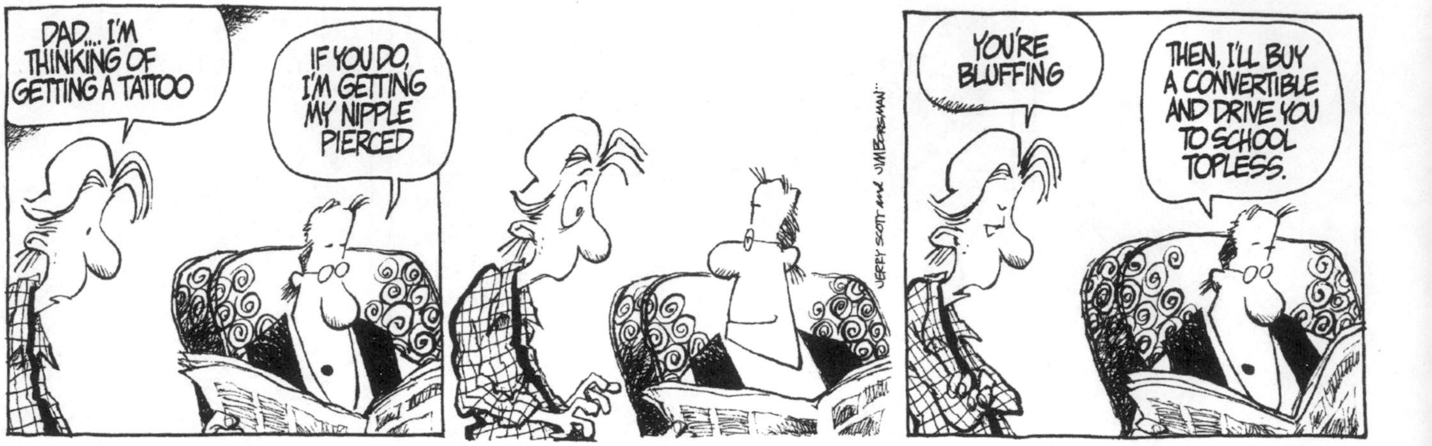
DAD... I'M THINKING OF GETTING A TATTOO
IF YOU DO, I'M GETTING MY NIPPLE PIERCED
YOU'RE BLUFFING
THEN, I'LL BUY A CONVERTIBLE AND DRIVE YOU TO SCHOOL TOPLESS.

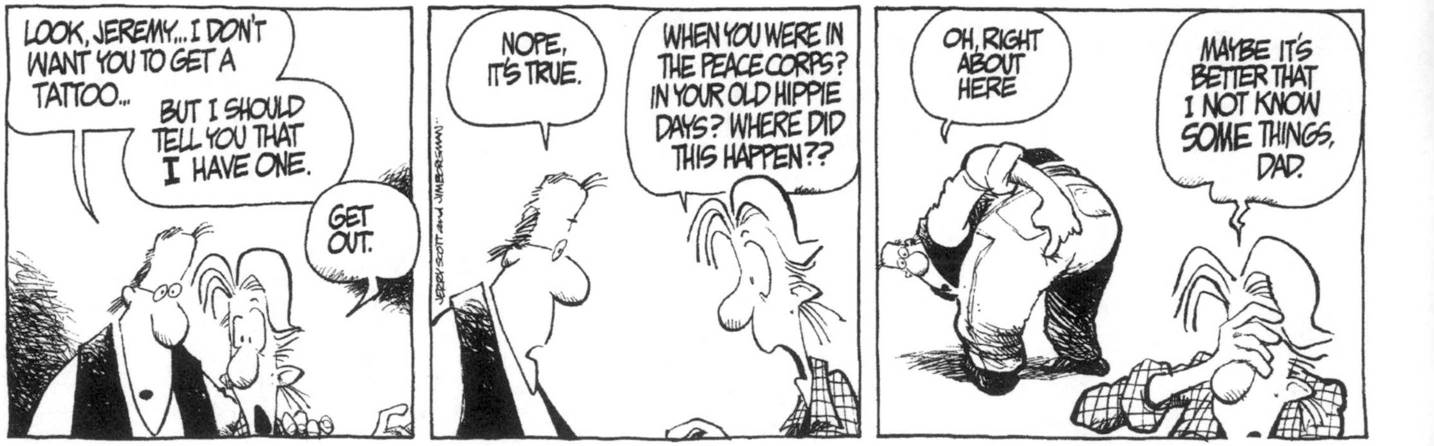
LOOK, JEREMY... I DON'T WANT YOU TO GET A TATTOO...
BUT I SHOULD TELL YOU THAT I HAVE ONE.
GET OUT.
NOPE, IT'S TRUE.
WHEN YOU WERE IN THE PEACE CORPS? IN YOUR OLD HIPPIE DAYS? WHERE DID THIS HAPPEN??
OH, RIGHT ABOUT HERE
MAYBE IT'S BETTER THAT I NOT KNOW SOME THINGS, DAD.

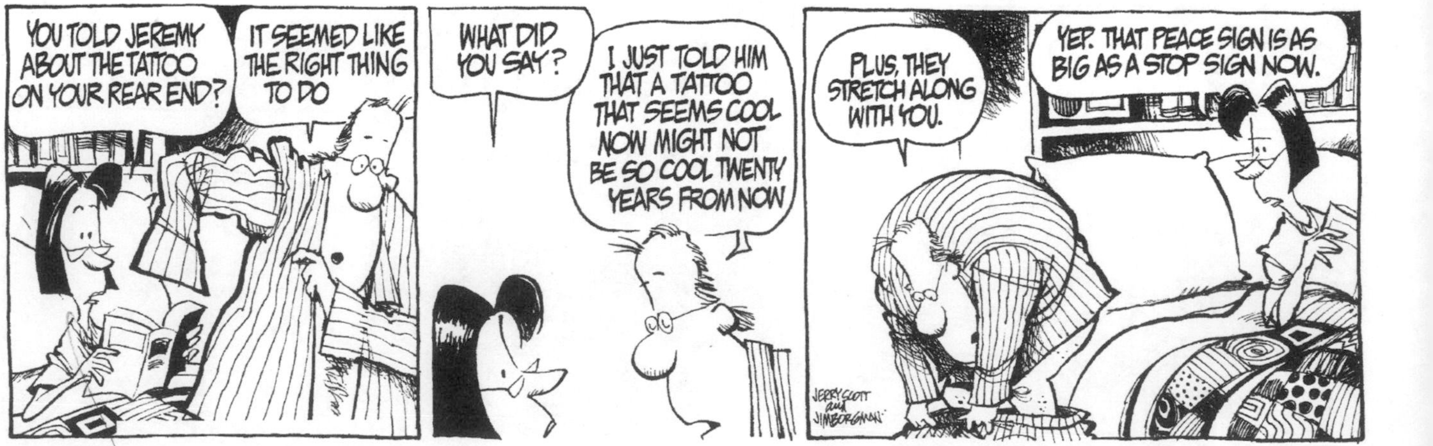
YOU TOLD JEREMY ABOUT THE TATTOO ON YOUR REAR END?
IT SEEMED LIKE THE RIGHT THING TO DO
WHAT DID YOU SAY?
I JUST TOLD HIM THAT A TATTOO THAT SEEMS COOL NOW MIGHT NOT BE SO COOL TWENTY YEARS FROM NOW
PLUS, THEY STRETCH ALONG WITH YOU.
YEP. THAT PEACE SIGN IS AS BIG AS A STOP SIGN NOW.

Zits®

by JERRY SCOTT and JIM BORGMAN

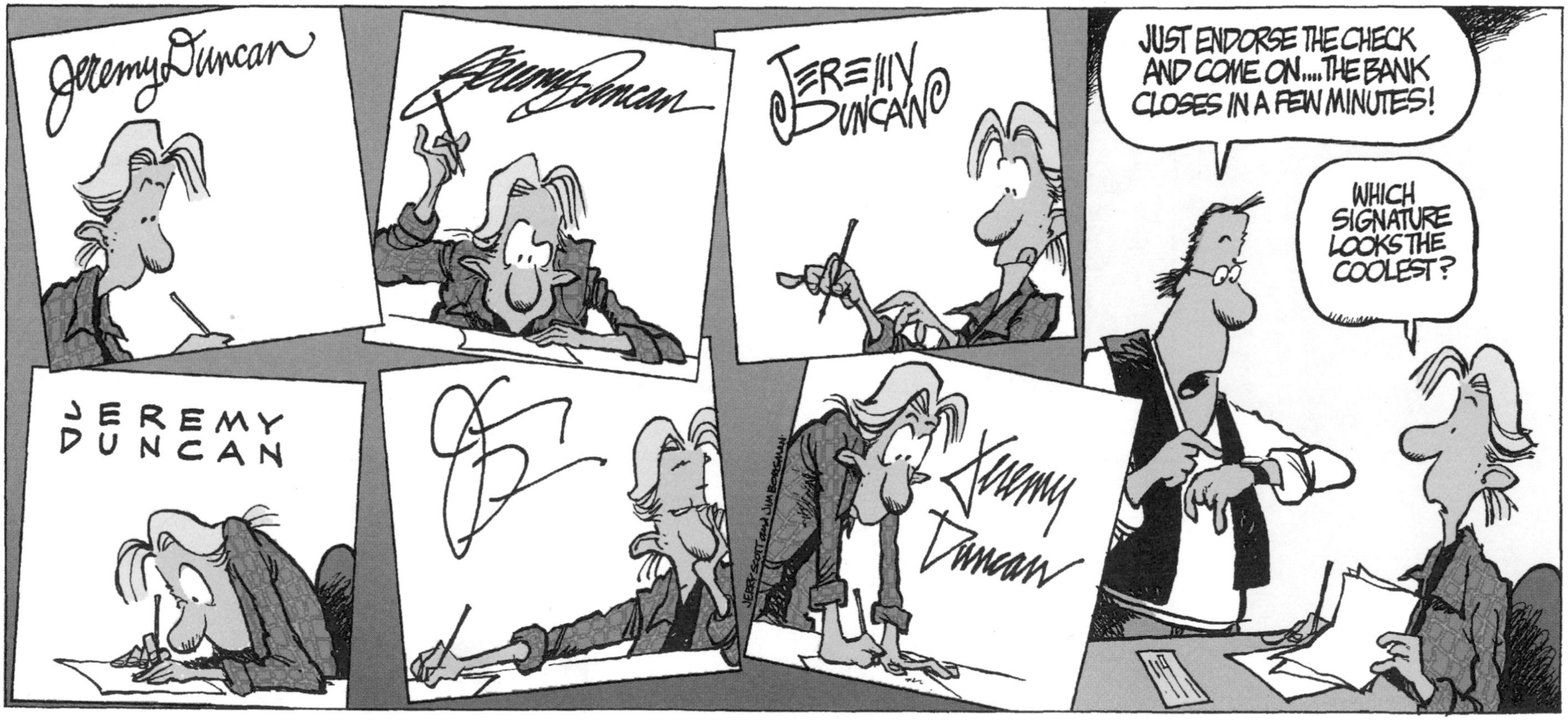

Jeremy Duncan
JEREMY DUNCAN
Jeremy Duncan
JERRY SCOTT and JIM BORGMAN
JUST ENDORSE THE CHECK AND COME ON.... THE BANK CLOSES IN A FEW MINUTES!
WHICH SIGNATURE LOOKS THE COOLEST?

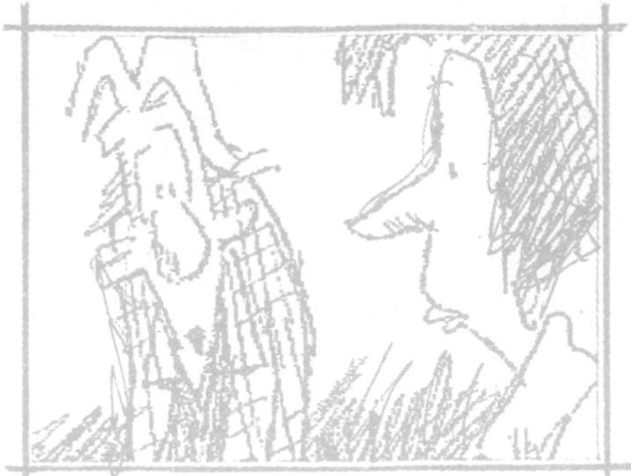

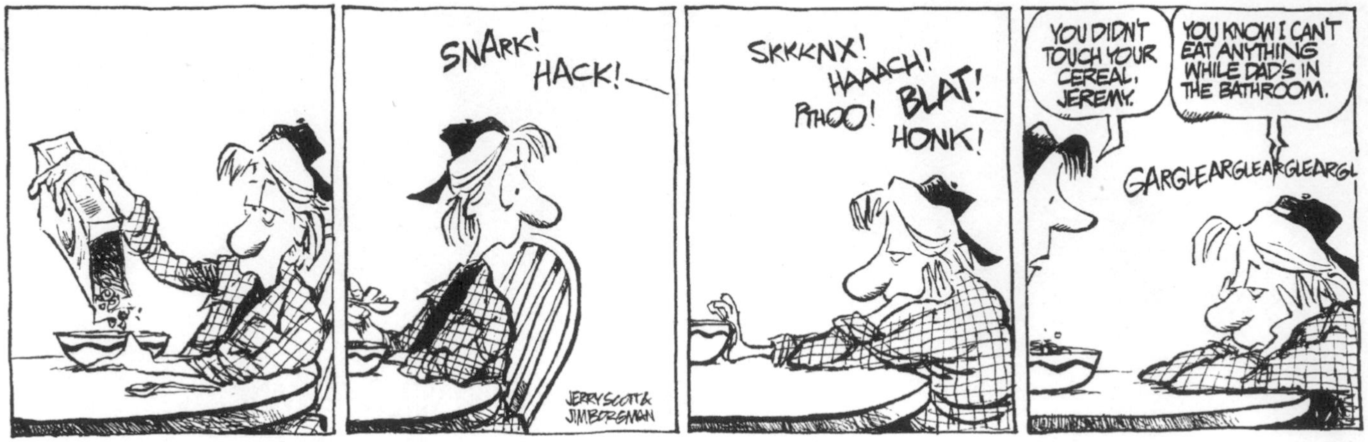
SNARK! HACK!
JERRY SCOTT & JIM BORGMAN
SKKKNX! HAAACH! PTHOO! BLAT! HONK!
YOU DIDN'T TOUCH YOUR CEREAL, JEREMY.
YOU KNOW I CAN'T EAT ANYTHING WHILE DAD'S IN THE BATHROOM.
GARGLEARGLEARGLEARGL

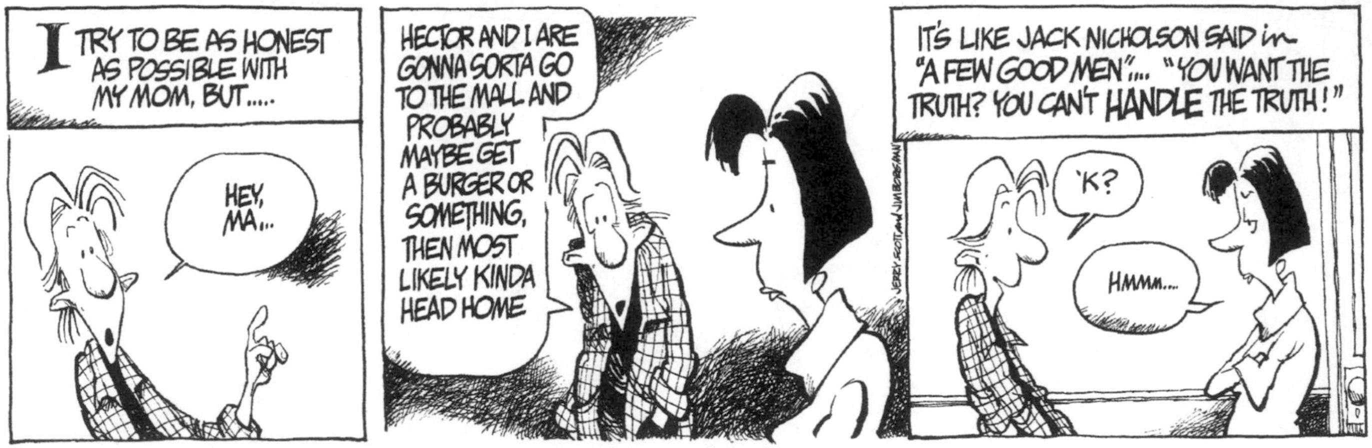
I TRY TO BE AS HONEST AS POSSIBLE WITH MY MOM, BUT.....
HEY, MA...
HECTOR AND I ARE GONNA SORTA GO TO THE MALL AND PROBABLY MAYBE GET A BURGER OR SOMETHING, THEN MOST LIKELY KINDA HEAD HOME
IT'S LIKE JACK NICHOLSON SAID in "A FEW GOOD MEN"... "YOU WANT THE TRUTH? YOU CAN'T HANDLE THE TRUTH!"
'K?
HMMM...

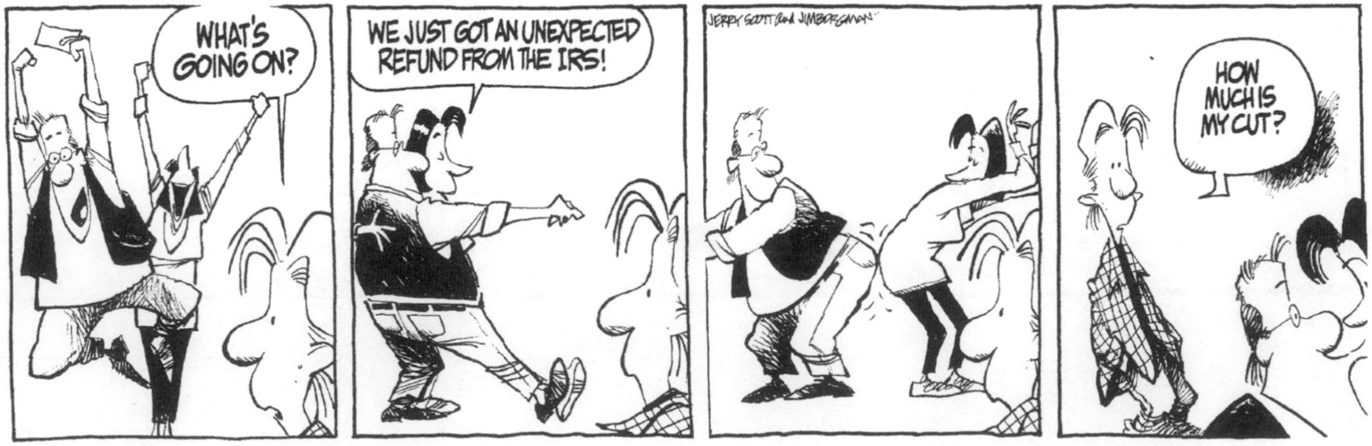
WHAT'S GOING ON?
WE JUST GOT AN UNEXPECTED REFUND FROM THE IRS!
HOW MUCH IS MY CUT?

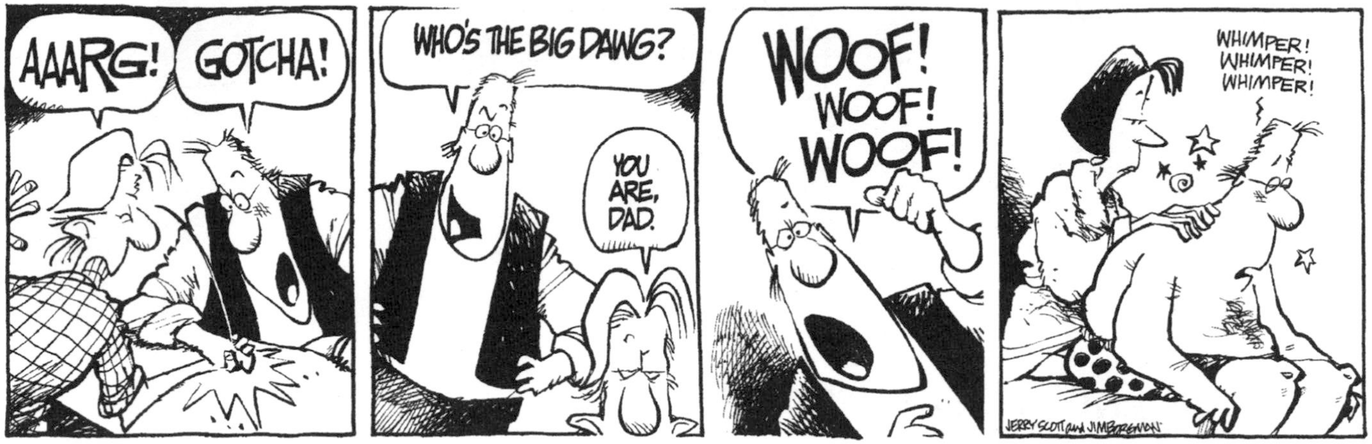
AAARG!
GOTCHA!
WHO'S THE BIG DAWG?
YOU ARE, DAD.
WOOF! WOOF! WOOF!
WHIMPER! WHIMPER! WHIMPER!
JERRY SCOTT and JIM BORGMAN

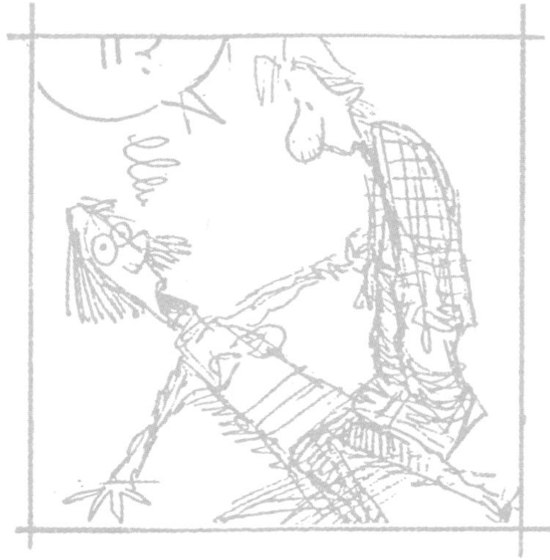

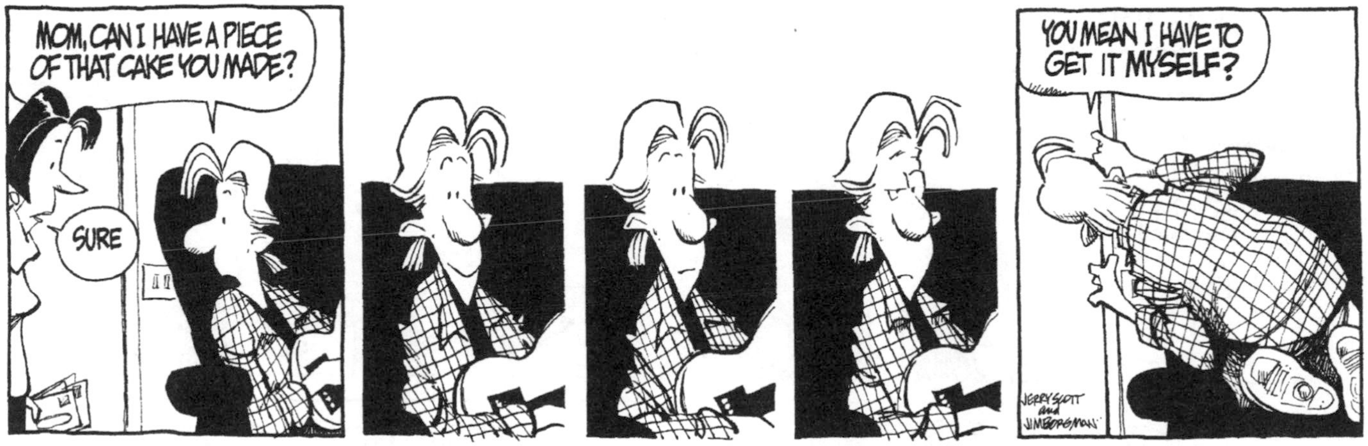
MOM, CAN I HAVE A PIECE OF THAT CAKE YOU MADE?
SURE
YOU MEAN I HAVE TO GET IT MYSELF?
JERRY SCOTT and JIM BORGMAN

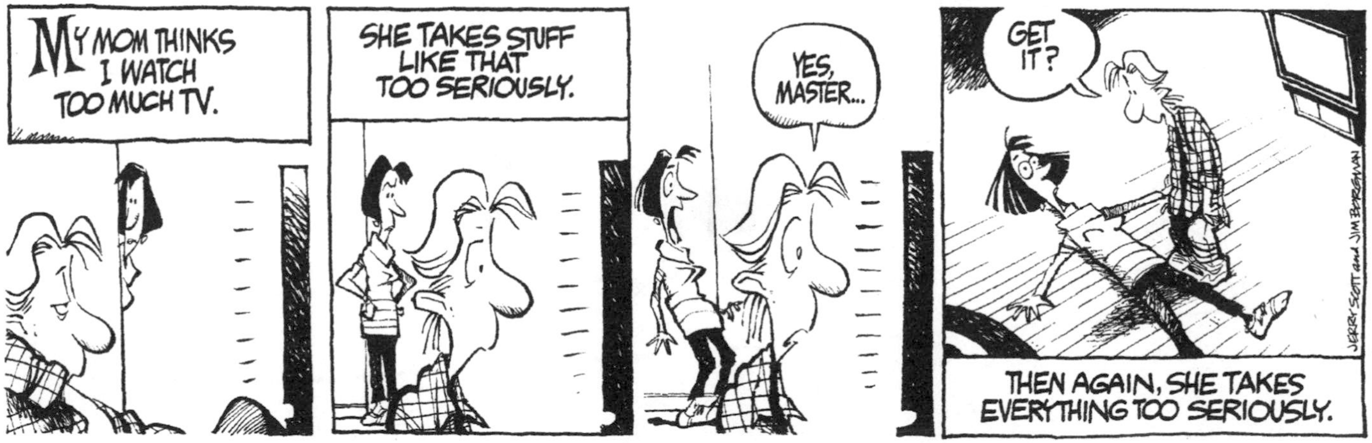
MY MOM THINKS I WATCH TOO MUCH TV.
SHE TAKES STUFF LIKE THAT TOO SERIOUSLY.
YES, MASTER...
GET IT?
THEN AGAIN, SHE TAKES EVERYTHING TOO SERIOUSLY.
JERRY SCOTT and JIM BORGMAN

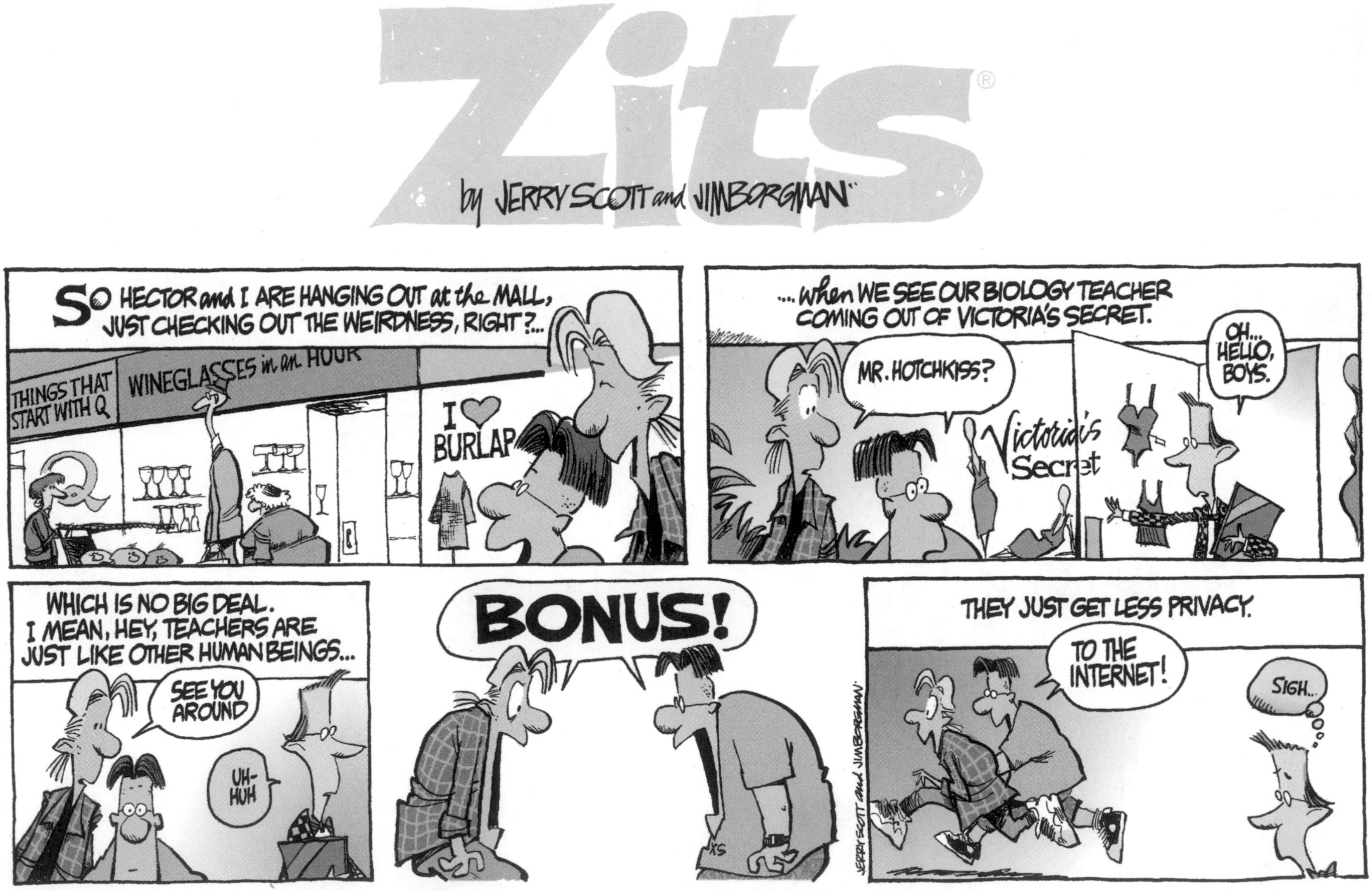
Zits®
by JERRY SCOTT and JIM BORGMAN
SO HECTOR and I ARE HANGING OUT at the MALL, JUST CHECKING OUT THE WEIRDNESS, RIGHT?...
THINGS THAT START WITH Q
WINEGLASSES in an HOUR
I ♥ BURLAP
...when WE SEE OUR BIOLOGY TEACHER COMING OUT OF VICTORIA'S SECRET.
MR. HOTCHKISS?
OH... HELLO, BOYS.
Victoria's Secret
WHICH IS NO BIG DEAL. I MEAN, HEY, TEACHERS ARE JUST LIKE OTHER HUMAN BEINGS...
SEE YOU AROUND
UH-HUH
BONUS!
THEY JUST GET LESS PRIVACY.
TO THE INTERNET!
SIGH...
JERRY SCOTT and JIM BORGMAN

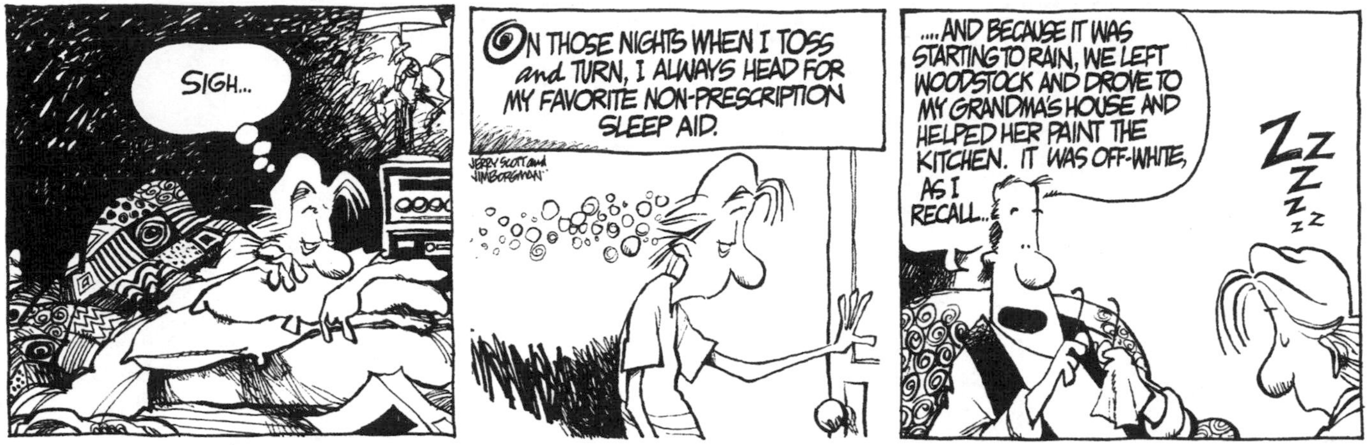
SIGH...
ON THOSE NIGHTS WHEN I TOSS and TURN, I ALWAYS HEAD FOR MY FAVORITE NON-PRESCRIPTION SLEEP AID.
JERRY SCOTT and JIMBORGMAN
....AND BECAUSE IT WAS STARTING TO RAIN, WE LEFT WOODSTOCK AND DROVE TO MY GRANDMA'S HOUSE AND HELPED HER PAINT THE KITCHEN. IT WAS OFF-WHITE, AS I RECALL...
ZZZZZZ

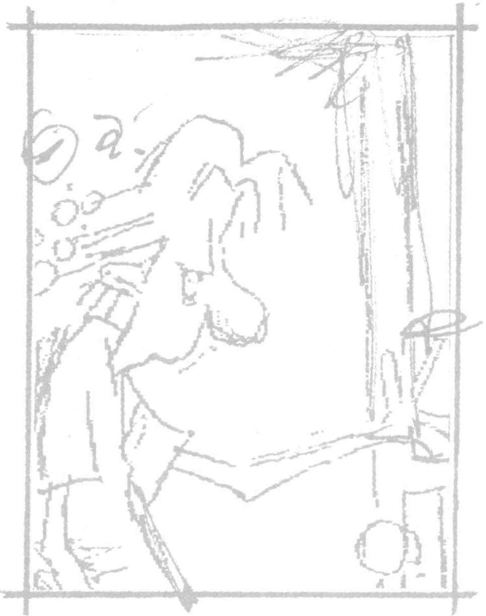

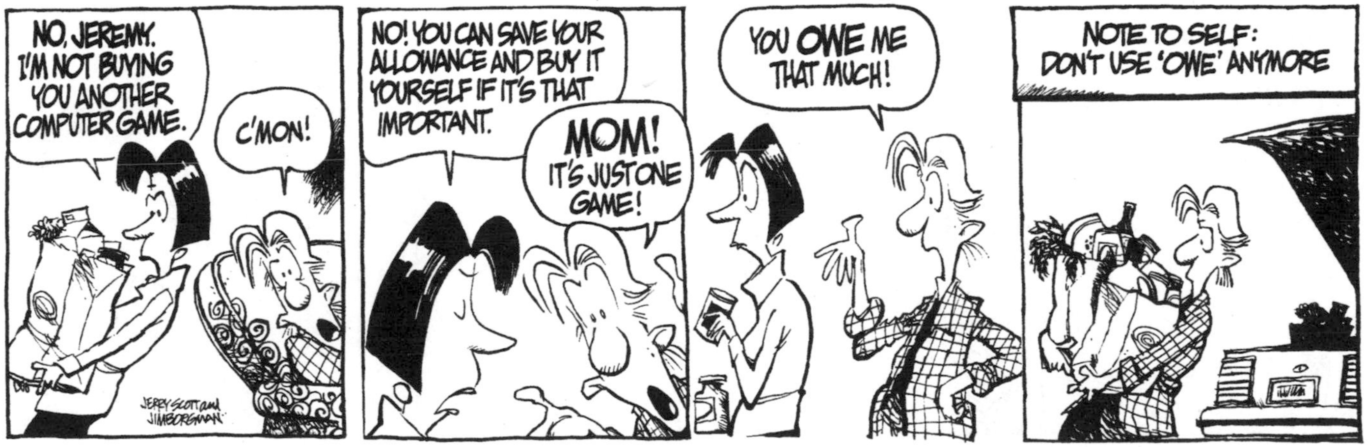
NO, JEREMY. I'M NOT BUYING YOU ANOTHER COMPUTER GAME.
C'MON!
JERRY SCOTT and JIMBORGMAN
NO! YOU CAN SAVE YOUR ALLOWANCE AND BUY IT YOURSELF IF IT'S THAT IMPORTANT.
MOM! IT'S JUST ONE GAME!
YOU OWE ME THAT MUCH!
NOTE TO SELF: DON'T USE 'OWE' ANYMORE

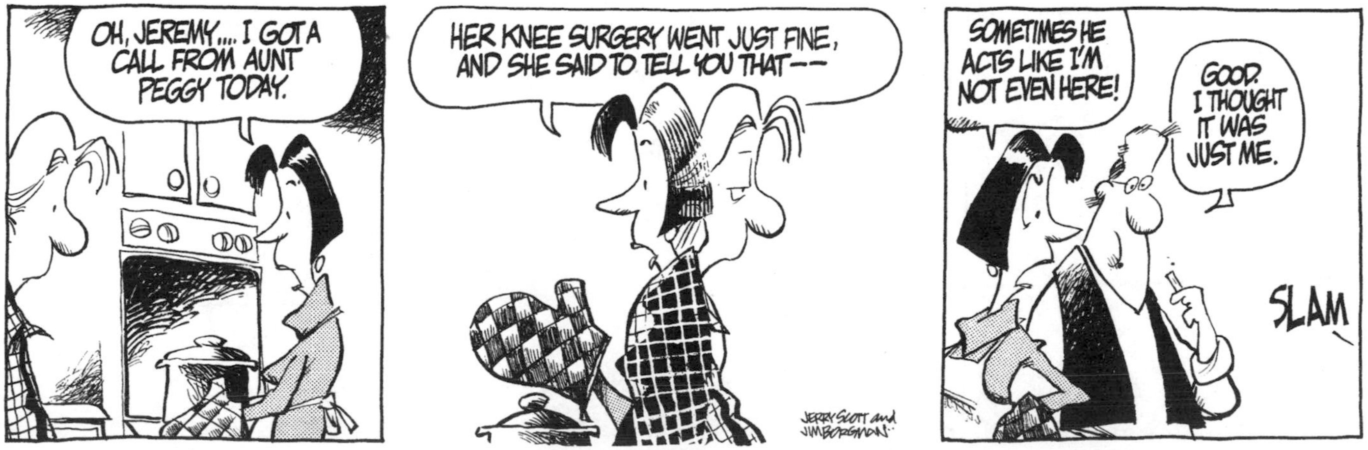
OH, JEREMY.... I GOT A CALL FROM AUNT PEGGY TODAY.
HER KNEE SURGERY WENT JUST FINE, AND SHE SAID TO TELL YOU THAT--
JERRY SCOTT and JIMBORGMAN
SOMETIMES HE ACTS LIKE I'M NOT EVEN HERE!
GOOD. I THOUGHT IT WAS JUST ME.
SLAM

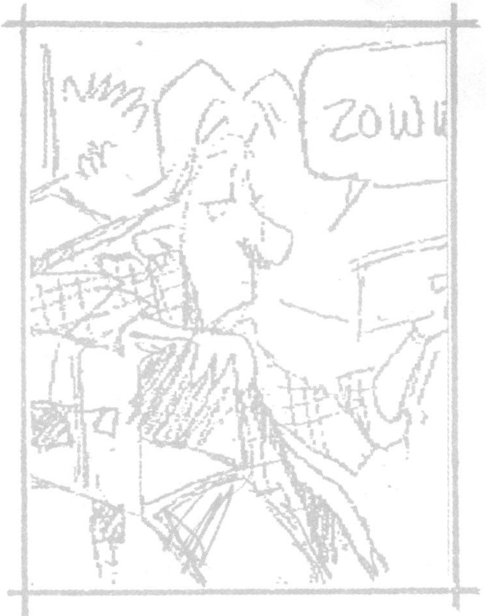

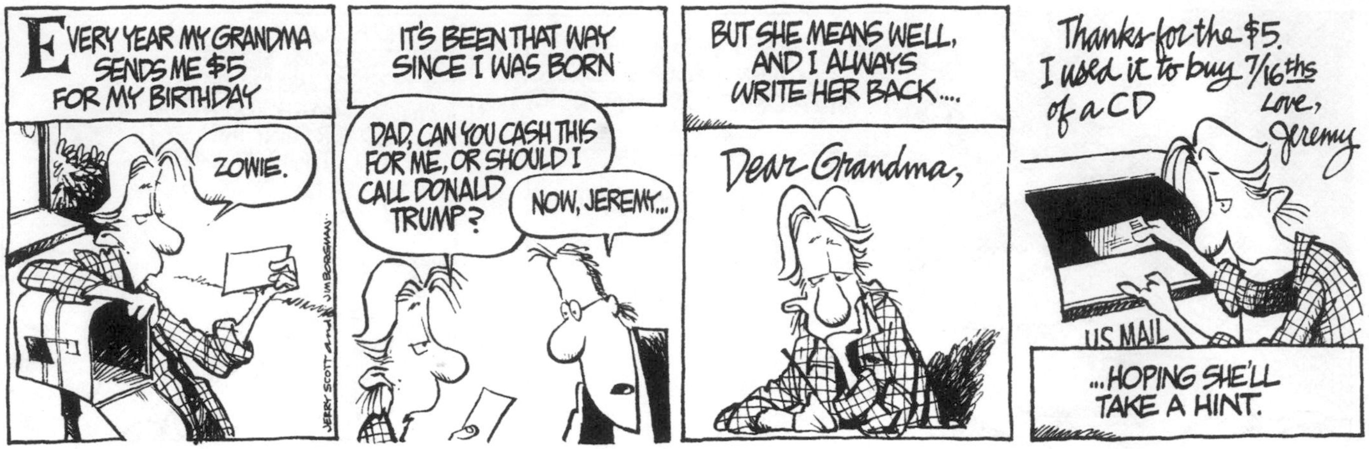
EVERY YEAR MY GRANDMA SENDS ME $5 FOR MY BIRTHDAY
ZOWIE.
JERRY SCOTT and JIM BORGMAN
IT'S BEEN THAT WAY SINCE I WAS BORN
DAD, CAN YOU CASH THIS FOR ME, OR SHOULD I CALL DONALD TRUMP?
NOW, JEREMY...
BUT SHE MEANS WELL, AND I ALWAYS WRITE HER BACK....
Dear Grandma,
Thanks for the $5. I used it to buy 7/16ths of a CD
Love, Jeremy
US MAIL
...HOPING SHE'LL TAKE A HINT.

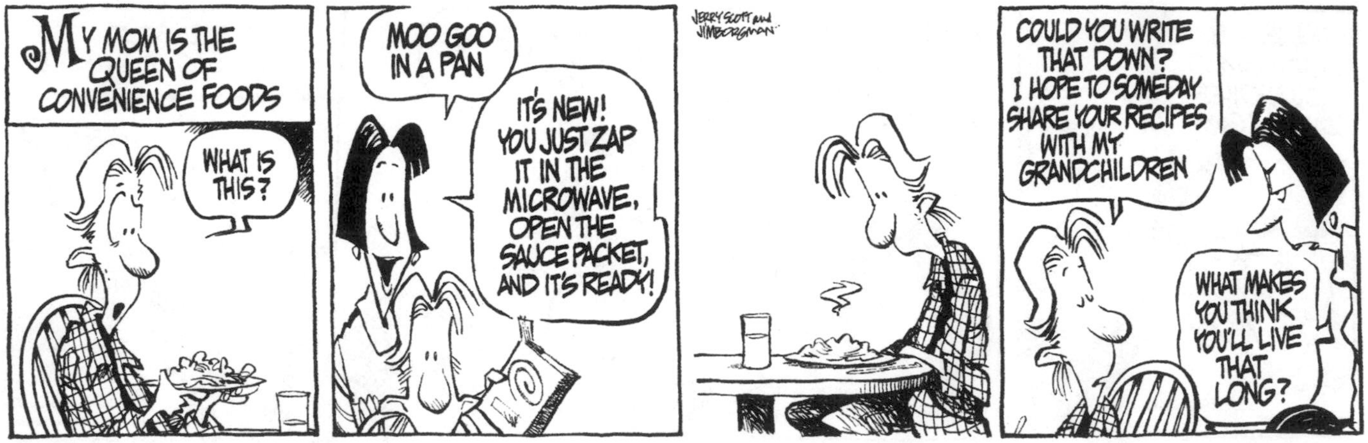
MY MOM IS THE QUEEN OF CONVENIENCE FOODS
WHAT IS THIS?
MOO GOO IN A PAN
IT'S NEW! YOU JUST ZAP IT IN THE MICROWAVE, OPEN THE SAUCE PACKET, AND IT'S READY!
JERRY SCOTT and JIM BORGMAN
COULD YOU WRITE THAT DOWN? I HOPE TO SOMEDAY SHARE YOUR RECIPES WITH MY GRANDCHILDREN
WHAT MAKES YOU THINK YOU'LL LIVE THAT LONG?

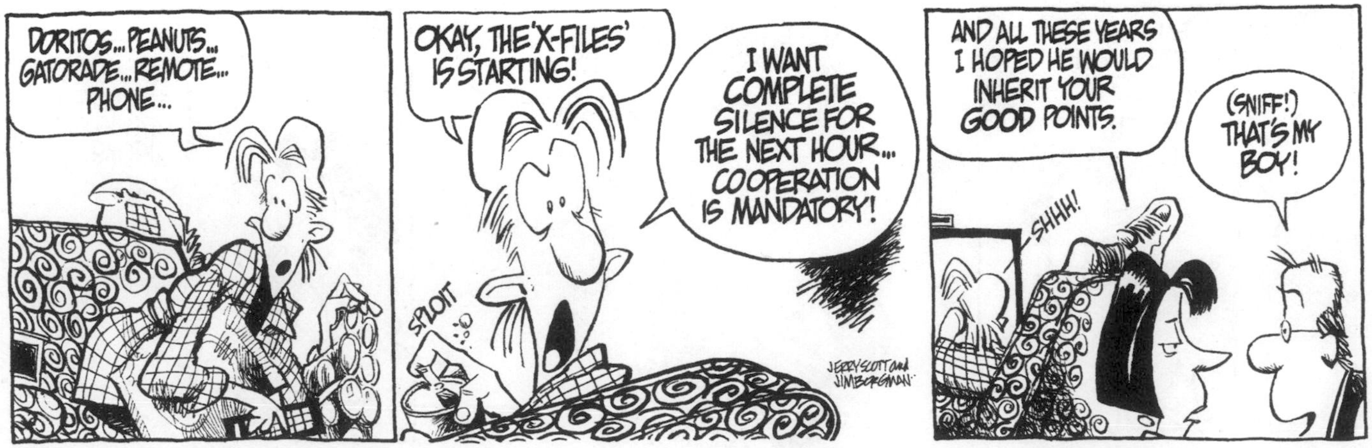
DORITOS... PEANUTS... GATORADE... REMOTE... PHONE...
OKAY, THE 'X-FILES' IS STARTING!
I WANT COMPLETE SILENCE FOR THE NEXT HOUR... COOPERATION IS MANDATORY!
SPLOIT
JERRY SCOTT and JIM BORGMAN
AND ALL THESE YEARS I HOPED HE WOULD INHERIT YOUR GOOD POINTS.
(SNIFF!) THAT'S MY BOY!
SHHH!

Zits®

by JERRY SCOTT and JIM BORGMAN

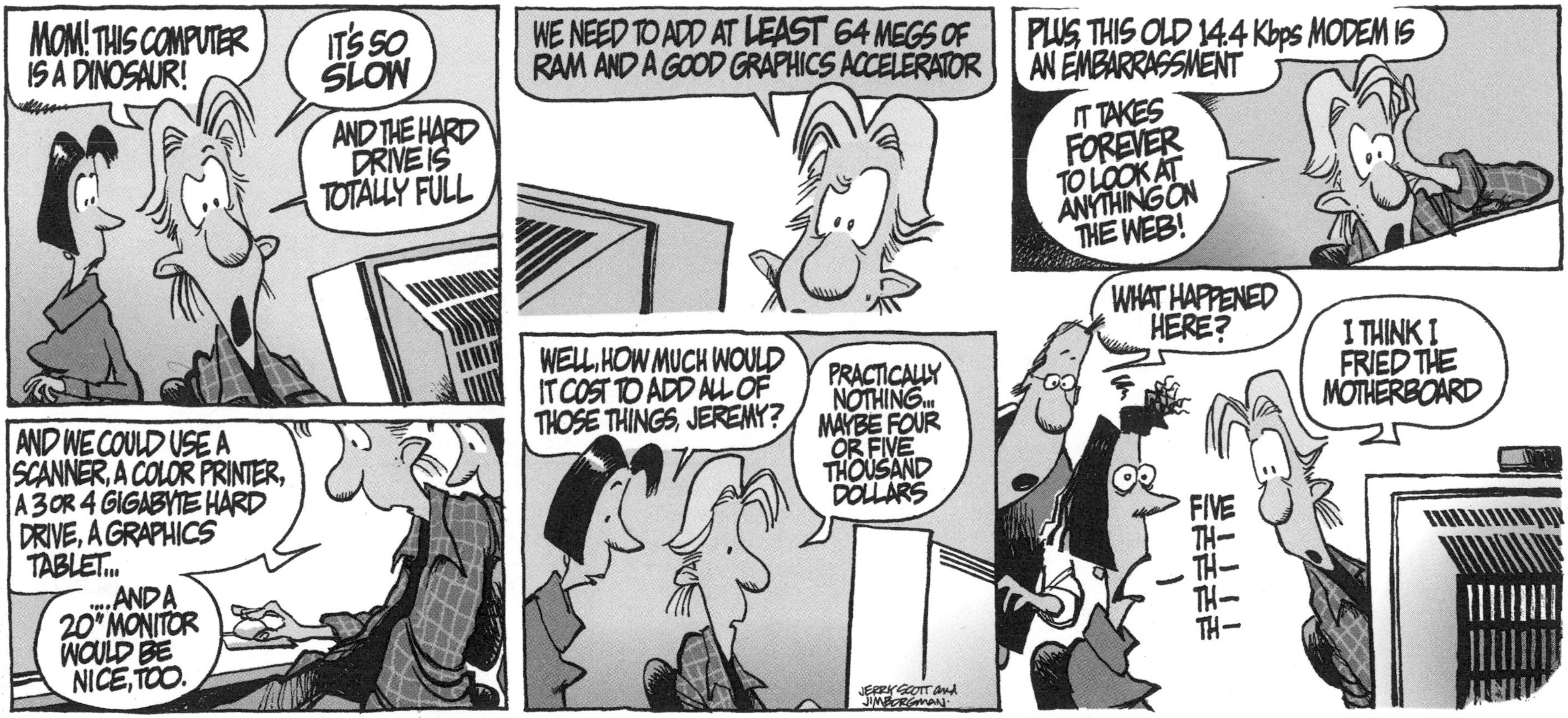

MOM! THIS COMPUTER IS A DINOSAUR!
IT'S SO SLOW
AND THE HARD DRIVE IS TOTALLY FULL
WE NEED TO ADD AT LEAST 64 MEGS OF RAM AND A GOOD GRAPHICS ACCELERATOR
PLUS, THIS OLD 14.4 Kbps MODEM IS AN EMBARRASSMENT
IT TAKES FOREVER TO LOOK AT ANYTHING ON THE WEB!
AND WE COULD USE A SCANNER, A COLOR PRINTER, A 3 OR 4 GIGABYTE HARD DRIVE, A GRAPHICS TABLET...
....AND A 20" MONITOR WOULD BE NICE, TOO.
WELL, HOW MUCH WOULD IT COST TO ADD ALL OF THOSE THINGS, JEREMY?
PRACTICALLY NOTHING... MAYBE FOUR OR FIVE THOUSAND DOLLARS
JERRY SCOTT and JIM BORGMAN
WHAT HAPPENED HERE?
I THINK I FRIED THE MOTHERBOARD
FIVE TH— TH— TH— TH—

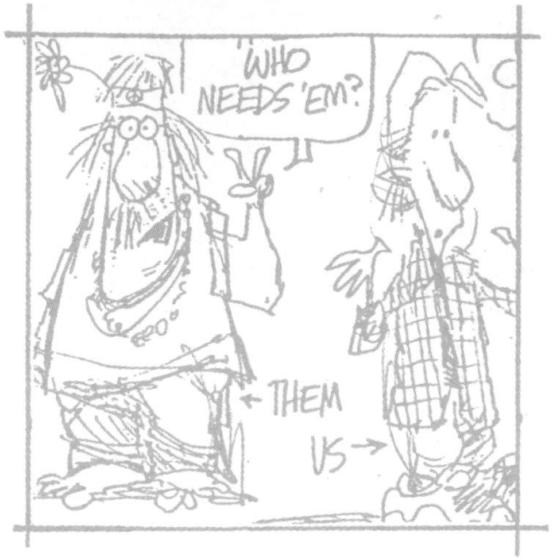
WHO NEEDS 'EM?
← THEM
US →

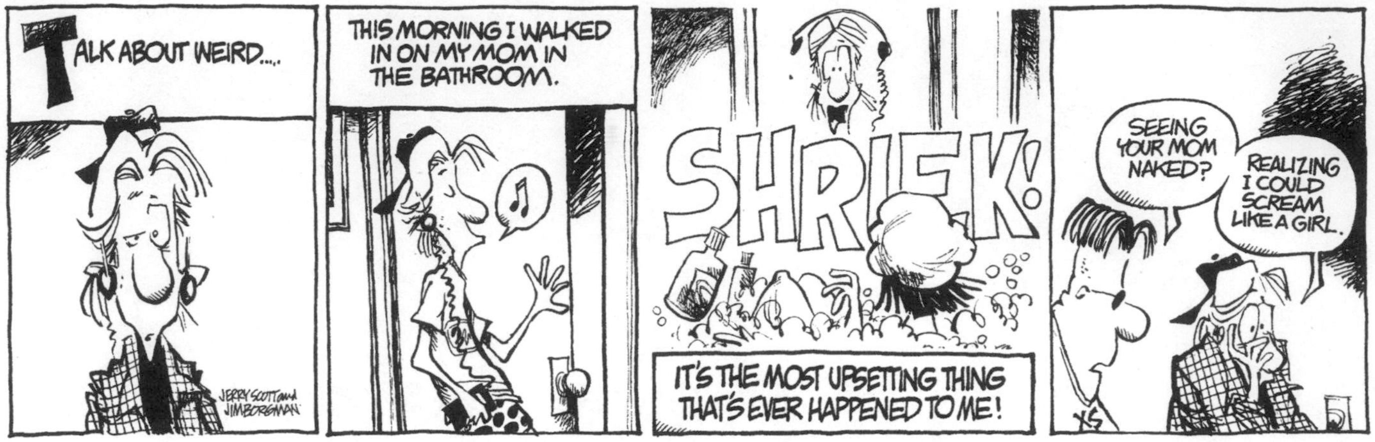
TALK ABOUT WEIRD....
JERRY SCOTT and JIM BORGMAN
THIS MORNING I WALKED IN ON MY MOM IN THE BATHROOM.
SHRIEK!
IT'S THE MOST UPSETTING THING THAT'S EVER HAPPENED TO ME!
SEEING YOUR MOM NAKED?
REALIZING I COULD SCREAM LIKE A GIRL.

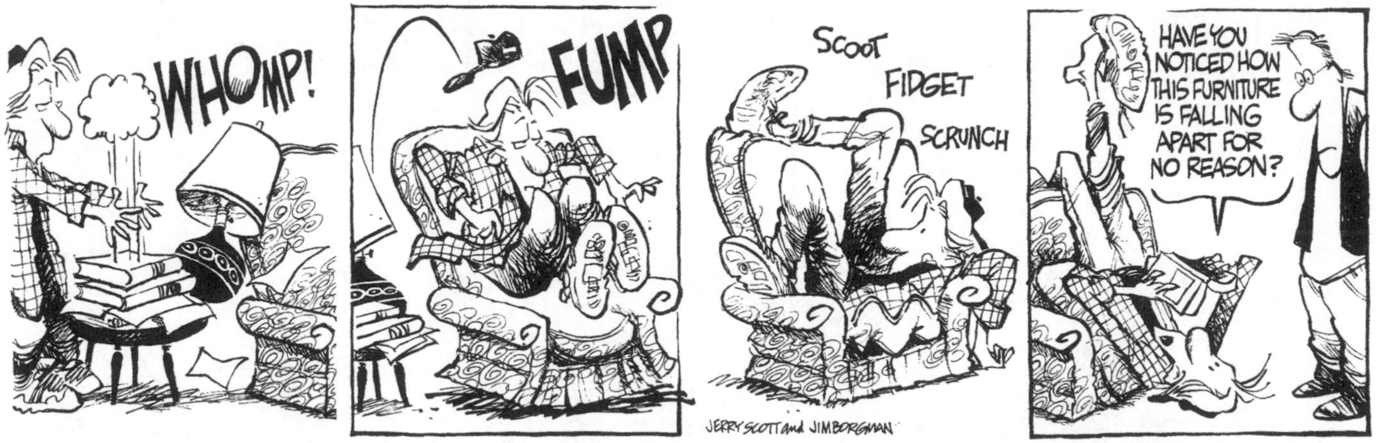
WHOMP!
FUMP
SCOOT
FIDGET
SCRUNCH
JERRY SCOTT and JIM BORGMAN
HAVE YOU NOTICED HOW THIS FURNITURE IS FALLING APART FOR NO REASON?

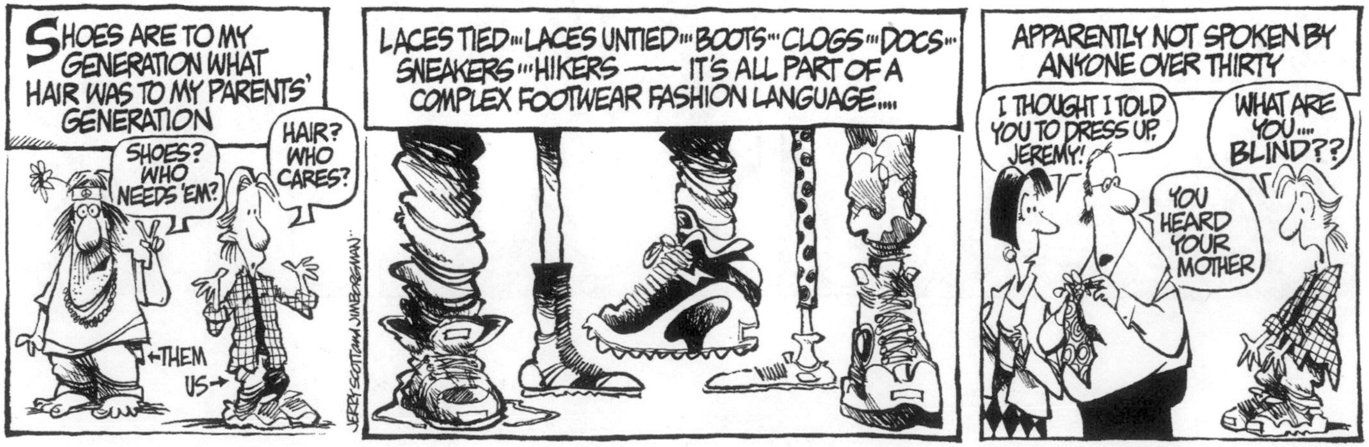
SHOES ARE TO MY GENERATION WHAT HAIR WAS TO MY PARENTS' GENERATION
SHOES? WHO NEEDS 'EM?
HAIR? WHO CARES?
←THEM
US→
JERRY SCOTT and JIM BORGMAN
LACES TIED... LACES UNTIED... BOOTS... CLOGS... DOCS... SNEAKERS... HIKERS — IT'S ALL PART OF A COMPLEX FOOTWEAR FASHION LANGUAGE....
APPARENTLY NOT SPOKEN BY ANYONE OVER THIRTY
I THOUGHT I TOLD YOU TO DRESS UP, JEREMY!
YOU HEARD YOUR MOTHER
WHAT ARE YOU.... BLIND??

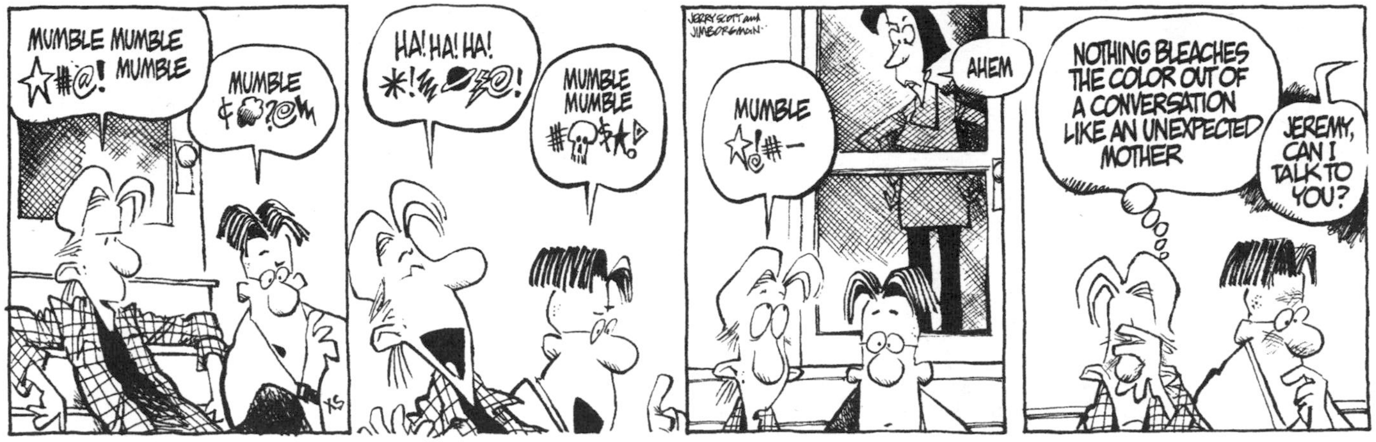
MUMBLE MUMBLE
MUMBLE
MUMBLE
HA! HA! HA!
MUMBLE MUMBLE
JERRY SCOTT and JIM BORGMAN
MUMBLE
AHEM
NOTHING BLEACHES THE COLOR OUT OF A CONVERSATION LIKE AN UNEXPECTED MOTHER
JEREMY, CAN I TALK TO YOU?

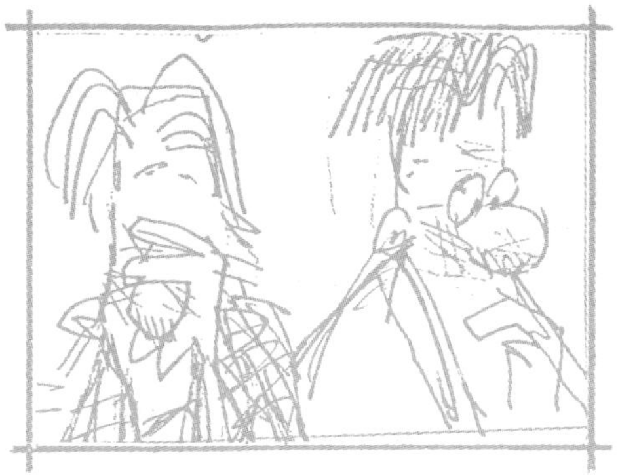

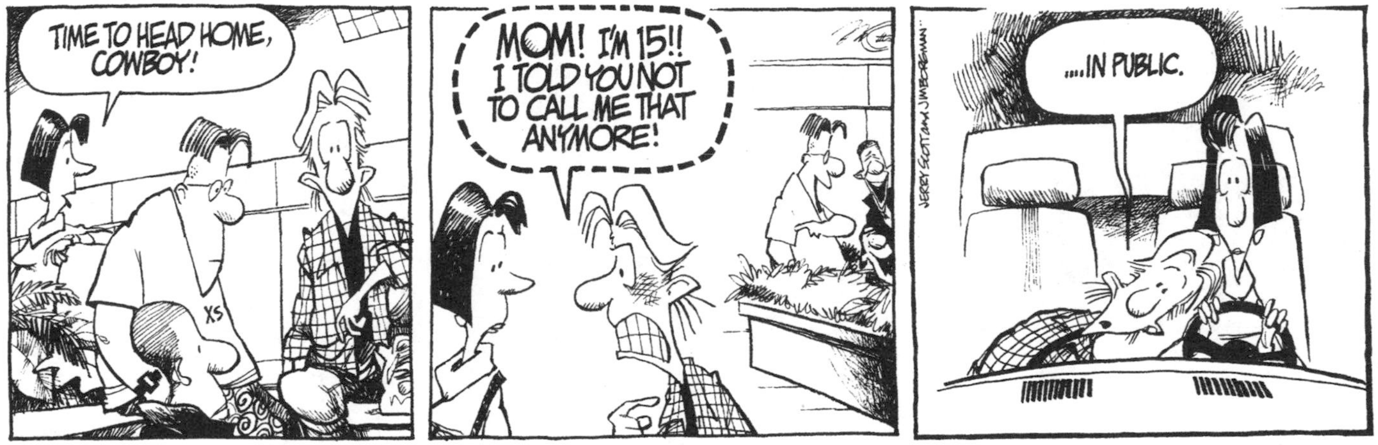
TIME TO HEAD HOME, COWBOY!
MOM! I'M 15!! I TOLD YOU NOT TO CALL ME THAT ANYMORE!
JERRY SCOTT and JIM BORGMAN
....IN PUBLIC.

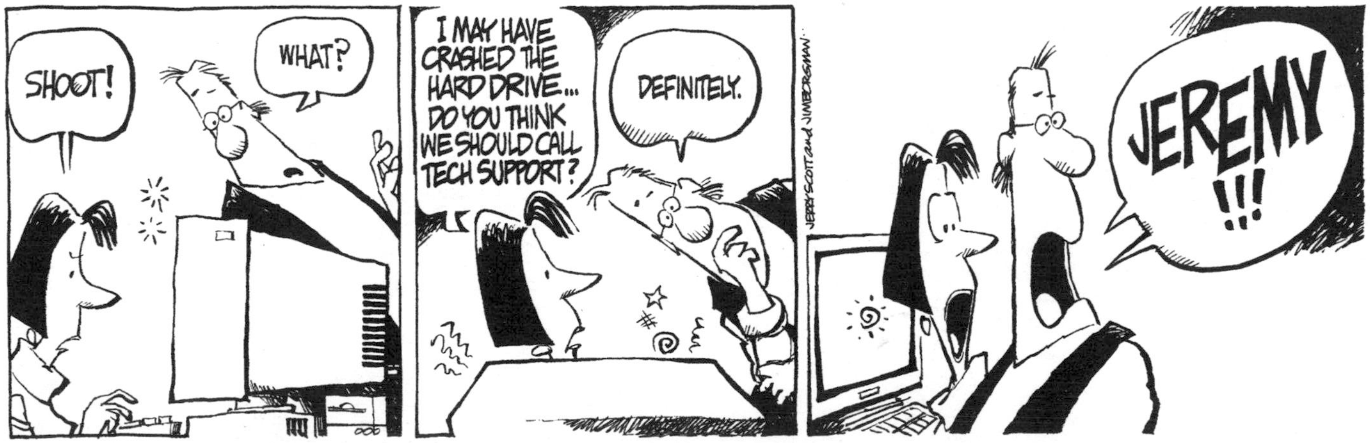
SHOOT!
WHAT?
I MAY HAVE CRASHED THE HARD DRIVE... DO YOU THINK WE SHOULD CALL TECH SUPPORT?
DEFINITELY.
JERRY SCOTT and JIM BORGMAN
JEREMY !!!

Zits®

by JERRY SCOTT and JIM BORGMAN

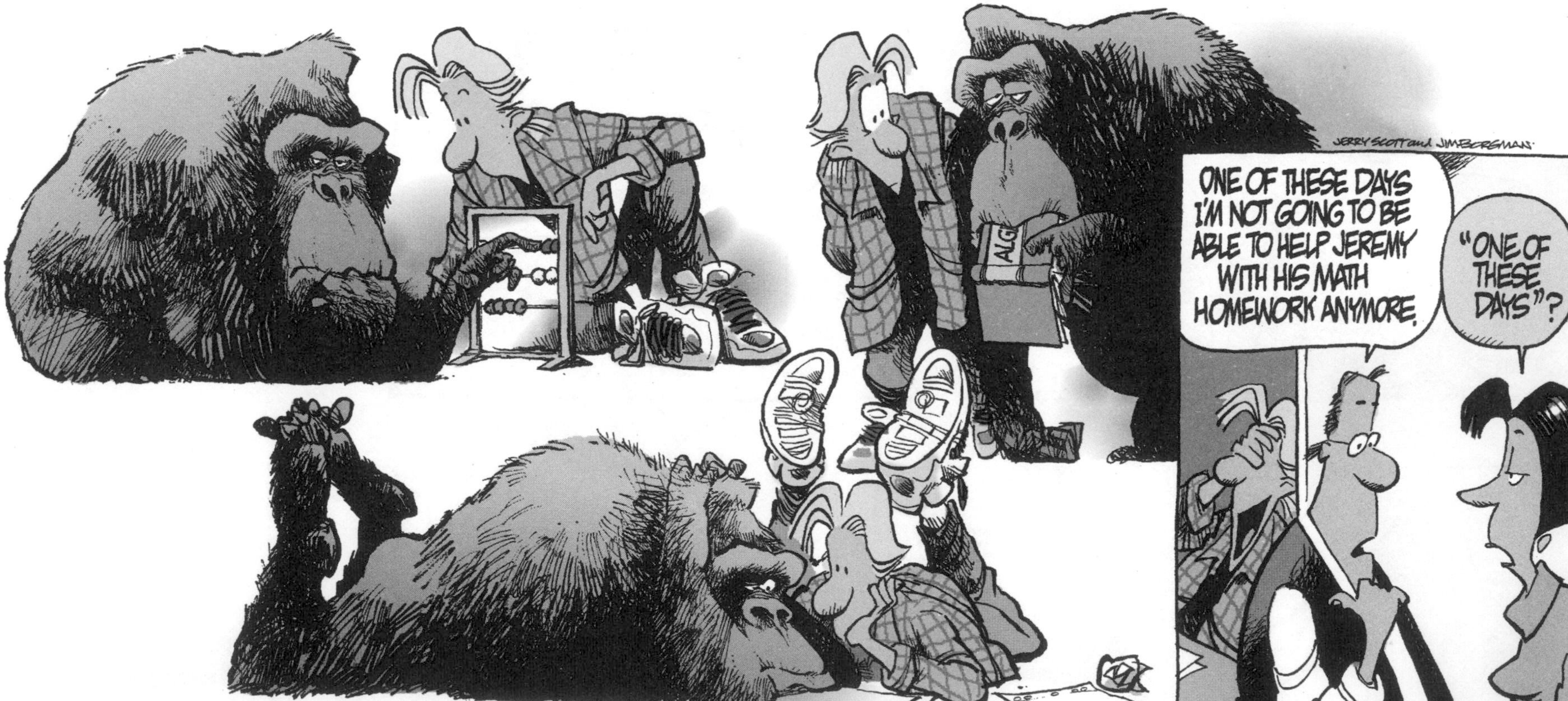
JERRY SCOTT and JIM BORGMAN
ONE OF THESE DAYS I'M NOT GOING TO BE ABLE TO HELP JEREMY WITH HIS MATH HOMEWORK ANYMORE.
"ONE OF THESE DAYS"?

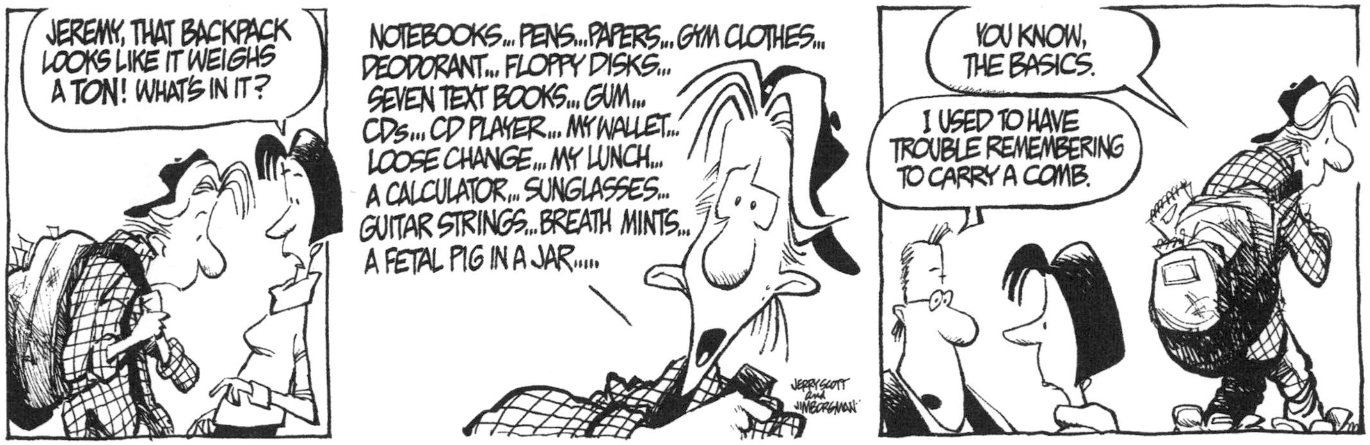
JEREMY, THAT BACKPACK LOOKS LIKE IT WEIGHS A TON! WHAT'S IN IT?
NOTEBOOKS... PENS... PAPERS... GYM CLOTHES... DEODORANT... FLOPPY DISKS... SEVEN TEXT BOOKS... GUM... CDs... CD PLAYER... MY WALLET... LOOSE CHANGE... MY LUNCH... A CALCULATOR... SUNGLASSES... GUITAR STRINGS... BREATH MINTS... A FETAL PIG IN A JAR.....
JERRY SCOTT and JIM BORGMAN
YOU KNOW, THE BASICS.
I USED TO HAVE TROUBLE REMEMBERING TO CARRY A COMB.

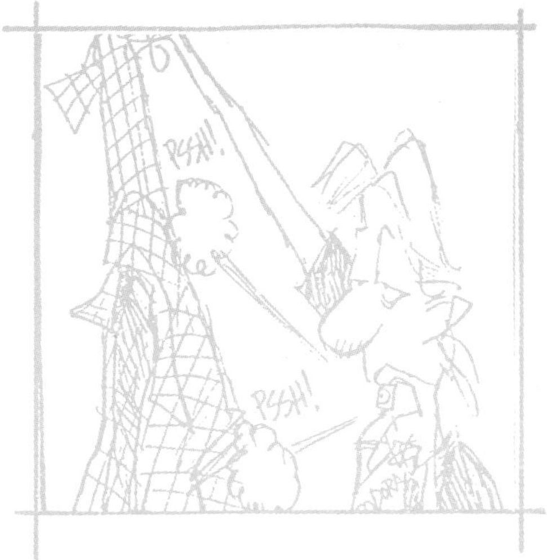
PSSH!
PSSH!

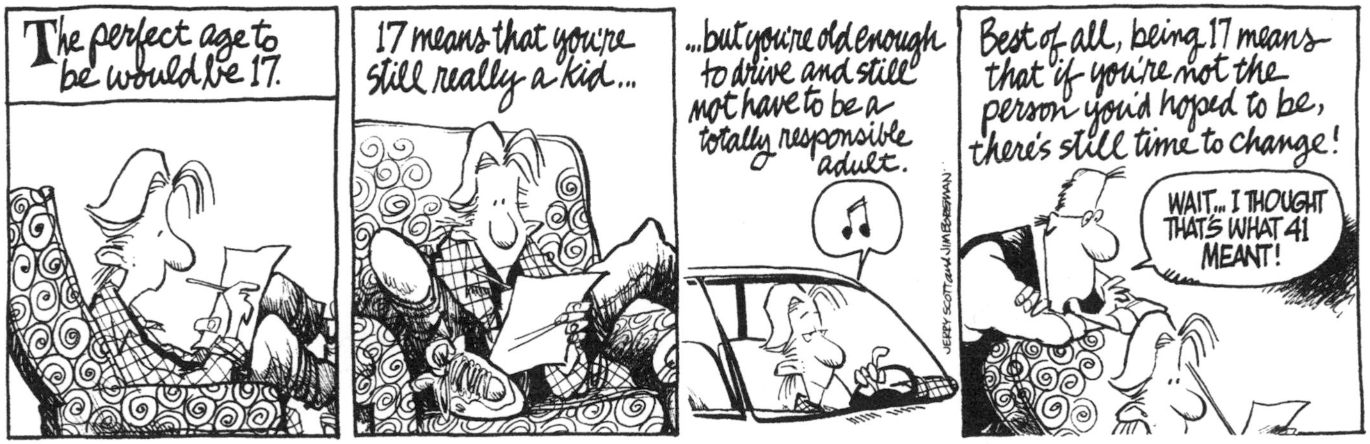
The perfect age to be would be 17.
17 means that you're still really a kid...
...but you're old enough to drive and still not have to be a totally responsible adult.
JERRY SCOTT and JIM BORGMAN
Best of all, being 17 means that if you're not the person you'd hoped to be, there's still time to change!
WAIT... I THOUGHT THAT'S WHAT 41 MEANT!

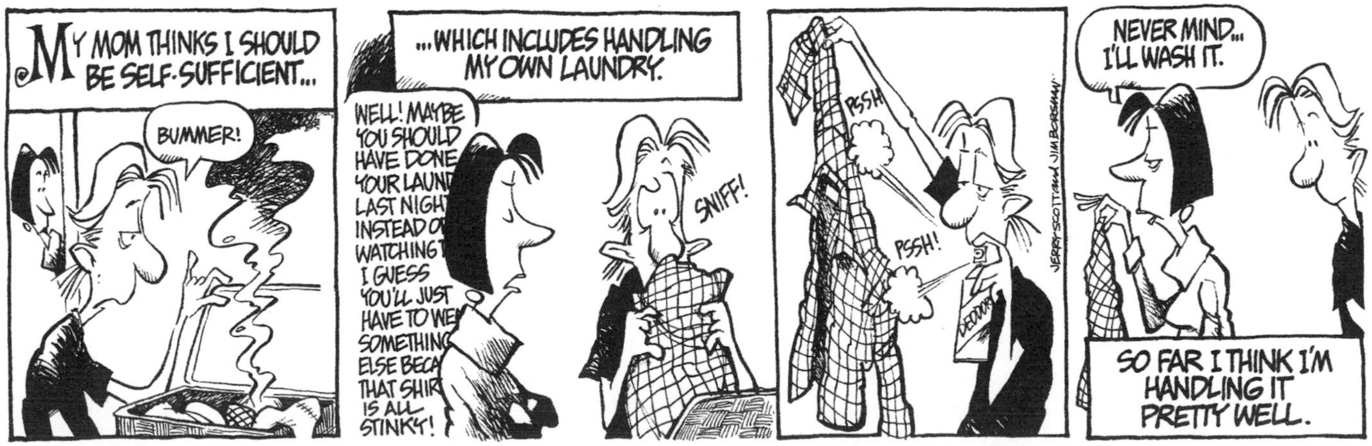
MY MOM THINKS I SHOULD BE SELF-SUFFICIENT...
BUMMER!
...WHICH INCLUDES HANDLING MY OWN LAUNDRY.
WELL! MAYBE YOU SHOULD HAVE DONE YOUR LAUND LAST NIGHT INSTEAD O WATCHING T I GUESS YOU'LL JUST HAVE TO WE SOMETHING ELSE BECA THAT SHIR IS ALL STINKY!
SNIFF!
PSSH!
PSSH!
DEODOR
JERRY SCOTT and JIM BORGMAN
NEVER MIND... I'LL WASH IT.
SO FAR I THINK I'M HANDLING IT PRETTY WELL.

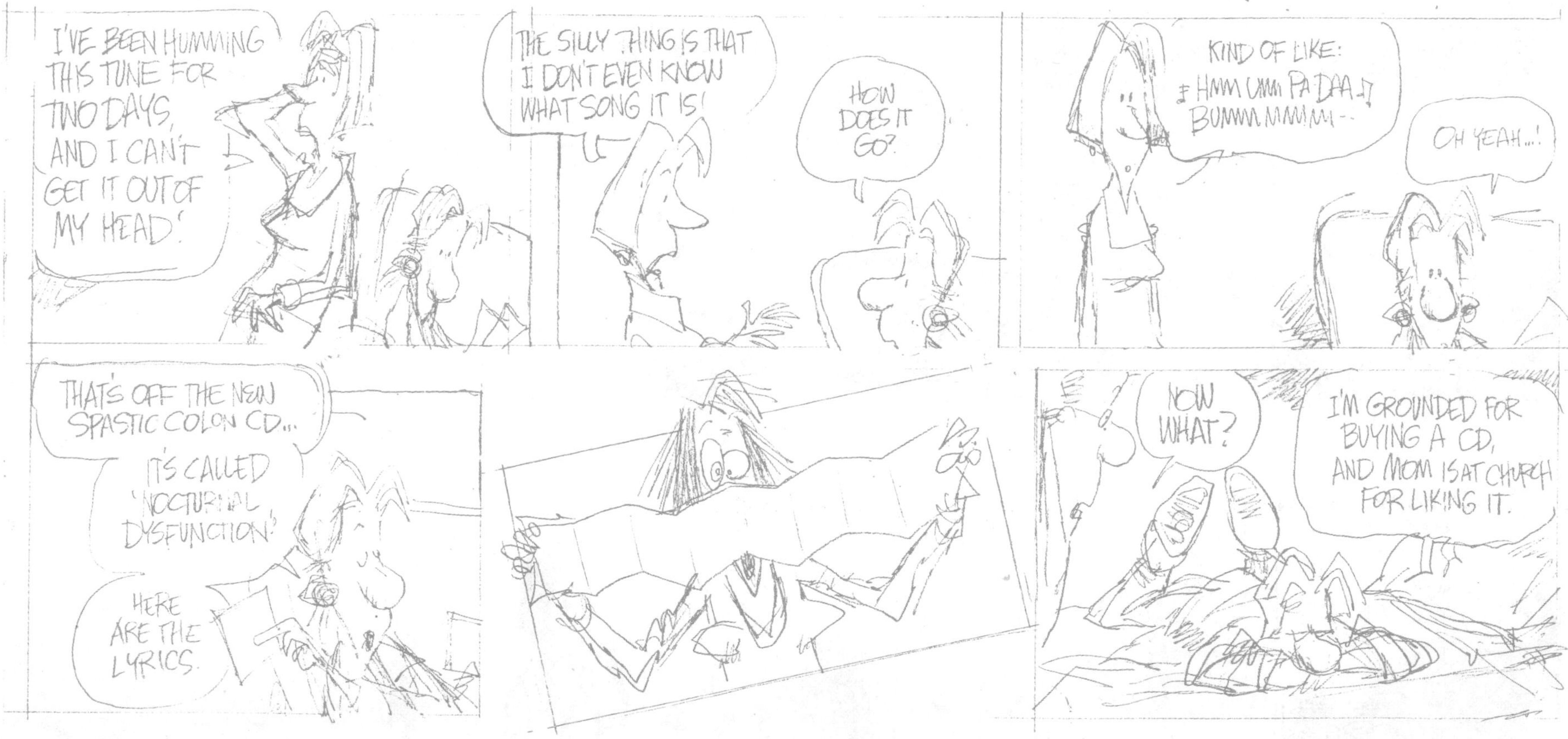
I'VE BEEN HUMMING THIS TUNE FOR TWO DAYS, AND I CAN'T GET IT OUT OF MY HEAD!
THE SILLY THING IS THAT I DON'T EVEN KNOW WHAT SONG IT IS!
HOW DOES IT GO?
KIND OF LIKE: ♪ HMM UMM PA DAA ♫ BUMMMMMMM--
OH YEAH...!
THAT'S OFF THE NEW SPASTIC COLON CD...
IT'S CALLED 'NOCTURNAL DYSFUNCTION.'
HERE ARE THE LYRICS.
NOW WHAT?
I'M GROUNDED FOR BUYING A CD, AND MOM IS AT CHURCH FOR LIKING IT.

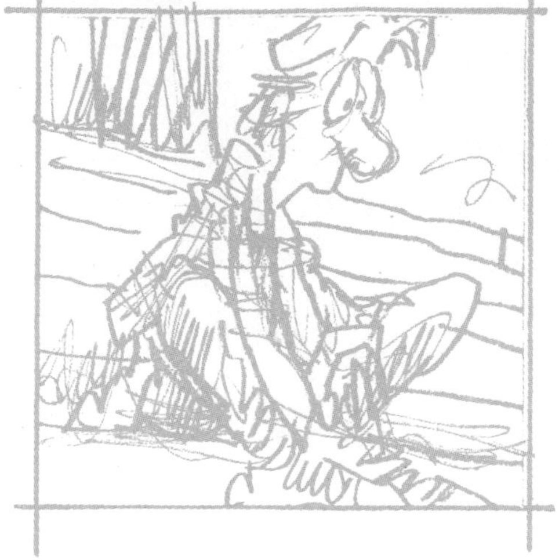

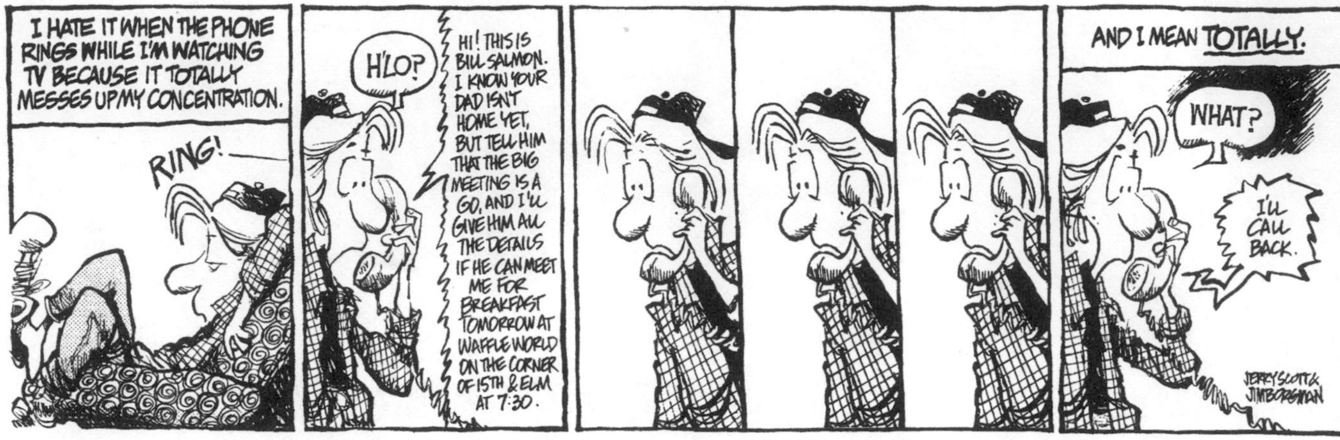

I HATE IT WHEN THE PHONE RINGS WHILE I'M WATCHING TV BECAUSE IT TOTALLY MESSES UP MY CONCENTRATION.
RING!
H'LO?
HI! THIS IS BILL SALMON. I KNOW YOUR DAD ISN'T HOME YET, BUT TELL HIM THAT THE BIG MEETING IS A GO, AND I'LL GIVE HIM ALL THE DETAILS IF HE CAN MEET ME FOR BREAKFAST TOMORROW AT WAFFLE WORLD ON THE CORNER OF 15TH & ELM AT 7:30.
AND I MEAN TOTALLY.
WHAT?
I'LL CALL BACK.
JERRY SCOTT & JIM BORGMAN

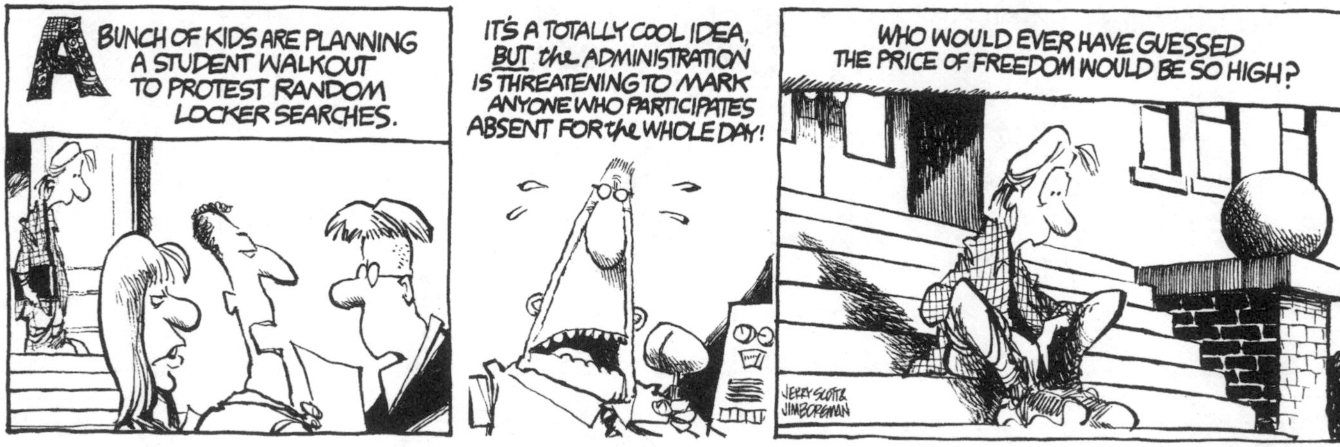

A BUNCH OF KIDS ARE PLANNING A STUDENT WALKOUT TO PROTEST RANDOM LOCKER SEARCHES.
IT'S A TOTALLY COOL IDEA, BUT the ADMINISTRATION IS THREATENING TO MARK ANYONE WHO PARTICIPATES ABSENT FOR the WHOLE DAY!
WHO WOULD EVER HAVE GUESSED THE PRICE OF FREEDOM WOULD BE SO HIGH?
JERRY SCOTT & JIM BORGMAN

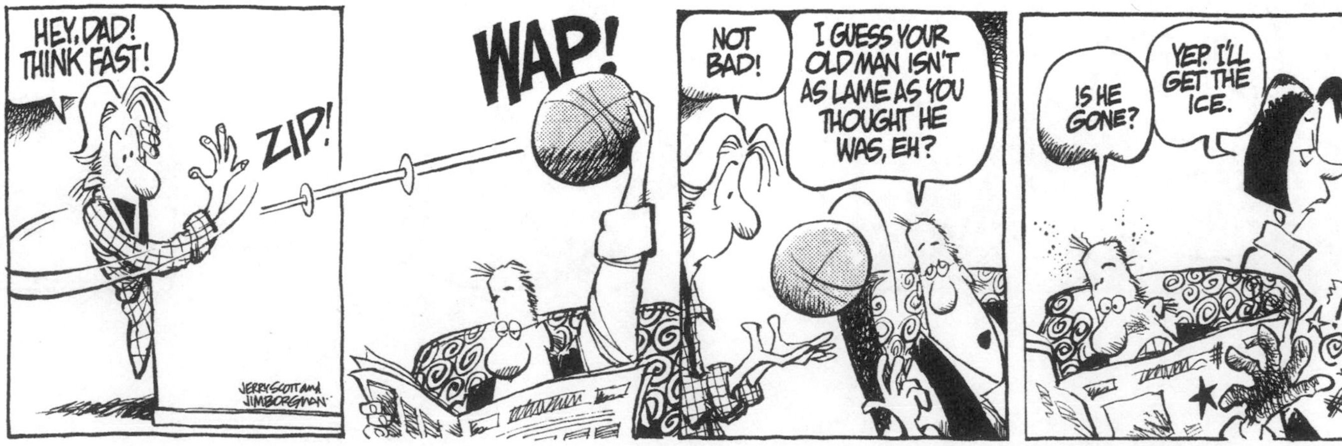

HEY, DAD! THINK FAST!
ZIP!
WAP!
JERRY SCOTT AND JIM BORGMAN
NOT BAD!
I GUESS YOUR OLD MAN ISN'T AS LAME AS YOU THOUGHT HE WAS, EH?
IS HE GONE?
YEP. I'LL GET THE ICE.

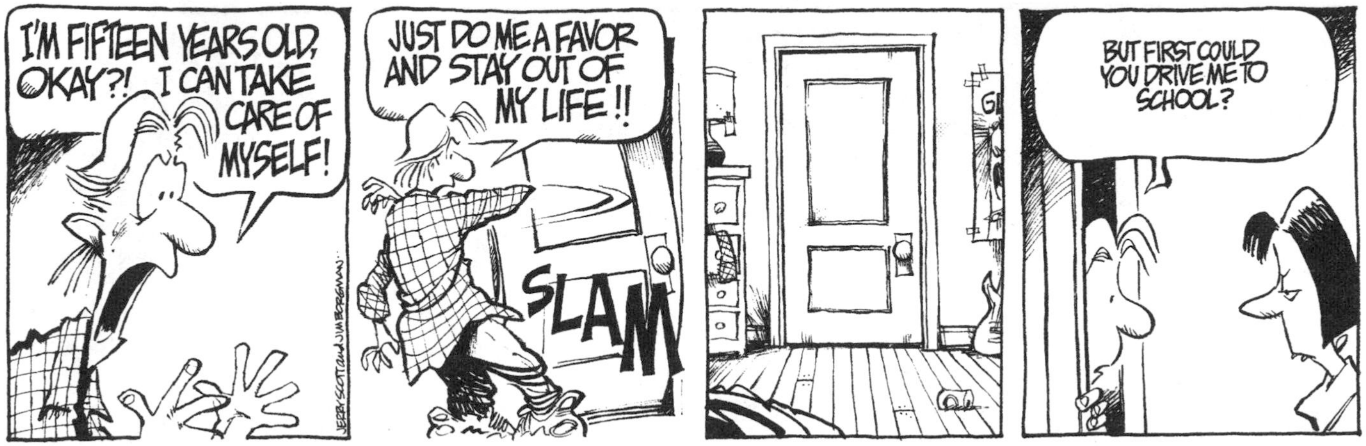
I'M FIFTEEN YEARS OLD, OKAY?! I CAN TAKE CARE OF MYSELF!
JUST DO ME A FAVOR AND STAY OUT OF MY LIFE!!
SLAM
JERRY SCOTT and JIM BORGMAN
BUT FIRST COULD YOU DRIVE ME TO SCHOOL?

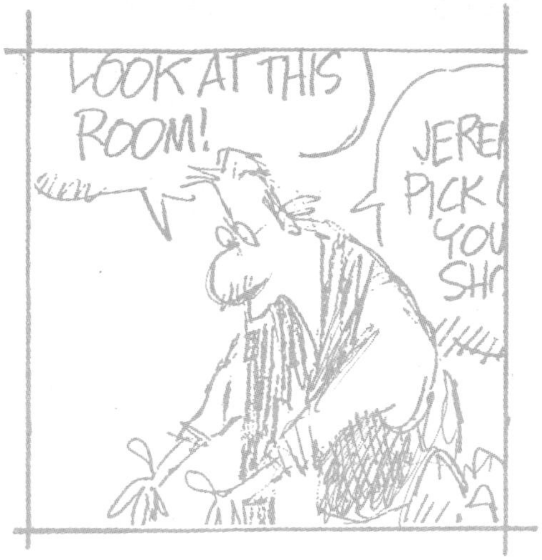
LOOK AT THIS ROOM!

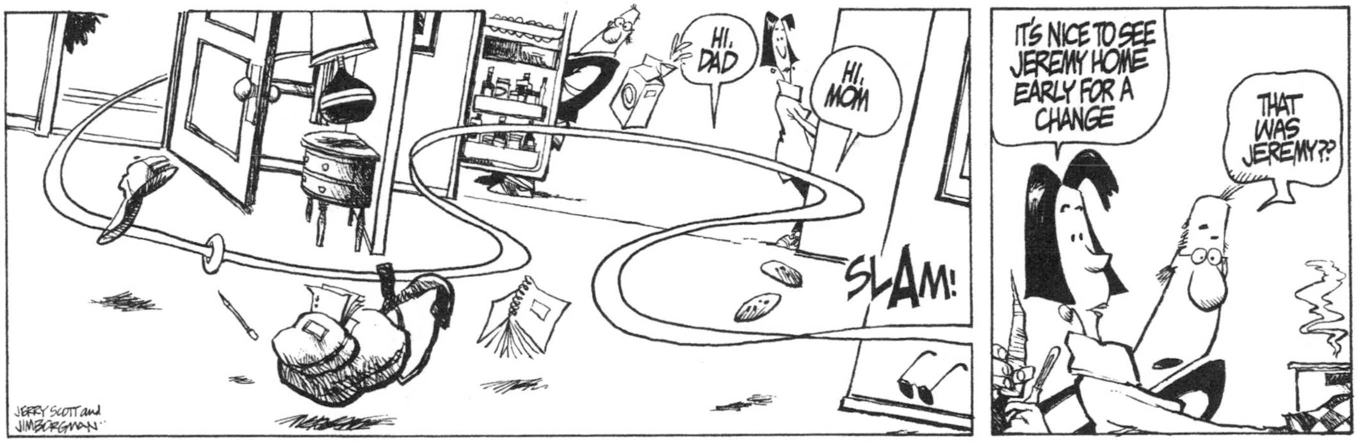
HI, DAD
HI, MOM
SLAM!
JERRY SCOTT and JIM BORGMAN
IT'S NICE TO SEE JEREMY HOME EARLY FOR A CHANGE
THAT WAS JEREMY??

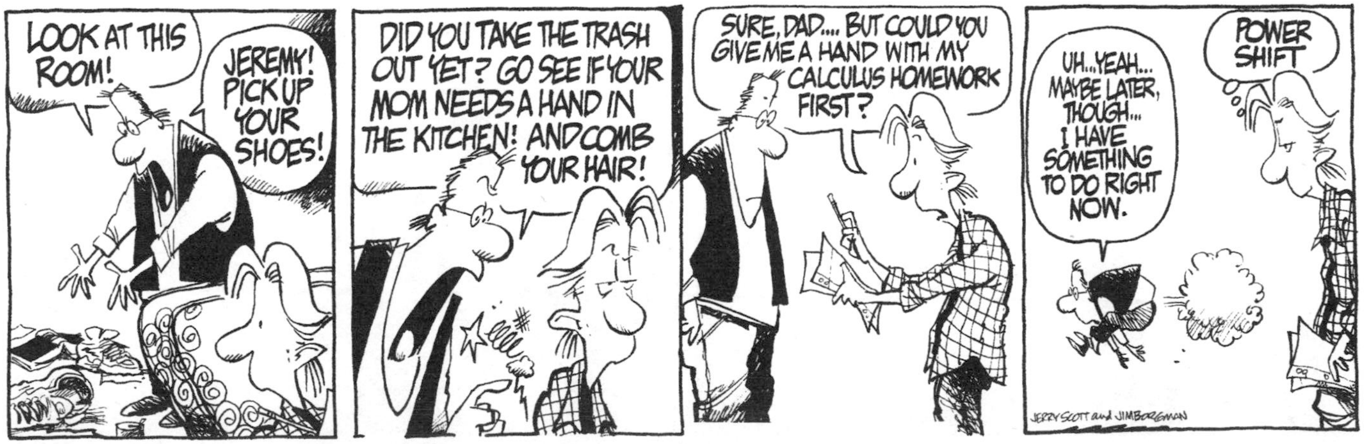
LOOK AT THIS ROOM!
JEREMY! PICK UP YOUR SHOES!
DID YOU TAKE THE TRASH OUT YET? GO SEE IF YOUR MOM NEEDS A HAND IN THE KITCHEN! AND COMB YOUR HAIR!
SURE, DAD.... BUT COULD YOU GIVE ME A HAND WITH MY CALCULUS HOMEWORK FIRST?
UH...YEAH... MAYBE LATER, THOUGH... I HAVE SOMETHING TO DO RIGHT NOW.
POWER SHIFT
JERRY SCOTT and JIM BORGMAN

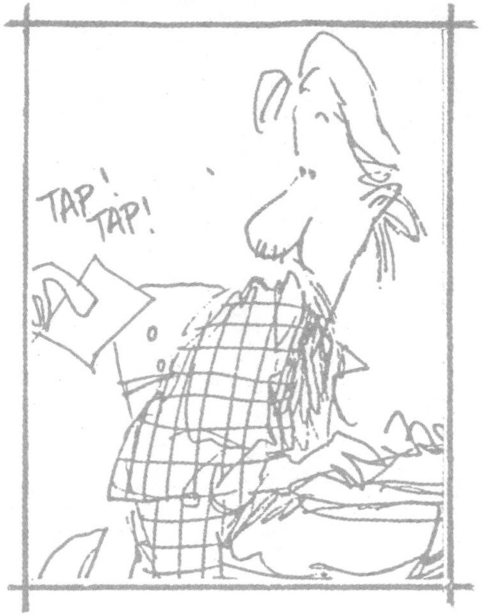

TAP! TAP!

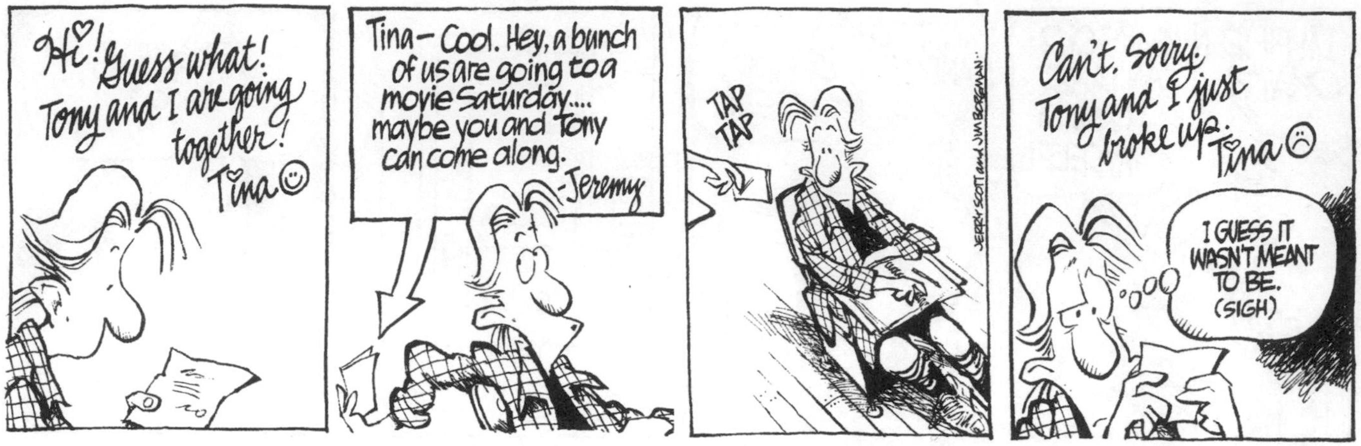

Hi! Guess what! Tony and I are going together! Tina ☺
Tina– Cool. Hey, a bunch of us are going to a movie Saturday.... maybe you and Tony can come along. -Jeremy
TAP TAP
JERRY SCOTT and JIM BORGMAN
Can't. Sorry. Tony and I just broke up. Tina ☹
I GUESS IT WASN'T MEANT TO BE. (SIGH)

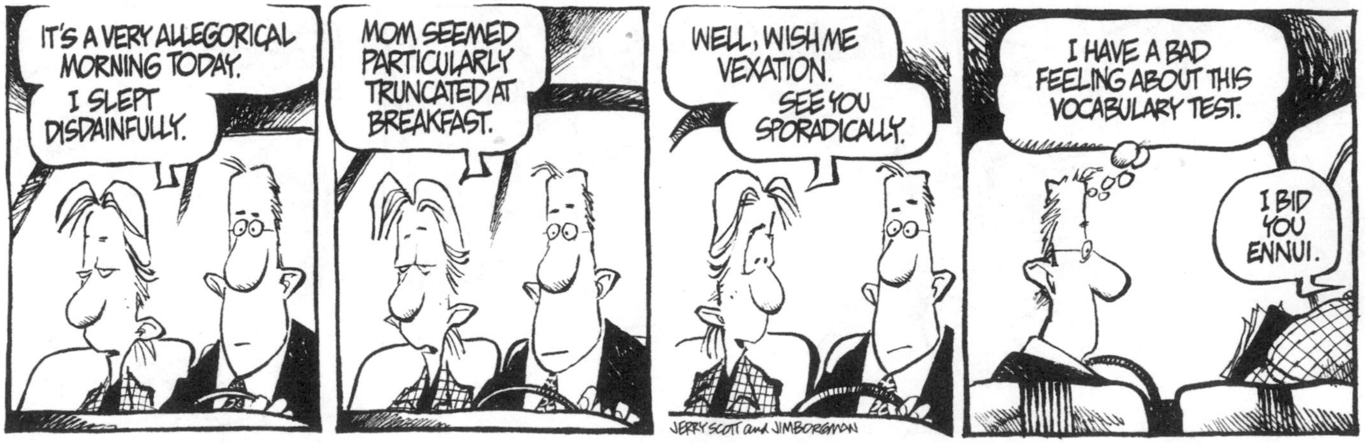

IT'S A VERY ALLEGORICAL MORNING TODAY.
I SLEPT DISDAINFULLY.
MOM SEEMED PARTICULARLY TRUNCATED AT BREAKFAST.
WELL, WISH ME VEXATION.
SEE YOU SPORADICALLY.
JERRY SCOTT and JIM BORGMAN
I HAVE A BAD FEELING ABOUT THIS VOCABULARY TEST.
I BID YOU ENNUI.

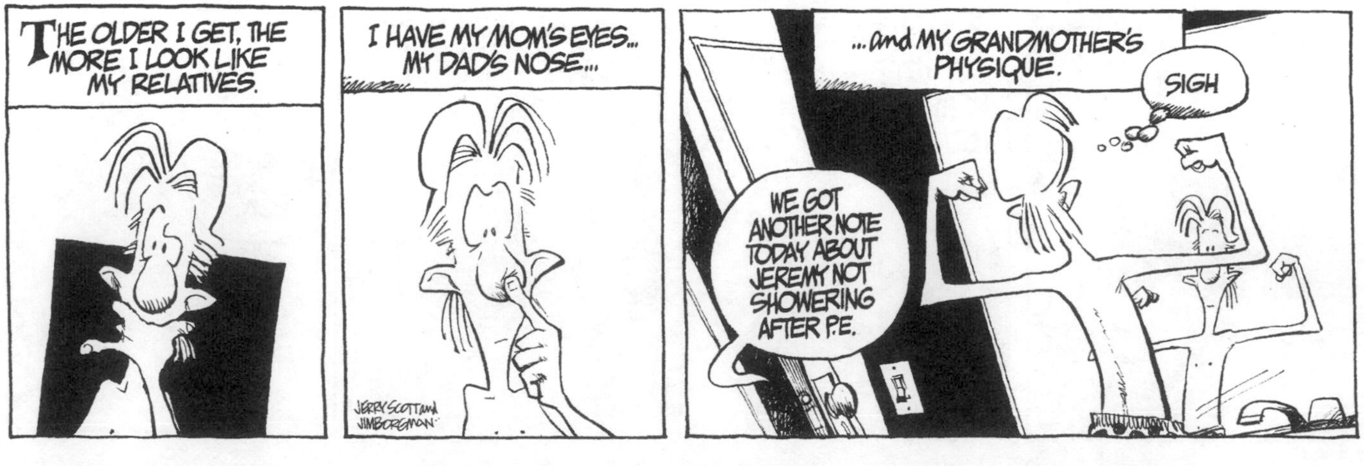

THE OLDER I GET, THE MORE I LOOK LIKE MY RELATIVES.
I HAVE MY MOM'S EYES... MY DAD'S NOSE...
JERRY SCOTT and JIM BORGMAN
...and MY GRANDMOTHER'S PHYSIQUE.
SIGH
WE GOT ANOTHER NOTE TODAY ABOUT JEREMY NOT SHOWERING AFTER P.E.

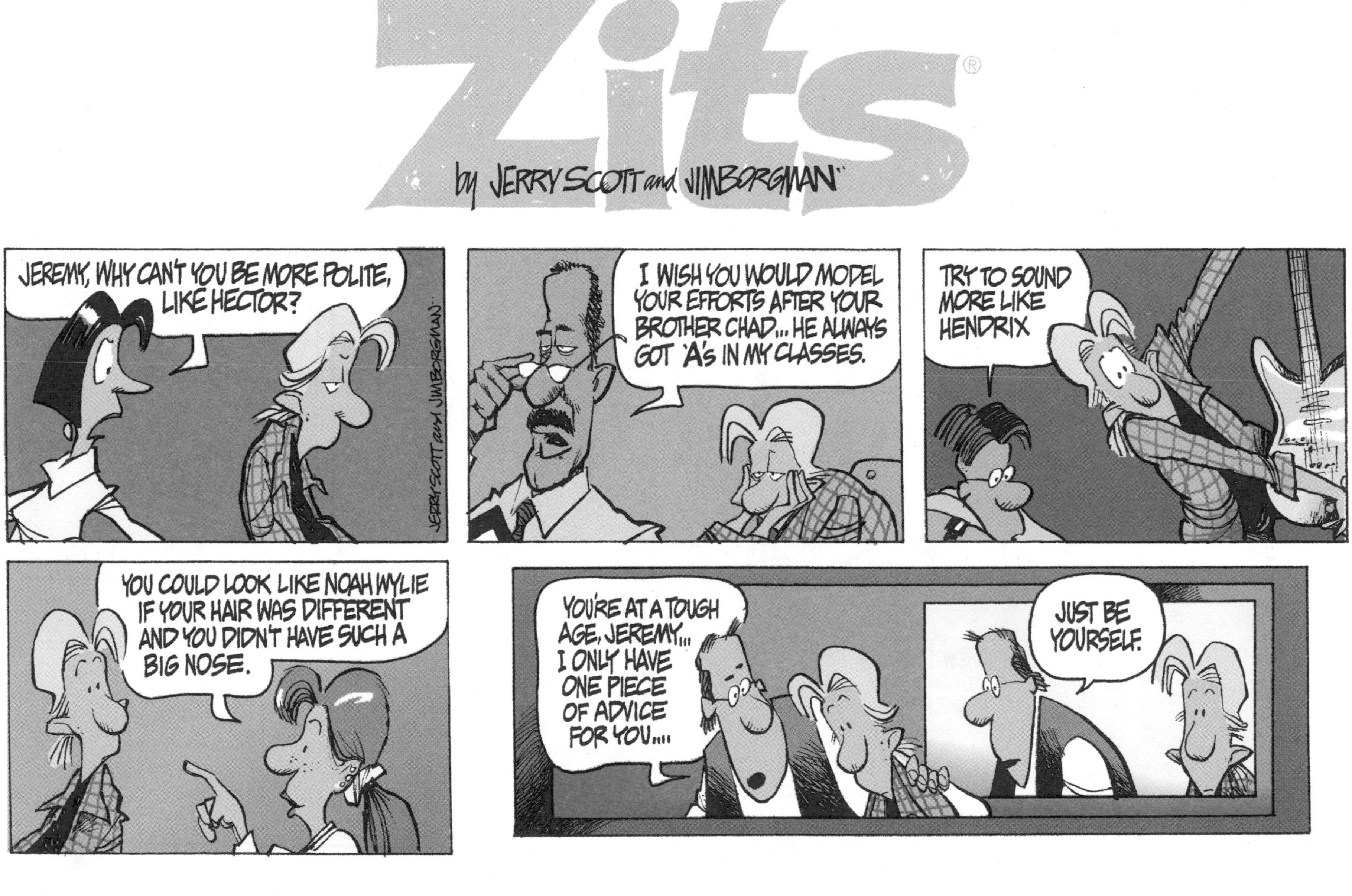
Zits
by JERRY SCOTT and JIM BORGMAN
JEREMY, WHY CAN'T YOU BE MORE POLITE, LIKE HECTOR?
I WISH YOU WOULD MODEL YOUR EFFORTS AFTER YOUR BROTHER CHAD... HE ALWAYS GOT 'A's IN MY CLASSES.
TRY TO SOUND MORE LIKE HENDRIX
YOU COULD LOOK LIKE NOAH WYLIE IF YOUR HAIR WAS DIFFERENT AND YOU DIDN'T HAVE SUCH A BIG NOSE.
YOU'RE AT A TOUGH AGE, JEREMY... I ONLY HAVE ONE PIECE OF ADVICE FOR YOU....
JUST BE YOURSELF.

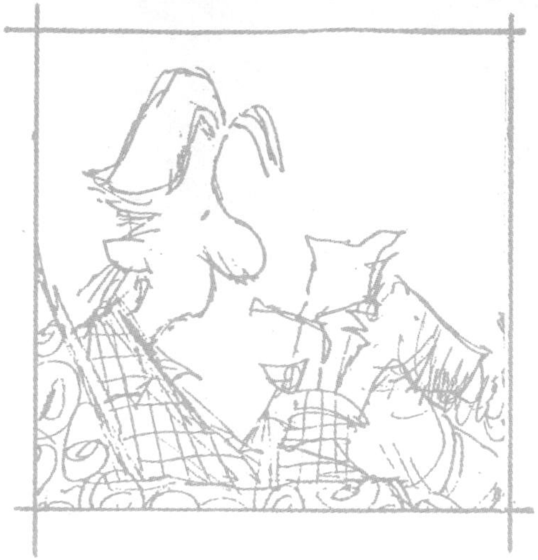

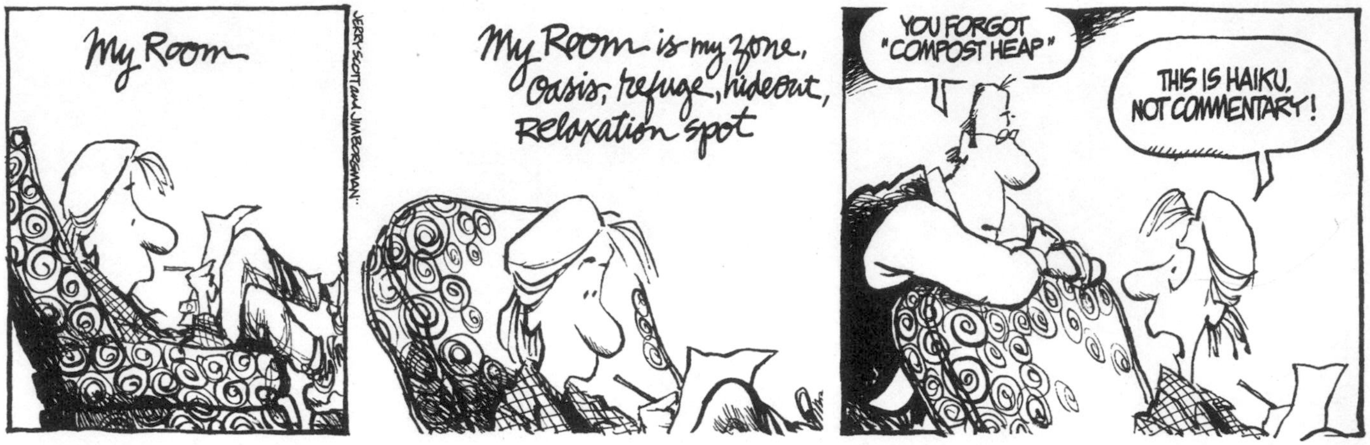
My Room
JERRY SCOTT and JIM BORGMAN
My Room is my zone, oasis, refuge, hideout, Relaxation spot
YOU FORGOT "COMPOST HEAP"
THIS IS HAIKU, NOT COMMENTARY!

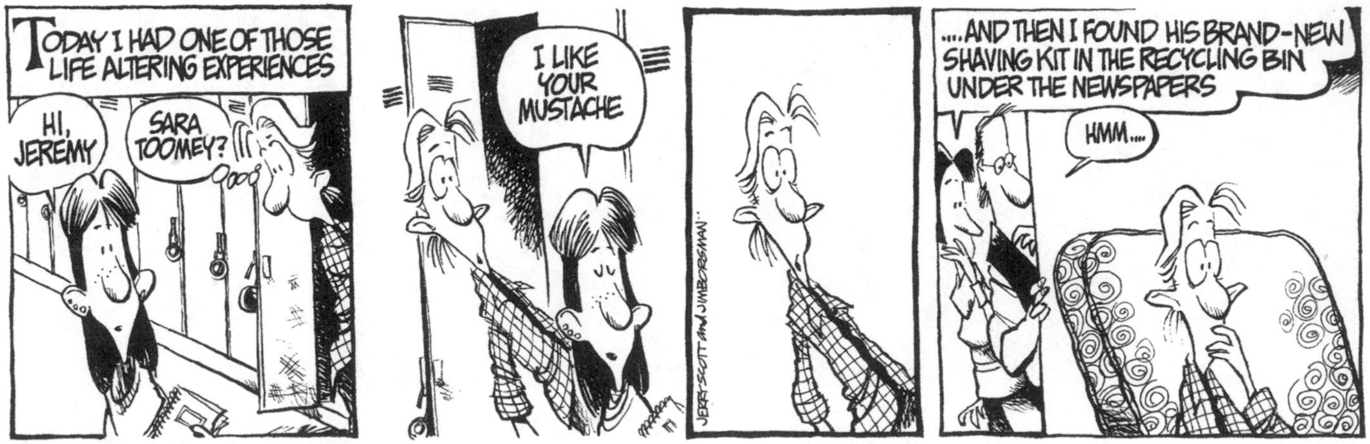
TODAY I HAD ONE OF THOSE LIFE ALTERING EXPERIENCES
HI, JEREMY
SARA TOOMEY?
I LIKE YOUR MUSTACHE
JERRY SCOTT and JIM BORGMAN
....AND THEN I FOUND HIS BRAND-NEW SHAVING KIT IN THE RECYCLING BIN UNDER THE NEWSPAPERS
HMM....

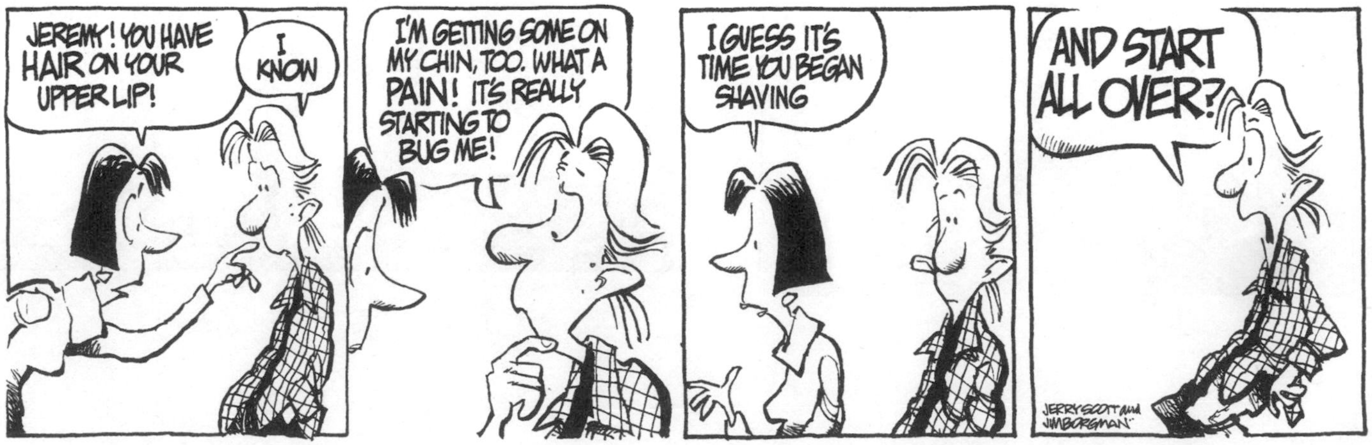
JEREMY! YOU HAVE HAIR ON YOUR UPPER LIP!
I KNOW
I'M GETTING SOME ON MY CHIN, TOO. WHAT A PAIN! IT'S REALLY STARTING TO BUG ME!
I GUESS IT'S TIME YOU BEGAN SHAVING
AND START ALL OVER?
JERRY SCOTT and JIM BORGMAN

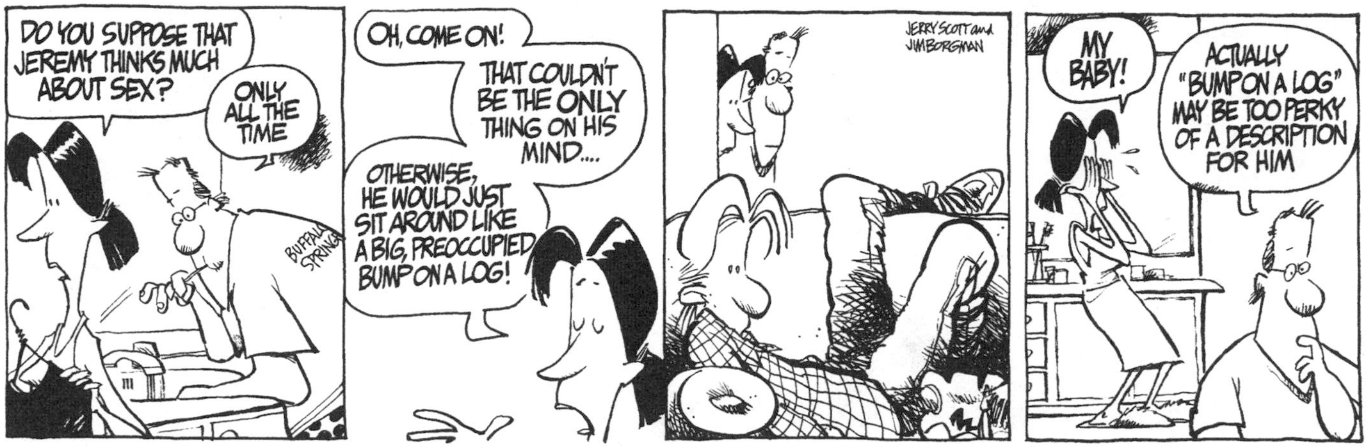
DO YOU SUPPOSE THAT JEREMY THINKS MUCH ABOUT SEX?
ONLY ALL THE TIME
BUFFALO SPRINGS
OH, COME ON!
THAT COULDN'T BE THE ONLY THING ON HIS MIND....
OTHERWISE, HE WOULD JUST SIT AROUND LIKE A BIG, PREOCCUPIED BUMP ON A LOG!
JERRY SCOTT and JIM BORGMAN
MY BABY!
ACTUALLY "BUMP ON A LOG" MAY BE TOO PERKY OF A DESCRIPTION FOR HIM

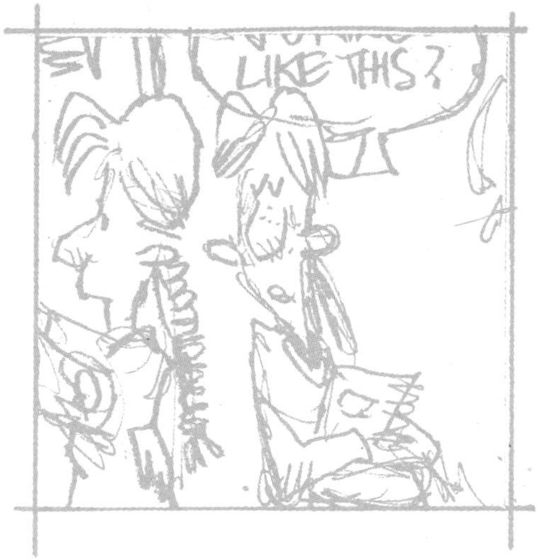
LIKE THIS?

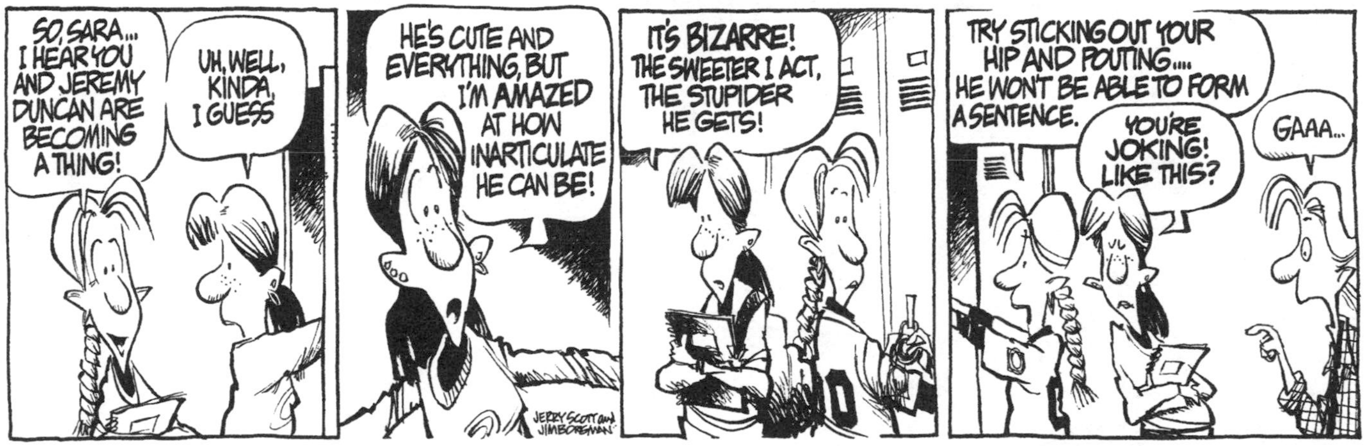
SO, SARA... I HEAR YOU AND JEREMY DUNCAN ARE BECOMING A THING!
UH, WELL, KINDA, I GUESS
HE'S CUTE AND EVERYTHING, BUT I'M AMAZED AT HOW INARTICULATE HE CAN BE!
JERRY SCOTT and JIM BORGMAN
IT'S BIZARRE! THE SWEETER I ACT, THE STUPIDER HE GETS!
TRY STICKING OUT YOUR HIP AND POUTING.... HE WON'T BE ABLE TO FORM A SENTENCE.
YOU'RE JOKING! LIKE THIS?
GAAA...

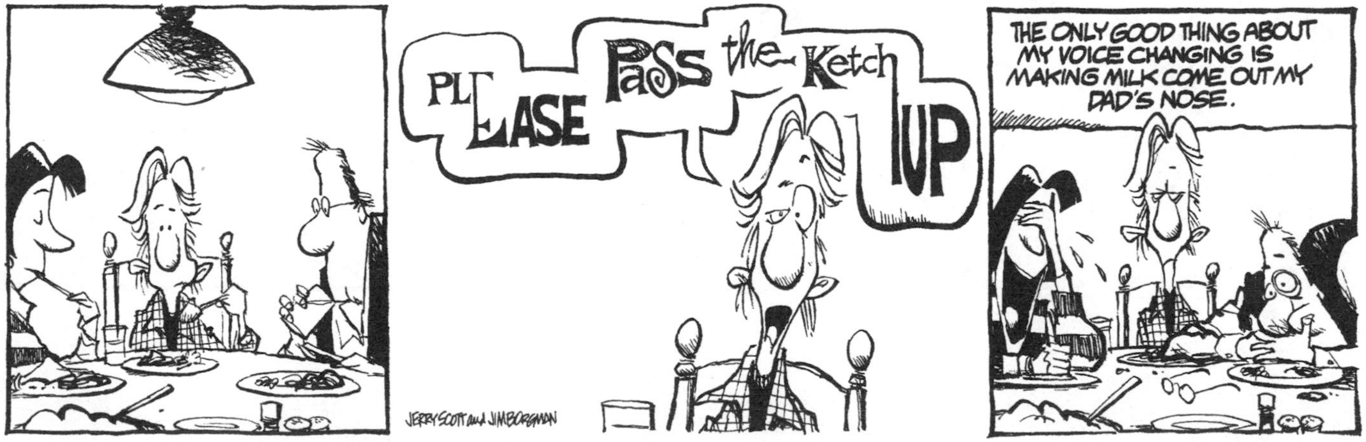
PLEASE PaSS the Ketch UP
JERRY SCOTT and JIM BORGMAN
THE ONLY GOOD THING ABOUT MY VOICE CHANGING IS MAKING MILK COME OUT MY DAD'S NOSE.

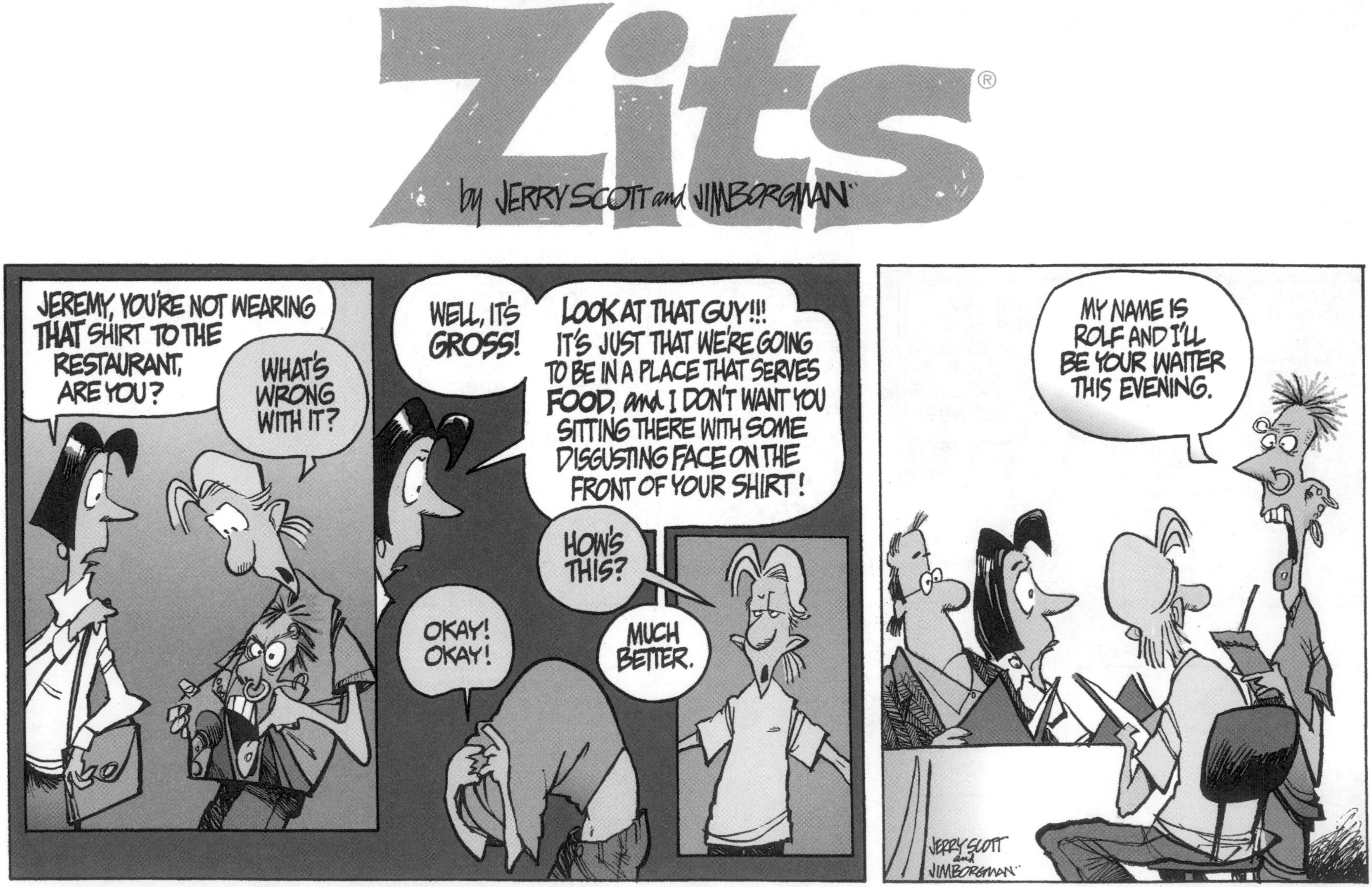
Zits®
by JERRY SCOTT and JIM BORGMAN
JEREMY, YOU'RE NOT WEARING THAT SHIRT TO THE RESTAURANT, ARE YOU?
WHAT'S WRONG WITH IT?
WELL, IT'S GROSS!
LOOK AT THAT GUY!!!
IT'S JUST THAT WE'RE GOING TO BE IN A PLACE THAT SERVES FOOD, and I DON'T WANT YOU SITTING THERE WITH SOME DISGUSTING FACE ON THE FRONT OF YOUR SHIRT!
OKAY! OKAY!
HOW'S THIS?
MUCH BETTER.
MY NAME IS ROLF AND I'LL BE YOUR WAITER THIS EVENING.
JERRY SCOTT and JIM BORGMAN

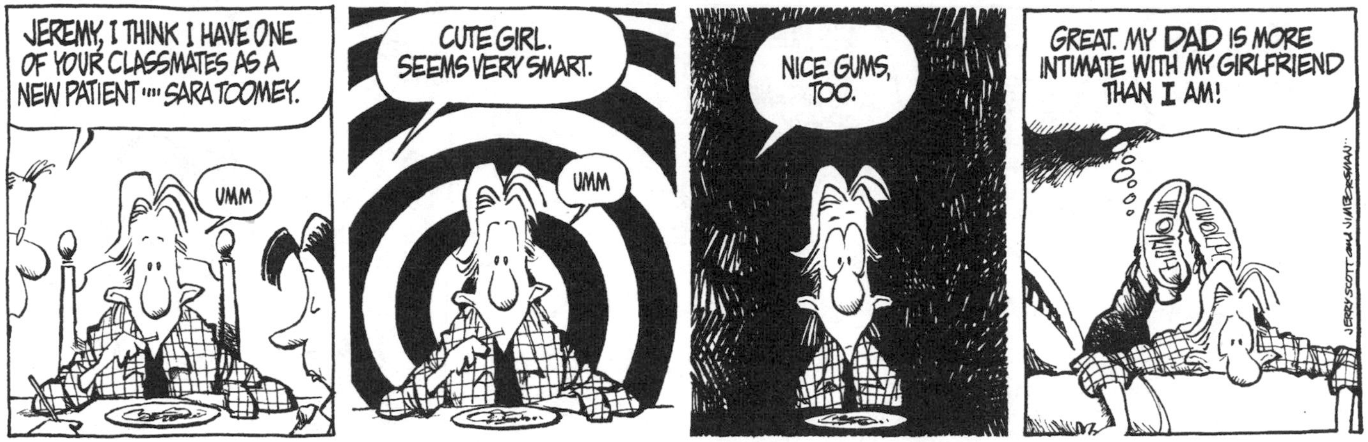
JEREMY, I THINK I HAVE ONE OF YOUR CLASSMATES AS A NEW PATIENT.... SARA TOOMEY.
UMM
CUTE GIRL. SEEMS VERY SMART.
UMM
NICE GUMS, TOO.
GREAT. MY DAD IS MORE INTIMATE WITH MY GIRLFRIEND THAN I AM!
JERRY SCOTT and JIM BORGMAN

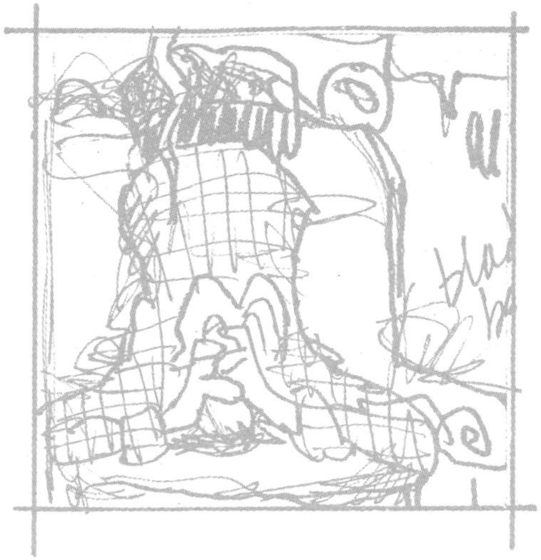

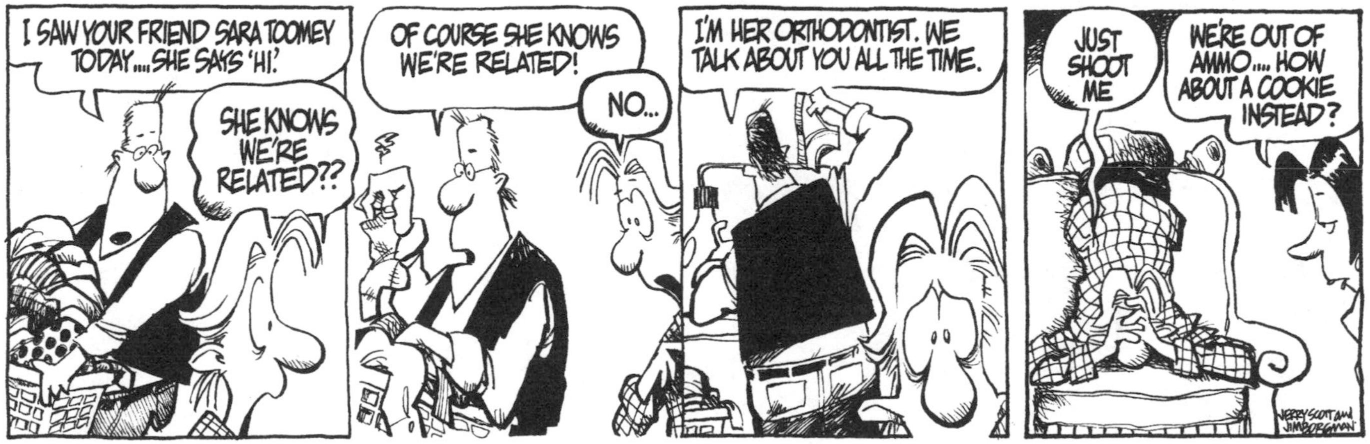
I SAW YOUR FRIEND SARA TOOMEY TODAY.... SHE SAYS 'HI.'
SHE KNOWS WE'RE RELATED??
OF COURSE SHE KNOWS WE'RE RELATED!
NO...
I'M HER ORTHODONTIST. WE TALK ABOUT YOU ALL THE TIME.
JUST SHOOT ME
WE'RE OUT OF AMMO.... HOW ABOUT A COOKIE INSTEAD?
JERRY SCOTT and JIM BORGMAN

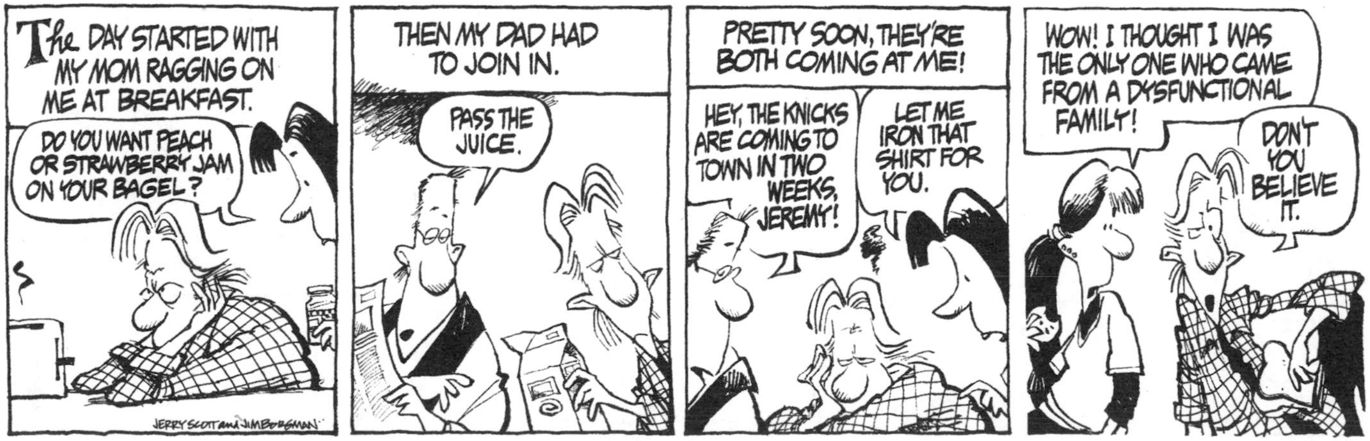
The DAY STARTED WITH MY MOM RAGGING ON ME AT BREAKFAST.
DO YOU WANT PEACH OR STRAWBERRY JAM ON YOUR BAGEL?
THEN MY DAD HAD TO JOIN IN.
PASS THE JUICE.
PRETTY SOON, THEY'RE BOTH COMING AT ME!
HEY, THE KNICKS ARE COMING TO TOWN IN TWO WEEKS, JEREMY!
LET ME IRON THAT SHIRT FOR YOU.
WOW! I THOUGHT I WAS THE ONLY ONE WHO CAME FROM A DYSFUNCTIONAL FAMILY!
DON'T YOU BELIEVE IT.
JERRY SCOTT and JIM BORGMAN

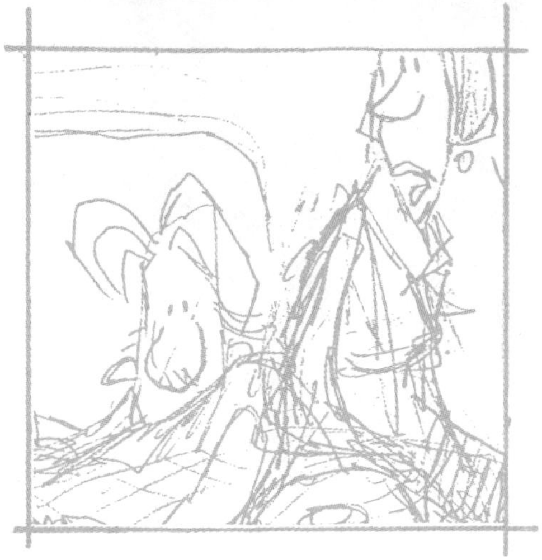

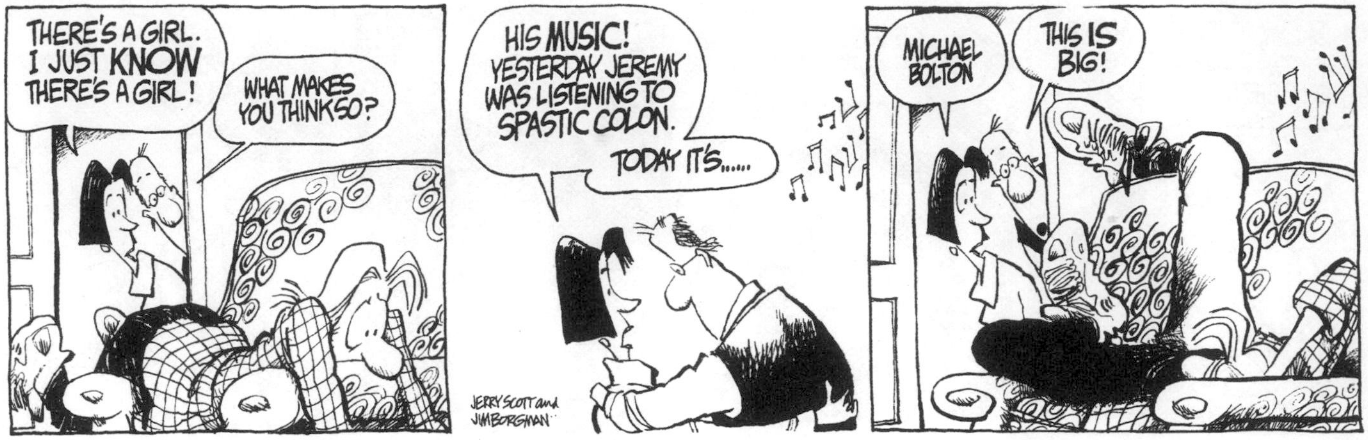

THERE'S A GIRL. I JUST KNOW THERE'S A GIRL!
WHAT MAKES YOU THINK SO?
HIS MUSIC! YESTERDAY JEREMY WAS LISTENING TO SPASTIC COLON.
TODAY IT'S......
JERRY SCOTT and JIM BORGMAN
MICHAEL BOLTON
THIS IS BIG!

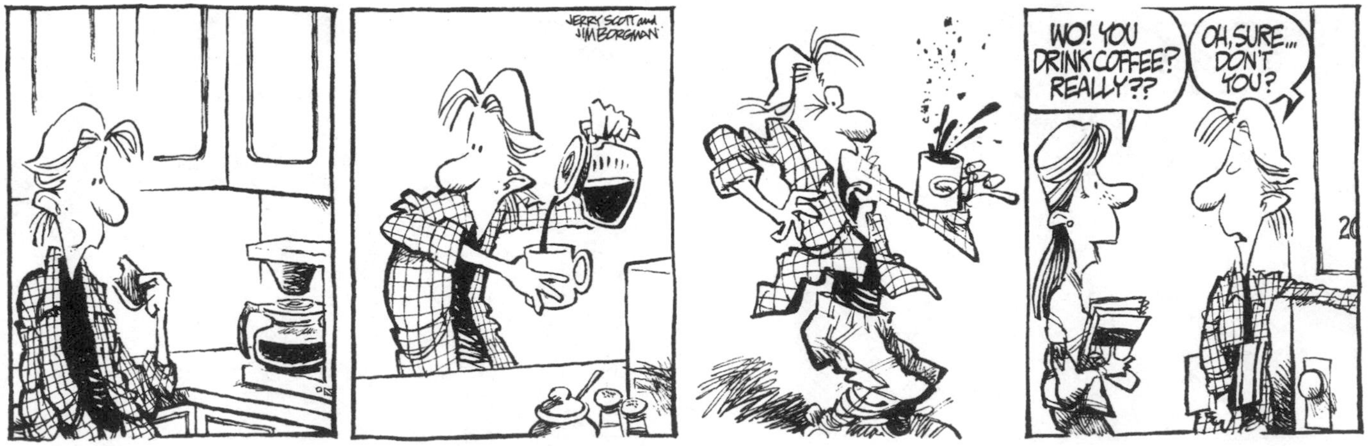

JERRY SCOTT and JIM BORGMAN
WO! YOU DRINK COFFEE? REALLY??
OH, SURE... DON'T YOU?

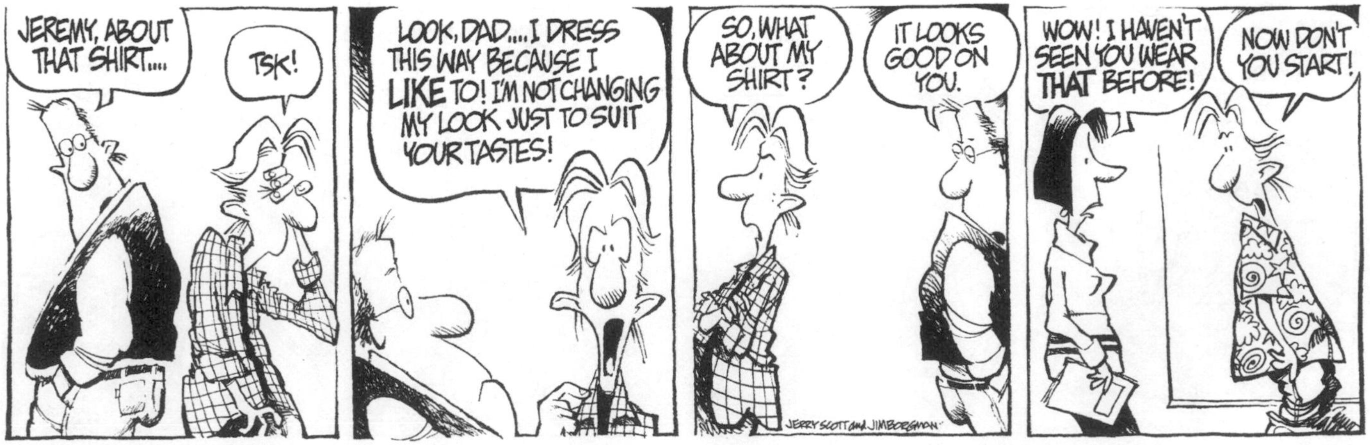

JEREMY, ABOUT THAT SHIRT....
TSK!
LOOK, DAD....I DRESS THIS WAY BECAUSE I LIKE TO! I'M NOT CHANGING MY LOOK JUST TO SUIT YOUR TASTES!
SO, WHAT ABOUT MY SHIRT?
IT LOOKS GOOD ON YOU.
JERRY SCOTT and JIM BORGMAN
WOW! I HAVEN'T SEEN YOU WEAR THAT BEFORE!
NOW DON'T YOU START!

Zits®

by JERRY SCOTT and JIM BORGMAN

HOW DID YOU DO ON THE HISTORY EXAM?
WHAT DID YOU HAVE FOR LUNCH TODAY?
BZZZZZZZZZZ
HAVE YOU FINISHED YOUR HOMEWORK YET?
ARE YOU GOING TO THE GAME ON FRIDAY?
WHAT'S NEW WITH YOU AND SARA?
JERRY SCOTT and JIM BORGMAN
WE'RE JUST TRYING TO MAKE CONVERSATION, JEREMY.
IT'S NOT LIKE WE'RE HOLDING AN INQUISITION.

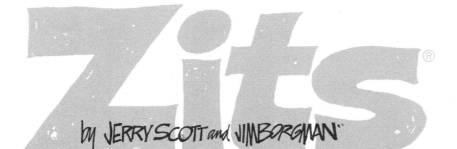

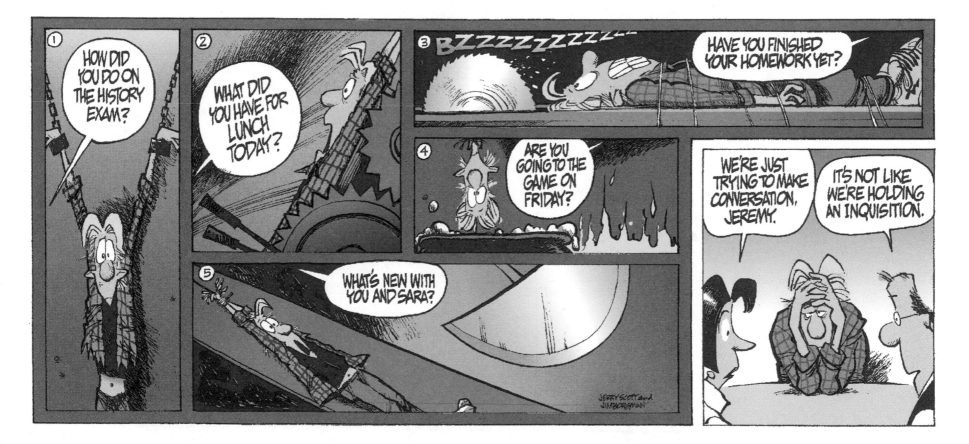

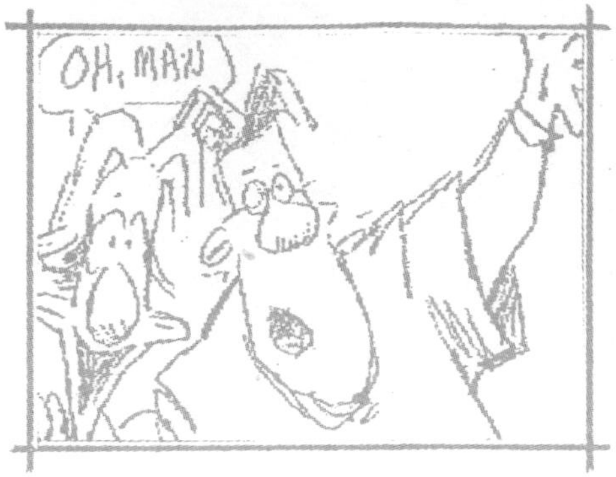
OH, MAN

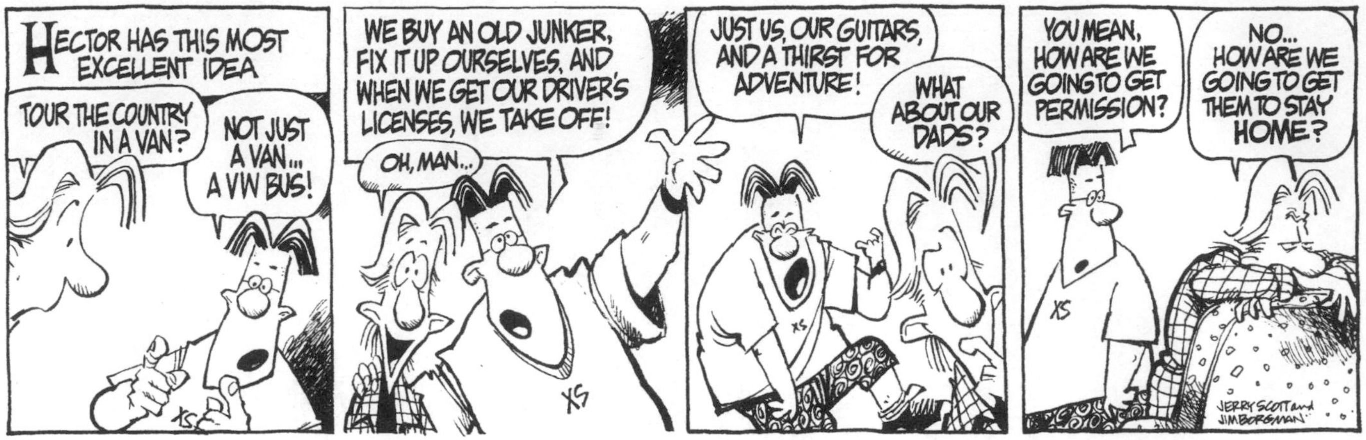
HECTOR HAS THIS MOST EXCELLENT IDEA
TOUR THE COUNTRY IN A VAN?
NOT JUST A VAN... A VW BUS!
WE BUY AN OLD JUNKER, FIX IT UP OURSELVES, AND WHEN WE GET OUR DRIVER'S LICENSES, WE TAKE OFF!
OH, MAN...
JUST US, OUR GUITARS, AND A THIRST FOR ADVENTURE!
WHAT ABOUT OUR DADS?
YOU MEAN, HOW ARE WE GOING TO GET PERMISSION?
NO... HOW ARE WE GOING TO GET THEM TO STAY HOME?
JERRY SCOTT and JIM BORGMAN

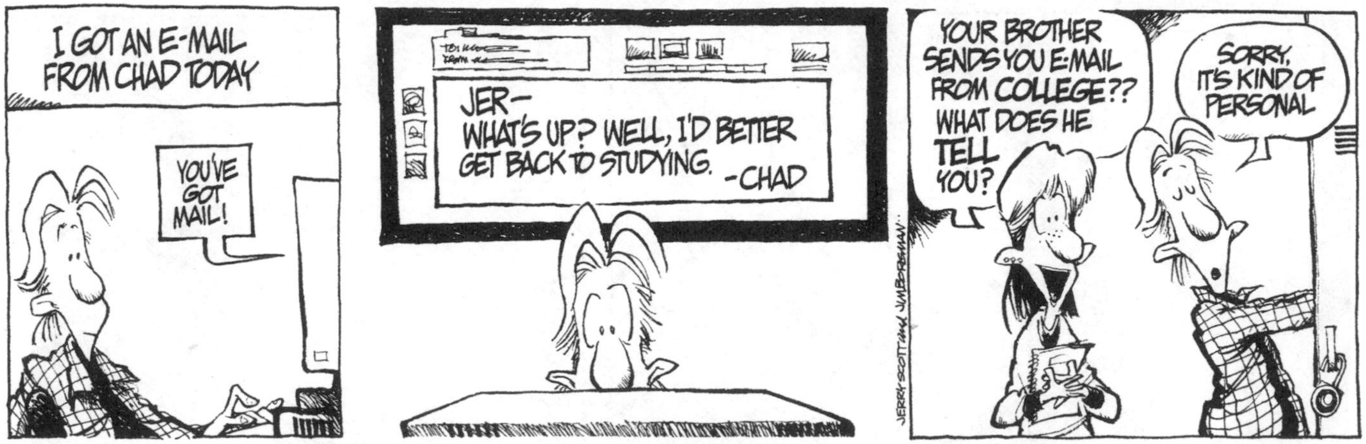
I GOT AN E-MAIL FROM CHAD TODAY
YOU'VE GOT MAIL!
JER—
WHAT'S UP? WELL, I'D BETTER GET BACK TO STUDYING. -CHAD
YOUR BROTHER SENDS YOU E-MAIL FROM COLLEGE?? WHAT DOES HE TELL YOU?
SORRY, IT'S KIND OF PERSONAL
JERRY SCOTT and JIM BORGMAN

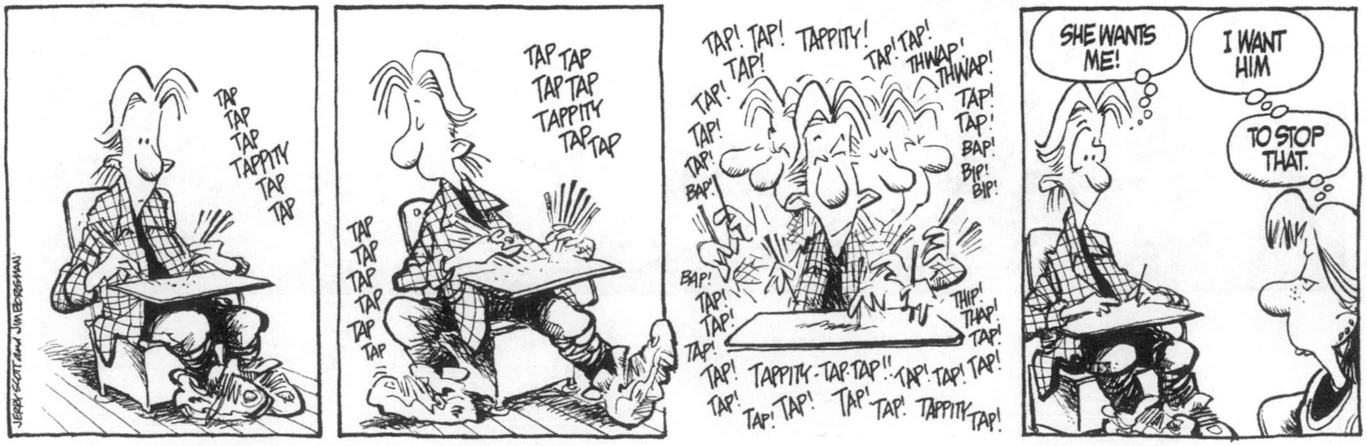
TAP TAP TAP TAPPITY TAP TAP
JERRY SCOTT and JIM BORGMAN
TAP TAP TAP TAP TAPPITY TAP TAP
TAP TAP TAP TAP TAP TAP
TAP! TAP! TAPPITY! TAP! TAP! THWAP! THWAP!
TAP! TAP! TAP! TAP! BAP!
TAP! TAP! BAP! BIP! BIP!
BAP! TAP! TAP! TAP! THIP! THAP! TAP!
TAP! TAPPITY-TAP TAP!! TAP! TAP! TAP!
TAP! TAP! TAP! TAP! TAP! TAPPITY TAP!
SHE WANTS ME!
I WANT HIM
TO STOP THAT.

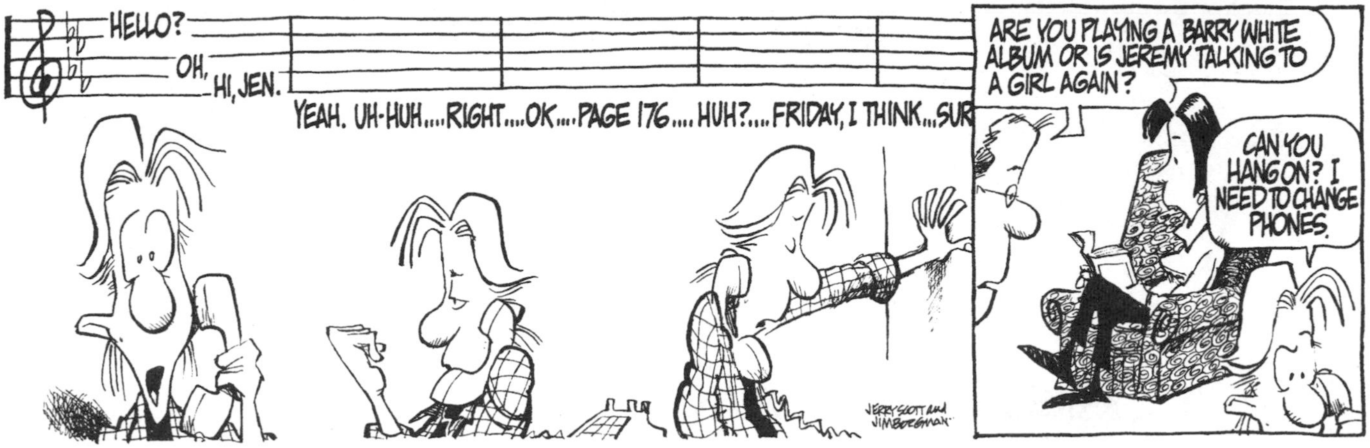
HELLO?
OH, HI, JEN.
YEAH. UH-HUH....RIGHT....OK....PAGE 176.... HUH?....FRIDAY, I THINK...SUR
ARE YOU PLAYING A BARRY WHITE ALBUM OR IS JEREMY TALKING TO A GIRL AGAIN?
CAN YOU HANG ON? I NEED TO CHANGE PHONES.
JERRY SCOTT and JIM BORGMAN

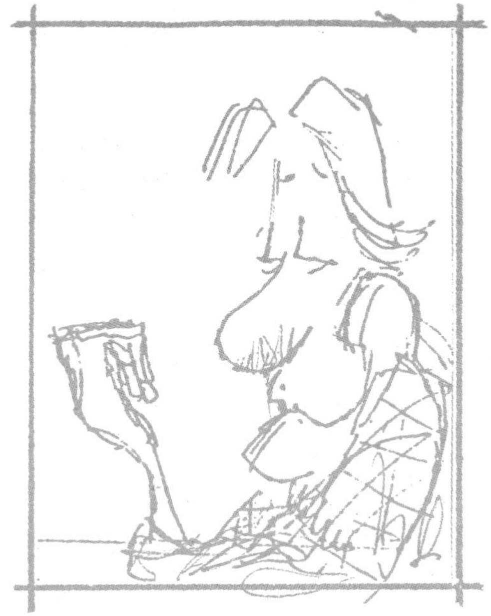

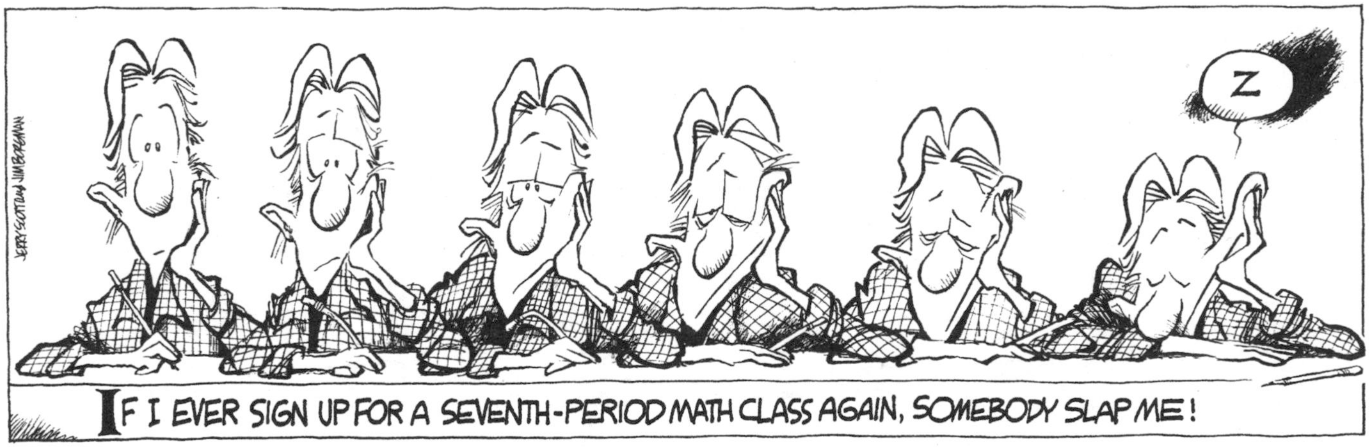
JERRY SCOTT and JIM BORGMAN
Z
IF I EVER SIGN UP FOR A SEVENTH-PERIOD MATH CLASS AGAIN, SOMEBODY SLAP ME!

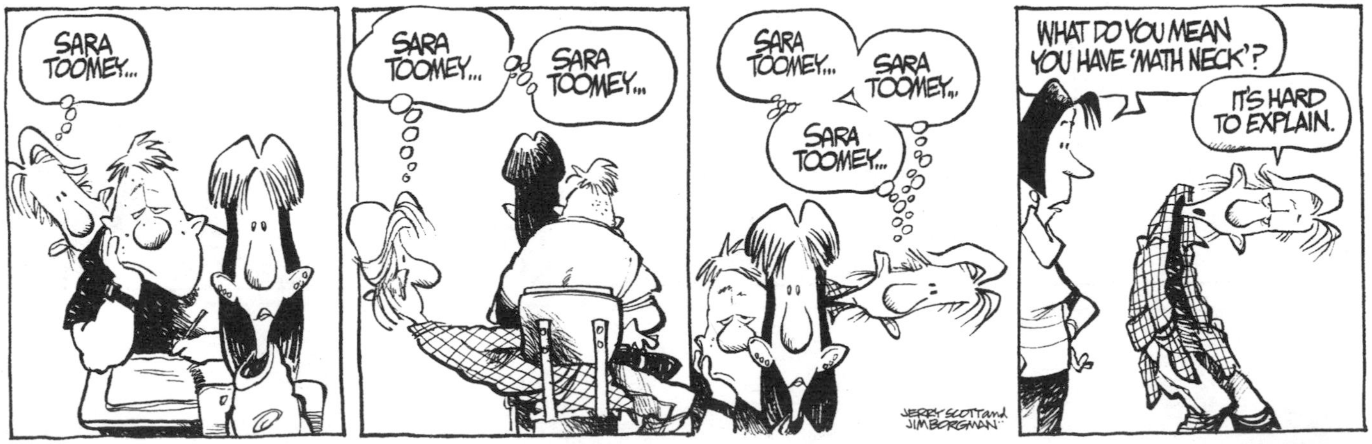
SARA TOOMEY...
SARA TOOMEY...
SARA TOOMEY...
SARA TOOMEY...
SARA TOOMEY...
SARA TOOMEY...
WHAT DO YOU MEAN YOU HAVE 'MATH NECK'?
IT'S HARD TO EXPLAIN.
JERRY SCOTT and JIM BORGMAN

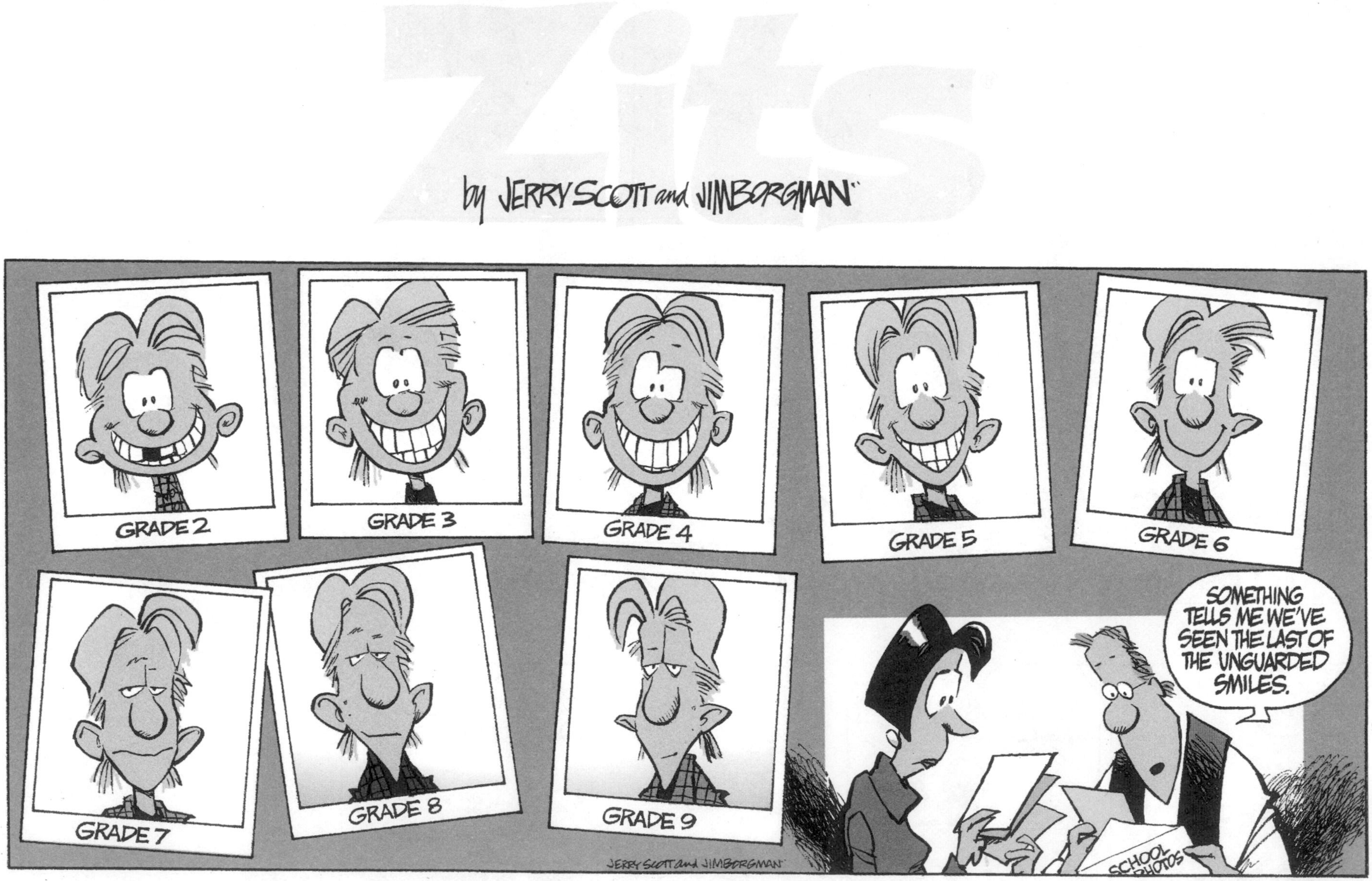
Zits
by JERRY SCOTT and JIM BORGMAN
GRADE 2
GRADE 3
GRADE 4
GRADE 5
GRADE 6
GRADE 7
GRADE 8
GRADE 9
SOMETHING TELLS ME WE'VE SEEN THE LAST OF THE UNGUARDED SMILES.
SCHOOL PHOTOS
JERRY SCOTT and JIM BORGMAN

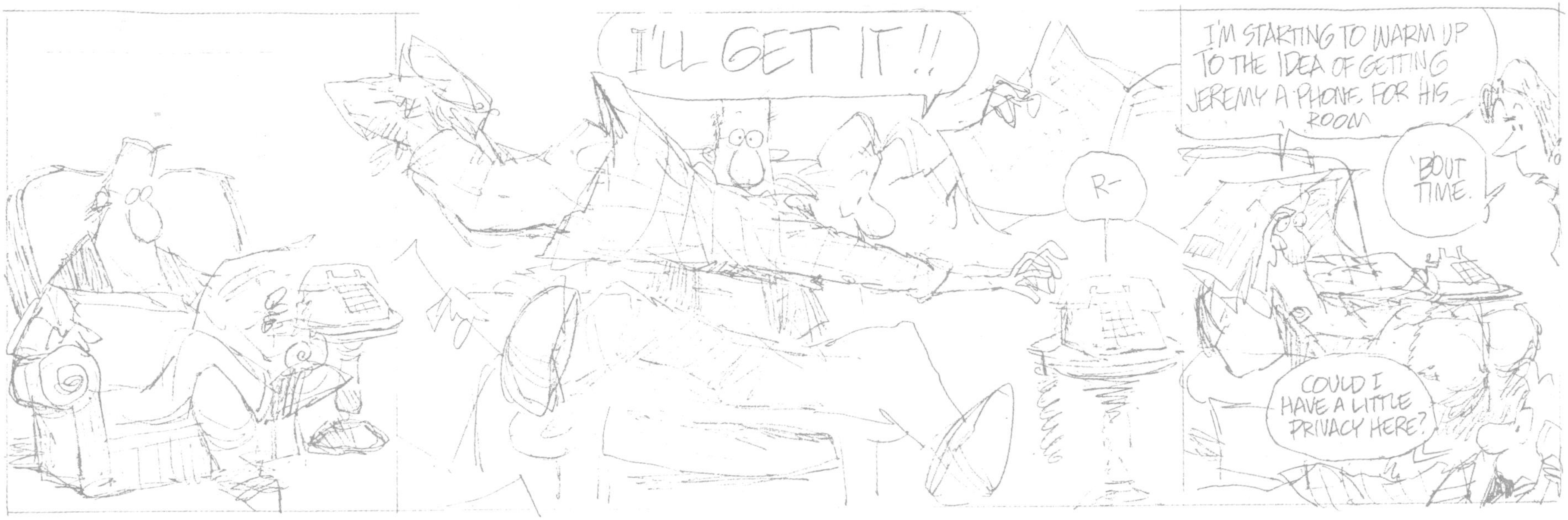
I'LL GET IT!!
R-
I'M STARTING TO WARM UP TO THE IDEA OF GETTING JEREMY A PHONE FOR HIS ROOM
'BOUT TIME.
COULD I HAVE A LITTLE PRIVACY HERE?

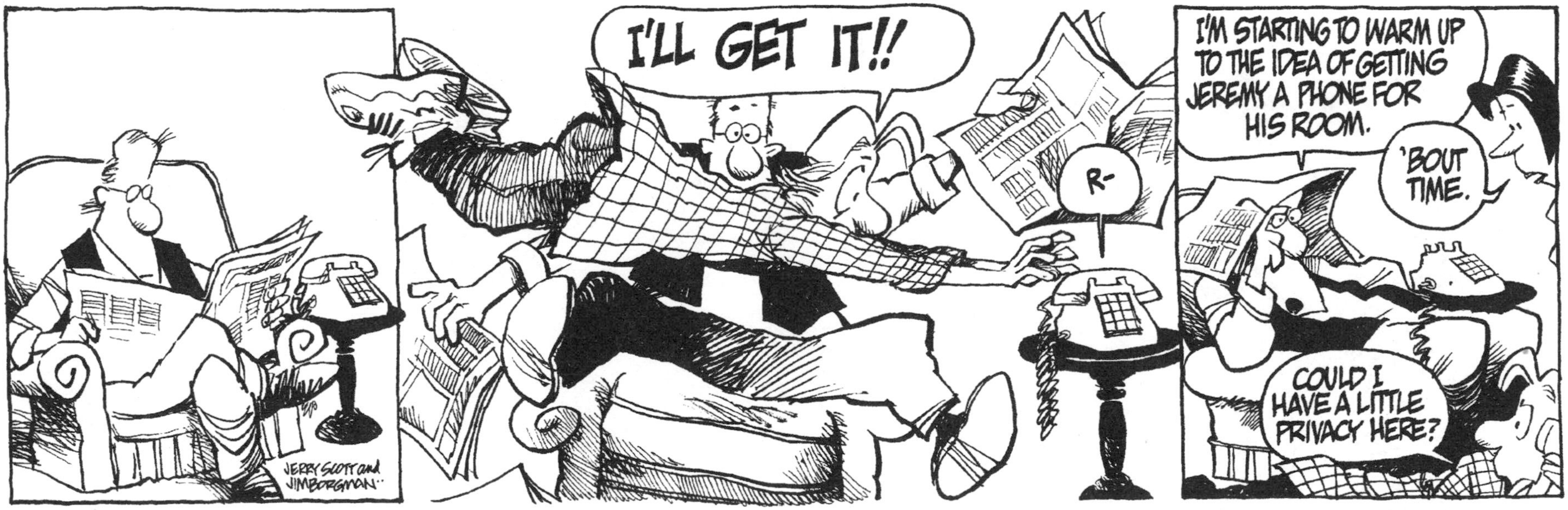
JERRY SCOTT and JIM BORGMAN
I'LL GET IT!!
R-
I'M STARTING TO WARM UP TO THE IDEA OF GETTING JEREMY A PHONE FOR HIS ROOM.
'BOUT TIME.
COULD I HAVE A LITTLE PRIVACY HERE?

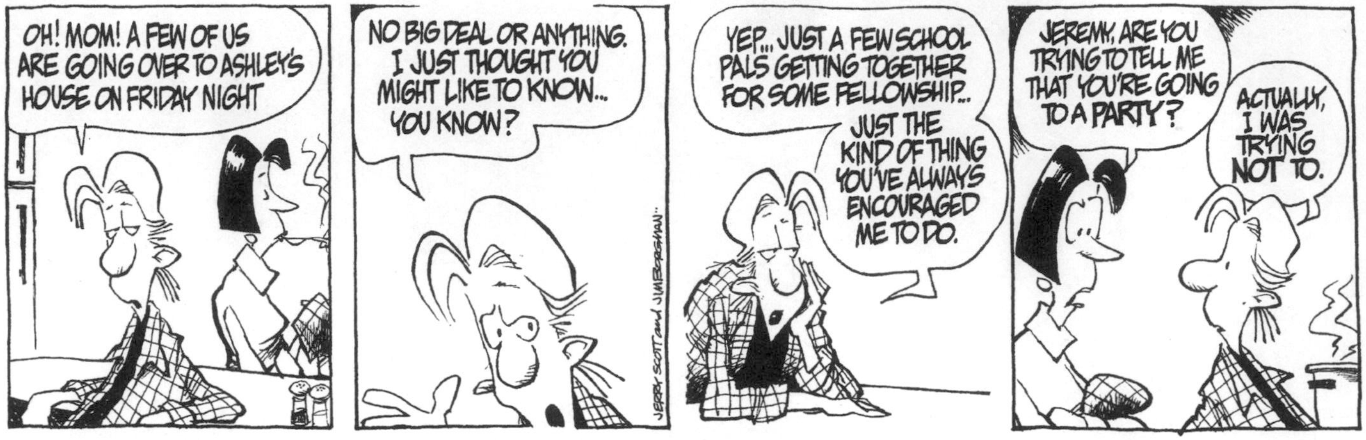
OH! MOM! A FEW OF US ARE GOING OVER TO ASHLEY'S HOUSE ON FRIDAY NIGHT
NO BIG DEAL OR ANYTHING. I JUST THOUGHT YOU MIGHT LIKE TO KNOW... YOU KNOW?
YEP... JUST A FEW SCHOOL PALS GETTING TOGETHER FOR SOME FELLOWSHIP...
JUST THE KIND OF THING YOU'VE ALWAYS ENCOURAGED ME TO DO.
JEREMY, ARE YOU TRYING TO TELL ME THAT YOU'RE GOING TO A PARTY?
ACTUALLY, I WAS TRYING NOT TO.

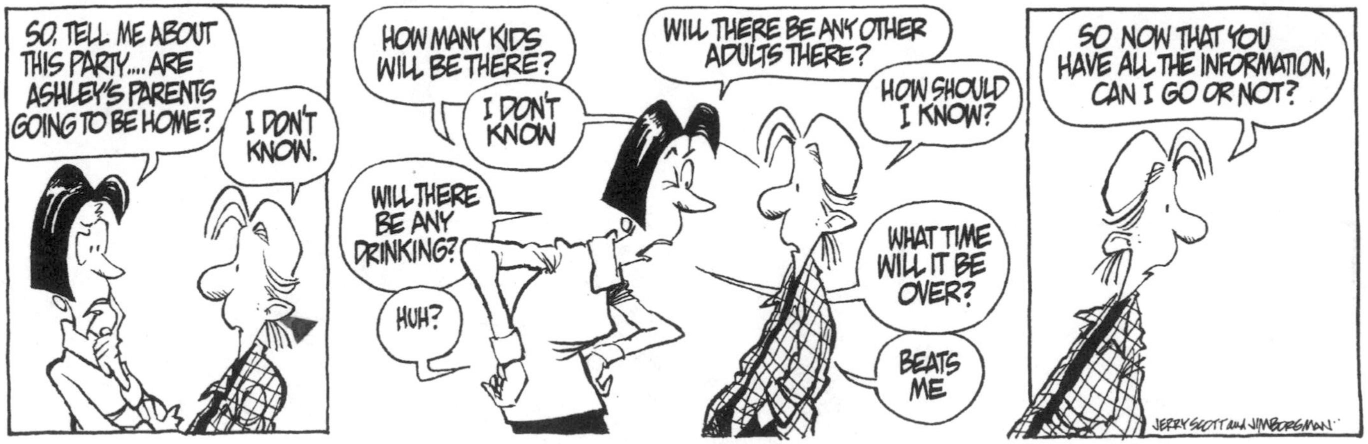
SO, TELL ME ABOUT THIS PARTY.... ARE ASHLEY'S PARENTS GOING TO BE HOME?
I DON'T KNOW.
HOW MANY KIDS WILL BE THERE?
I DON'T KNOW
WILL THERE BE ANY OTHER ADULTS THERE?
HOW SHOULD I KNOW?
WILL THERE BE ANY DRINKING?
HUH?
WHAT TIME WILL IT BE OVER?
BEATS ME
SO NOW THAT YOU HAVE ALL THE INFORMATION, CAN I GO OR NOT?
JERRY SCOTT AND JIM BORGMAN

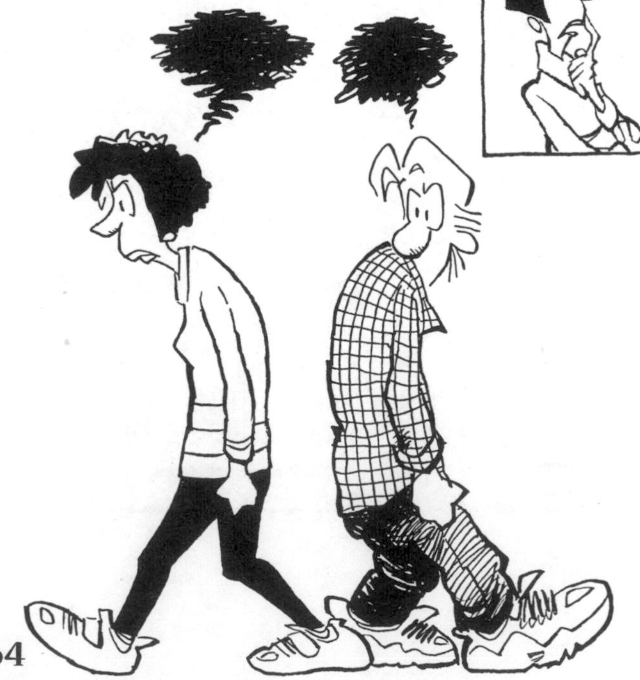

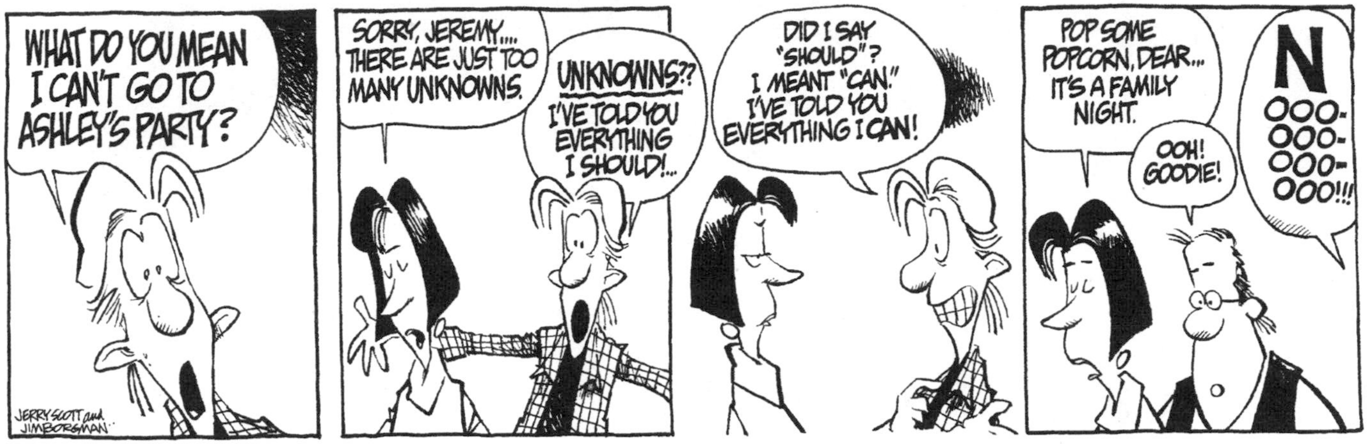
WHAT DO YOU MEAN I CAN'T GO TO ASHLEY'S PARTY?
JERRY SCOTT and JIM BORGMAN
SORRY, JEREMY.... THERE ARE JUST TOO MANY UNKNOWNS.
UNKNOWNS?? I'VE TOLD YOU EVERYTHING I SHOULD!...
DID I SAY "SHOULD"? I MEANT "CAN." I'VE TOLD YOU EVERYTHING I CAN!
POP SOME POPCORN, DEAR... IT'S A FAMILY NIGHT.
OOH! GOODIE!
N OOO-OOO-OOO-OOO-OOO!!!

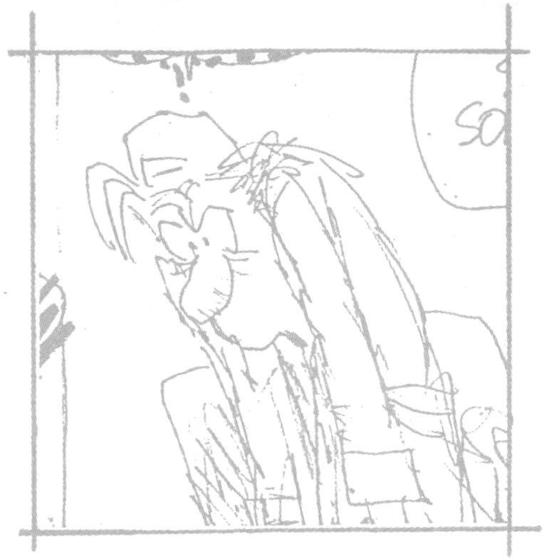

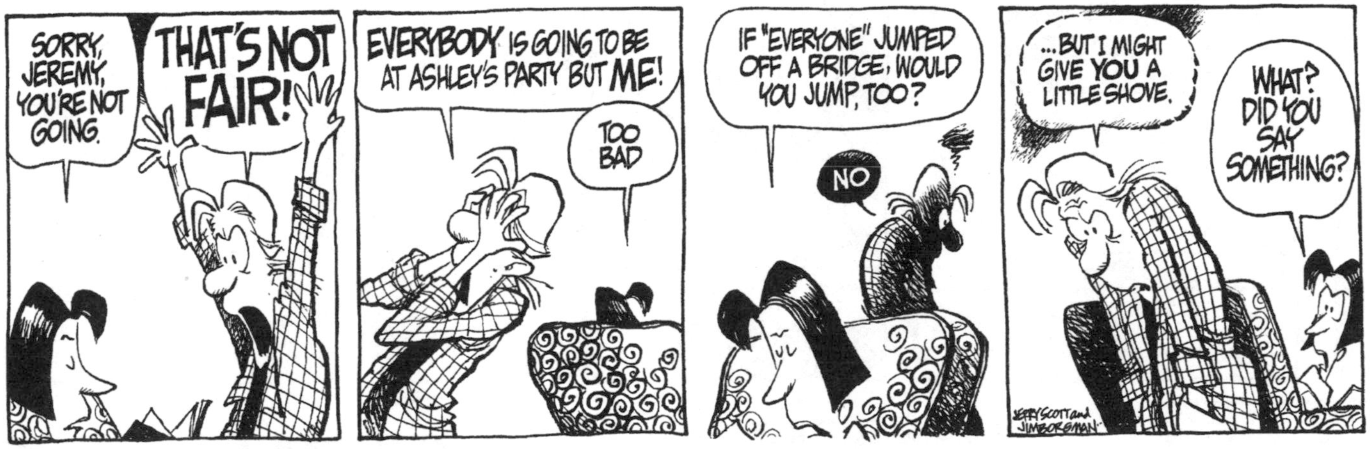
SORRY, JEREMY, YOU'RE NOT GOING.
THAT'S NOT FAIR!
EVERYBODY IS GOING TO BE AT ASHLEY'S PARTY BUT ME!
TOO BAD
IF "EVERYONE" JUMPED OFF A BRIDGE, WOULD YOU JUMP, TOO?
NO
...BUT I MIGHT GIVE YOU A LITTLE SHOVE.
WHAT? DID YOU SAY SOMETHING?
JERRY SCOTT and JIM BORGMAN

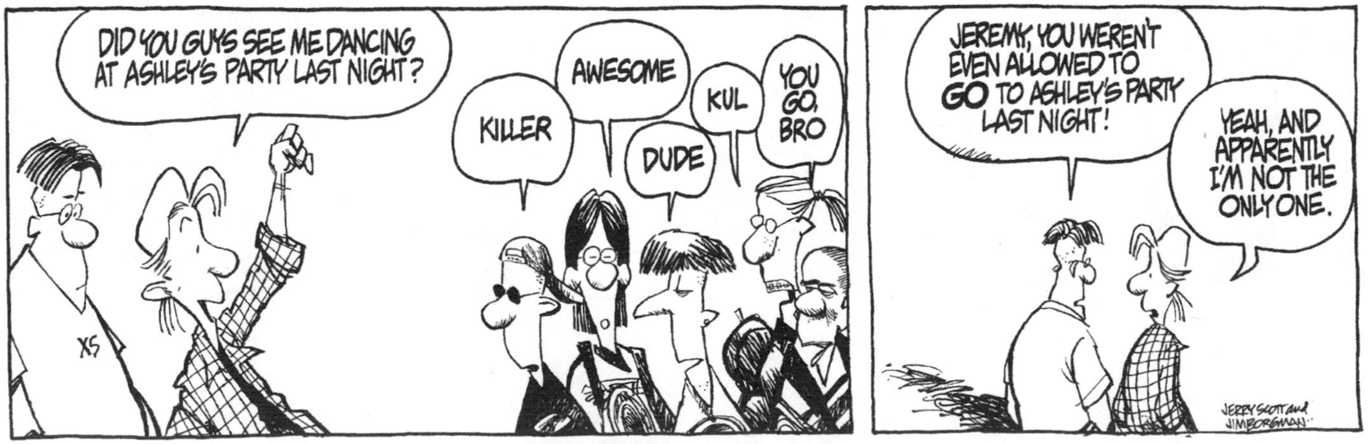
DID YOU GUYS SEE ME DANCING AT ASHLEY'S PARTY LAST NIGHT?
KILLER
AWESOME
DUDE
KUL
YOU GO, BRO
XS
JEREMY, YOU WEREN'T EVEN ALLOWED TO GO TO ASHLEY'S PARTY LAST NIGHT!
YEAH, AND APPARENTLY I'M NOT THE ONLY ONE.
JERRY SCOTT and JIM BORGMAN

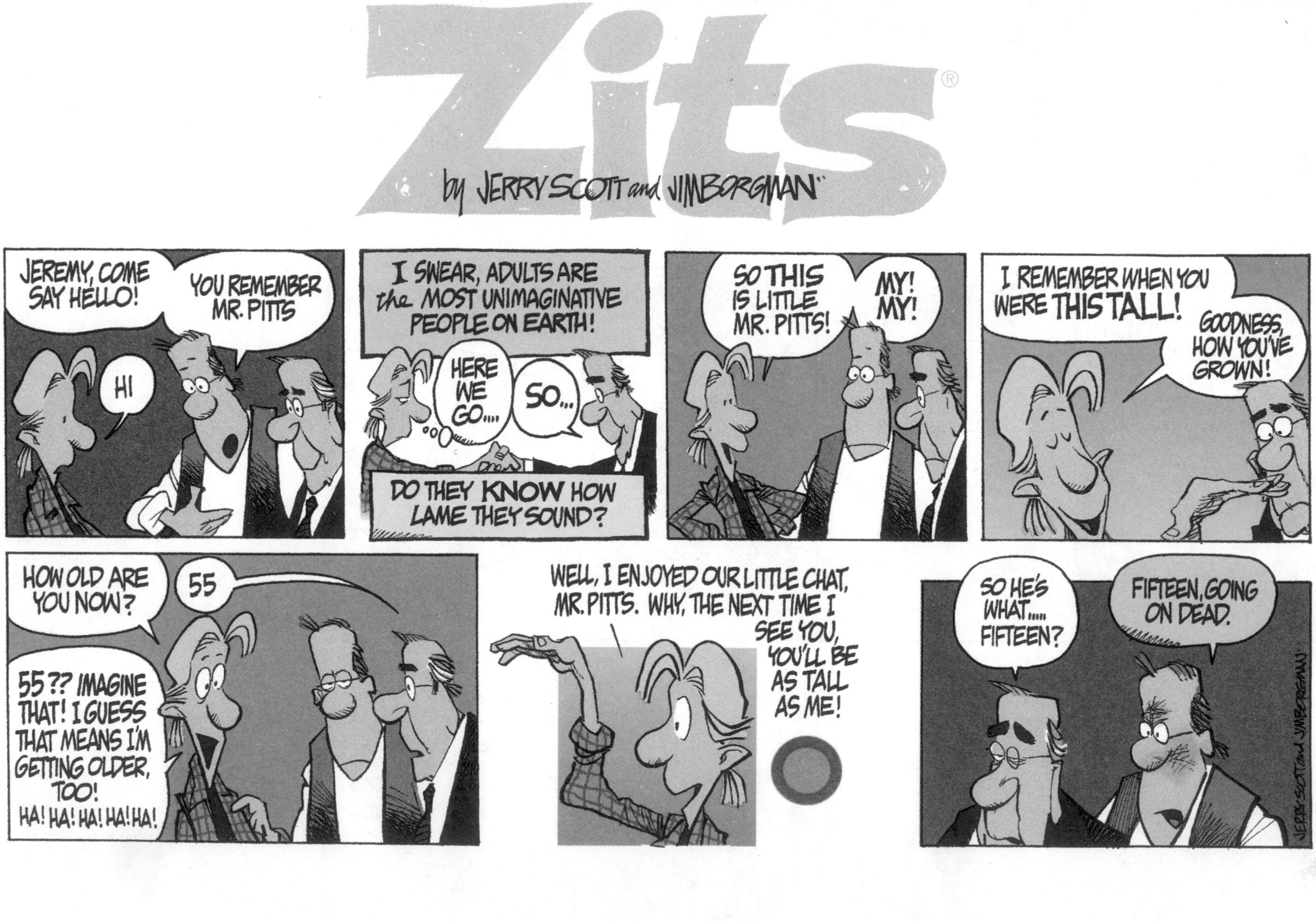
Zits
by JERRY SCOTT and JIM BORGMAN
JEREMY, COME SAY HELLO!
YOU REMEMBER MR. PITTS
HI
I SWEAR, ADULTS ARE the MOST UNIMAGINATIVE PEOPLE ON EARTH!
HERE WE GO.....
SO...
DO THEY KNOW HOW LAME THEY SOUND?
SO THIS IS LITTLE MR. PITTS!
MY! MY!
I REMEMBER WHEN YOU WERE THIS TALL!
GOODNESS, HOW YOU'VE GROWN!
HOW OLD ARE YOU NOW?
55
55?? IMAGINE THAT! I GUESS THAT MEANS I'M GETTING OLDER, TOO! HA! HA! HA! HA! HA!
WELL, I ENJOYED OUR LITTLE CHAT, MR. PITTS. WHY, THE NEXT TIME I SEE YOU, YOU'LL BE AS TALL AS ME!
SO HE'S WHAT..... FIFTEEN?
FIFTEEN, GOING ON DEAD.

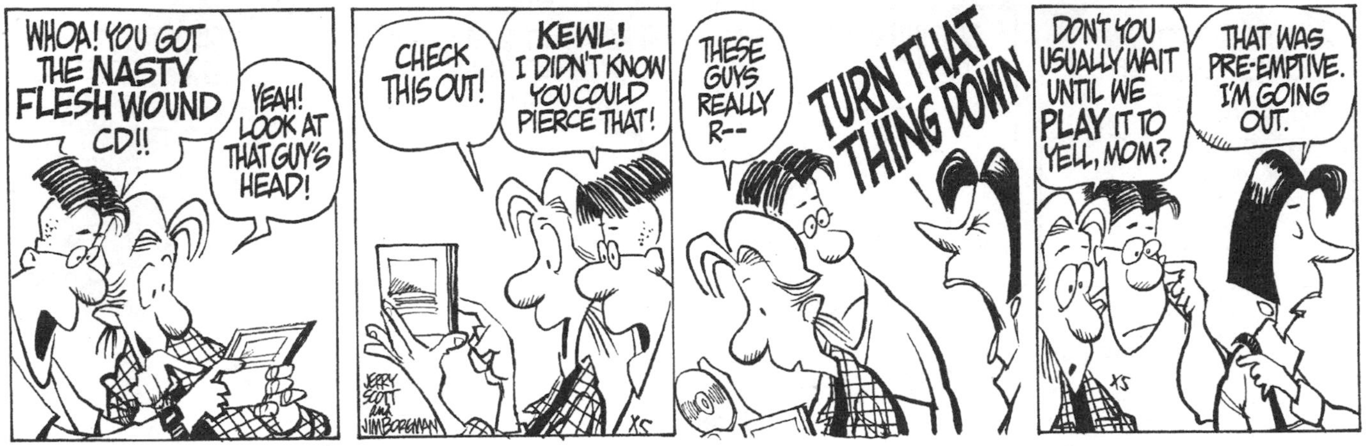
WHOA! YOU GOT THE NASTY FLESH WOUND CD!!
YEAH! LOOK AT THAT GUY'S HEAD!
CHECK THIS OUT!
KEWL! I DIDN'T KNOW YOU COULD PIERCE THAT!
JERRY SCOTT and JIM BORGMAN
THESE GUYS REALLY R--
TURN THAT THING DOWN
DON'T YOU USUALLY WAIT UNTIL WE PLAY IT TO YELL, MOM?
THAT WAS PRE-EMPTIVE. I'M GOING OUT.

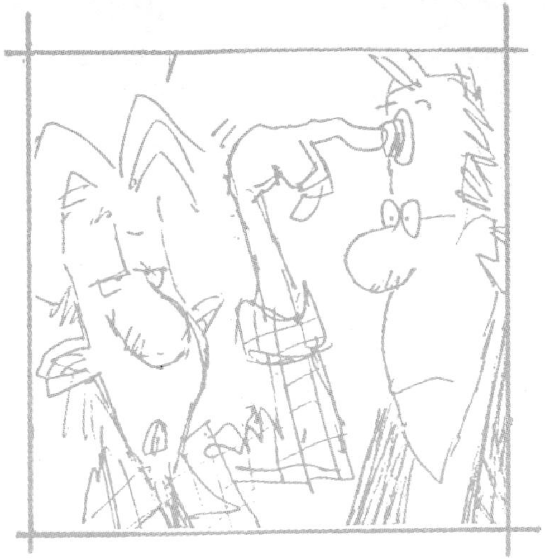

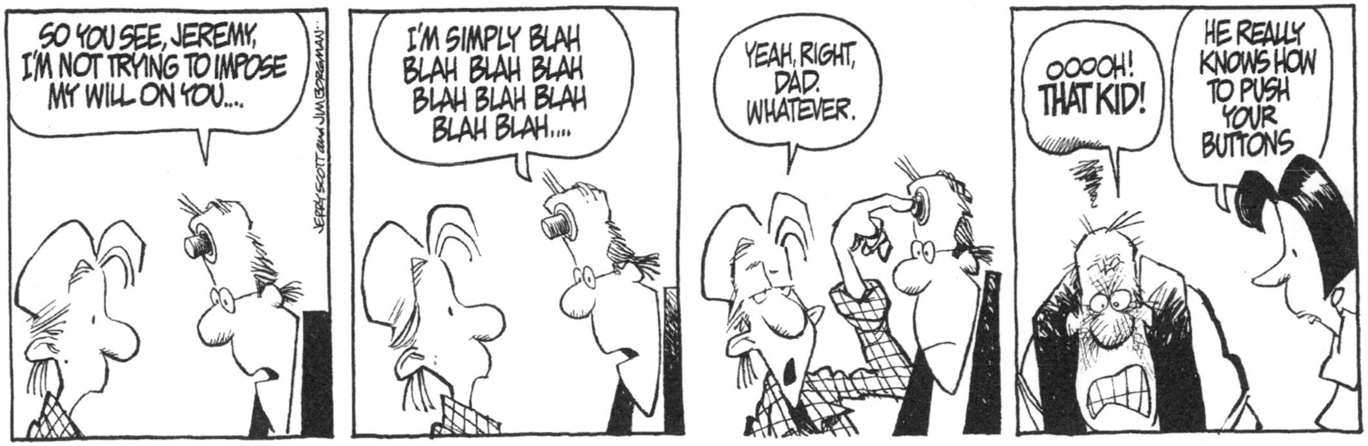
SO YOU SEE, JEREMY, I'M NOT TRYING TO IMPOSE MY WILL ON YOU....
JERRY SCOTT and JIM BORGMAN
I'M SIMPLY BLAH BLAH BLAH BLAH BLAH BLAH BLAH BLAH BLAH....
YEAH, RIGHT, DAD. WHATEVER.
OOOOH! THAT KID!
HE REALLY KNOWS HOW TO PUSH YOUR BUTTONS

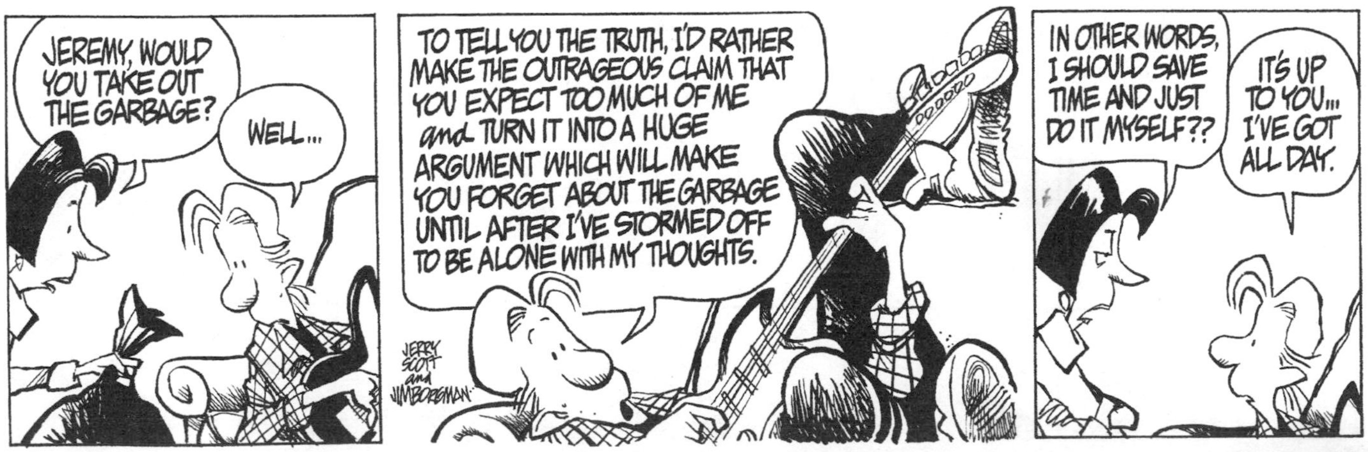
JEREMY, WOULD YOU TAKE OUT THE GARBAGE?
WELL...
TO TELL YOU THE TRUTH, I'D RATHER MAKE THE OUTRAGEOUS CLAIM THAT YOU EXPECT TOO MUCH OF ME and TURN IT INTO A HUGE ARGUMENT WHICH WILL MAKE YOU FORGET ABOUT THE GARBAGE UNTIL AFTER I'VE STORMED OFF TO BE ALONE WITH MY THOUGHTS.
JERRY SCOTT and JIM BORGMAN
IN OTHER WORDS, I SHOULD SAVE TIME AND JUST DO IT MYSELF??
IT'S UP TO YOU... I'VE GOT ALL DAY.

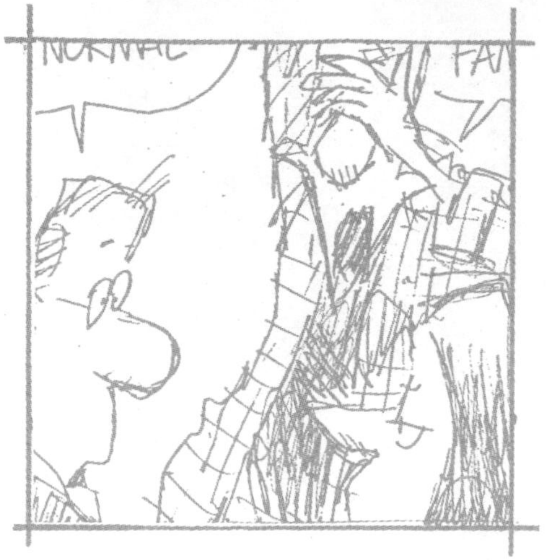

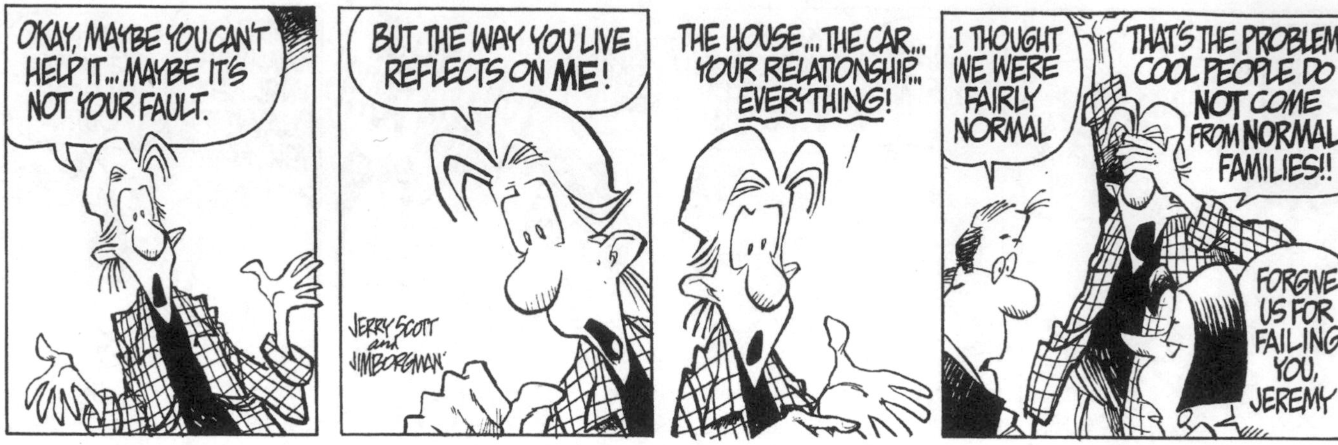

OKAY, MAYBE YOU CAN'T HELP IT... MAYBE IT'S NOT YOUR FAULT.
BUT THE WAY YOU LIVE REFLECTS ON ME!
JERRY SCOTT and JIMBORGMAN
THE HOUSE... THE CAR... YOUR RELATIONSHIP... EVERYTHING!
I THOUGHT WE WERE FAIRLY NORMAL
THAT'S THE PROBLEM! COOL PEOPLE DO NOT COME FROM NORMAL FAMILIES!!
FORGIVE US FOR FAILING YOU, JEREMY

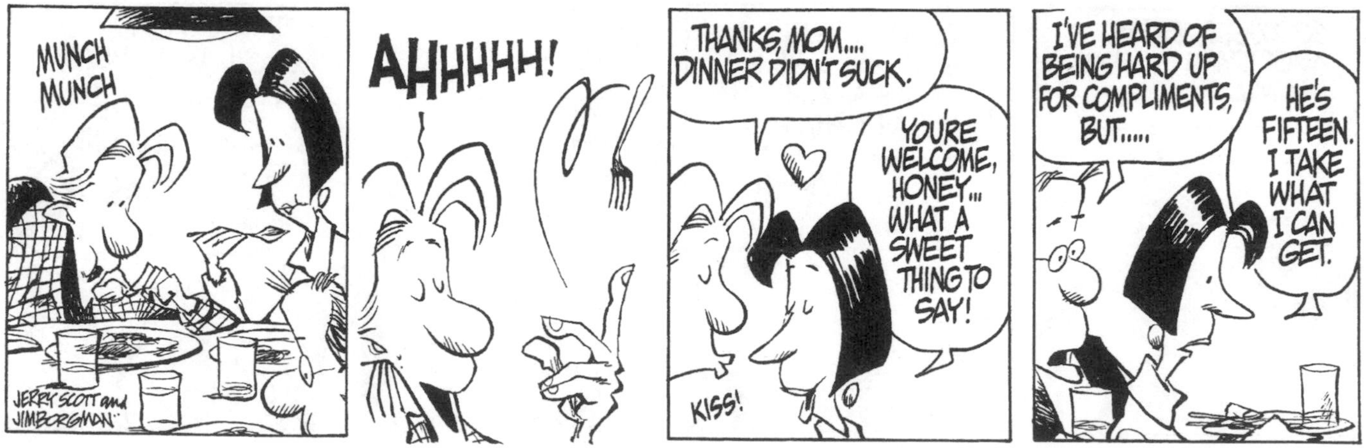

MUNCH MUNCH
JERRY SCOTT and JIMBORGMAN
AHHHHH!
THANKS, MOM.... DINNER DIDN'T SUCK.
YOU'RE WELCOME, HONEY... WHAT A SWEET THING TO SAY!
KISS!
I'VE HEARD OF BEING HARD UP FOR COMPLIMENTS, BUT.....
HE'S FIFTEEN. I TAKE WHAT I CAN GET.

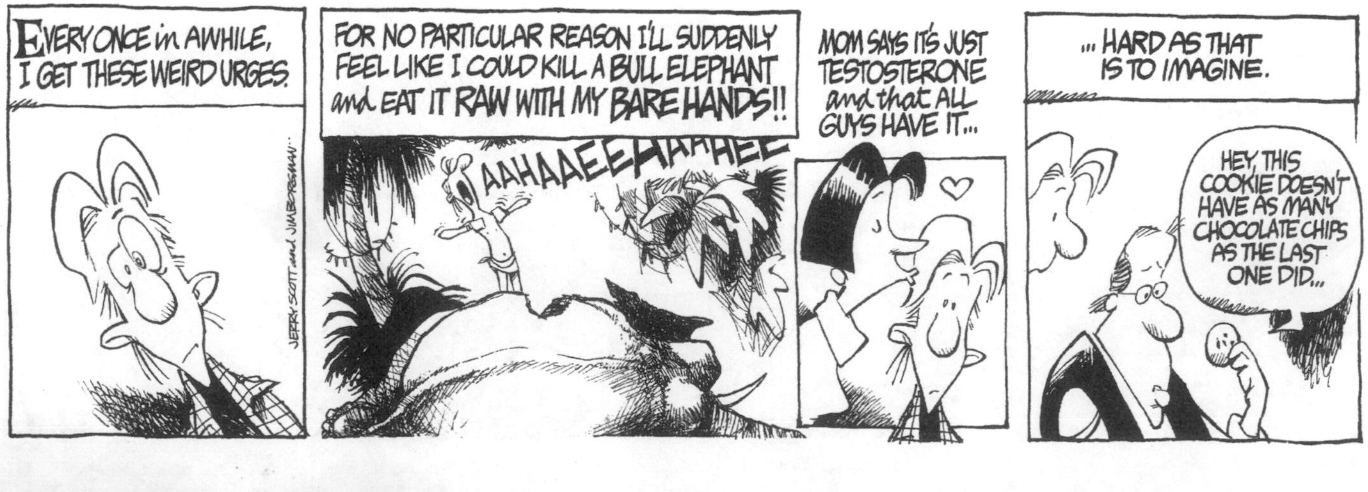

EVERY ONCE in AWHILE, I GET THESE WEIRD URGES.
JERRY SCOTT and JIMBORGMAN
FOR NO PARTICULAR REASON I'LL SUDDENLY FEEL LIKE I COULD KILL A BULL ELEPHANT and EAT IT RAW WITH MY BARE HANDS!!
MOM SAYS IT'S JUST TESTOSTERONE and that ALL GUYS HAVE IT...
... HARD AS THAT IS TO IMAGINE.
HEY, THIS COOKIE DOESN'T HAVE AS MANY CHOCOLATE CHIPS AS THE LAST ONE DID...

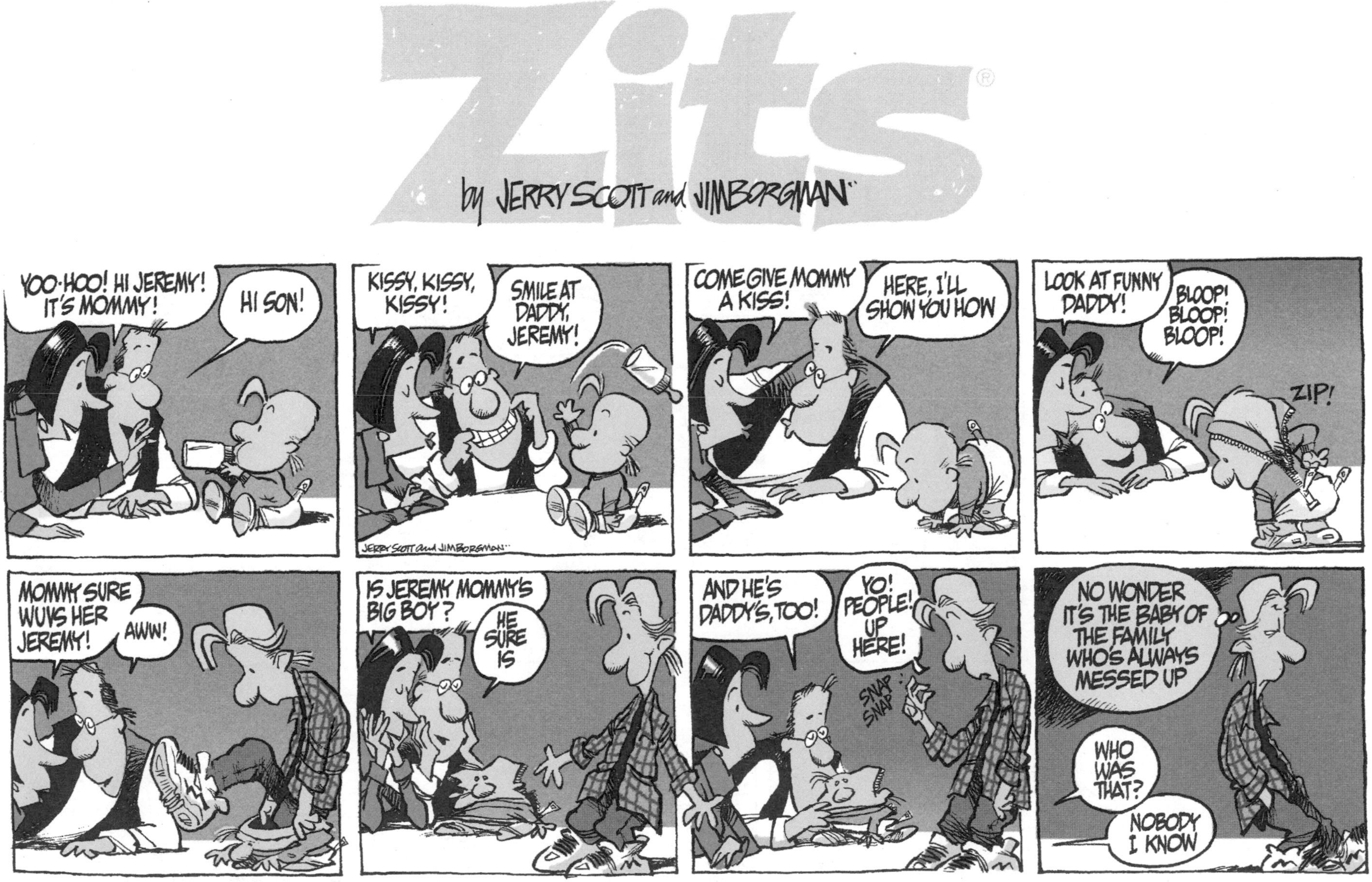
Zits®
by JERRY SCOTT and JIM BORGMAN
YOO-HOO! HI JEREMY! IT'S MOMMY!
HI SON!
KISSY, KISSY, KISSY!
SMILE AT DADDY, JEREMY!
JERRY SCOTT and JIM BORGMAN
COME GIVE MOMMY A KISS!
HERE, I'LL SHOW YOU HOW
LOOK AT FUNNY DADDY!
BLOOP! BLOOP! BLOOP!
ZIP!
MOMMY SURE WUVS HER JEREMY!
AWW!
IS JEREMY MOMMY'S BIG BOY?
HE SURE IS
AND HE'S DADDY'S, TOO!
YO! PEOPLE! UP HERE!
SNAP SNAP
NO WONDER IT'S THE BABY OF THE FAMILY WHO'S ALWAYS MESSED UP
WHO WAS THAT?
NOBODY I KNOW

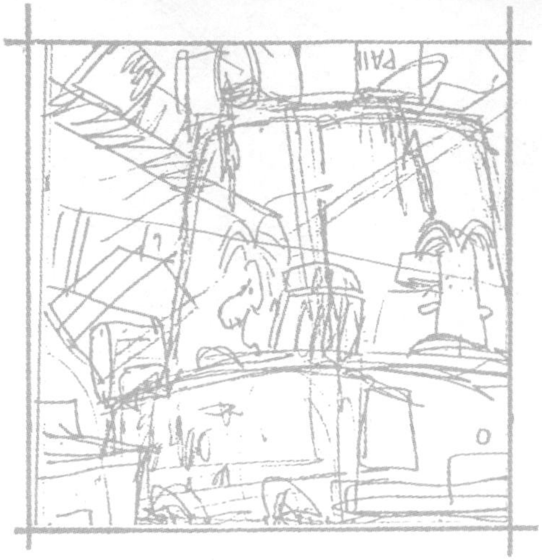

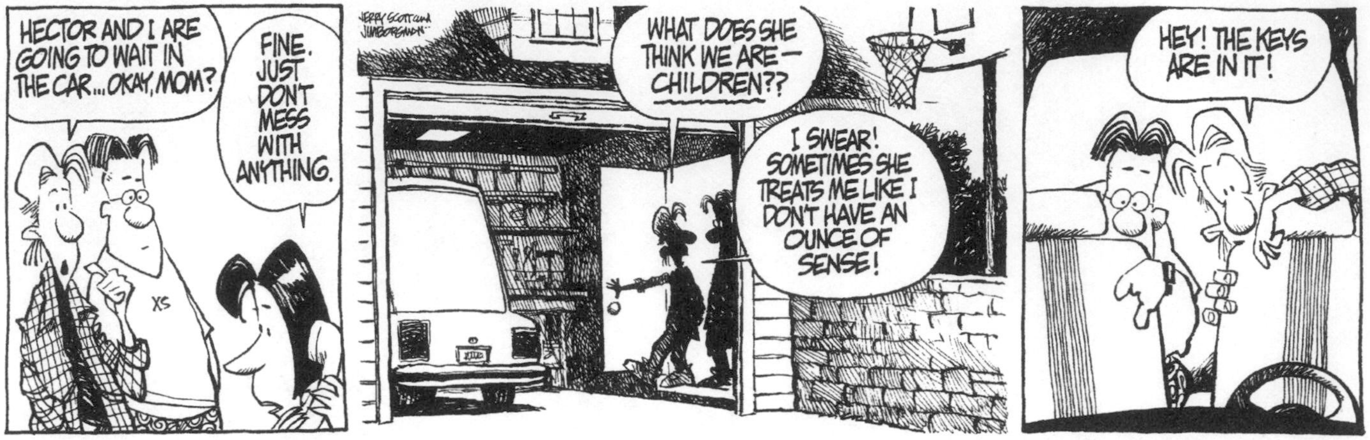
HECTOR AND I ARE GOING TO WAIT IN THE CAR... OKAY, MOM?
FINE. JUST DON'T MESS WITH ANYTHING.
WHAT DOES SHE THINK WE ARE— CHILDREN??
I SWEAR! SOMETIMES SHE TREATS ME LIKE I DON'T HAVE AN OUNCE OF SENSE!
HEY! THE KEYS ARE IN IT!

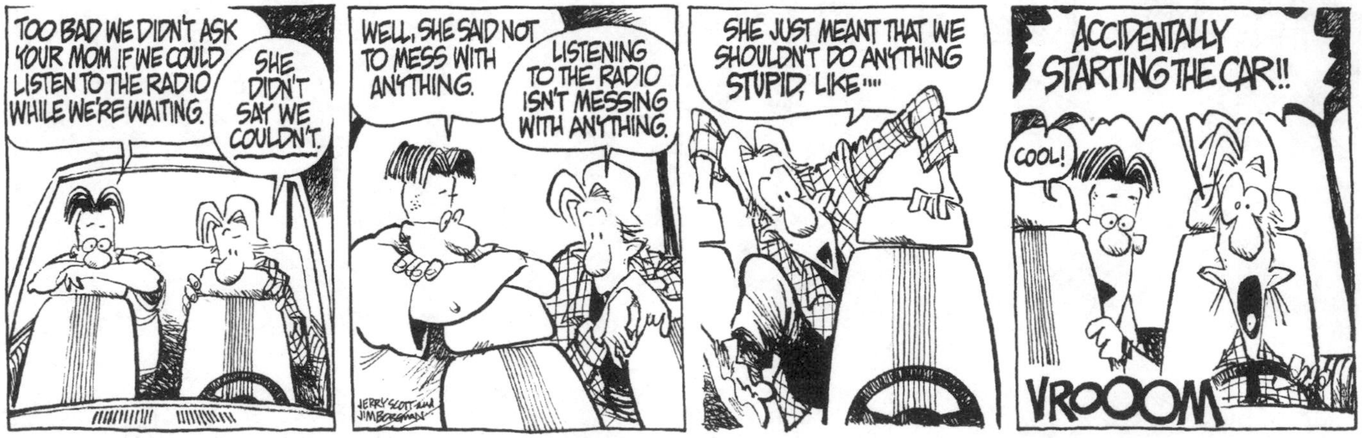
TOO BAD WE DIDN'T ASK YOUR MOM IF WE COULD LISTEN TO THE RADIO WHILE WE'RE WAITING.
SHE DIDN'T SAY WE COULDN'T.
WELL, SHE SAID NOT TO MESS WITH ANYTHING.
LISTENING TO THE RADIO ISN'T MESSING WITH ANYTHING.
SHE JUST MEANT THAT WE SHOULDN'T DO ANYTHING STUPID, LIKE....
ACCIDENTALLY STARTING THE CAR!!
COOL!
VROOOM

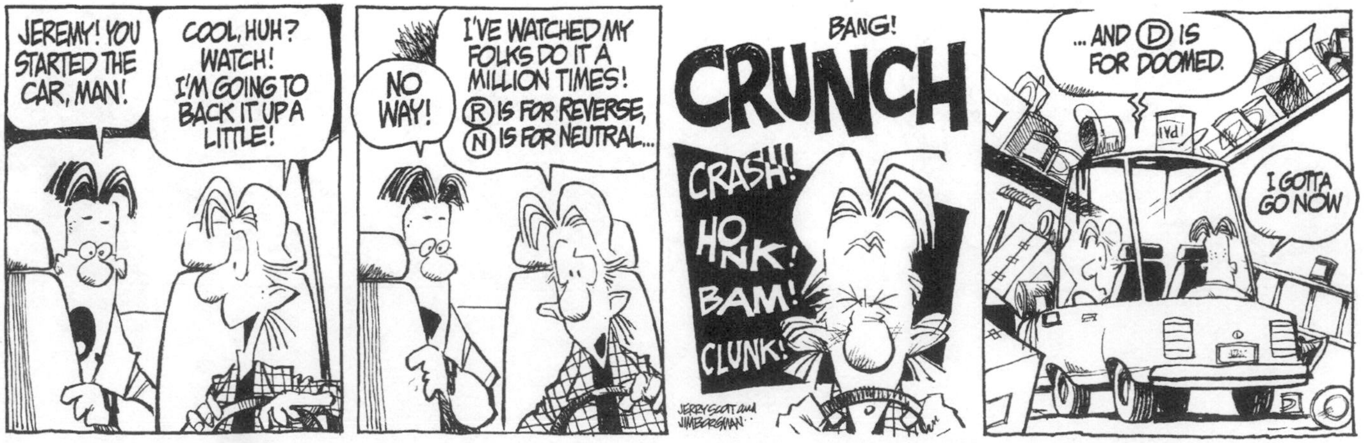
JEREMY! YOU STARTED THE CAR, MAN!
COOL, HUH? WATCH! I'M GOING TO BACK IT UP A LITTLE!
NO WAY!
I'VE WATCHED MY FOLKS DO IT A MILLION TIMES! (R) IS FOR REVERSE, (N) IS FOR NEUTRAL...
BANG!
CRUNCH
CRASH!
HONK!
BAM!
CLUNK!
...AND (D) IS FOR DOOMED.
I GOTTA GO NOW

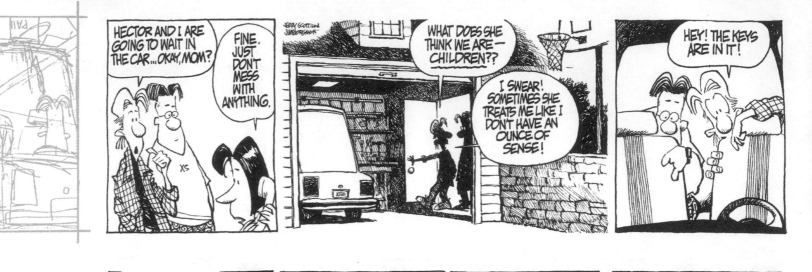

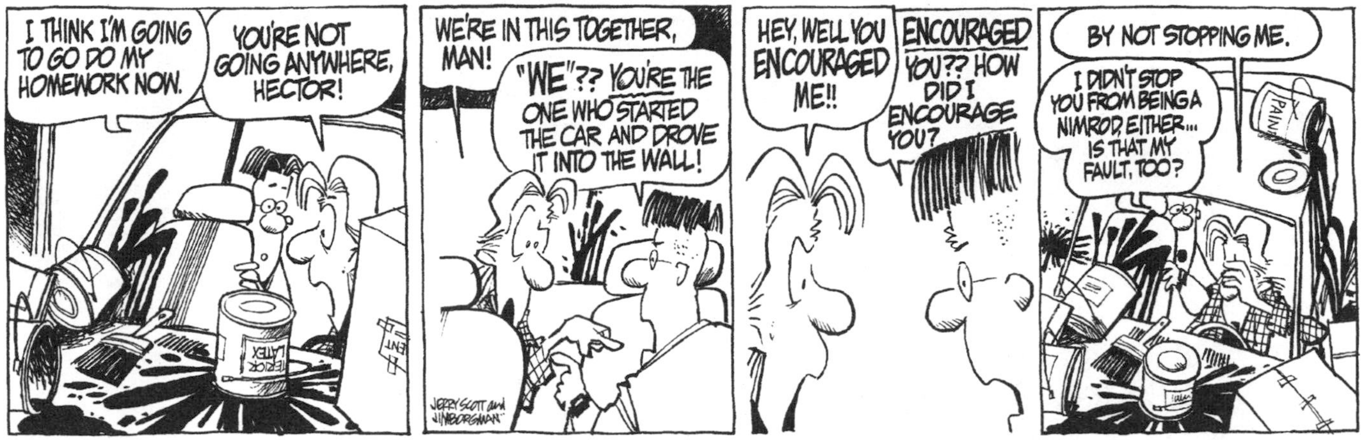
I THINK I'M GOING TO GO DO MY HOMEWORK NOW.
YOU'RE NOT GOING ANYWHERE, HECTOR!
WE'RE IN THIS TOGETHER, MAN!
"WE"?? YOU'RE THE ONE WHO STARTED THE CAR AND DROVE IT INTO THE WALL!
JERRY SCOTT and JIM BORGMAN
HEY, WELL YOU ENCOURAGED ME!!
ENCOURAGED YOU?? HOW DID I ENCOURAGE YOU?
BY NOT STOPPING ME.
I DIDN'T STOP YOU FROM BEING A NIMROD, EITHER... IS THAT MY FAULT, TOO?

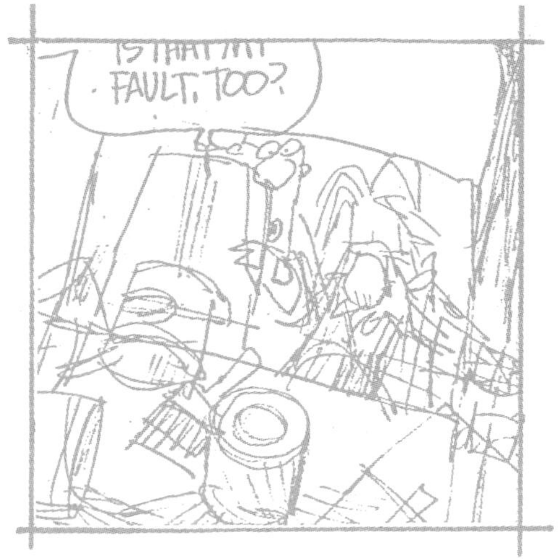
FAULT, TOO?

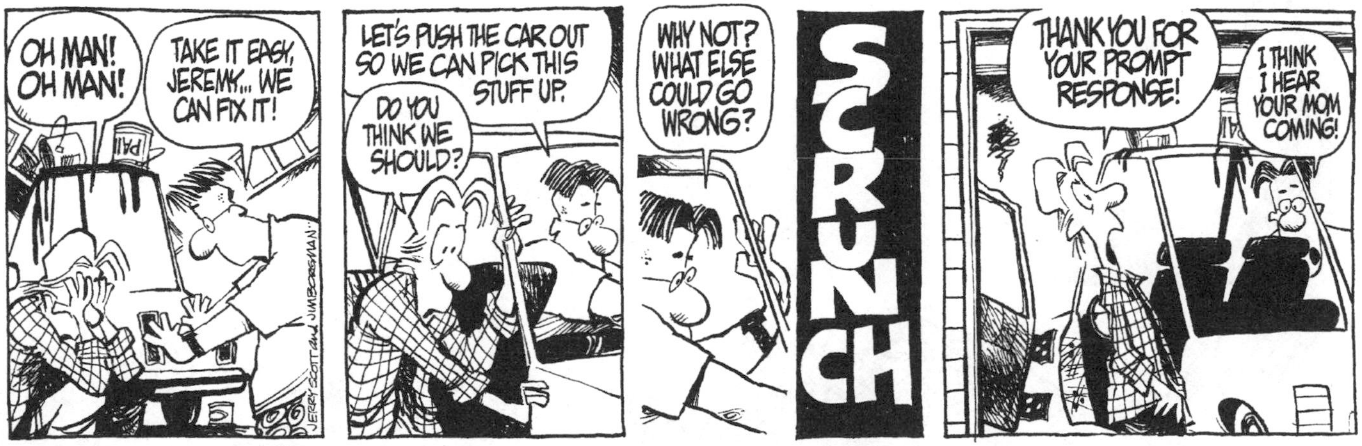
OH MAN! OH MAN!
TAKE IT EASY, JEREMY... WE CAN FIX IT!
JERRY SCOTT and JIM BORGMAN
LET'S PUSH THE CAR OUT SO WE CAN PICK THIS STUFF UP.
DO YOU THINK WE SHOULD?
WHY NOT? WHAT ELSE COULD GO WRONG?
SCRUNCH
THANK YOU FOR YOUR PROMPT RESPONSE!
I THINK I HEAR YOUR MOM COMING!

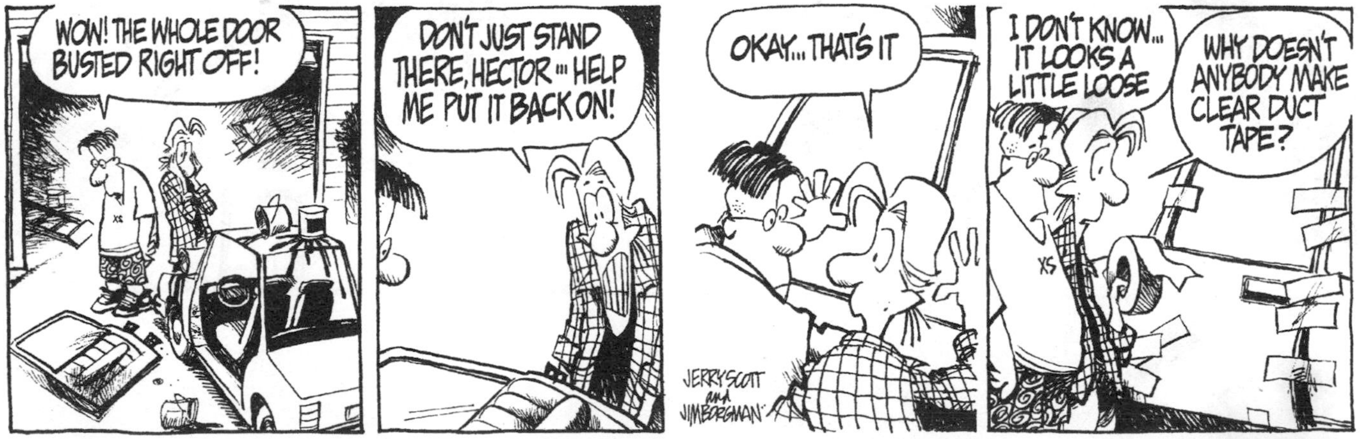
WOW! THE WHOLE DOOR BUSTED RIGHT OFF!
DON'T JUST STAND THERE, HECTOR... HELP ME PUT IT BACK ON!
OKAY... THAT'S IT
JERRY SCOTT and JIM BORGMAN
I DON'T KNOW... IT LOOKS A LITTLE LOOSE
WHY DOESN'T ANYBODY MAKE CLEAR DUCT TAPE?

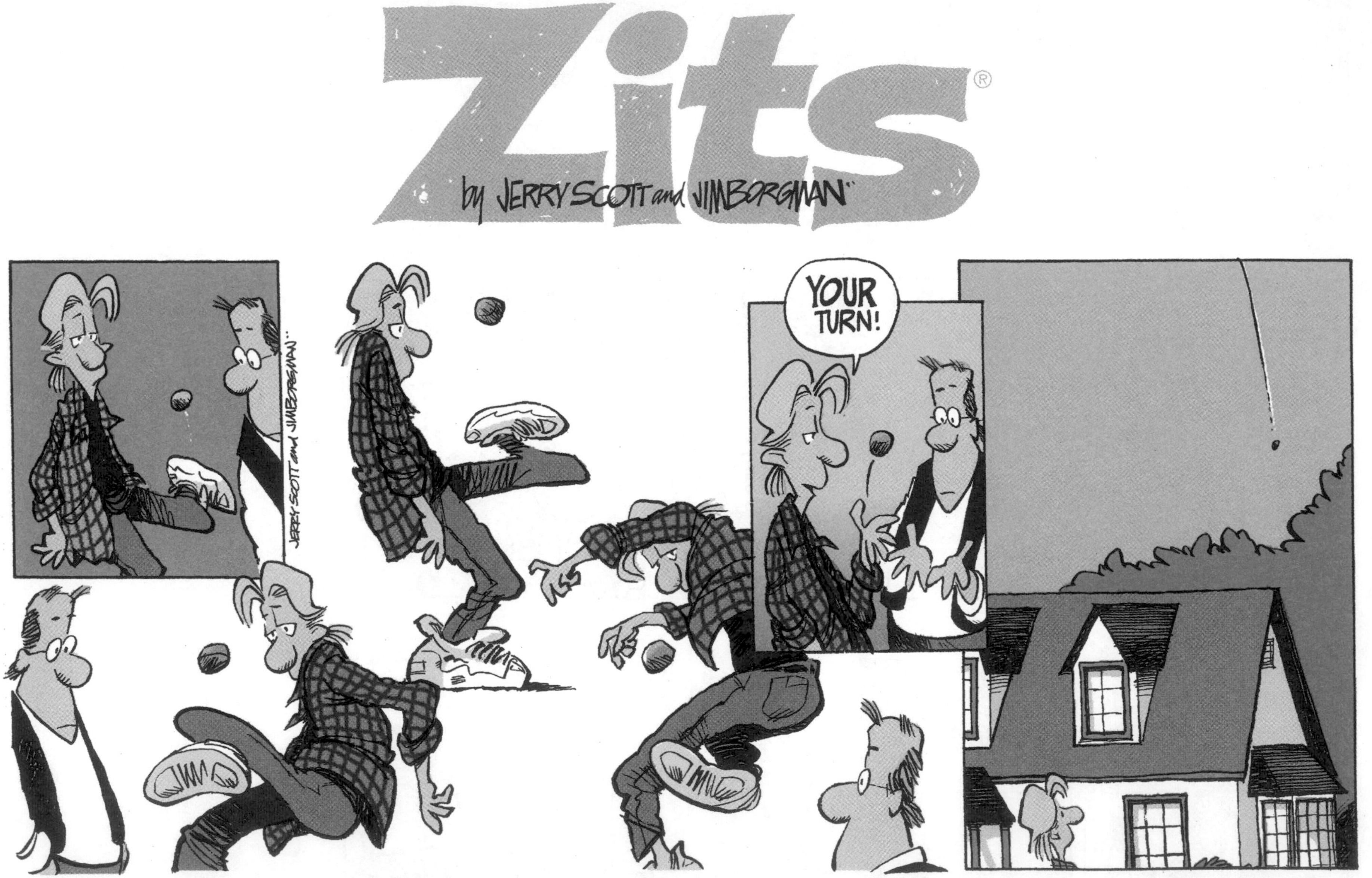
Zits®
by JERRY SCOTT and JIM BORGMAN
JERRY SCOTT and JIM BORGMAN
YOUR TURN!

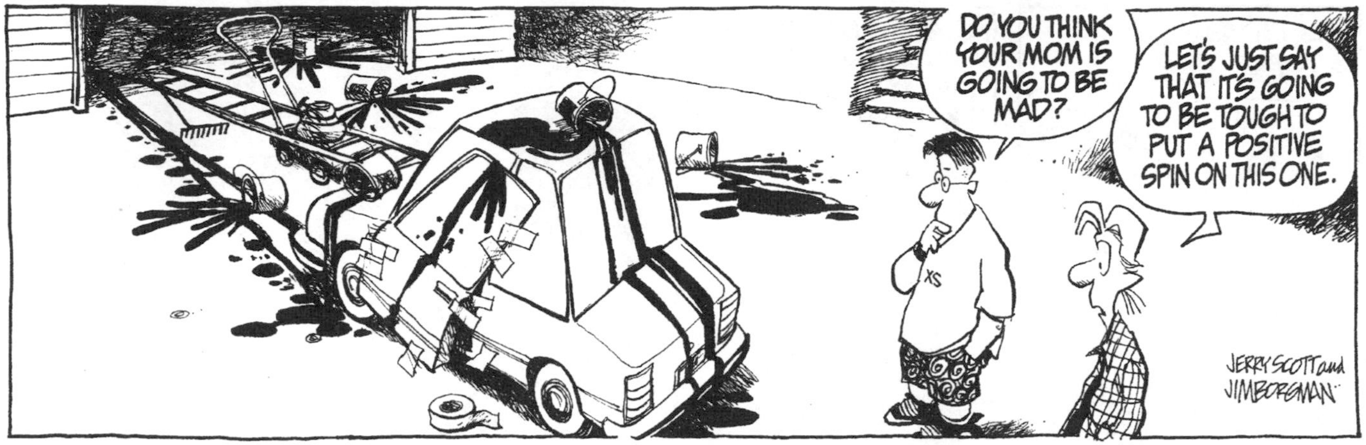
DO YOU THINK YOUR MOM IS GOING TO BE MAD?
LET'S JUST SAY THAT IT'S GOING TO BE TOUGH TO PUT A POSITIVE SPIN ON THIS ONE.
JERRY SCOTT and JIMBORGMAN

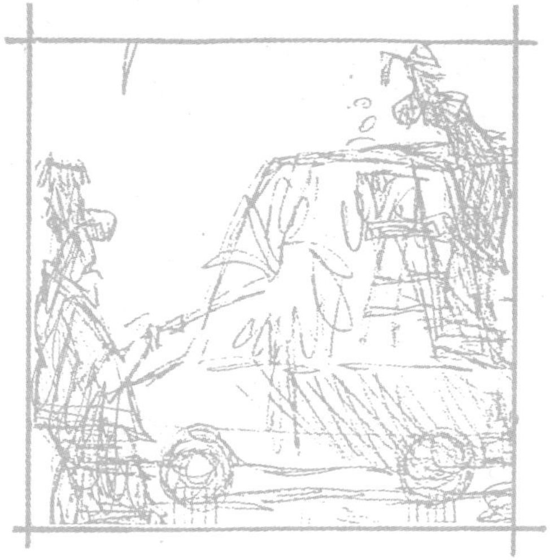

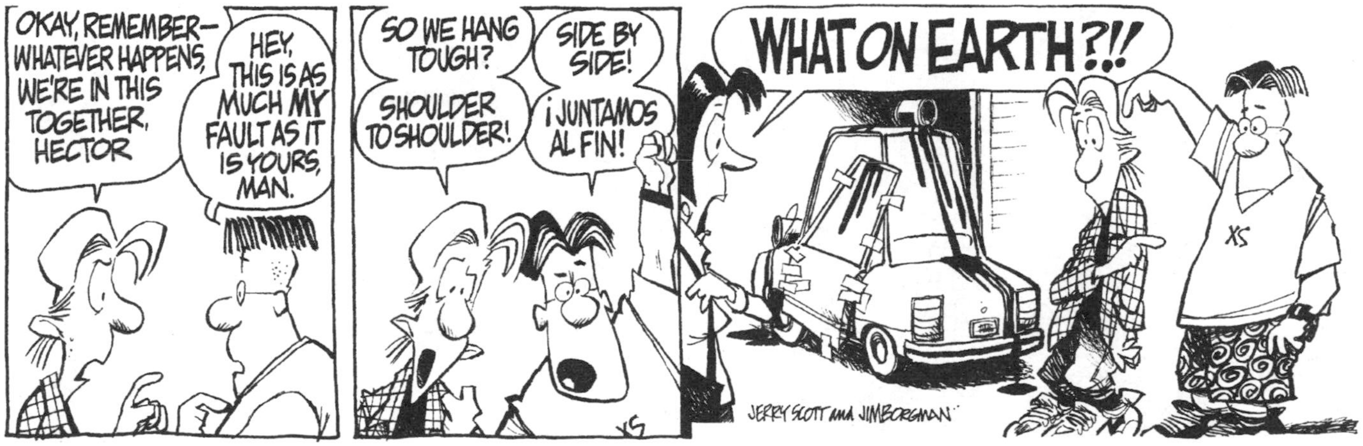
OKAY, REMEMBER— WHATEVER HAPPENS, WE'RE IN THIS TOGETHER, HECTOR
HEY, THIS IS AS MUCH MY FAULT AS IT IS YOURS, MAN.
SO WE HANG TOUGH?
SIDE BY SIDE!
SHOULDER TO SHOULDER!
¡JUNTAMOS AL FIN!
WHAT ON EARTH?!!
JERRY SCOTT and JIMBORGMAN

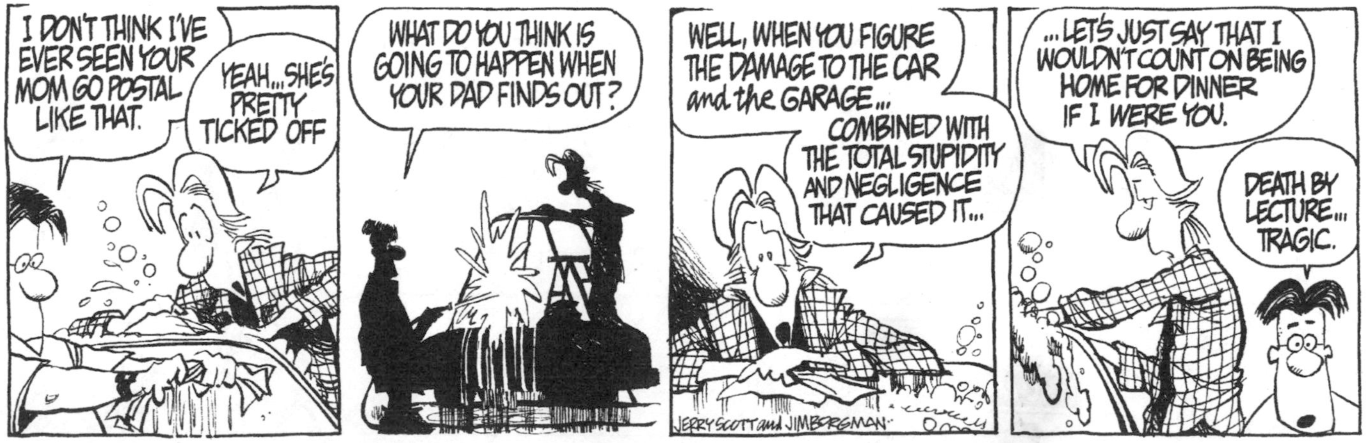
I DON'T THINK I'VE EVER SEEN YOUR MOM GO POSTAL LIKE THAT.
YEAH... SHE'S PRETTY TICKED OFF
WHAT DO YOU THINK IS GOING TO HAPPEN WHEN YOUR DAD FINDS OUT?
WELL, WHEN YOU FIGURE THE DAMAGE TO THE CAR and the GARAGE...
COMBINED WITH THE TOTAL STUPIDITY AND NEGLIGENCE THAT CAUSED IT...
...LET'S JUST SAY THAT I WOULDN'T COUNT ON BEING HOME FOR DINNER IF I WERE YOU.
DEATH BY LECTURE... TRAGIC.
JERRY SCOTT and JIMBORGMAN

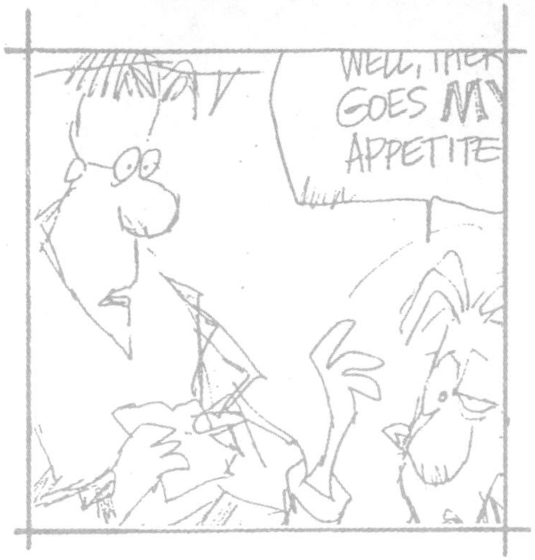
WELL, THER
GOES MY
APPETITE

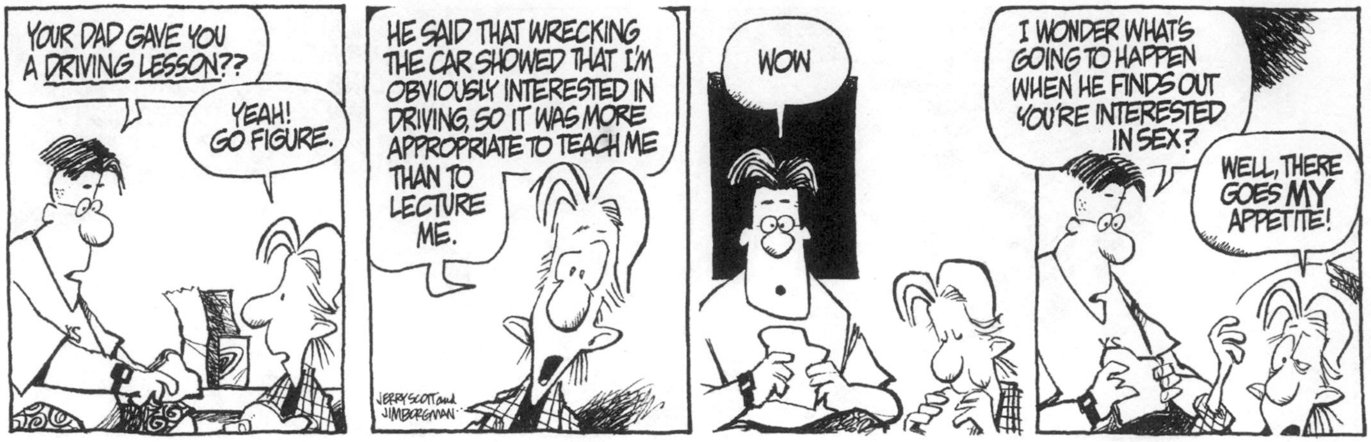
YOUR DAD GAVE YOU A DRIVING LESSON??
YEAH! GO FIGURE.
HE SAID THAT WRECKING THE CAR SHOWED THAT I'M OBVIOUSLY INTERESTED IN DRIVING, SO IT WAS MORE APPROPRIATE TO TEACH ME THAN TO LECTURE ME.
JERRY SCOTT and JIM BORGMAN
WOW
I WONDER WHAT'S GOING TO HAPPEN WHEN HE FINDS OUT YOU'RE INTERESTED IN SEX?
WELL, THERE GOES MY APPETITE!

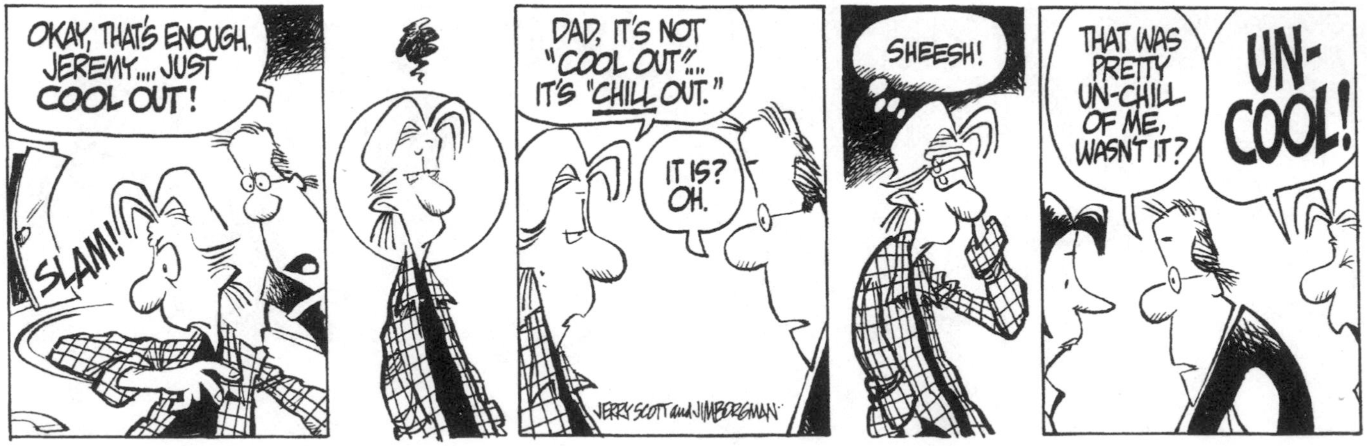
OKAY, THAT'S ENOUGH, JEREMY.... JUST COOL OUT!
SLAM!
DAD, IT'S NOT "COOL OUT".... IT'S "CHILL OUT."
IT IS? OH.
JERRY SCOTT and JIM BORGMAN
SHEESH!
THAT WAS PRETTY UN-CHILL OF ME, WASN'T IT?
UN-COOL!

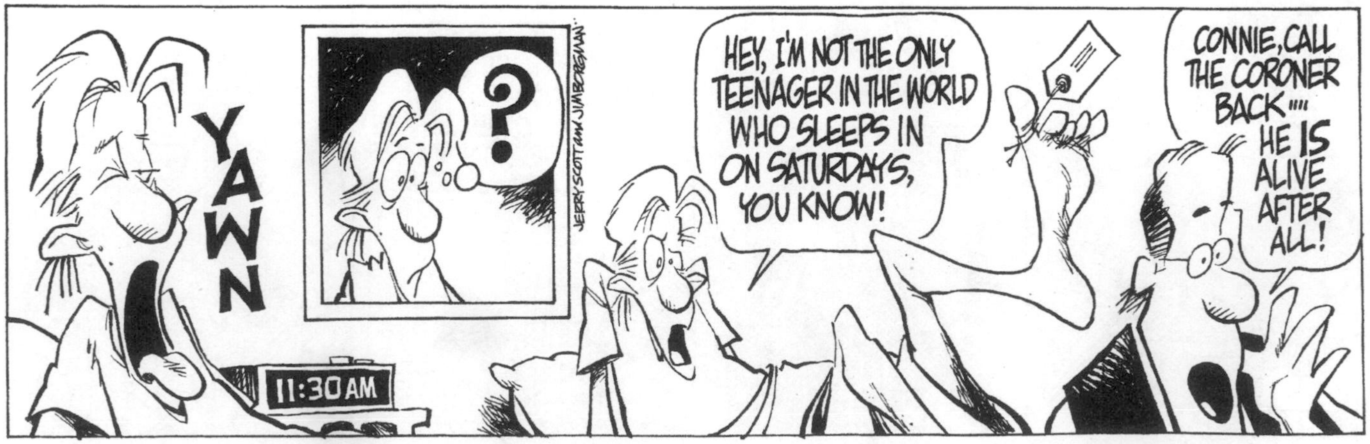
YAWN
11:30 AM
?
JERRY SCOTT and JIM BORGMAN
HEY, I'M NOT THE ONLY TEENAGER IN THE WORLD WHO SLEEPS IN ON SATURDAYS, YOU KNOW!
CONNIE, CALL THE CORONER BACK.... HE IS ALIVE AFTER ALL!

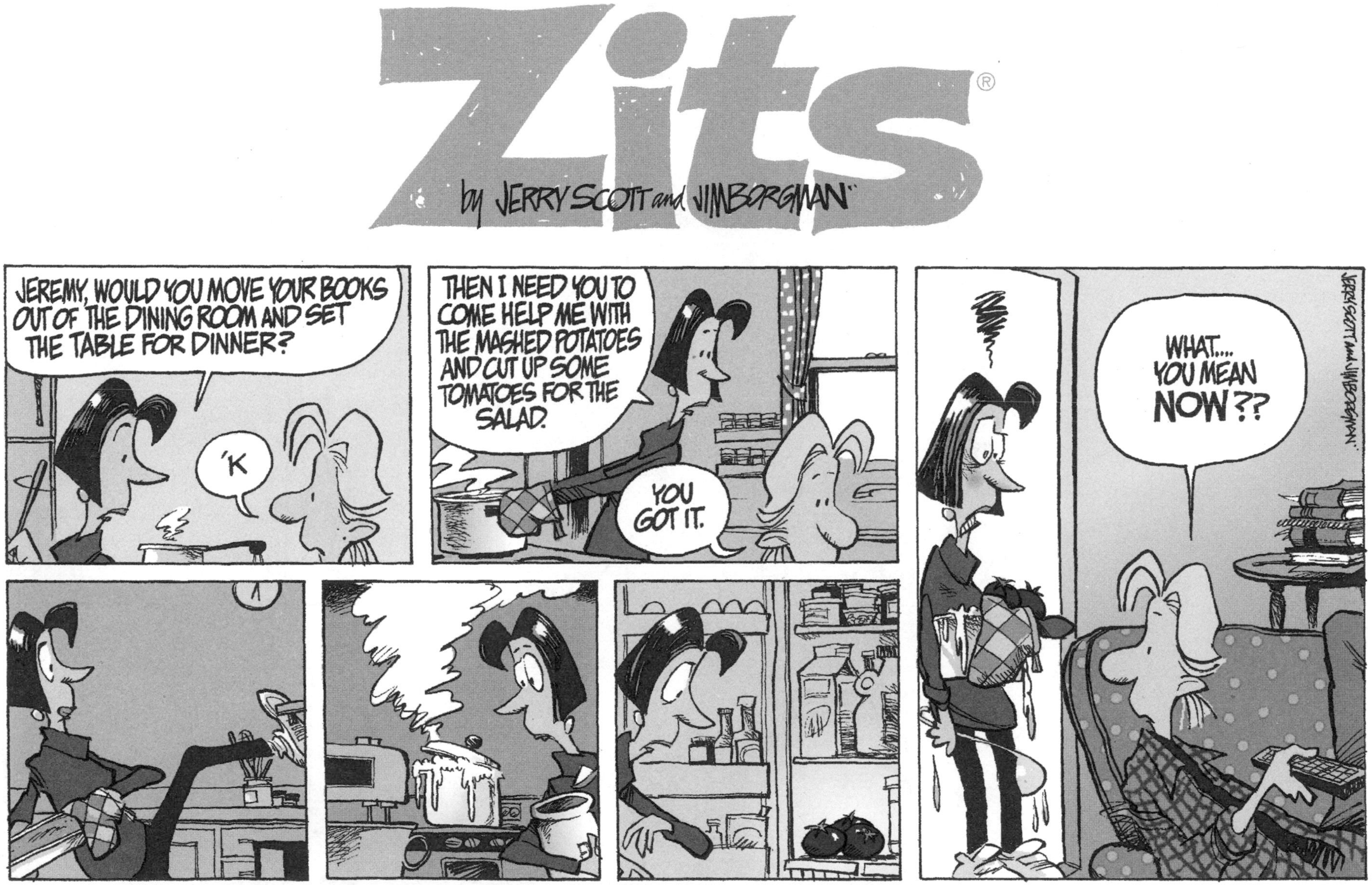
Zits®
by JERRY SCOTT and JIM BORGMAN
JEREMY, WOULD YOU MOVE YOUR BOOKS OUT OF THE DINING ROOM AND SET THE TABLE FOR DINNER?
'K
THEN I NEED YOU TO COME HELP ME WITH THE MASHED POTATOES AND CUT UP SOME TOMATOES FOR THE SALAD.
YOU GOT IT.
JERRY SCOTT and JIM BORGMAN
WHAT.... YOU MEAN NOW??

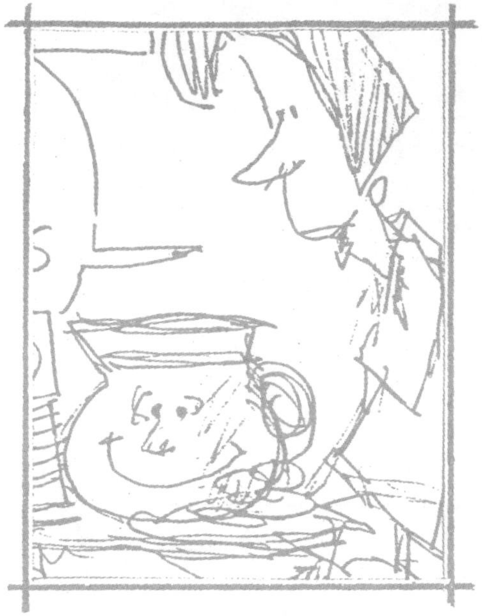

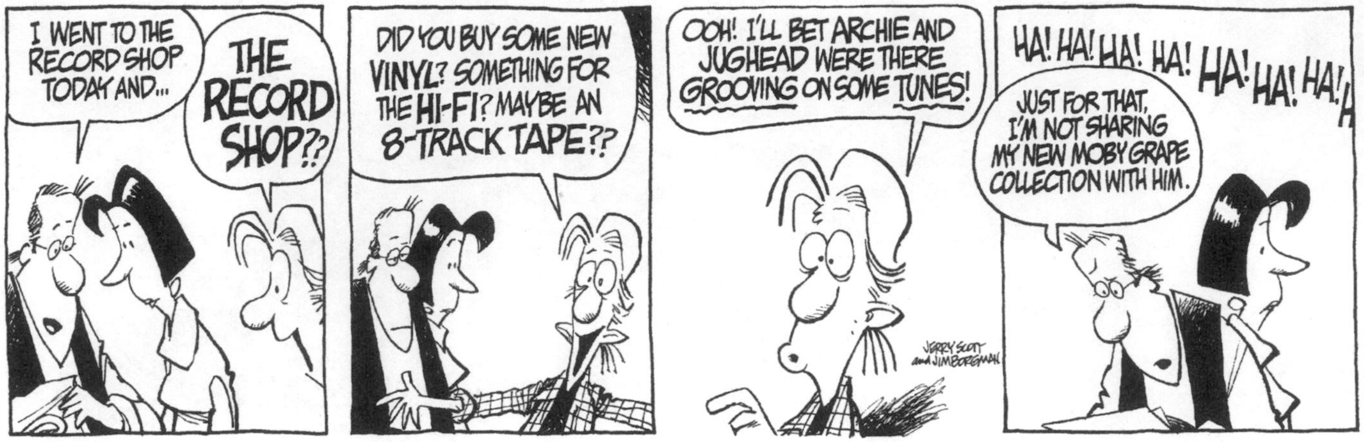

I WENT TO THE RECORD SHOP TODAY AND...
THE RECORD SHOP??
DID YOU BUY SOME NEW VINYL? SOMETHING FOR THE HI-FI? MAYBE AN 8-TRACK TAPE??
OOH! I'LL BET ARCHIE AND JUGHEAD WERE THERE GROOVING ON SOME TUNES!
JERRY SCOTT and JIM BORGMAN
HA! HA! HA! HA! HA! HA! HA!
JUST FOR THAT, I'M NOT SHARING MY NEW MOBY GRAPE COLLECTION WITH HIM.

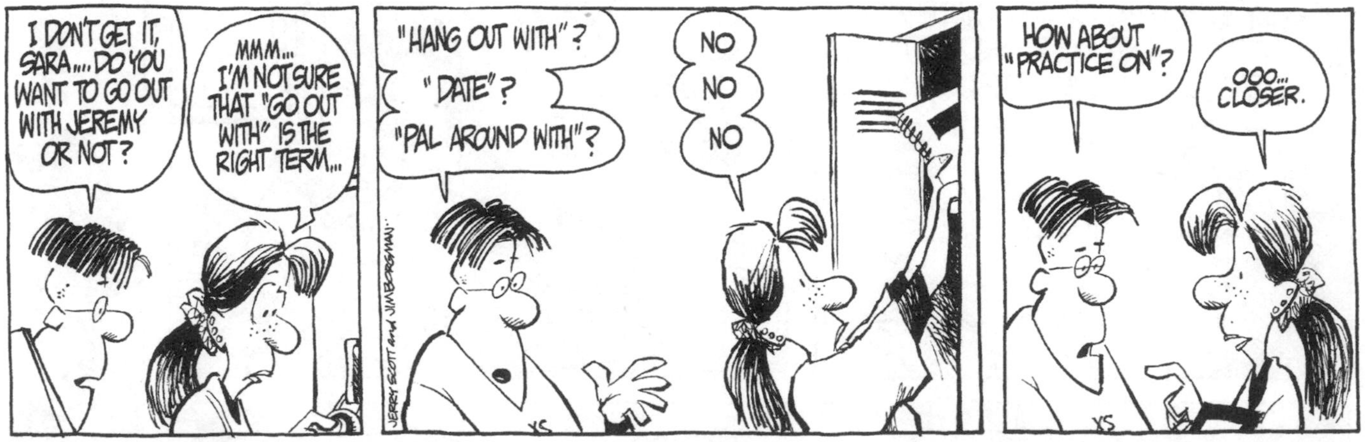

I DON'T GET IT, SARA.... DO YOU WANT TO GO OUT WITH JEREMY OR NOT?
MMM... I'M NOT SURE THAT "GO OUT WITH" IS THE RIGHT TERM...
JERRY SCOTT and JIM BORGMAN
"HANG OUT WITH"?
"DATE"?
"PAL AROUND WITH"?
NO
NO
NO
HOW ABOUT "PRACTICE ON"?
OOO... CLOSER.

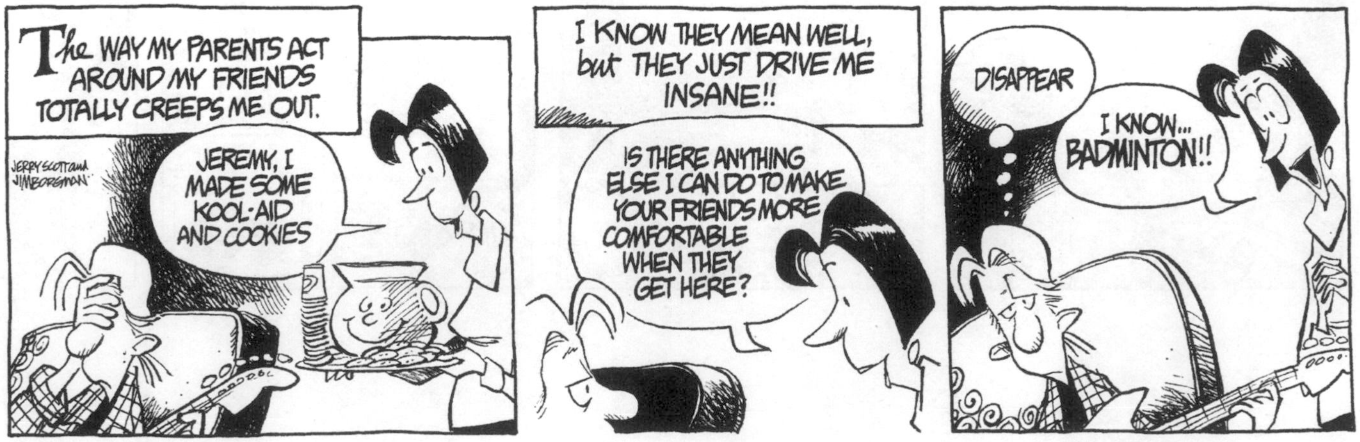

The WAY MY PARENTS ACT AROUND MY FRIENDS TOTALLY CREEPS ME OUT.
JERRY SCOTT and JIM BORGMAN
JEREMY, I MADE SOME KOOL-AID AND COOKIES
I KNOW THEY MEAN WELL, but THEY JUST DRIVE ME INSANE!!
IS THERE ANYTHING ELSE I CAN DO TO MAKE YOUR FRIENDS MORE COMFORTABLE WHEN THEY GET HERE?
DISAPPEAR
I KNOW... BADMINTON!!

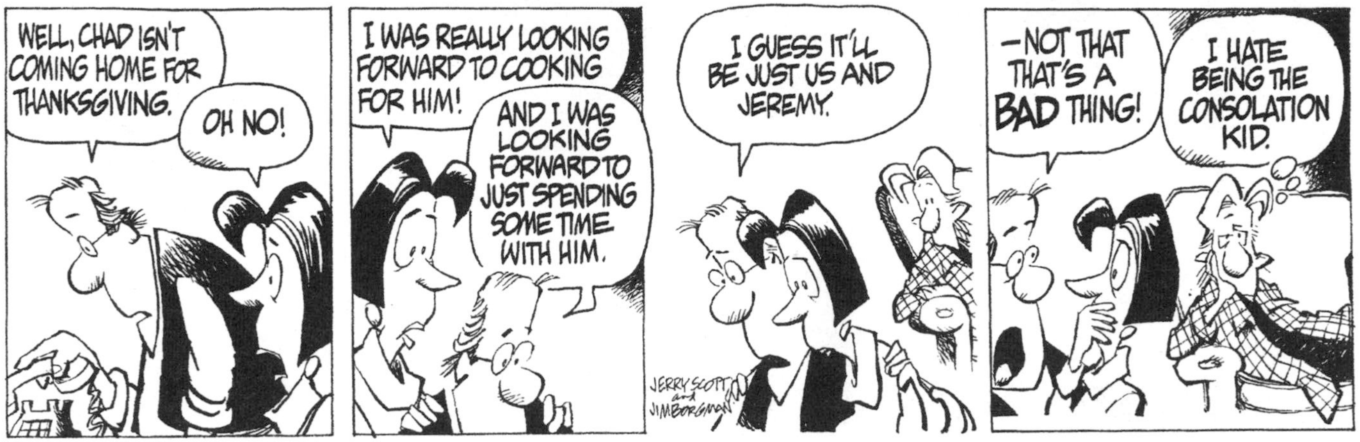
WELL, CHAD ISN'T COMING HOME FOR THANKSGIVING.
OH NO!
I WAS REALLY LOOKING FORWARD TO COOKING FOR HIM!
AND I WAS LOOKING FORWARD TO JUST SPENDING SOME TIME WITH HIM.
I GUESS IT'LL BE JUST US AND JEREMY.
—NOT THAT THAT'S A BAD THING!
I HATE BEING THE CONSOLATION KID.

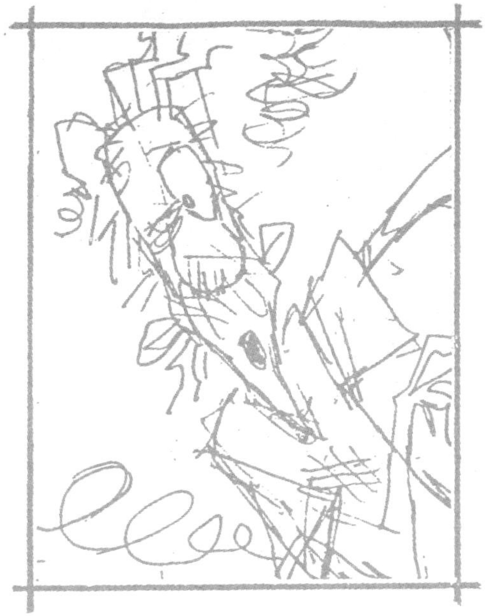

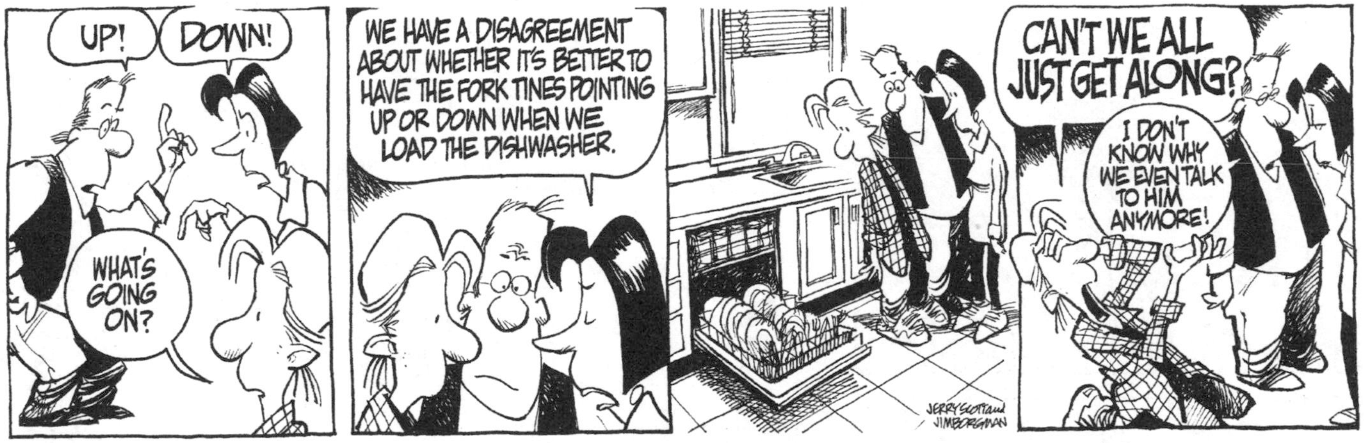
UP!
DOWN!
WHAT'S GOING ON?
WE HAVE A DISAGREEMENT ABOUT WHETHER IT'S BETTER TO HAVE THE FORK TINES POINTING UP OR DOWN WHEN WE LOAD THE DISHWASHER.
CAN'T WE ALL JUST GET ALONG?
I DON'T KNOW WHY WE EVEN TALK TO HIM ANYMORE!

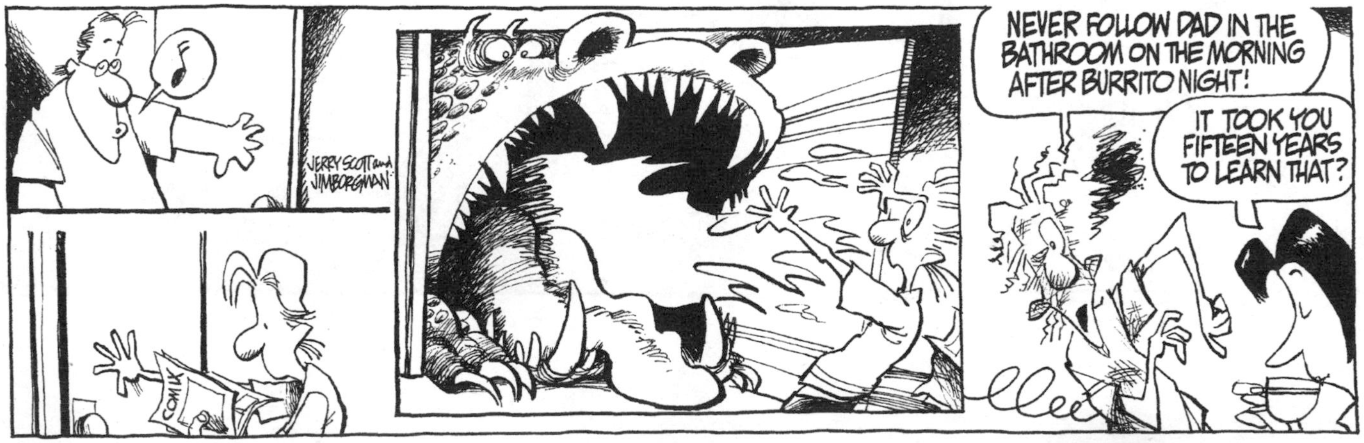
COMIX
NEVER FOLLOW DAD IN THE BATHROOM ON THE MORNING AFTER BURRITO NIGHT!
IT TOOK YOU FIFTEEN YEARS TO LEARN THAT?

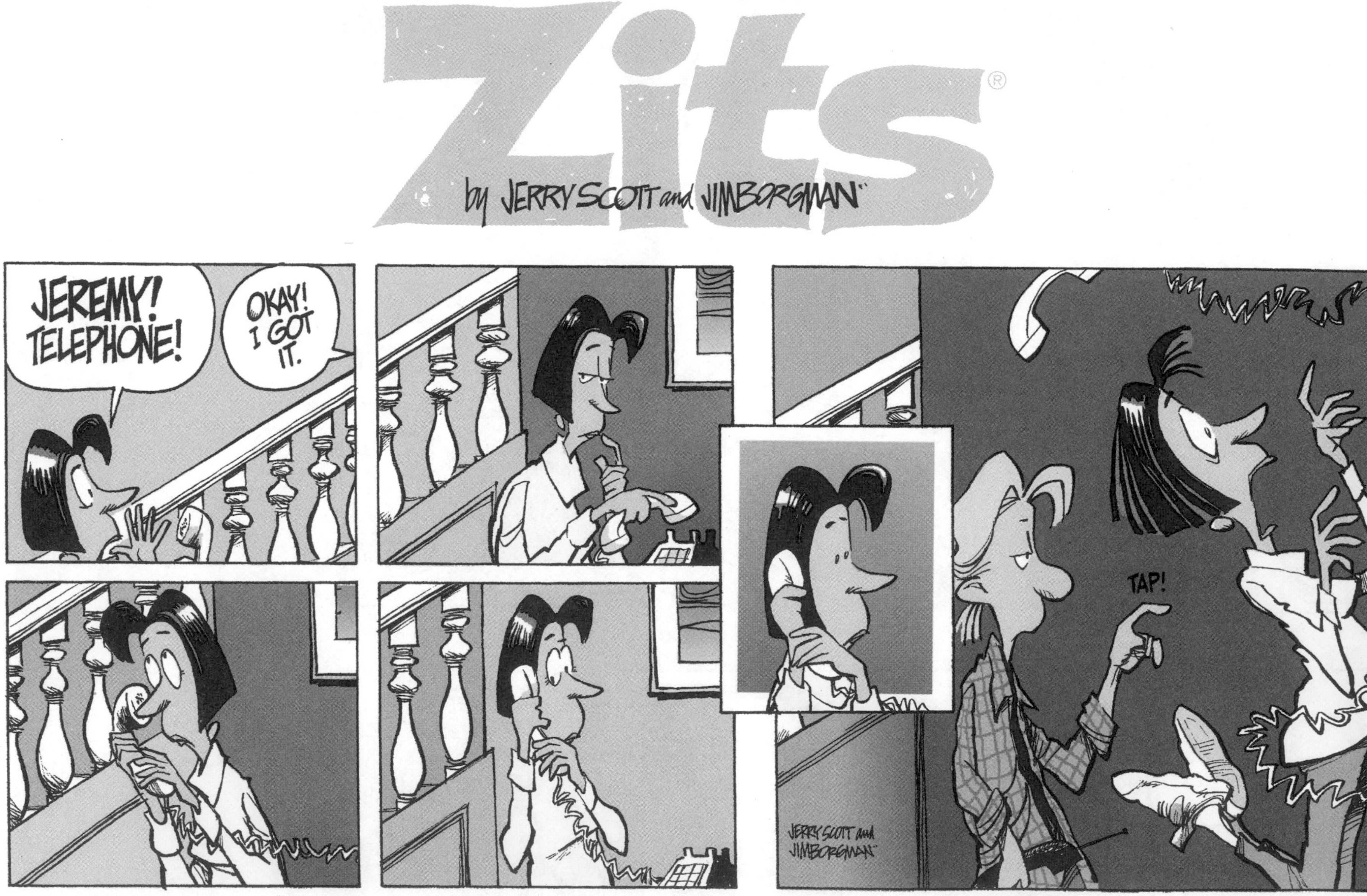
Zits®
by JERRY SCOTT and JIMBORGMAN
JEREMY! TELEPHONE!
OKAY! I GOT IT.
TAP!
JERRY SCOTT and JIMBORGMAN

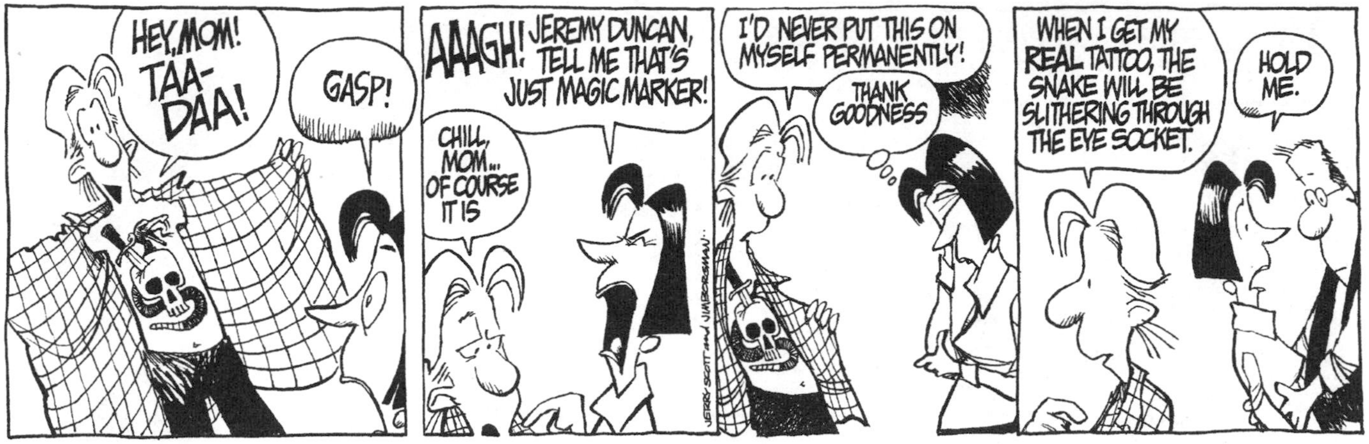
HEY, MOM! TAA-DAA!
GASP!
AAAGH! JEREMY DUNCAN, TELL ME THAT'S JUST MAGIC MARKER!
CHILL, MOM... OF COURSE IT IS
JERRY SCOTT and JIMBORGMAN
I'D NEVER PUT THIS ON MYSELF PERMANENTLY!
THANK GOODNESS
WHEN I GET MY REAL TATTOO, THE SNAKE WILL BE SLITHERING THROUGH THE EYE SOCKET.
HOLD ME.

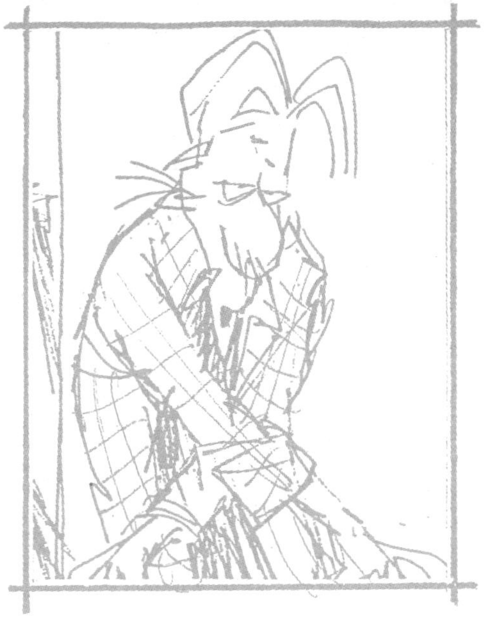

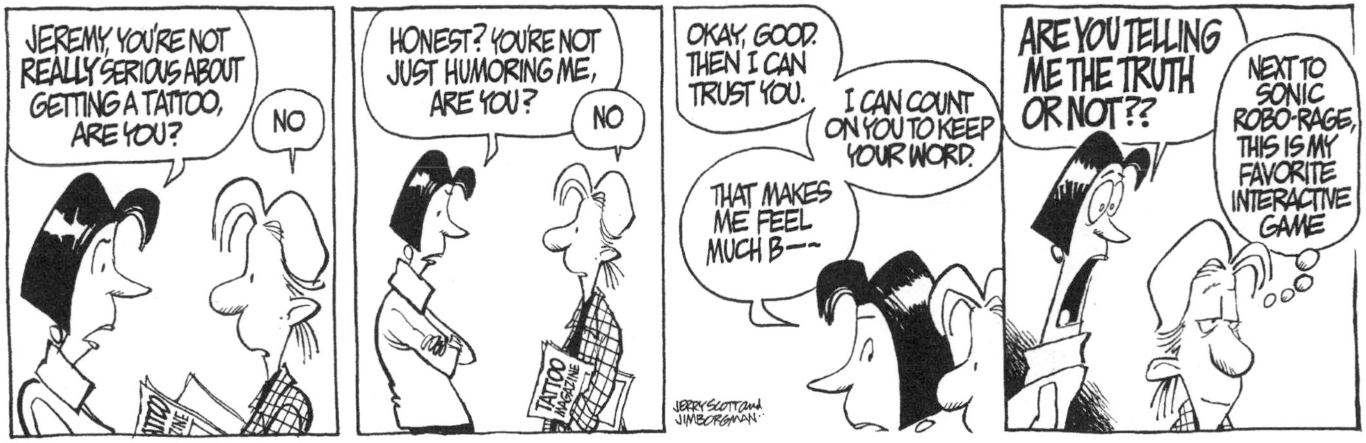
JEREMY, YOU'RE NOT REALLY SERIOUS ABOUT GETTING A TATTOO, ARE YOU?
NO
HONEST? YOU'RE NOT JUST HUMORING ME, ARE YOU?
NO
TATTOO MAGAZINE
OKAY, GOOD. THEN I CAN TRUST YOU.
I CAN COUNT ON YOU TO KEEP YOUR WORD.
THAT MAKES ME FEEL MUCH B---
JERRY SCOTT and JIMBORGMAN
ARE YOU TELLING ME THE TRUTH OR NOT??
NEXT TO SONIC ROBO-RAGE, THIS IS MY FAVORITE INTERACTIVE GAME

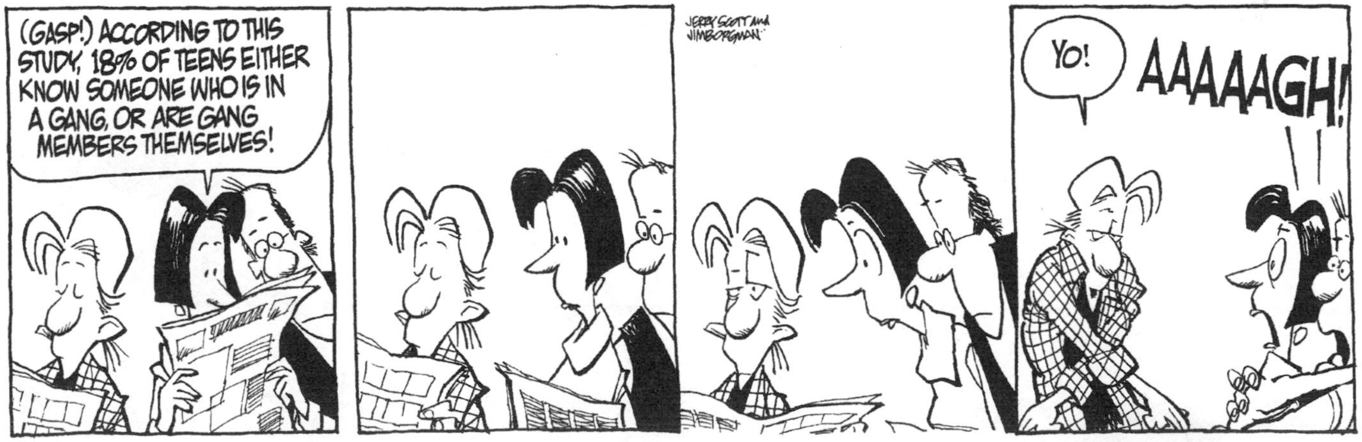
(GASP!) ACCORDING TO THIS STUDY, 18% OF TEENS EITHER KNOW SOMEONE WHO IS IN A GANG, OR ARE GANG MEMBERS THEMSELVES!
JERRY SCOTT and JIMBORGMAN
YO!
AAAAAGH!

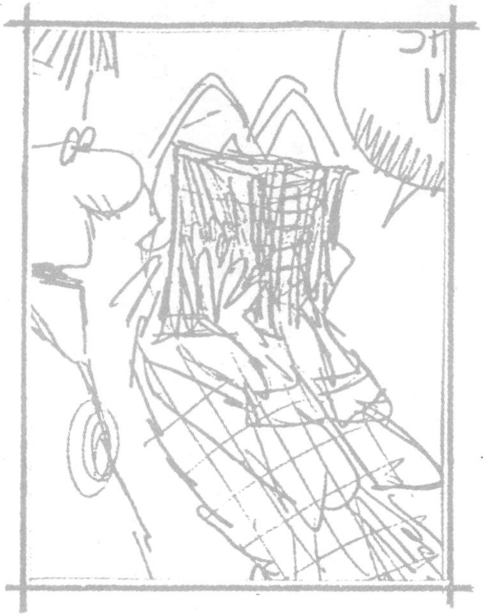

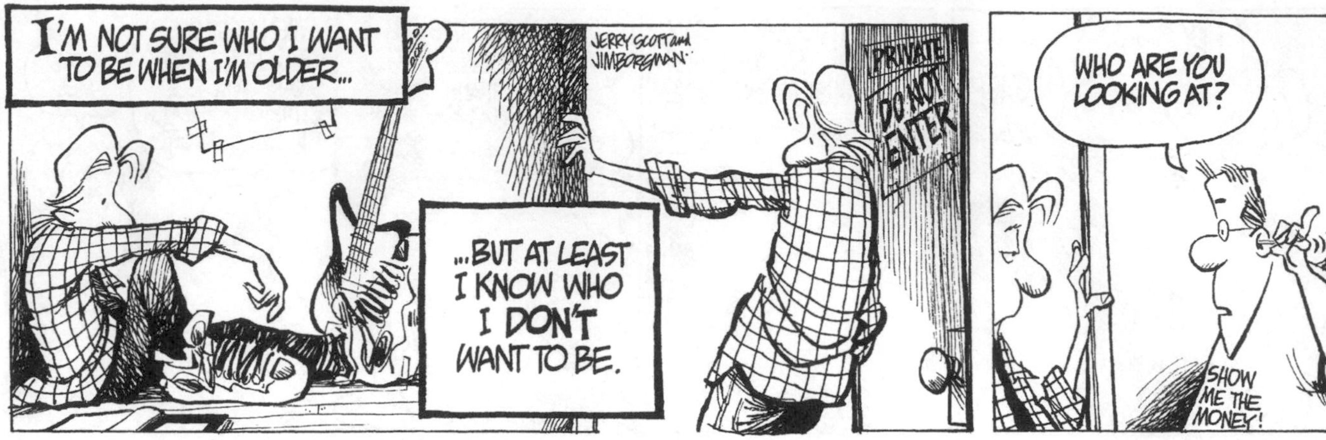
I'M NOT SURE WHO I WANT TO BE WHEN I'M OLDER...
JERRY SCOTT and JIMBORGMAN
PRIVATE
DO NOT ENTER
...BUT AT LEAST I KNOW WHO I DON'T WANT TO BE.
WHO ARE YOU LOOKING AT?
SHOW ME THE MONEY!

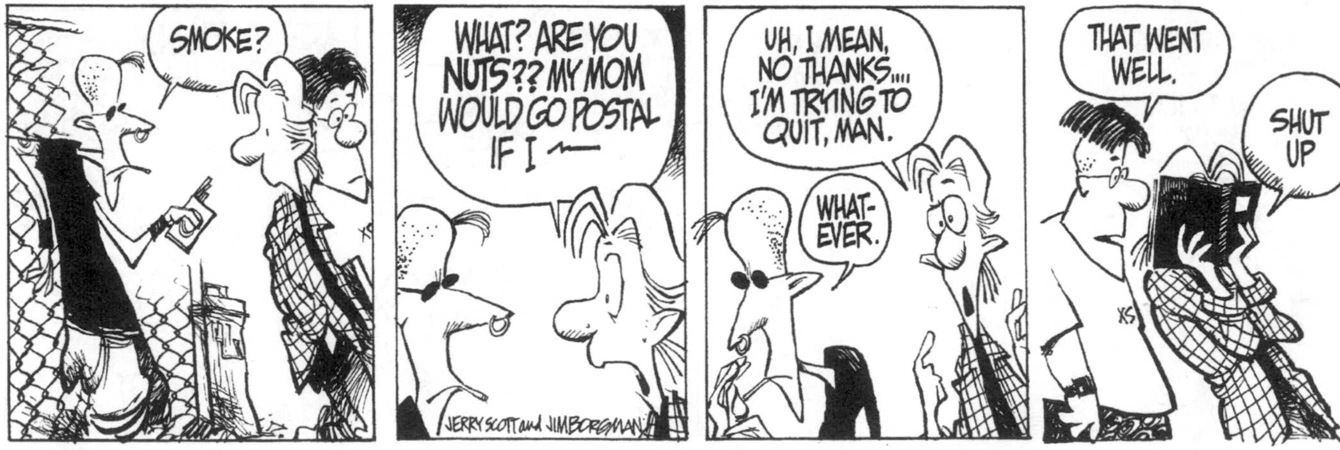
SMOKE?
WHAT? ARE YOU NUTS?? MY MOM WOULD GO POSTAL IF I —
JERRY SCOTT and JIMBORGMAN
UH, I MEAN, NO THANKS.... I'M TRYING TO QUIT, MAN.
WHAT-EVER.
THAT WENT WELL.
SHUT UP

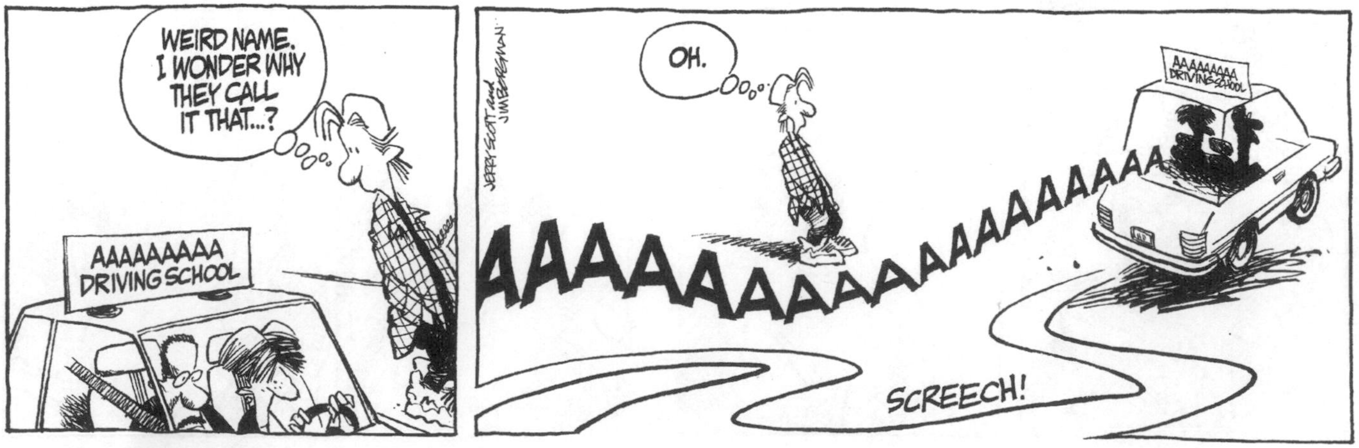
WEIRD NAME. I WONDER WHY THEY CALL IT THAT...?
AAAAAAAAA DRIVING SCHOOL
JERRY SCOTT and JIMBORGMAN
OH.
AAAAAAAA DRIVING SCHOOL
AAAAAAAAAAAAAAAAAAAAA
SCREECH!

Zits®

by JERRY SCOTT and JIM BORGMAN

WOW! THIS LOOKS GOOD!
AHEM!
INHALE!!
I HATE THESE GROWTH SPURTS
CAN I BE EXCUSED?
COUNT THE PLATES
JERRY SCOTT and JIMBORGMAN

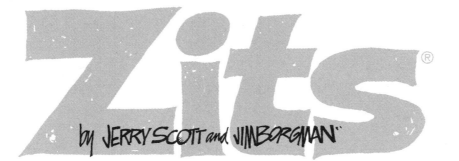

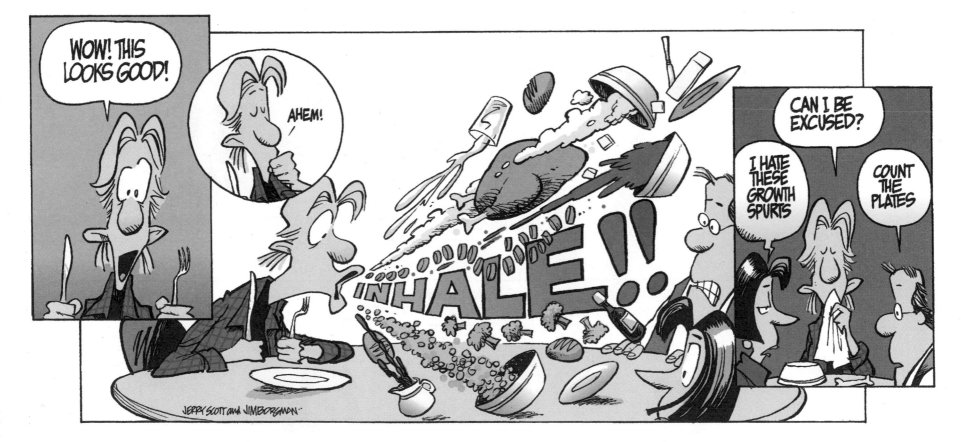

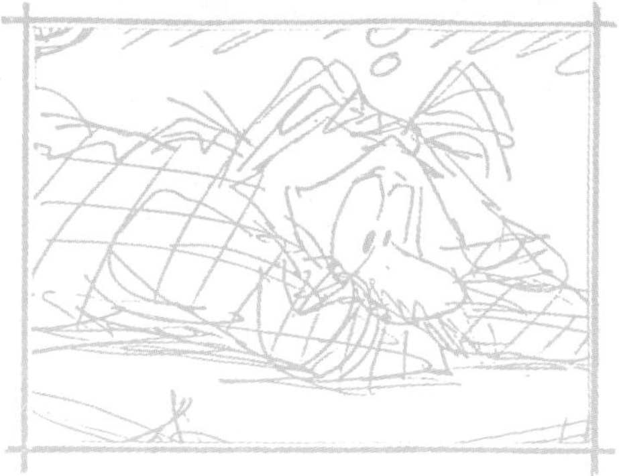

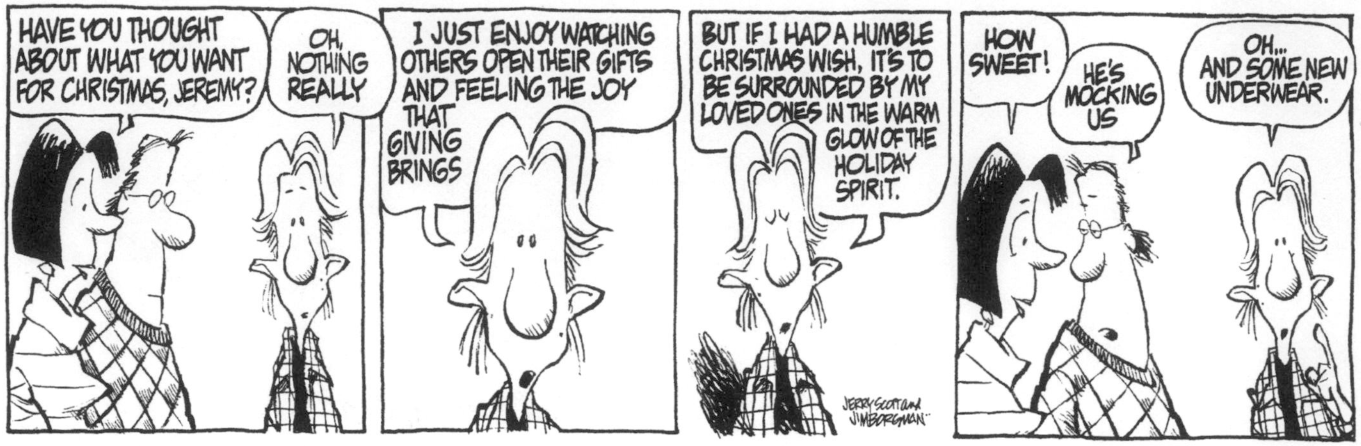
HAVE YOU THOUGHT ABOUT WHAT YOU WANT FOR CHRISTMAS, JEREMY?
OH, NOTHING REALLY
I JUST ENJOY WATCHING OTHERS OPEN THEIR GIFTS AND FEELING THE JOY THAT GIVING BRINGS
BUT IF I HAD A HUMBLE CHRISTMAS WISH, IT'S TO BE SURROUNDED BY MY LOVED ONES IN THE WARM GLOW OF THE HOLIDAY SPIRIT.
JERRY SCOTT and JIMBORGMAN
HOW SWEET!
HE'S MOCKING US
OH... AND SOME NEW UNDERWEAR.

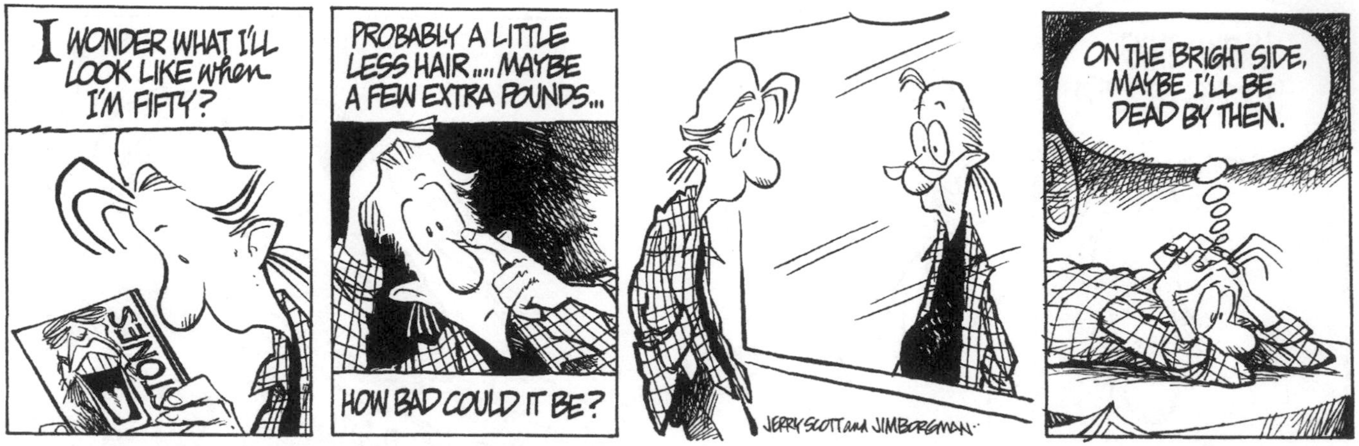
I WONDER WHAT I'LL LOOK LIKE when I'M FIFTY?
STONES
PROBABLY A LITTLE LESS HAIR.... MAYBE A FEW EXTRA POUNDS...
HOW BAD COULD IT BE?
JERRY SCOTT and JIMBORGMAN
ON THE BRIGHT SIDE, MAYBE I'LL BE DEAD BY THEN.

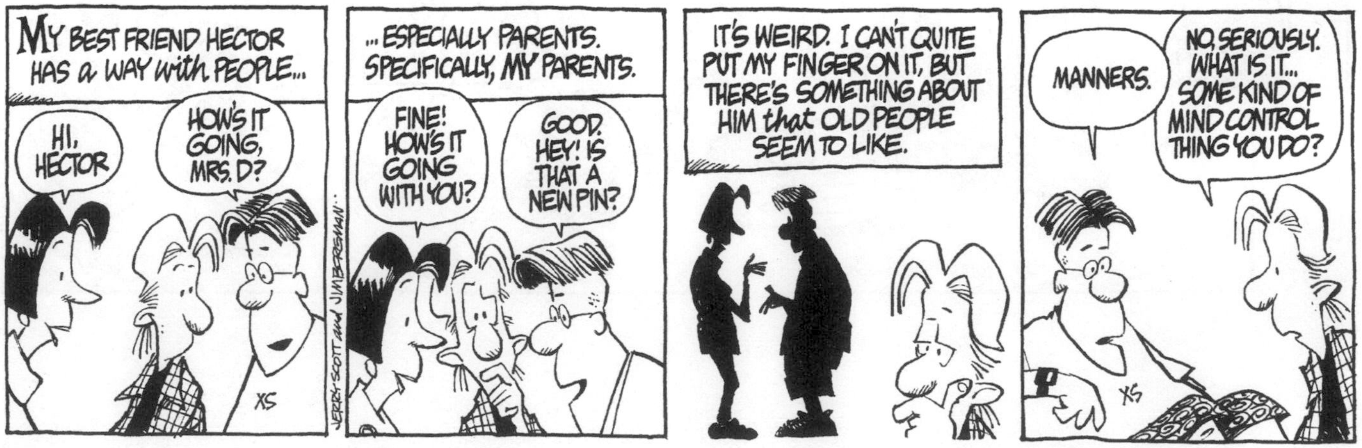
MY BEST FRIEND HECTOR HAS a WAY with PEOPLE...
HI, HECTOR
HOW'S IT GOING, MRS. D?
XS
JERRY SCOTT and JIMBORGMAN
...ESPECIALLY PARENTS. SPECIFICALLY, MY PARENTS.
FINE! HOW'S IT GOING WITH YOU?
GOOD. HEY! IS THAT A NEW PIN?
IT'S WEIRD. I CAN'T QUITE PUT MY FINGER ON IT, BUT THERE'S SOMETHING ABOUT HIM that OLD PEOPLE SEEM TO LIKE.
MANNERS.
NO, SERIOUSLY. WHAT IS IT... SOME KIND OF MIND CONTROL THING YOU DO?
XS

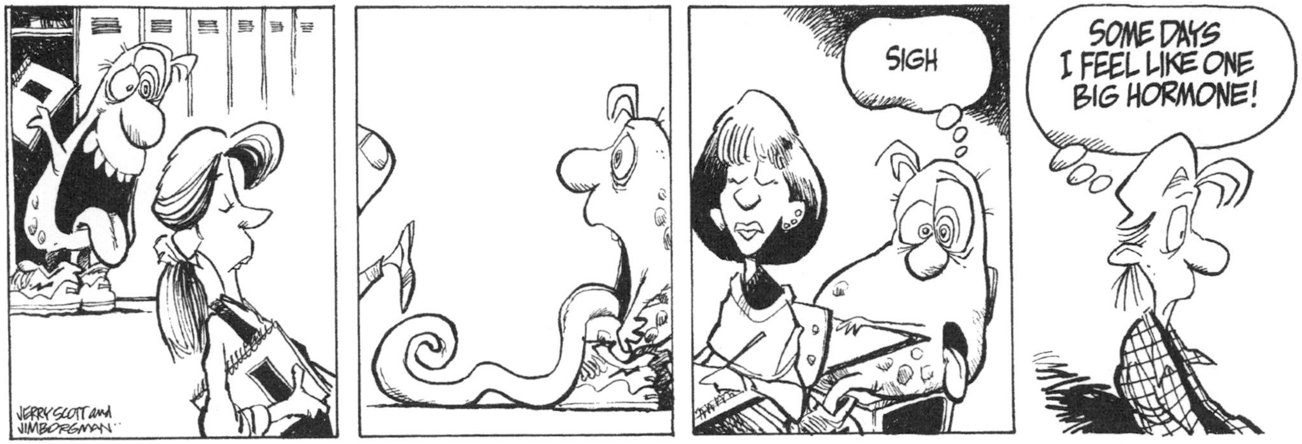
JERRY SCOTT and JIM BORGMAN
SIGH
SOME DAYS I FEEL LIKE ONE BIG HORMONE!

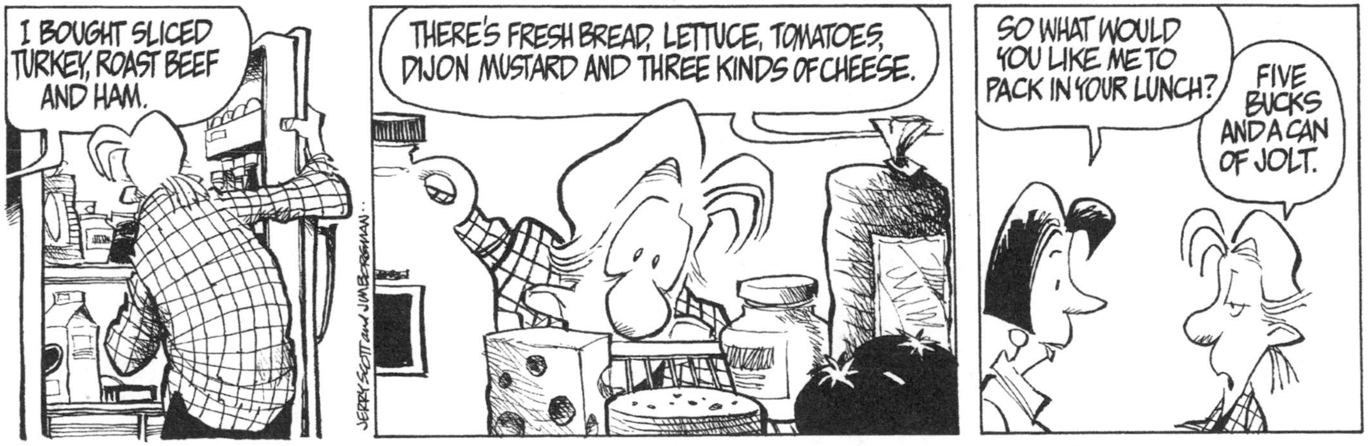
I BOUGHT SLICED TURKEY, ROAST BEEF AND HAM.
JERRY SCOTT and JIM BORGMAN
THERE'S FRESH BREAD, LETTUCE, TOMATOES, DIJON MUSTARD AND THREE KINDS OF CHEESE.
SO WHAT WOULD YOU LIKE ME TO PACK IN YOUR LUNCH?
FIVE BUCKS AND A CAN OF JOLT.

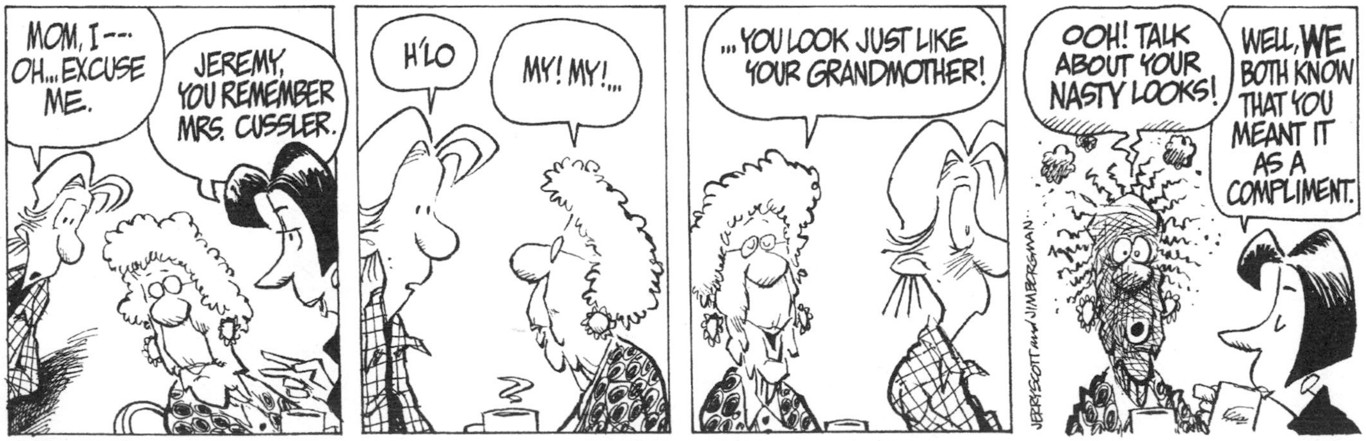
MOM, I--- OH... EXCUSE ME.
JEREMY, YOU REMEMBER MRS. CUSSLER.
H'LO
MY! MY!...
...YOU LOOK JUST LIKE YOUR GRANDMOTHER!
JERRY SCOTT and JIM BORGMAN
OOH! TALK ABOUT YOUR NASTY LOOKS!
WELL, WE BOTH KNOW THAT YOU MEANT IT AS A COMPLIMENT.

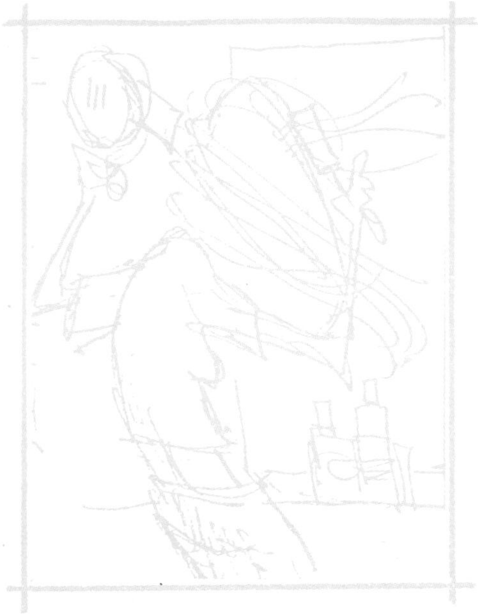

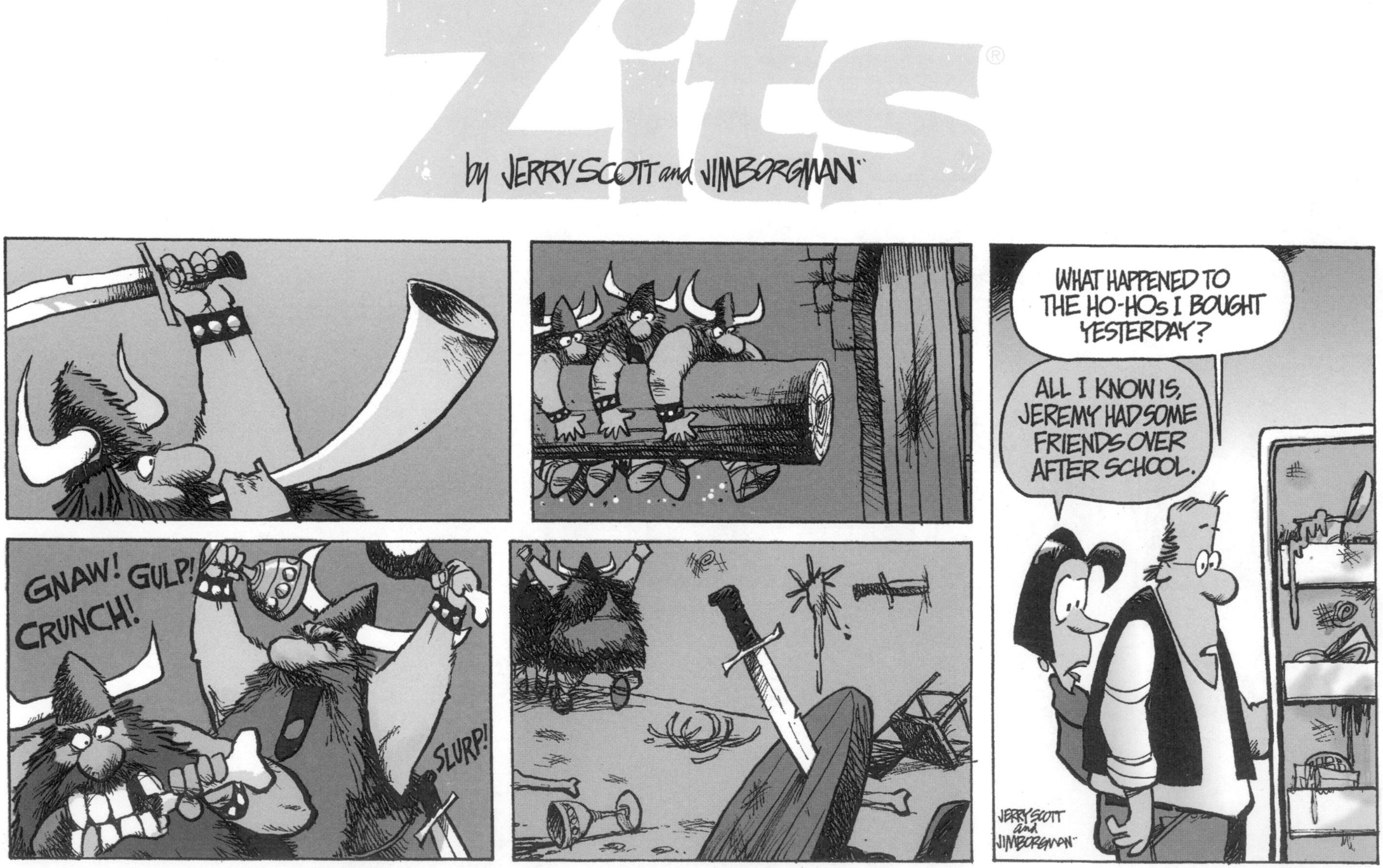
Zits
by JERRY SCOTT and JIMBORGMAN
GNAW! GULP!
CRUNCH!
SLURP!
WHAT HAPPENED TO THE HO-HOs I BOUGHT YESTERDAY?
ALL I KNOW IS, JEREMY HAD SOME FRIENDS OVER AFTER SCHOOL.
JERRY SCOTT and JIMBORGMAN

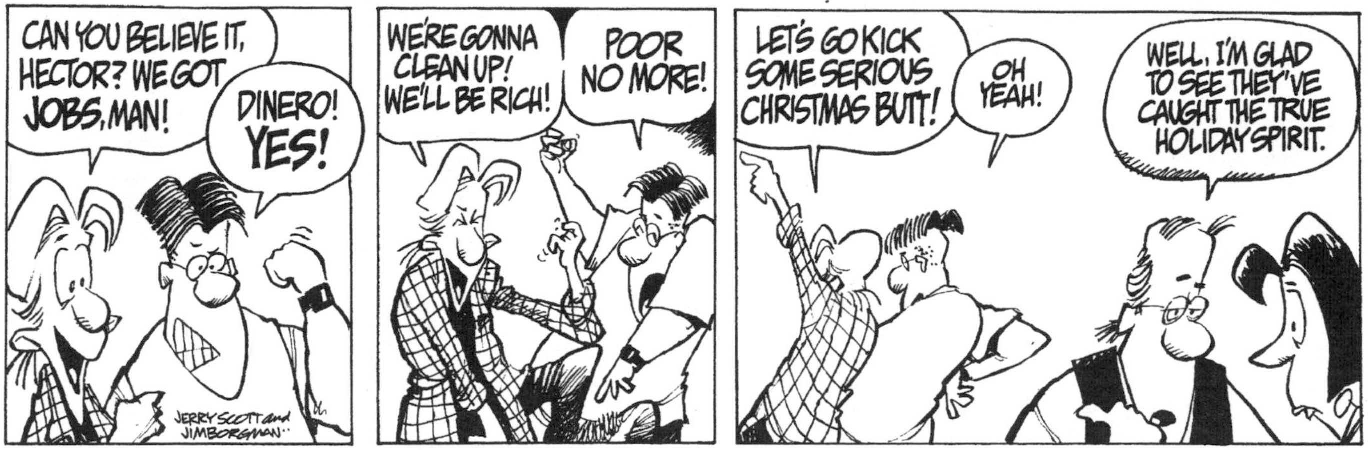
CAN YOU BELIEVE IT, HECTOR? WE GOT JOBS, MAN!
DINERO! YES!
JERRY SCOTT and JIM BORGMAN
WE'RE GONNA CLEAN UP! WE'LL BE RICH!
POOR NO MORE!
LET'S GO KICK SOME SERIOUS CHRISTMAS BUTT!
OH YEAH!
WELL, I'M GLAD TO SEE THEY'VE CAUGHT THE TRUE HOLIDAY SPIRIT.

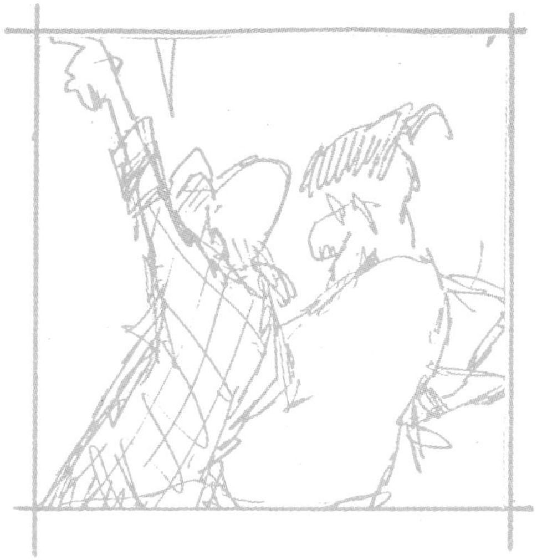

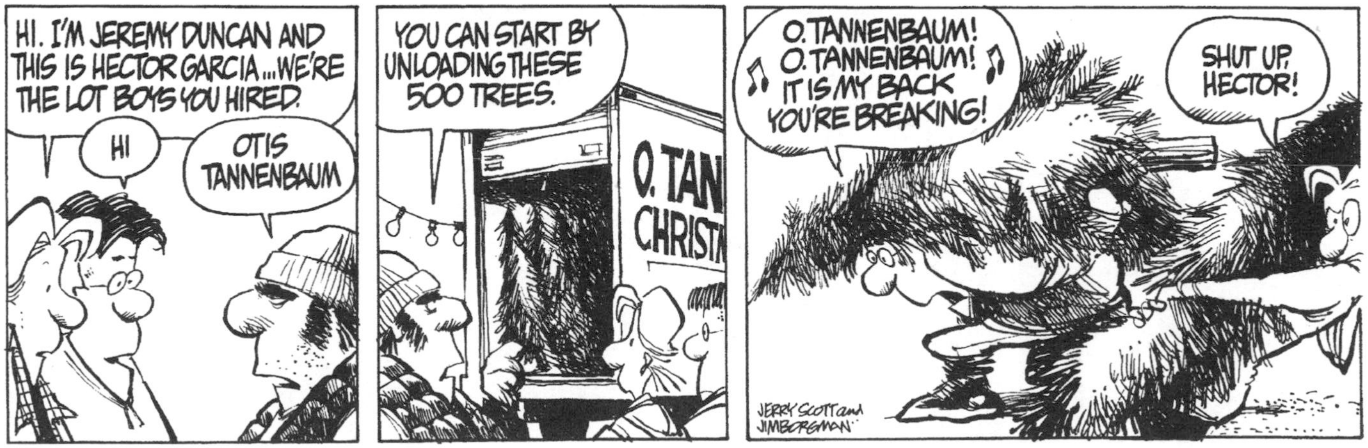
HI. I'M JEREMY DUNCAN AND THIS IS HECTOR GARCIA...WE'RE THE LOT BOYS YOU HIRED.
HI
OTIS TANNENBAUM
YOU CAN START BY UNLOADING THESE 500 TREES.
O. TAN
CHRIST
O. TANNENBAUM! O. TANNENBAUM! IT IS MY BACK YOU'RE BREAKING!
SHUT UP, HECTOR!
JERRY SCOTT and JIM BORGMAN

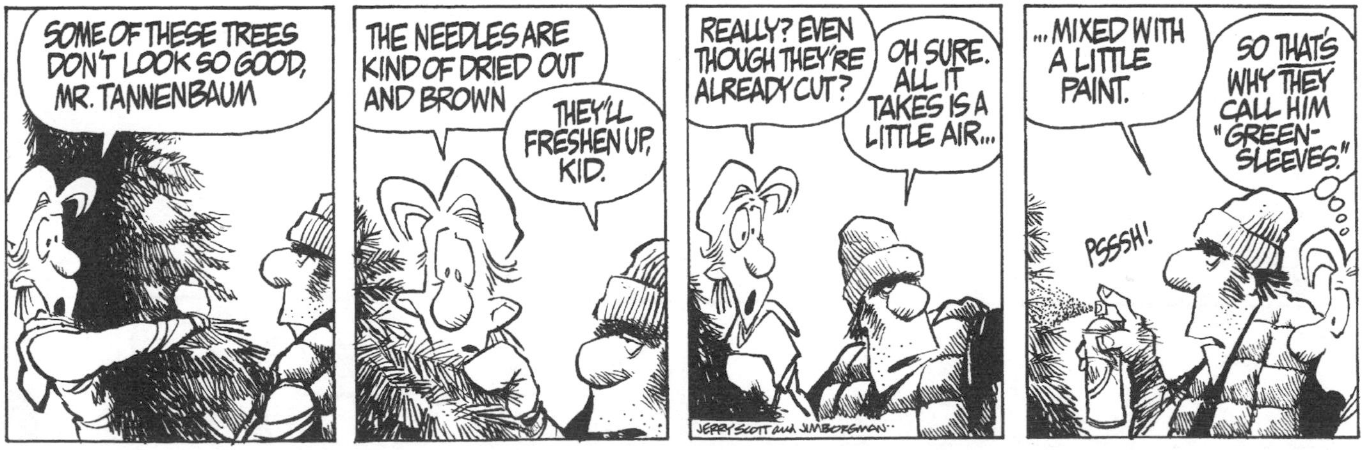
SOME OF THESE TREES DON'T LOOK SO GOOD, MR. TANNENBAUM
THE NEEDLES ARE KIND OF DRIED OUT AND BROWN
THEY'LL FRESHEN UP, KID.
REALLY? EVEN THOUGH THEY'RE ALREADY CUT?
OH SURE. ALL IT TAKES IS A LITTLE AIR...
JERRY SCOTT and JIM BORGMAN
...MIXED WITH A LITTLE PAINT.
PSSSH!
SO THAT'S WHY THEY CALL HIM "GREEN-SLEEVES."

IT'S FREEZING OUT HERE, JEREMY!
I KNOW IT'S COLD, HECTOR, BUT IT'S BETTER THAN SOME FAST-FOOD JOB!
CHRISTMA TREES $25 AND UP
WE'RE OUTSIDE IN THE FRESH AIR, WE'RE GETTING SOME EXERCISE....
LOT BOY!
PLUS, THEY DON'T MAKE US WEAR SOME RIDICULOUS UNIFORM.
YOU HAVE A POINT THERE.
JERRY SCOTT and JIMBORGMAN

CAN I HELP YOU?
YES. I CAN'T DECIDE BETWEEN THESE TWO TREES.
JERRY SCOTT and JIMBORGMAN
IT'S SO DIFFICULT TO DECIDE.
IMAGINE HOW HARD IT IS TO CARE.

OKAY, NOW WRAP IT AROUND THE TRUNK A FEW MORE TIMES...
I CAN'T. IT'S TOO SHORT.
HEY, MR. TANNENBAUM, WE NEED MORE TWINE!
DIDN'T I JUST GIVE YOU A NEW BALL?
YEAH, BUT THAT WAS TWO CARS AGO.
HELP!
JERRY SCOTT and JIMBORGMAN

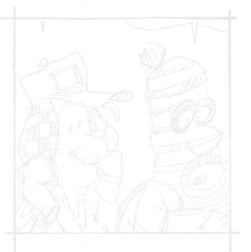

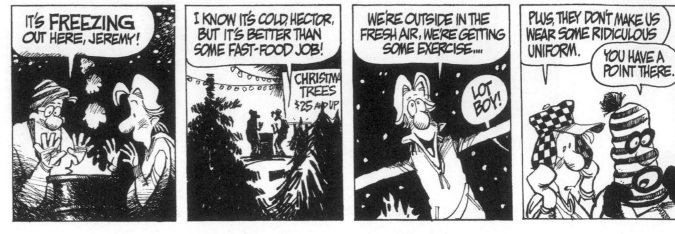

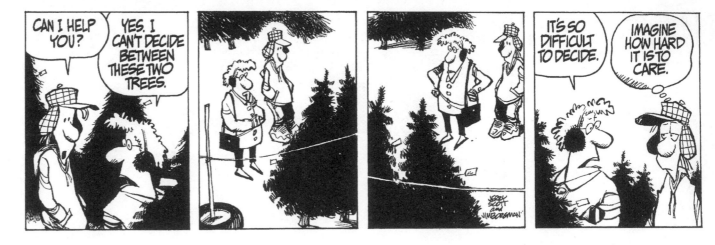

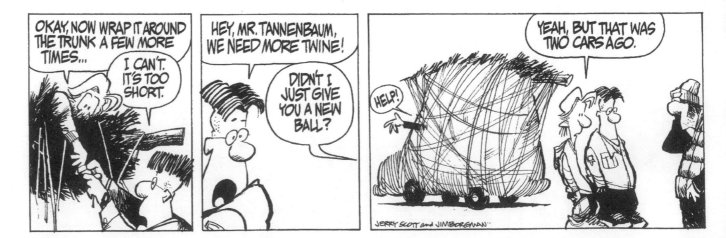

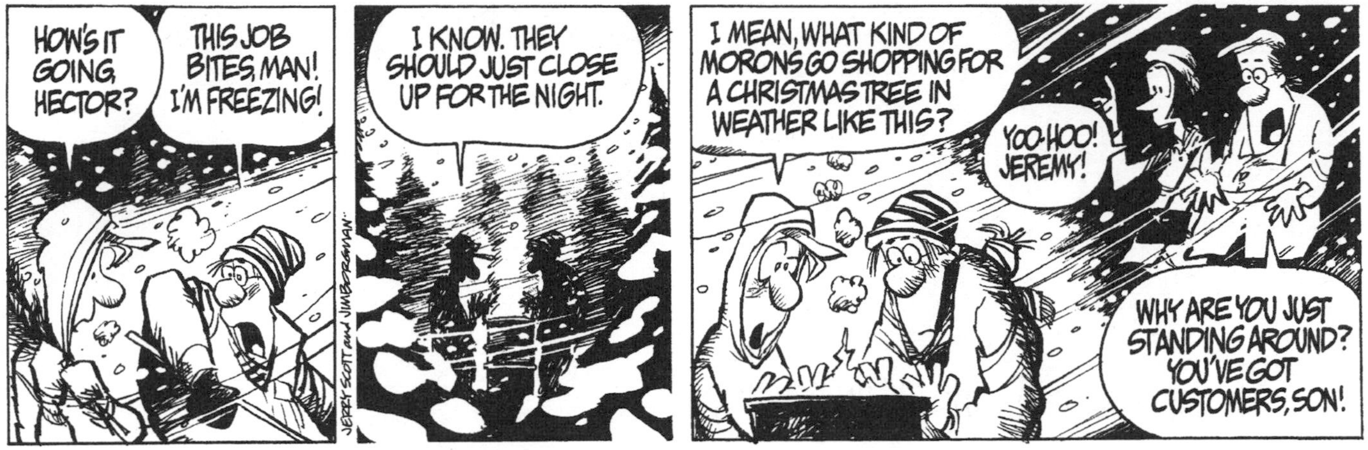
HOW'S IT GOING, HECTOR?
THIS JOB BITES, MAN! I'M FREEZING!
JERRY SCOTT and JIM BORGMAN
I KNOW. THEY SHOULD JUST CLOSE UP FOR THE NIGHT.
I MEAN, WHAT KIND OF MORONS GO SHOPPING FOR A CHRISTMAS TREE IN WEATHER LIKE THIS?
YOO-HOO! JEREMY!
WHY ARE YOU JUST STANDING AROUND? YOU'VE GOT CUSTOMERS, SON!

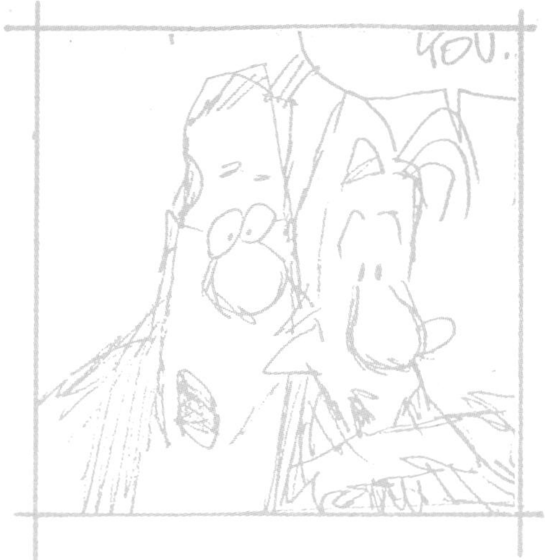
YOU.

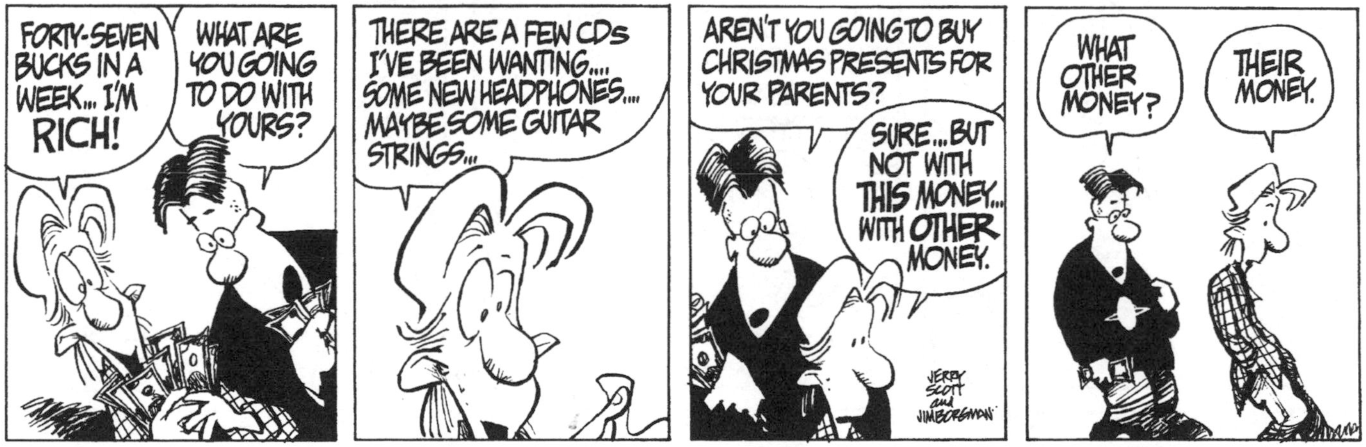
FORTY-SEVEN BUCKS IN A WEEK... I'M RICH!
WHAT ARE YOU GOING TO DO WITH YOURS?
THERE ARE A FEW CDs I'VE BEEN WANTING.... SOME NEW HEADPHONES.... MAYBE SOME GUITAR STRINGS...
AREN'T YOU GOING TO BUY CHRISTMAS PRESENTS FOR YOUR PARENTS?
SURE... BUT NOT WITH THIS MONEY... WITH OTHER MONEY.
JERRY SCOTT and JIM BORGMAN
WHAT OTHER MONEY?
THEIR MONEY.

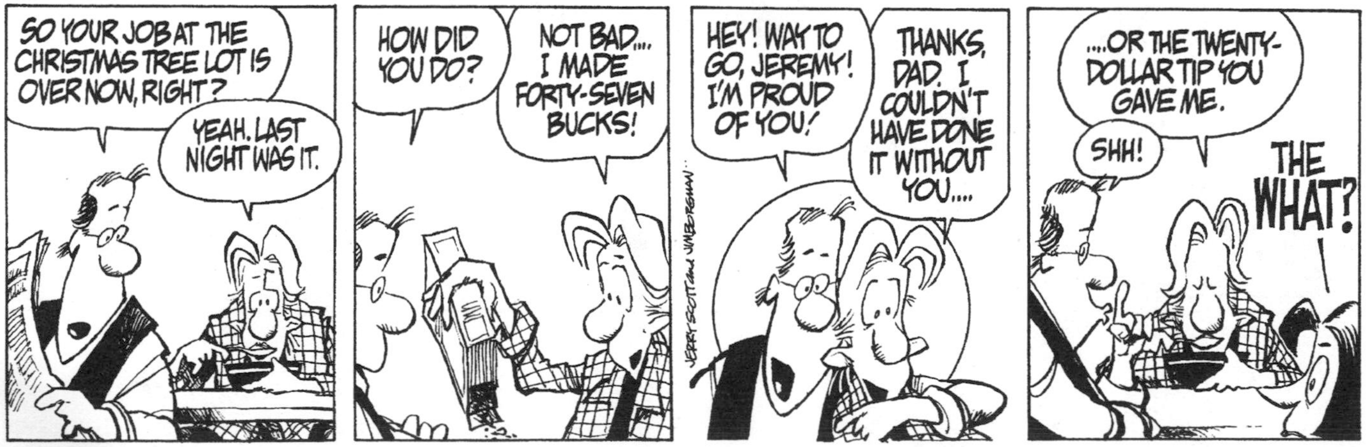
SO YOUR JOB AT THE CHRISTMAS TREE LOT IS OVER NOW, RIGHT?
YEAH. LAST NIGHT WAS IT.
HOW DID YOU DO?
NOT BAD.... I MADE FORTY-SEVEN BUCKS!
JERRY SCOTT and JIM BORGMAN
HEY! WAY TO GO, JEREMY! I'M PROUD OF YOU!
THANKS, DAD. I COULDN'T HAVE DONE IT WITHOUT YOU....
....OR THE TWENTY-DOLLAR TIP YOU GAVE ME.
SHH!
THE WHAT?

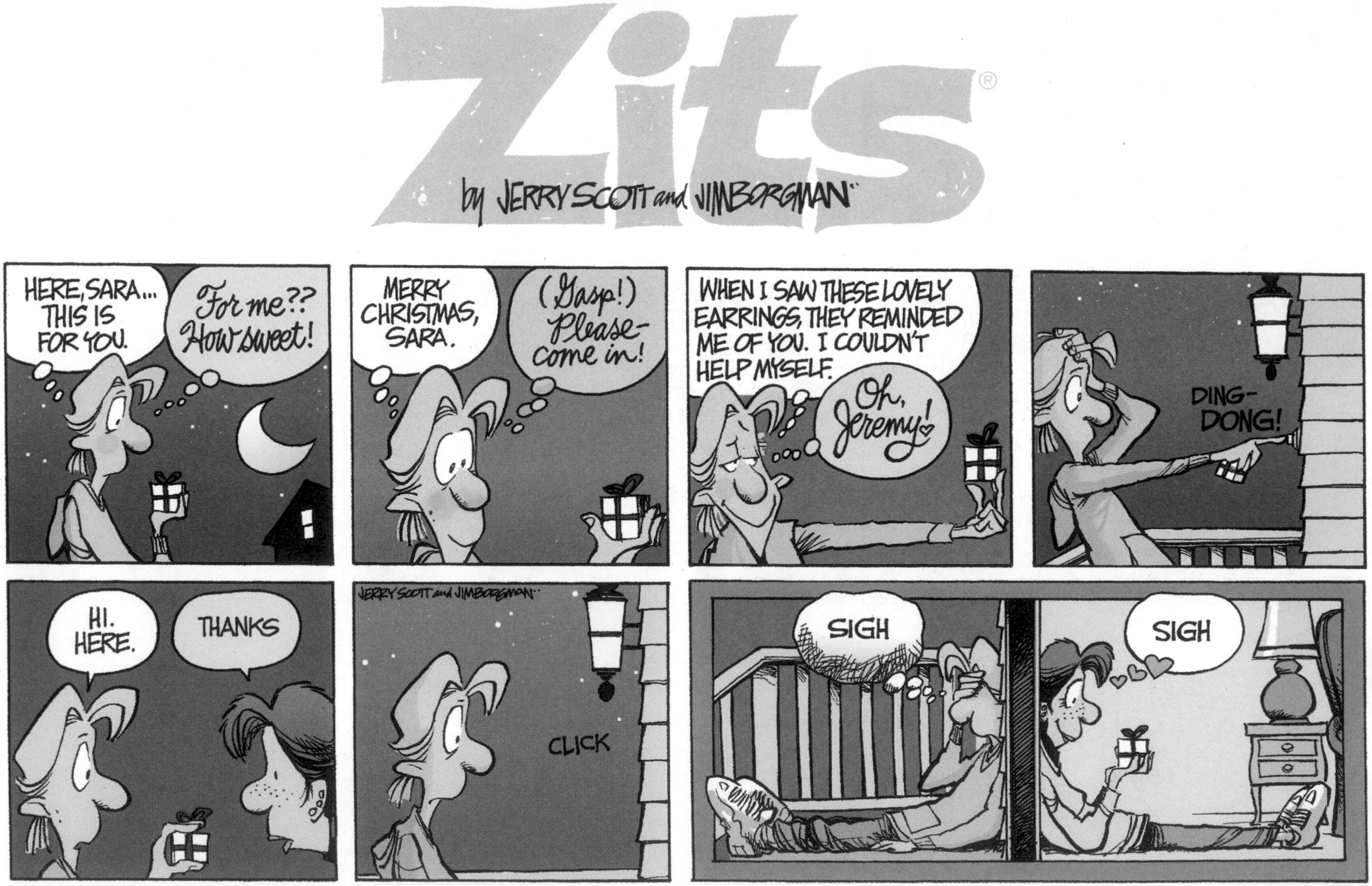
Zits
by JERRY SCOTT and JIM BORGMAN
HERE, SARA... THIS IS FOR YOU.
For me?? How sweet!
MERRY CHRISTMAS, SARA.
(Gasp!) Please-come in!
WHEN I SAW THESE LOVELY EARRINGS, THEY REMINDED ME OF YOU. I COULDN'T HELP MYSELF.
Oh, Jeremy!
DING-DONG!
HI. HERE.
THANKS
JERRY SCOTT and JIM BORGMAN
CLICK
SIGH
SIGH

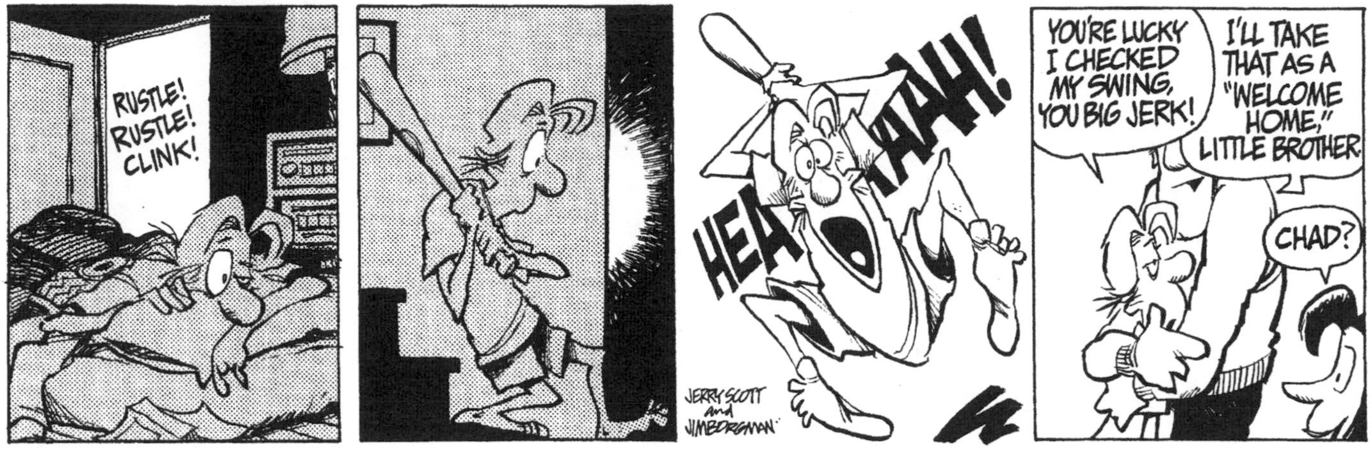
RUSTLE! RUSTLE! CLINK!
HEA
AAH!
JERRY SCOTT and JIM BORGMAN
YOU'RE LUCKY I CHECKED MY SWING, YOU BIG JERK!
I'LL TAKE THAT AS A "WELCOME HOME," LITTLE BROTHER.
CHAD?

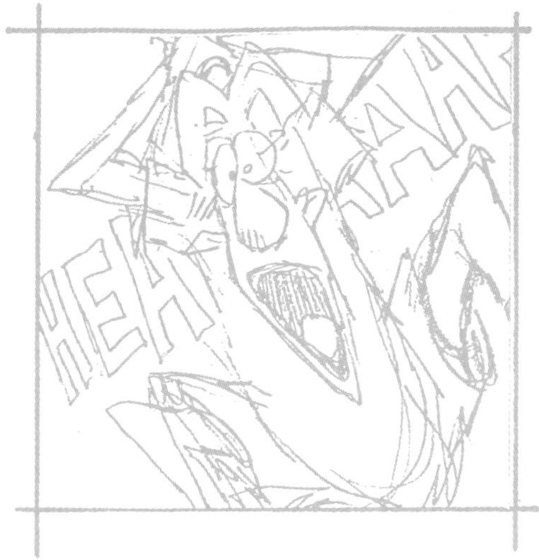

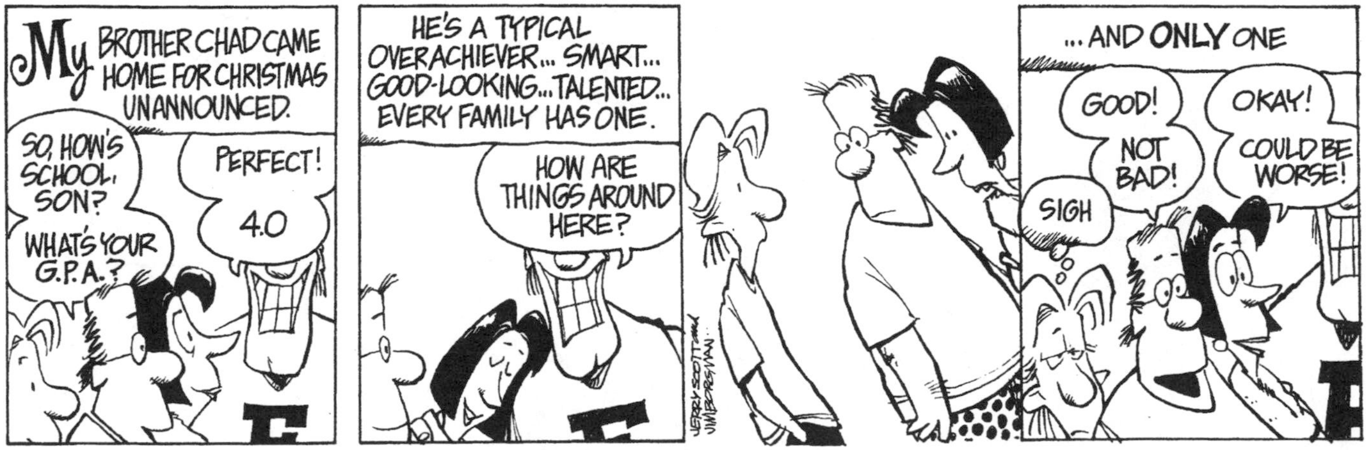
My BROTHER CHAD CAME HOME FOR CHRISTMAS UNANNOUNCED.
SO, HOW'S SCHOOL, SON?
WHAT'S YOUR G.P.A.?
PERFECT!
4.0
HE'S A TYPICAL OVERACHIEVER... SMART... GOOD-LOOKING... TALENTED... EVERY FAMILY HAS ONE.
HOW ARE THINGS AROUND HERE?
JERRY SCOTT and JIM BORGMAN
... AND ONLY ONE
GOOD!
OKAY!
NOT BAD!
COULD BE WORSE!
SIGH

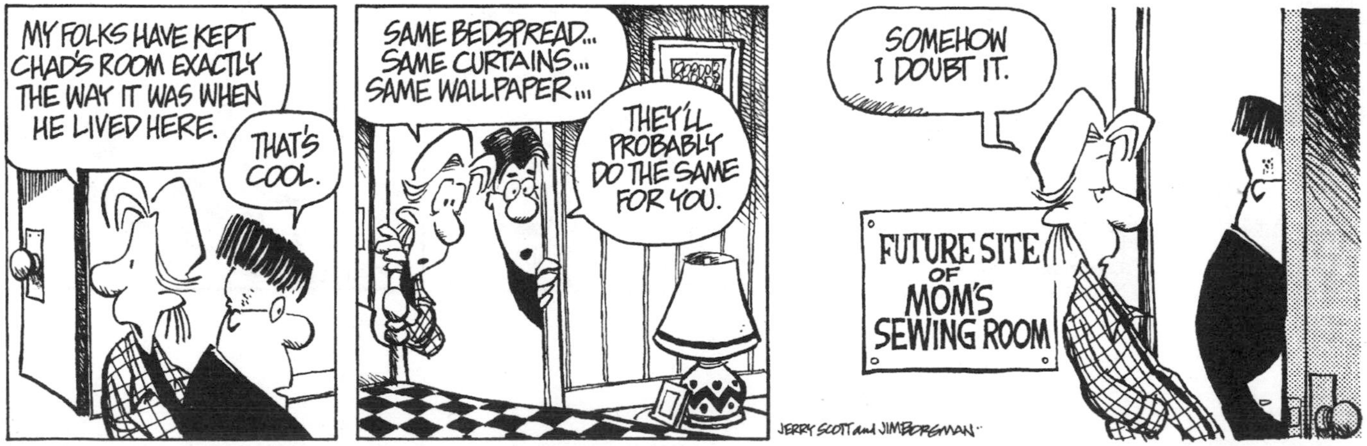
MY FOLKS HAVE KEPT CHAD'S ROOM EXACTLY THE WAY IT WAS WHEN HE LIVED HERE.
THAT'S COOL.
SAME BEDSPREAD... SAME CURTAINS... SAME WALLPAPER...
THEY'LL PROBABLY DO THE SAME FOR YOU.
SOMEHOW I DOUBT IT.
FUTURE SITE OF MOM'S SEWING ROOM
JERRY SCOTT and JIM BORGMAN

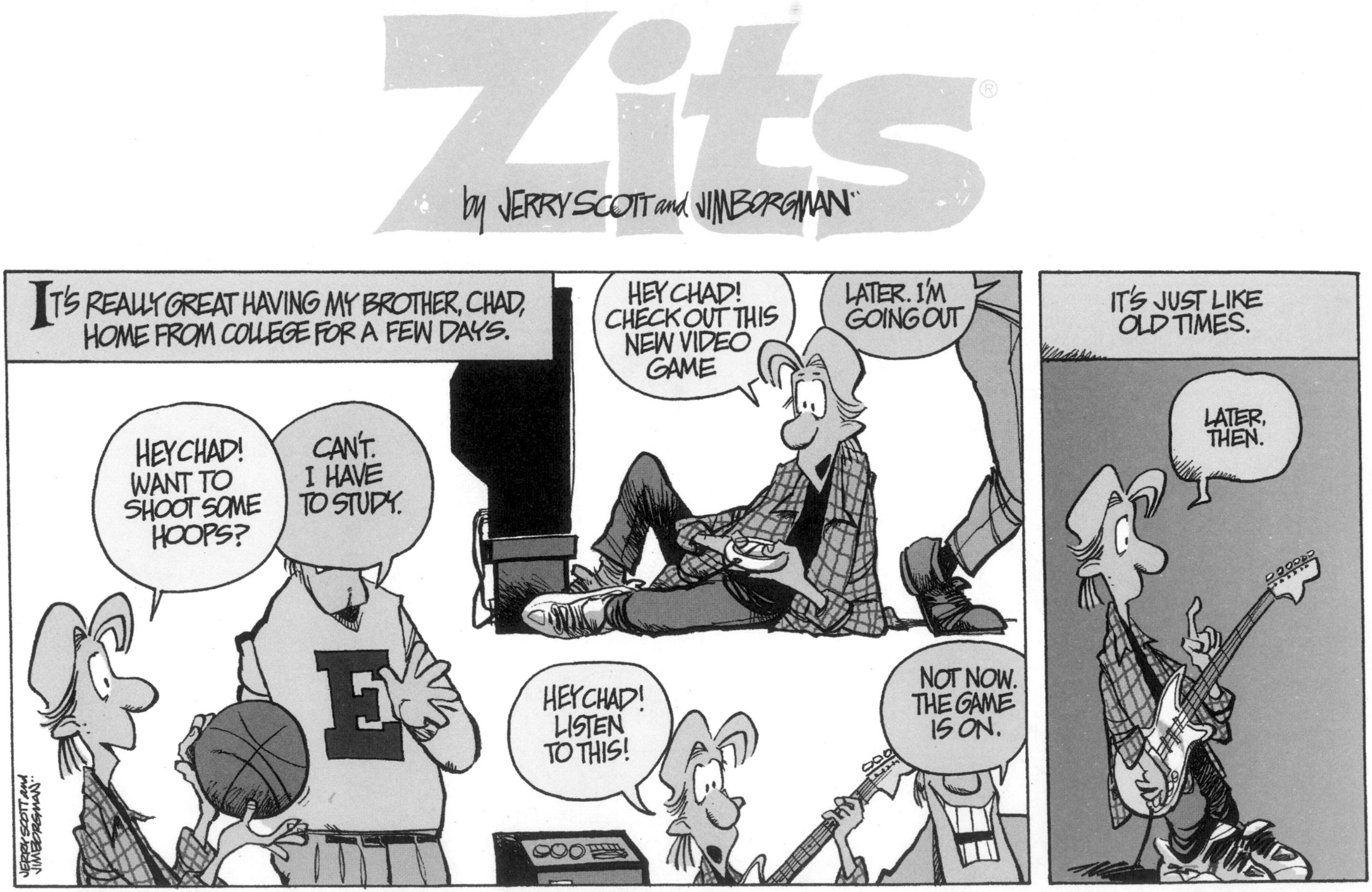
Zits®
by JERRY SCOTT and JIMBORGMAN
IT'S REALLY GREAT HAVING MY BROTHER, CHAD, HOME FROM COLLEGE FOR A FEW DAYS.
HEY CHAD! WANT TO SHOOT SOME HOOPS?
CAN'T. I HAVE TO STUDY.
HEY CHAD! CHECK OUT THIS NEW VIDEO GAME
LATER. I'M GOING OUT
HEY CHAD! LISTEN TO THIS!
NOT NOW. THE GAME IS ON.
IT'S JUST LIKE OLD TIMES.
LATER, THEN.
JERRY SCOTT and JIMBORGMAN

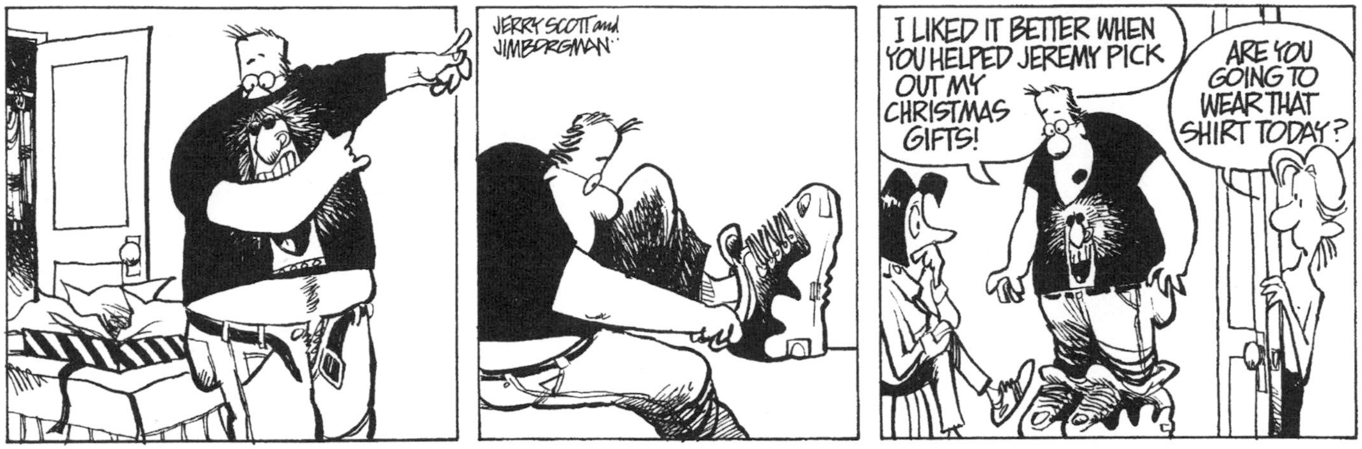
JERRY SCOTT and JIMBORGMAN
I LIKED IT BETTER WHEN YOU HELPED JEREMY PICK OUT MY CHRISTMAS GIFTS!
ARE YOU GOING TO WEAR THAT SHIRT TODAY?

CHRISTMAS GIFTS

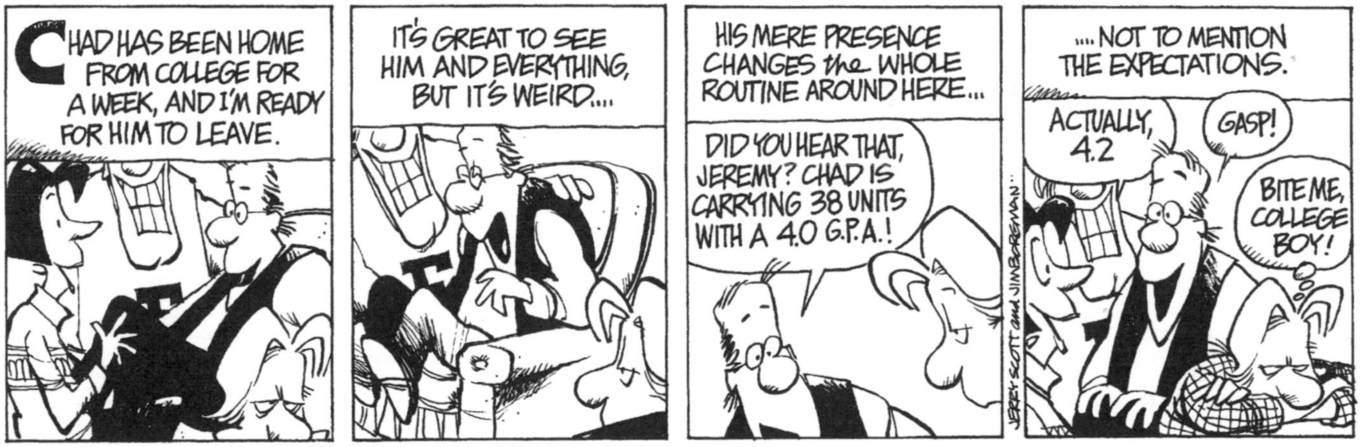
CHAD HAS BEEN HOME FROM COLLEGE FOR A WEEK, AND I'M READY FOR HIM TO LEAVE.
IT'S GREAT TO SEE HIM AND EVERYTHING, BUT IT'S WEIRD....
HIS MERE PRESENCE CHANGES the WHOLE ROUTINE AROUND HERE...
DID YOU HEAR THAT, JEREMY? CHAD IS CARRYING 38 UNITS WITH A 4.0 G.P.A.!
JERRY SCOTT and JIMBORGMAN
....NOT TO MENTION THE EXPECTATIONS.
ACTUALLY, 4.2
GASP!
BITE ME, COLLEGE BOY!

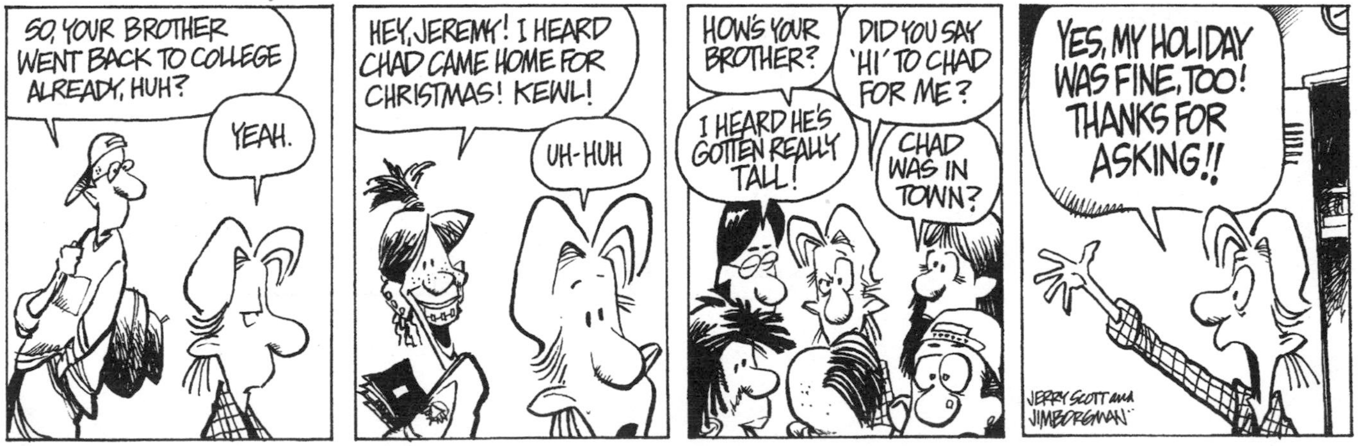
SO, YOUR BROTHER WENT BACK TO COLLEGE ALREADY, HUH?
YEAH.
HEY, JEREMY! I HEARD CHAD CAME HOME FOR CHRISTMAS! KEWL!
UH-HUH
HOW'S YOUR BROTHER?
DID YOU SAY 'HI' TO CHAD FOR ME?
I HEARD HE'S GOTTEN REALLY TALL!
CHAD WAS IN TOWN?
YES, MY HOLIDAY WAS FINE, TOO! THANKS FOR ASKING!!
JERRY SCOTT and JIMBORGMAN

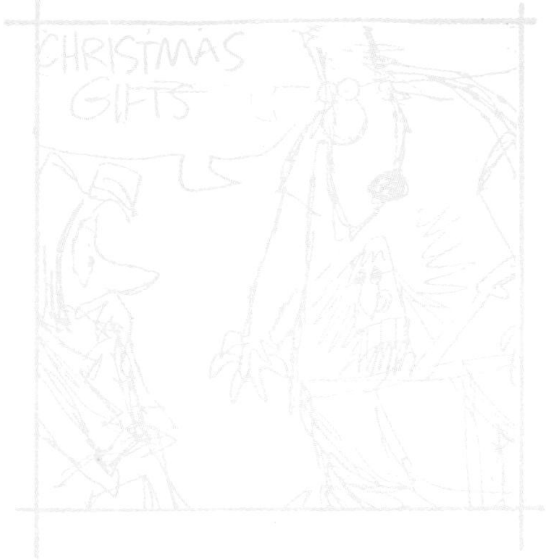

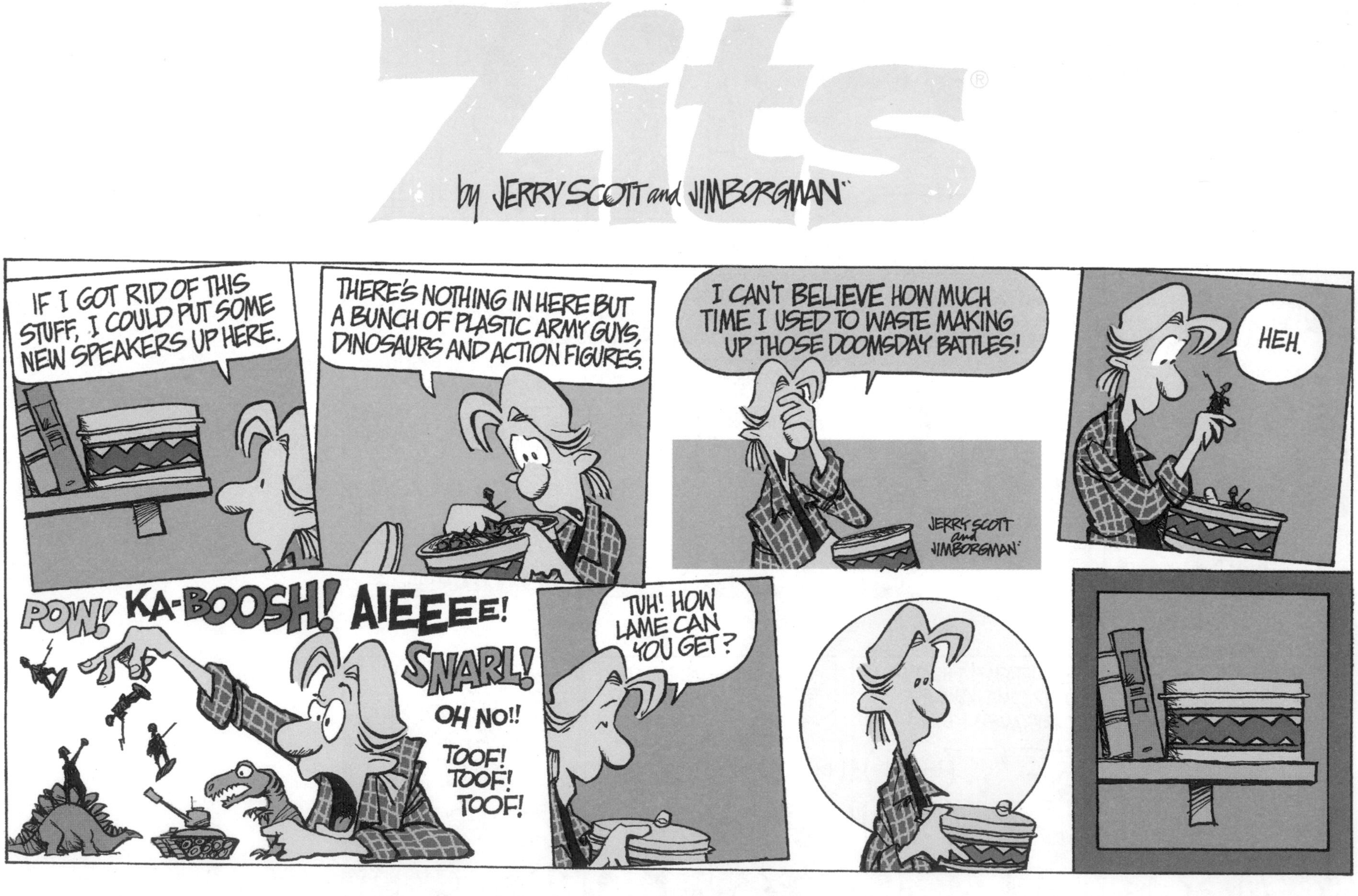
Zits®
by JERRY SCOTT and JIM BORGMAN
IF I GOT RID OF THIS STUFF, I COULD PUT SOME NEW SPEAKERS UP HERE.
THERE'S NOTHING IN HERE BUT A BUNCH OF PLASTIC ARMY GUYS, DINOSAURS AND ACTION FIGURES.
I CAN'T BELIEVE HOW MUCH TIME I USED TO WASTE MAKING UP THOSE DOOMSDAY BATTLES!
JERRY SCOTT and JIM BORGMAN
HEH.
POW! KA-BOOSH! AIEEEEE!
SNARL!
OH NO!!
TOOF! TOOF! TOOF!
TUH! HOW LAME CAN YOU GET?

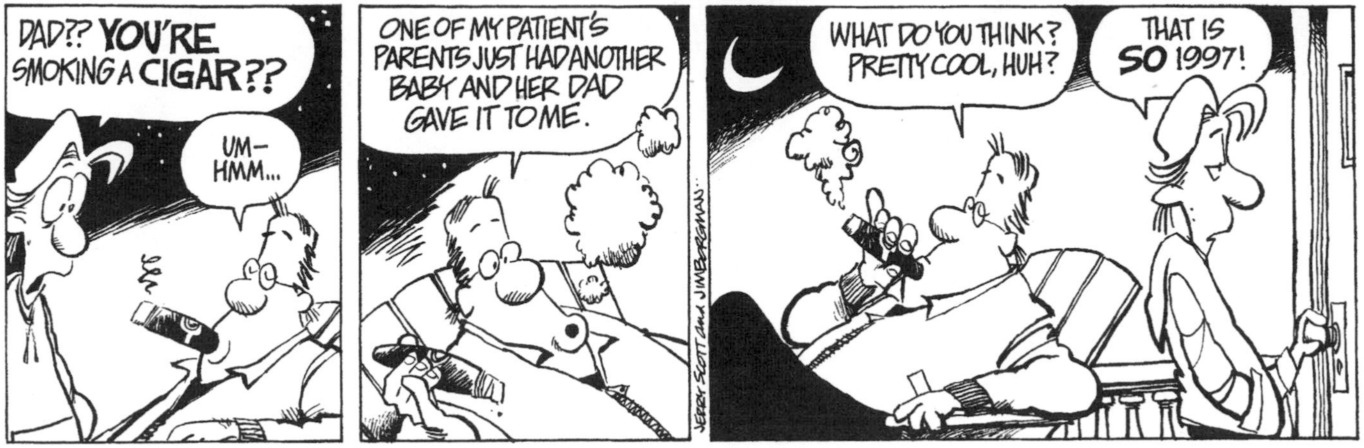
DAD?? YOU'RE SMOKING A CIGAR??
UM-HMM...
ONE OF MY PATIENT'S PARENTS JUST HAD ANOTHER BABY AND HER DAD GAVE IT TO ME.
JERRY SCOTT and JIM BORGMAN
WHAT DO YOU THINK? PRETTY COOL, HUH?
THAT IS SO 1997!

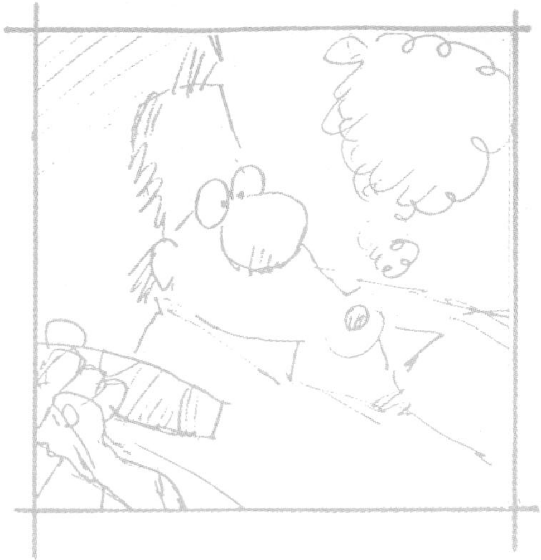

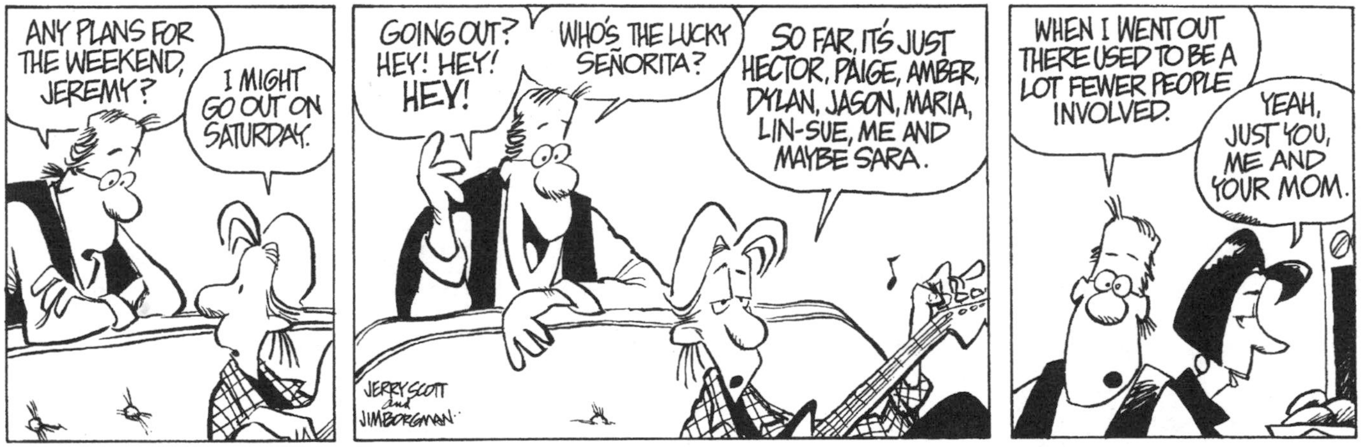
ANY PLANS FOR THE WEEKEND, JEREMY?
I MIGHT GO OUT ON SATURDAY.
GOING OUT? HEY! HEY! HEY!
WHO'S THE LUCKY SEÑORITA?
SO FAR, IT'S JUST HECTOR, PAIGE, AMBER, DYLAN, JASON, MARIA, LIN-SUE, ME AND MAYBE SARA.
JERRY SCOTT and JIM BORGMAN
WHEN I WENT OUT THERE USED TO BE A LOT FEWER PEOPLE INVOLVED.
YEAH, JUST YOU, ME AND YOUR MOM.

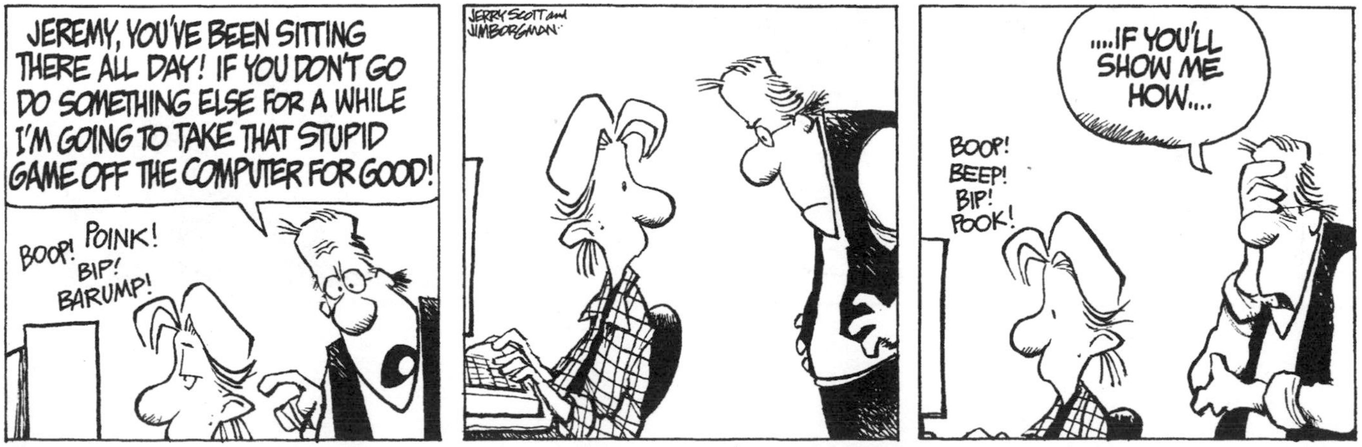
JEREMY, YOU'VE BEEN SITTING THERE ALL DAY! IF YOU DON'T GO DO SOMETHING ELSE FOR A WHILE I'M GOING TO TAKE THAT STUPID GAME OFF THE COMPUTER FOR GOOD!
BOOP! POINK! BIP! BARUMP!
JERRY SCOTT and JIM BORGMAN
BOOP! BEEP! BIP! POOK!
....IF YOU'LL SHOW ME HOW....

PUFF! PUFF!
WHEEZE!
COUGH!
GASP! COUGH!
HACK! HACK! HACK! HACK! HACK!
SO THAT'S WHY THEY CALL IT 'HACKYSACK'!
MAYBE THEY SHOULD CHANGE IT TO 'HEART-ATTACKY SACK'.

PUFF! PUFF!
WHEEZE!
JERRY SCOTT AND JIM BORGMAN
COUGH!
GASP! COUGH!
HACK! HACK! HACK! HACK! HACK!
SO THAT'S WHY THEY CALL IT 'HACKYSACK'!
MAYBE THEY SHOULD CHANGE IT TO 'HEART-ATTACKY SACK'.

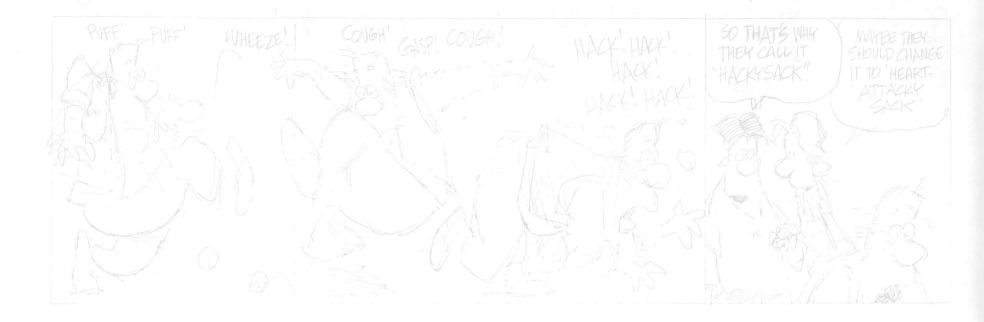

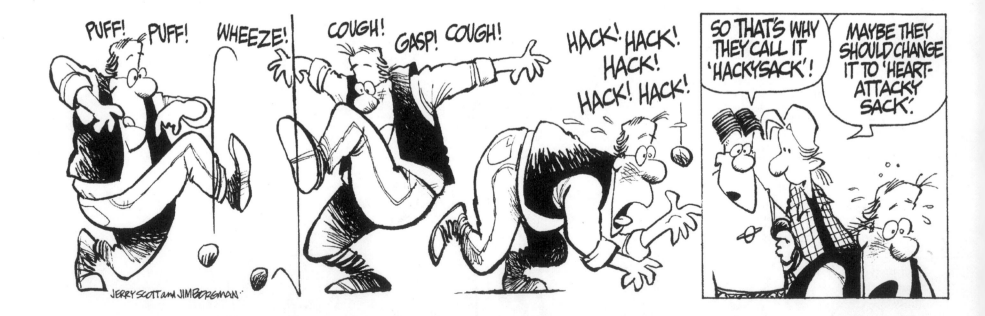

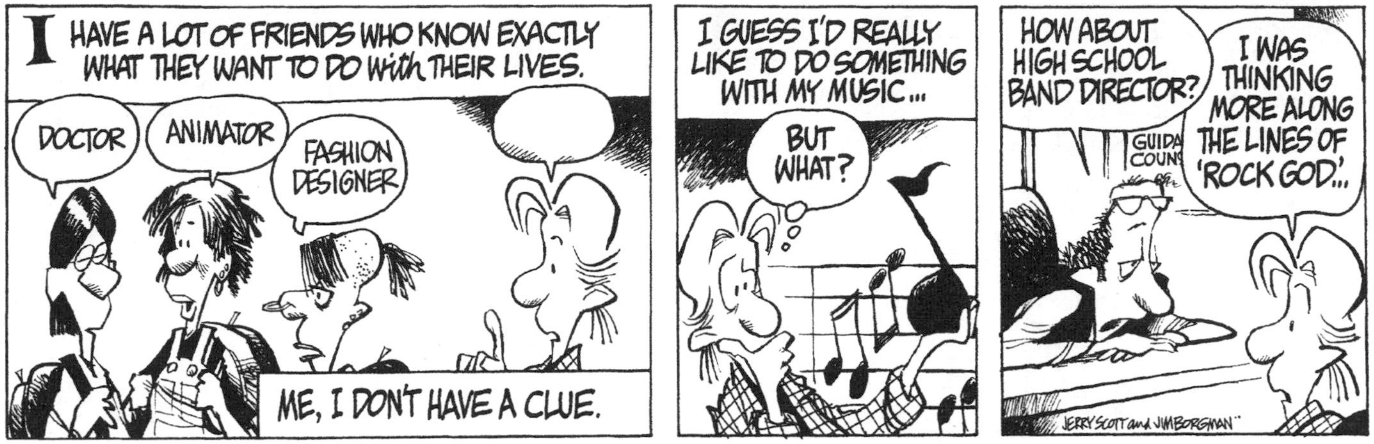
I HAVE A LOT OF FRIENDS WHO KNOW EXACTLY WHAT THEY WANT TO DO *with* THEIR LIVES.
DOCTOR
ANIMATOR
FASHION DESIGNER
ME, I DON'T HAVE A CLUE.
I GUESS I'D REALLY LIKE TO DO SOMETHING WITH MY MUSIC...
BUT WHAT?
HOW ABOUT HIGH SCHOOL BAND DIRECTOR?
I WAS THINKING MORE ALONG THE LINES OF 'ROCK GOD'...
JERRY SCOTT and JIM BORGMAN

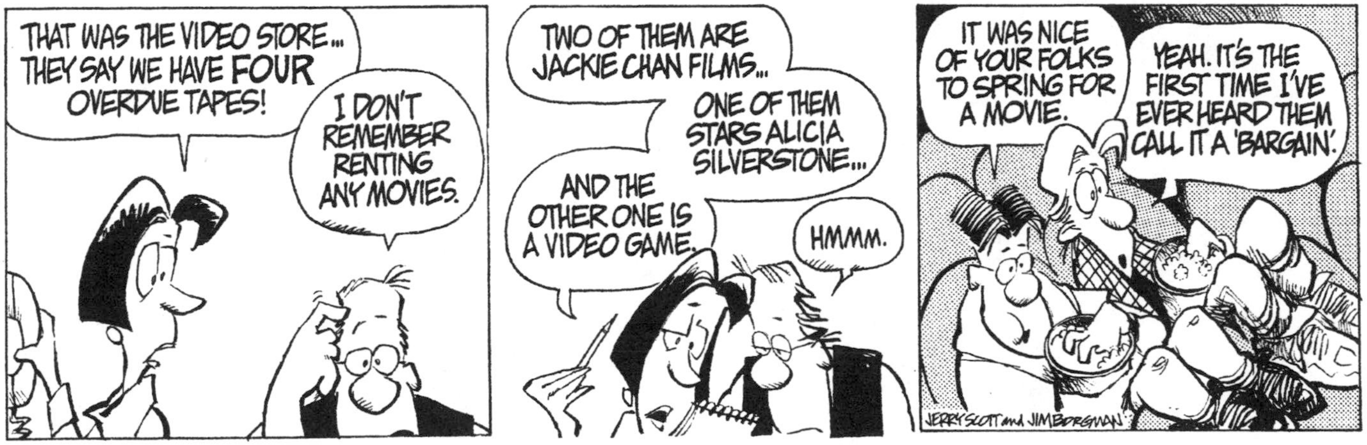
THAT WAS THE VIDEO STORE... THEY SAY WE HAVE FOUR OVERDUE TAPES!
I DON'T REMEMBER RENTING ANY MOVIES.
TWO OF THEM ARE JACKIE CHAN FILMS...
ONE OF THEM STARS ALICIA SILVERSTONE...
AND THE OTHER ONE IS A VIDEO GAME.
HMMM.
IT WAS NICE OF YOUR FOLKS TO SPRING FOR A MOVIE.
YEAH. IT'S THE FIRST TIME I'VE EVER HEARD THEM CALL IT A 'BARGAIN'.
JERRY SCOTT and JIM BORGMAN

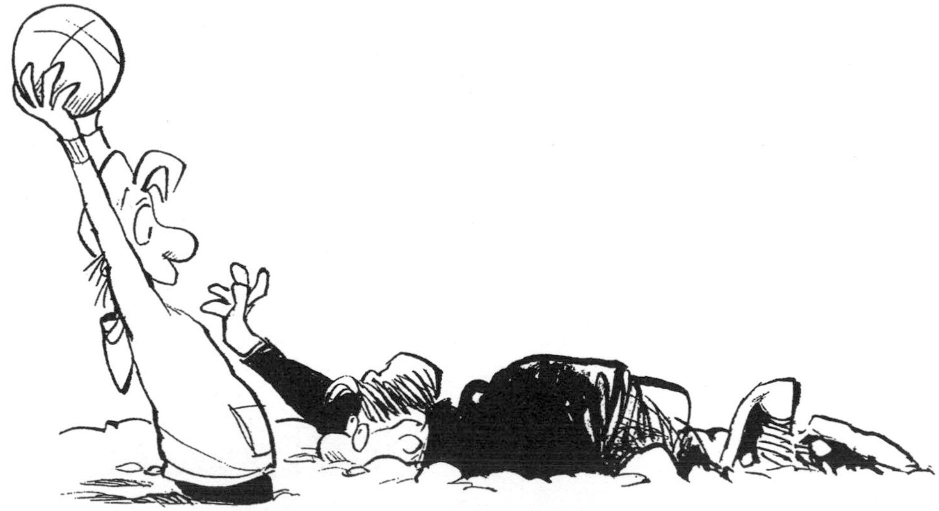

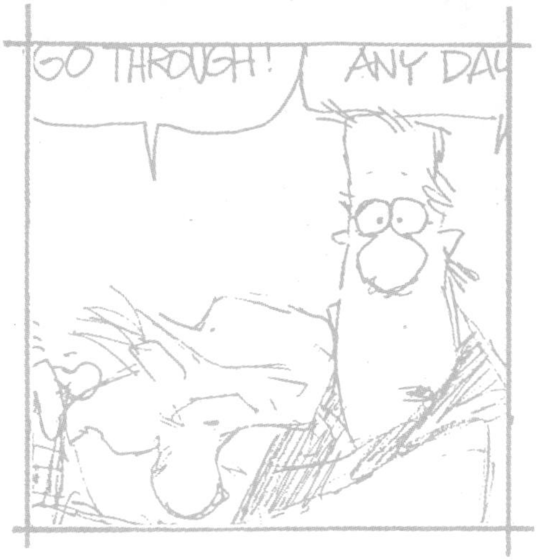
GO THROUGH!
ANY DAY

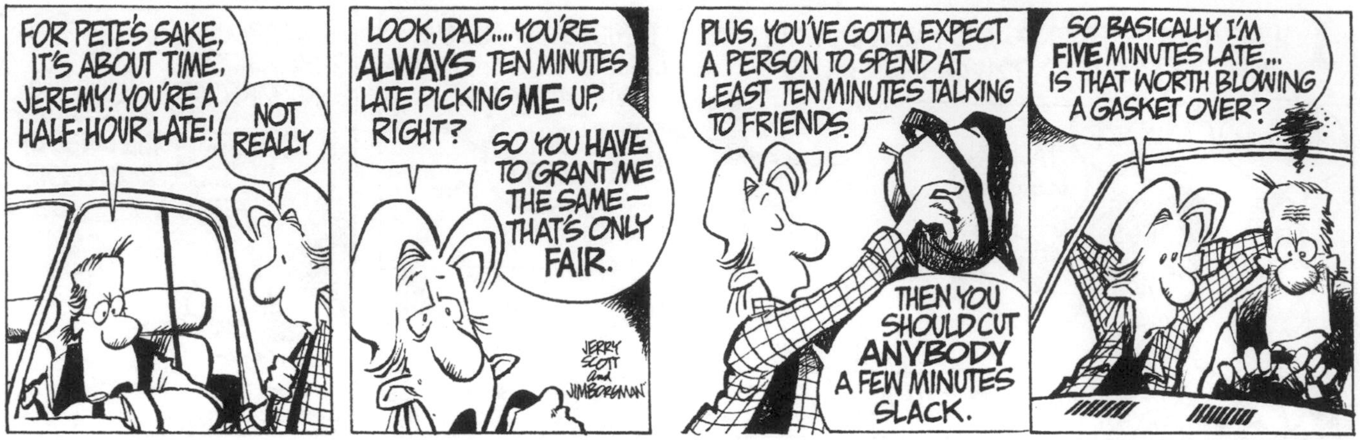
FOR PETE'S SAKE, IT'S ABOUT TIME, JEREMY! YOU'RE A HALF-HOUR LATE!
NOT REALLY
LOOK, DAD.... YOU'RE ALWAYS TEN MINUTES LATE PICKING ME UP, RIGHT?
SO YOU HAVE TO GRANT ME THE SAME— THAT'S ONLY FAIR.
JERRY SCOTT and JIM BORGMAN
PLUS, YOU'VE GOTTA EXPECT A PERSON TO SPEND AT LEAST TEN MINUTES TALKING TO FRIENDS.
THEN YOU SHOULD CUT ANYBODY A FEW MINUTES SLACK.
SO BASICALLY I'M FIVE MINUTES LATE... IS THAT WORTH BLOWING A GASKET OVER?

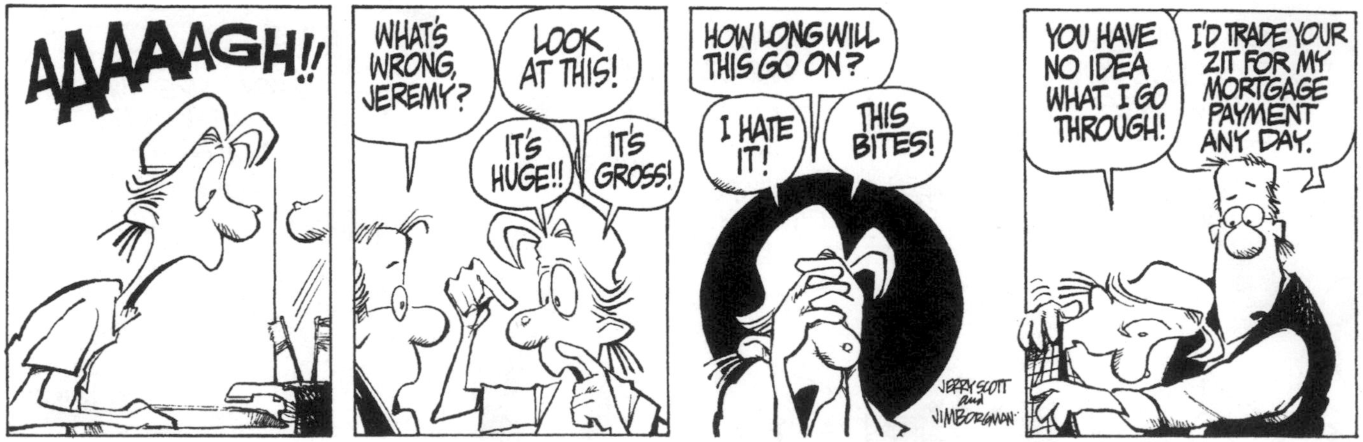
AAAAAGH!!
WHAT'S WRONG, JEREMY?
LOOK AT THIS!
IT'S HUGE!!
IT'S GROSS!
HOW LONG WILL THIS GO ON?
I HATE IT!
THIS BITES!
JERRY SCOTT and JIM BORGMAN
YOU HAVE NO IDEA WHAT I GO THROUGH!
I'D TRADE YOUR ZIT FOR MY MORTGAGE PAYMENT ANY DAY.

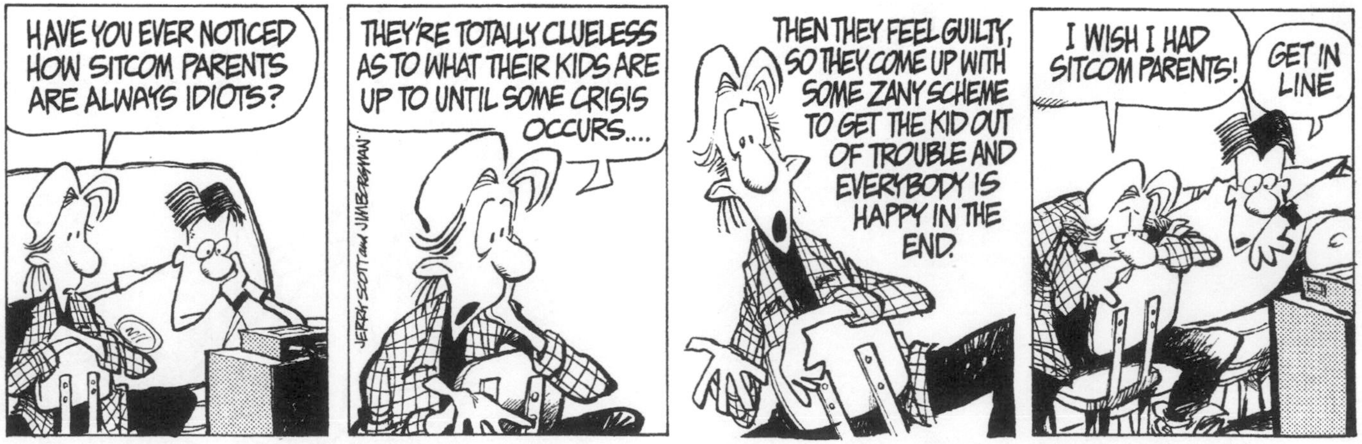
HAVE YOU EVER NOTICED HOW SITCOM PARENTS ARE ALWAYS IDIOTS?
JERRY SCOTT and JIM BORGMAN
THEY'RE TOTALLY CLUELESS AS TO WHAT THEIR KIDS ARE UP TO UNTIL SOME CRISIS OCCURS....
THEN THEY FEEL GUILTY, SO THEY COME UP WITH SOME ZANY SCHEME TO GET THE KID OUT OF TROUBLE AND EVERYBODY IS HAPPY IN THE END.
I WISH I HAD SITCOM PARENTS!
GET IN LINE

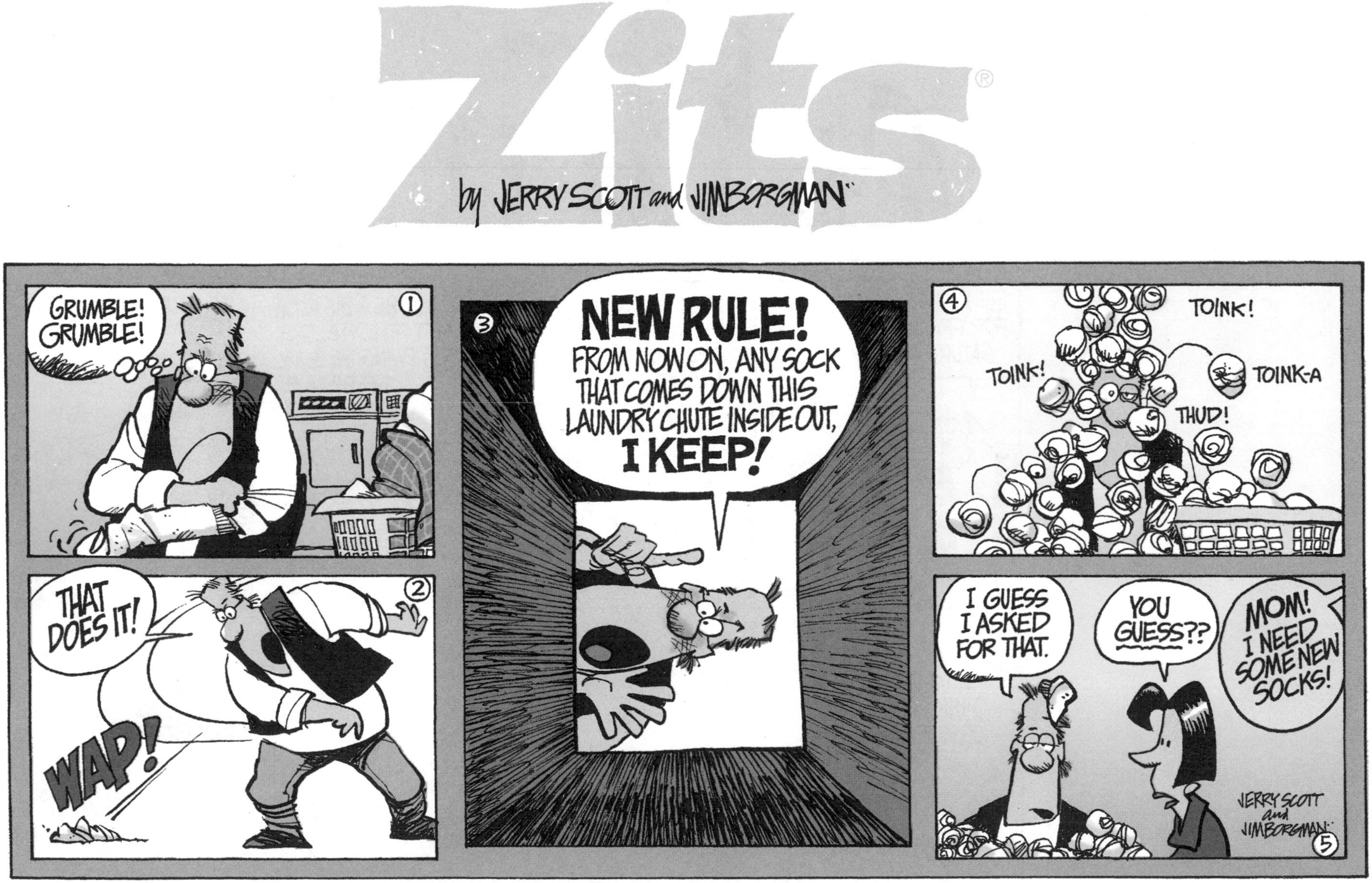
Zits
by JERRY SCOTT and JIM BORGMAN
GRUMBLE! GRUMBLE!
THAT DOES IT!
WAP!
NEW RULE! FROM NOW ON, ANY SOCK THAT COMES DOWN THIS LAUNDRY CHUTE INSIDE OUT, I KEEP!
TOINK!
TOINK!
TOINK-A
THUD!
I GUESS I ASKED FOR THAT.
YOU GUESS??
MOM! I NEED SOME NEW SOCKS!
JERRY SCOTT and JIM BORGMAN

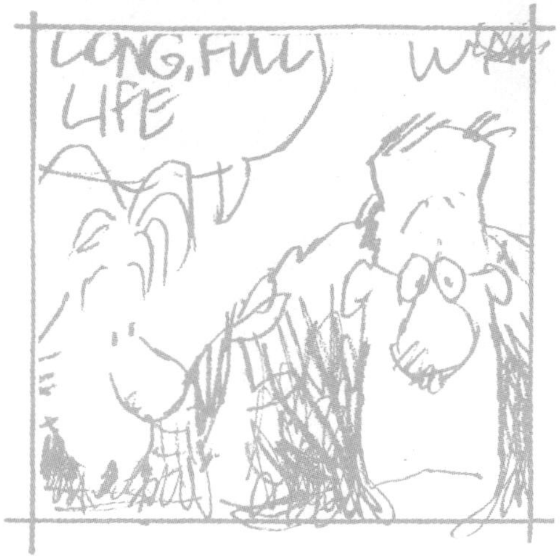
LONG, FULL
LIFE

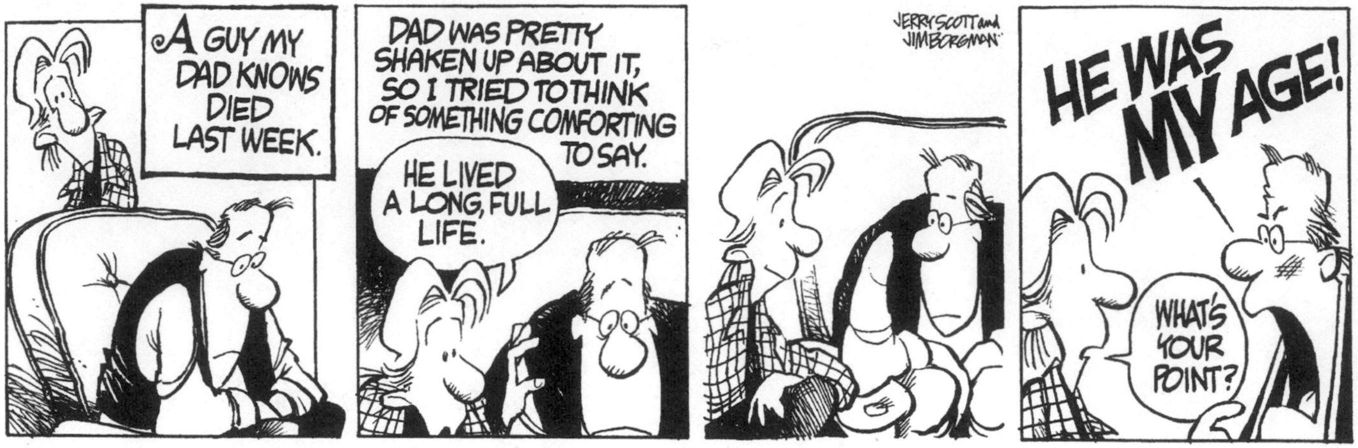
A GUY MY DAD KNOWS DIED LAST WEEK.
DAD WAS PRETTY SHAKEN UP ABOUT IT, SO I TRIED TO THINK OF SOMETHING COMFORTING TO SAY.
HE LIVED A LONG, FULL LIFE.
JERRY SCOTT and JIM BORGMAN
HE WAS MY AGE!
WHAT'S YOUR POINT?

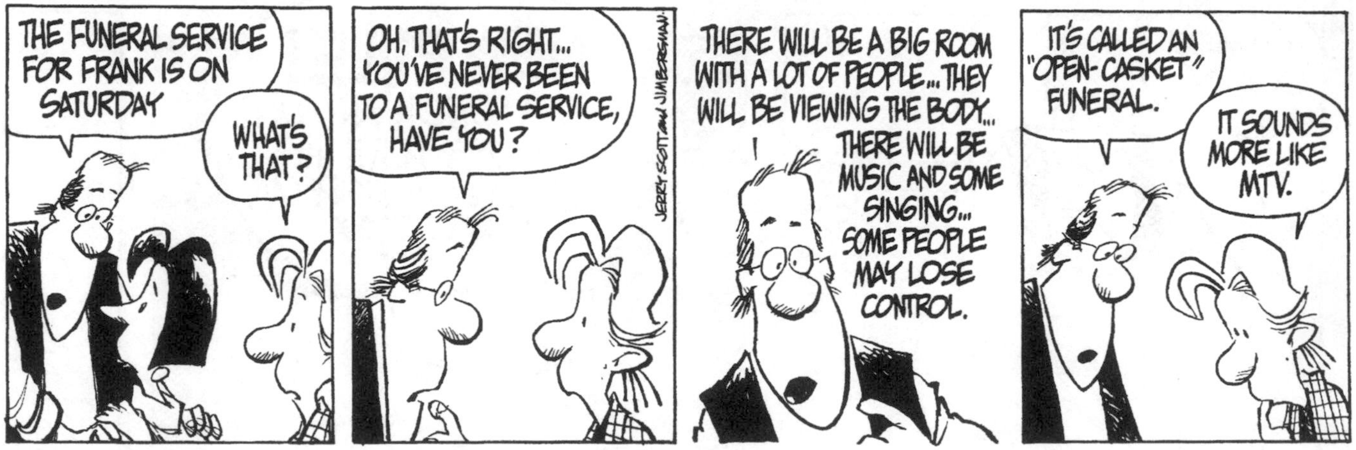
THE FUNERAL SERVICE FOR FRANK IS ON SATURDAY
WHAT'S THAT?
OH, THAT'S RIGHT... YOU'VE NEVER BEEN TO A FUNERAL SERVICE, HAVE YOU?
JERRY SCOTT and JIM BORGMAN
THERE WILL BE A BIG ROOM WITH A LOT OF PEOPLE... THEY WILL BE VIEWING THE BODY...
THERE WILL BE MUSIC AND SOME SINGING... SOME PEOPLE MAY LOSE CONTROL.
IT'S CALLED AN "OPEN-CASKET" FUNERAL.
IT SOUNDS MORE LIKE MTV.

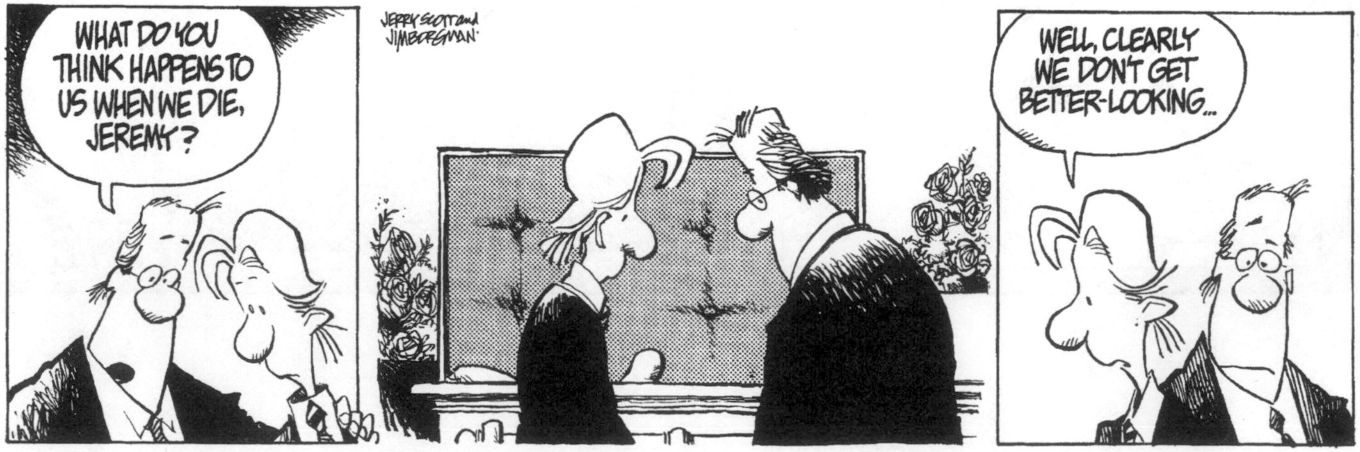
WHAT DO YOU THINK HAPPENS TO US WHEN WE DIE, JEREMY?
JERRY SCOTT and JIM BORGMAN
WELL, CLEARLY WE DON'T GET BETTER-LOOKING...

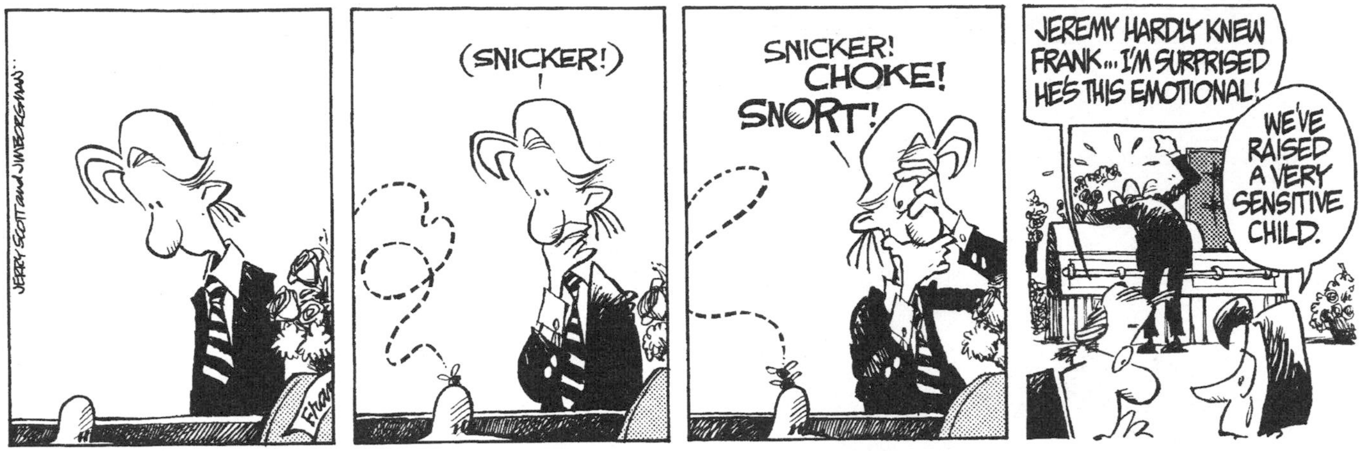
JERRY SCOTT and JIM BORGMAN
(SNICKER!)
SNICKER! CHOKE! SNORT!
JEREMY HARDLY KNEW FRANK... I'M SURPRISED HE'S THIS EMOTIONAL!
WE'VE RAISED A VERY SENSITIVE CHILD.

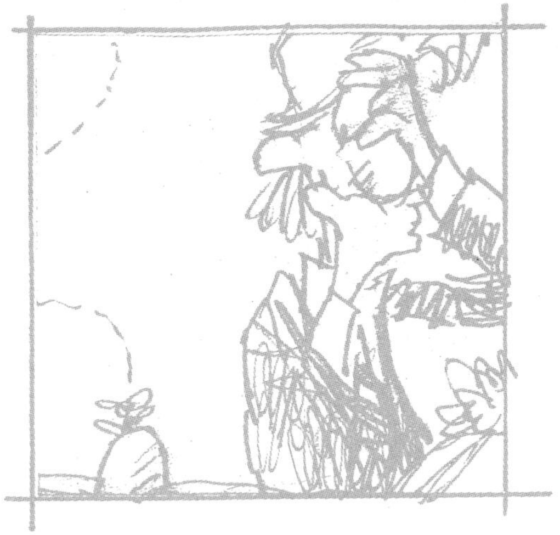

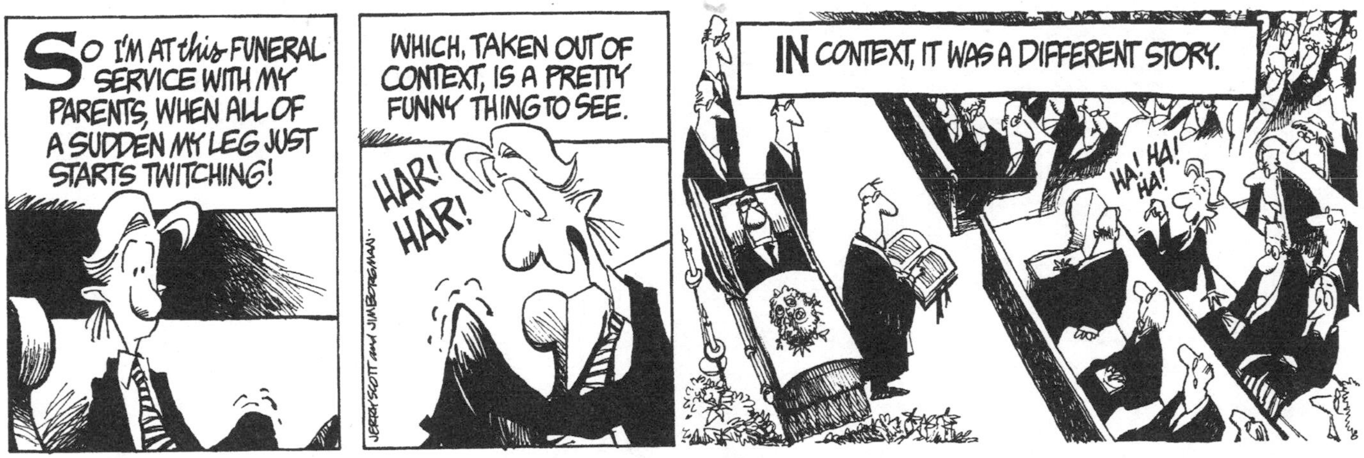
SO I'M AT this FUNERAL SERVICE WITH MY PARENTS, WHEN ALL OF A SUDDEN MY LEG JUST STARTS TWITCHING!
WHICH, TAKEN OUT OF CONTEXT, IS A PRETTY FUNNY THING TO SEE.
HAR! HAR!
JERRY SCOTT and JIM BORGMAN
IN CONTEXT, IT WAS A DIFFERENT STORY.
HA! HA! HA!

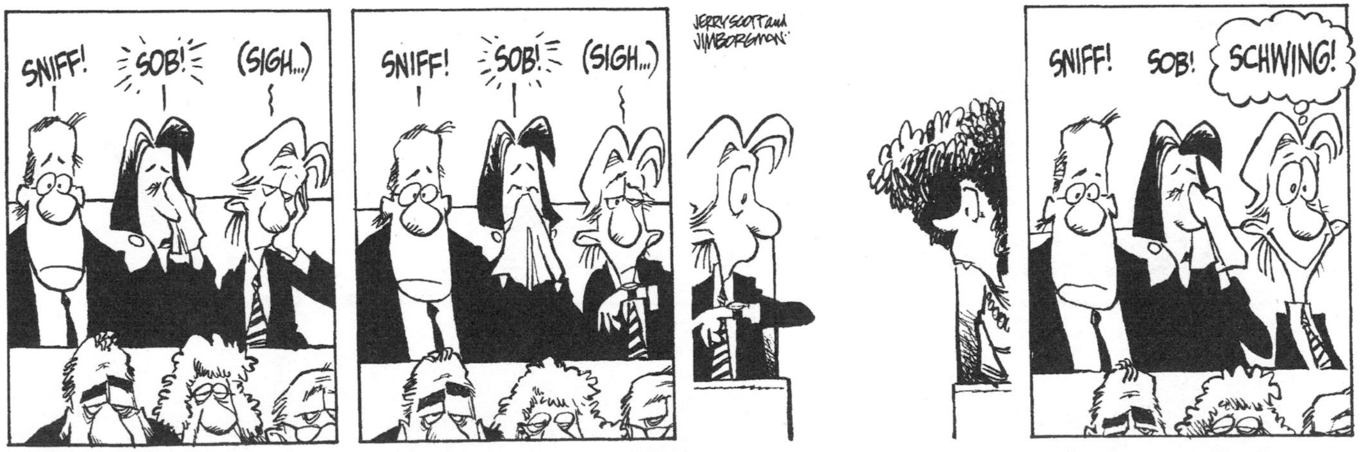
SNIFF! SOB! (SIGH...)
SNIFF! SOB! (SIGH...)
JERRY SCOTT and JIM BORGMAN
SNIFF! SOB! SCHWING!

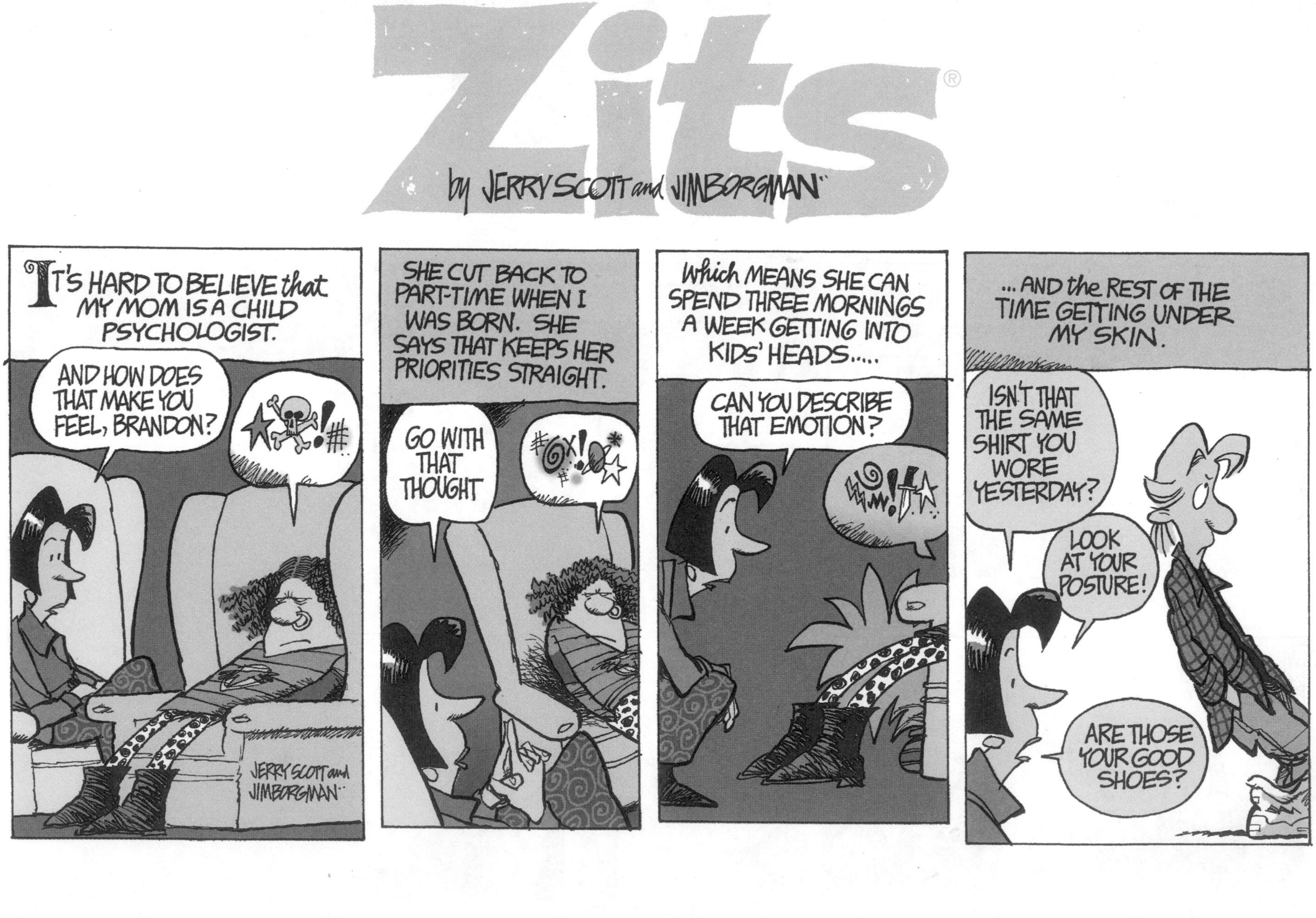
Zits®
by JERRY SCOTT and JIM BORGMAN
IT'S HARD TO BELIEVE that MY MOM IS A CHILD PSYCHOLOGIST.
AND HOW DOES THAT MAKE YOU FEEL, BRANDON?
JERRY SCOTT and JIM BORGMAN
SHE CUT BACK TO PART-TIME WHEN I WAS BORN. SHE SAYS THAT KEEPS HER PRIORITIES STRAIGHT.
GO WITH THAT THOUGHT
Which MEANS SHE CAN SPEND THREE MORNINGS A WEEK GETTING INTO KIDS' HEADS.....
CAN YOU DESCRIBE THAT EMOTION?
... AND the REST OF THE TIME GETTING UNDER MY SKIN.
ISN'T THAT THE SAME SHIRT YOU WORE YESTERDAY?
LOOK AT YOUR POSTURE!
ARE THOSE YOUR GOOD SHOES?

Panel 1:
SO HOW WAS THAT GUY'S FUNERAL YOU WENT TO?
AWESOME!

Panel 2:
THERE WAS THE MOST BEAUTIFUL GIRL THERE!

Panel 3:
I'M TELLING YOU, HECTOR, SHE WAS SUPREME! IT MAY HAVE BEEN THE BEST TWO HOURS OF MY LIFE!

Panel 4:
EXCEPT FOR THE DEATH THING.
YEAH. WHY DO THEY ALWAYS HAVE TO DRAG THAT INTO FUNERALS?

Panel 5:
I JUST SAW JEREMY ORDERING SOMETHING OVER THE PHONE WITH YOUR CREDIT CARD.

Panel 6:
YEAH, HE NEEDED SOME KIND OF SOFTWARE, AND I SAID HE COULD GET IT.
THAT'S PRETTY TRUSTING OF YOU.

Panel 7:
LOOK, JEREMY IS A RESPONSIBLE KID... BESIDES, HE'S JUST IN THE NEXT ROOM!

Panel 8:
DON'T YOU TRUST YOUR OWN SON?
I LOST YOUR CREDIT CARD.

Panel 9:
WHAT DO YOU MEAN YOU LOST MY VISA CARD?? I JUST GAVE IT TO YOU THREE MINUTES AGO!

Panel 10:
HOW COULD YOU LOSE IT?
I DON'T KNOW... IT'S JUST GONE!

Panel 11:
IT WAS REALLY STUPID AND CARELESS OF ME, AND I FEEL REALLY BAD...

Panel 12:
... CAN I HAVE YOUR AMERICAN EXPRESS?

JERRY SCOTT and JIM BORGMAN

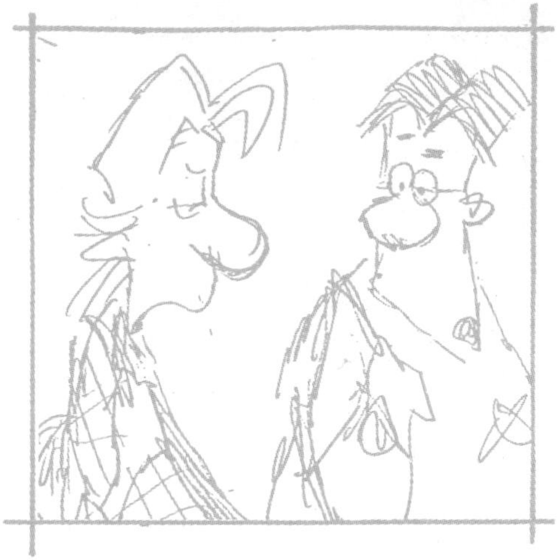

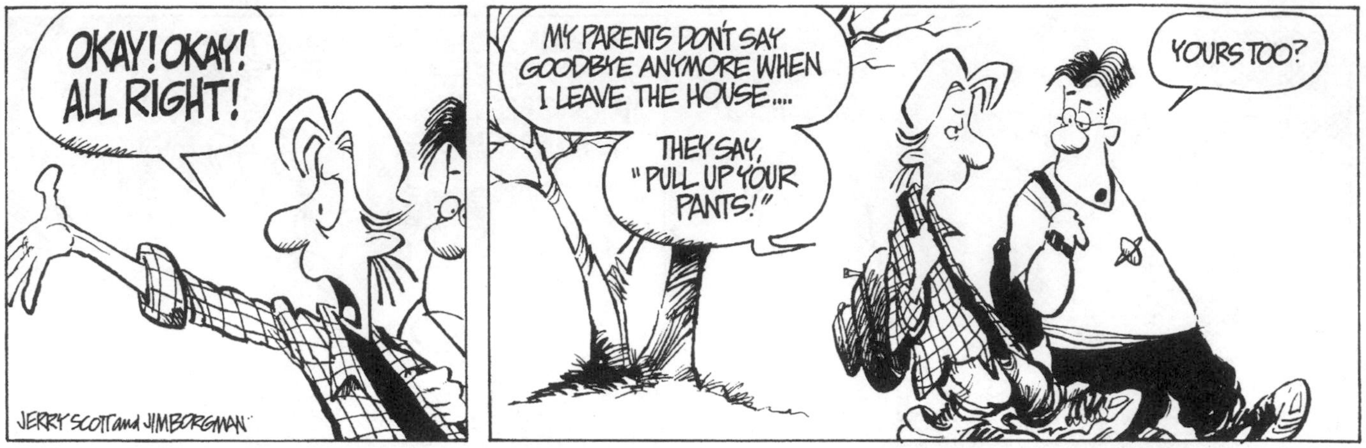

OKAY! OKAY! ALL RIGHT!
JERRY SCOTT and JIM BORGMAN
MY PARENTS DON'T SAY GOODBYE ANYMORE WHEN I LEAVE THE HOUSE....
THEY SAY, "PULL UP YOUR PANTS!"
YOURS TOO?

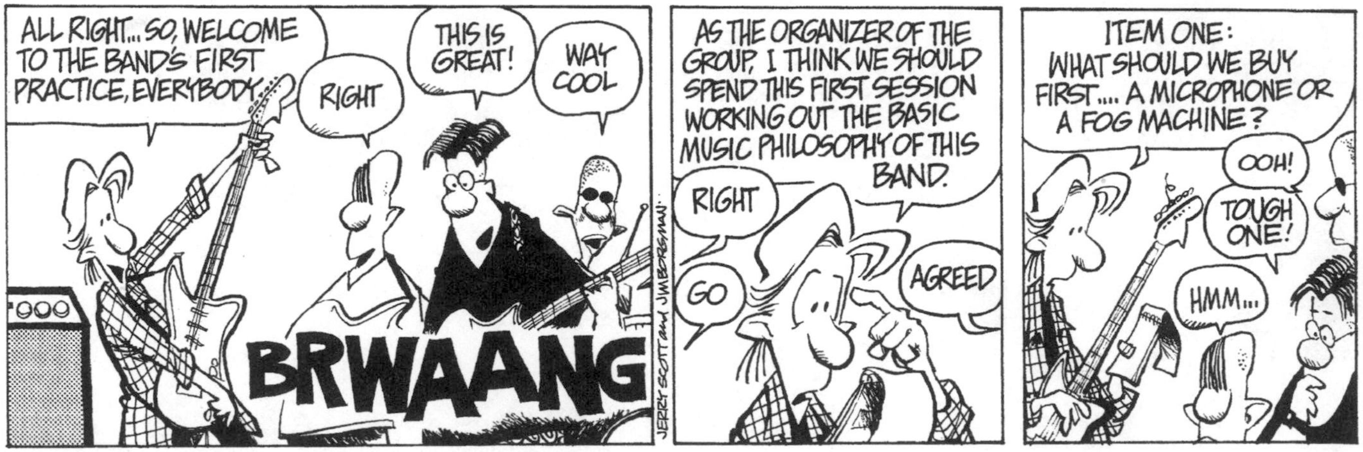

ALL RIGHT... SO, WELCOME TO THE BAND'S FIRST PRACTICE, EVERYBODY...
RIGHT
THIS IS GREAT!
WAY COOL
BRWAANG
JERRY SCOTT and JIM BORGMAN
AS THE ORGANIZER OF THE GROUP, I THINK WE SHOULD SPEND THIS FIRST SESSION WORKING OUT THE BASIC MUSIC PHILOSOPHY OF THIS BAND.
RIGHT
GO
AGREED
ITEM ONE: WHAT SHOULD WE BUY FIRST.... A MICROPHONE OR A FOG MACHINE?
OOH!
TOUGH ONE!
HMM...

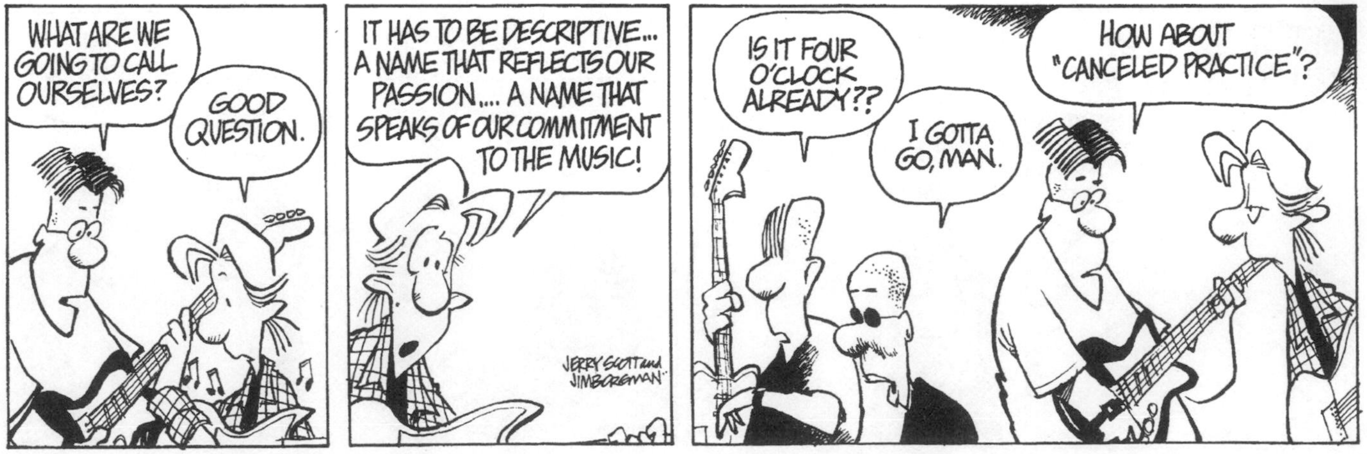

WHAT ARE WE GOING TO CALL OURSELVES?
GOOD QUESTION.
IT HAS TO BE DESCRIPTIVE... A NAME THAT REFLECTS OUR PASSION.... A NAME THAT SPEAKS OF OUR COMMITMENT TO THE MUSIC!
JERRY SCOTT and JIM BORGMAN
IS IT FOUR O'CLOCK ALREADY??
I GOTTA GO, MAN.
HOW ABOUT "CANCELED PRACTICE"?

Zits®
by JERRY SCOTT and JIM BORGMAN

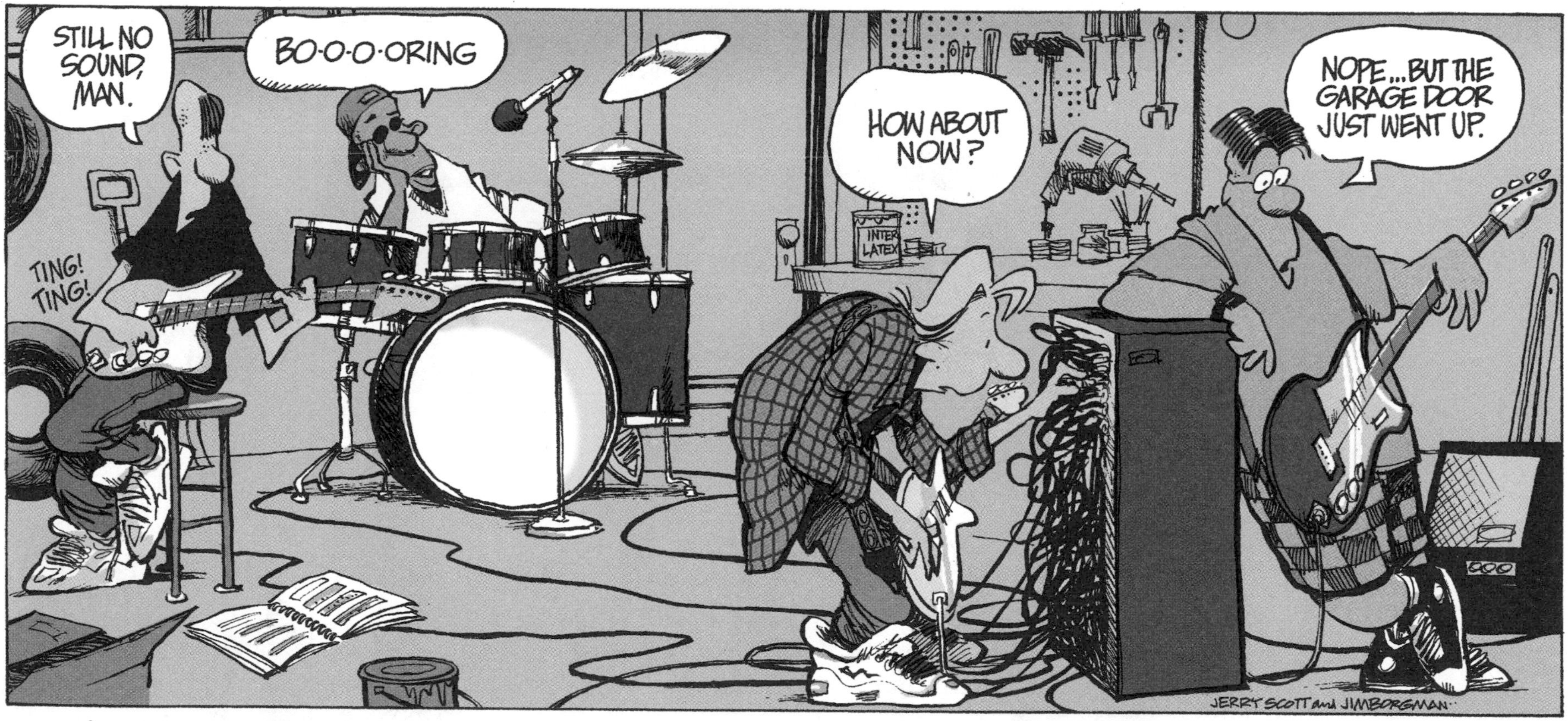
STILL NO SOUND, MAN.
BO-O-O-ORING
TING! TING!
HOW ABOUT NOW?
NOPE...BUT THE GARAGE DOOR JUST WENT UP.
INTER LATEX
JERRY SCOTT and JIM BORGMAN

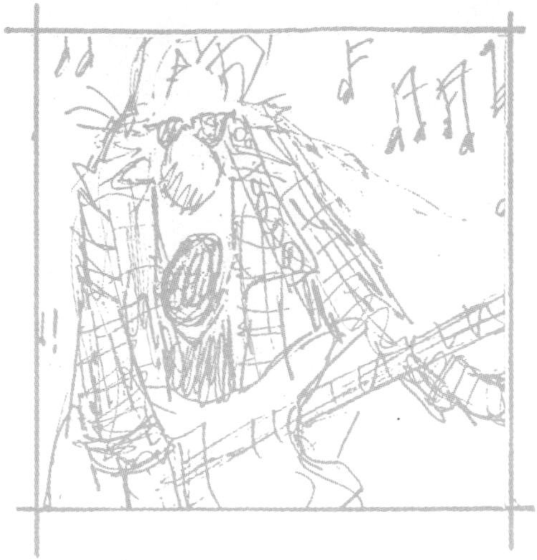

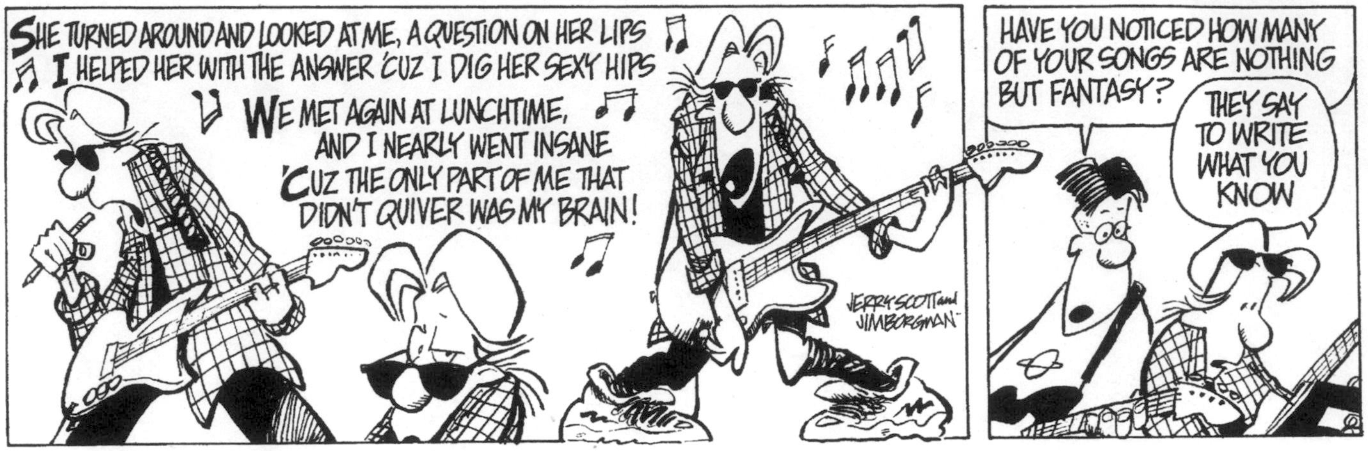
SHE TURNED AROUND AND LOOKED AT ME, A QUESTION ON HER LIPS
I HELPED HER WITH THE ANSWER 'CUZ I DIG HER SEXY HIPS
WE MET AGAIN AT LUNCHTIME, AND I NEARLY WENT INSANE
'CUZ THE ONLY PART OF ME THAT DIDN'T QUIVER WAS MY BRAIN!
JERRY SCOTT and JIM BORGMAN
HAVE YOU NOTICED HOW MANY OF YOUR SONGS ARE NOTHING BUT FANTASY?
THEY SAY TO WRITE WHAT YOU KNOW

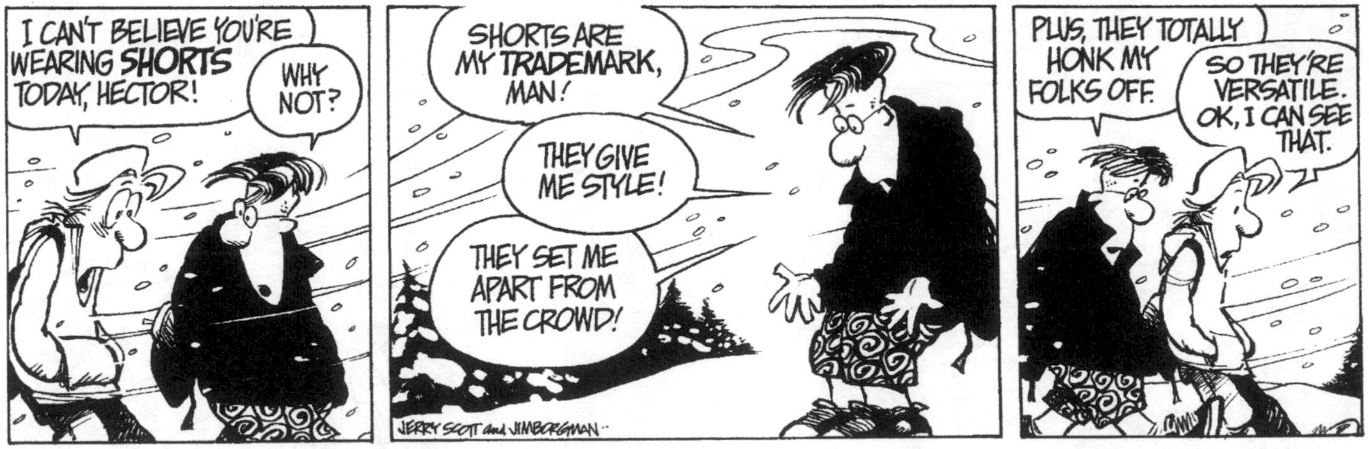
I CAN'T BELIEVE YOU'RE WEARING SHORTS TODAY, HECTOR!
WHY NOT?
SHORTS ARE MY TRADEMARK, MAN!
THEY GIVE ME STYLE!
THEY SET ME APART FROM THE CROWD!
JERRY SCOTT and JIM BORGMAN
PLUS, THEY TOTALLY HONK MY FOLKS OFF.
SO THEY'RE VERSATILE. OK, I CAN SEE THAT.

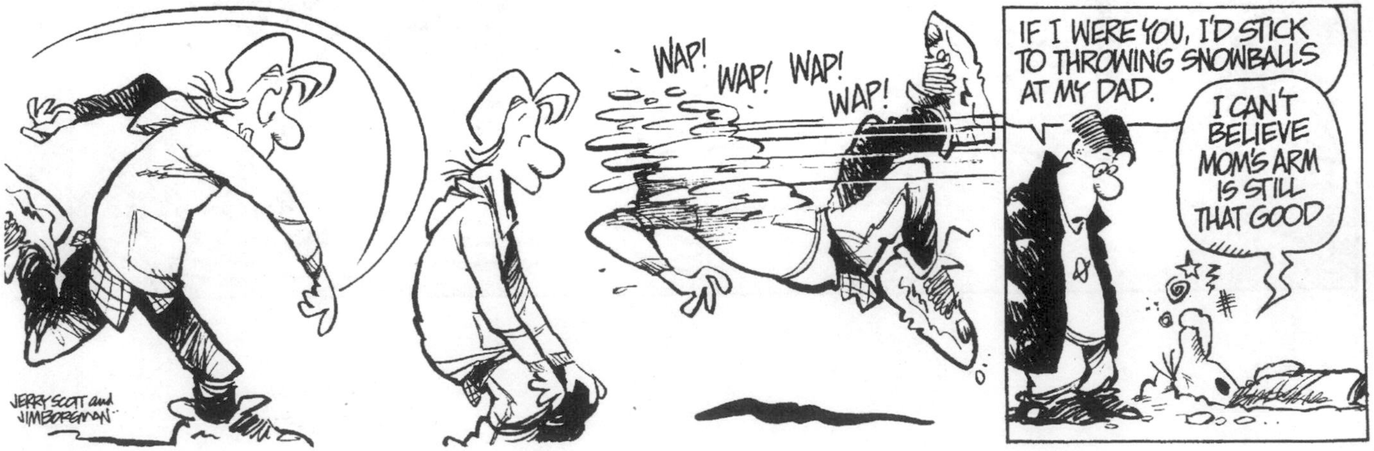
JERRY SCOTT and JIM BORGMAN
WAP!
WAP!
WAP!
WAP!
IF I WERE YOU, I'D STICK TO THROWING SNOWBALLS AT MY DAD.
I CAN'T BELIEVE MOM'S ARM IS STILL THAT GOOD

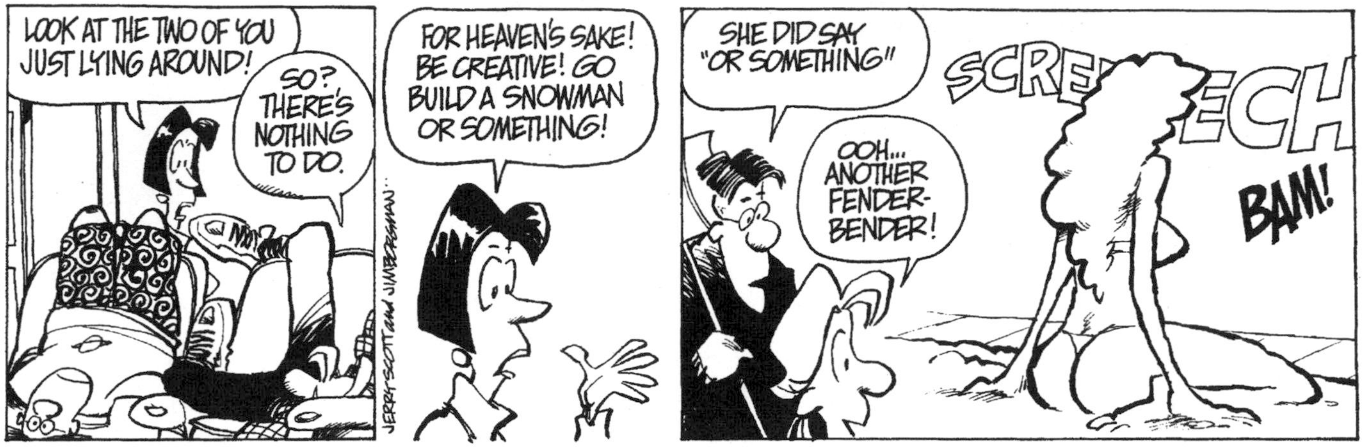
LOOK AT THE TWO OF YOU JUST LYING AROUND!
SO? THERE'S NOTHING TO DO.
JERRY SCOTT and JIM BORGMAN
FOR HEAVEN'S SAKE! BE CREATIVE! GO BUILD A SNOWMAN OR SOMETHING!
SHE DID SAY "OR SOMETHING"
SCREECH
OOH... ANOTHER FENDER-BENDER!
BAM!

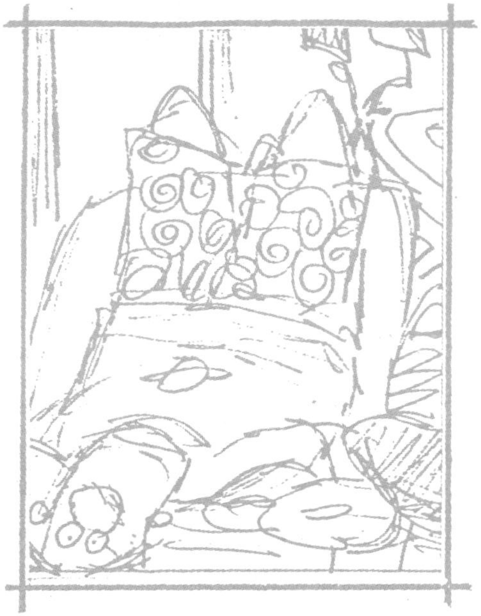

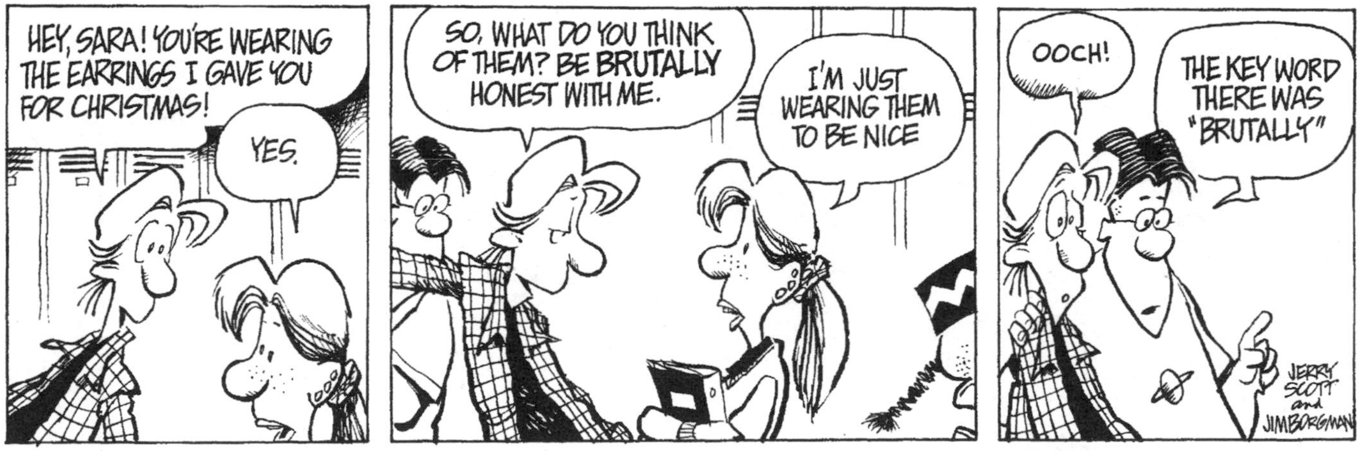
HEY, SARA! YOU'RE WEARING THE EARRINGS I GAVE YOU FOR CHRISTMAS!
YES.
SO, WHAT DO YOU THINK OF THEM? BE BRUTALLY HONEST WITH ME.
I'M JUST WEARING THEM TO BE NICE
OOCH!
THE KEY WORD THERE WAS "BRUTALLY"
JERRY SCOTT and JIM BORGMAN

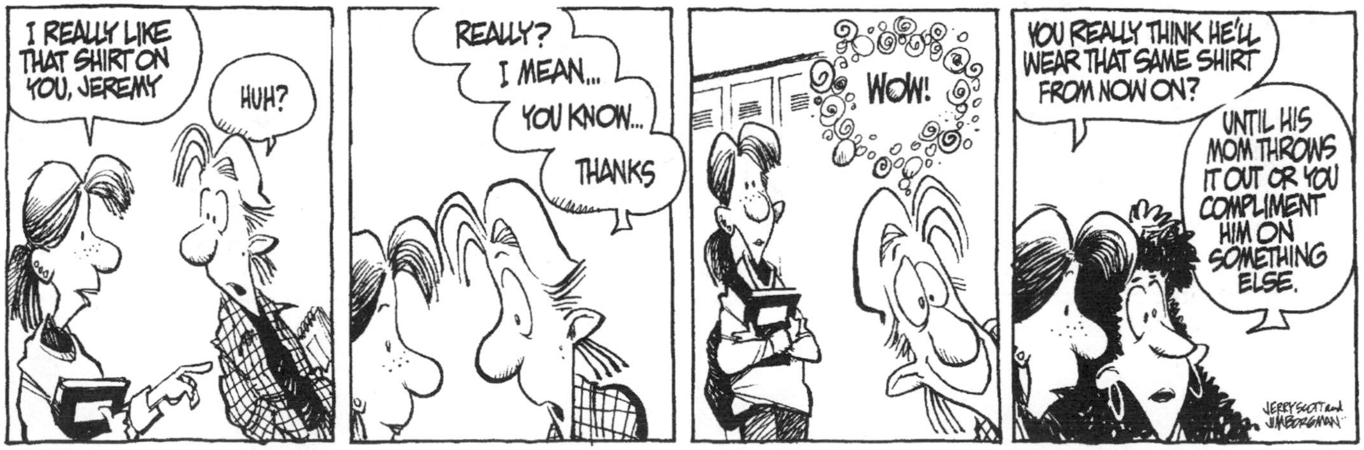
I REALLY LIKE THAT SHIRT ON YOU, JEREMY
HUH?
REALLY? I MEAN... YOU KNOW... THANKS
WOW!
YOU REALLY THINK HE'LL WEAR THAT SAME SHIRT FROM NOW ON?
UNTIL HIS MOM THROWS IT OUT OR YOU COMPLIMENT HIM ON SOMETHING ELSE.
JERRY SCOTT and JIM BORGMAN

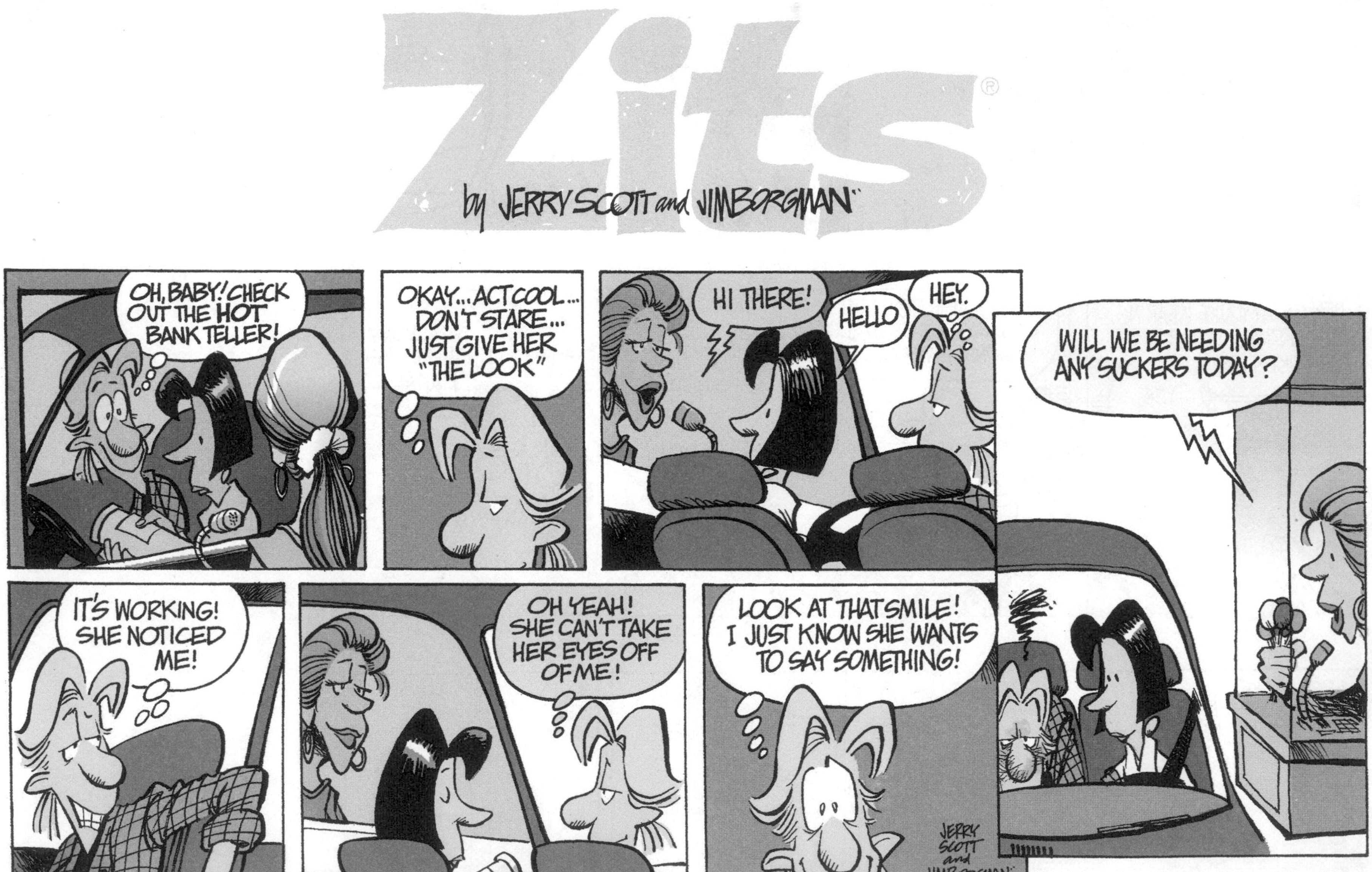
Zits®
by JERRY SCOTT and JIM BORGMAN
OH, BABY! CHECK OUT THE HOT BANK TELLER!
OKAY... ACT COOL... DON'T STARE... JUST GIVE HER "THE LOOK"
HI THERE!
HELLO
HEY.
WILL WE BE NEEDING ANY SUCKERS TODAY?
IT'S WORKING! SHE NOTICED ME!
OH YEAH! SHE CAN'T TAKE HER EYES OFF OF ME!
LOOK AT THAT SMILE! I JUST KNOW SHE WANTS TO SAY SOMETHING!
JERRY SCOTT and JIM BORGMAN

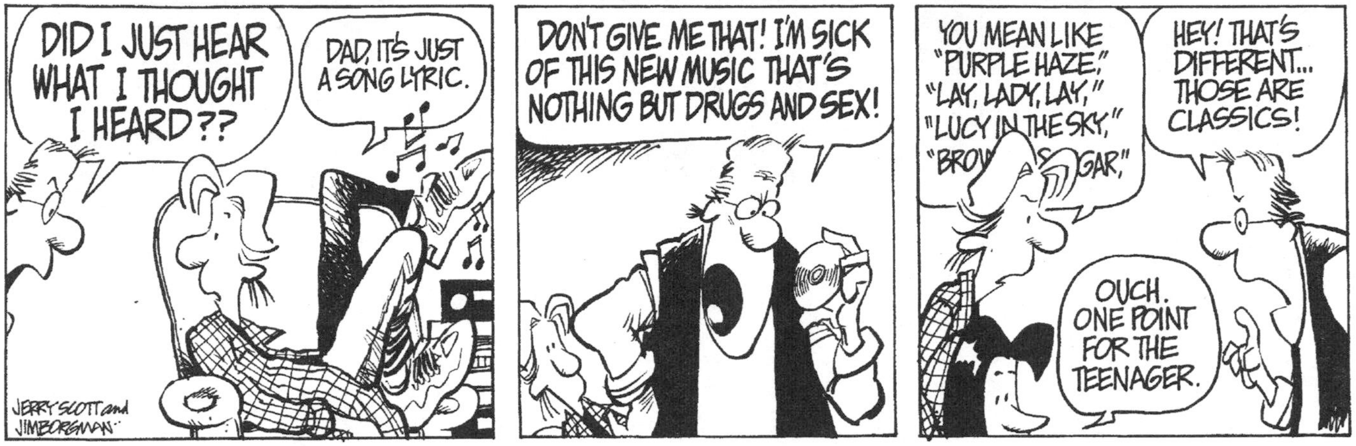
DID I JUST HEAR WHAT I THOUGHT I HEARD??
DAD, IT'S JUST A SONG LYRIC.
JERRY SCOTT and JIM BORGMAN
DON'T GIVE ME THAT! I'M SICK OF THIS NEW MUSIC THAT'S NOTHING BUT DRUGS AND SEX!
YOU MEAN LIKE "PURPLE HAZE," "LAY, LADY, LAY," "LUCY IN THE SKY," "BROW S GAR,"
HEY! THAT'S DIFFERENT... THOSE ARE CLASSICS!
OUCH. ONE POINT FOR THE TEENAGER.

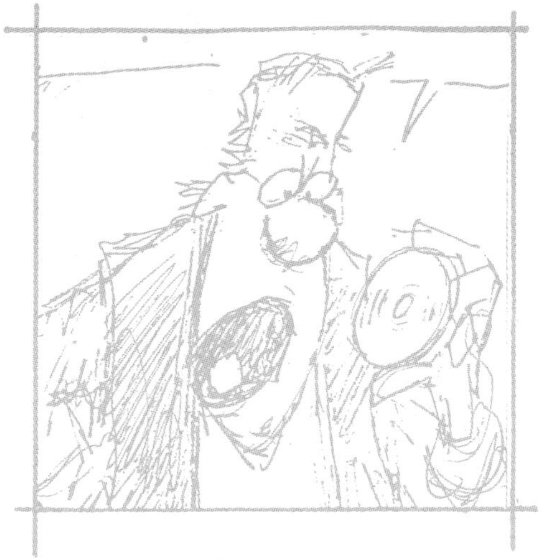

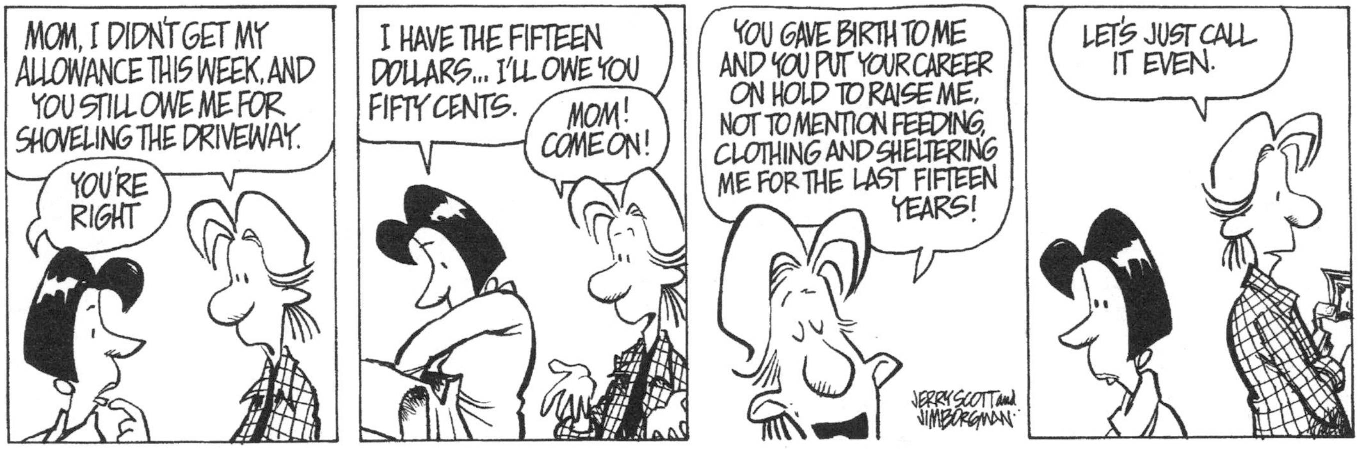
MOM, I DIDN'T GET MY ALLOWANCE THIS WEEK, AND YOU STILL OWE ME FOR SHOVELING THE DRIVEWAY.
YOU'RE RIGHT
I HAVE THE FIFTEEN DOLLARS... I'LL OWE YOU FIFTY CENTS.
MOM! COME ON!
YOU GAVE BIRTH TO ME AND YOU PUT YOUR CAREER ON HOLD TO RAISE ME, NOT TO MENTION FEEDING, CLOTHING AND SHELTERING ME FOR THE LAST FIFTEEN YEARS!
JERRY SCOTT and JIM BORGMAN
LET'S JUST CALL IT EVEN.

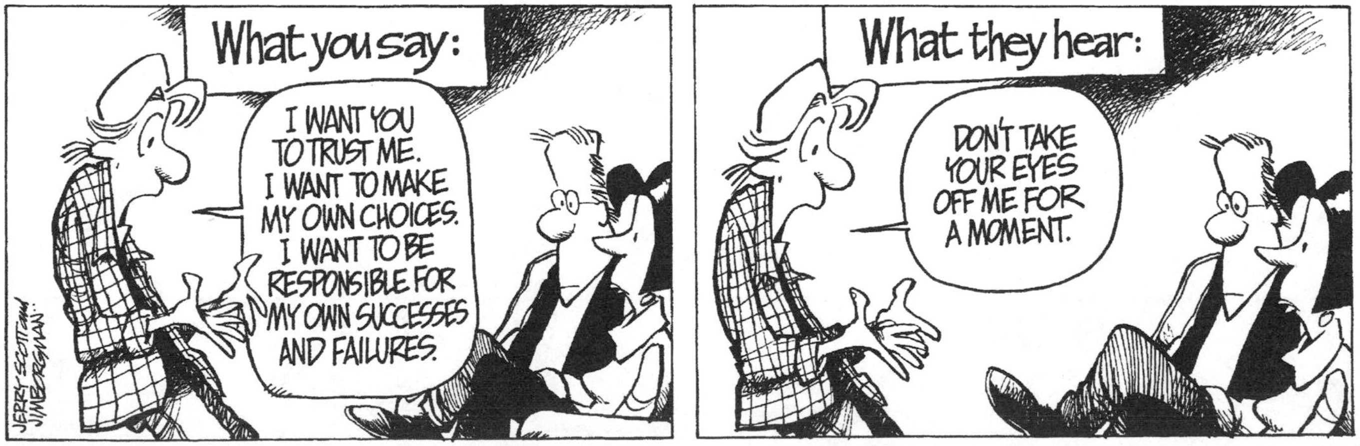
What you say:
I WANT YOU TO TRUST ME. I WANT TO MAKE MY OWN CHOICES. I WANT TO BE RESPONSIBLE FOR MY OWN SUCCESSES AND FAILURES.
JERRY SCOTT and JIM BORGMAN
What they hear:
DON'T TAKE YOUR EYES OFF ME FOR A MOMENT.

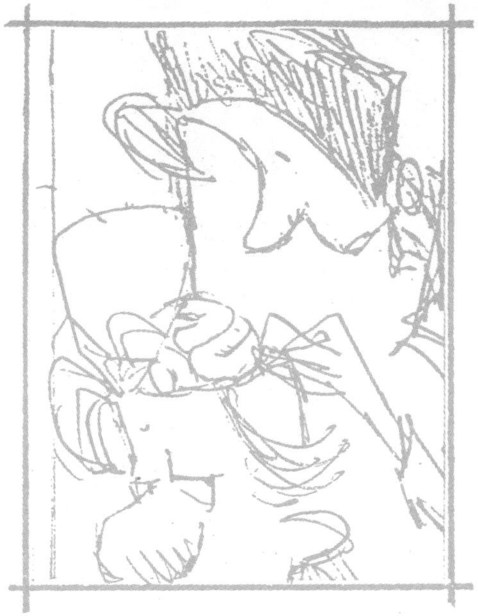

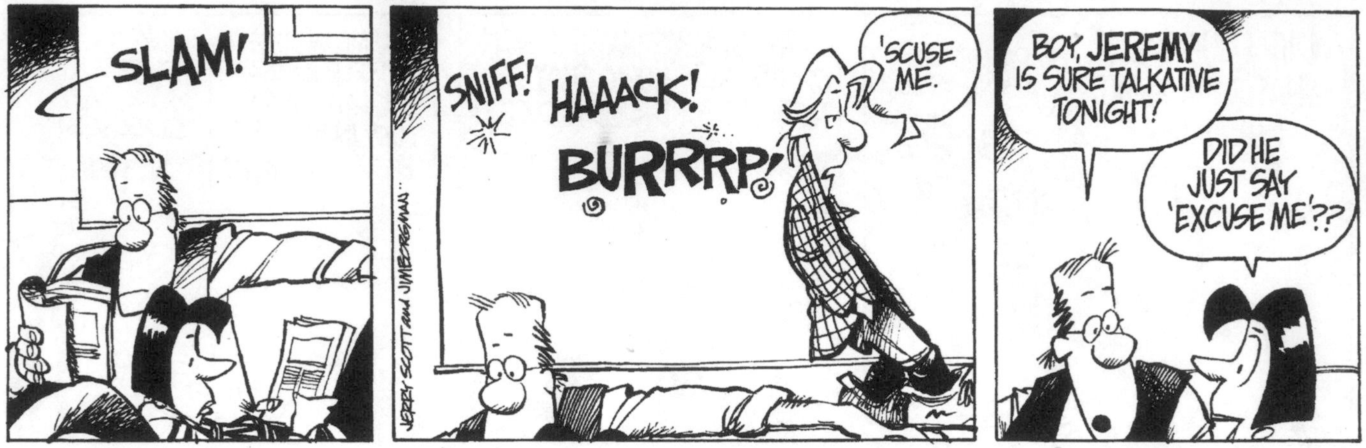
SLAM!
SNIFF!
HAAACK!
BURRRP!
'SCUSE ME.
JERRY SCOTT AND JIM BORGMAN
BOY, JEREMY IS SURE TALKATIVE TONIGHT!
DID HE JUST SAY 'EXCUSE ME'??

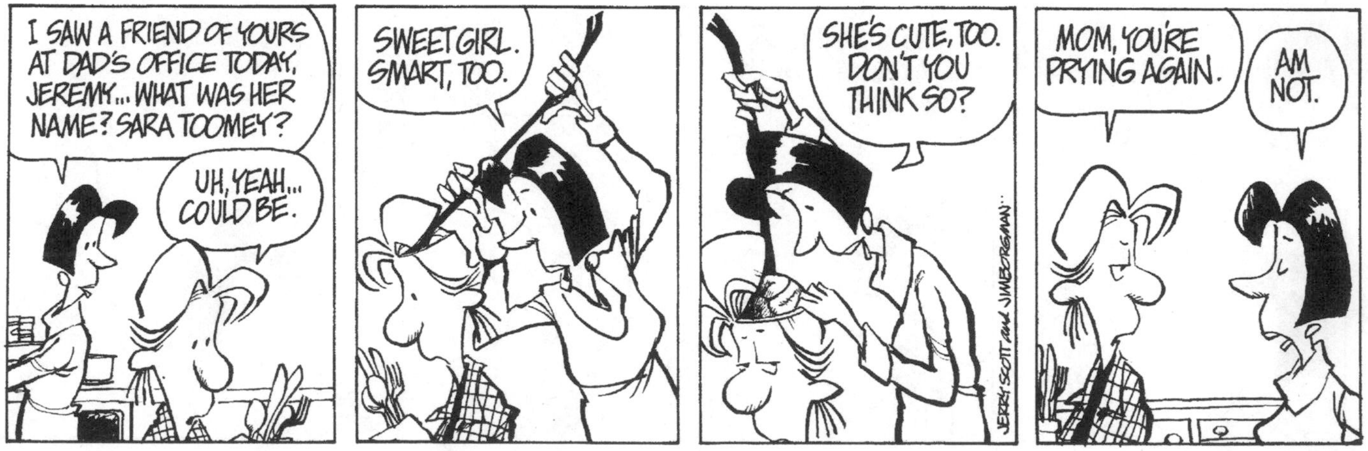
I SAW A FRIEND OF YOURS AT DAD'S OFFICE TODAY, JEREMY... WHAT WAS HER NAME? SARA TOOMEY?
UH, YEAH... COULD BE.
SWEET GIRL. SMART, TOO.
SHE'S CUTE, TOO. DON'T YOU THINK SO?
JERRY SCOTT AND JIM BORGMAN
MOM, YOU'RE PRYING AGAIN.
AM NOT.

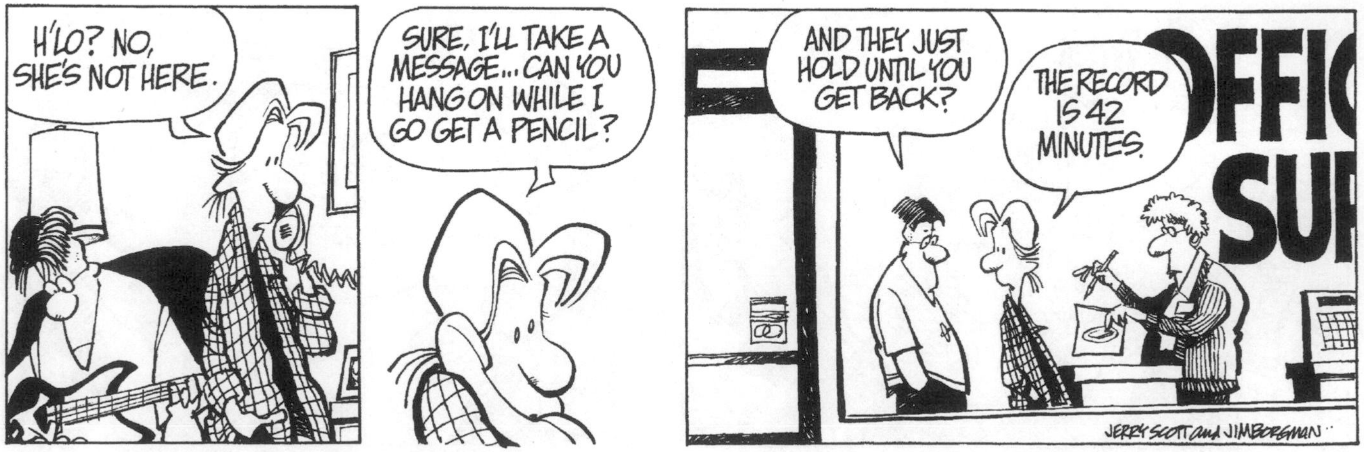
H'LO? NO, SHE'S NOT HERE.
SURE, I'LL TAKE A MESSAGE... CAN YOU HANG ON WHILE I GO GET A PENCIL?
AND THEY JUST HOLD UNTIL YOU GET BACK?
THE RECORD IS 42 MINUTES.
OFFIC
SU
JERRY SCOTT AND JIM BORGMAN

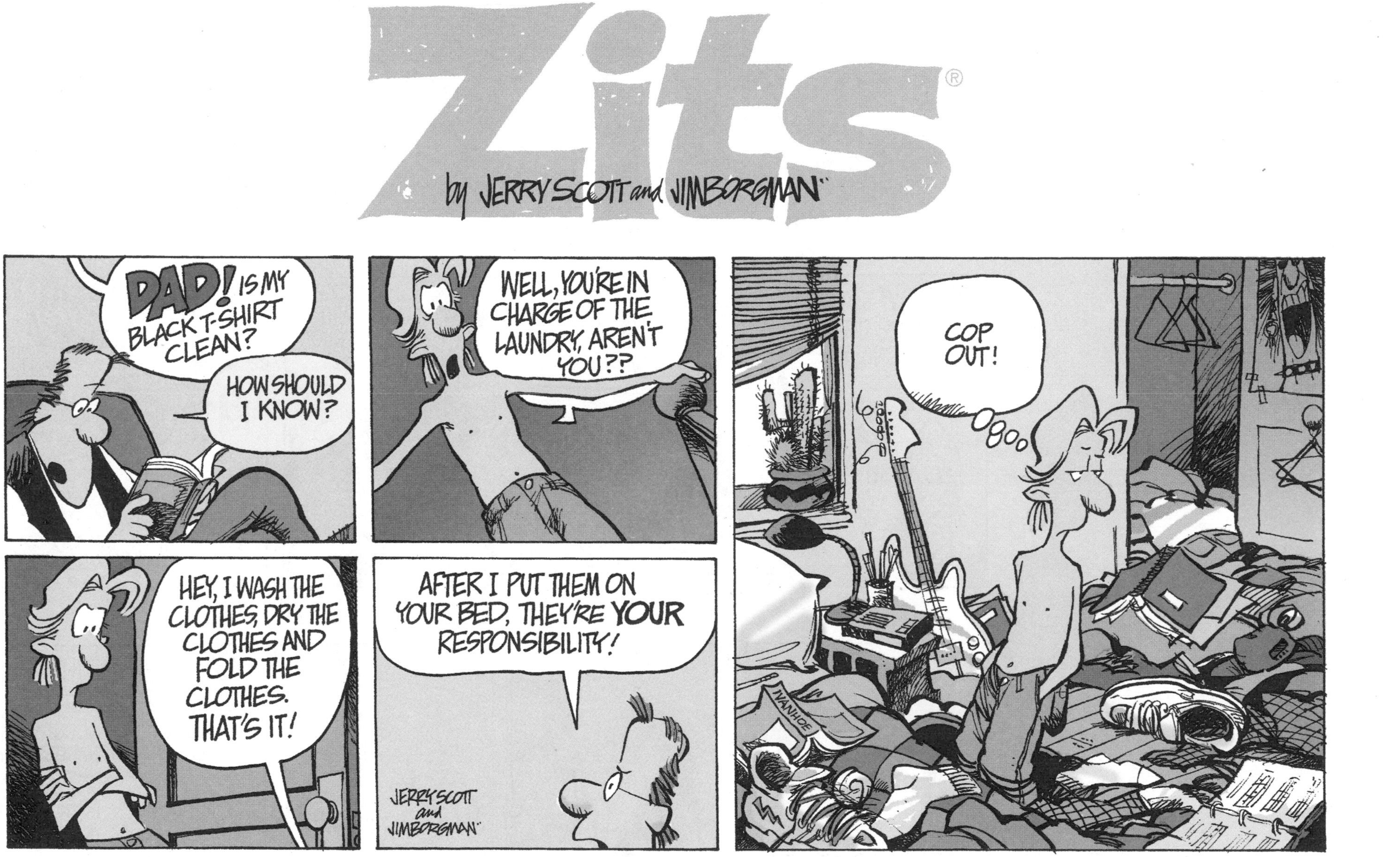
Zits®
by JERRY SCOTT and JIM BORGMAN
DAD! IS MY BLACK T-SHIRT CLEAN?
HOW SHOULD I KNOW?
WELL, YOU'RE IN CHARGE OF THE LAUNDRY, AREN'T YOU??
HEY, I WASH THE CLOTHES, DRY THE CLOTHES AND FOLD THE CLOTHES. THAT'S IT!
AFTER I PUT THEM ON YOUR BED, THEY'RE **YOUR** RESPONSIBILITY!
JERRY SCOTT and JIM BORGMAN
COP OUT!
IVANHOE

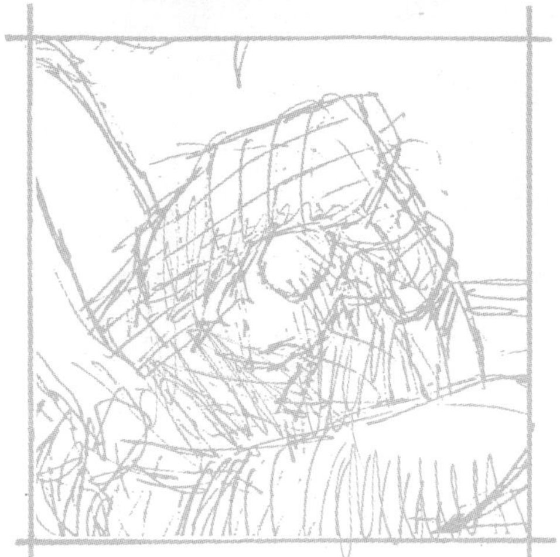

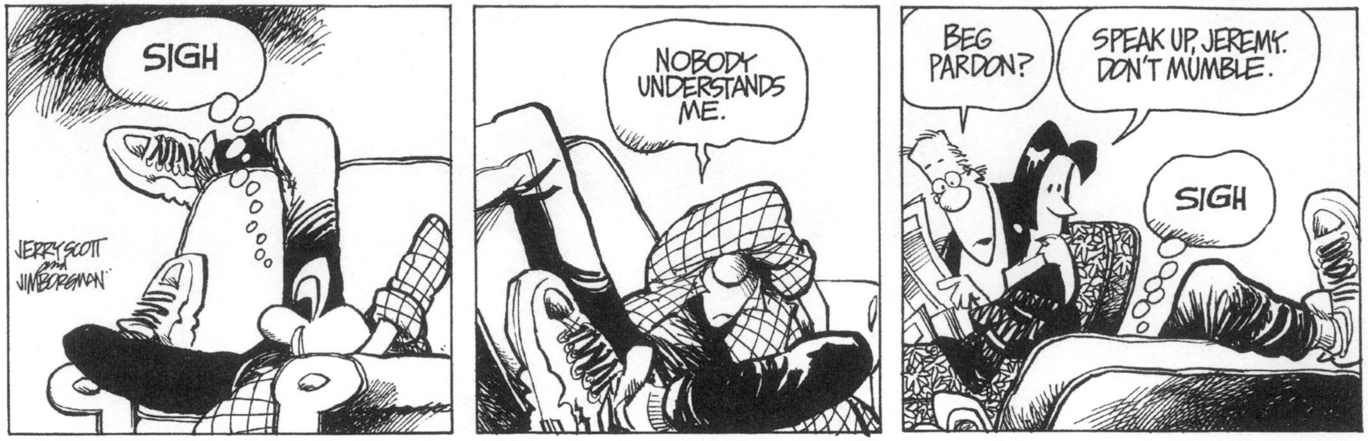
SIGH
JERRY SCOTT and JIM BORGMAN
NOBODY UNDERSTANDS ME.
BEG PARDON?
SPEAK UP, JEREMY. DON'T MUMBLE.
SIGH

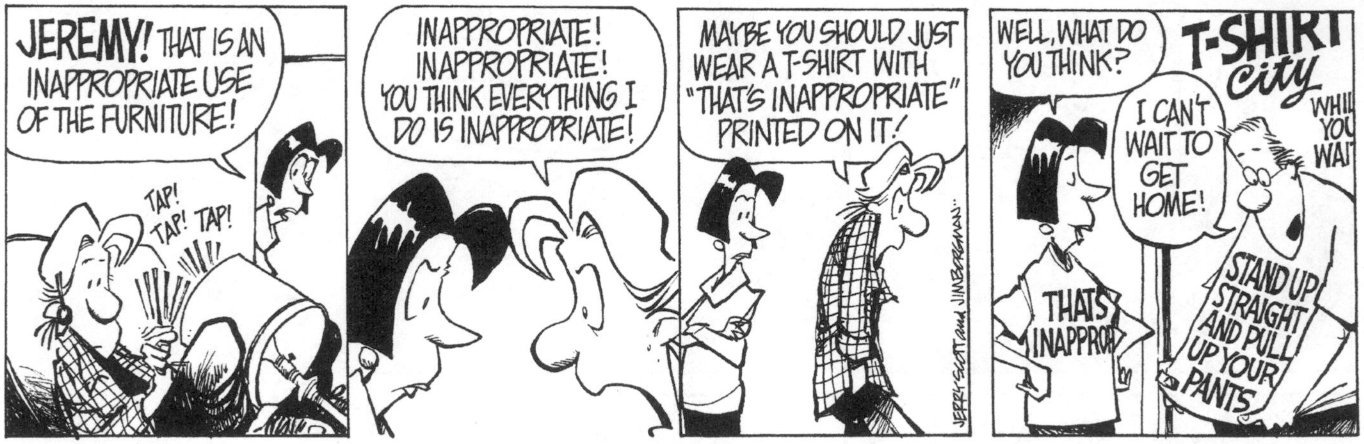
JEREMY! THAT IS AN INAPPROPRIATE USE OF THE FURNITURE!
TAP! TAP! TAP!
INAPPROPRIATE! INAPPROPRIATE! YOU THINK EVERYTHING I DO IS INAPPROPRIATE!
MAYBE YOU SHOULD JUST WEAR A T-SHIRT WITH "THAT'S INAPPROPRIATE" PRINTED ON IT!
JERRY SCOTT and JIM BORGMAN
WELL, WHAT DO YOU THINK?
T-SHIRT city
I CAN'T WAIT TO GET HOME!
THAT'S INAPPROP
STAND UP STRAIGHT AND PULL UP YOUR PANTS

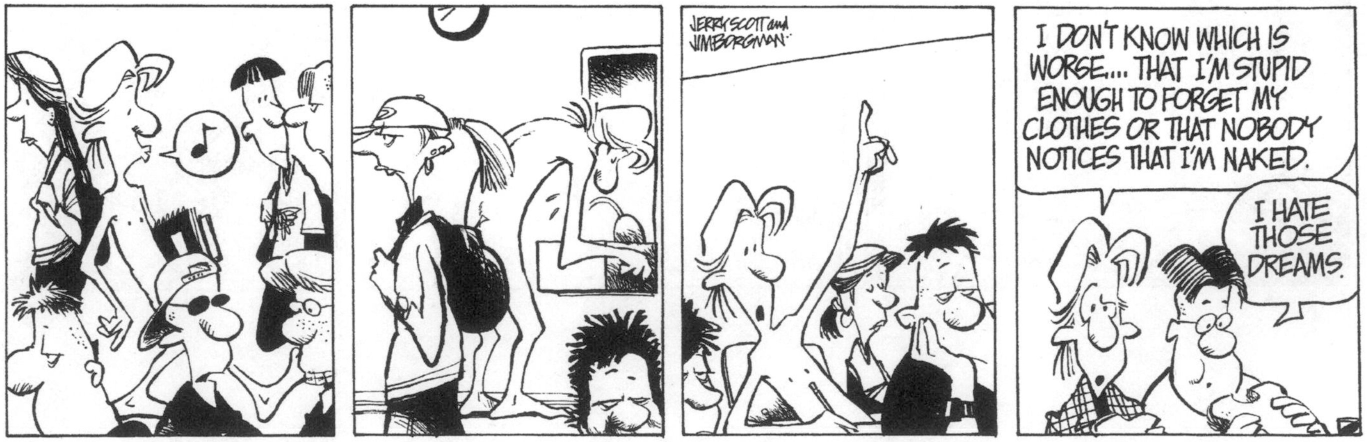
JERRY SCOTT and JIM BORGMAN
I DON'T KNOW WHICH IS WORSE.... THAT I'M STUPID ENOUGH TO FORGET MY CLOTHES OR THAT NOBODY NOTICES THAT I'M NAKED.
I HATE THOSE DREAMS.

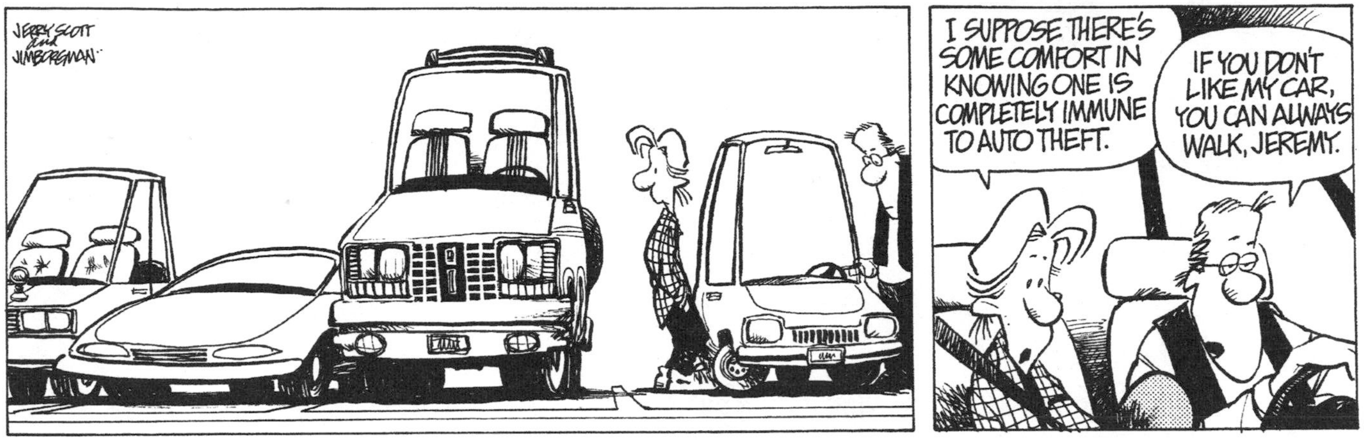
JERRY SCOTT and JIM BORGMAN
I SUPPOSE THERE'S SOME COMFORT IN KNOWING ONE IS COMPLETELY IMMUNE TO AUTO THEFT.
IF YOU DON'T LIKE MY CAR, YOU CAN ALWAYS WALK, JEREMY.

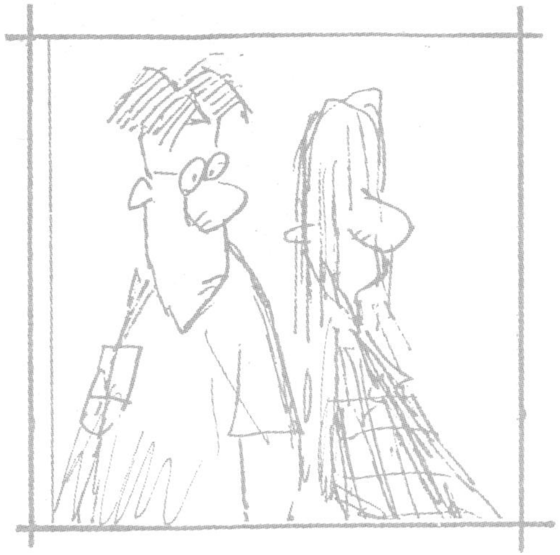

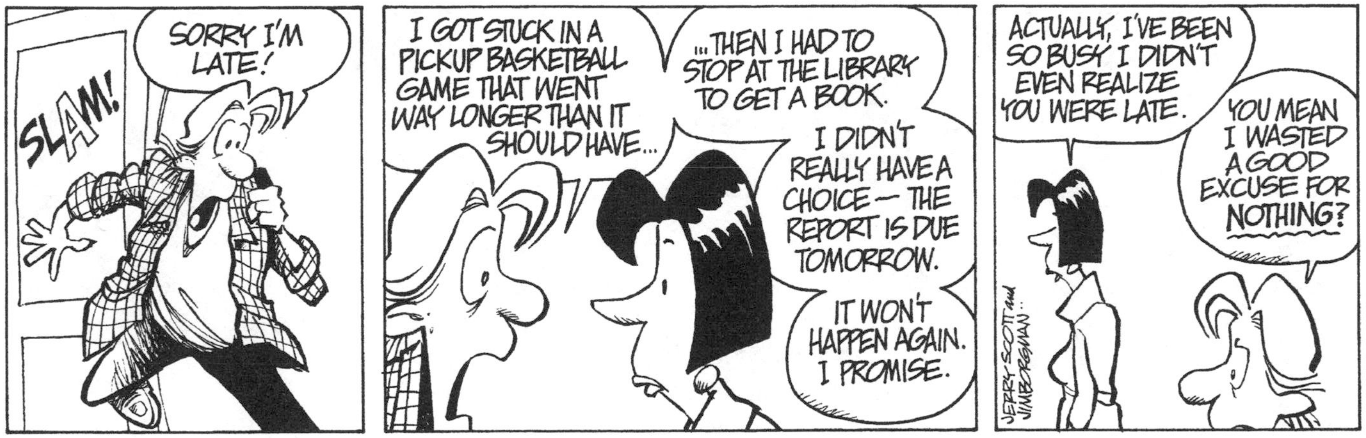
SORRY I'M LATE!
SLAM!
I GOT STUCK IN A PICKUP BASKETBALL GAME THAT WENT WAY LONGER THAN IT SHOULD HAVE...
...THEN I HAD TO STOP AT THE LIBRARY TO GET A BOOK.
I DIDN'T REALLY HAVE A CHOICE — THE REPORT IS DUE TOMORROW.
IT WON'T HAPPEN AGAIN. I PROMISE.
JERRY SCOTT and JIM BORGMAN
ACTUALLY, I'VE BEEN SO BUSY I DIDN'T EVEN REALIZE YOU WERE LATE.
YOU MEAN I WASTED A GOOD EXCUSE FOR NOTHING?

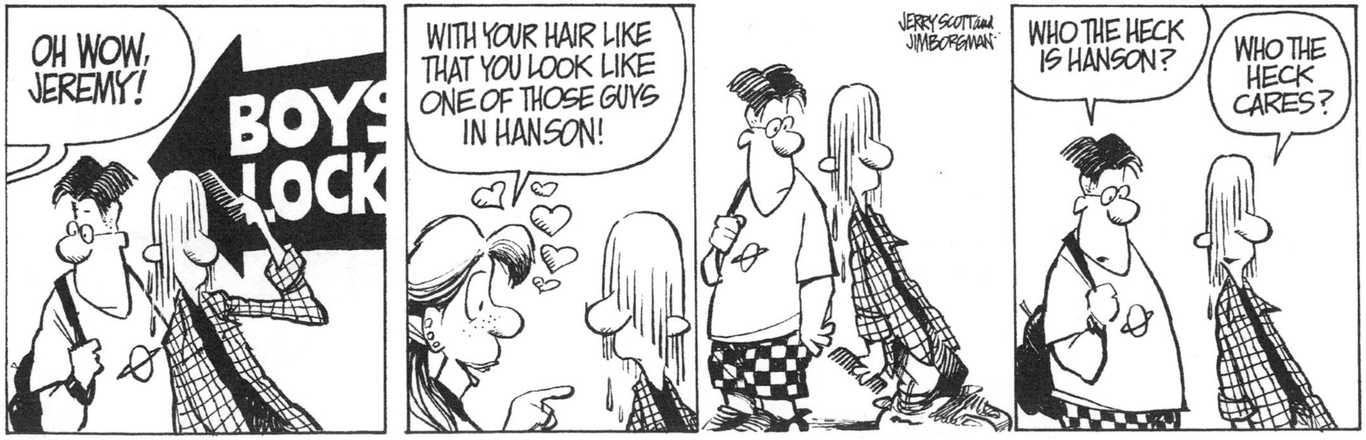
OH WOW, JEREMY!
BOYS
LOCK
WITH YOUR HAIR LIKE THAT YOU LOOK LIKE ONE OF THOSE GUYS IN HANSON!
JERRY SCOTT and JIM BORGMAN
WHO THE HECK IS HANSON?
WHO THE HECK CARES?

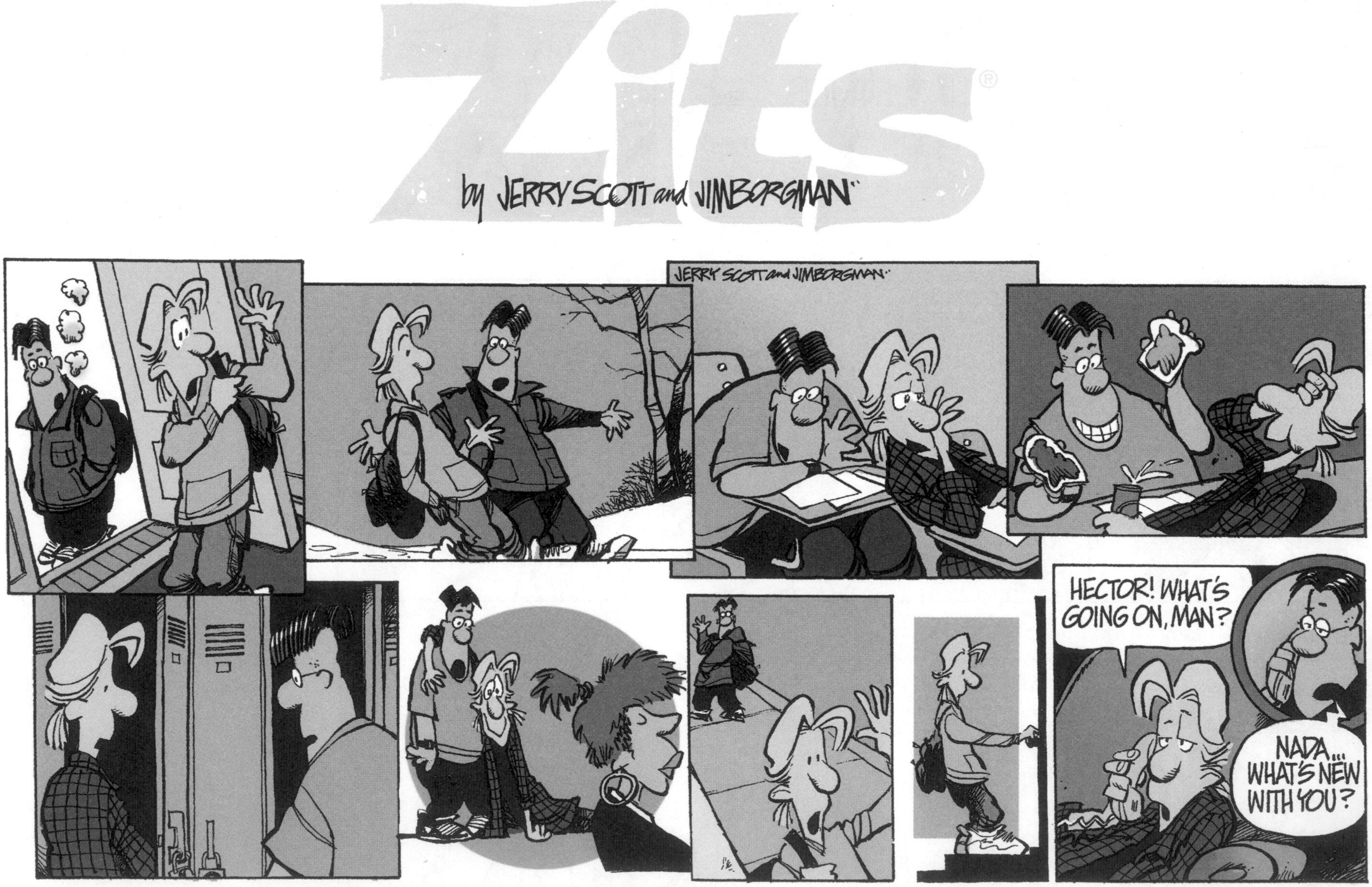
Zits
by JERRY SCOTT and JIMBORGMAN
JERRY SCOTT and JIMBORGMAN
HECTOR! WHAT'S GOING ON, MAN?
NADA... WHAT'S NEW WITH YOU?

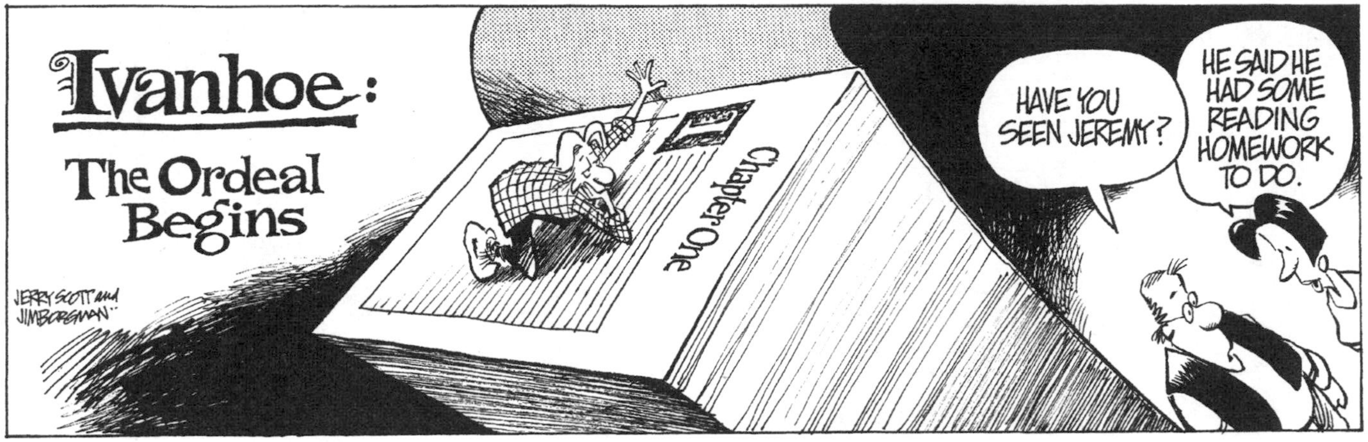
Ivanhoe:
The Ordeal Begins
JERRY SCOTT and JIM BORGMAN
Chapter One
HAVE YOU SEEN JEREMY?
HE SAID HE HAD SOME READING HOMEWORK TO DO.

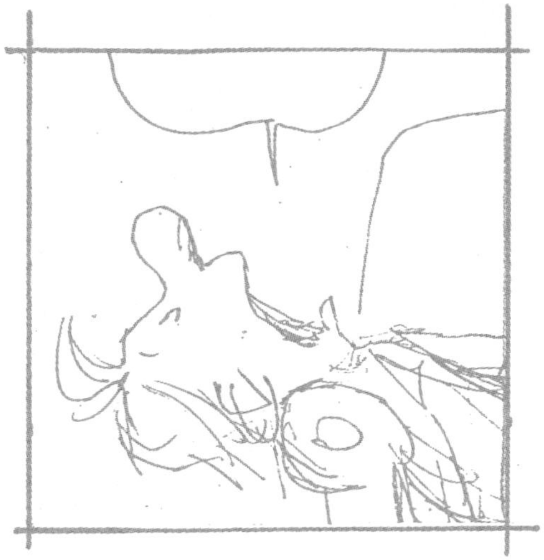

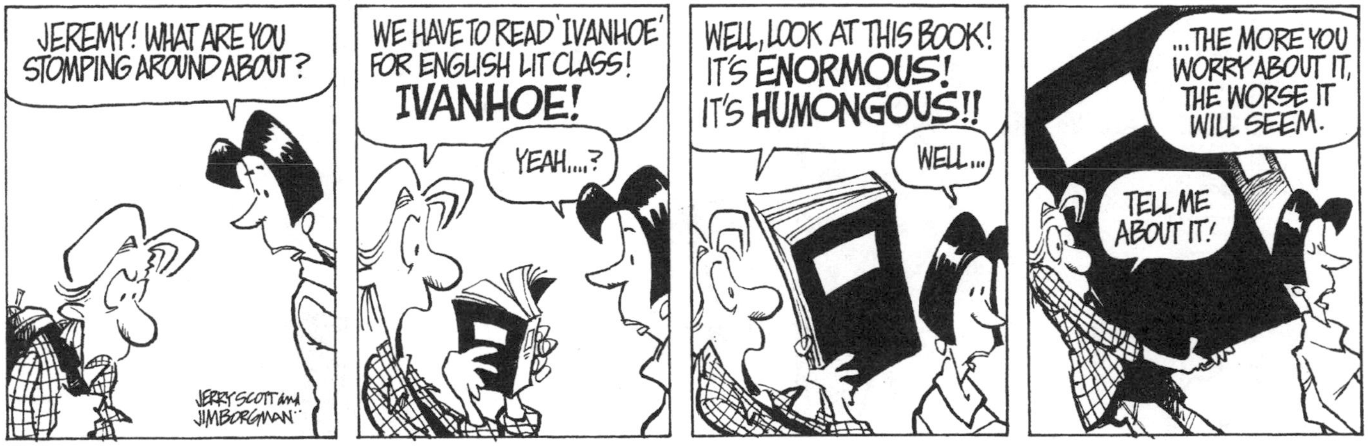
JEREMY! WHAT ARE YOU STOMPING AROUND ABOUT?
JERRY SCOTT and JIM BORGMAN
WE HAVE TO READ 'IVANHOE' FOR ENGLISH LIT CLASS! IVANHOE!
YEAH....?
WELL, LOOK AT THIS BOOK! IT'S ENORMOUS! IT'S HUMONGOUS!!
WELL...
...THE MORE YOU WORRY ABOUT IT, THE WORSE IT WILL SEEM.
TELL ME ABOUT IT!

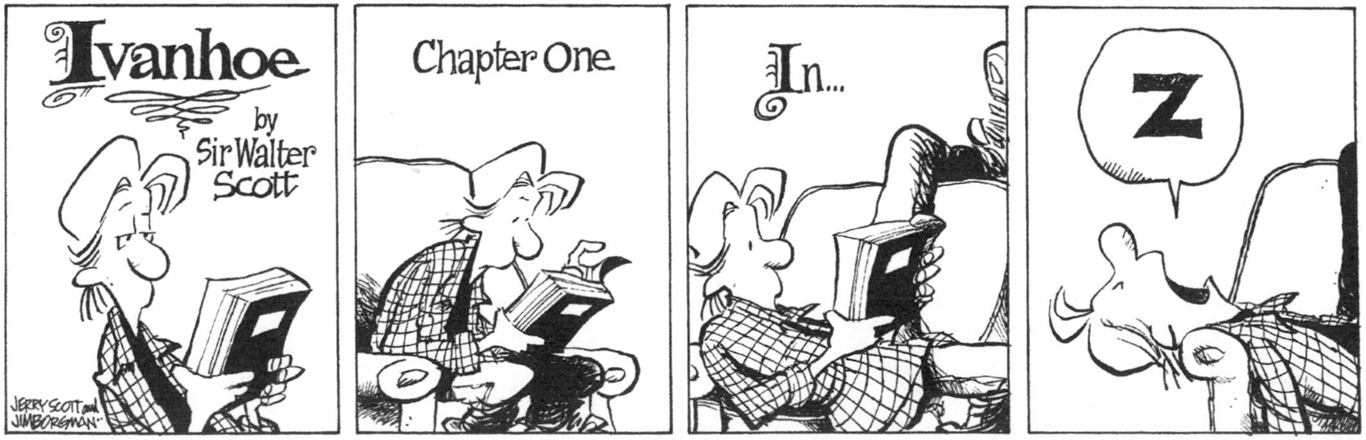
Ivanhoe
by Sir Walter Scott
JERRY SCOTT and JIM BORGMAN
Chapter One
In...
Z

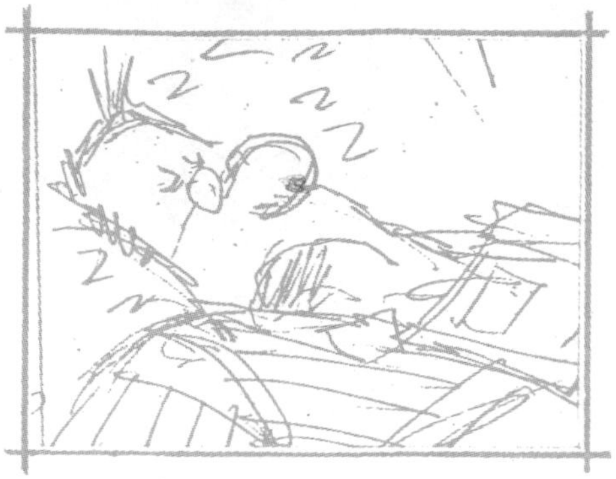

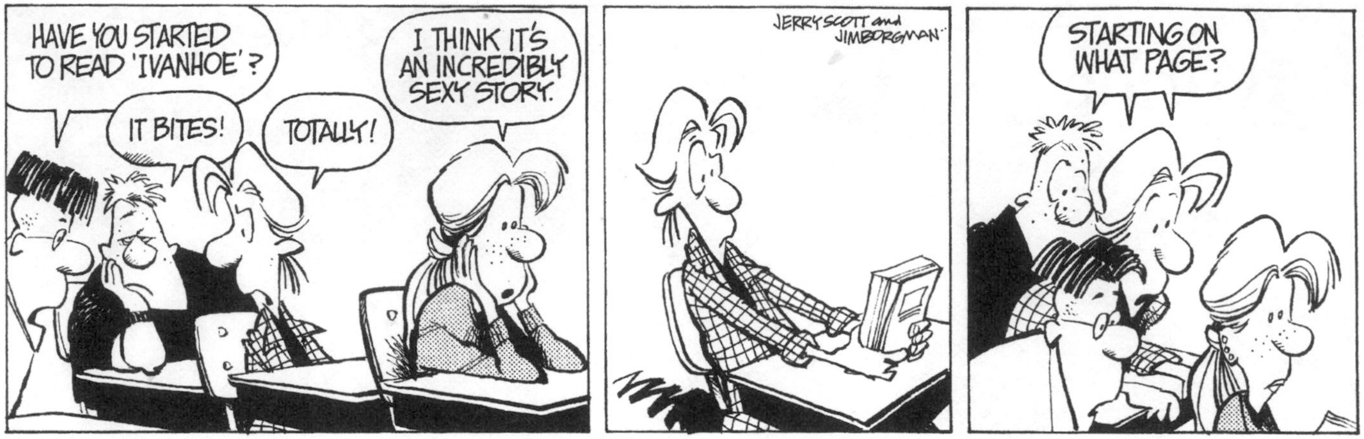
HAVE YOU STARTED TO READ 'IVANHOE'?
IT BITES!
TOTALLY!
I THINK IT'S AN INCREDIBLY SEXY STORY.
JERRY SCOTT and JIM BORGMAN
STARTING ON WHAT PAGE?

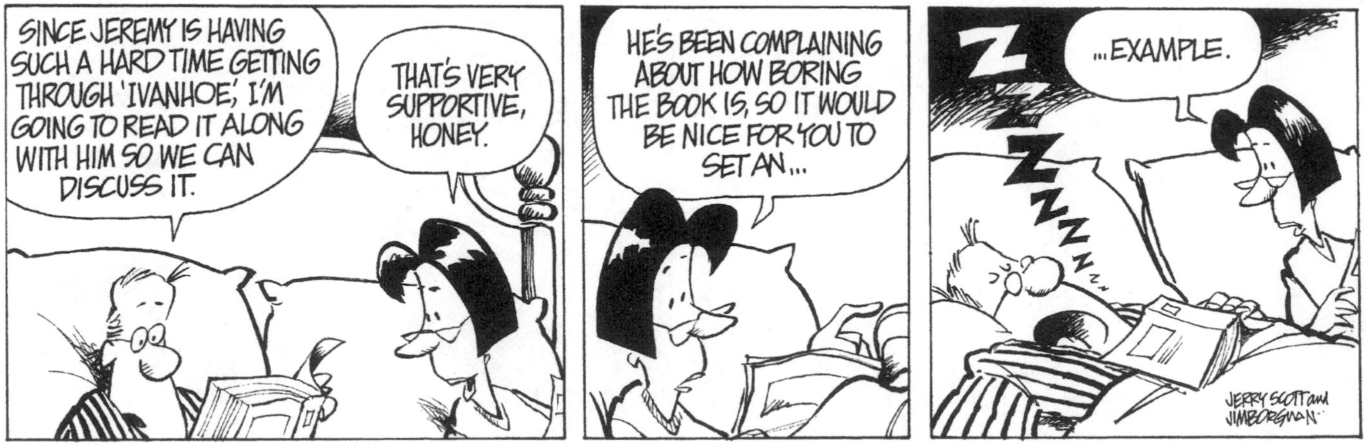
SINCE JEREMY IS HAVING SUCH A HARD TIME GETTING THROUGH 'IVANHOE,' I'M GOING TO READ IT ALONG WITH HIM SO WE CAN DISCUSS IT.
THAT'S VERY SUPPORTIVE, HONEY.
HE'S BEEN COMPLAINING ABOUT HOW BORING THE BOOK IS, SO IT WOULD BE NICE FOR YOU TO SET AN...
Z Z Z Z Z Z Z
...EXAMPLE.
JERRY SCOTT and JIM BORGMAN

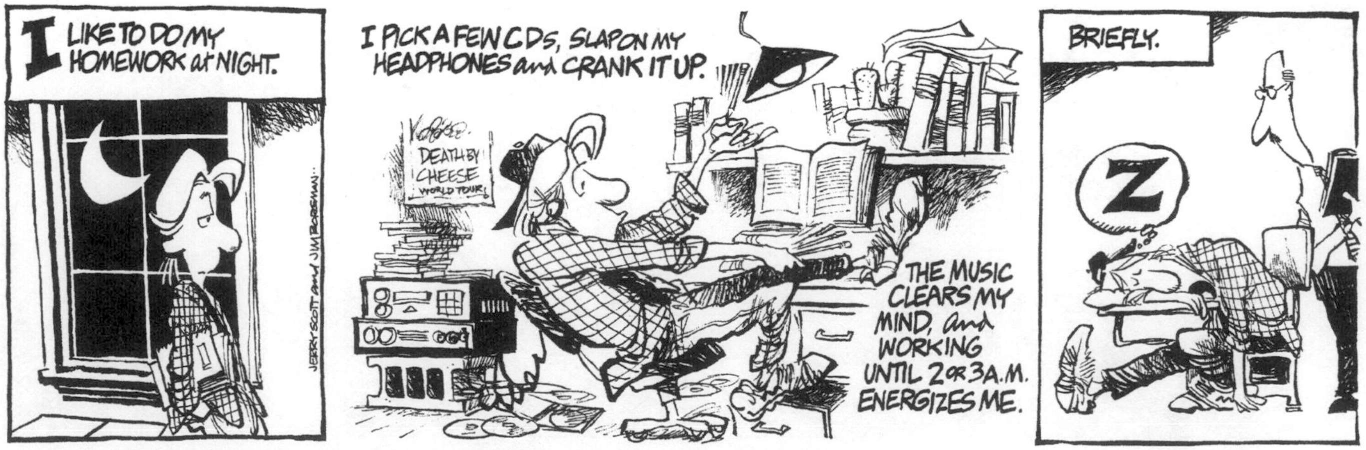
I LIKE TO DO MY HOMEWORK at NIGHT.
JERRY SCOTT and JIM BORGMAN
I PICK A FEW CDs, SLAP ON MY HEADPHONES and CRANK IT UP.
DEATH BY CHEESE WORLD TOUR
THE MUSIC CLEARS MY MIND, and WORKING UNTIL 2 OR 3 A.M. ENERGIZES ME.
BRIEFLY.
Z

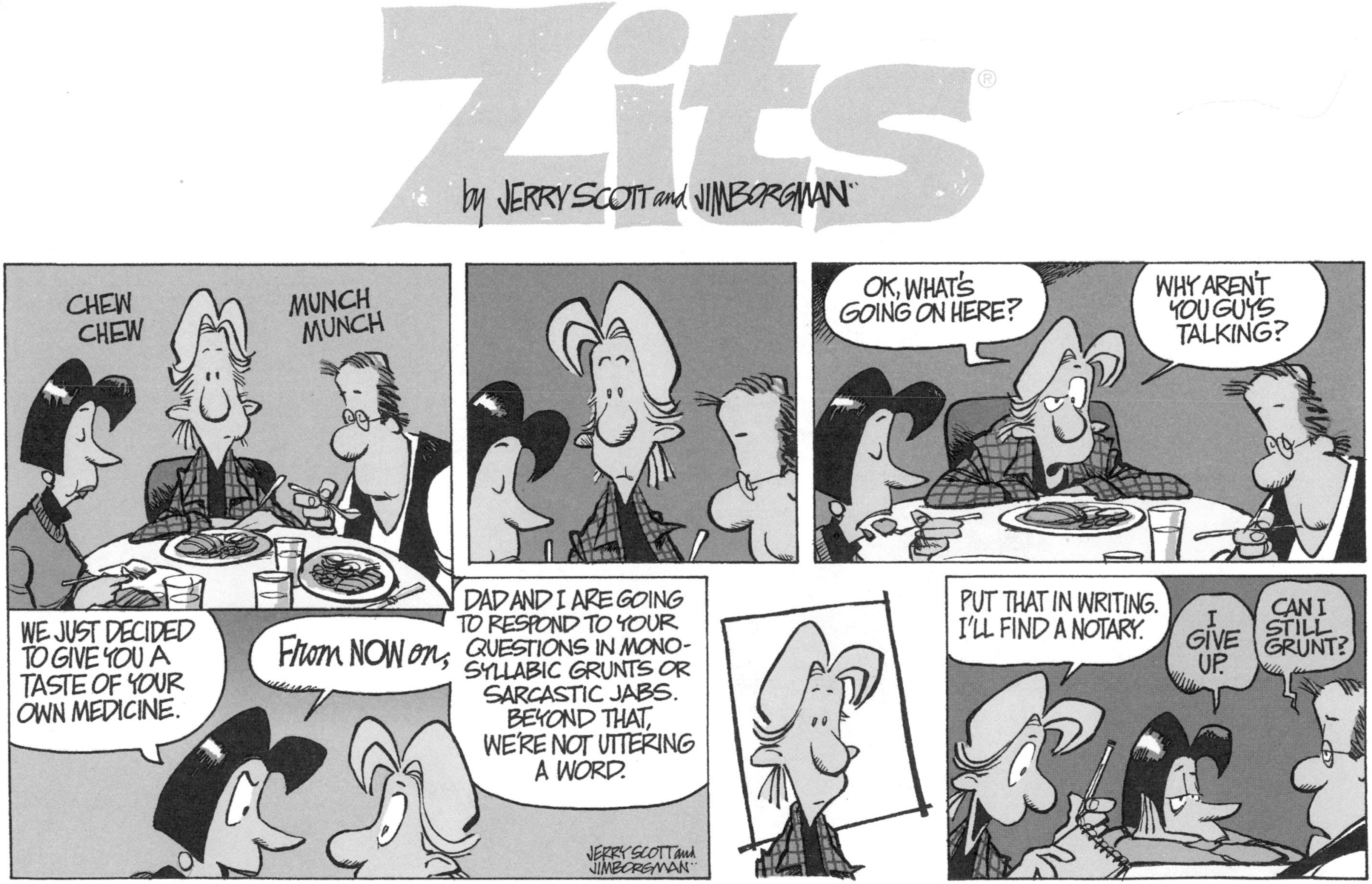
Zits®
by JERRY SCOTT and JIM BORGMAN
CHEW CHEW
MUNCH MUNCH
OK, WHAT'S GOING ON HERE?
WHY AREN'T YOU GUYS TALKING?
WE JUST DECIDED TO GIVE YOU A TASTE OF YOUR OWN MEDICINE.
From NOW on,
DAD AND I ARE GOING TO RESPOND TO YOUR QUESTIONS IN MONO-SYLLABIC GRUNTS OR SARCASTIC JABS. BEYOND THAT, WE'RE NOT UTTERING A WORD.
JERRY SCOTT and JIM BORGMAN
PUT THAT IN WRITING. I'LL FIND A NOTARY.
I GIVE UP.
CAN I STILL GRUNT?

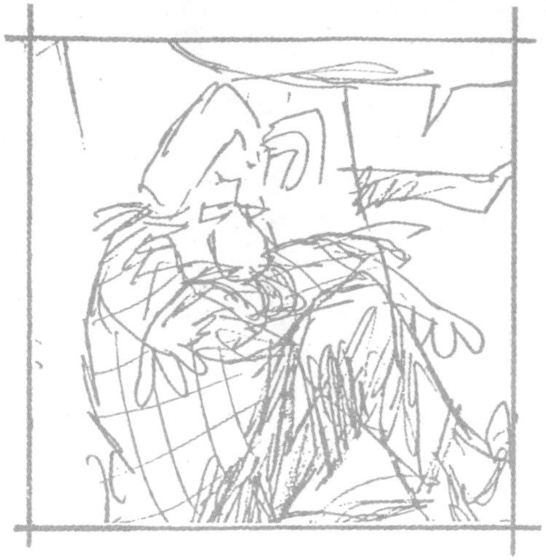

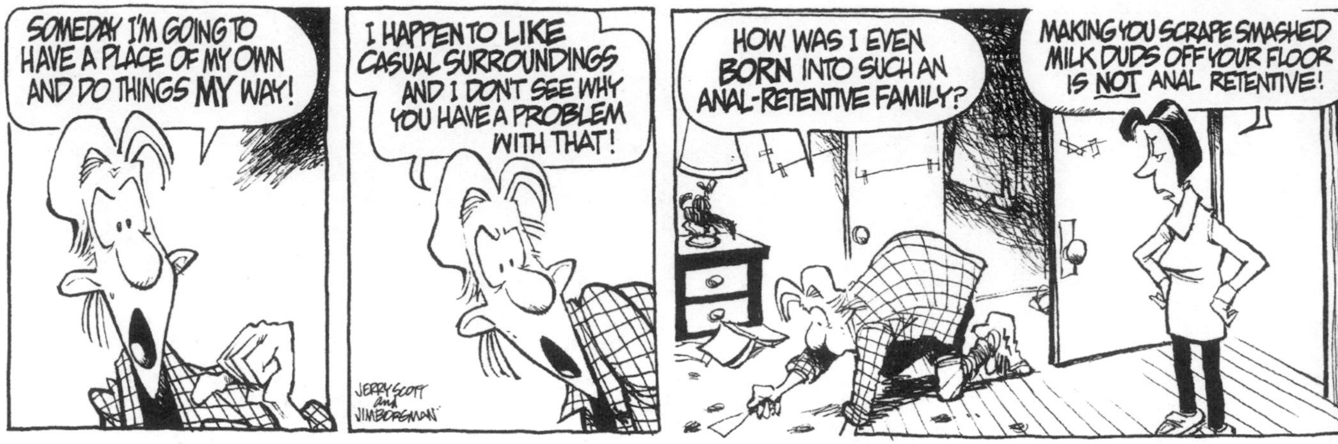
SOMEDAY I'M GOING TO HAVE A PLACE OF MY OWN AND DO THINGS MY WAY!
I HAPPEN TO LIKE CASUAL SURROUNDINGS AND I DON'T SEE WHY YOU HAVE A PROBLEM WITH THAT!
JERRY SCOTT and JIMBORGMAN
HOW WAS I EVEN BORN INTO SUCH AN ANAL-RETENTIVE FAMILY?
MAKING YOU SCRAPE SMASHED MILK DUDS OFF YOUR FLOOR IS NOT ANAL RETENTIVE!

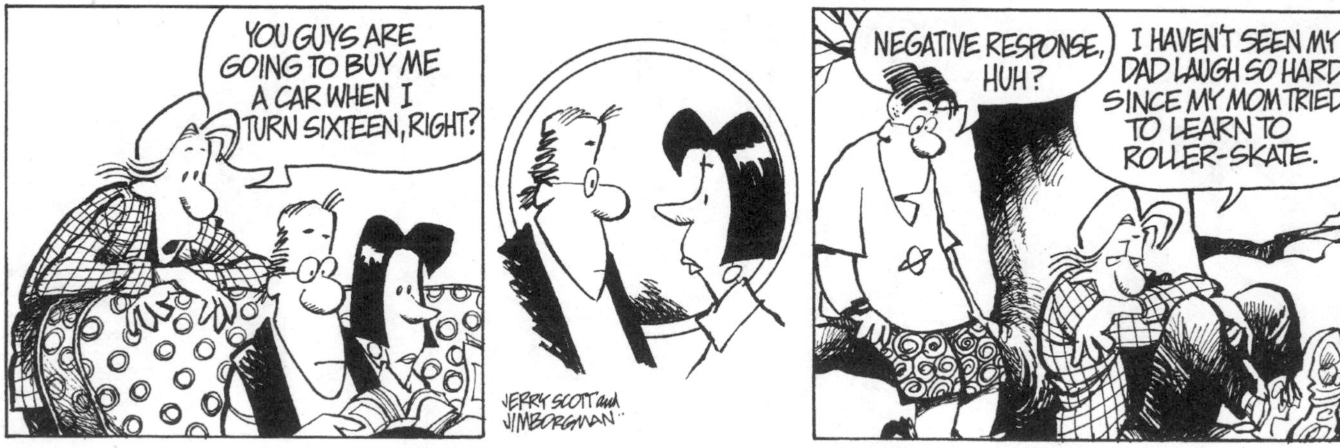
YOU GUYS ARE GOING TO BUY ME A CAR WHEN I TURN SIXTEEN, RIGHT?
JERRY SCOTT and JIMBORGMAN
NEGATIVE RESPONSE, HUH?
I HAVEN'T SEEN MY DAD LAUGH SO HARD SINCE MY MOM TRIED TO LEARN TO ROLLER-SKATE.

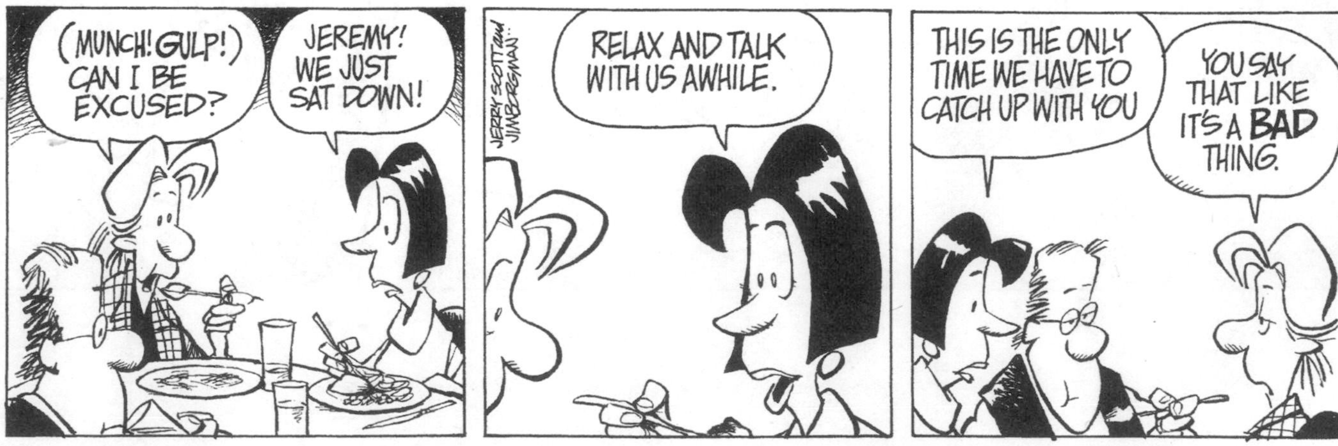
(MUNCH! GULP!) CAN I BE EXCUSED?
JEREMY! WE JUST SAT DOWN!
JERRY SCOTT and JIMBORGMAN
RELAX AND TALK WITH US AWHILE.
THIS IS THE ONLY TIME WE HAVE TO CATCH UP WITH YOU
YOU SAY THAT LIKE IT'S A BAD THING.

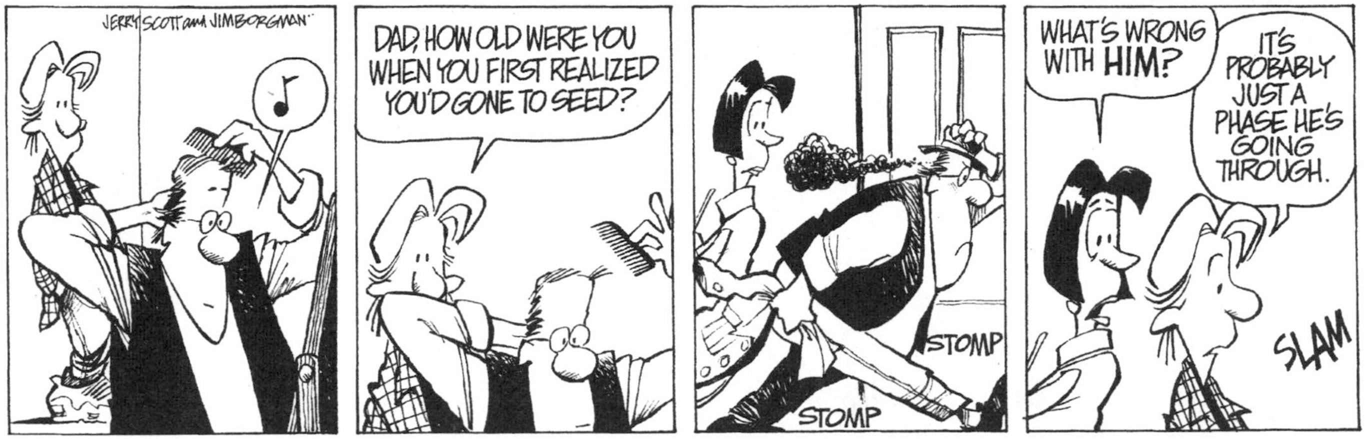
JERRY SCOTT and JIM BORGMAN
DAD, HOW OLD WERE YOU WHEN YOU FIRST REALIZED YOU'D GONE TO SEED?
STOMP
STOMP
WHAT'S WRONG WITH HIM?
IT'S PROBABLY JUST A PHASE HE'S GOING THROUGH.
SLAM

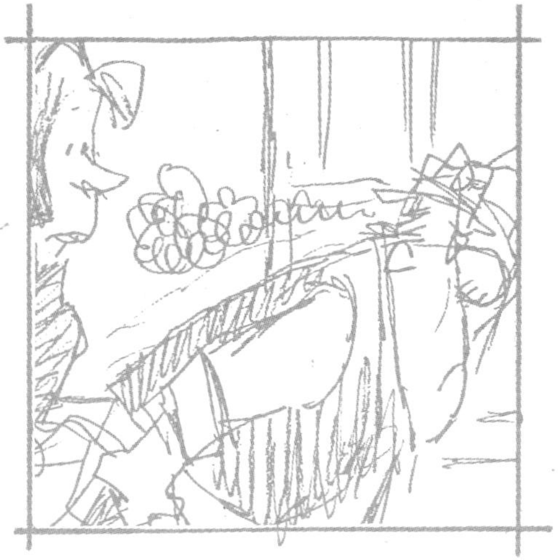

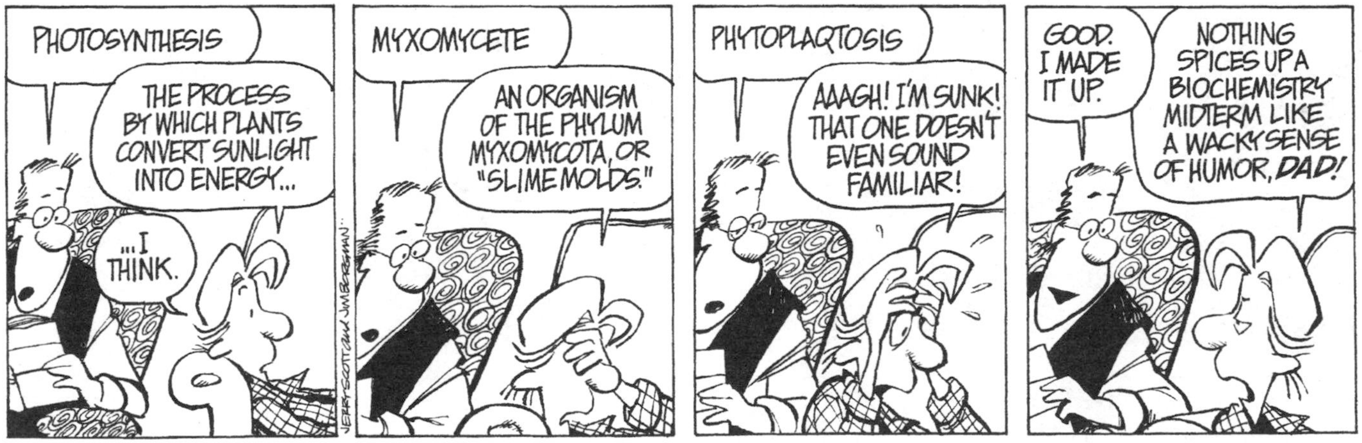
PHOTOSYNTHESIS
THE PROCESS BY WHICH PLANTS CONVERT SUNLIGHT INTO ENERGY...
...I THINK.
JERRY SCOTT and JIM BORGMAN
MYXOMYCETE
AN ORGANISM OF THE PHYLUM MYXOMYCOTA, OR "SLIME MOLDS."
PHYTOPLAQTOSIS
AAAGH! I'M SUNK! THAT ONE DOESN'T EVEN SOUND FAMILIAR!
GOOD. I MADE IT UP.
NOTHING SPICES UP A BIOCHEMISTRY MIDTERM LIKE A WACKY SENSE OF HUMOR, DAD!

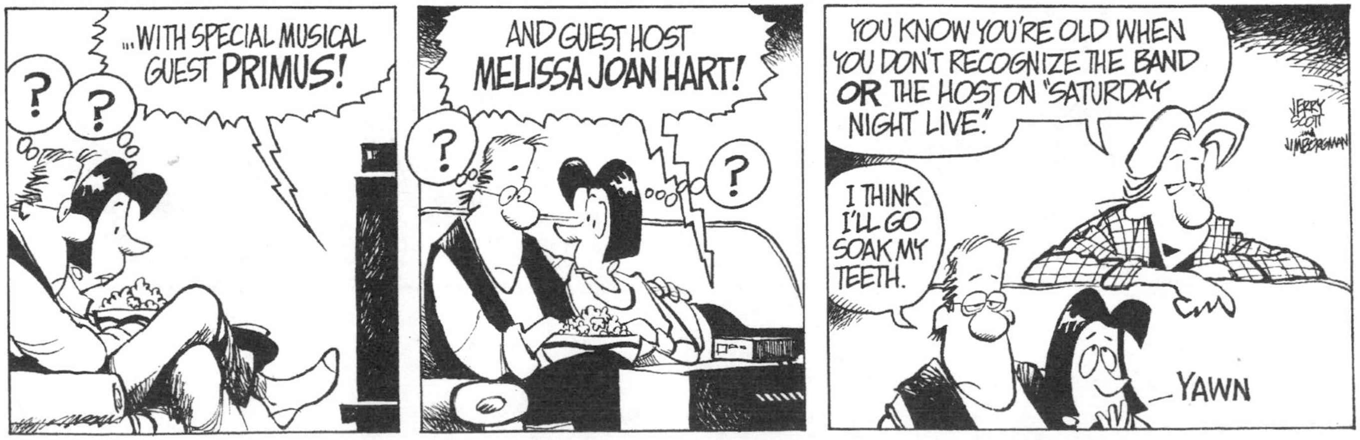
...WITH SPECIAL MUSICAL GUEST PRIMUS!
?
?
AND GUEST HOST MELISSA JOAN HART!
?
?
YOU KNOW YOU'RE OLD WHEN YOU DON'T RECOGNIZE THE BAND OR THE HOST ON "SATURDAY NIGHT LIVE."
JERRY SCOTT and JIM BORGMAN
I THINK I'LL GO SOAK MY TEETH.
YAWN

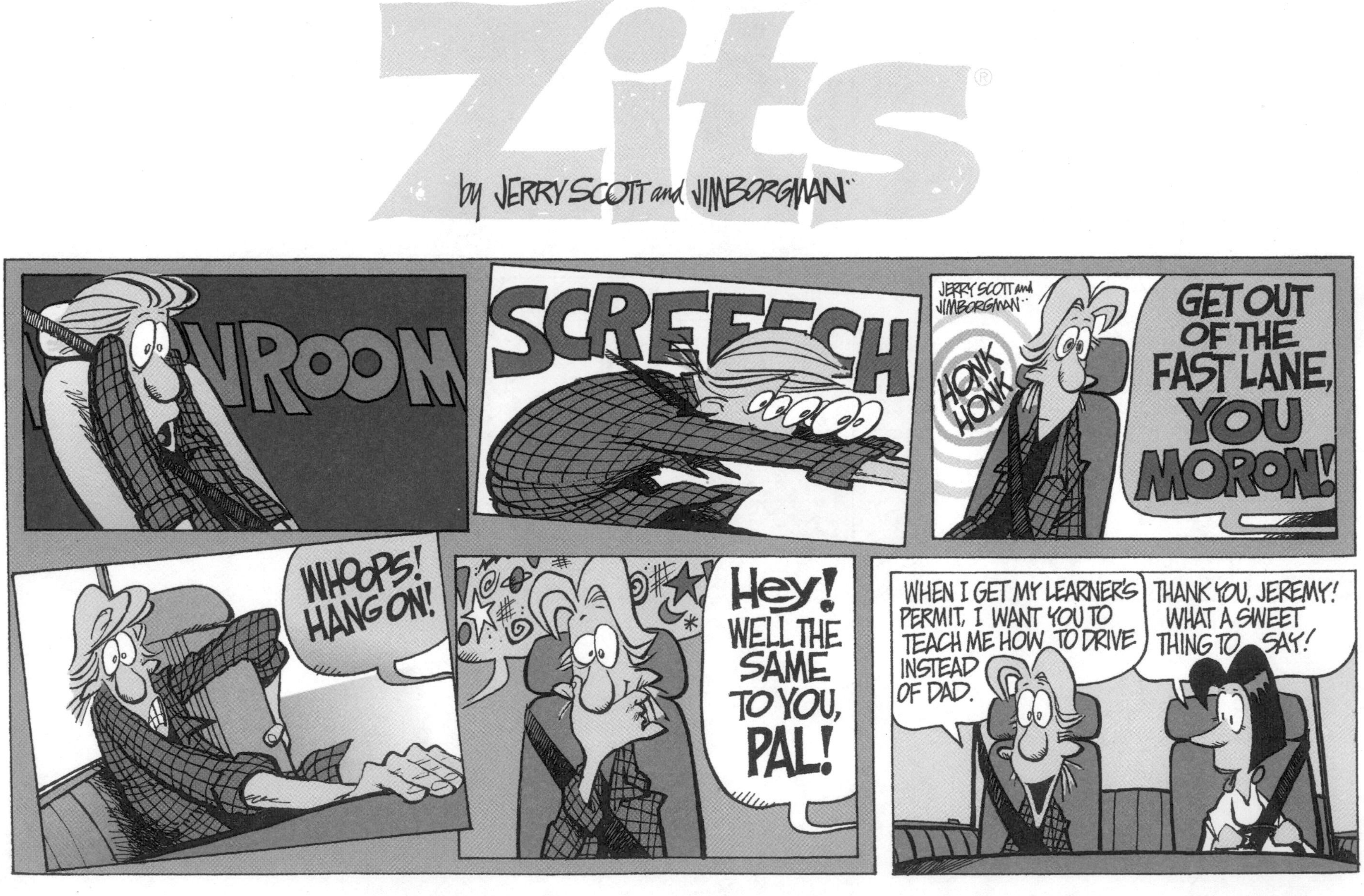
Zits®
by JERRY SCOTT and JIM BORGMAN
VROOOM
SCREEECH
JERRY SCOTT and JIM BORGMAN
HONK HONK
GET OUT OF THE FAST LANE, YOU MORON!
WHOOPS! HANG ON!
Hey! WELL THE SAME TO YOU, PAL!
WHEN I GET MY LEARNER'S PERMIT, I WANT YOU TO TEACH ME HOW TO DRIVE INSTEAD OF DAD.
THANK YOU, JEREMY! WHAT A SWEET THING TO SAY!

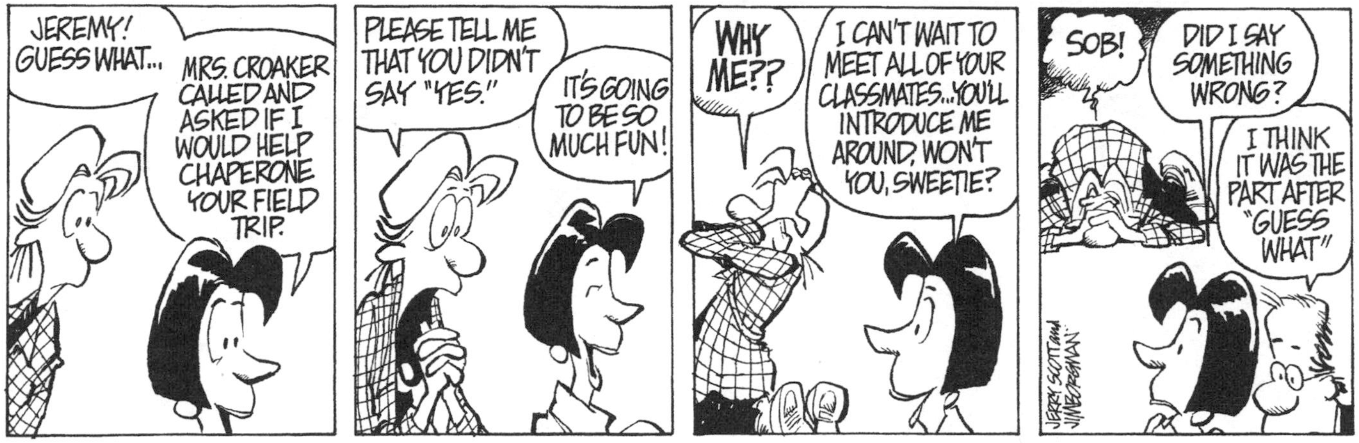
JEREMY! GUESS WHAT...
MRS. CROAKER CALLED AND ASKED IF I WOULD HELP CHAPERONE YOUR FIELD TRIP.
PLEASE TELL ME THAT YOU DIDN'T SAY "YES."
IT'S GOING TO BE SO MUCH FUN!
WHY ME??
I CAN'T WAIT TO MEET ALL OF YOUR CLASSMATES...YOU'LL INTRODUCE ME AROUND, WON'T YOU, SWEETIE?
SOB!
DID I SAY SOMETHING WRONG?
I THINK IT WAS THE PART AFTER "GUESS WHAT"
JERRY SCOTT and JIM BORGMAN

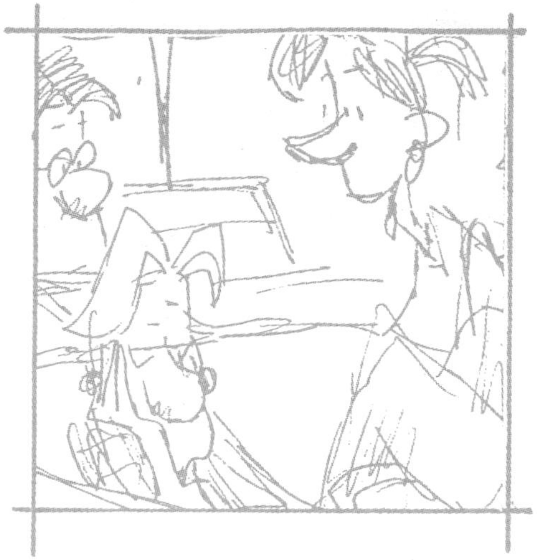

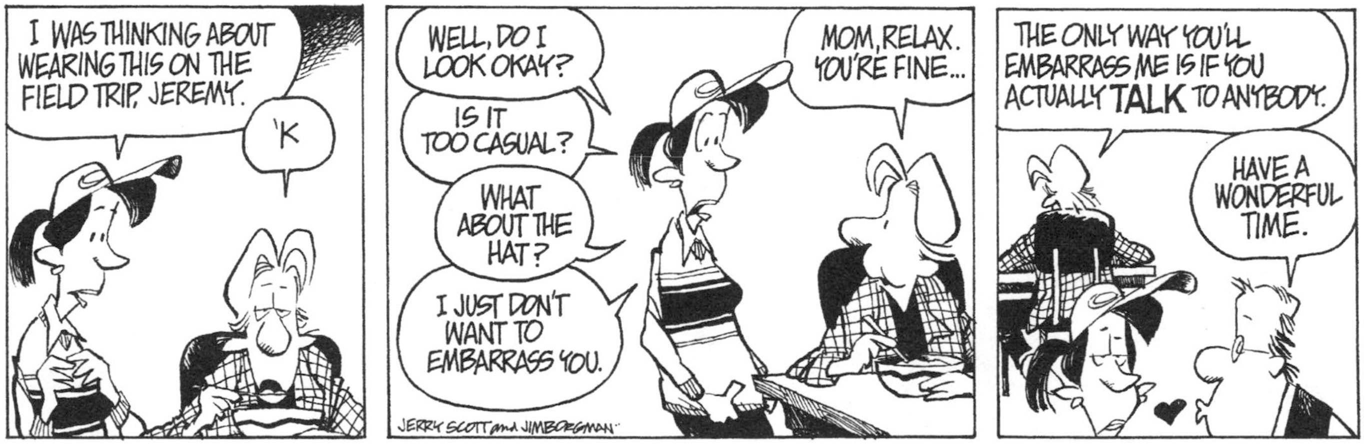
I WAS THINKING ABOUT WEARING THIS ON THE FIELD TRIP, JEREMY.
'K
WELL, DO I LOOK OKAY?
IS IT TOO CASUAL?
WHAT ABOUT THE HAT?
I JUST DON'T WANT TO EMBARRASS YOU.
MOM, RELAX. YOU'RE FINE...
JERRY SCOTT and JIM BORGMAN
THE ONLY WAY YOU'LL EMBARRASS ME IS IF YOU ACTUALLY TALK TO ANYBODY.
HAVE A WONDERFUL TIME.

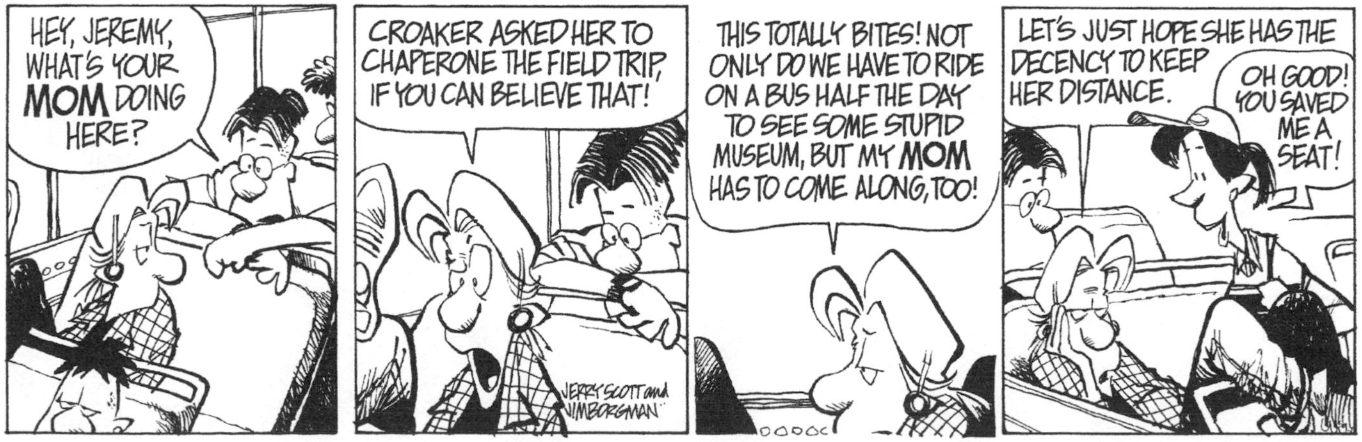
HEY, JEREMY, WHAT'S YOUR MOM DOING HERE?
CROAKER ASKED HER TO CHAPERONE THE FIELD TRIP, IF YOU CAN BELIEVE THAT!
JERRY SCOTT and JIM BORGMAN
THIS TOTALLY BITES! NOT ONLY DO WE HAVE TO RIDE ON A BUS HALF THE DAY TO SEE SOME STUPID MUSEUM, BUT MY MOM HAS TO COME ALONG, TOO!
LET'S JUST HOPE SHE HAS THE DECENCY TO KEEP HER DISTANCE.
OH GOOD! YOU SAVED ME A SEAT!

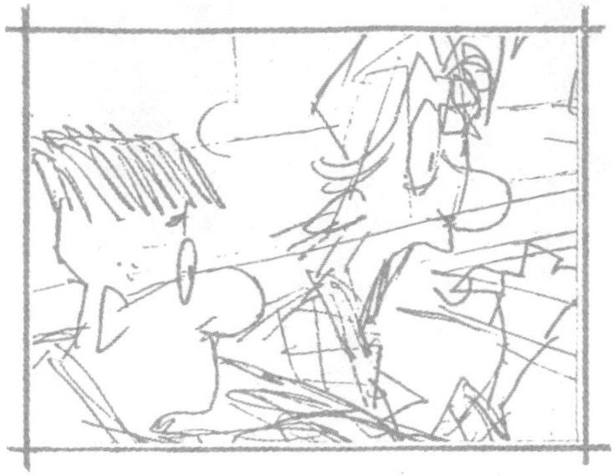

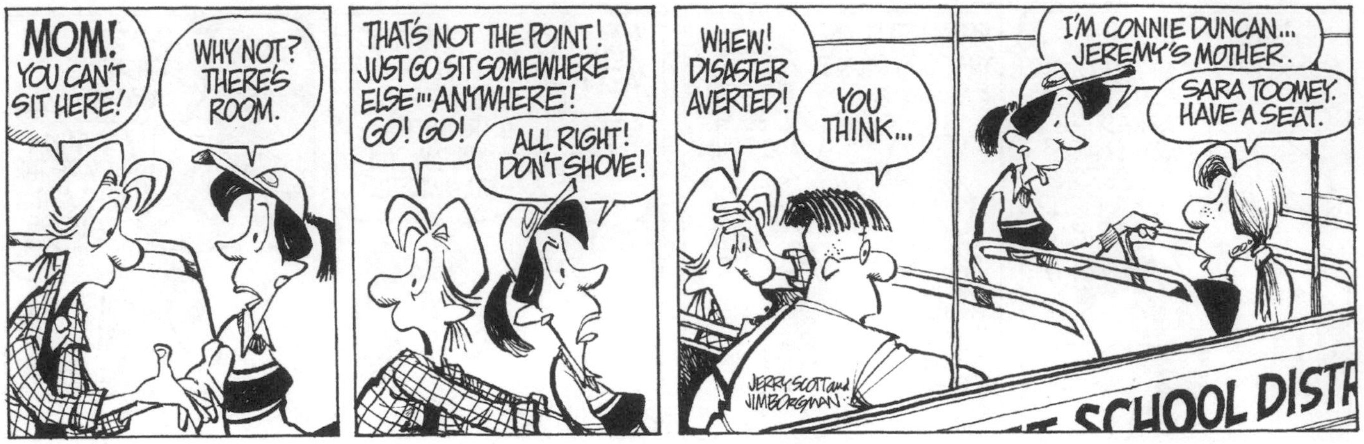

MOM! YOU CAN'T SIT HERE!
WHY NOT? THERE'S ROOM.
THAT'S NOT THE POINT! JUST GO SIT SOMEWHERE ELSE ... ANYWHERE! GO! GO!
ALL RIGHT! DON'T SHOVE!
WHEW! DISASTER AVERTED!
YOU THINK...
I'M CONNIE DUNCAN... JEREMY'S MOTHER.
SARA TOOMEY. HAVE A SEAT.
JERRY SCOTT and JIMBORGMAN
SCHOOL DISTR

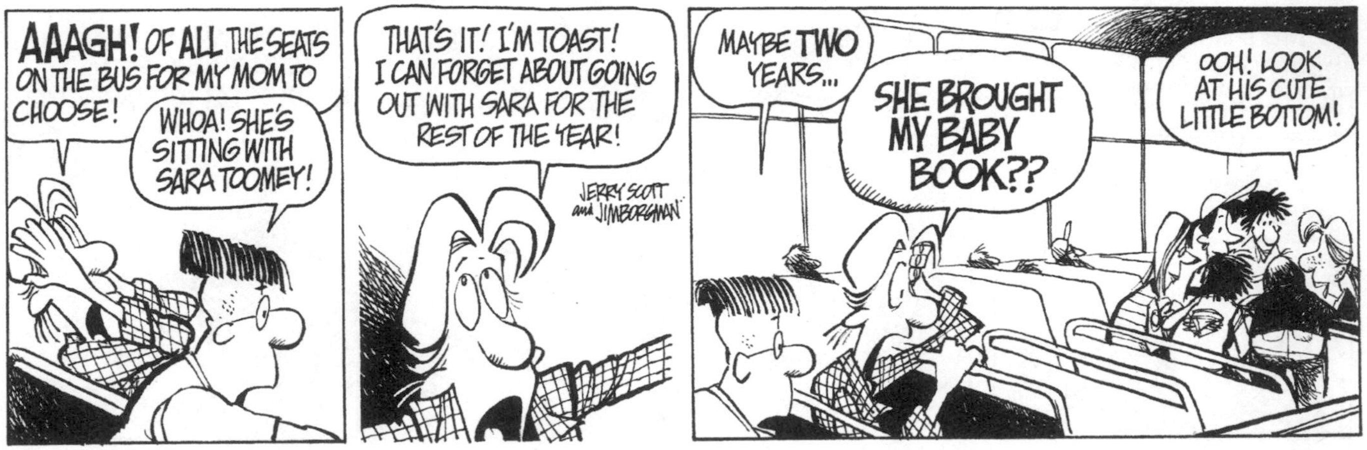

AAAGH! OF ALL THE SEATS ON THE BUS FOR MY MOM TO CHOOSE!
WHOA! SHE'S SITTING WITH SARA TOOMEY!
THAT'S IT! I'M TOAST! I CAN FORGET ABOUT GOING OUT WITH SARA FOR THE REST OF THE YEAR!
JERRY SCOTT and JIMBORGMAN
MAYBE TWO YEARS...
SHE BROUGHT MY BABY BOOK??
OOH! LOOK AT HIS CUTE LITTLE BOTTOM!

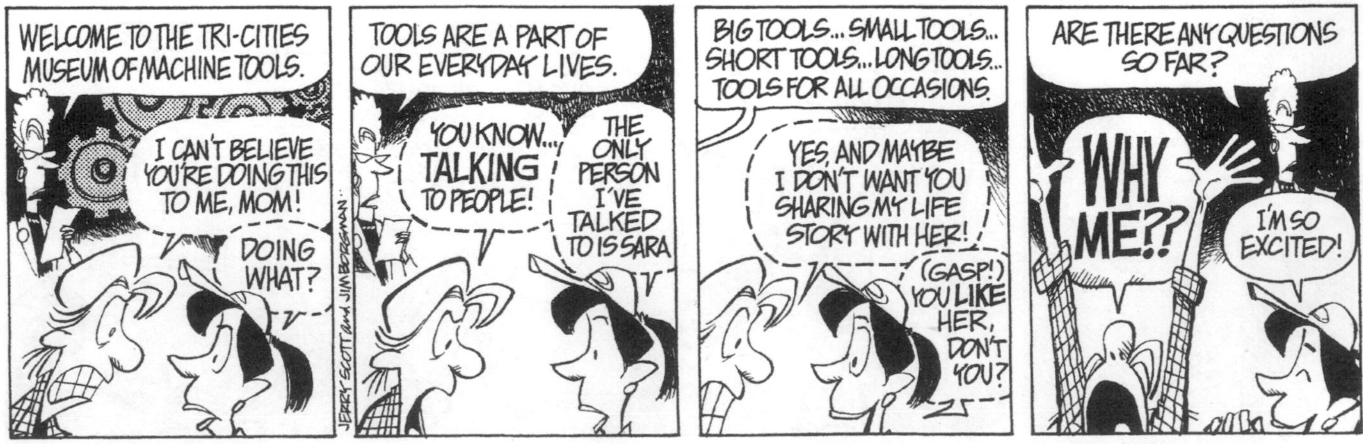

WELCOME TO THE TRI-CITIES MUSEUM OF MACHINE TOOLS.
I CAN'T BELIEVE YOU'RE DOING THIS TO ME, MOM!
DOING WHAT?
JERRY SCOTT and JIMBORGMAN
TOOLS ARE A PART OF OUR EVERYDAY LIVES.
YOU KNOW... TALKING TO PEOPLE!
THE ONLY PERSON I'VE TALKED TO IS SARA
BIG TOOLS... SMALL TOOLS... SHORT TOOLS... LONG TOOLS... TOOLS FOR ALL OCCASIONS.
YES, AND MAYBE I DON'T WANT YOU SHARING MY LIFE STORY WITH HER!
(GASP!) YOU LIKE HER, DON'T YOU?
ARE THERE ANY QUESTIONS SO FAR?
WHY ME??
I'M SO EXCITED!

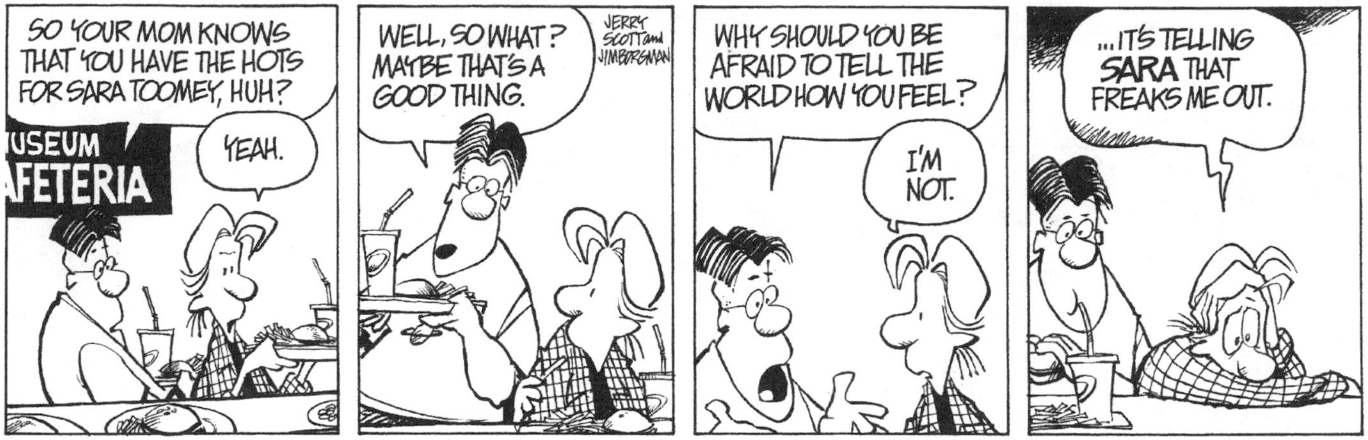
SO YOUR MOM KNOWS THAT YOU HAVE THE HOTS FOR SARA TOOMEY, HUH?
USEUM
AFETERIA
YEAH.
WELL, SO WHAT? MAYBE THAT'S A GOOD THING.
JERRY SCOTT and JIMBORGMAN
WHY SHOULD YOU BE AFRAID TO TELL THE WORLD HOW YOU FEEL?
I'M NOT.
...IT'S TELLING SARA THAT FREAKS ME OUT.

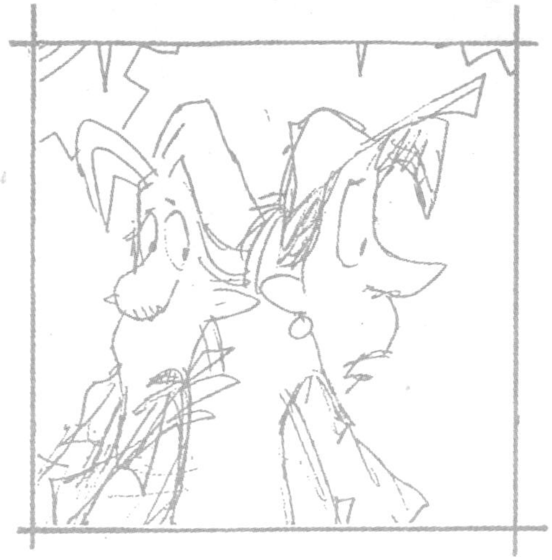

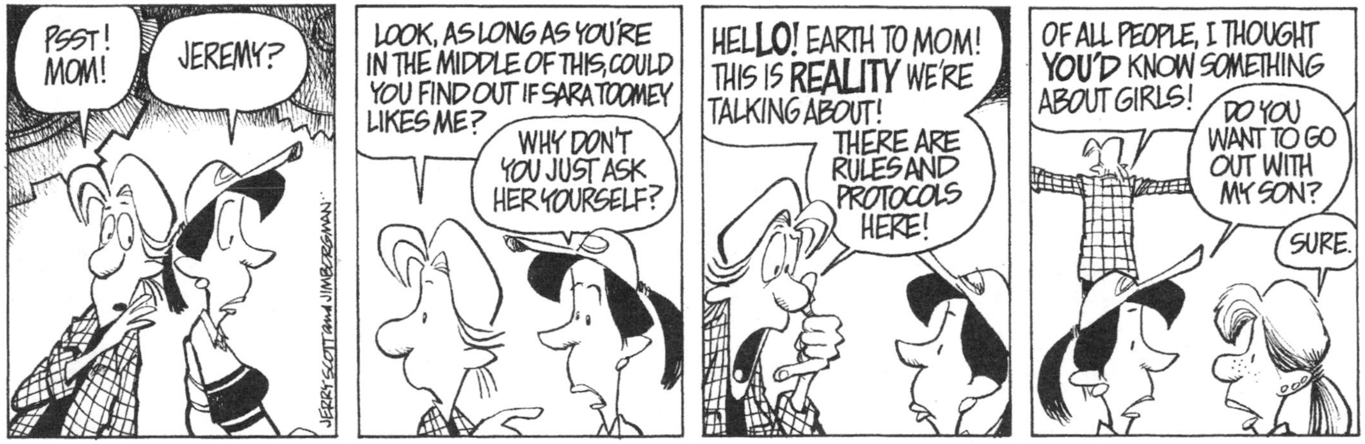
PSST! MOM!
JEREMY?
JERRY SCOTT and JIMBORGMAN
LOOK, AS LONG AS YOU'RE IN THE MIDDLE OF THIS, COULD YOU FIND OUT IF SARA TOOMEY LIKES ME?
WHY DON'T YOU JUST ASK HER YOURSELF?
HELLO! EARTH TO MOM! THIS IS REALITY WE'RE TALKING ABOUT!
THERE ARE RULES AND PROTOCOLS HERE!
OF ALL PEOPLE, I THOUGHT YOU'D KNOW SOMETHING ABOUT GIRLS!
DO YOU WANT TO GO OUT WITH MY SON?
SURE.

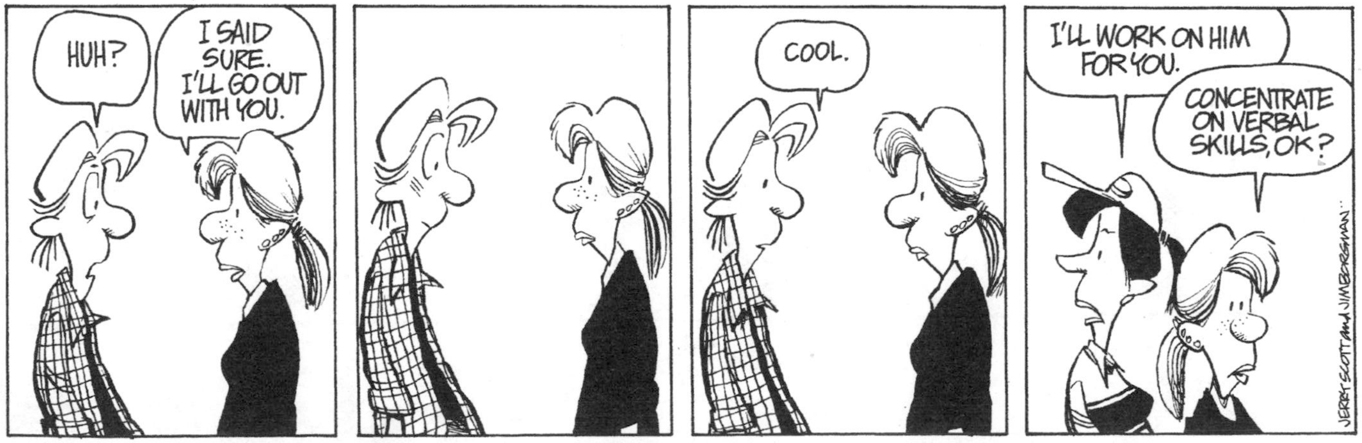
HUH?
I SAID SURE. I'LL GO OUT WITH YOU.
COOL.
I'LL WORK ON HIM FOR YOU.
CONCENTRATE ON VERBAL SKILLS, OK?
JERRY SCOTT and JIMBORGMAN

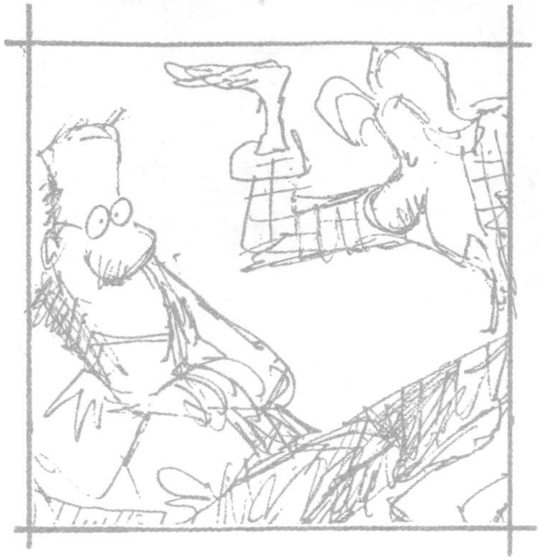

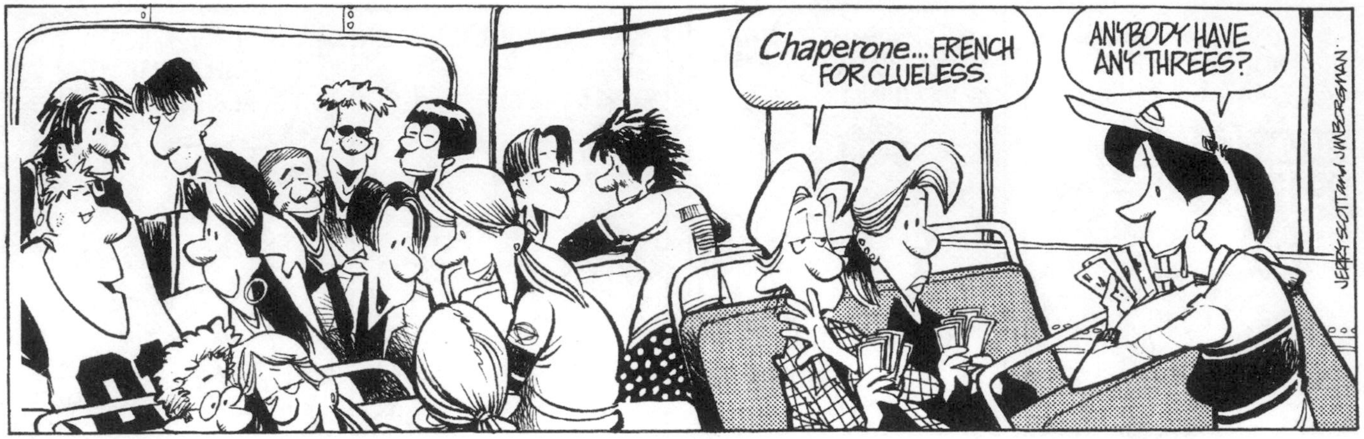
Chaperone... FRENCH FOR CLUELESS.
ANYBODY HAVE ANY THREES?
JERRY SCOTT and JIM BORGMAN

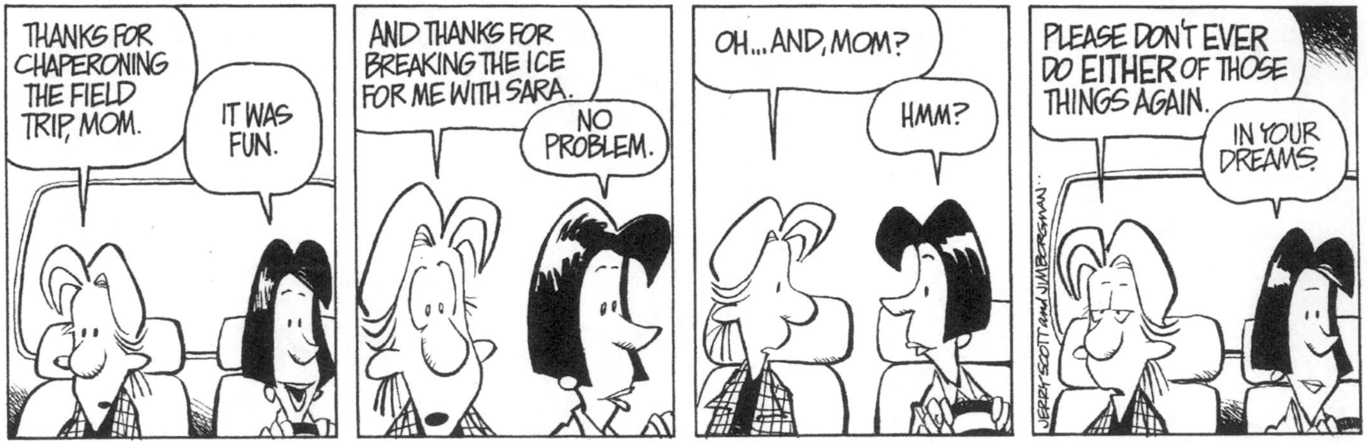
THANKS FOR CHAPERONING THE FIELD TRIP, MOM.
IT WAS FUN.
AND THANKS FOR BREAKING THE ICE FOR ME WITH SARA.
NO PROBLEM.
OH... AND, MOM?
HMM?
PLEASE DON'T EVER DO EITHER OF THOSE THINGS AGAIN.
IN YOUR DREAMS.
JERRY SCOTT and JIM BORGMAN

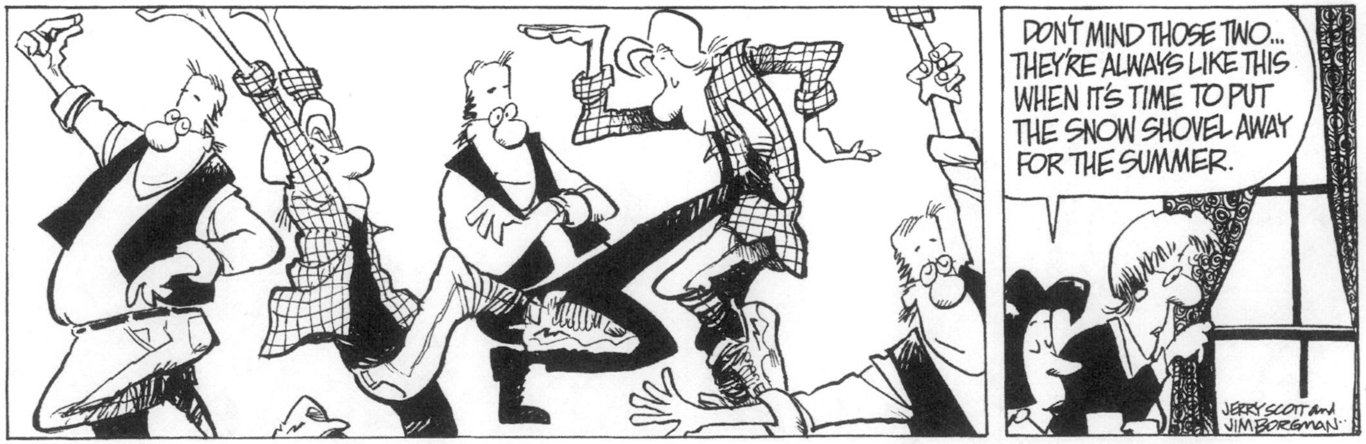
DON'T MIND THOSE TWO... THEY'RE ALWAYS LIKE THIS WHEN IT'S TIME TO PUT THE SNOW SHOVEL AWAY FOR THE SUMMER.
JERRY SCOTT and JIM BORGMAN

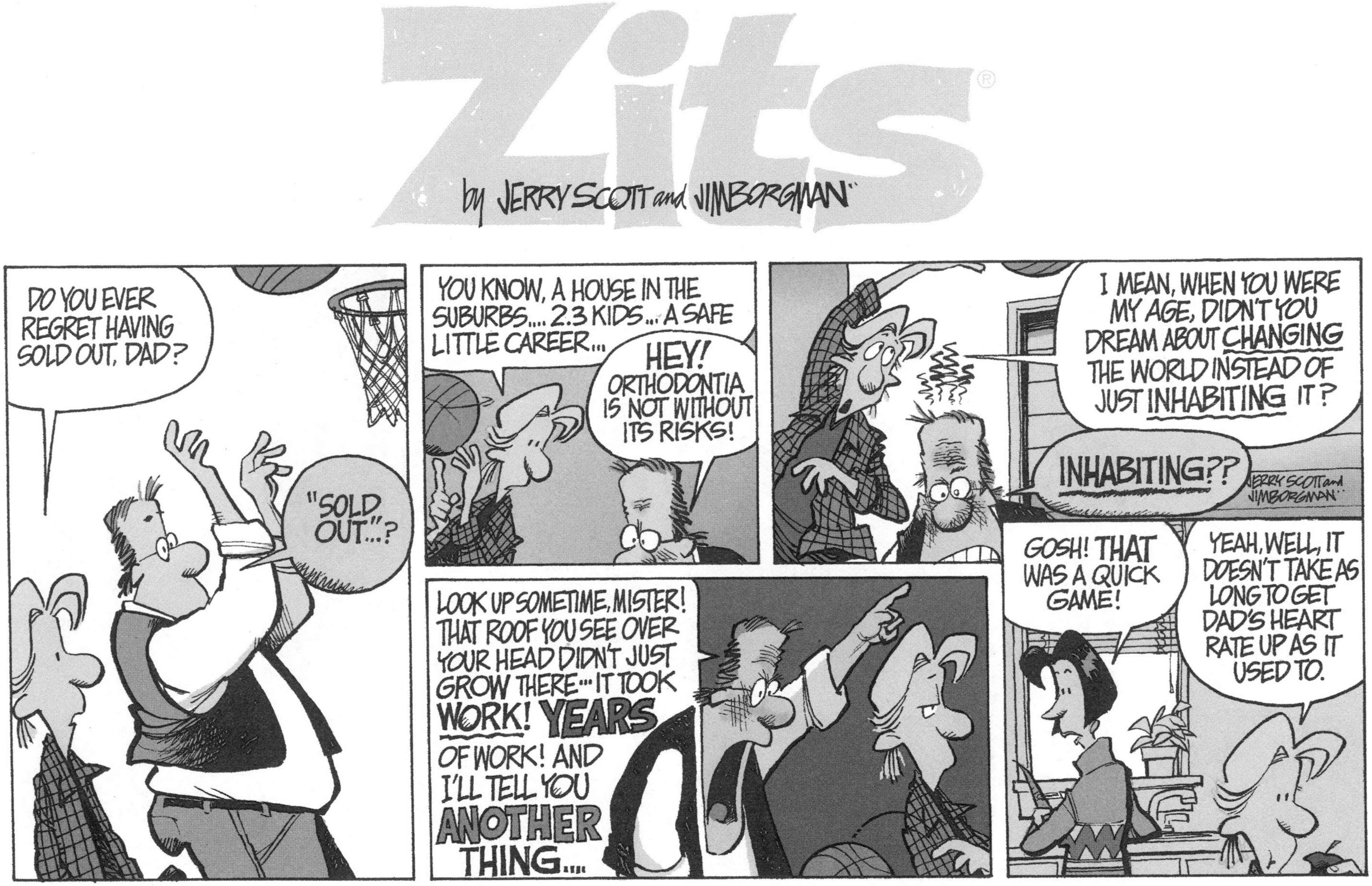
Zits
by JERRY SCOTT and JIM BORGMAN
DO YOU EVER REGRET HAVING SOLD OUT, DAD?
"SOLD OUT"...?
YOU KNOW, A HOUSE IN THE SUBURBS.... 2.3 KIDS... A SAFE LITTLE CAREER...
HEY! ORTHODONTIA IS NOT WITHOUT ITS RISKS!
I MEAN, WHEN YOU WERE MY AGE, DIDN'T YOU DREAM ABOUT CHANGING THE WORLD INSTEAD OF JUST INHABITING IT?
INHABITING??
JERRY SCOTT and JIM BORGMAN
LOOK UP SOMETIME, MISTER! THAT ROOF YOU SEE OVER YOUR HEAD DIDN'T JUST GROW THERE... IT TOOK WORK! YEARS OF WORK! AND I'LL TELL YOU ANOTHER THING....
GOSH! THAT WAS A QUICK GAME!
YEAH, WELL, IT DOESN'T TAKE AS LONG TO GET DAD'S HEART RATE UP AS IT USED TO.

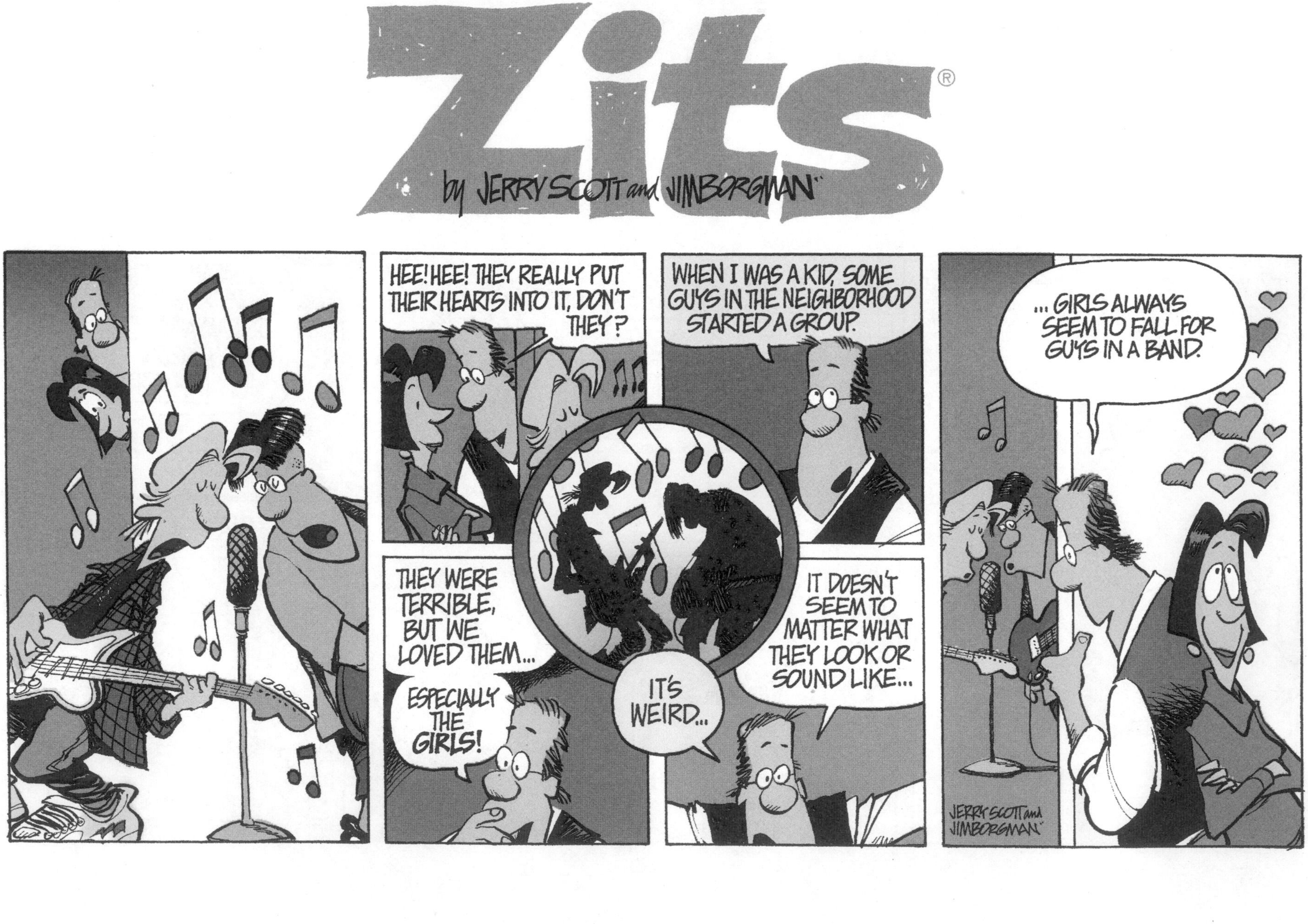
Zits®
by JERRY SCOTT and JIM BORGMAN
HEE! HEE! THEY REALLY PUT THEIR HEARTS INTO IT, DON'T THEY?
WHEN I WAS A KID, SOME GUYS IN THE NEIGHBORHOOD STARTED A GROUP.
THEY WERE TERRIBLE, BUT WE LOVED THEM...
ESPECIALLY THE GIRLS!
IT'S WEIRD...
IT DOESN'T SEEM TO MATTER WHAT THEY LOOK OR SOUND LIKE...
...GIRLS ALWAYS SEEM TO FALL FOR GUYS IN A BAND.
JERRY SCOTT and JIM BORGMAN

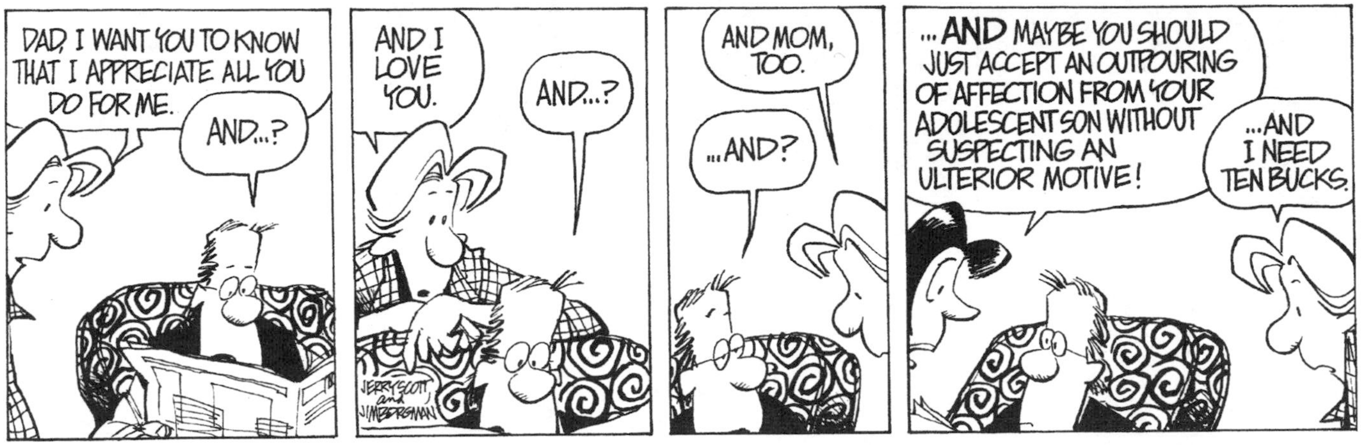
DAD, I WANT YOU TO KNOW THAT I APPRECIATE ALL YOU DO FOR ME.
AND...?
AND I LOVE YOU.
AND...?
AND MOM, TOO.
...AND?
...AND MAYBE YOU SHOULD JUST ACCEPT AN OUTPOURING OF AFFECTION FROM YOUR ADOLESCENT SON WITHOUT SUSPECTING AN ULTERIOR MOTIVE!
...AND I NEED TEN BUCKS.
JERRY SCOTT and JIM BORGMAN

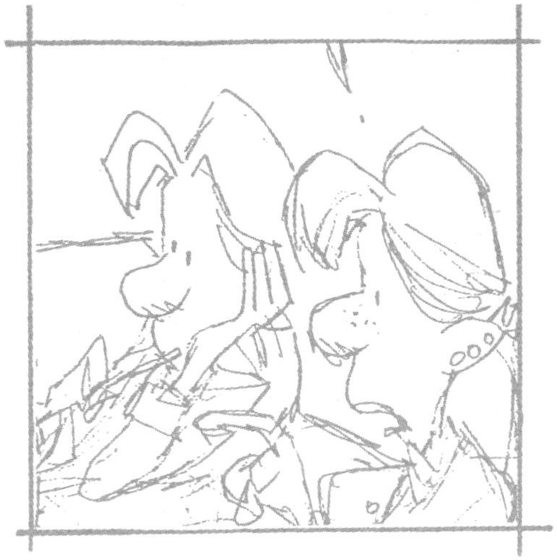

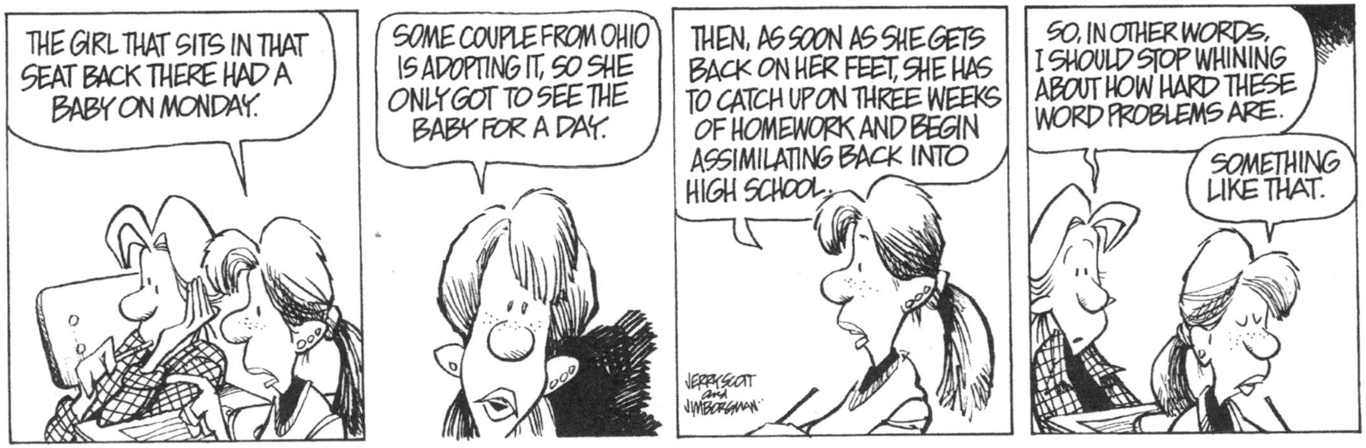
THE GIRL THAT SITS IN THAT SEAT BACK THERE HAD A BABY ON MONDAY.
SOME COUPLE FROM OHIO IS ADOPTING IT, SO SHE ONLY GOT TO SEE THE BABY FOR A DAY.
THEN, AS SOON AS SHE GETS BACK ON HER FEET, SHE HAS TO CATCH UP ON THREE WEEKS OF HOMEWORK AND BEGIN ASSIMILATING BACK INTO HIGH SCHOOL.
SO, IN OTHER WORDS, I SHOULD STOP WHINING ABOUT HOW HARD THESE WORD PROBLEMS ARE.
SOMETHING LIKE THAT.
JERRY SCOTT and JIM BORGMAN

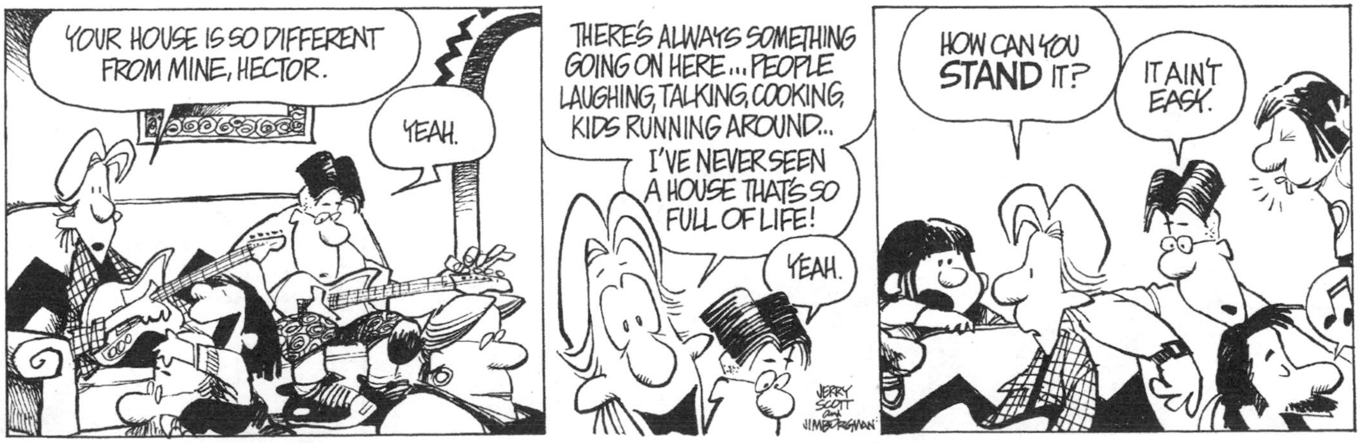
YOUR HOUSE IS SO DIFFERENT FROM MINE, HECTOR.
YEAH.
THERE'S ALWAYS SOMETHING GOING ON HERE... PEOPLE LAUGHING, TALKING, COOKING, KIDS RUNNING AROUND...
I'VE NEVER SEEN A HOUSE THAT'S SO FULL OF LIFE!
YEAH.
HOW CAN YOU STAND IT?
IT AIN'T EASY.
JERRY SCOTT and JIM BORGMAN

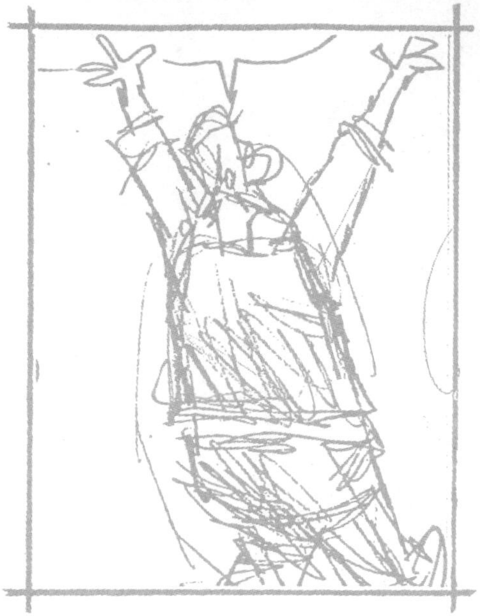

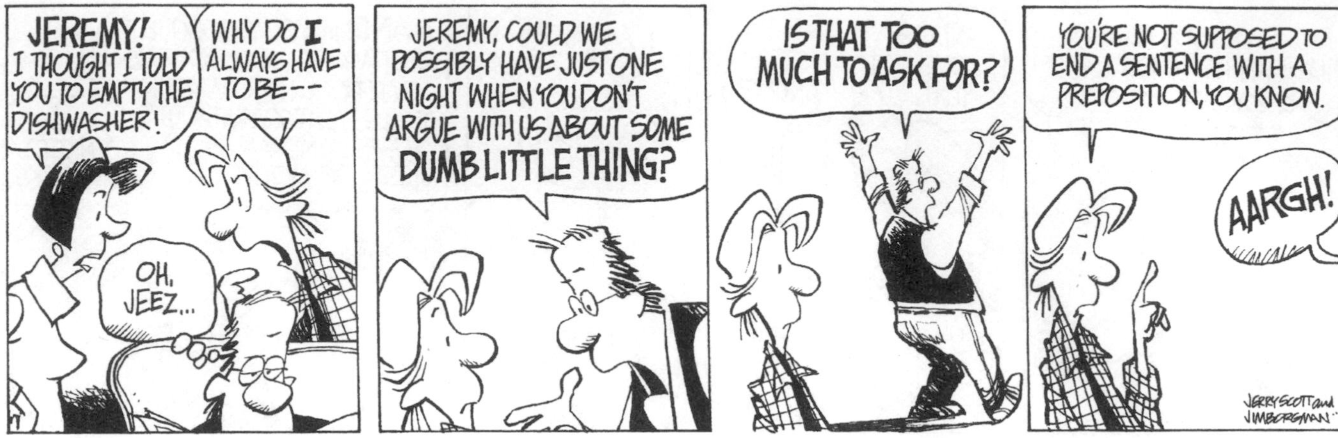

JEREMY! I THOUGHT I TOLD YOU TO EMPTY THE DISHWASHER!
WHY DO I ALWAYS HAVE TO BE--
OH, JEEZ...
JEREMY, COULD WE POSSIBLY HAVE JUST ONE NIGHT WHEN YOU DON'T ARGUE WITH US ABOUT SOME DUMB LITTLE THING?
IS THAT TOO MUCH TO ASK FOR?
YOU'RE NOT SUPPOSED TO END A SENTENCE WITH A PREPOSITION, YOU KNOW.
AARGH!
JERRY SCOTT and JIM BORGMAN

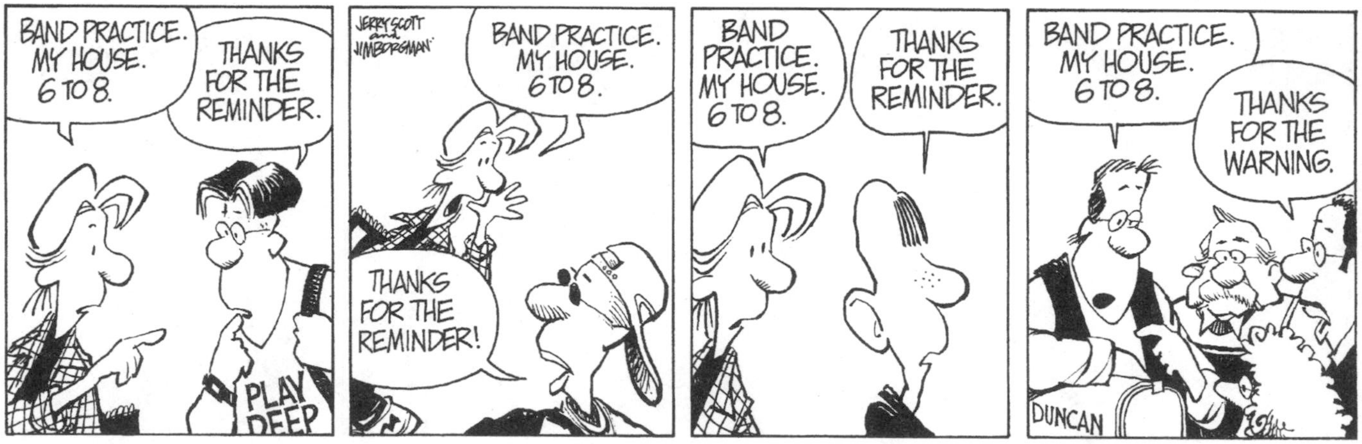

BAND PRACTICE. MY HOUSE. 6 TO 8.
THANKS FOR THE REMINDER.
PLAY DEEP
JERRY SCOTT and JIM BORGMAN
BAND PRACTICE. MY HOUSE. 6 TO 8.
THANKS FOR THE REMINDER!
BAND PRACTICE. MY HOUSE. 6 TO 8.
THANKS FOR THE REMINDER.
BAND PRACTICE. MY HOUSE. 6 TO 8.
THANKS FOR THE WARNING.
DUNCAN

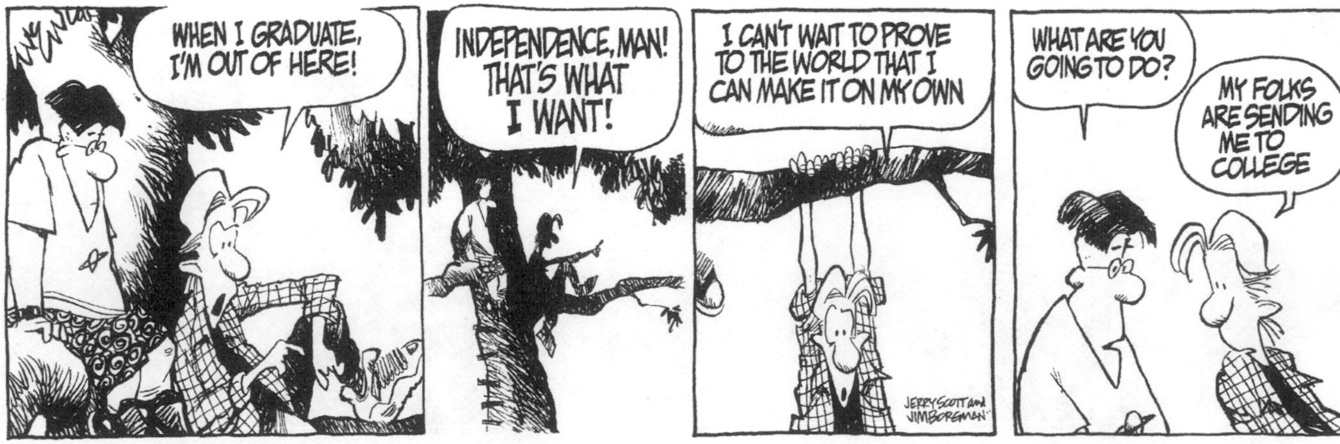

WHEN I GRADUATE, I'M OUT OF HERE!
INDEPENDENCE, MAN! THAT'S WHAT I WANT!
I CAN'T WAIT TO PROVE TO THE WORLD THAT I CAN MAKE IT ON MY OWN
JERRY SCOTT and JIM BORGMAN
WHAT ARE YOU GOING TO DO?
MY FOLKS ARE SENDING ME TO COLLEGE

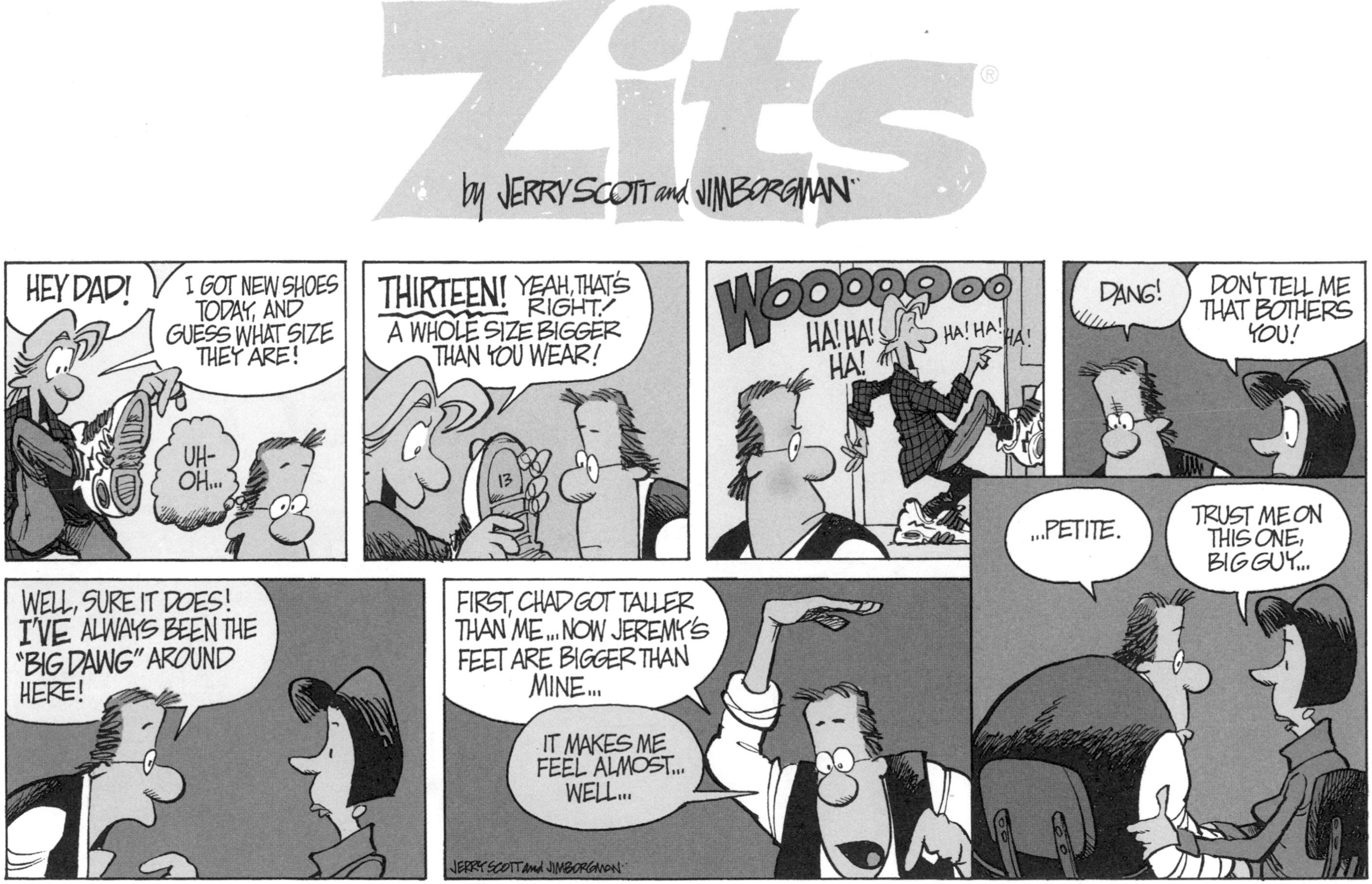
Zits
by JERRY SCOTT and JIM BORGMAN
HEY DAD!
I GOT NEW SHOES TODAY, AND GUESS WHAT SIZE THEY ARE!
UH-OH...
THIRTEEN! YEAH, THAT'S RIGHT! A WHOLE SIZE BIGGER THAN YOU WEAR!
13
WOOOOOOOO
HA! HA! HA!
HA! HA! HA!
DANG!
DON'T TELL ME THAT BOTHERS YOU!
WELL, SURE IT DOES! I'VE ALWAYS BEEN THE "BIG DAWG" AROUND HERE!
FIRST, CHAD GOT TALLER THAN ME... NOW JEREMY'S FEET ARE BIGGER THAN MINE...
IT MAKES ME FEEL ALMOST... WELL...
...PETITE.
TRUST ME ON THIS ONE, BIG GUY...
JERRY SCOTT and JIM BORGMAN

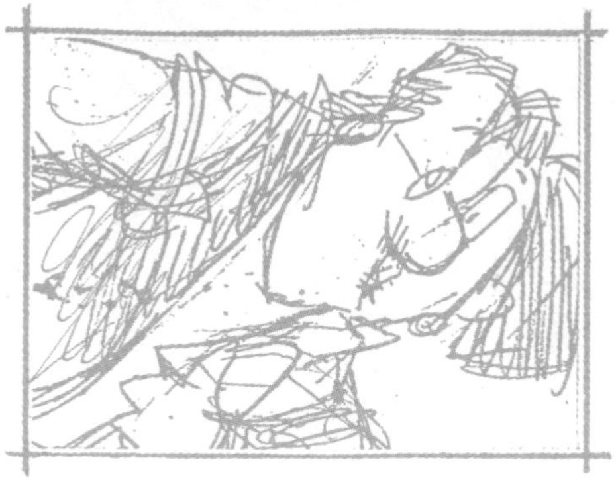

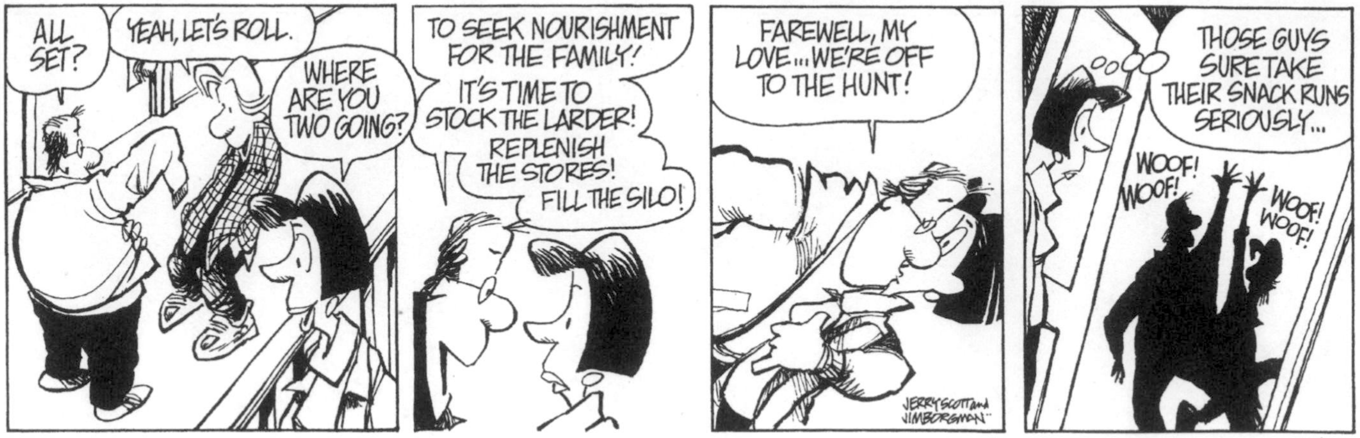
ALL SET?
YEAH, LET'S ROLL.
WHERE ARE YOU TWO GOING?
TO SEEK NOURISHMENT FOR THE FAMILY!
IT'S TIME TO STOCK THE LARDER!
REPLENISH THE STORES!
FILL THE SILO!
FAREWELL, MY LOVE... WE'RE OFF TO THE HUNT!
JERRY SCOTT and JIMBORGMAN
THOSE GUYS SURE TAKE THEIR SNACK RUNS SERIOUSLY...
WOOF! WOOF!
WOOF! WOOF!

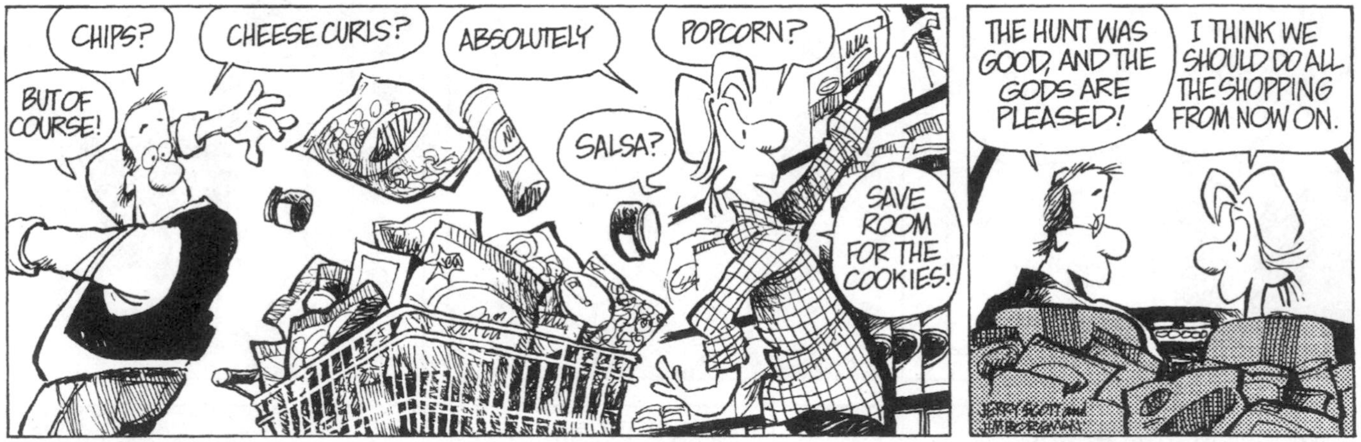
CHIPS?
BUT OF COURSE!
CHEESE CURLS?
ABSOLUTELY
POPCORN?
SALSA?
SAVE ROOM FOR THE COOKIES!
THE HUNT WAS GOOD, AND THE GODS ARE PLEASED!
I THINK WE SHOULD DO ALL THE SHOPPING FROM NOW ON.
JERRY SCOTT and JIMBORGMAN

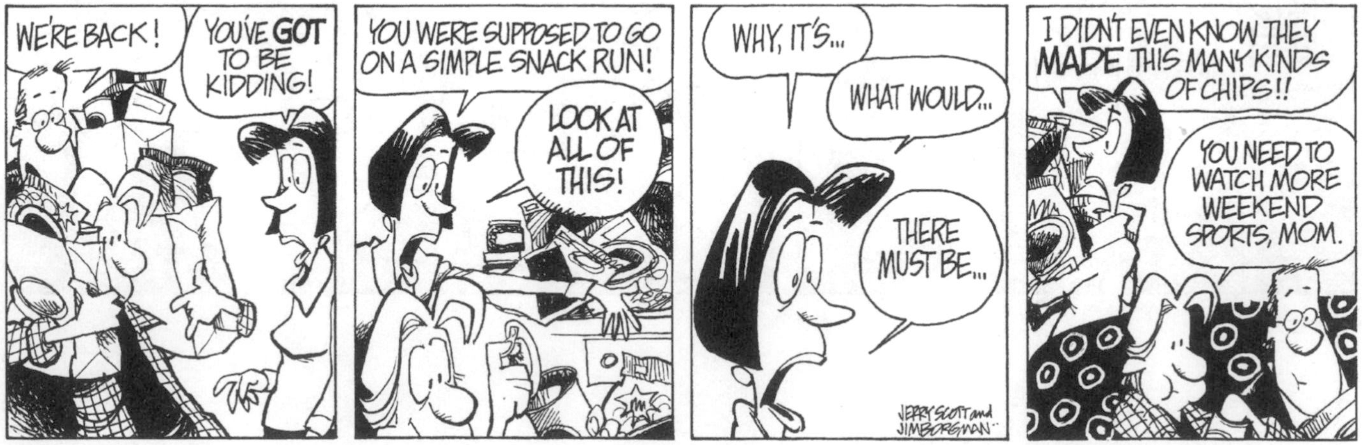
WE'RE BACK!
YOU'VE GOT TO BE KIDDING!
YOU WERE SUPPOSED TO GO ON A SIMPLE SNACK RUN!
LOOK AT ALL OF THIS!
WHY, IT'S...
WHAT WOULD...
THERE MUST BE...
JERRY SCOTT and JIMBORGMAN
I DIDN'T EVEN KNOW THEY MADE THIS MANY KINDS OF CHIPS!!
YOU NEED TO WATCH MORE WEEKEND SPORTS, MOM.

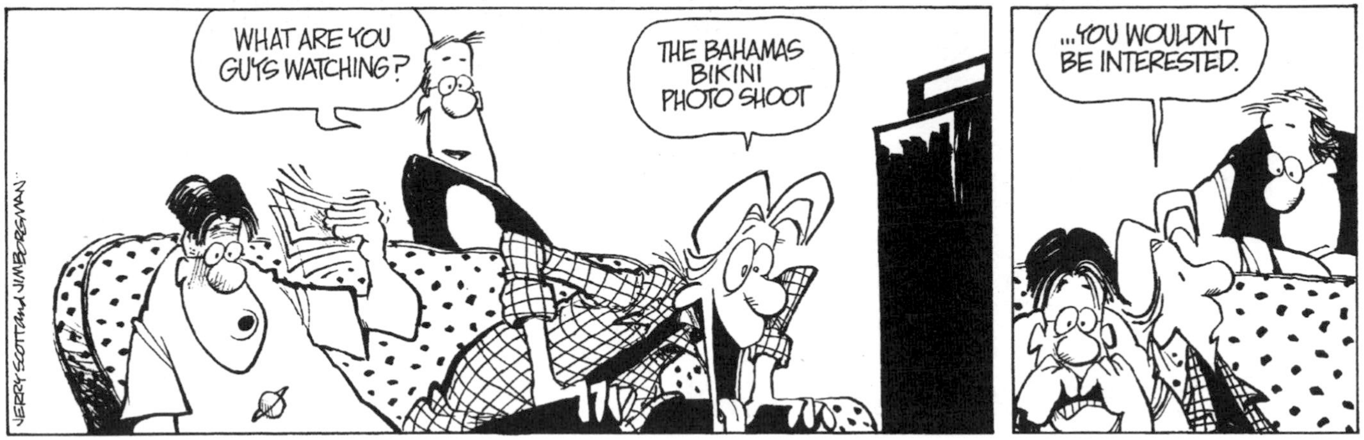

WHAT ARE YOU GUYS WATCHING?
THE BAHAMAS BIKINI PHOTO SHOOT
...YOU WOULDN'T BE INTERESTED.
JERRY SCOTT and JIM BORGMAN

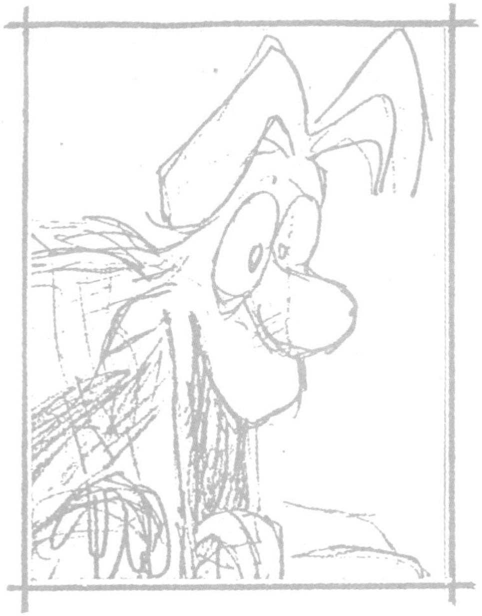

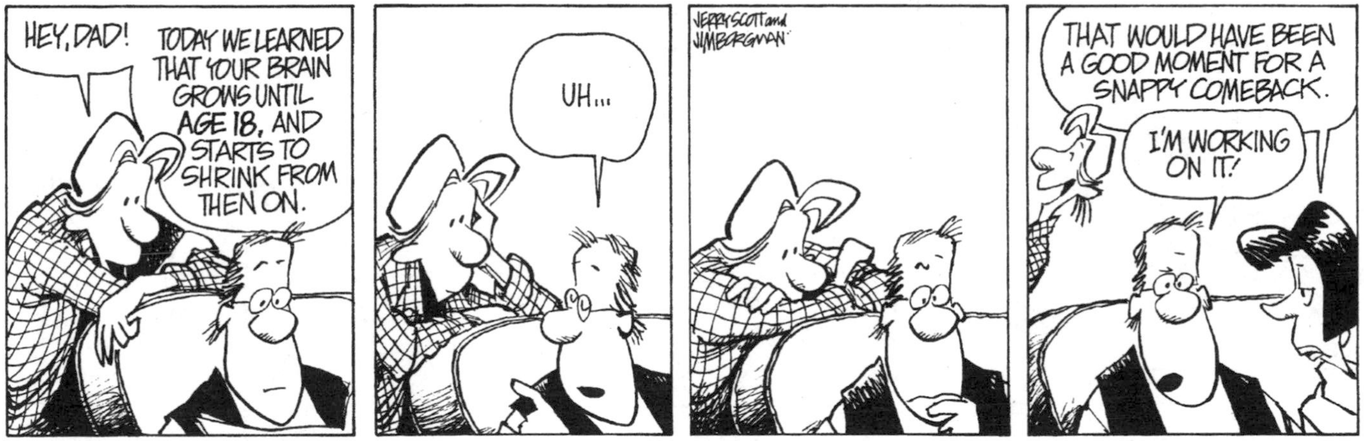

HEY, DAD!
TODAY WE LEARNED THAT YOUR BRAIN GROWS UNTIL AGE 18, AND STARTS TO SHRINK FROM THEN ON.
UH...
JERRY SCOTT and JIM BORGMAN
THAT WOULD HAVE BEEN A GOOD MOMENT FOR A SNAPPY COMEBACK.
I'M WORKING ON IT!

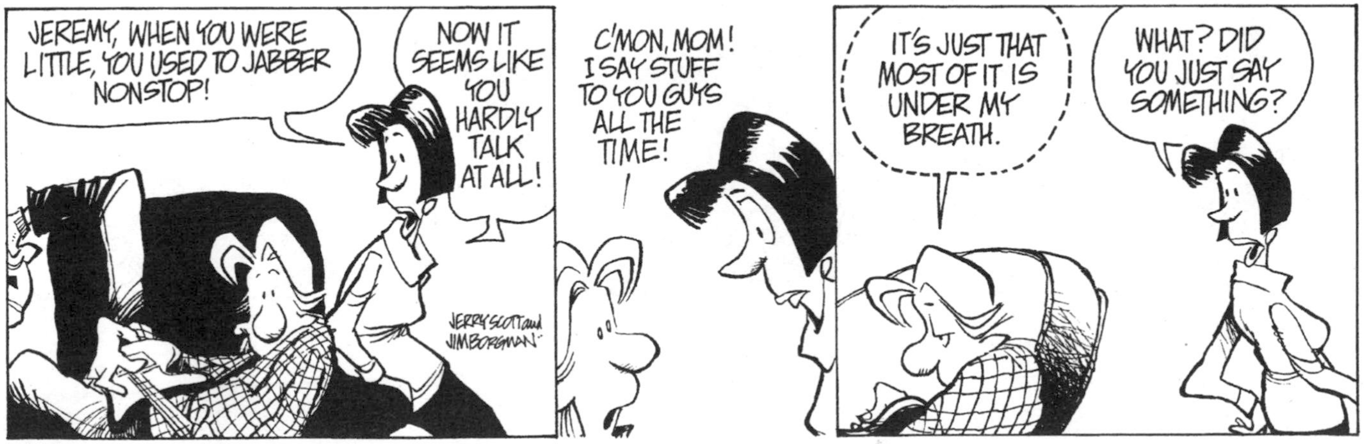

JEREMY, WHEN YOU WERE LITTLE, YOU USED TO JABBER NONSTOP!
NOW IT SEEMS LIKE YOU HARDLY TALK AT ALL!
JERRY SCOTT and JIM BORGMAN
C'MON, MOM! I SAY STUFF TO YOU GUYS ALL THE TIME!
IT'S JUST THAT MOST OF IT IS UNDER MY BREATH.
WHAT? DID YOU JUST SAY SOMETHING?

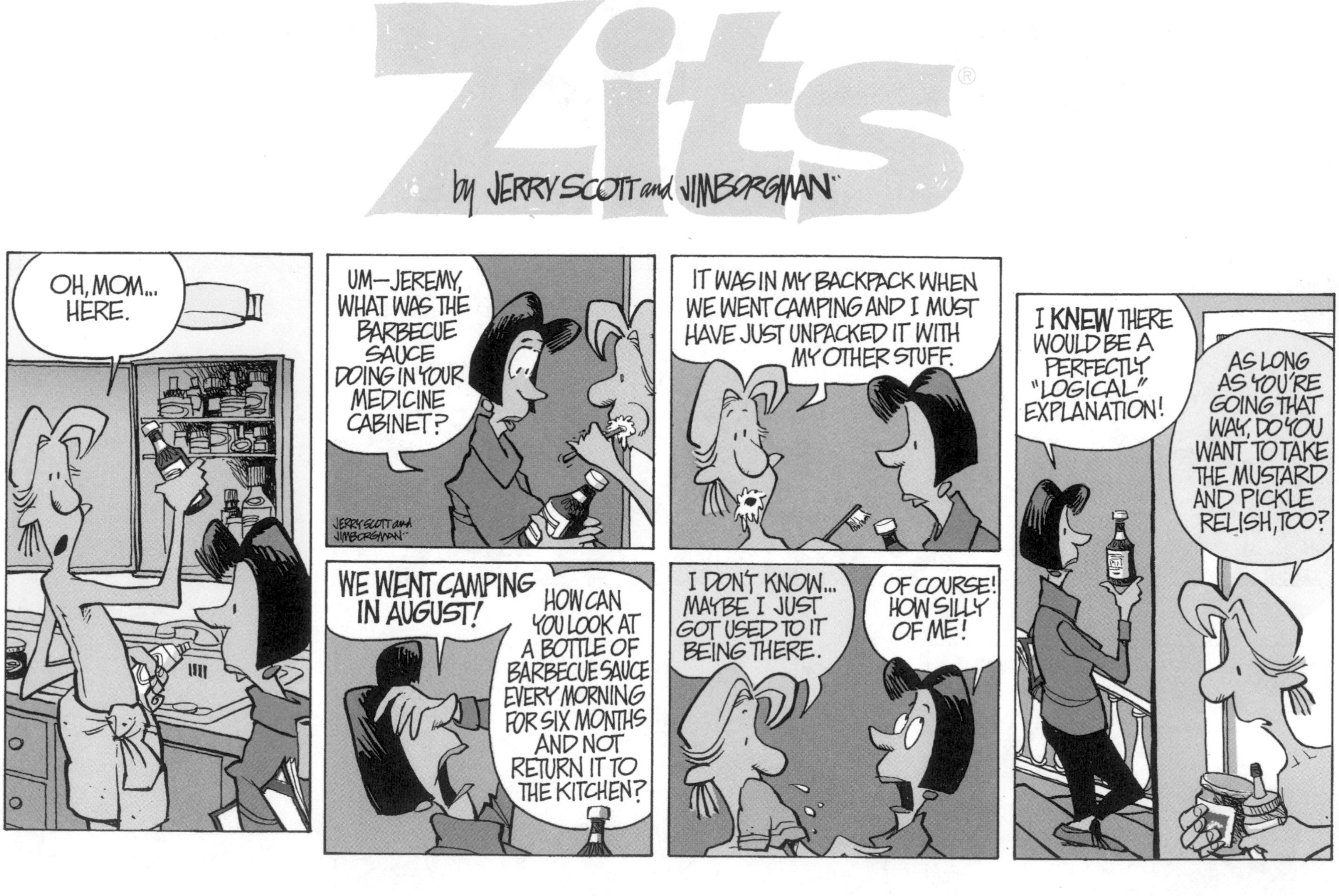
Zits®
by JERRY SCOTT and JIMBORGMAN™
OH, MOM... HERE.
UM—JEREMY, WHAT WAS THE BARBECUE SAUCE DOING IN YOUR MEDICINE CABINET?
JERRY SCOTT and JIMBORGMAN™
IT WAS IN MY BACKPACK WHEN WE WENT CAMPING AND I MUST HAVE JUST UNPACKED IT WITH MY OTHER STUFF.
WE WENT CAMPING IN AUGUST!
HOW CAN YOU LOOK AT A BOTTLE OF BARBECUE SAUCE EVERY MORNING FOR SIX MONTHS AND NOT RETURN IT TO THE KITCHEN?
I DON'T KNOW... MAYBE I JUST GOT USED TO IT BEING THERE.
OF COURSE! HOW SILLY OF ME!
I KNEW THERE WOULD BE A PERFECTLY "LOGICAL" EXPLANATION!
AS LONG AS YOU'RE GOING THAT WAY, DO YOU WANT TO TAKE THE MUSTARD AND PICKLE RELISH, TOO?

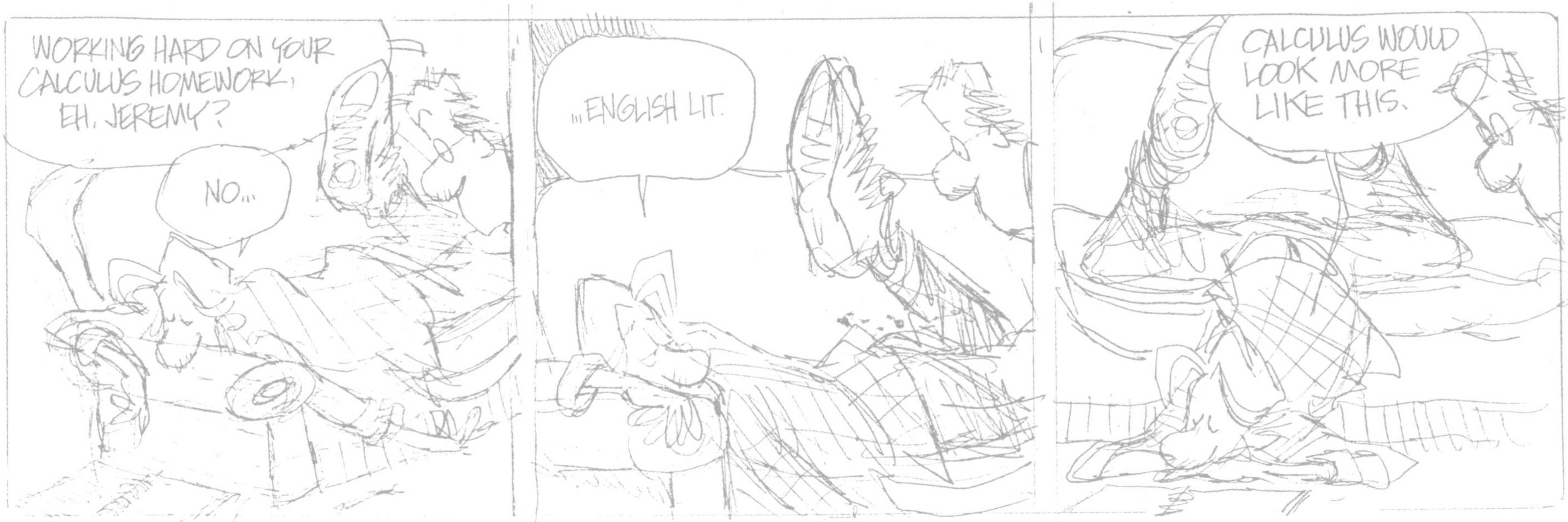
WORKING HARD ON YOUR CALCULUS HOMEWORK, EH, JEREMY?
NO...
...ENGLISH LIT.
CALCULUS WOULD LOOK MORE LIKE THIS.

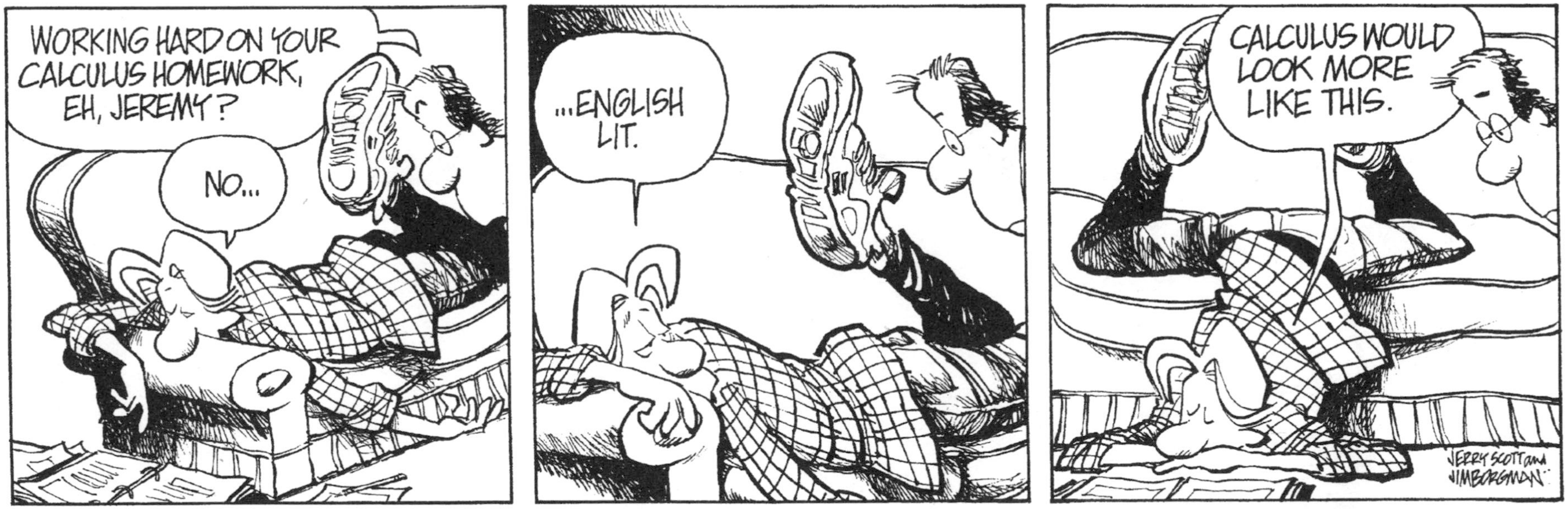
WORKING HARD ON YOUR CALCULUS HOMEWORK, EH, JEREMY?
NO...
...ENGLISH LIT.
CALCULUS WOULD LOOK MORE LIKE THIS.
JERRY SCOTT and JIMBORGMAN

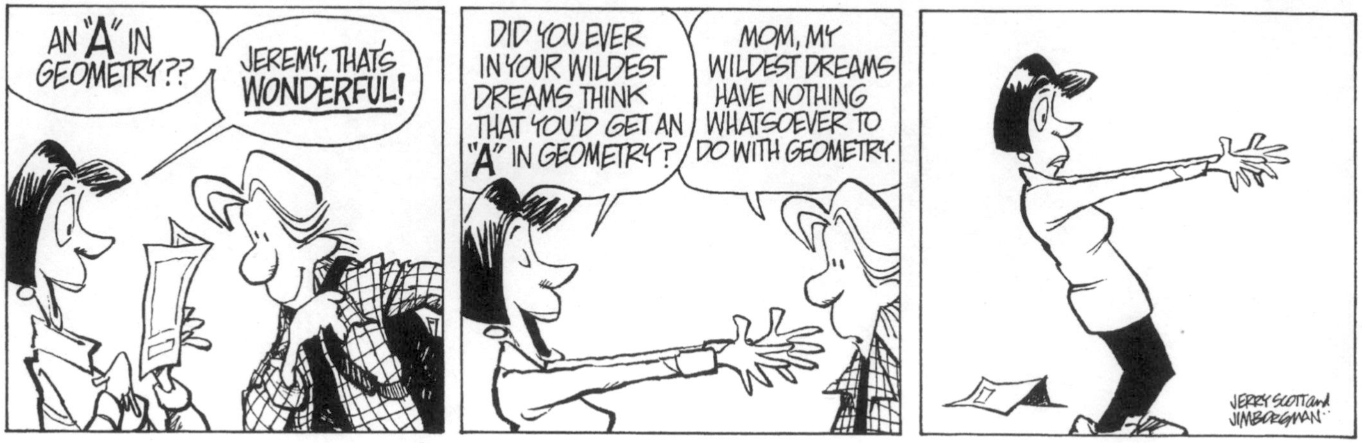
AN "A" IN GEOMETRY??
JEREMY, THAT'S WONDERFUL!
DID YOU EVER IN YOUR WILDEST DREAMS THINK THAT YOU'D GET AN "A" IN GEOMETRY?
MOM, MY WILDEST DREAMS HAVE NOTHING WHATSOEVER TO DO WITH GEOMETRY.
JERRY SCOTT and JIM BORGMAN

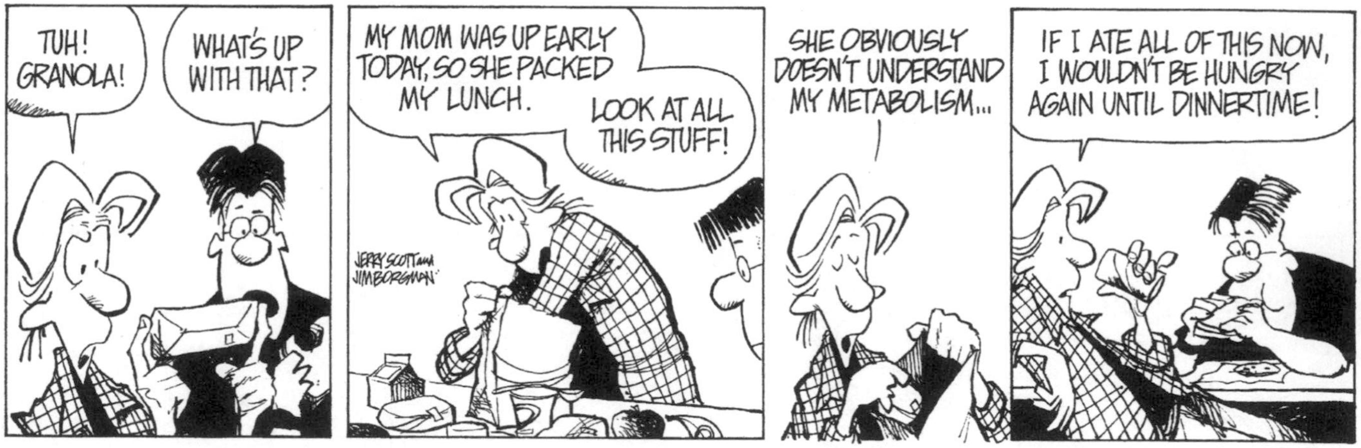
TUH! GRANOLA!
WHAT'S UP WITH THAT?
MY MOM WAS UP EARLY TODAY, SO SHE PACKED MY LUNCH.
LOOK AT ALL THIS STUFF!
JERRY SCOTT and JIM BORGMAN
SHE OBVIOUSLY DOESN'T UNDERSTAND MY METABOLISM...
IF I ATE ALL OF THIS NOW, I WOULDN'T BE HUNGRY AGAIN UNTIL DINNERTIME!

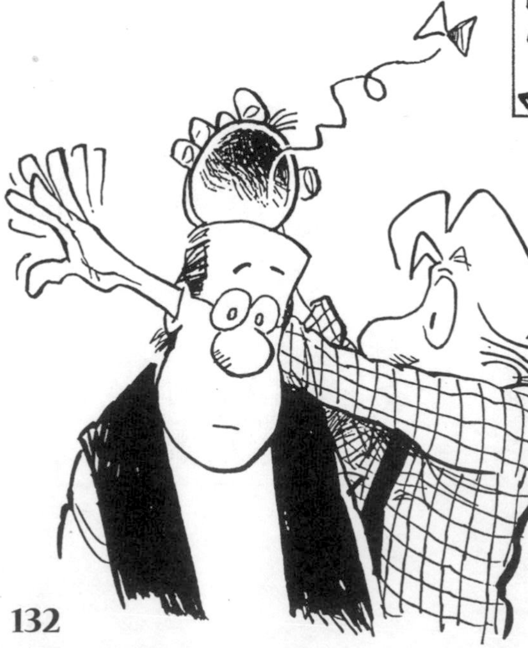

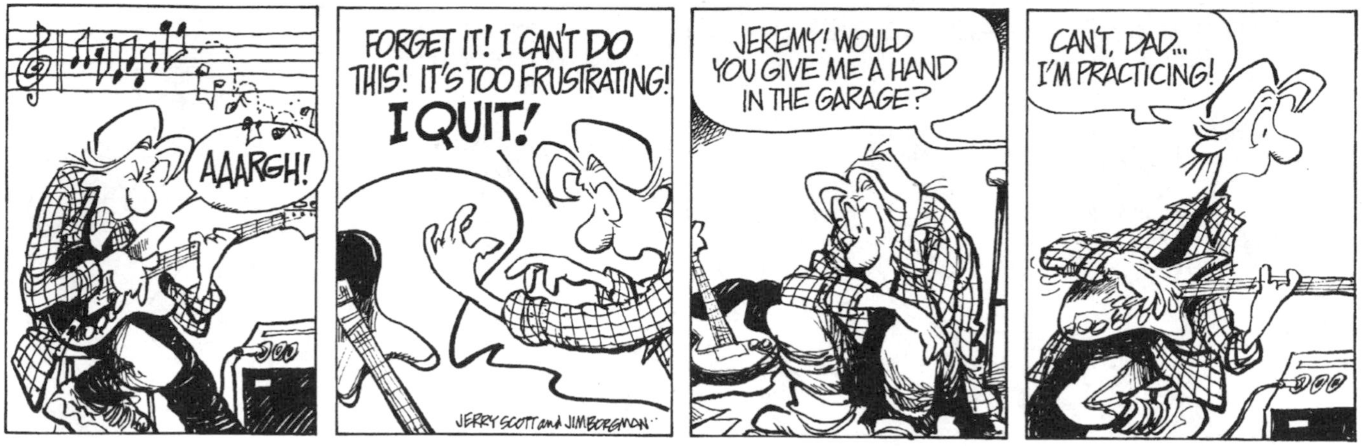
AAARGH!
FORGET IT! I CAN'T DO THIS! IT'S TOO FRUSTRATING!
I QUIT!
JERRY SCOTT and JIM BORGMAN
JEREMY! WOULD YOU GIVE ME A HAND IN THE GARAGE?
CAN'T, DAD... I'M PRACTICING!

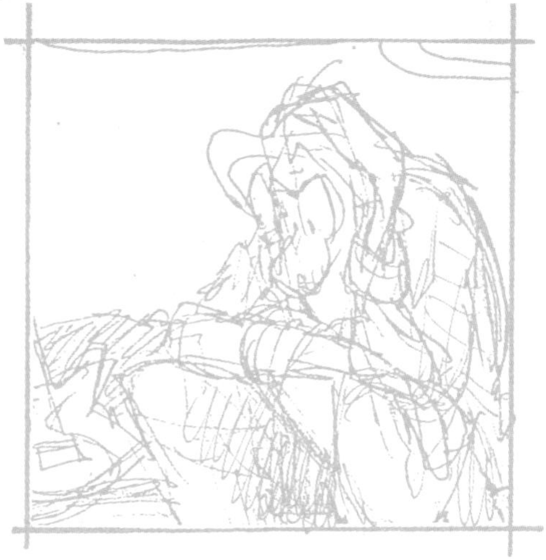

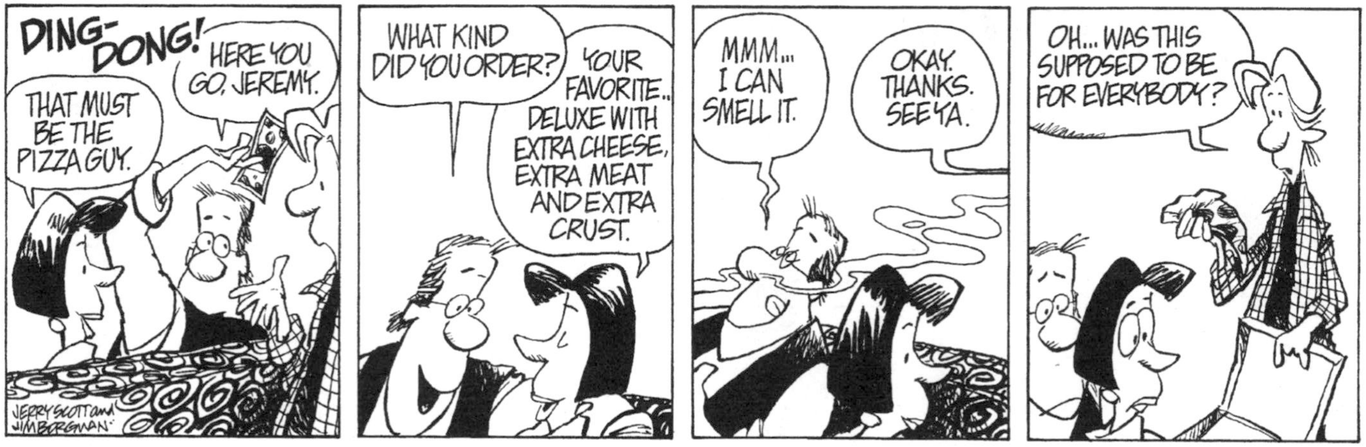
DING-DONG!
THAT MUST BE THE PIZZA GUY.
HERE YOU GO, JEREMY.
JERRY SCOTT and JIM BORGMAN
WHAT KIND DID YOU ORDER?
YOUR FAVORITE... DELUXE WITH EXTRA CHEESE, EXTRA MEAT AND EXTRA CRUST.
MMM... I CAN SMELL IT.
OKAY. THANKS. SEE YA.
OH... WAS THIS SUPPOSED TO BE FOR EVERYBODY?

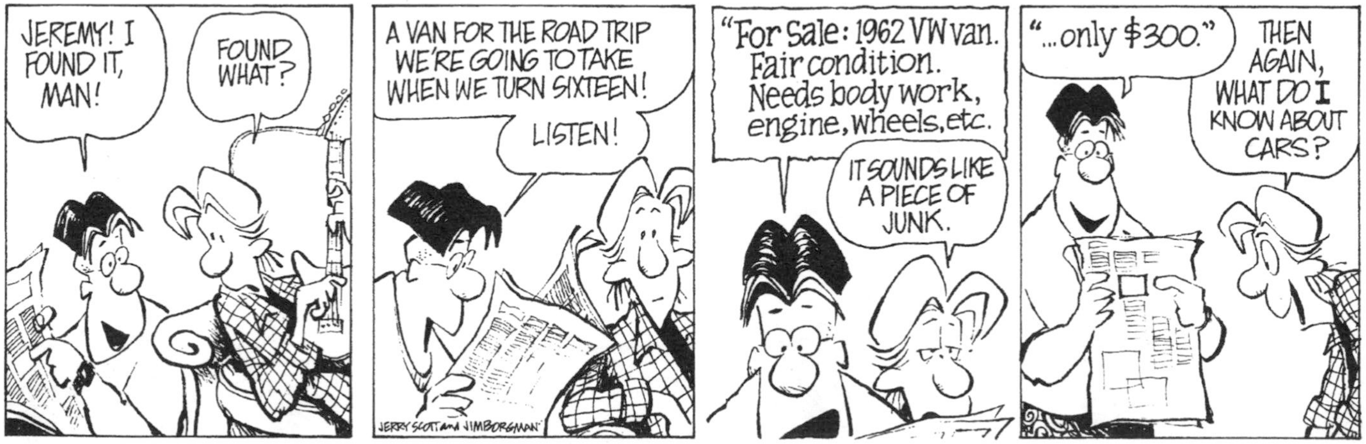
JEREMY! I FOUND IT, MAN!
FOUND WHAT?
A VAN FOR THE ROAD TRIP WE'RE GOING TO TAKE WHEN WE TURN SIXTEEN!
LISTEN!
JERRY SCOTT and JIM BORGMAN
"For Sale: 1962 VW van. Fair condition. Needs body work, engine, wheels, etc.
IT SOUNDS LIKE A PIECE OF JUNK.
"...only $300."
THEN AGAIN, WHAT DO I KNOW ABOUT CARS?

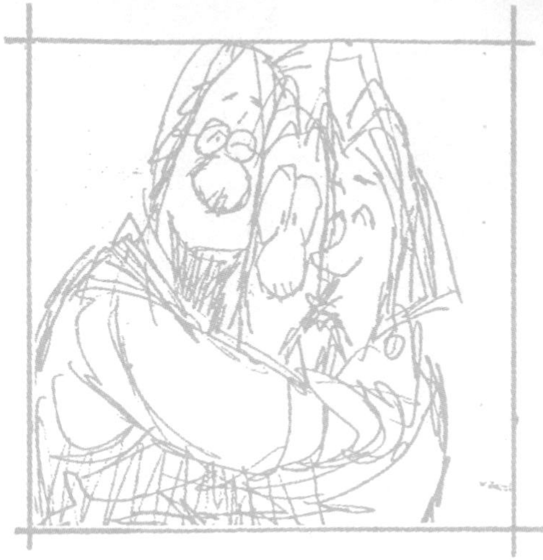

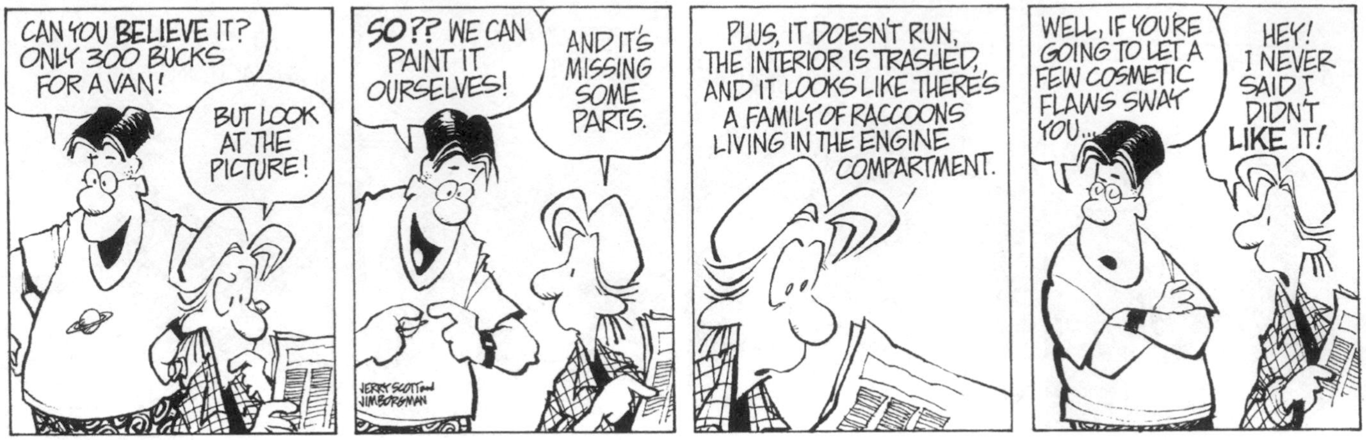
CAN YOU BELIEVE IT? ONLY 300 BUCKS FOR A VAN!
BUT LOOK AT THE PICTURE!
SO?? WE CAN PAINT IT OURSELVES!
AND IT'S MISSING SOME PARTS.
JERRY SCOTT and JIMBORGMAN
PLUS, IT DOESN'T RUN, THE INTERIOR IS TRASHED, AND IT LOOKS LIKE THERE'S A FAMILY OF RACCOONS LIVING IN THE ENGINE COMPARTMENT.
WELL, IF YOU'RE GOING TO LET A FEW COSMETIC FLAWS SWAY YOU...
HEY! I NEVER SAID I DIDN'T LIKE IT!

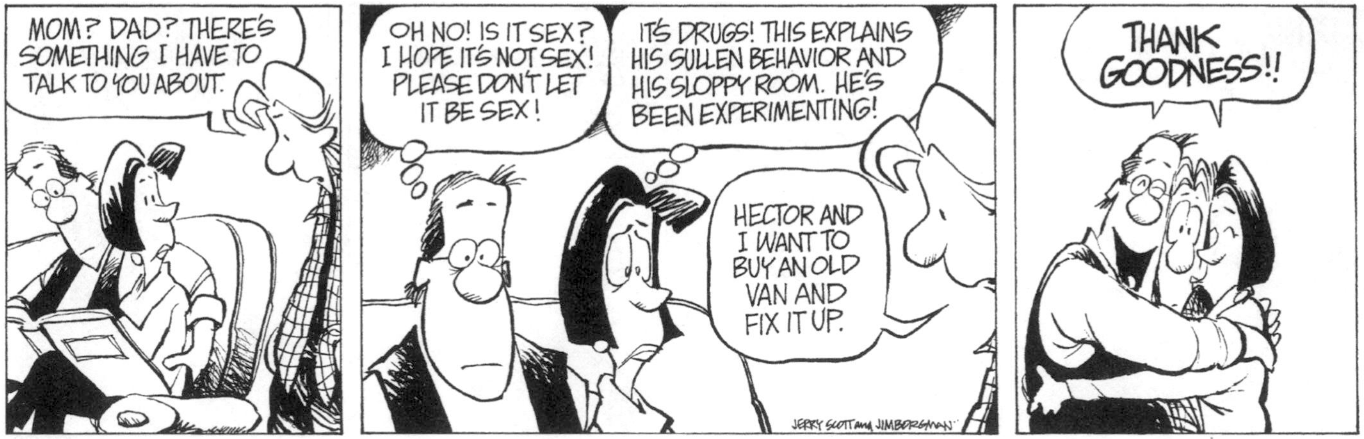
MOM? DAD? THERE'S SOMETHING I HAVE TO TALK TO YOU ABOUT.
OH NO! IS IT SEX? I HOPE IT'S NOT SEX! PLEASE DON'T LET IT BE SEX!
IT'S DRUGS! THIS EXPLAINS HIS SULLEN BEHAVIOR AND HIS SLOPPY ROOM. HE'S BEEN EXPERIMENTING!
HECTOR AND I WANT TO BUY AN OLD VAN AND FIX IT UP.
JERRY SCOTT and JIMBORGMAN
THANK GOODNESS!!

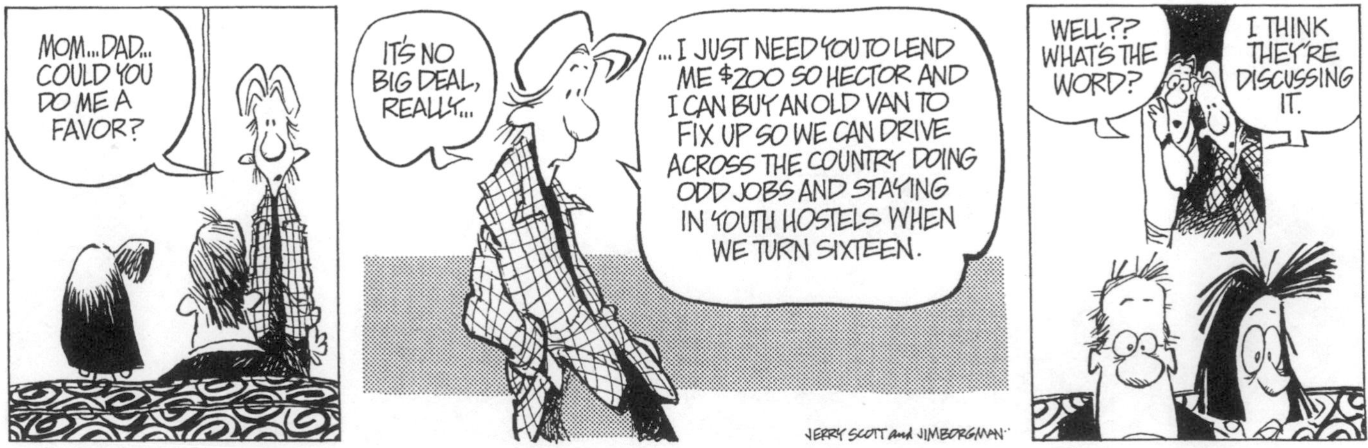
MOM...DAD... COULD YOU DO ME A FAVOR?
IT'S NO BIG DEAL, REALLY...
...I JUST NEED YOU TO LEND ME $200 SO HECTOR AND I CAN BUY AN OLD VAN TO FIX UP SO WE CAN DRIVE ACROSS THE COUNTRY DOING ODD JOBS AND STAYING IN YOUTH HOSTELS WHEN WE TURN SIXTEEN.
JERRY SCOTT and JIMBORGMAN
WELL?? WHAT'S THE WORD?
I THINK THEY'RE DISCUSSING IT.

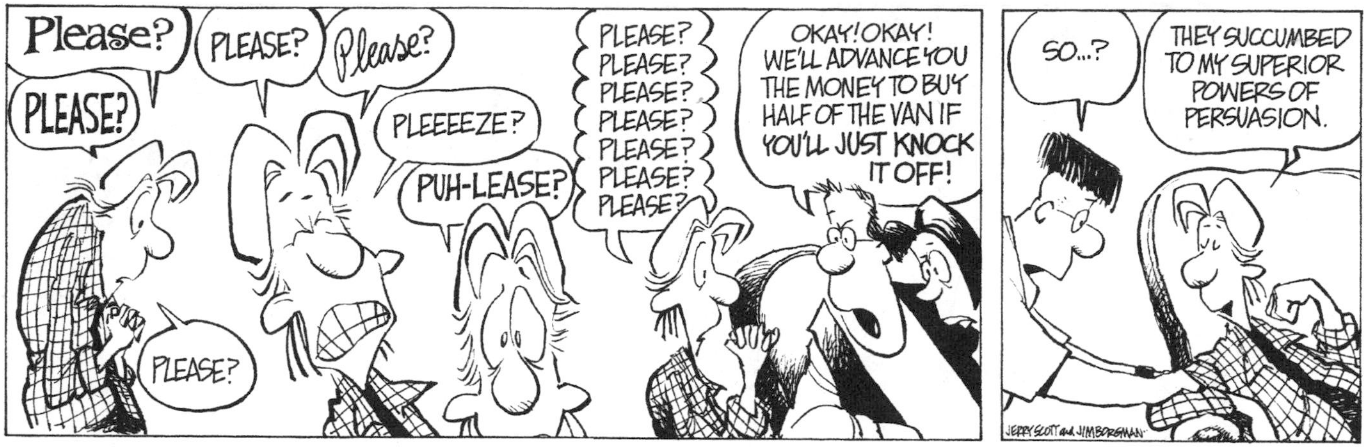
Please?
PLEASE?
PLEASE?
PLEASE?
Please?
PLEEEEZE?
PUH-LEASE?
PLEASE?
PLEASE?
PLEASE?
PLEASE?
PLEASE?
PLEASE?
PLEASE?
OKAY! OKAY! WE'LL ADVANCE YOU THE MONEY TO BUY HALF OF THE VAN IF YOU'LL JUST KNOCK IT OFF!
SO...?
THEY SUCCUMBED TO MY SUPERIOR POWERS OF PERSUASION.
JERRY SCOTT and JIM BORGMAN

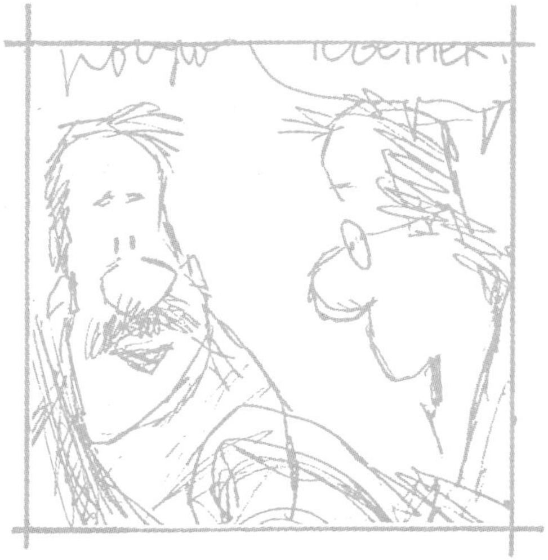

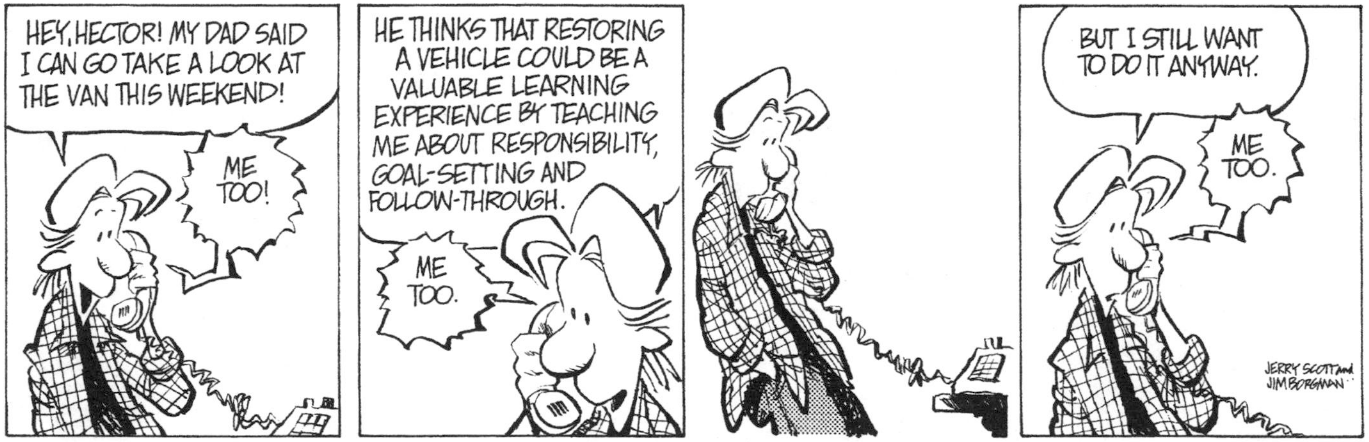
HEY, HECTOR! MY DAD SAID I CAN GO TAKE A LOOK AT THE VAN THIS WEEKEND!
ME TOO!
HE THINKS THAT RESTORING A VEHICLE COULD BE A VALUABLE LEARNING EXPERIENCE BY TEACHING ME ABOUT RESPONSIBILITY, GOAL-SETTING AND FOLLOW-THROUGH.
ME TOO.
BUT I STILL WANT TO DO IT ANYWAY.
ME TOO.
JERRY SCOTT and JIM BORGMAN

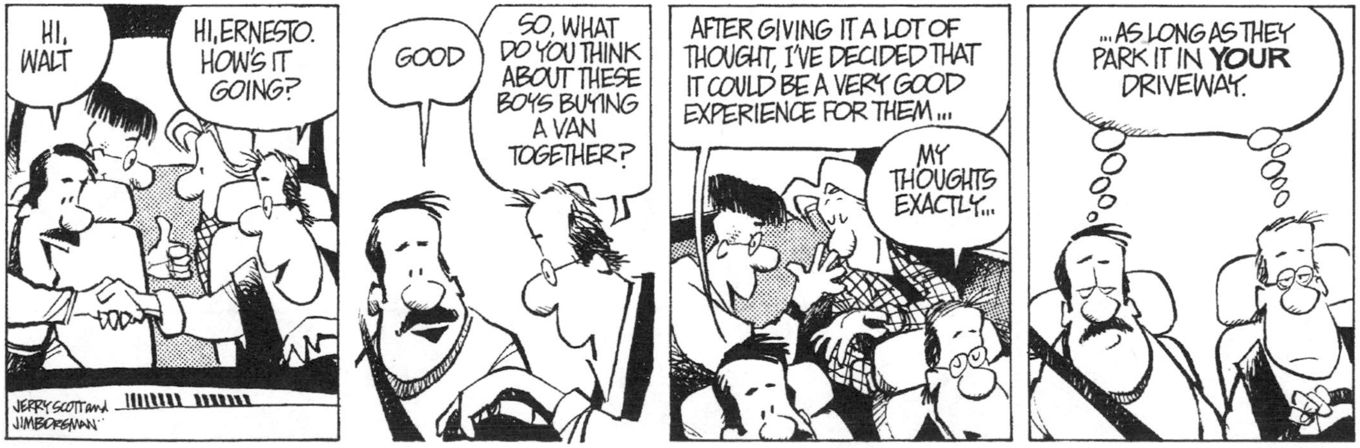
HI, WALT
HI, ERNESTO. HOW'S IT GOING?
JERRY SCOTT and JIM BORGMAN
GOOD
SO, WHAT DO YOU THINK ABOUT THESE BOYS BUYING A VAN TOGETHER?
AFTER GIVING IT A LOT OF THOUGHT, I'VE DECIDED THAT IT COULD BE A VERY GOOD EXPERIENCE FOR THEM...
MY THOUGHTS EXACTLY...
...AS LONG AS THEY PARK IT IN **YOUR** DRIVEWAY.

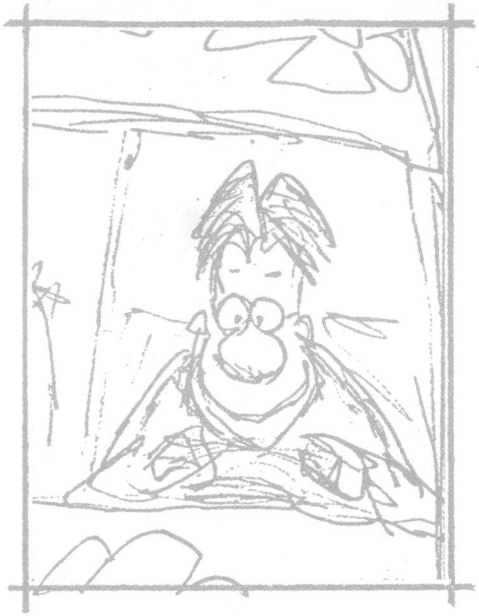

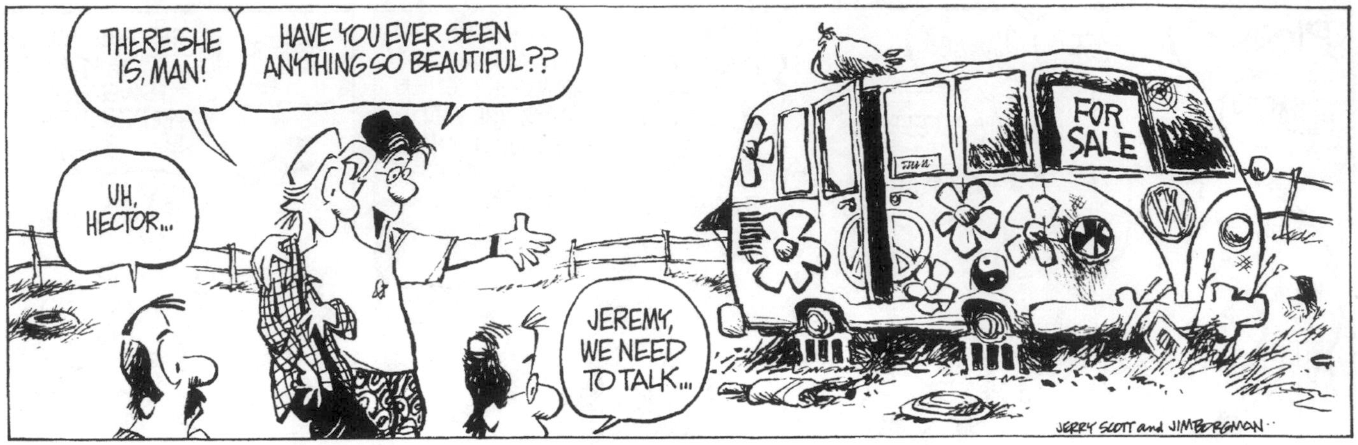

THERE SHE IS, MAN!
HAVE YOU EVER SEEN ANYTHING SO BEAUTIFUL??
UH, HECTOR...
JEREMY, WE NEED TO TALK...
FOR SALE
JERRY SCOTT and JIM BORGMAN

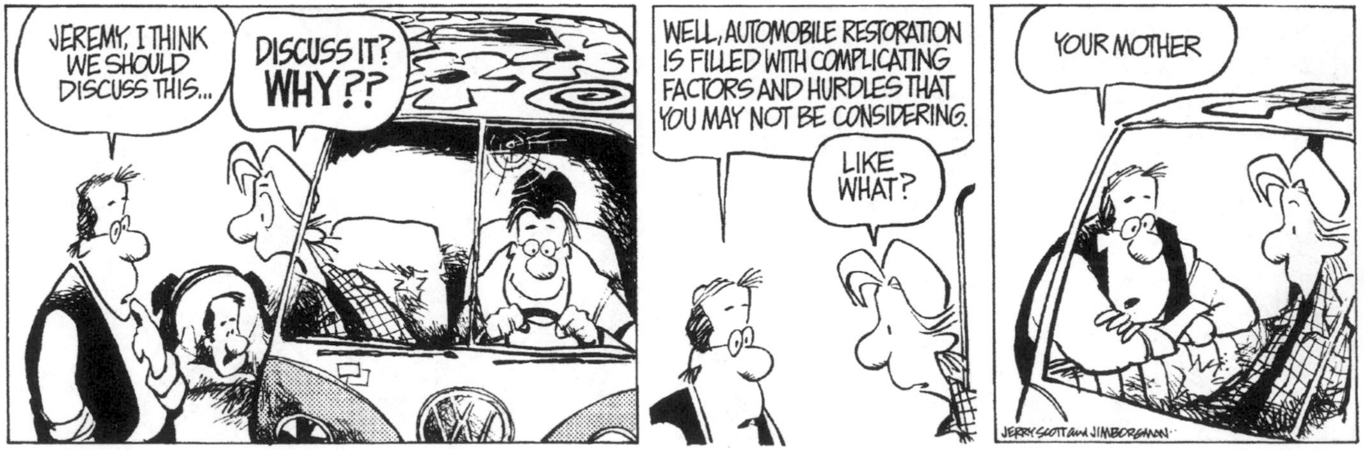

JEREMY, I THINK WE SHOULD DISCUSS THIS...
DISCUSS IT? WHY??
WELL, AUTOMOBILE RESTORATION IS FILLED WITH COMPLICATING FACTORS AND HURDLES THAT YOU MAY NOT BE CONSIDERING.
LIKE WHAT?
YOUR MOTHER
JERRY SCOTT and JIM BORGMAN

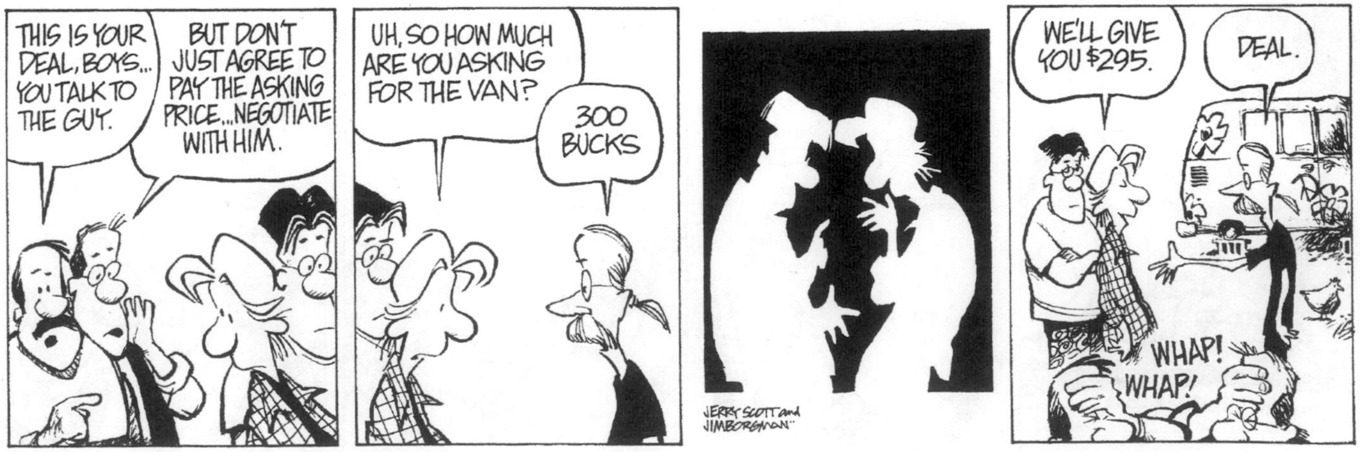

THIS IS YOUR DEAL, BOYS... YOU TALK TO THE GUY.
BUT DON'T JUST AGREE TO PAY THE ASKING PRICE... NEGOTIATE WITH HIM.
UH, SO HOW MUCH ARE YOU ASKING FOR THE VAN?
300 BUCKS
JERRY SCOTT and JIM BORGMAN
WE'LL GIVE YOU $295.
DEAL.
WHAP!
WHAP!

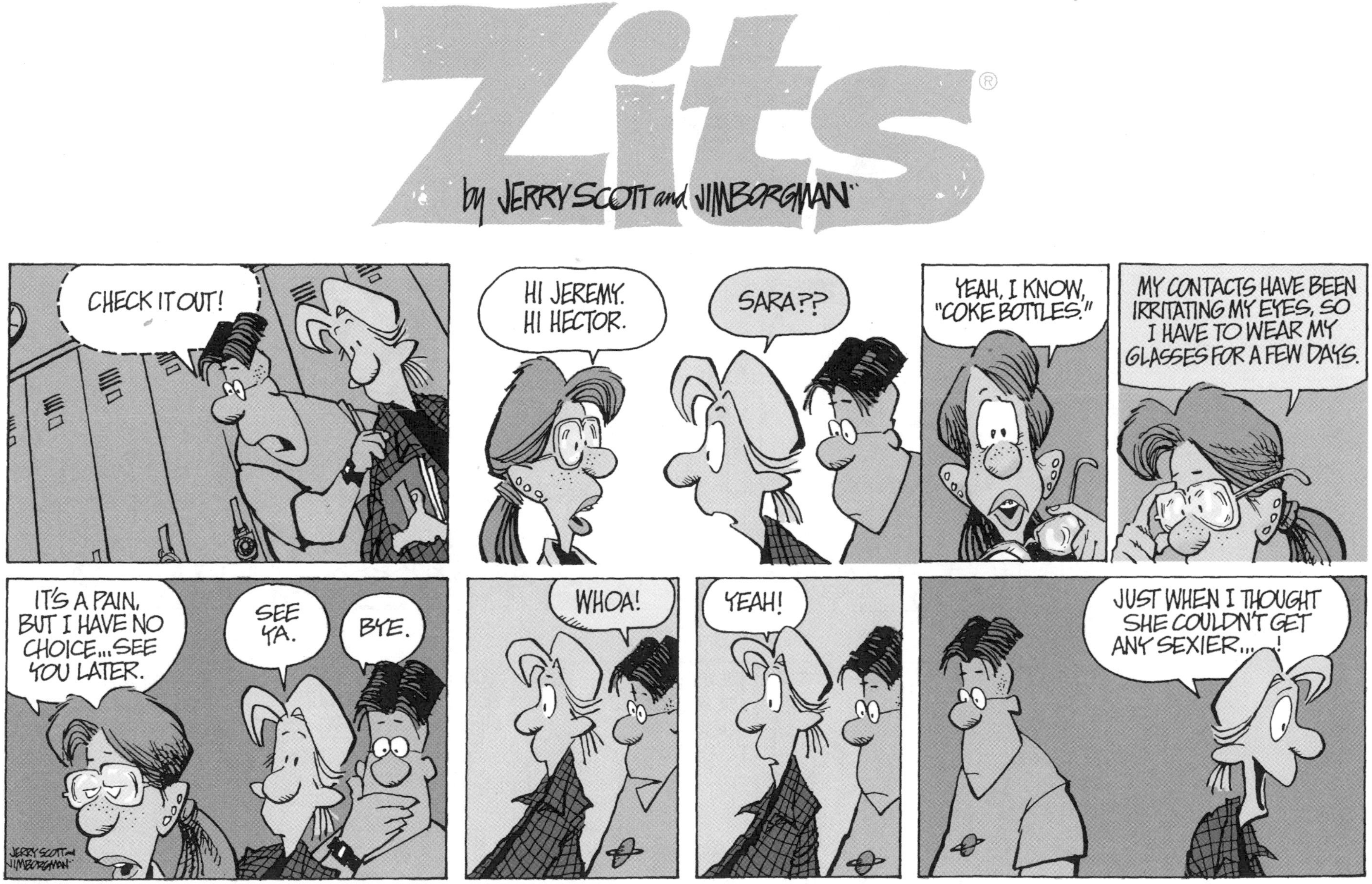

Zits®
by JERRY SCOTT and JIM BORGMAN
CHECK IT OUT!
HI JEREMY. HI HECTOR.
SARA??
YEAH, I KNOW, "COKE BOTTLES."
MY CONTACTS HAVE BEEN IRRITATING MY EYES, SO I HAVE TO WEAR MY GLASSES FOR A FEW DAYS.
IT'S A PAIN, BUT I HAVE NO CHOICE... SEE YOU LATER.
SEE YA.
BYE.
WHOA!
YEAH!
JUST WHEN I THOUGHT SHE COULDN'T GET ANY SEXIER... !

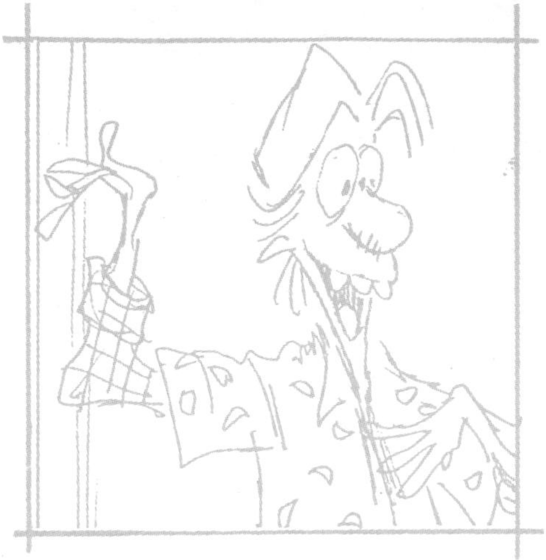

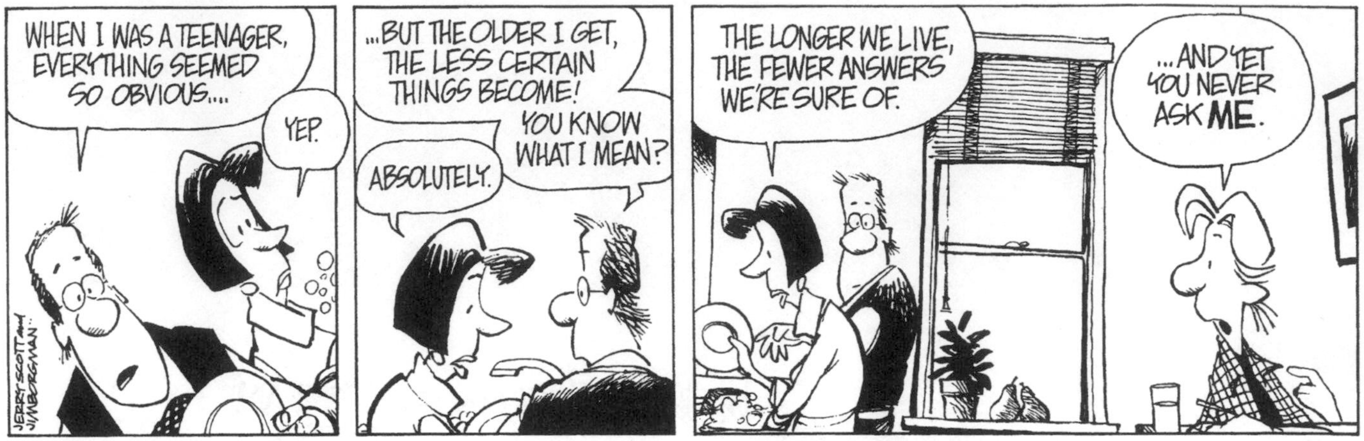
WHEN I WAS A TEENAGER, EVERYTHING SEEMED SO OBVIOUS....
YEP.
...BUT THE OLDER I GET, THE LESS CERTAIN THINGS BECOME!
ABSOLUTELY.
YOU KNOW WHAT I MEAN?
THE LONGER WE LIVE, THE FEWER ANSWERS WE'RE SURE OF.
...AND YET YOU NEVER ASK **ME**.

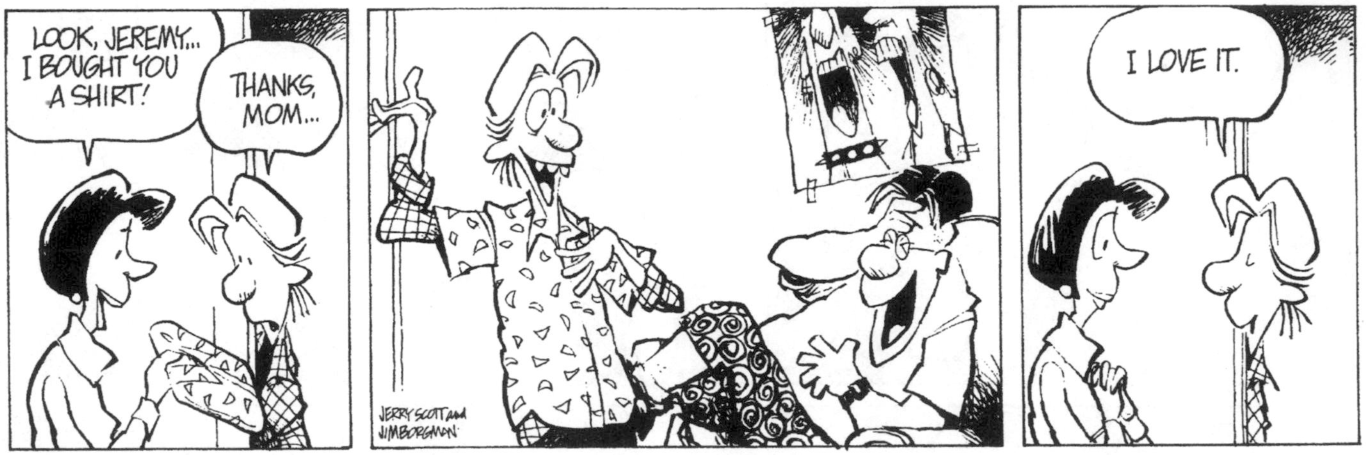
LOOK, JEREMY... I BOUGHT YOU A SHIRT!
THANKS, MOM...
I LOVE IT.

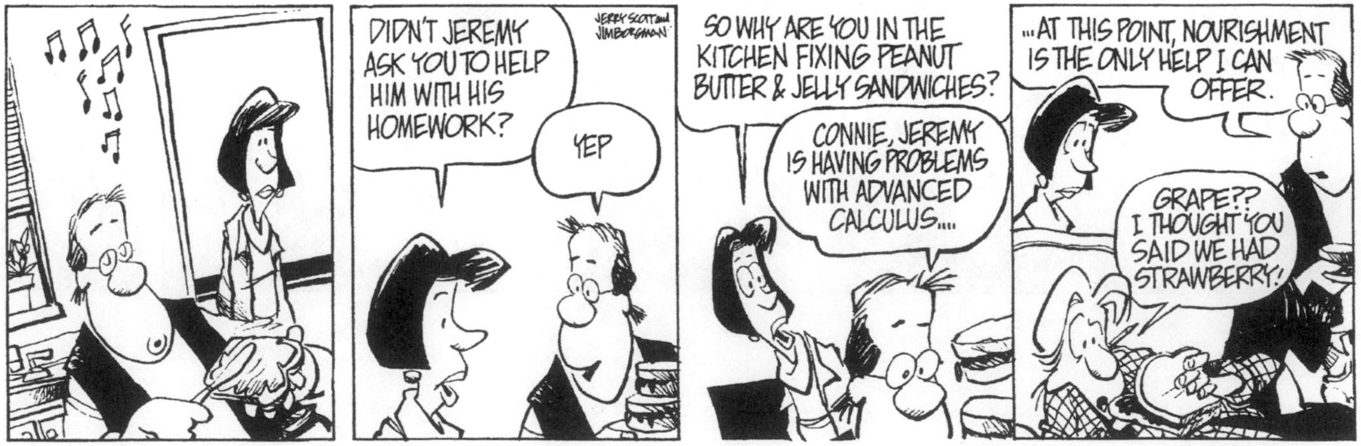
DIDN'T JEREMY ASK YOU TO HELP HIM WITH HIS HOMEWORK?
YEP
SO WHY ARE YOU IN THE KITCHEN FIXING PEANUT BUTTER & JELLY SANDWICHES?
CONNIE, JEREMY IS HAVING PROBLEMS WITH ADVANCED CALCULUS....
...AT THIS POINT, NOURISHMENT IS THE ONLY HELP I CAN OFFER.
GRAPE?? I THOUGHT YOU SAID WE HAD STRAWBERRY!

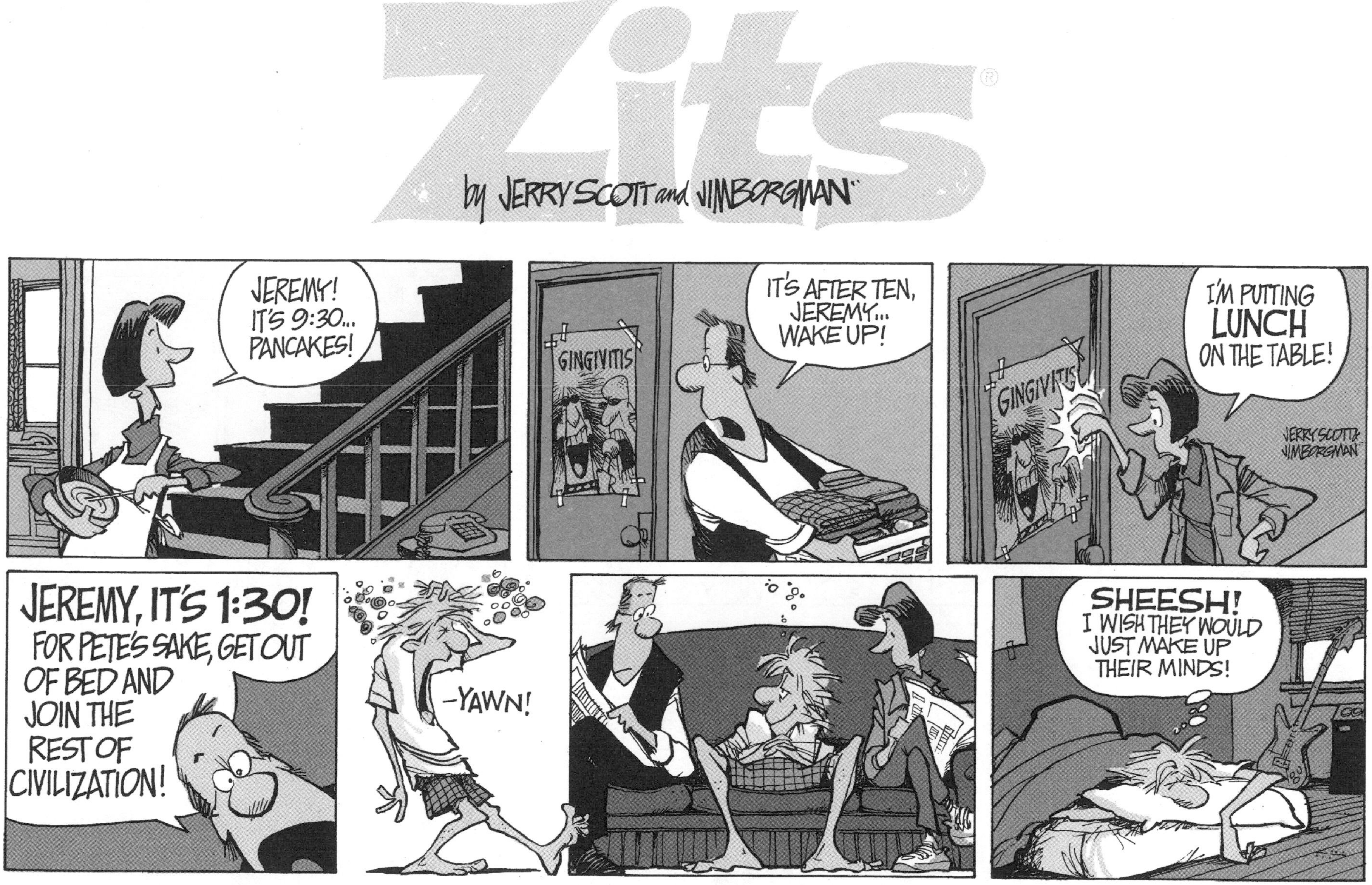

Zits®
by JERRY SCOTT and JIM BORGMAN
JEREMY! IT'S 9:30... PANCAKES!
GINGIVITIS
IT'S AFTER TEN, JEREMY... WAKE UP!
GINGIVITIS
I'M PUTTING LUNCH ON THE TABLE!
JERRY SCOTT & JIM BORGMAN
JEREMY, IT'S 1:30! FOR PETE'S SAKE, GET OUT OF BED AND JOIN THE REST OF CIVILIZATION!
-YAWN!
SHEESH! I WISH THEY WOULD JUST MAKE UP THEIR MINDS!

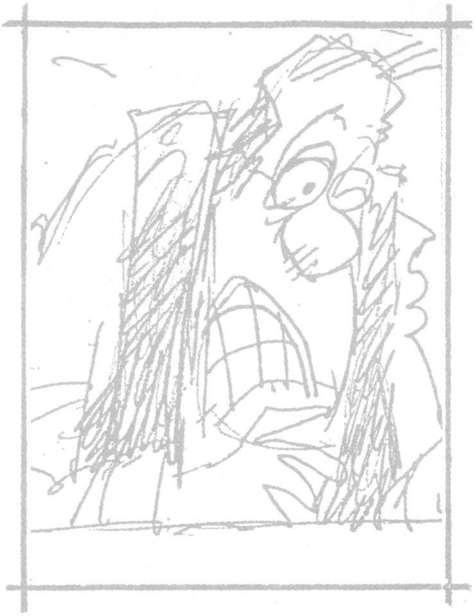

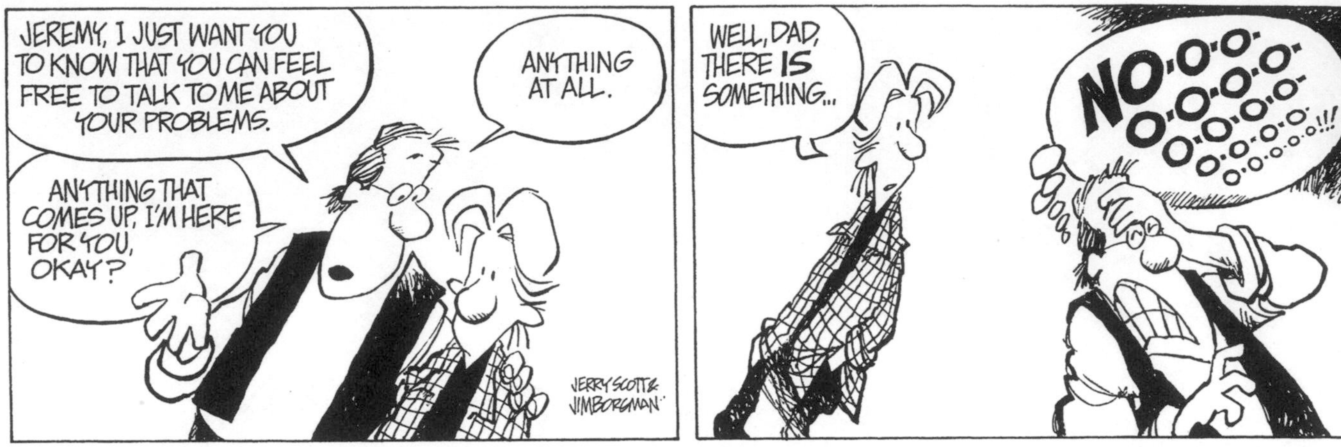
JEREMY, I JUST WANT YOU TO KNOW THAT YOU CAN FEEL FREE TO TALK TO ME ABOUT YOUR PROBLEMS.
ANYTHING THAT COMES UP, I'M HERE FOR YOU, OKAY?
ANYTHING AT ALL.
JERRY SCOTT & JIMBORGMAN
WELL, DAD, THERE IS SOMETHING...
NO-O-O-O-O-O-O-O-O-O-O-O-O-O-O-O-O-O-O!!!

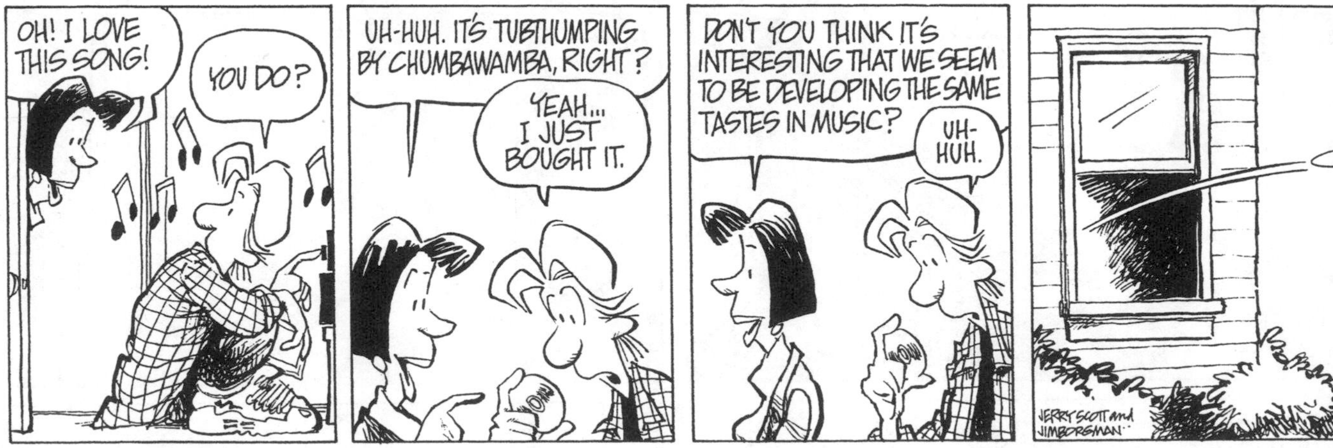
OH! I LOVE THIS SONG!
YOU DO?
UH-HUH. IT'S TUBTHUMPING BY CHUMBAWAMBA, RIGHT?
YEAH... I JUST BOUGHT IT.
DON'T YOU THINK IT'S INTERESTING THAT WE SEEM TO BE DEVELOPING THE SAME TASTES IN MUSIC?
UH-HUH.
JERRY SCOTT and JIMBORGMAN

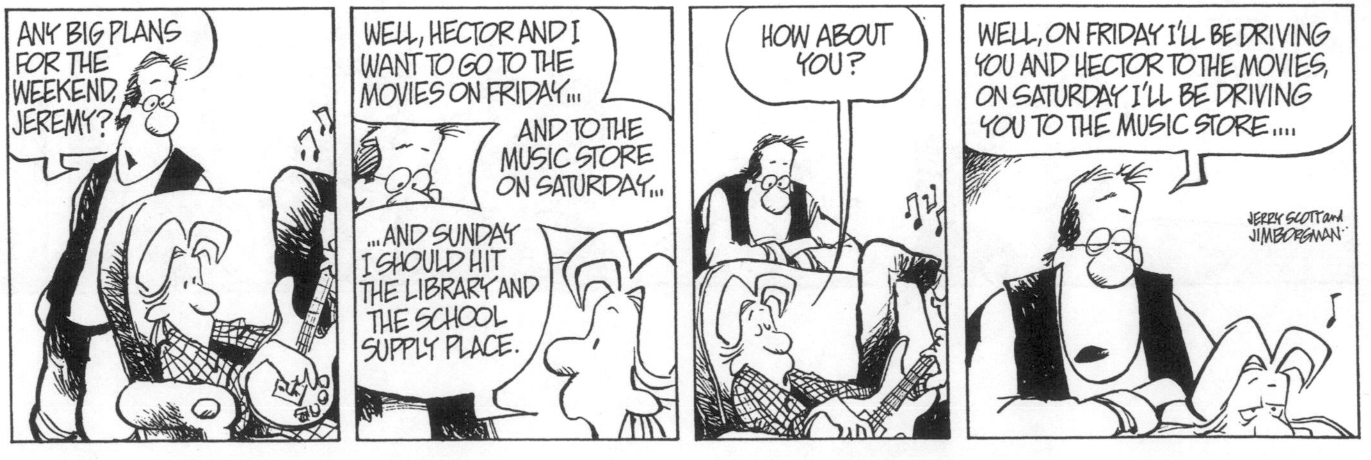
ANY BIG PLANS FOR THE WEEKEND, JEREMY?
WELL, HECTOR AND I WANT TO GO TO THE MOVIES ON FRIDAY...
AND TO THE MUSIC STORE ON SATURDAY...
...AND SUNDAY I SHOULD HIT THE LIBRARY AND THE SCHOOL SUPPLY PLACE.
HOW ABOUT YOU?
WELL, ON FRIDAY I'LL BE DRIVING YOU AND HECTOR TO THE MOVIES, ON SATURDAY I'LL BE DRIVING YOU TO THE MUSIC STORE....
JERRY SCOTT and JIMBORGMAN

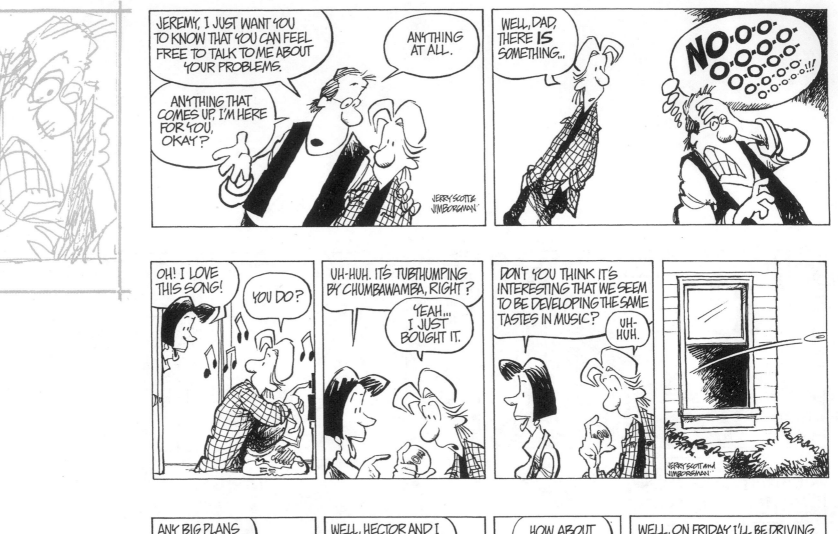

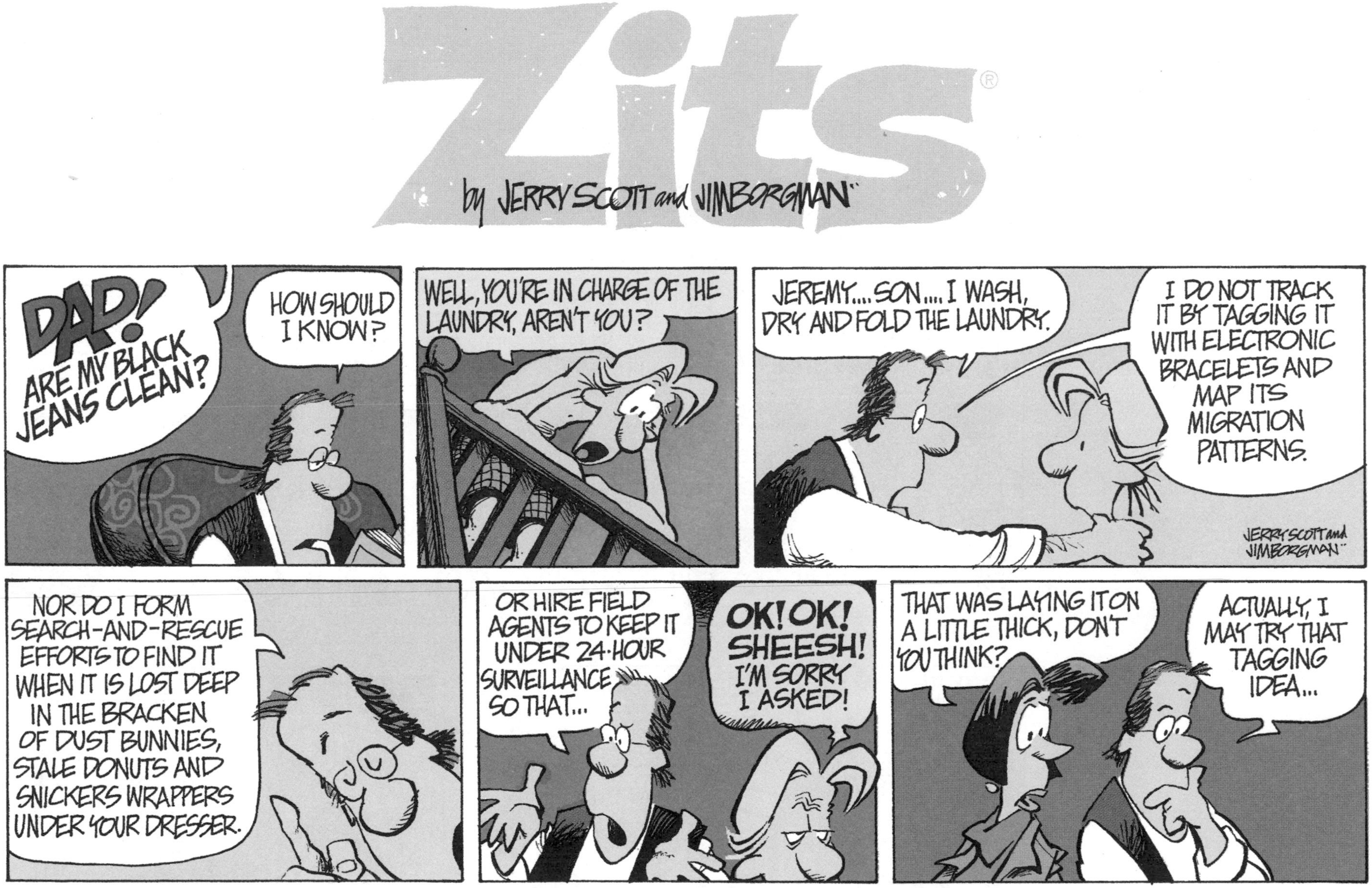
Zits
by JERRY SCOTT and JIM BORGMAN
DAD! ARE MY BLACK JEANS CLEAN?
HOW SHOULD I KNOW?
WELL, YOU'RE IN CHARGE OF THE LAUNDRY, AREN'T YOU?
JEREMY.... SON.... I WASH, DRY AND FOLD THE LAUNDRY.
I DO NOT TRACK IT BY TAGGING IT WITH ELECTRONIC BRACELETS AND MAP ITS MIGRATION PATTERNS.
JERRY SCOTT and JIM BORGMAN
NOR DO I FORM SEARCH-AND-RESCUE EFFORTS TO FIND IT WHEN IT IS LOST DEEP IN THE BRACKEN OF DUST BUNNIES, STALE DONUTS AND SNICKERS WRAPPERS UNDER YOUR DRESSER.
OR HIRE FIELD AGENTS TO KEEP IT UNDER 24-HOUR SURVEILLANCE SO THAT...
OK! OK! SHEESH! I'M SORRY I ASKED!
THAT WAS LAYING IT ON A LITTLE THICK, DON'T YOU THINK?
ACTUALLY, I MAY TRY THAT TAGGING IDEA...

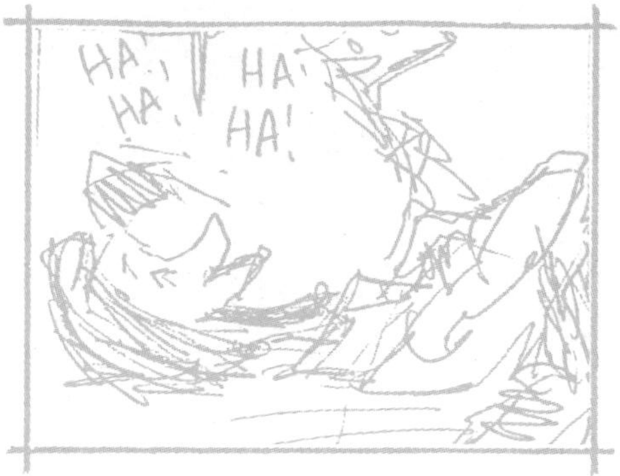

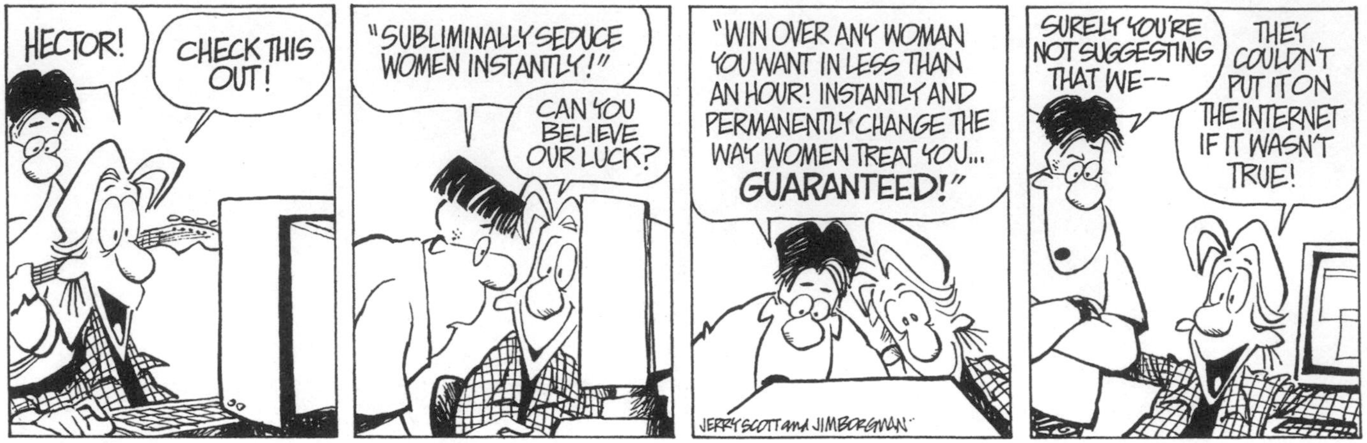

HECTOR!
CHECK THIS OUT!
"SUBLIMINALLY SEDUCE WOMEN INSTANTLY!"
CAN YOU BELIEVE OUR LUCK?
"WIN OVER ANY WOMAN YOU WANT IN LESS THAN AN HOUR! INSTANTLY AND PERMANENTLY CHANGE THE WAY WOMEN TREAT YOU... GUARANTEED!"
JERRY SCOTT and JIM BORGMAN
SURELY YOU'RE NOT SUGGESTING THAT WE--
THEY COULDN'T PUT IT ON THE INTERNET IF IT WASN'T TRUE!

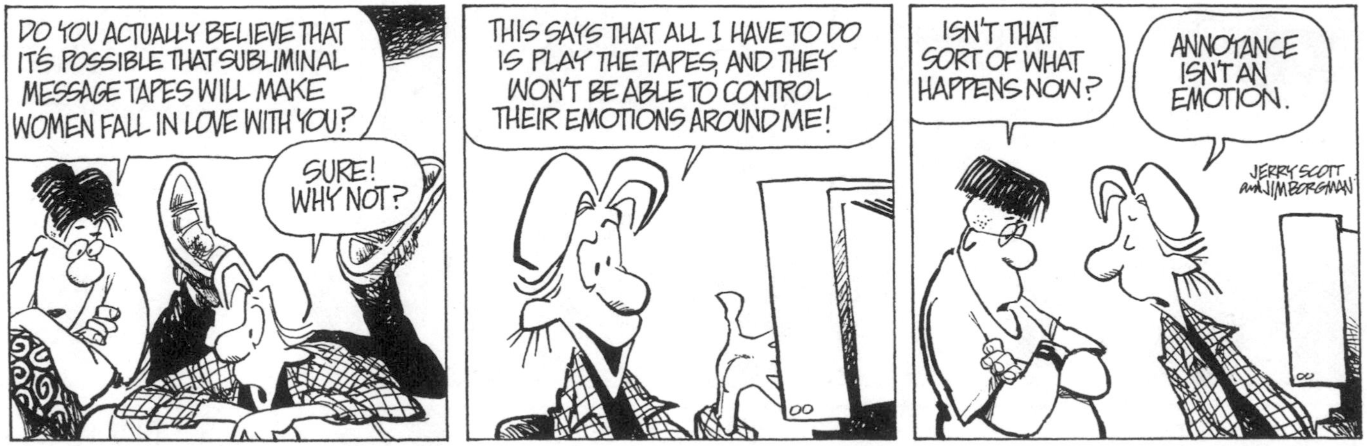

DO YOU ACTUALLY BELIEVE THAT IT'S POSSIBLE THAT SUBLIMINAL MESSAGE TAPES WILL MAKE WOMEN FALL IN LOVE WITH YOU?
SURE! WHY NOT?
THIS SAYS THAT ALL I HAVE TO DO IS PLAY THE TAPES, AND THEY WON'T BE ABLE TO CONTROL THEIR EMOTIONS AROUND ME!
ISN'T THAT SORT OF WHAT HAPPENS NOW?
ANNOYANCE ISN'T AN EMOTION.
JERRY SCOTT and JIM BORGMAN

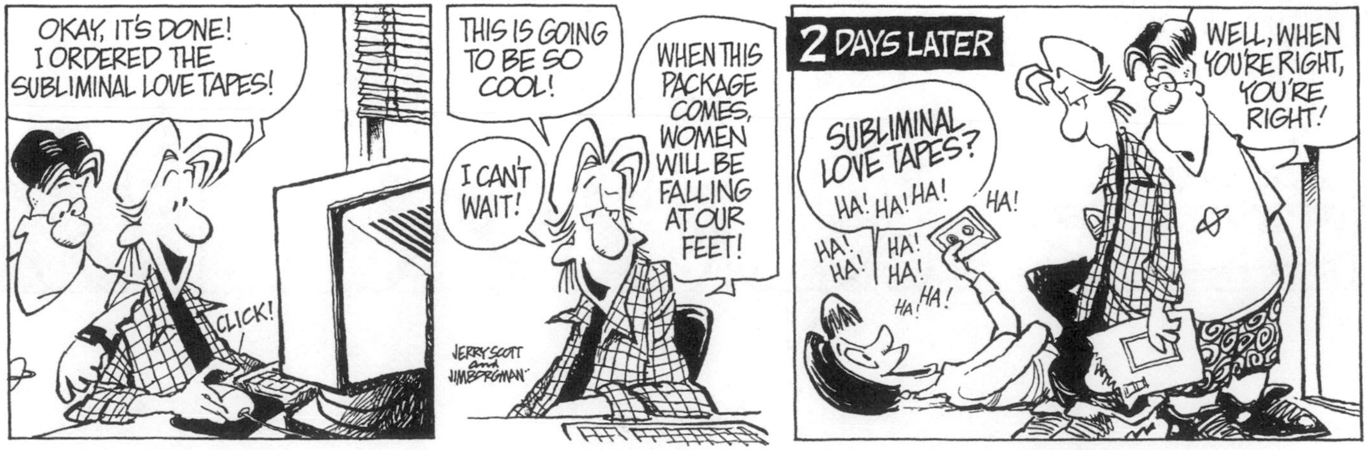

OKAY, IT'S DONE! I ORDERED THE SUBLIMINAL LOVE TAPES!
CLICK!
THIS IS GOING TO BE SO COOL!
I CAN'T WAIT!
WHEN THIS PACKAGE COMES, WOMEN WILL BE FALLING AT OUR FEET!
JERRY SCOTT and JIM BORGMAN
2 DAYS LATER
SUBLIMINAL LOVE TAPES? HA! HA! HA! HA! HA! HA! HA! HA! HA! HA! HA!
WELL, WHEN YOU'RE RIGHT, YOU'RE RIGHT!

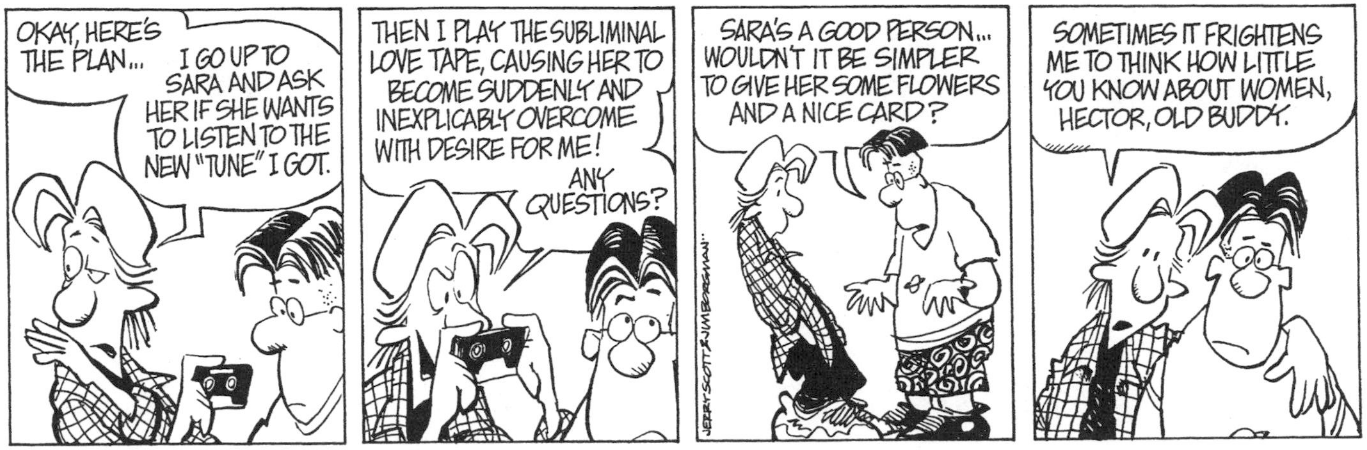
OKAY, HERE'S THE PLAN...
I GO UP TO SARA AND ASK HER IF SHE WANTS TO LISTEN TO THE NEW "TUNE" I GOT.
THEN I PLAY THE SUBLIMINAL LOVE TAPE, CAUSING HER TO BECOME SUDDENLY AND INEXPLICABLY OVERCOME WITH DESIRE FOR ME!
ANY QUESTIONS?
SARA'S A GOOD PERSON... WOULDN'T IT BE SIMPLER TO GIVE HER SOME FLOWERS AND A NICE CARD?
SOMETIMES IT FRIGHTENS ME TO THINK HOW LITTLE YOU KNOW ABOUT WOMEN, HECTOR, OLD BUDDY.

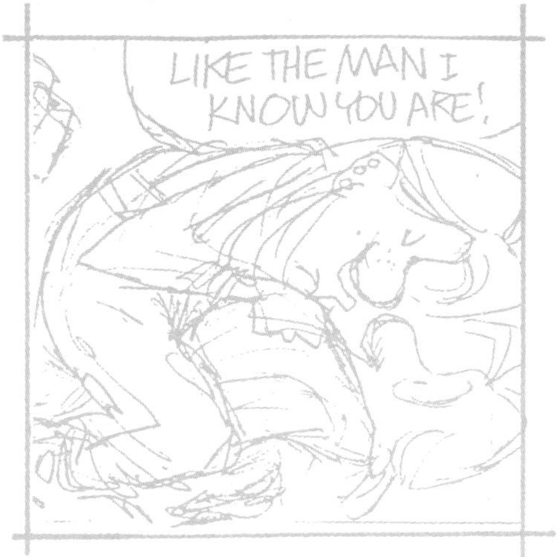
LIKE THE MAN I KNOW YOU ARE!

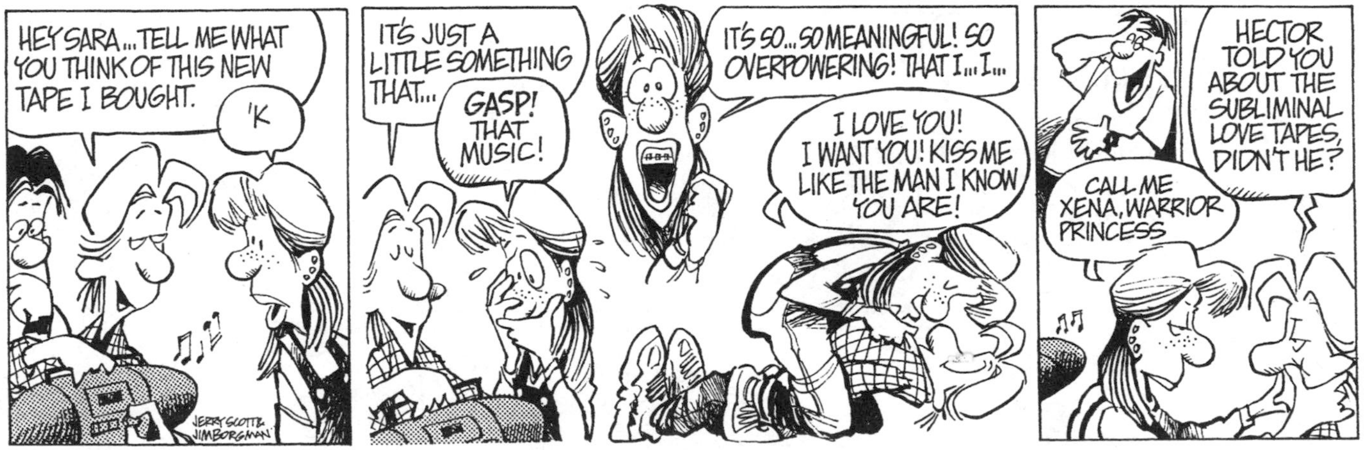
HEY SARA... TELL ME WHAT YOU THINK OF THIS NEW TAPE I BOUGHT.
'K
IT'S JUST A LITTLE SOMETHING THAT...
GASP! THAT MUSIC!
IT'S SO... SO MEANINGFUL! SO OVERPOWERING! THAT I... I...
I LOVE YOU! I WANT YOU! KISS ME LIKE THE MAN I KNOW YOU ARE!
HECTOR TOLD YOU ABOUT THE SUBLIMINAL LOVE TAPES, DIDN'T HE?
CALL ME XENA, WARRIOR PRINCESS

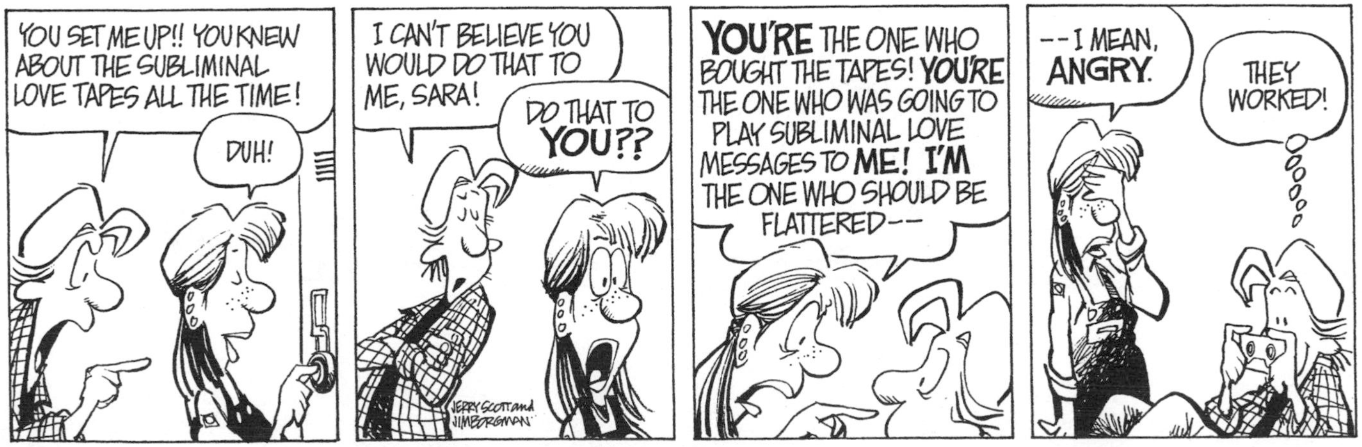
YOU SET ME UP!! YOU KNEW ABOUT THE SUBLIMINAL LOVE TAPES ALL THE TIME!
DUH!
I CAN'T BELIEVE YOU WOULD DO THAT TO ME, SARA!
DO THAT TO YOU??
YOU'RE THE ONE WHO BOUGHT THE TAPES! YOU'RE THE ONE WHO WAS GOING TO PLAY SUBLIMINAL LOVE MESSAGES TO ME! I'M THE ONE WHO SHOULD BE FLATTERED--
--I MEAN, ANGRY.
THEY WORKED!

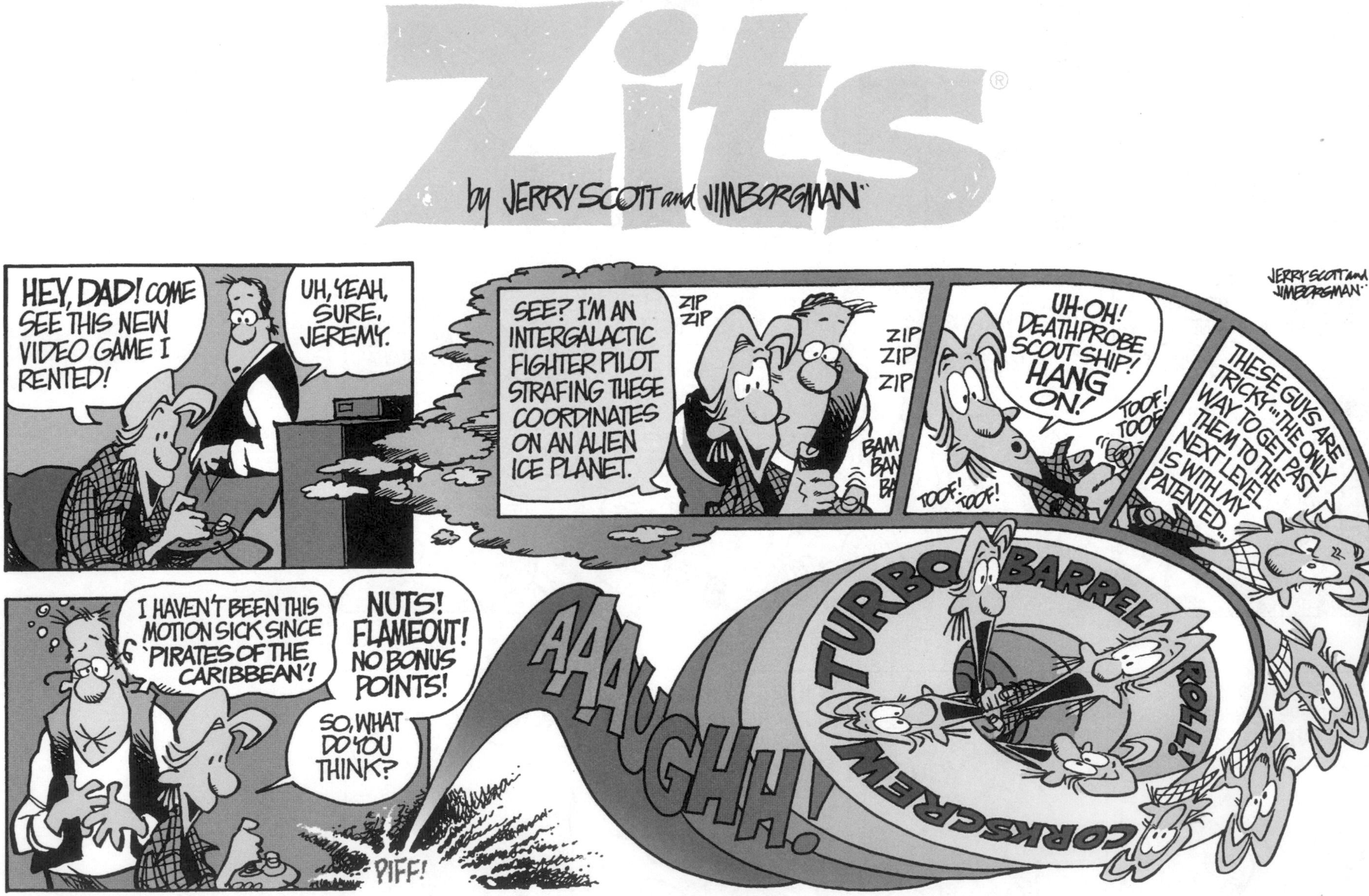
Zits®
by JERRY SCOTT and JIM BORGMAN
JERRY SCOTT and JIM BORGMAN
HEY, DAD! COME SEE THIS NEW VIDEO GAME I RENTED!
UH, YEAH, SURE, JEREMY.
SEE? I'M AN INTERGALACTIC FIGHTER PILOT STRAFING THESE COORDINATES ON AN ALIEN ICE PLANET.
ZIP ZIP
ZIP ZIP ZIP
BAM BAM BA
UH-OH! DEATHPROBE SCOUT SHIP! HANG ON!
TOOF! TOOF!
TOOF! TOOF!
THESE GUYS ARE TRICKY... THE ONLY WAY TO GET PAST THEM TO THE NEXT LEVEL IS WITH MY PATENTED...
TURBO BARREL ROLL!
CORKSCREW
AAAUGHH!
PIFF!
I HAVEN'T BEEN THIS MOTION SICK SINCE 'PIRATES OF THE CARIBBEAN'!
NUTS! FLAMEOUT! NO BONUS POINTS!
SO, WHAT DO YOU THINK?

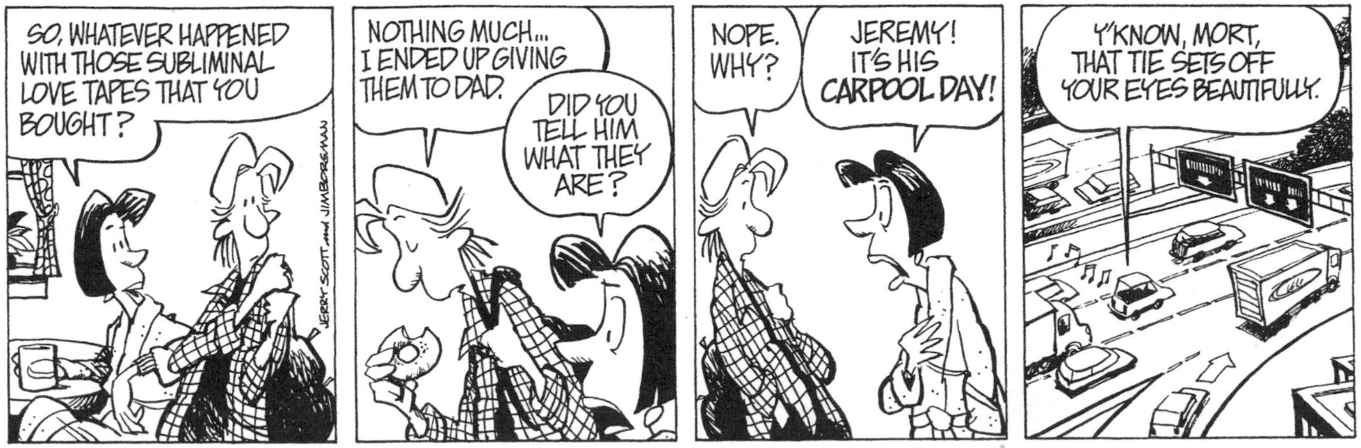
SO, WHATEVER HAPPENED WITH THOSE SUBLIMINAL LOVE TAPES THAT YOU BOUGHT?
JERRY SCOTT and JIM BORGMAN
NOTHING MUCH... I ENDED UP GIVING THEM TO DAD.
DID YOU TELL HIM WHAT THEY ARE?
NOPE. WHY?
JEREMY! IT'S HIS CARPOOL DAY!
Y'KNOW, MORT, THAT TIE SETS OFF YOUR EYES BEAUTIFULLY.

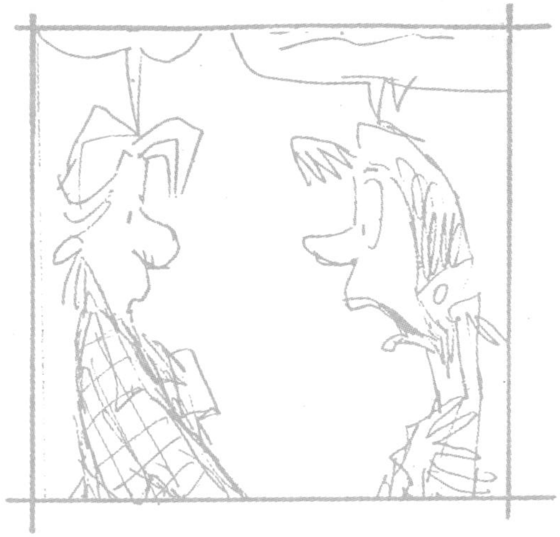

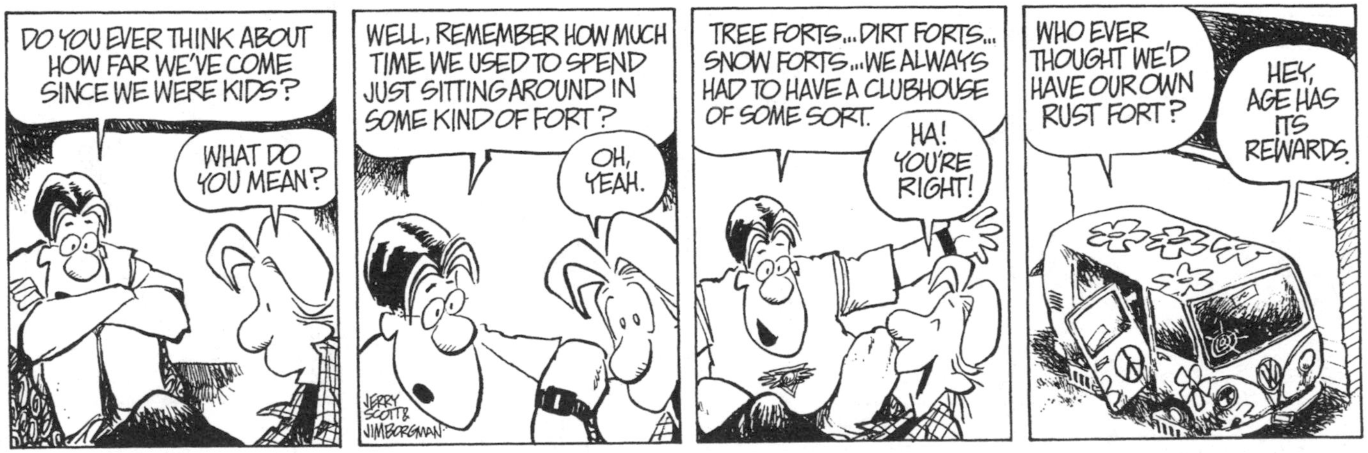
DO YOU EVER THINK ABOUT HOW FAR WE'VE COME SINCE WE WERE KIDS?
WHAT DO YOU MEAN?
WELL, REMEMBER HOW MUCH TIME WE USED TO SPEND JUST SITTING AROUND IN SOME KIND OF FORT?
OH, YEAH.
JERRY SCOTT & JIM BORGMAN
TREE FORTS... DIRT FORTS... SNOW FORTS... WE ALWAYS HAD TO HAVE A CLUBHOUSE OF SOME SORT.
HA! YOU'RE RIGHT!
WHO EVER THOUGHT WE'D HAVE OUR OWN RUST FORT?
HEY, AGE HAS ITS REWARDS.

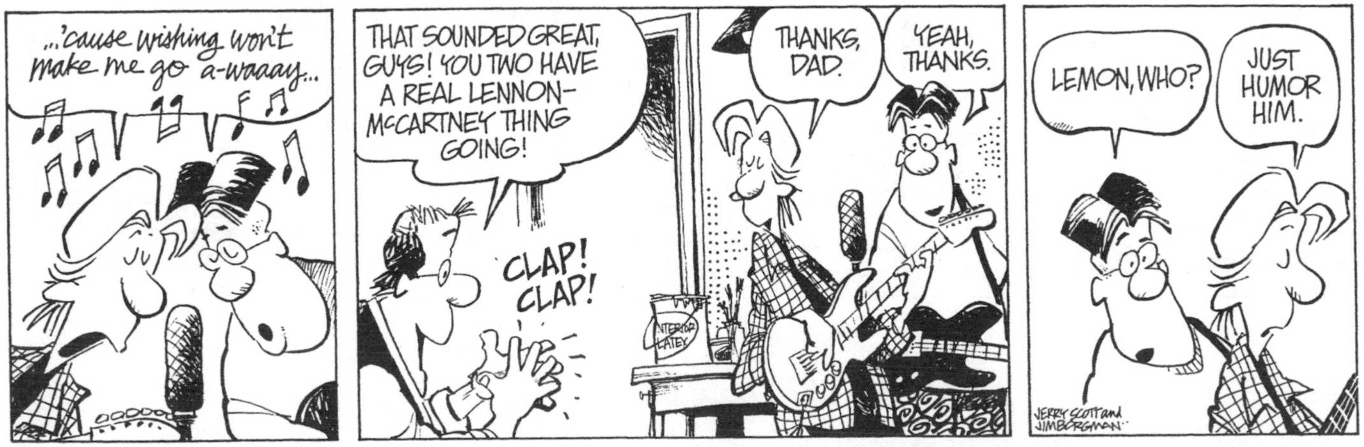
...'cause wishing won't make me go a-waaay...
THAT SOUNDED GREAT, GUYS! YOU TWO HAVE A REAL LENNON-McCARTNEY THING GOING!
CLAP! CLAP!
INTERIOR LATEX
THANKS, DAD.
YEAH, THANKS.
LEMON, WHO?
JUST HUMOR HIM.
JERRY SCOTT and JIM BORGMAN

Zits

by JERRY SCOTT and JIMBORGMAN

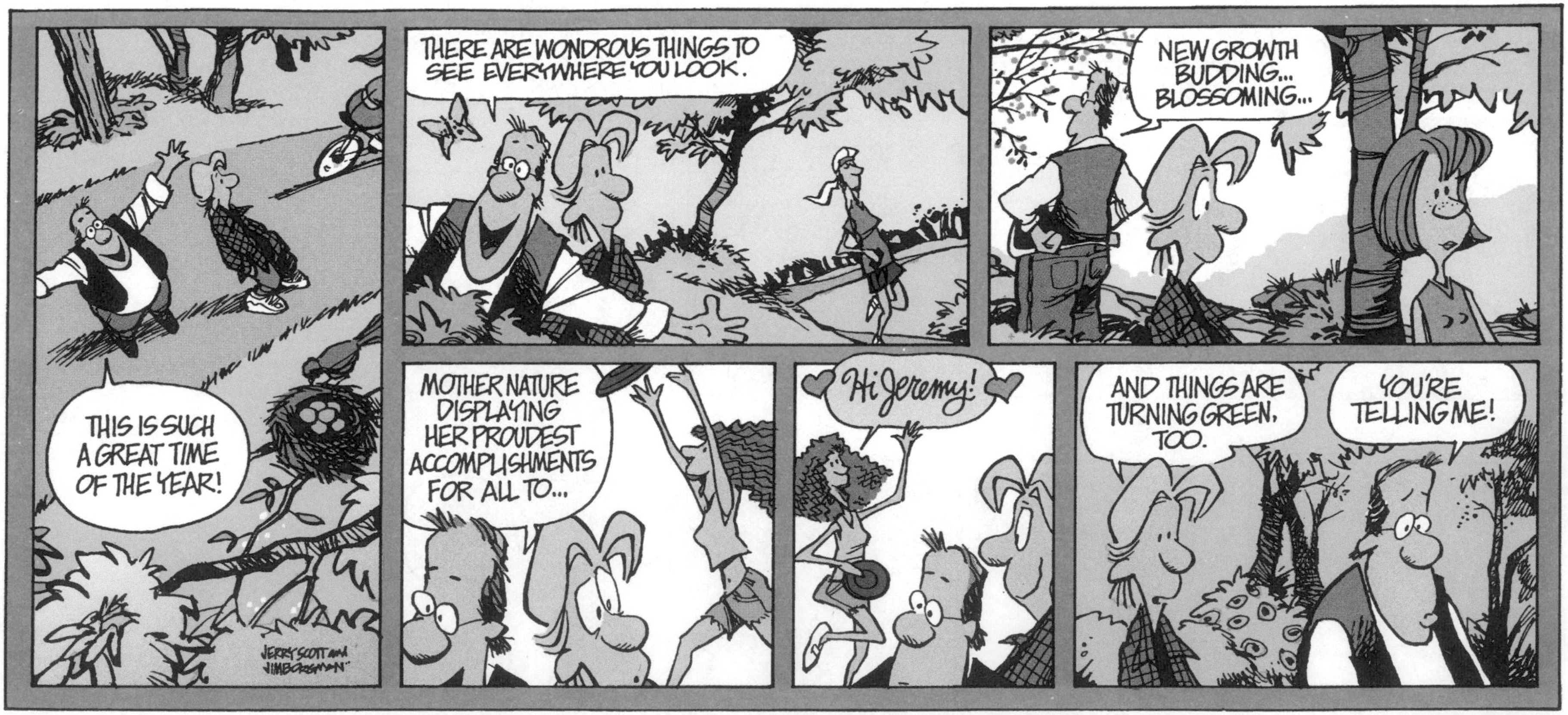

THIS IS SUCH A GREAT TIME OF THE YEAR!
JERRY SCOTT and JIMBORGMAN
THERE ARE WONDROUS THINGS TO SEE EVERYWHERE YOU LOOK.
NEW GROWTH BUDDING... BLOSSOMING...
MOTHER NATURE DISPLAYING HER PROUDEST ACCOMPLISHMENTS FOR ALL TO...
Hi Jeremy!
AND THINGS ARE TURNING GREEN, TOO.
YOU'RE TELLING ME!

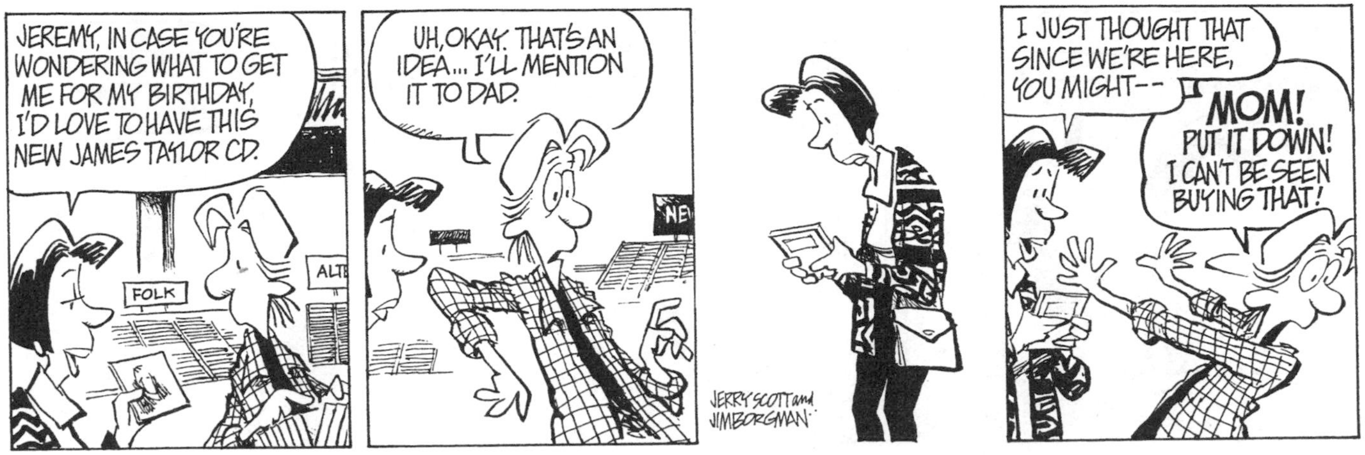
JEREMY, IN CASE YOU'RE WONDERING WHAT TO GET ME FOR MY BIRTHDAY, I'D LOVE TO HAVE THIS NEW JAMES TAYLOR CD.
FOLK
UH, OKAY. THAT'S AN IDEA... I'LL MENTION IT TO DAD.
JERRY SCOTT and JIM BORGMAN
I JUST THOUGHT THAT SINCE WE'RE HERE, YOU MIGHT--
MOM! PUT IT DOWN! I CAN'T BE SEEN BUYING THAT!

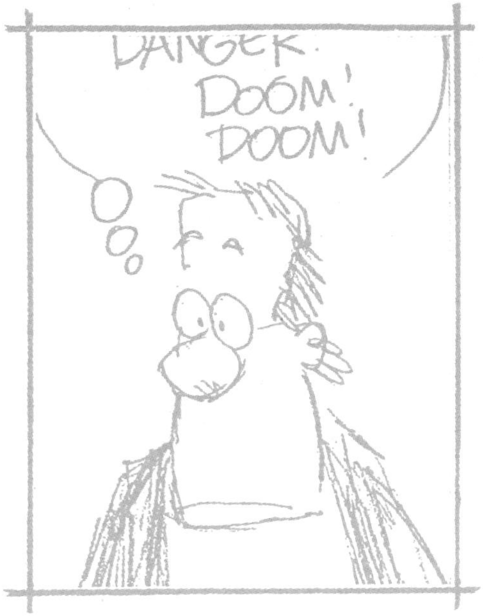
DOOM! DOOM!

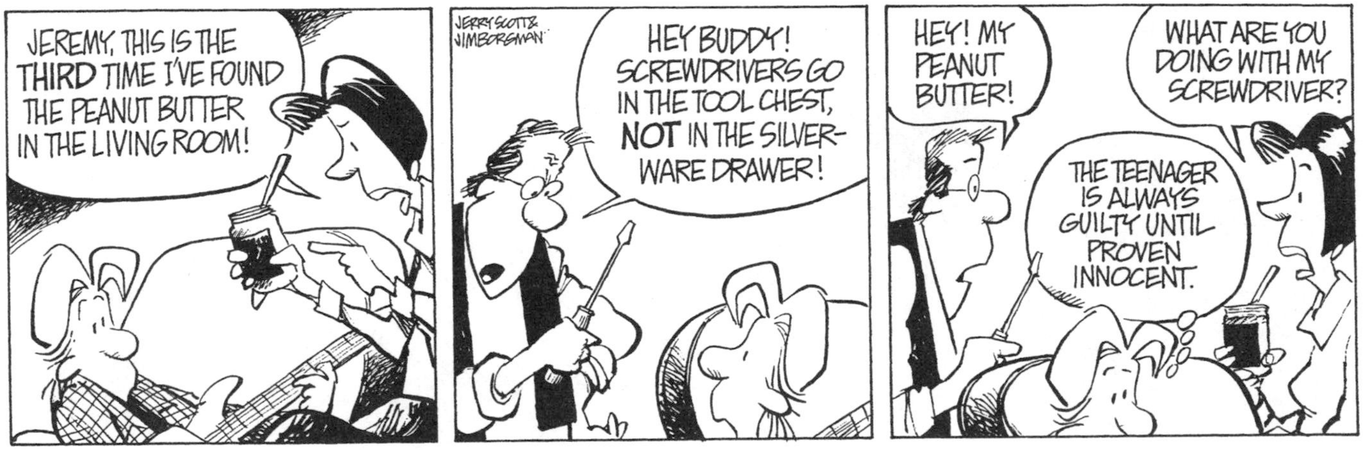
JEREMY, THIS IS THE THIRD TIME I'VE FOUND THE PEANUT BUTTER IN THE LIVING ROOM!
JERRY SCOTT & JIM BORGMAN
HEY BUDDY! SCREWDRIVERS GO IN THE TOOL CHEST, NOT IN THE SILVERWARE DRAWER!
HEY! MY PEANUT BUTTER!
WHAT ARE YOU DOING WITH MY SCREWDRIVER?
THE TEENAGER IS ALWAYS GUILTY UNTIL PROVEN INNOCENT.

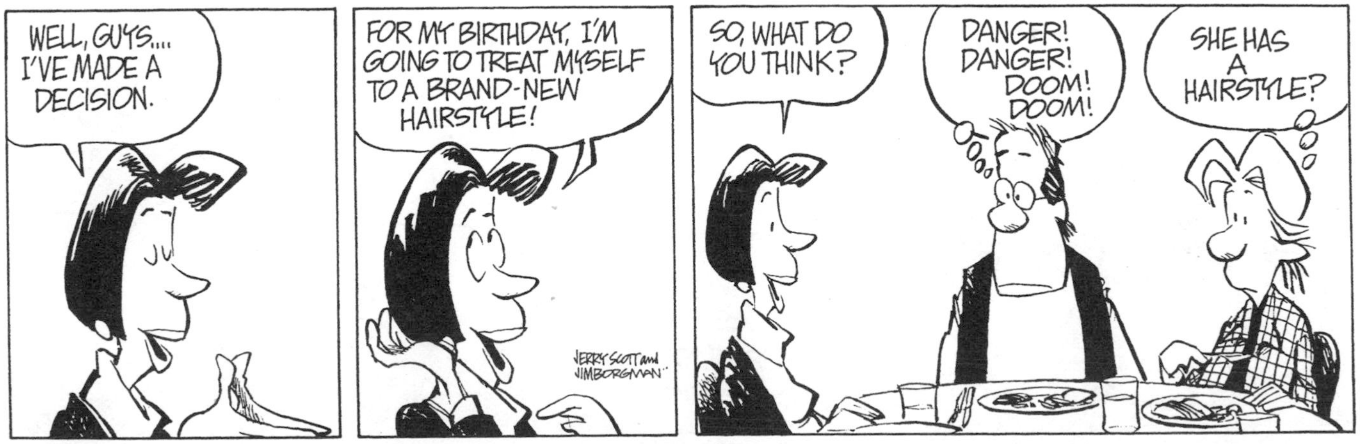
WELL, GUYS.... I'VE MADE A DECISION.
FOR MY BIRTHDAY, I'M GOING TO TREAT MYSELF TO A BRAND-NEW HAIRSTYLE!
JERRY SCOTT and JIM BORGMAN
SO, WHAT DO YOU THINK?
DANGER! DANGER! DOOM! DOOM!
SHE HAS A HAIRSTYLE?

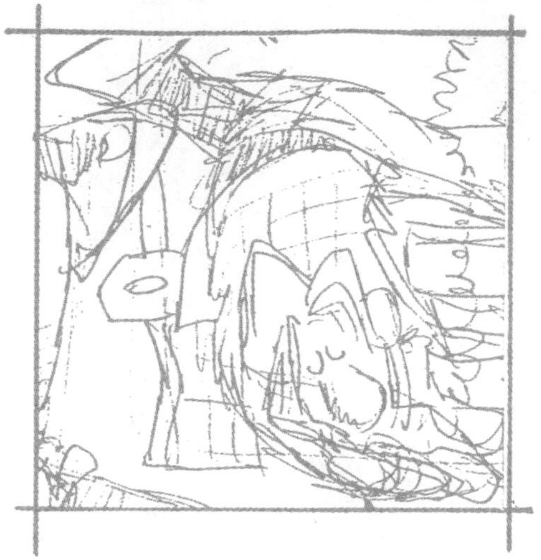

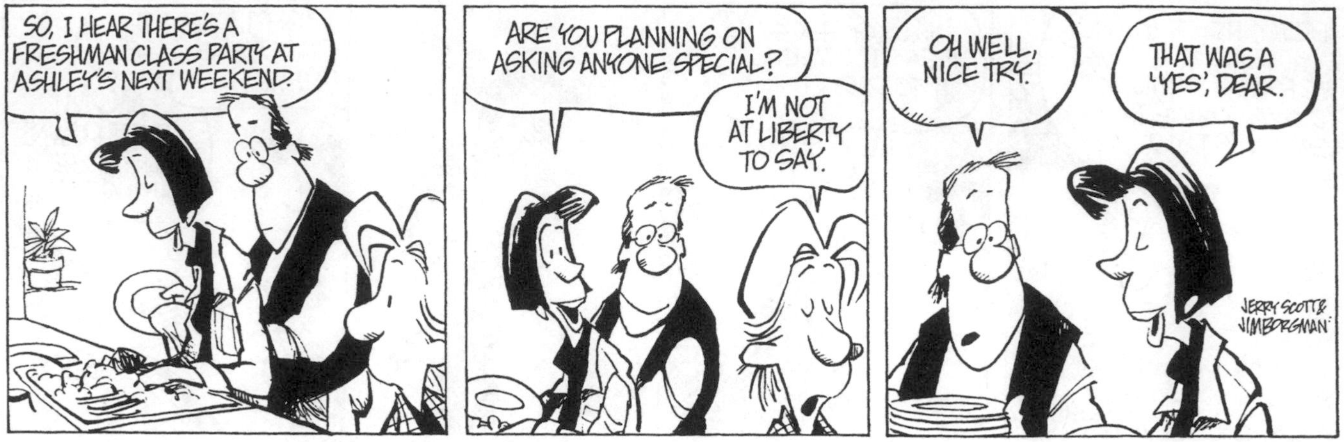

SO, I HEAR THERE'S A FRESHMAN CLASS PARTY AT ASHLEY'S NEXT WEEKEND.
ARE YOU PLANNING ON ASKING ANYONE SPECIAL?
I'M NOT AT LIBERTY TO SAY.
OH WELL, NICE TRY.
THAT WAS A 'YES', DEAR.
JERRY SCOTT & JIMBORGMAN

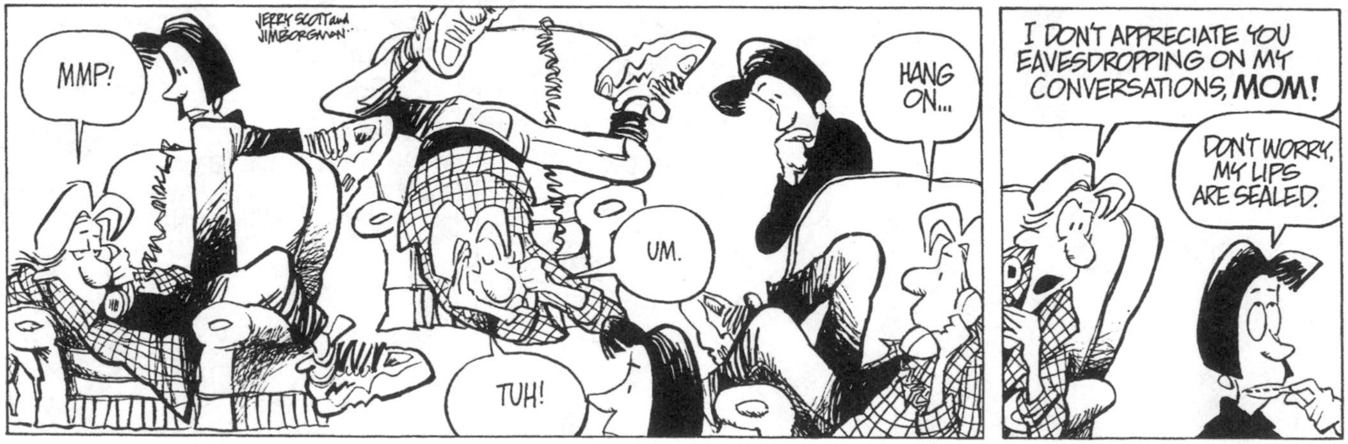

JERRY SCOTT and JIMBORGMAN
MMP!
HANG ON...
UM.
TUH!
I DON'T APPRECIATE YOU EAVESDROPPING ON MY CONVERSATIONS, MOM!
DON'T WORRY, MY LIPS ARE SEALED.

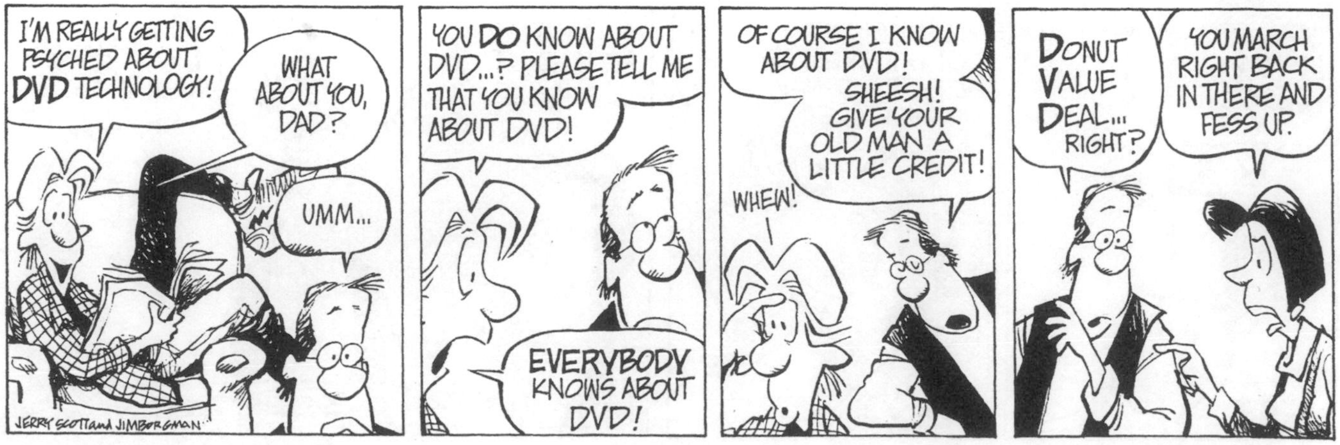

I'M REALLY GETTING PSYCHED ABOUT DVD TECHNOLOGY!
WHAT ABOUT YOU, DAD?
UMM...
JERRY SCOTT and JIMBORGMAN
YOU DO KNOW ABOUT DVD...? PLEASE TELL ME THAT YOU KNOW ABOUT DVD!
EVERYBODY KNOWS ABOUT DVD!
OF COURSE I KNOW ABOUT DVD!
SHEESH! GIVE YOUR OLD MAN A LITTLE CREDIT!
WHEW!
DONUT VALUE DEAL... RIGHT?
YOU MARCH RIGHT BACK IN THERE AND FESS UP.

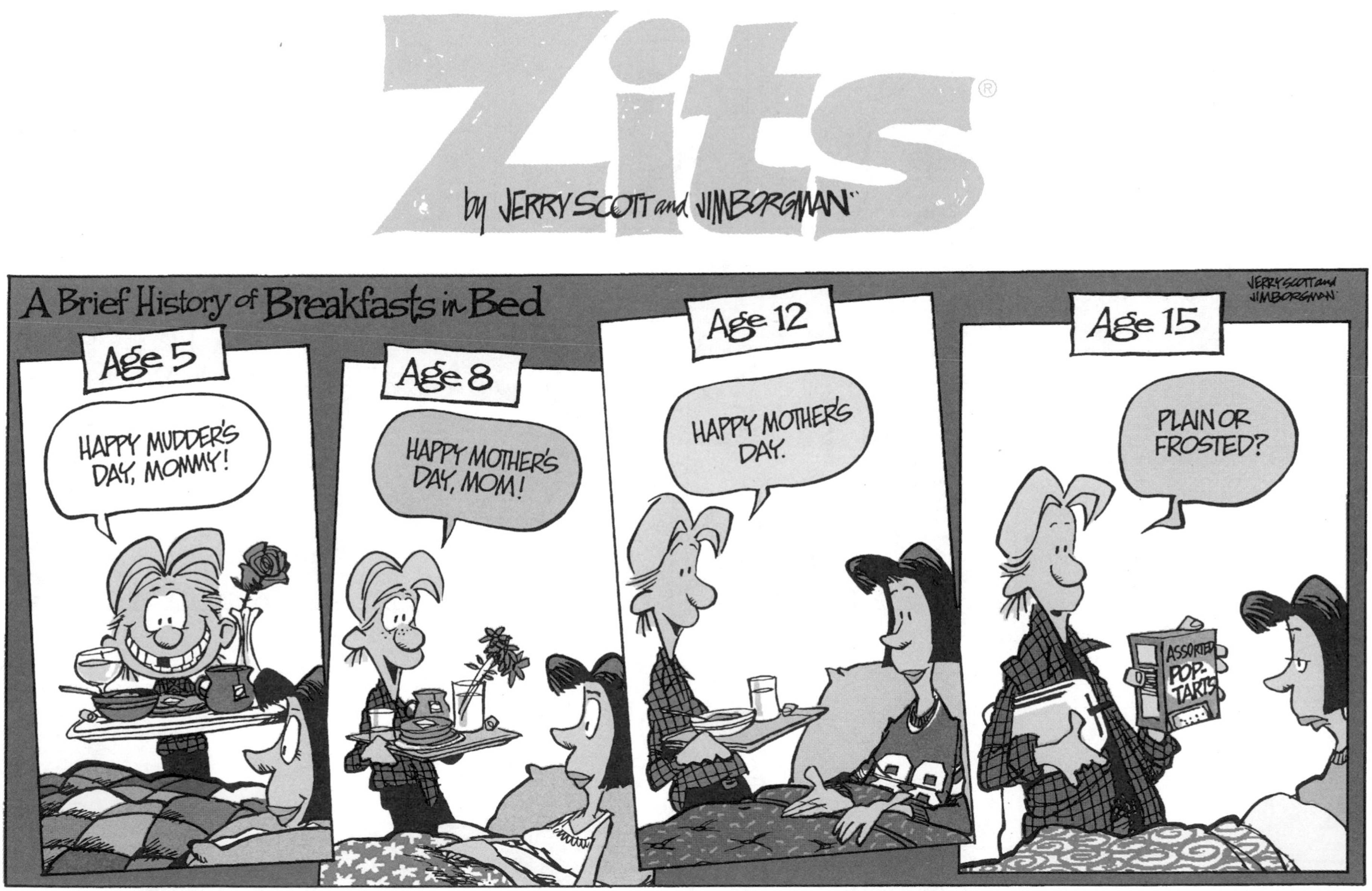
Zits
by JERRY SCOTT and JIM BORGMAN
A Brief History of Breakfasts in Bed
JERRY SCOTT and JIM BORGMAN
Age 5
HAPPY MUDDER'S DAY, MOMMY!
Age 8
HAPPY MOTHER'S DAY, MOM!
Age 12
HAPPY MOTHER'S DAY.
Age 15
PLAIN OR FROSTED?
ASSORTED POP-TARTS

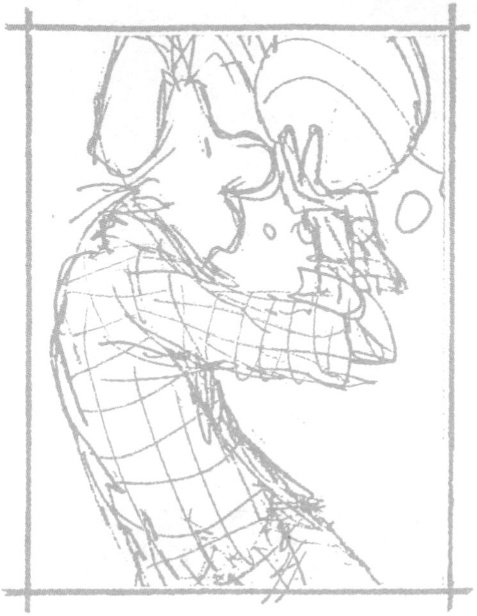

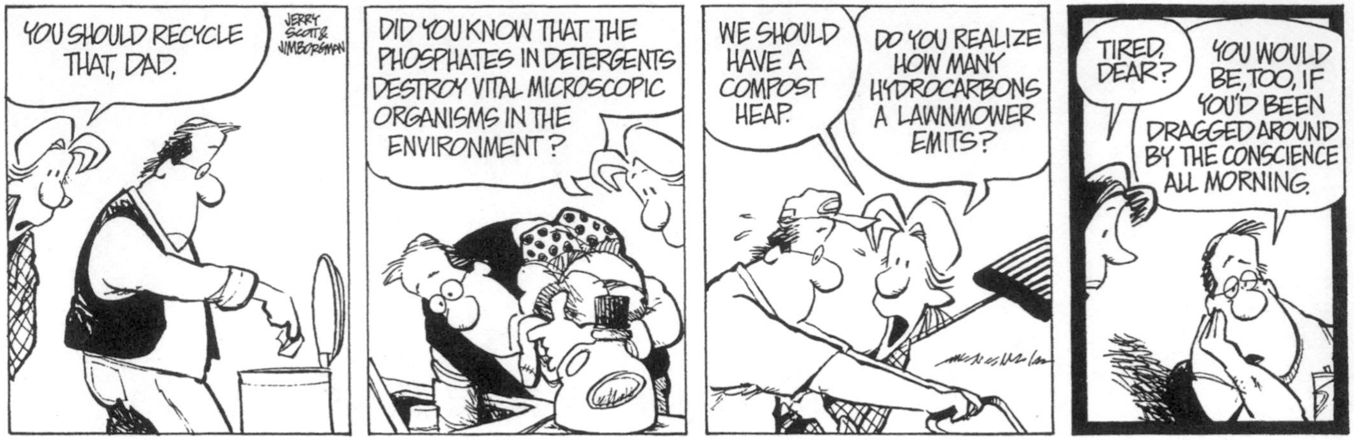

YOU SHOULD RECYCLE THAT, DAD.
JERRY SCOTT & JIM BORGMAN
DID YOU KNOW THAT THE PHOSPHATES IN DETERGENTS DESTROY VITAL MICROSCOPIC ORGANISMS IN THE ENVIRONMENT?
WE SHOULD HAVE A COMPOST HEAP.
DO YOU REALIZE HOW MANY HYDROCARBONS A LAWNMOWER EMITS?
TIRED, DEAR?
YOU WOULD BE, TOO, IF YOU'D BEEN DRAGGED AROUND BY THE CONSCIENCE ALL MORNING.

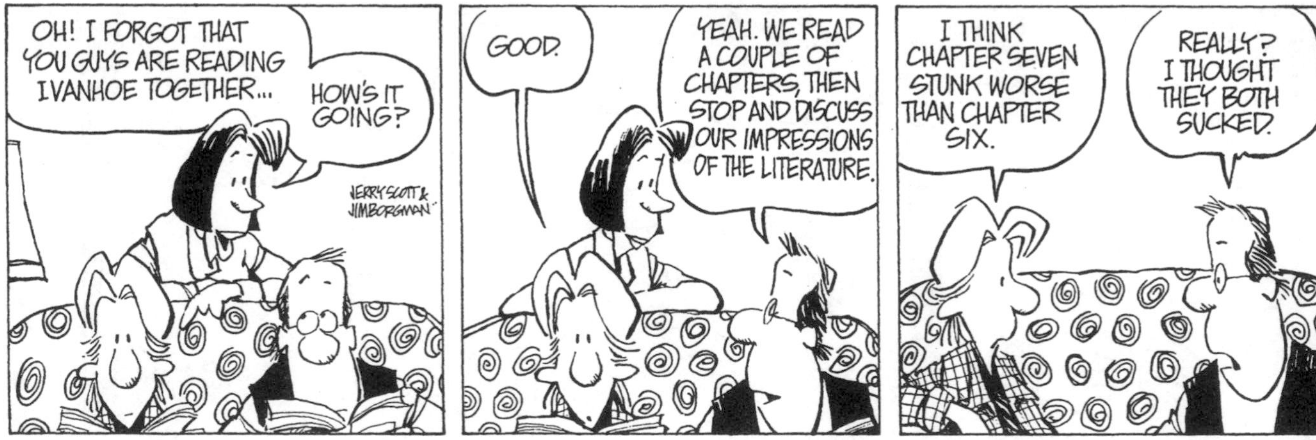

OH! I FORGOT THAT YOU GUYS ARE READING IVANHOE TOGETHER...
HOW'S IT GOING?
JERRY SCOTT & JIM BORGMAN
GOOD.
YEAH. WE READ A COUPLE OF CHAPTERS, THEN STOP AND DISCUSS OUR IMPRESSIONS OF THE LITERATURE.
I THINK CHAPTER SEVEN STUNK WORSE THAN CHAPTER SIX.
REALLY? I THOUGHT THEY BOTH SUCKED.

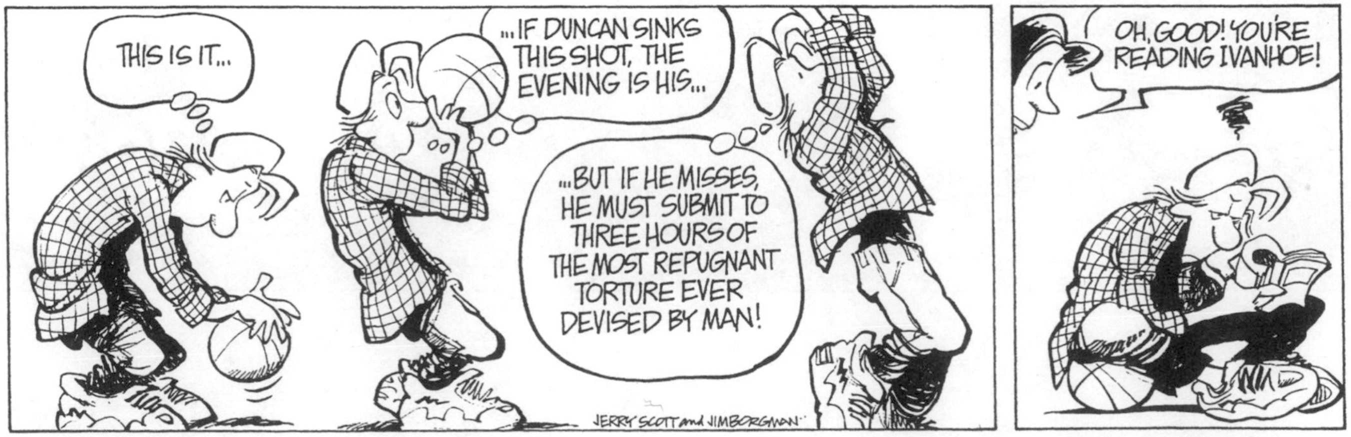

THIS IS IT...
...IF DUNCAN SINKS THIS SHOT, THE EVENING IS HIS...
...BUT IF HE MISSES, HE MUST SUBMIT TO THREE HOURS OF THE MOST REPUGNANT TORTURE EVER DEVISED BY MAN!
JERRY SCOTT and JIM BORGMAN
OH, GOOD! YOU'RE READING IVANHOE!

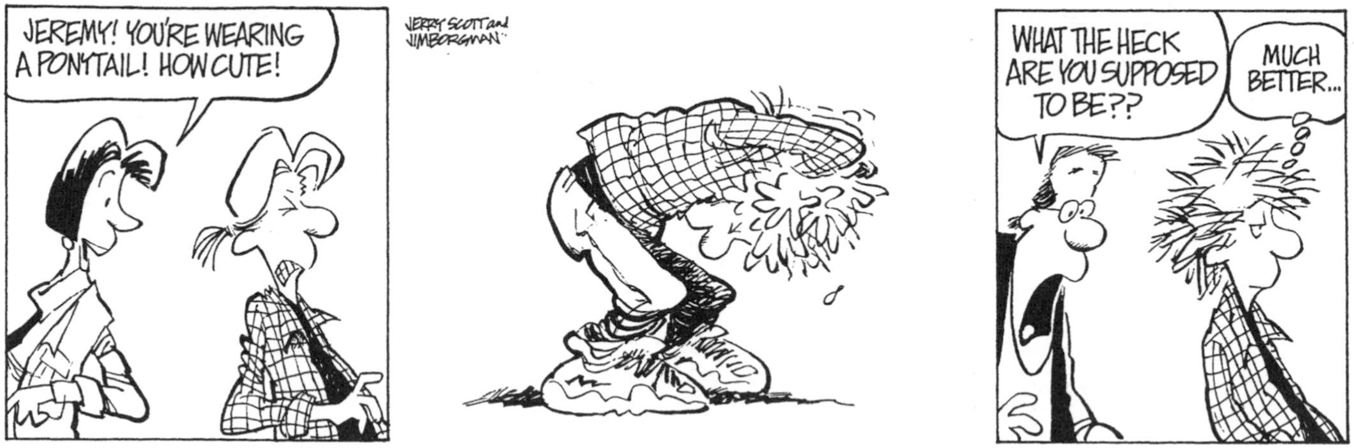
JEREMY! YOU'RE WEARING A PONYTAIL! HOW CUTE!
JERRY SCOTT and JIM BORGMAN
WHAT THE HECK ARE YOU SUPPOSED TO BE??
MUCH BETTER...

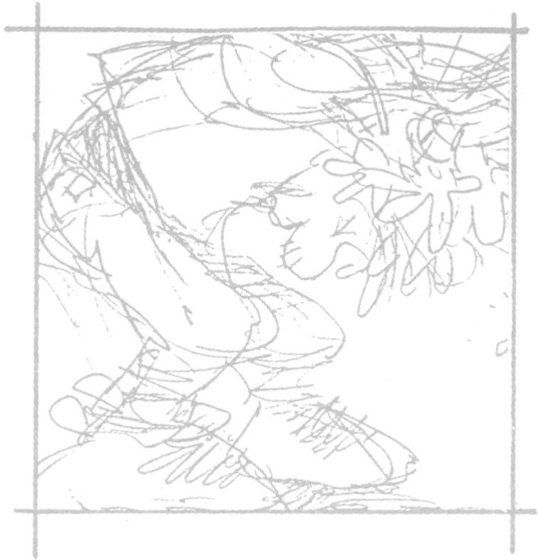

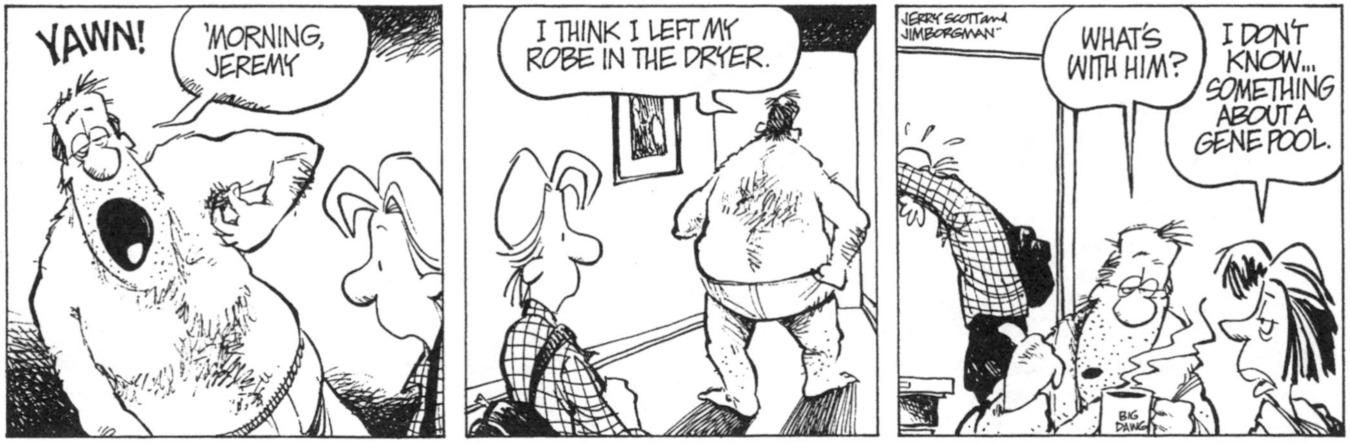
YAWN!
'MORNING, JEREMY
I THINK I LEFT MY ROBE IN THE DRYER.
JERRY SCOTT and JIM BORGMAN
WHAT'S WITH HIM?
I DON'T KNOW... SOMETHING ABOUT A GENE POOL.
BIG DAWG

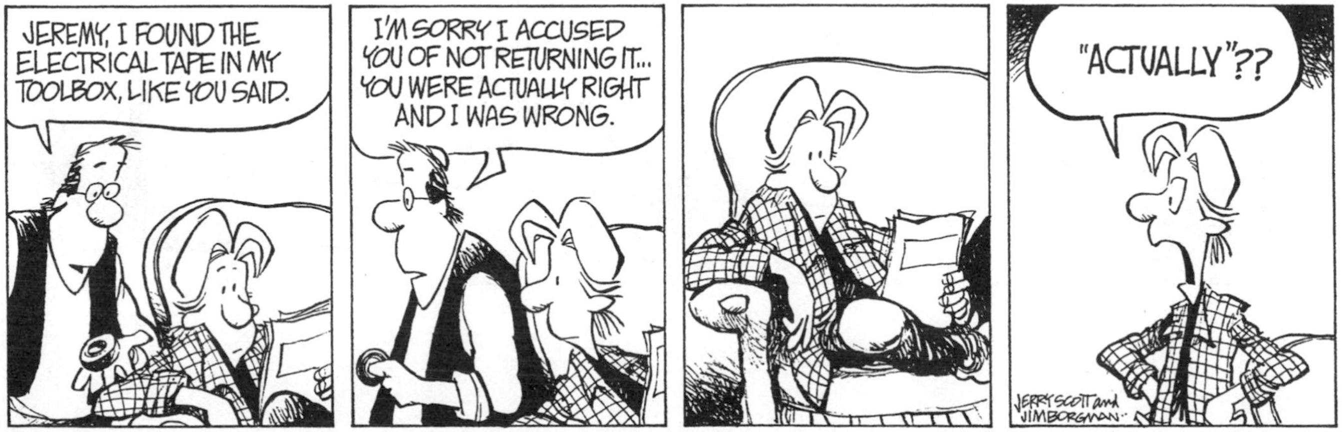
JEREMY, I FOUND THE ELECTRICAL TAPE IN MY TOOLBOX, LIKE YOU SAID.
I'M SORRY I ACCUSED YOU OF NOT RETURNING IT... YOU WERE ACTUALLY RIGHT AND I WAS WRONG.
"ACTUALLY"??
JERRY SCOTT and JIM BORGMAN

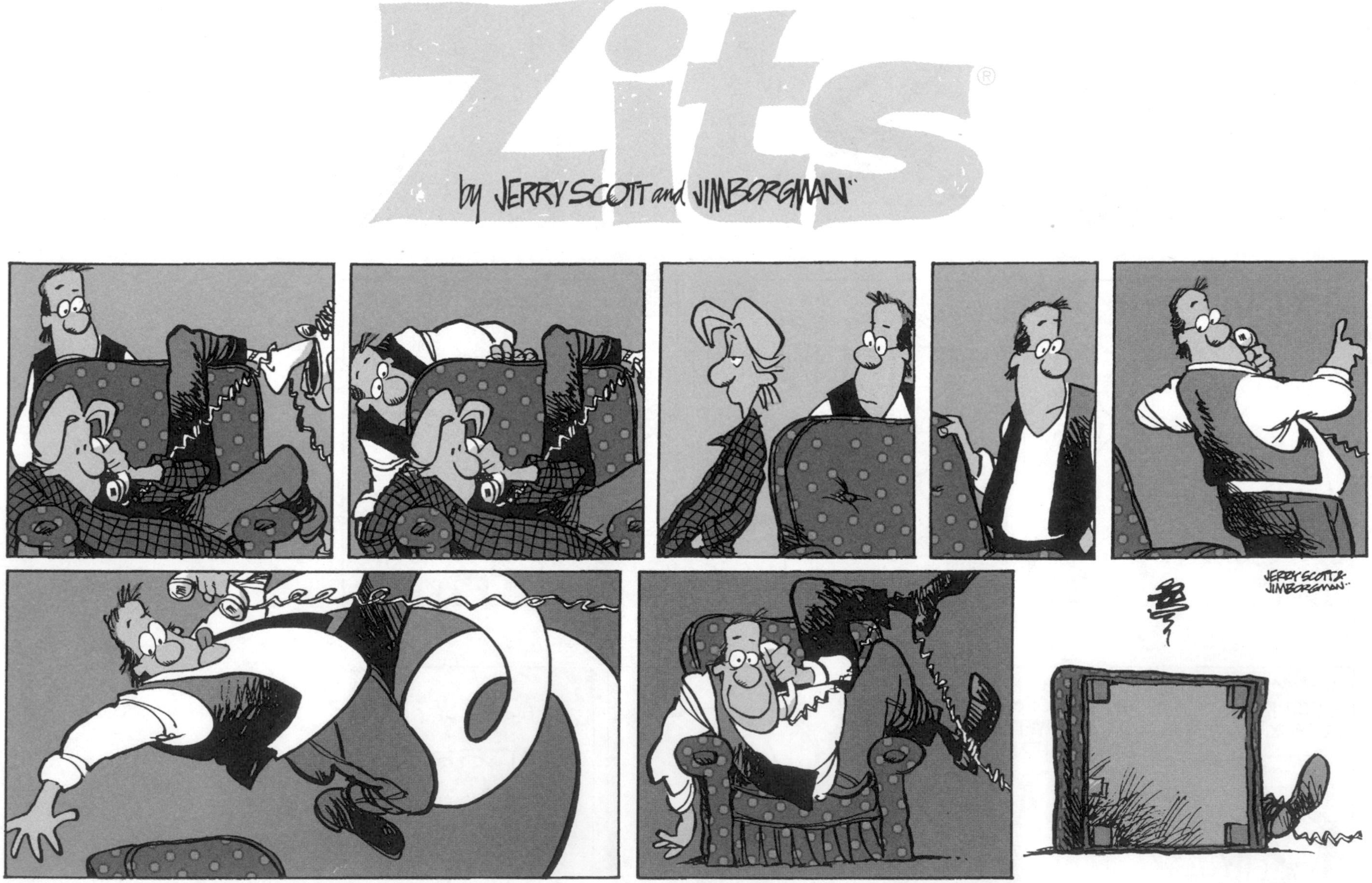
Zits®
by JERRY SCOTT and JIM BORGMAN
JERRY SCOTT & JIM BORGMAN

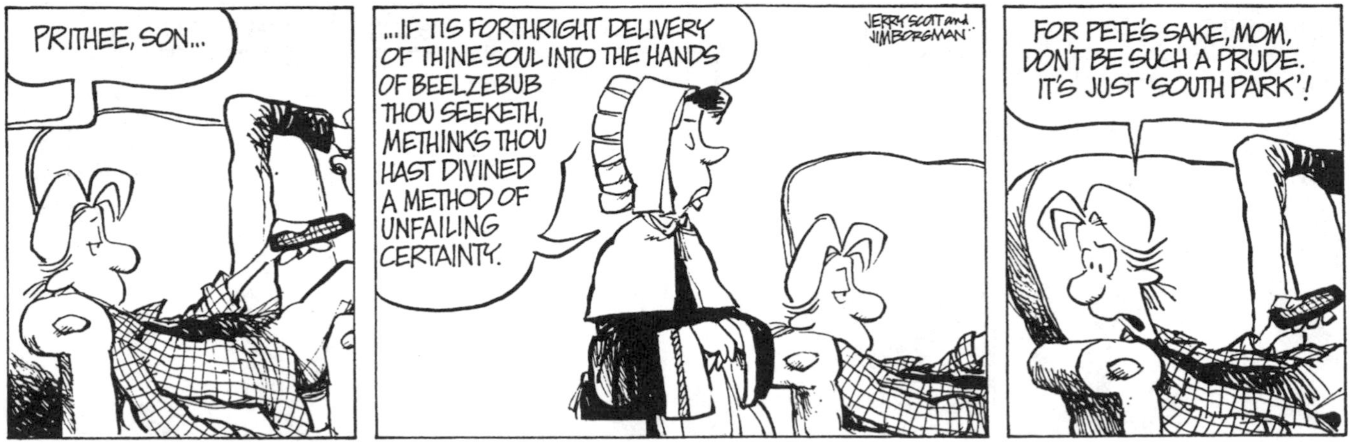
PRITHEE, SON...
...IF TIS FORTHRIGHT DELIVERY OF THINE SOUL INTO THE HANDS OF BEELZEBUB THOU SEEKETH, METHINKS THOU HAST DIVINED A METHOD OF UNFAILING CERTAINTY.
JERRY SCOTT and JIM BORGMAN
FOR PETE'S SAKE, MOM, DON'T BE SUCH A PRUDE. IT'S JUST 'SOUTH PARK'!

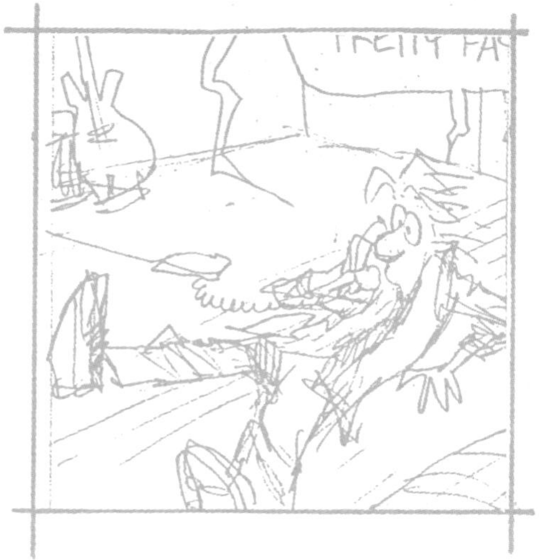

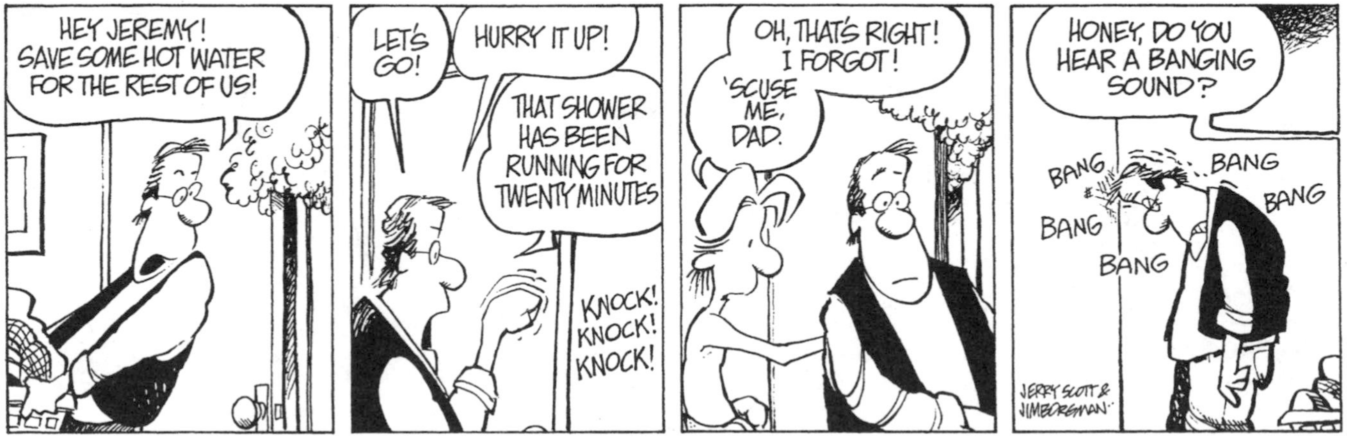
HEY JEREMY! SAVE SOME HOT WATER FOR THE REST OF US!
LET'S GO!
HURRY IT UP!
THAT SHOWER HAS BEEN RUNNING FOR TWENTY MINUTES
KNOCK! KNOCK! KNOCK!
OH, THAT'S RIGHT! I FORGOT!
'SCUSE ME, DAD.
HONEY, DO YOU HEAR A BANGING SOUND?
BANG BANG BANG BANG BANG
JERRY SCOTT & JIM BORGMAN

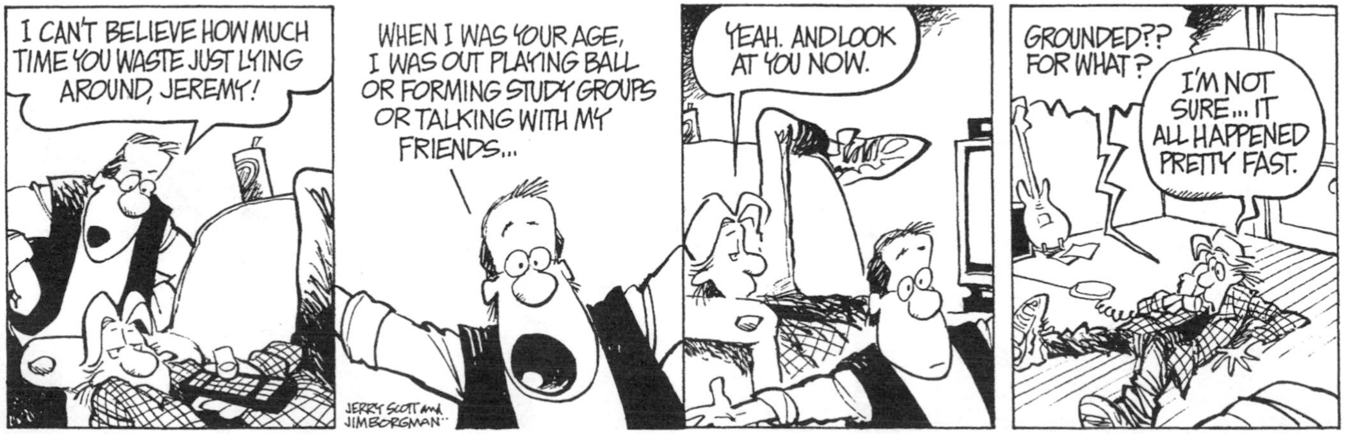
I CAN'T BELIEVE HOW MUCH TIME YOU WASTE JUST LYING AROUND, JEREMY!
WHEN I WAS YOUR AGE, I WAS OUT PLAYING BALL OR FORMING STUDY GROUPS OR TALKING WITH MY FRIENDS...
JERRY SCOTT and JIM BORGMAN
YEAH. AND LOOK AT YOU NOW.
GROUNDED?? FOR WHAT?
I'M NOT SURE... IT ALL HAPPENED PRETTY FAST.

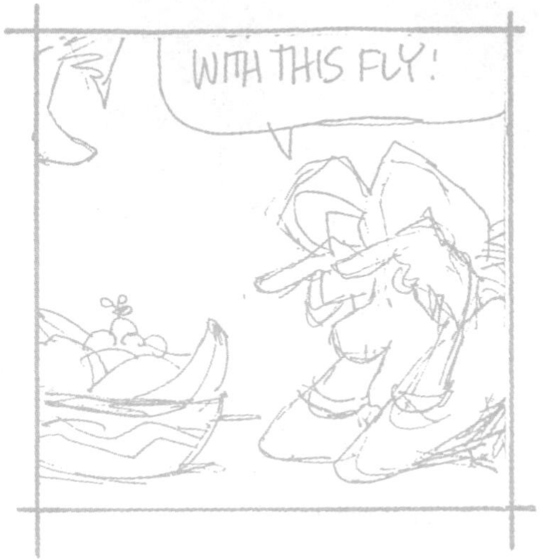
WITH THIS FLY!

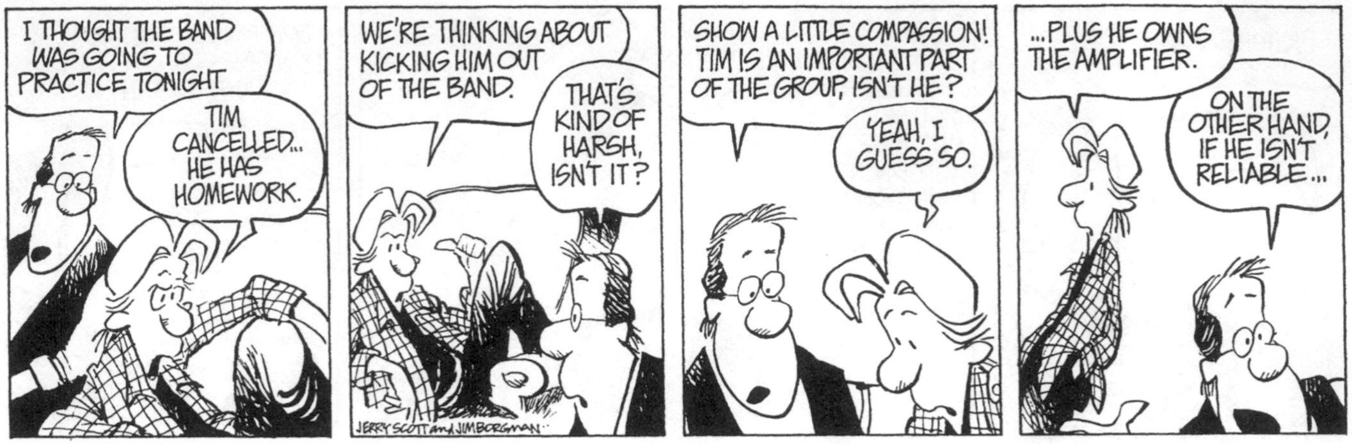
I THOUGHT THE BAND WAS GOING TO PRACTICE TONIGHT
TIM CANCELLED... HE HAS HOMEWORK.
WE'RE THINKING ABOUT KICKING HIM OUT OF THE BAND.
THAT'S KIND OF HARSH, ISN'T IT?
JERRY SCOTT and JIM BORGMAN
SHOW A LITTLE COMPASSION! TIM IS AN IMPORTANT PART OF THE GROUP, ISN'T HE?
YEAH, I GUESS SO.
...PLUS HE OWNS THE AMPLIFIER.
ON THE OTHER HAND, IF HE ISN'T RELIABLE...

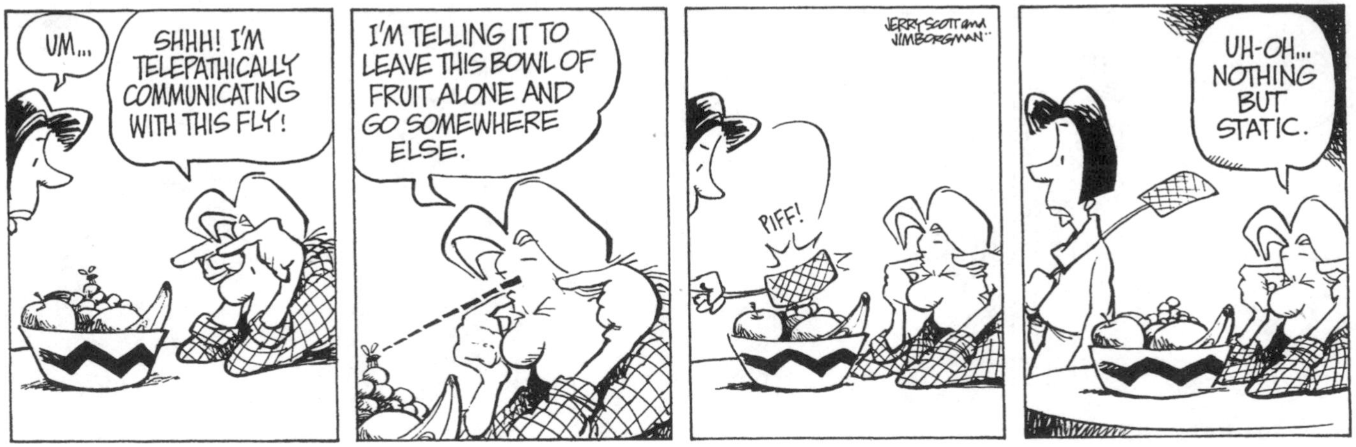
UM...
SHHH! I'M TELEPATHICALLY COMMUNICATING WITH THIS FLY!
I'M TELLING IT TO LEAVE THIS BOWL OF FRUIT ALONE AND GO SOMEWHERE ELSE.
JERRY SCOTT and JIM BORGMAN
PIFF!
UH-OH... NOTHING BUT STATIC.

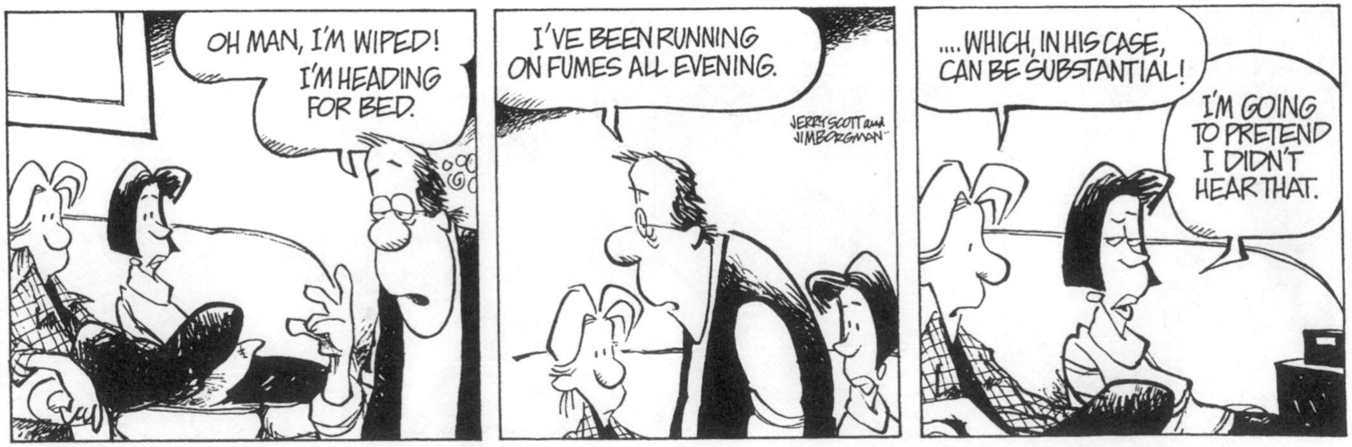
OH MAN, I'M WIPED! I'M HEADING FOR BED.
I'VE BEEN RUNNING ON FUMES ALL EVENING.
JERRY SCOTT and JIM BORGMAN
....WHICH, IN HIS CASE, CAN BE SUBSTANTIAL!
I'M GOING TO PRETEND I DIDN'T HEAR THAT.

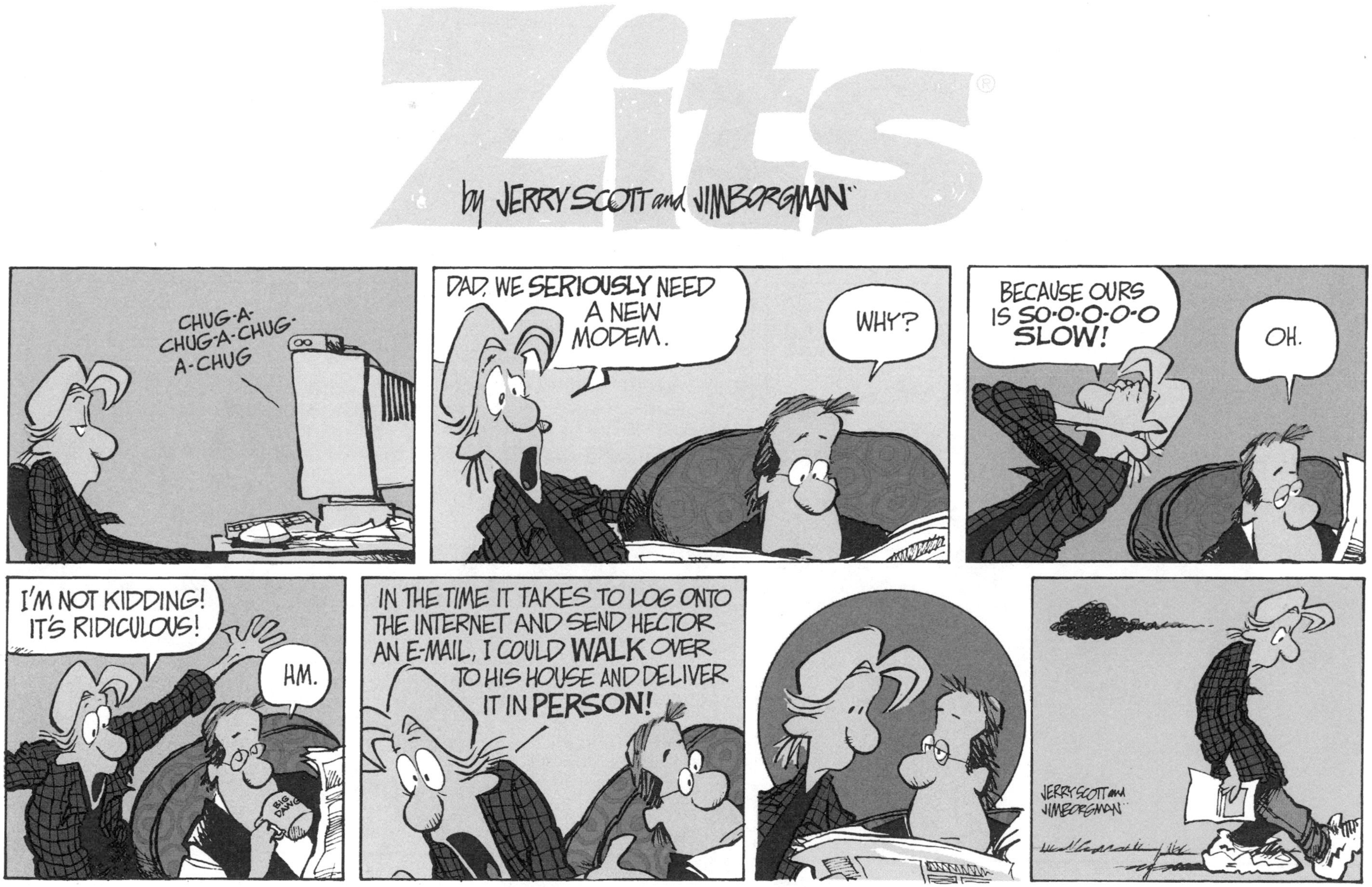
Zits®
by JERRY SCOTT and JIM BORGMAN
CHUG-A-CHUG-A-CHUG-A-CHUG
DAD, WE SERIOUSLY NEED A NEW MODEM.
WHY?
BECAUSE OURS IS SO-O-O-O-O-O SLOW!
OH.
I'M NOT KIDDING! IT'S RIDICULOUS!
HM.
IN THE TIME IT TAKES TO LOG ONTO THE INTERNET AND SEND HECTOR AN E-MAIL, I COULD WALK OVER TO HIS HOUSE AND DELIVER IT IN PERSON!

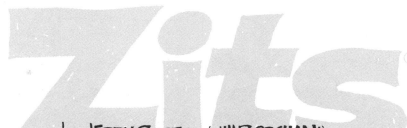

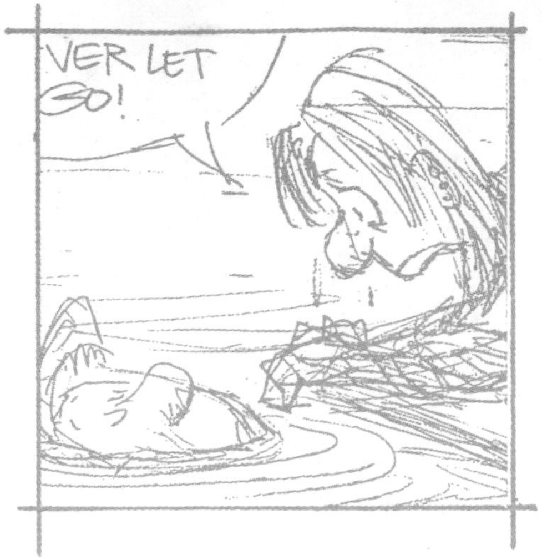
VER LET GO!

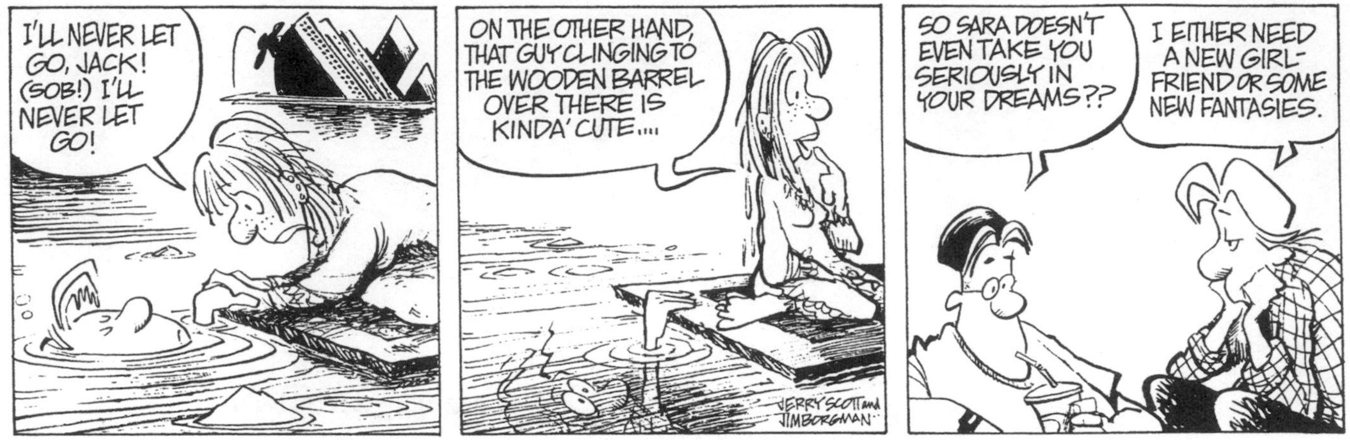
I'LL NEVER LET GO, JACK! (SOB!) I'LL NEVER LET GO!
ON THE OTHER HAND, THAT GUY CLINGING TO THE WOODEN BARREL OVER THERE IS KINDA' CUTE....
JERRY SCOTT and JIM BORGMAN
SO SARA DOESN'T EVEN TAKE YOU SERIOUSLY IN YOUR DREAMS??
I EITHER NEED A NEW GIRL-FRIEND OR SOME NEW FANTASIES.

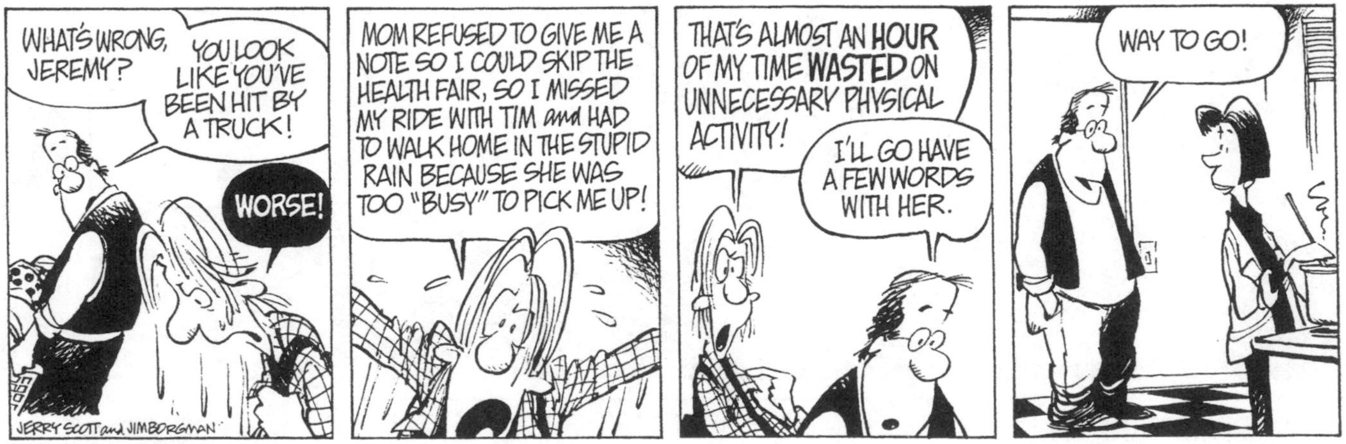
WHAT'S WRONG, JEREMY?
YOU LOOK LIKE YOU'VE BEEN HIT BY A TRUCK!
WORSE!
JERRY SCOTT and JIM BORGMAN
MOM REFUSED TO GIVE ME A NOTE SO I COULD SKIP THE HEALTH FAIR, SO I MISSED MY RIDE WITH TIM and HAD TO WALK HOME IN THE STUPID RAIN BECAUSE SHE WAS TOO "BUSY" TO PICK ME UP!
THAT'S ALMOST AN HOUR OF MY TIME WASTED ON UNNECESSARY PHYSICAL ACTIVITY!
I'LL GO HAVE A FEW WORDS WITH HER.
WAY TO GO!

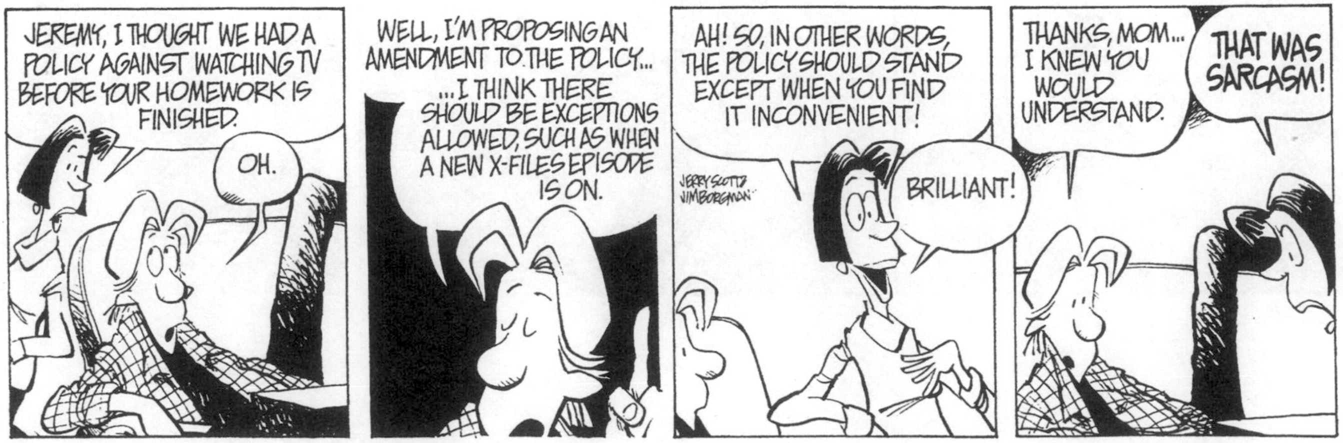
JEREMY, I THOUGHT WE HAD A POLICY AGAINST WATCHING TV BEFORE YOUR HOMEWORK IS FINISHED.
OH.
WELL, I'M PROPOSING AN AMENDMENT TO THE POLICY...
...I THINK THERE SHOULD BE EXCEPTIONS ALLOWED, SUCH AS WHEN A NEW X-FILES EPISODE IS ON.
AH! SO, IN OTHER WORDS, THE POLICY SHOULD STAND EXCEPT WHEN YOU FIND IT INCONVENIENT!
JERRY SCOTT JIM BORGMAN
BRILLIANT!
THANKS, MOM... I KNEW YOU WOULD UNDERSTAND.
THAT WAS SARCASM!

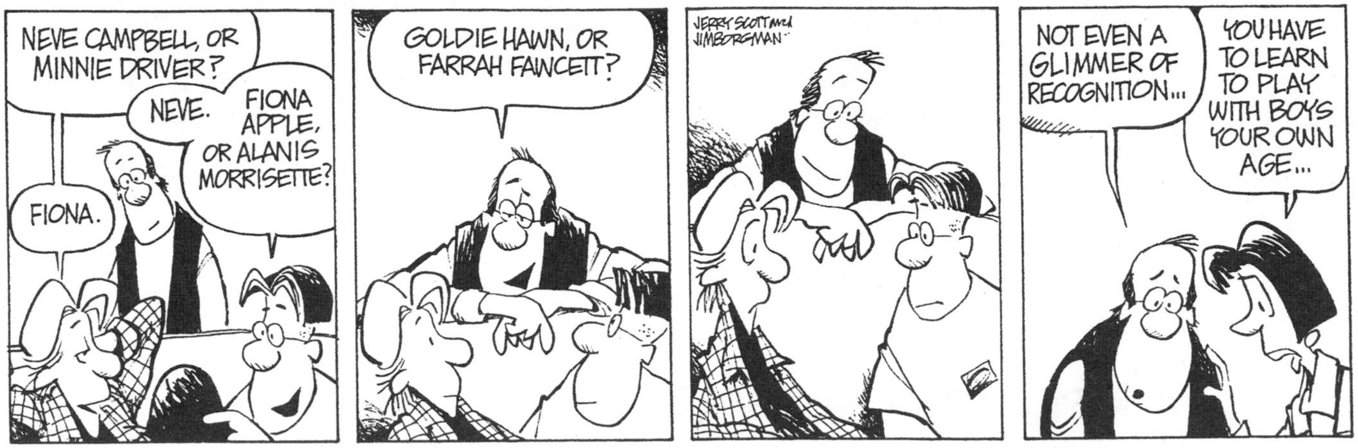
NEVE CAMPBELL, OR MINNIE DRIVER?
NEVE.
FIONA APPLE, OR ALANIS MORRISETTE?
FIONA.
GOLDIE HAWN, OR FARRAH FAWCETT?
JERRY SCOTT and JIM BORGMAN
NOT EVEN A GLIMMER OF RECOGNITION...
YOU HAVE TO LEARN TO PLAY WITH BOYS YOUR OWN AGE...

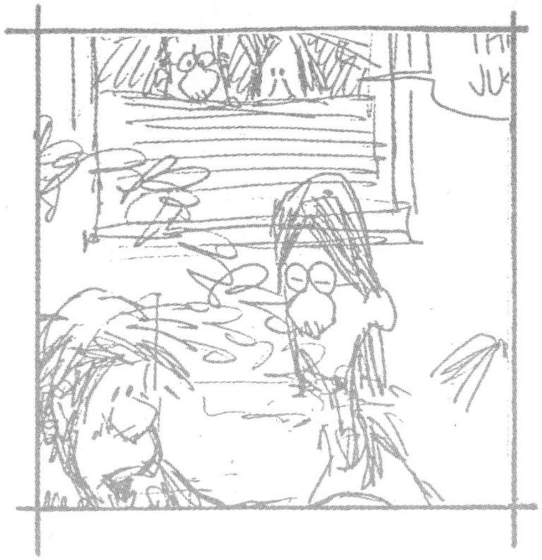

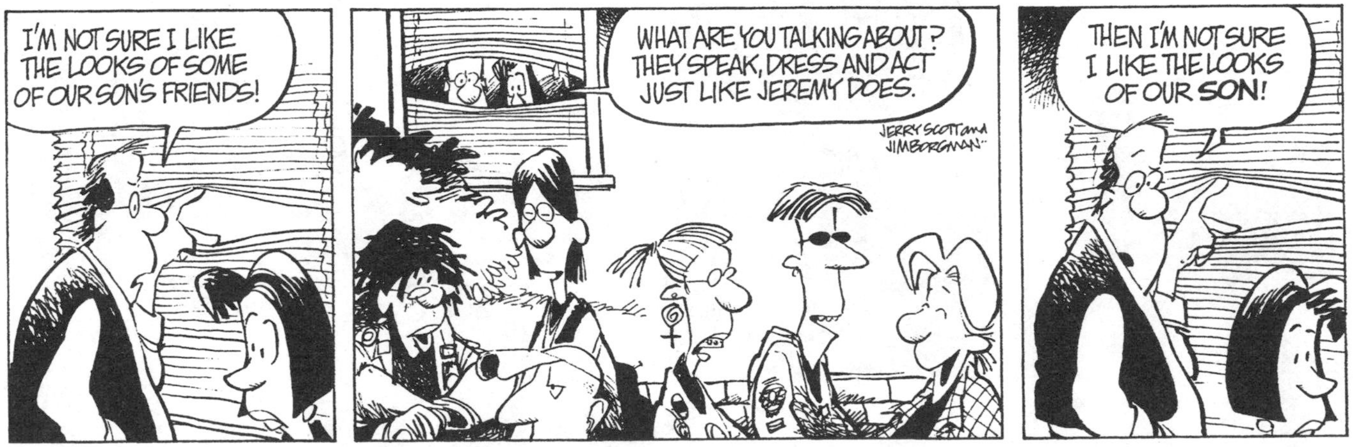
I'M NOT SURE I LIKE THE LOOKS OF SOME OF OUR SON'S FRIENDS!
WHAT ARE YOU TALKING ABOUT? THEY SPEAK, DRESS AND ACT JUST LIKE JEREMY DOES.
JERRY SCOTT and JIM BORGMAN
THEN I'M NOT SURE I LIKE THE LOOKS OF OUR **SON**!

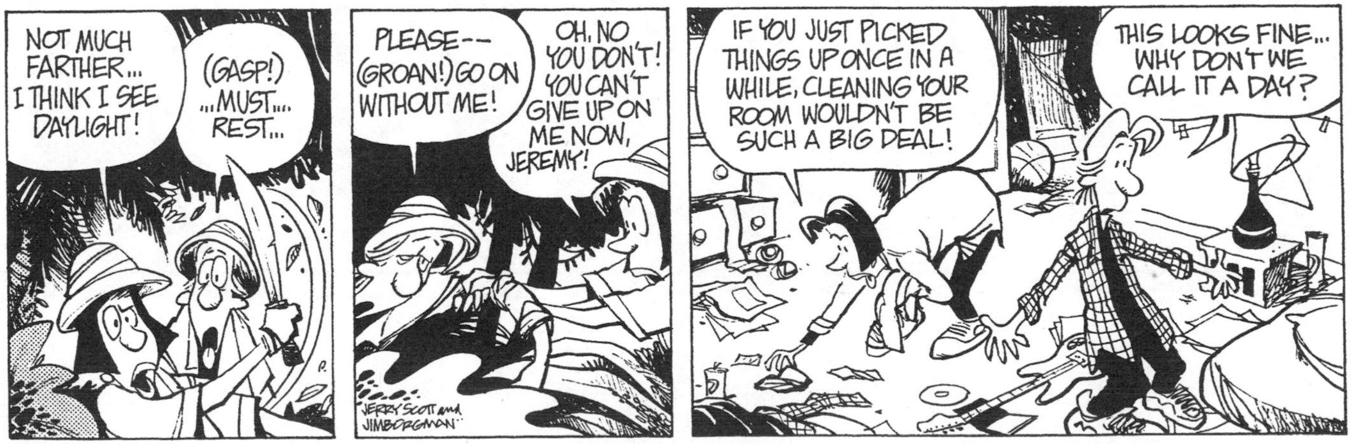
NOT MUCH FARTHER... I THINK I SEE DAYLIGHT!
(GASP!) ...MUST.... REST...
PLEASE-- (GROAN!) GO ON WITHOUT ME!
OH, NO YOU DON'T! YOU CAN'T GIVE UP ON ME NOW, JEREMY!
JERRY SCOTT and JIM BORGMAN
IF YOU JUST PICKED THINGS UP ONCE IN A WHILE, CLEANING YOUR ROOM WOULDN'T BE SUCH A BIG DEAL!
THIS LOOKS FINE... WHY DON'T WE CALL IT A DAY?

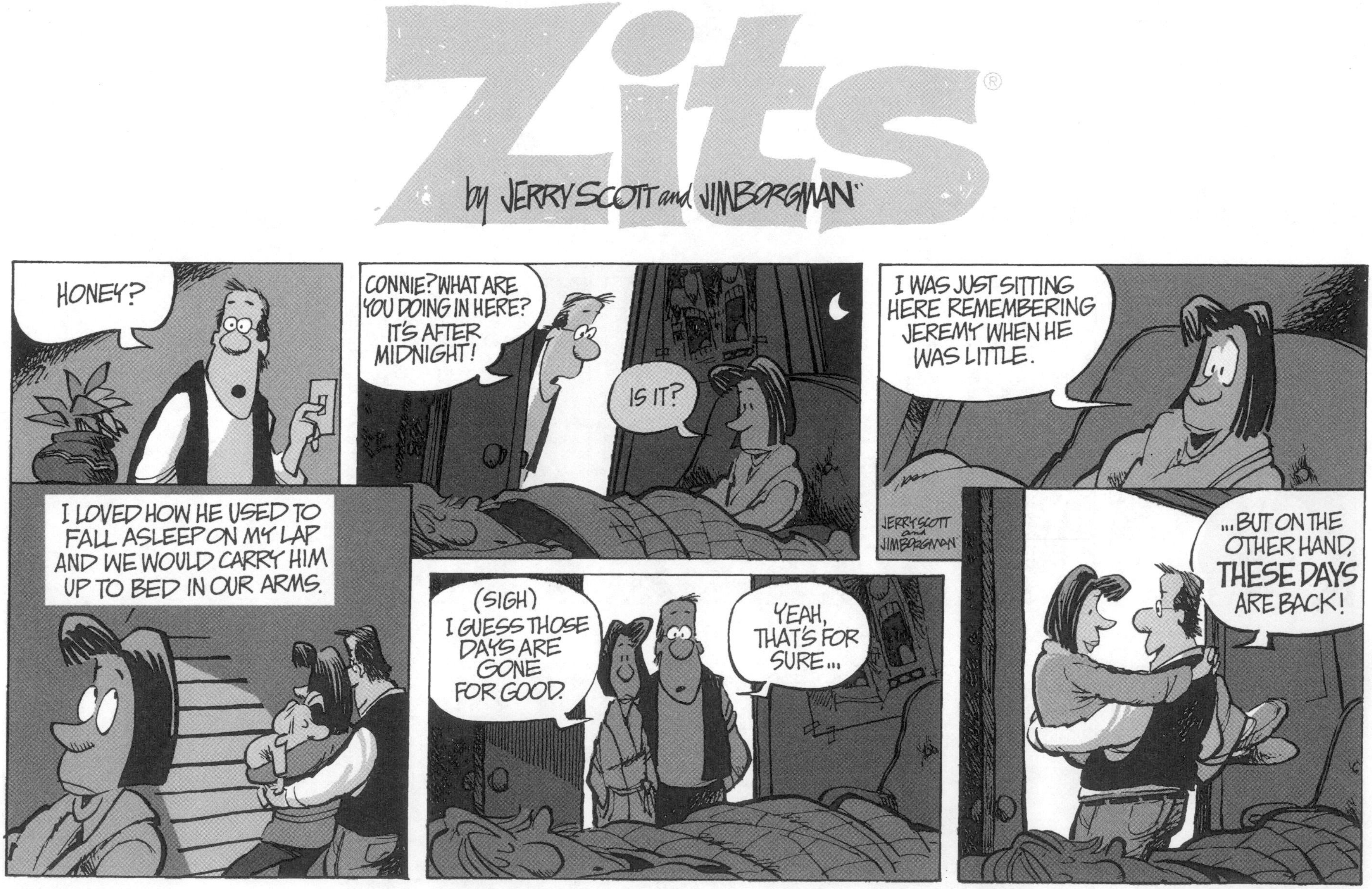

Zits®
by JERRY SCOTT and JIM BORGMAN
HONEY?
CONNIE? WHAT ARE YOU DOING IN HERE? IT'S AFTER MIDNIGHT!
IS IT?
I WAS JUST SITTING HERE REMEMBERING JEREMY WHEN HE WAS LITTLE.
JERRY SCOTT and JIM BORGMAN
I LOVED HOW HE USED TO FALL ASLEEP ON MY LAP AND WE WOULD CARRY HIM UP TO BED IN OUR ARMS.
(SIGH) I GUESS THOSE DAYS ARE GONE FOR GOOD.
YEAH, THAT'S FOR SURE...
...BUT ON THE OTHER HAND, THESE DAYS ARE BACK!

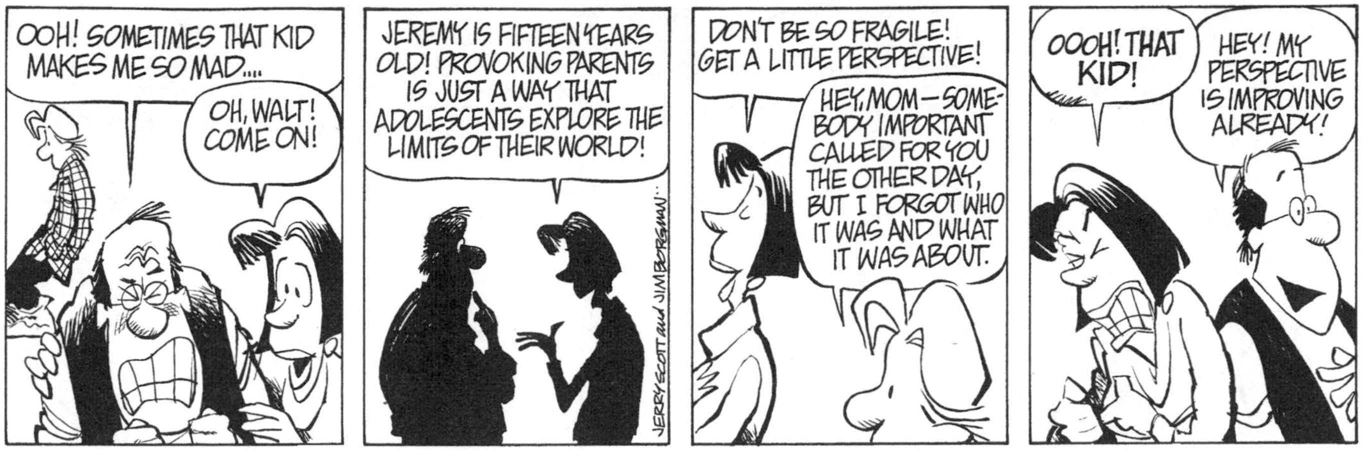
OOH! SOMETIMES THAT KID MAKES ME SO MAD....
OH, WALT! COME ON!
JEREMY IS FIFTEEN YEARS OLD! PROVOKING PARENTS IS JUST A WAY THAT ADOLESCENTS EXPLORE THE LIMITS OF THEIR WORLD!
JERRY SCOTT and JIM BORGMAN
DON'T BE SO FRAGILE! GET A LITTLE PERSPECTIVE!
HEY, MOM — SOMEBODY IMPORTANT CALLED FOR YOU THE OTHER DAY, BUT I FORGOT WHO IT WAS AND WHAT IT WAS ABOUT.
OOOH! THAT KID!
HEY! MY PERSPECTIVE IS IMPROVING ALREADY!

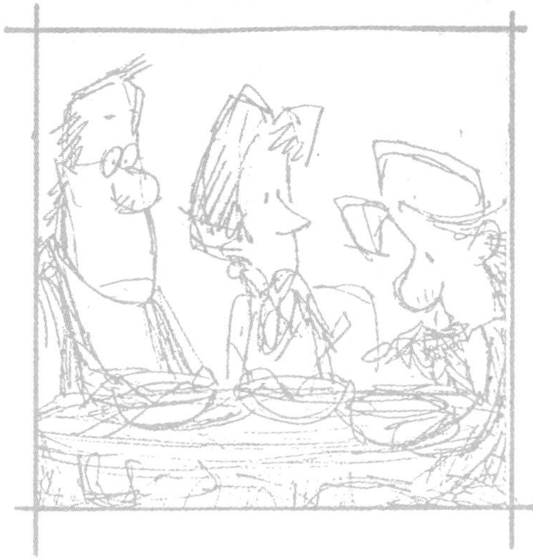

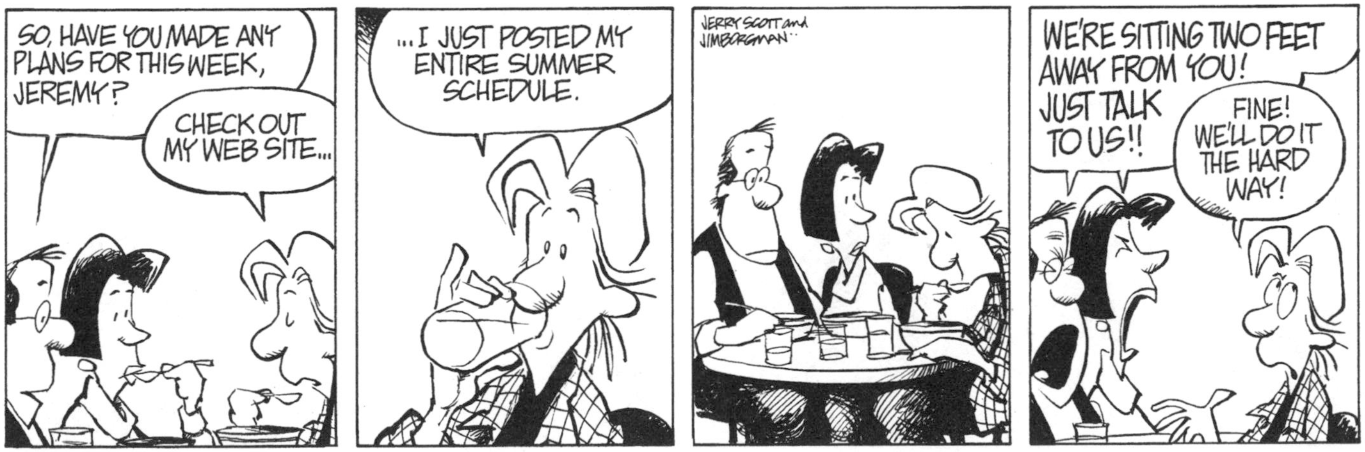
SO, HAVE YOU MADE ANY PLANS FOR THIS WEEK, JEREMY?
CHECK OUT MY WEB SITE...
...I JUST POSTED MY ENTIRE SUMMER SCHEDULE.
JERRY SCOTT and JIM BORGMAN
WE'RE SITTING TWO FEET AWAY FROM YOU! JUST TALK TO US!!
FINE! WE'LL DO IT THE HARD WAY!

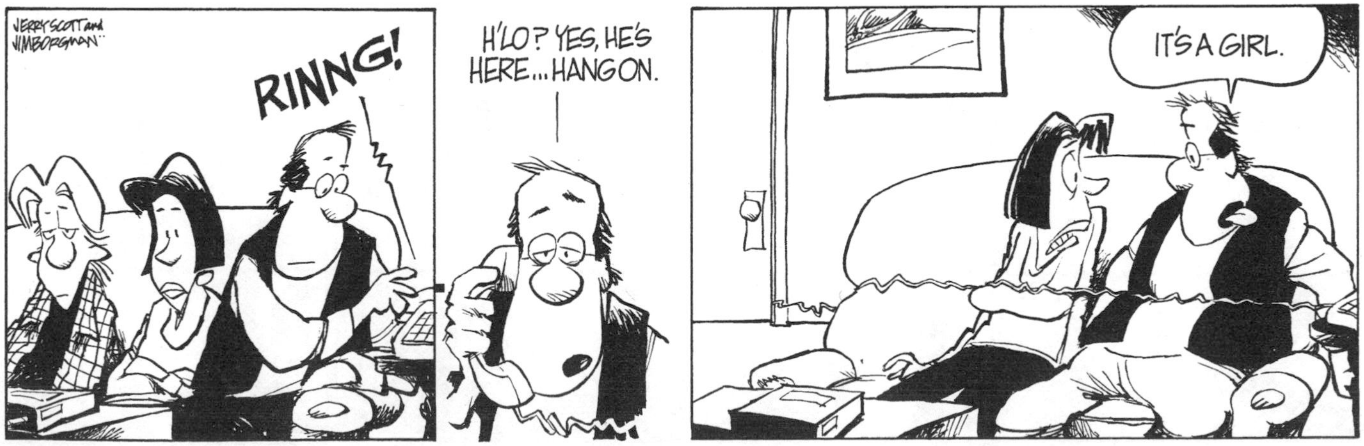
JERRY SCOTT and JIM BORGMAN
RINNG!
H'LO? YES, HE'S HERE... HANG ON.
IT'S A GIRL.

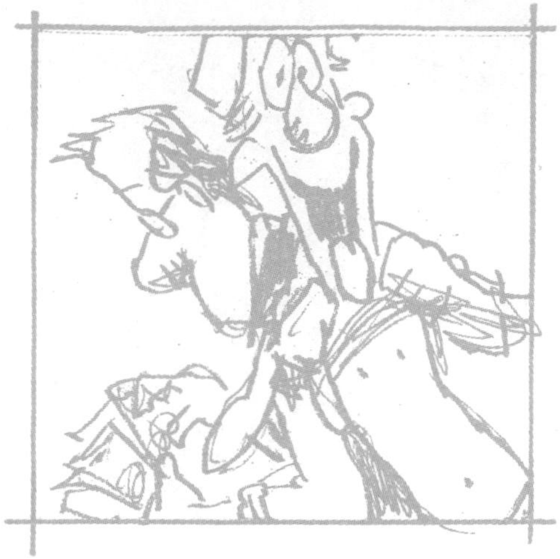

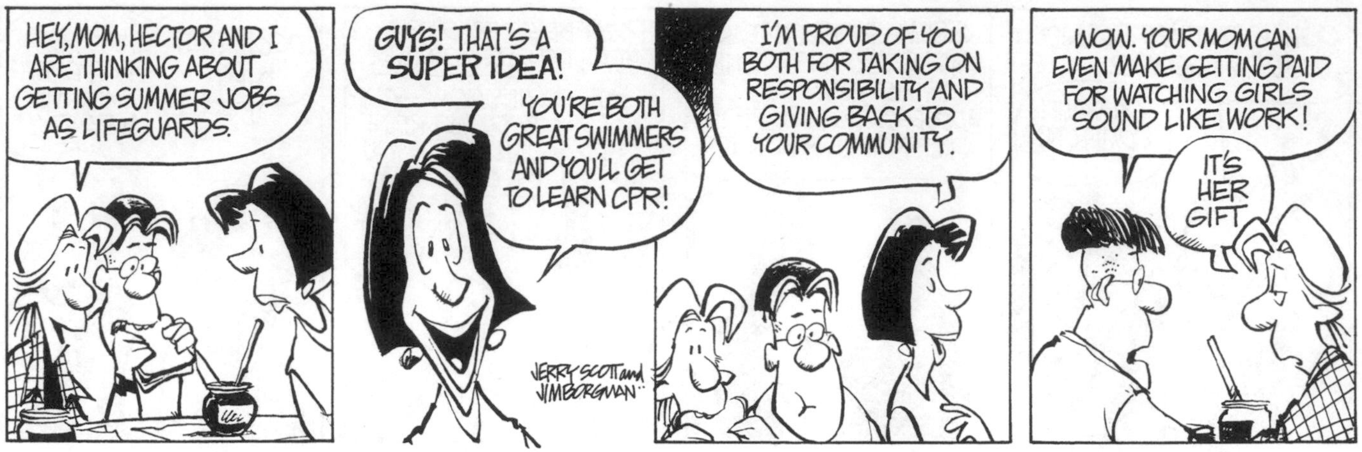
HEY, MOM, HECTOR AND I ARE THINKING ABOUT GETTING SUMMER JOBS AS LIFEGUARDS.
GUYS! THAT'S A SUPER IDEA!
YOU'RE BOTH GREAT SWIMMERS AND YOU'LL GET TO LEARN CPR!
JERRY SCOTT and JIM BORGMAN
I'M PROUD OF YOU BOTH FOR TAKING ON RESPONSIBILITY AND GIVING BACK TO YOUR COMMUNITY.
WOW. YOUR MOM CAN EVEN MAKE GETTING PAID FOR WATCHING GIRLS SOUND LIKE WORK!
IT'S HER GIFT.

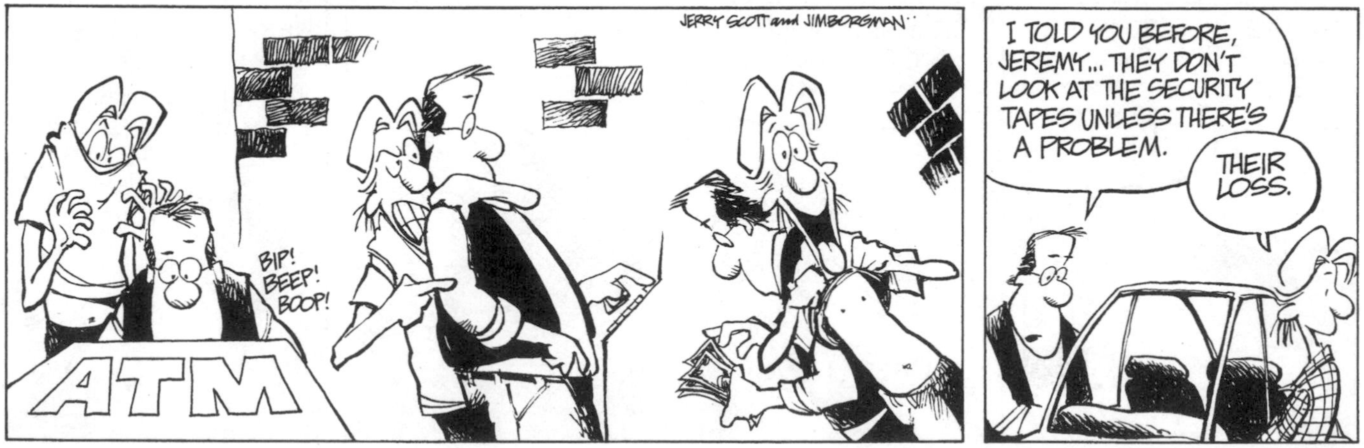
JERRY SCOTT and JIM BORGMAN
ATM
BIP! BEEP! BOOP!
I TOLD YOU BEFORE, JEREMY... THEY DON'T LOOK AT THE SECURITY TAPES UNLESS THERE'S A PROBLEM.
THEIR LOSS.

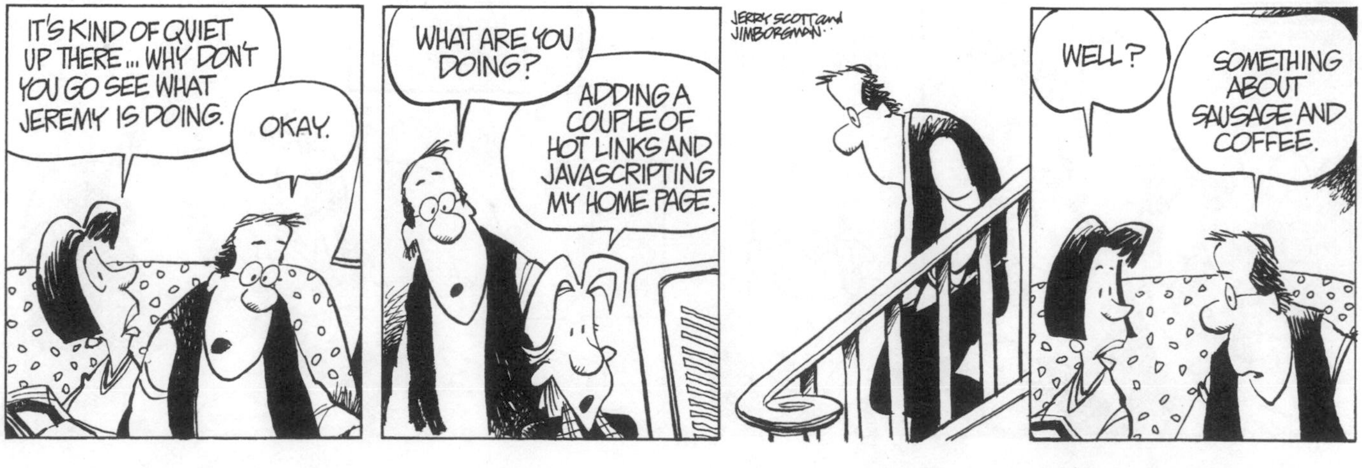
IT'S KIND OF QUIET UP THERE... WHY DON'T YOU GO SEE WHAT JEREMY IS DOING.
OKAY.
WHAT ARE YOU DOING?
ADDING A COUPLE OF HOT LINKS AND JAVASCRIPTING MY HOME PAGE.
JERRY SCOTT and JIM BORGMAN
WELL?
SOMETHING ABOUT SAUSAGE AND COFFEE.

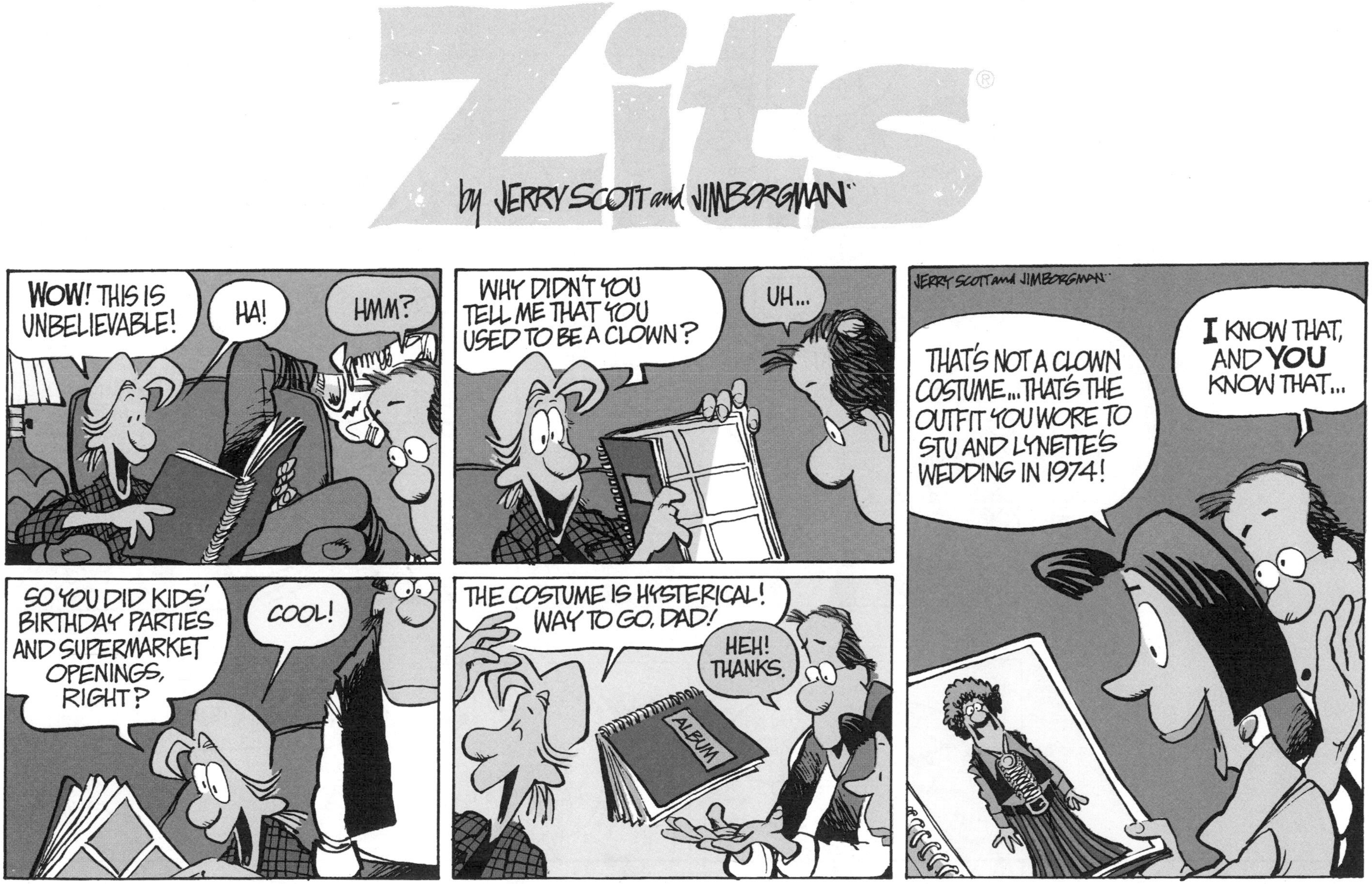
Zits®
by JERRY SCOTT and JIM BORGMAN
WOW! THIS IS UNBELIEVABLE!
HA!
HMM?
WHY DIDN'T YOU TELL ME THAT YOU USED TO BE A CLOWN?
UH...
SO YOU DID KIDS' BIRTHDAY PARTIES AND SUPERMARKET OPENINGS, RIGHT?
COOL!
THE COSTUME IS HYSTERICAL! WAY TO GO, DAD!
HEH! THANKS.
ALBUM
JERRY SCOTT and JIM BORGMAN
THAT'S NOT A CLOWN COSTUME... THAT'S THE OUTFIT YOU WORE TO STU AND LYNETTE'S WEDDING IN 1974!
I KNOW THAT, AND YOU KNOW THAT...

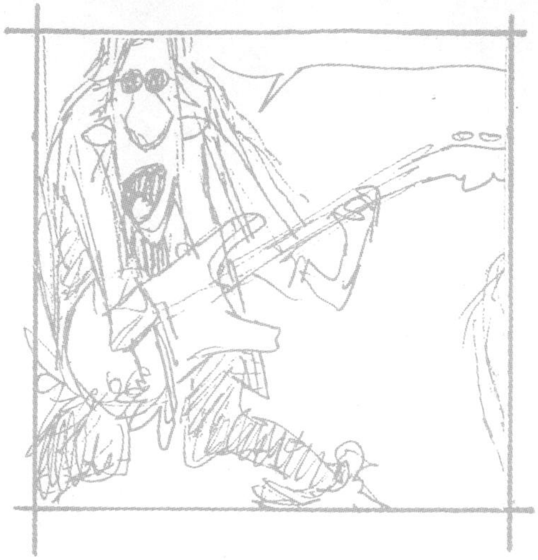

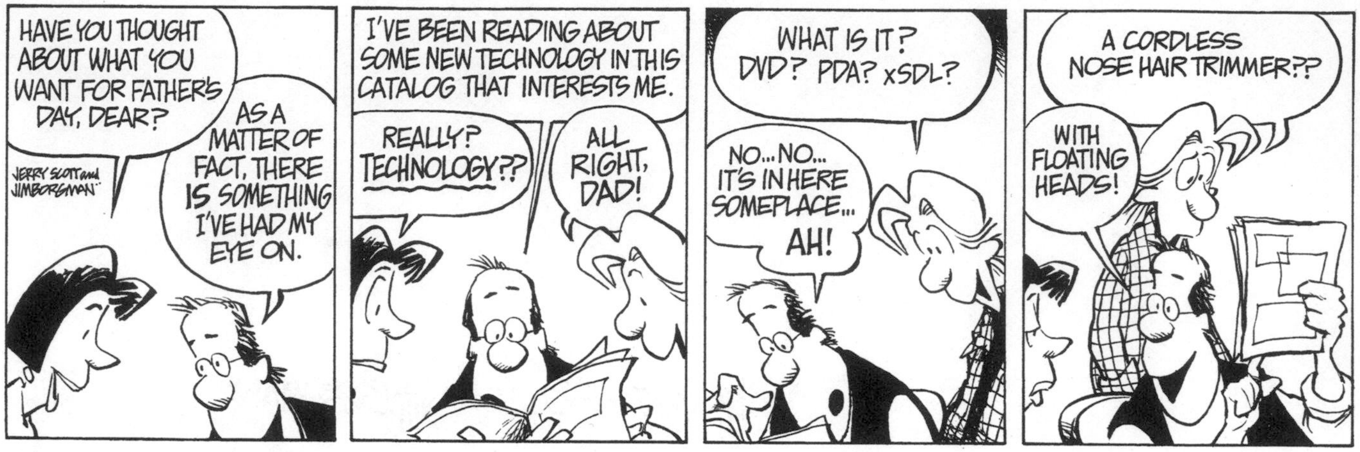
HAVE YOU THOUGHT ABOUT WHAT YOU WANT FOR FATHER'S DAY, DEAR?
JERRY SCOTT and JIMBORGMAN
AS A MATTER OF FACT, THERE IS SOMETHING I'VE HAD MY EYE ON.
I'VE BEEN READING ABOUT SOME NEW TECHNOLOGY IN THIS CATALOG THAT INTERESTS ME.
REALLY? TECHNOLOGY??
ALL RIGHT, DAD!
WHAT IS IT? DVD? PDA? xSDL?
NO... NO... IT'S IN HERE SOMEPLACE... AH!
A CORDLESS NOSE HAIR TRIMMER??
WITH FLOATING HEADS!

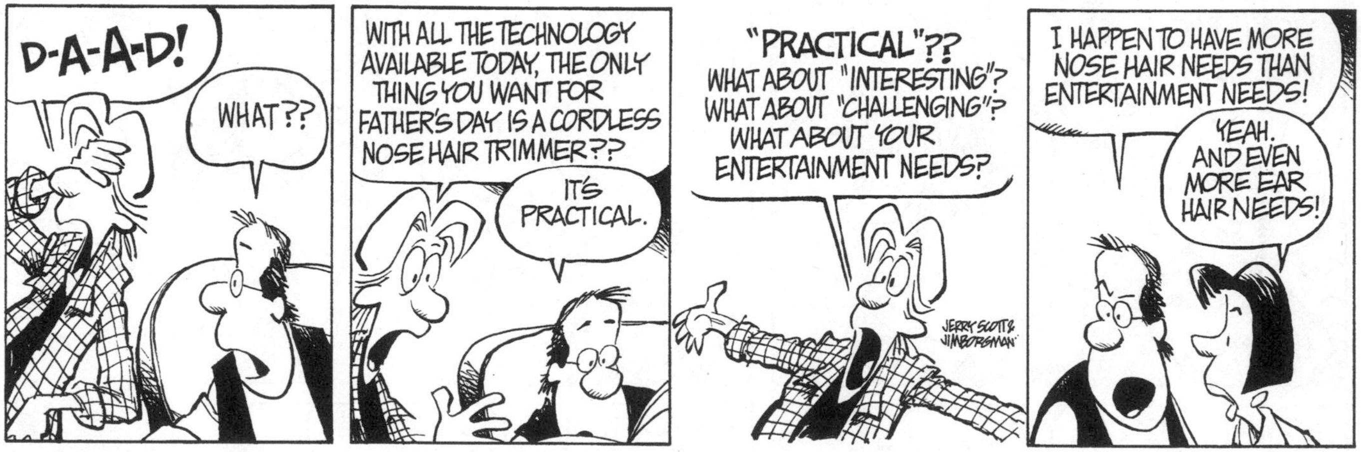
D-A-A-D!
WHAT??
WITH ALL THE TECHNOLOGY AVAILABLE TODAY, THE ONLY THING YOU WANT FOR FATHER'S DAY IS A CORDLESS NOSE HAIR TRIMMER??
IT'S PRACTICAL.
"PRACTICAL"?? WHAT ABOUT "INTERESTING"? WHAT ABOUT "CHALLENGING"? WHAT ABOUT YOUR ENTERTAINMENT NEEDS?
JERRY SCOTT & JIMBORGMAN
I HAPPEN TO HAVE MORE NOSE HAIR NEEDS THAN ENTERTAINMENT NEEDS!
YEAH. AND EVEN MORE EAR HAIR NEEDS!

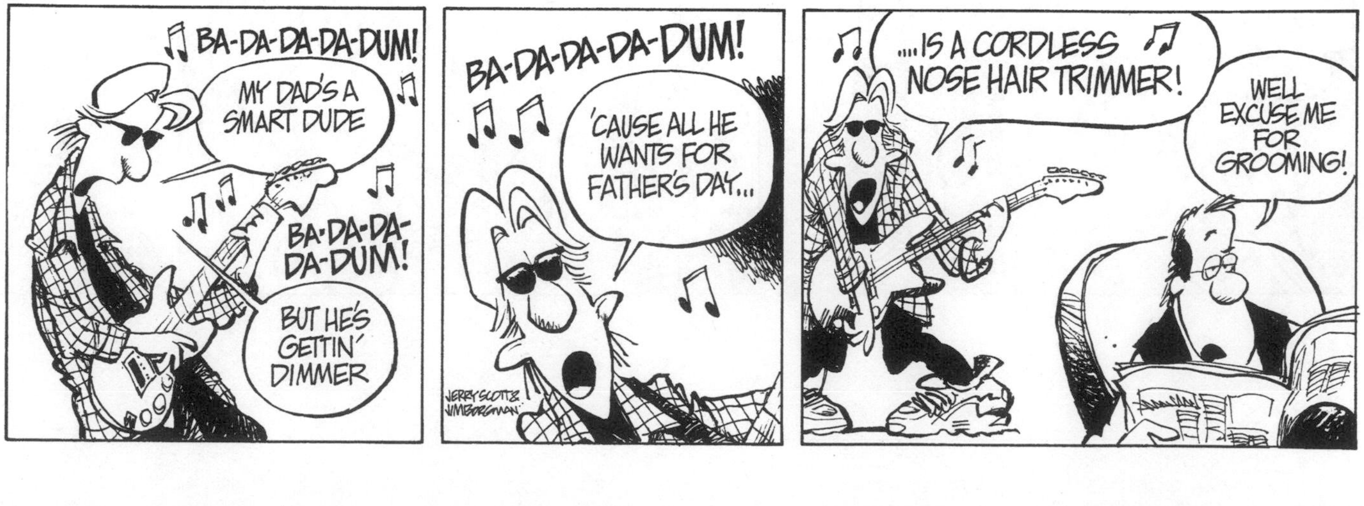
BA-DA-DA-DA-DUM!
MY DAD'S A SMART DUDE
BA-DA-DA-DA-DUM!
BUT HE'S GETTIN' DIMMER
BA-DA-DA-DA-DUM!
'CAUSE ALL HE WANTS FOR FATHER'S DAY...
JERRY SCOTT & JIMBORGMAN
....IS A CORDLESS NOSE HAIR TRIMMER!
WELL EXCUSE ME FOR GROOMING!

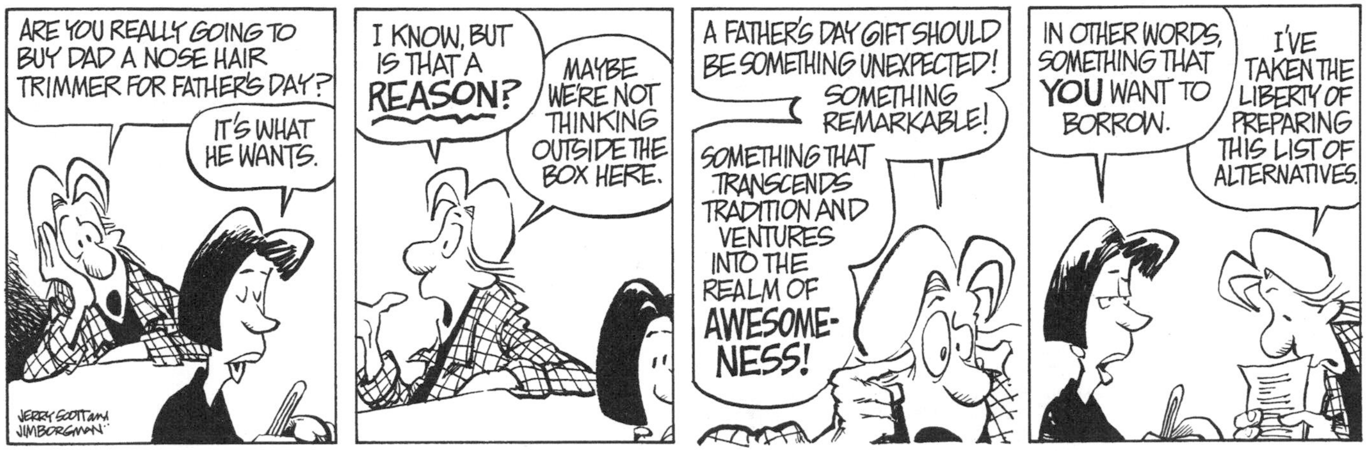
ARE YOU REALLY GOING TO BUY DAD A NOSE HAIR TRIMMER FOR FATHER'S DAY?
IT'S WHAT HE WANTS.
JERRY SCOTT and JIM BORGMAN
I KNOW, BUT IS THAT A REASON?
MAYBE WE'RE NOT THINKING OUTSIDE THE BOX HERE.
A FATHER'S DAY GIFT SHOULD BE SOMETHING UNEXPECTED!
SOMETHING REMARKABLE!
SOMETHING THAT TRANSCENDS TRADITION AND VENTURES INTO THE REALM OF AWESOME-NESS!
IN OTHER WORDS, SOMETHING THAT YOU WANT TO BORROW.
I'VE TAKEN THE LIBERTY OF PREPARING THIS LIST OF ALTERNATIVES.

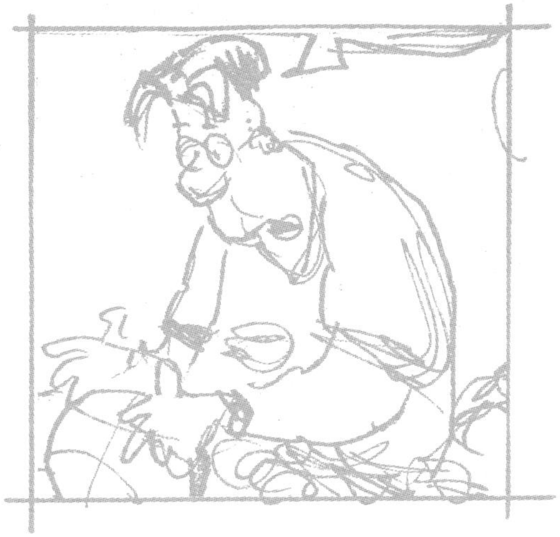

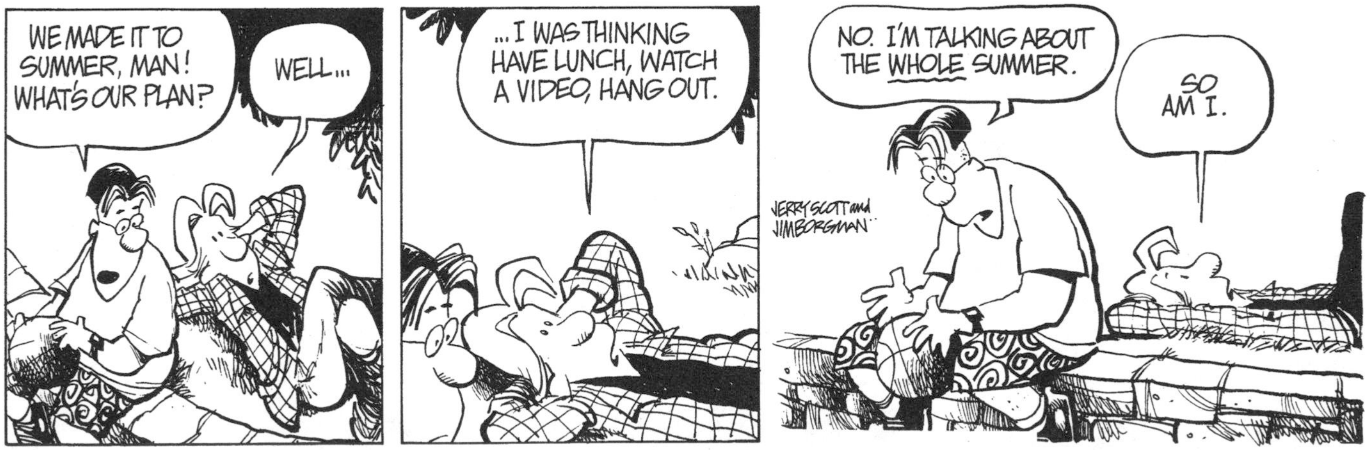
WE MADE IT TO SUMMER, MAN! WHAT'S OUR PLAN?
WELL...
...I WAS THINKING HAVE LUNCH, WATCH A VIDEO, HANG OUT.
JERRY SCOTT and JIM BORGMAN
NO. I'M TALKING ABOUT THE WHOLE SUMMER.
SO AM I.

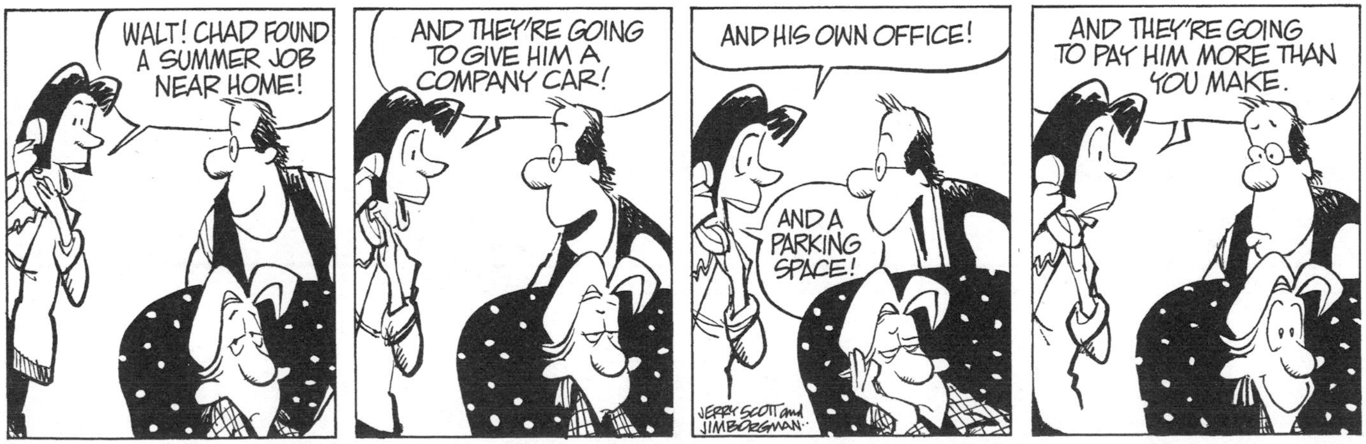
WALT! CHAD FOUND A SUMMER JOB NEAR HOME!
AND THEY'RE GOING TO GIVE HIM A COMPANY CAR!
AND HIS OWN OFFICE!
AND A PARKING SPACE!
JERRY SCOTT and JIM BORGMAN
AND THEY'RE GOING TO PAY HIM MORE THAN YOU MAKE.

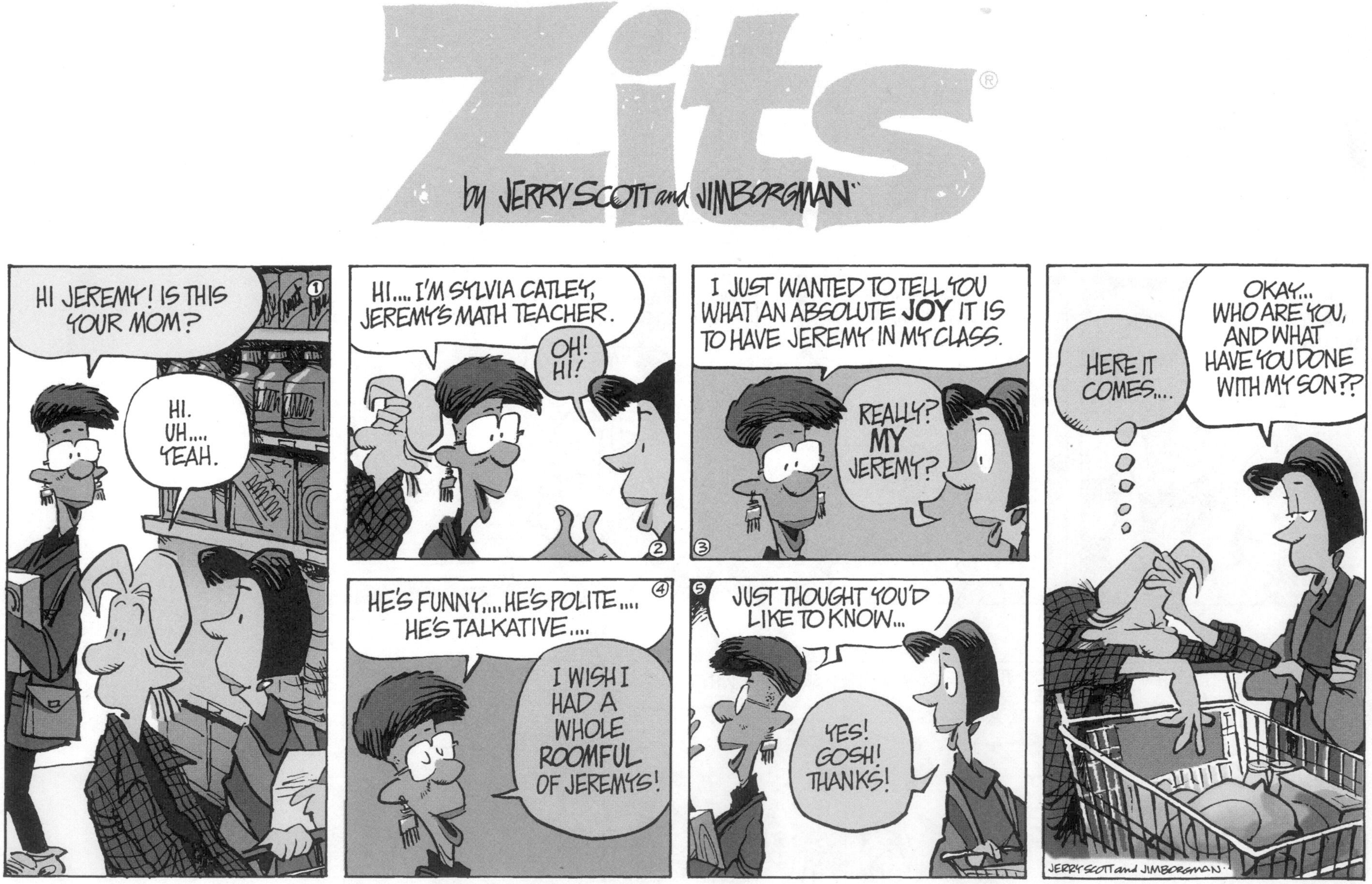
Zits®
by JERRY SCOTT and JIM BORGMAN
HI JEREMY! IS THIS YOUR MOM?
HI. UH.... YEAH.
HI.... I'M SYLVIA CATLEY, JEREMY'S MATH TEACHER.
OH! HI!
I JUST WANTED TO TELL YOU WHAT AN ABSOLUTE JOY IT IS TO HAVE JEREMY IN MY CLASS.
REALLY? MY JEREMY?
HE'S FUNNY.... HE'S POLITE.... HE'S TALKATIVE....
I WISH I HAD A WHOLE ROOMFUL OF JEREMYS!
JUST THOUGHT YOU'D LIKE TO KNOW...
YES! GOSH! THANKS!
HERE IT COMES....
OKAY... WHO ARE YOU, AND WHAT HAVE YOU DONE WITH MY SON??
JERRY SCOTT and JIM BORGMAN

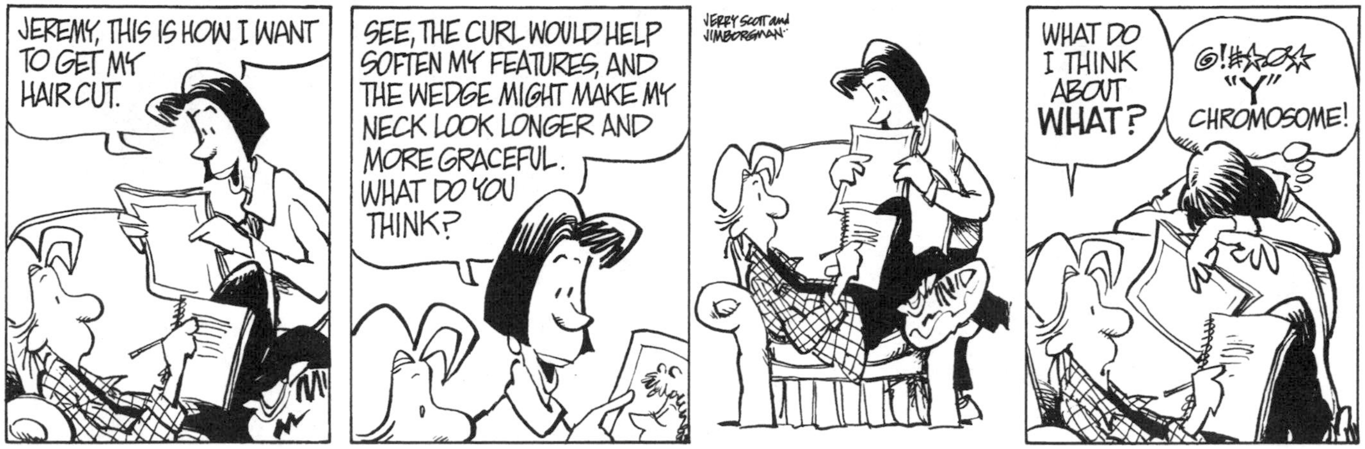
JEREMY, THIS IS HOW I WANT TO GET MY HAIRCUT.
SEE, THE CURL WOULD HELP SOFTEN MY FEATURES, AND THE WEDGE MIGHT MAKE MY NECK LOOK LONGER AND MORE GRACEFUL. WHAT DO YOU THINK?
JERRY SCOTT and JIM BORGMAN
WHAT DO I THINK ABOUT WHAT?
"Y" CHROMOSOME!

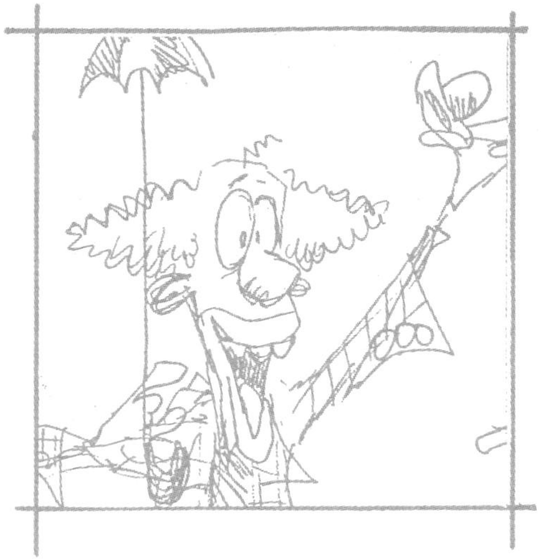

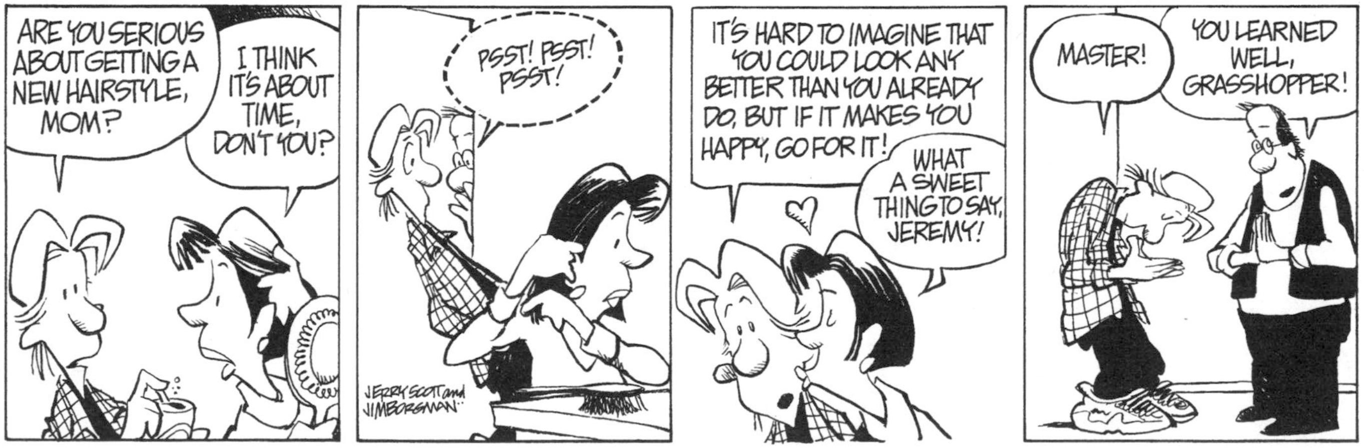
ARE YOU SERIOUS ABOUT GETTING A NEW HAIRSTYLE, MOM?
I THINK IT'S ABOUT TIME, DON'T YOU?
PSST! PSST! PSST!
JERRY SCOTT and JIM BORGMAN
IT'S HARD TO IMAGINE THAT YOU COULD LOOK ANY BETTER THAN YOU ALREADY DO, BUT IF IT MAKES YOU HAPPY, GO FOR IT!
WHAT A SWEET THING TO SAY, JEREMY!
MASTER!
YOU LEARNED WELL, GRASSHOPPER!

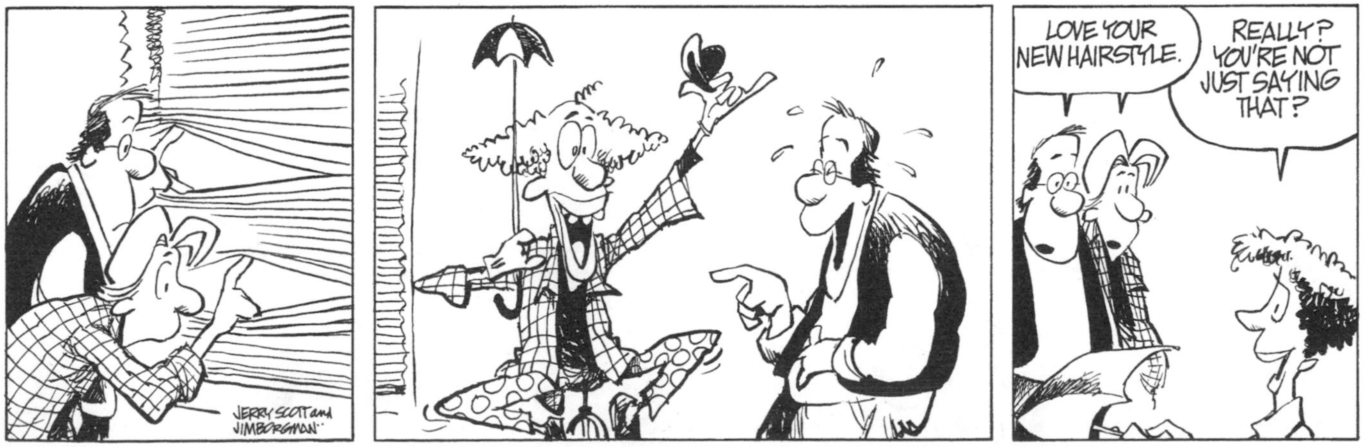
JERRY SCOTT and JIM BORGMAN
LOVE YOUR NEW HAIRSTYLE.
REALLY? YOU'RE NOT JUST SAYING THAT?

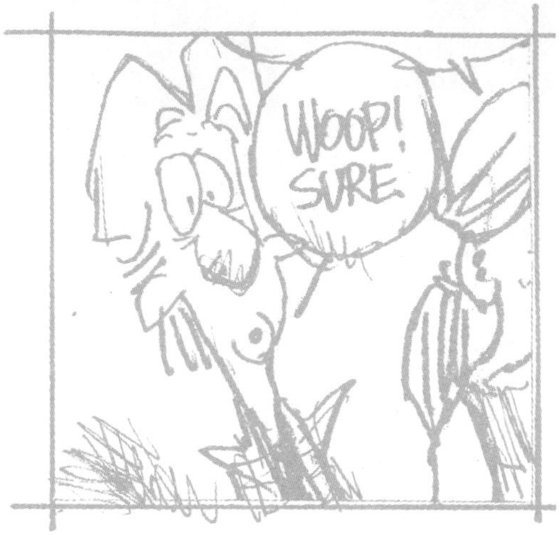
WOOP! SURE.

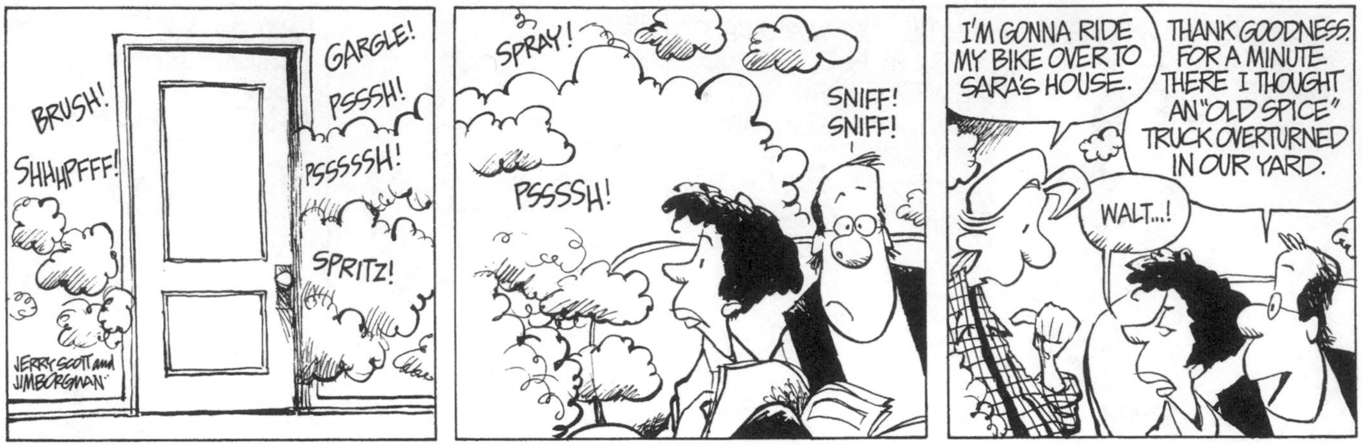
BRUSH!
SHHHPFFF!
GARGLE!
PSSSH!
PSSSSSH!
SPRITZ!
JERRY SCOTT and JIM BORGMAN
SPRAY!
PSSSSH!
SNIFF! SNIFF!
I'M GONNA RIDE MY BIKE OVER TO SARA'S HOUSE.
THANK GOODNESS. FOR A MINUTE THERE I THOUGHT AN "OLD SPICE" TRUCK OVERTURNED IN OUR YARD.
WALT...!

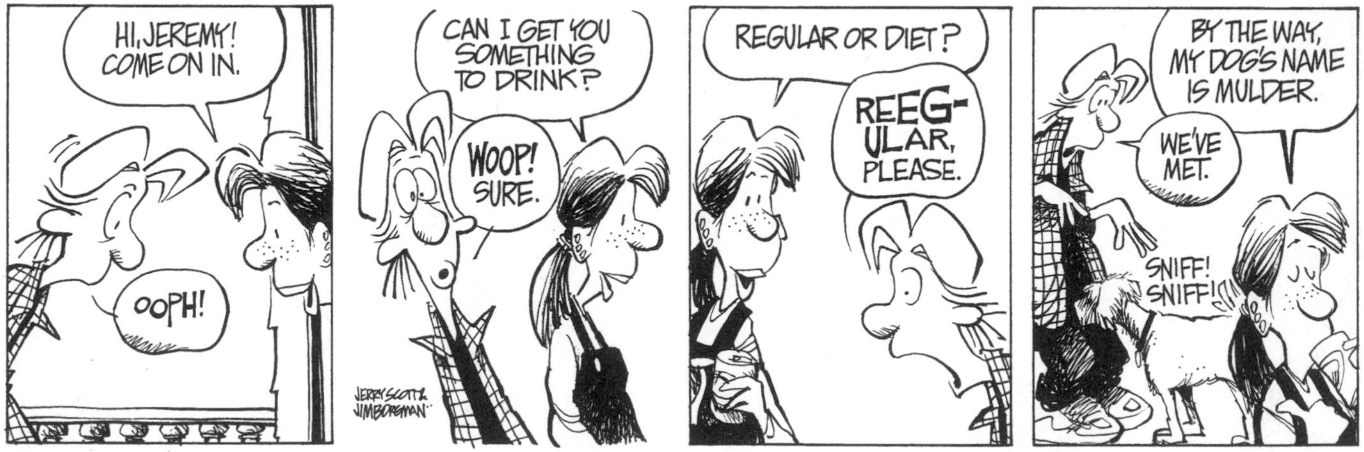
HI, JEREMY! COME ON IN.
OOPH!
CAN I GET YOU SOMETHING TO DRINK?
WOOP! SURE.
JERRY SCOTT & JIM BORGMAN
REGULAR OR DIET?
REEG-ULAR, PLEASE.
BY THE WAY, MY DOG'S NAME IS MULDER.
WE'VE MET.
SNIFF! SNIFF!

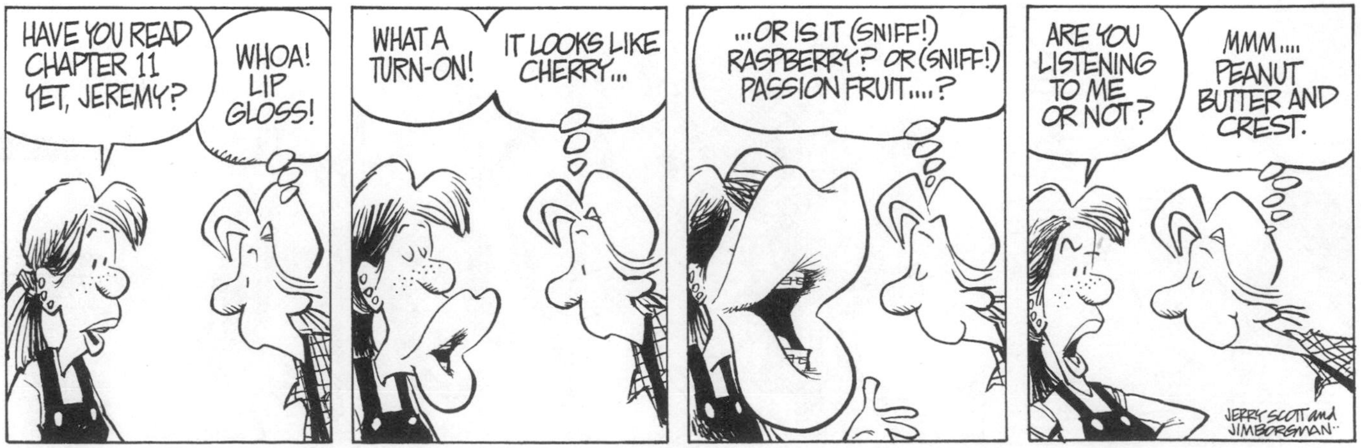
HAVE YOU READ CHAPTER 11 YET, JEREMY?
WHOA! LIP GLOSS!
WHAT A TURN-ON!
IT LOOKS LIKE CHERRY...
...OR IS IT (SNIFF!) RASPBERRY? OR (SNIFF!) PASSION FRUIT....?
ARE YOU LISTENING TO ME OR NOT?
MMM.... PEANUT BUTTER AND CREST.
JERRY SCOTT and JIM BORGMAN

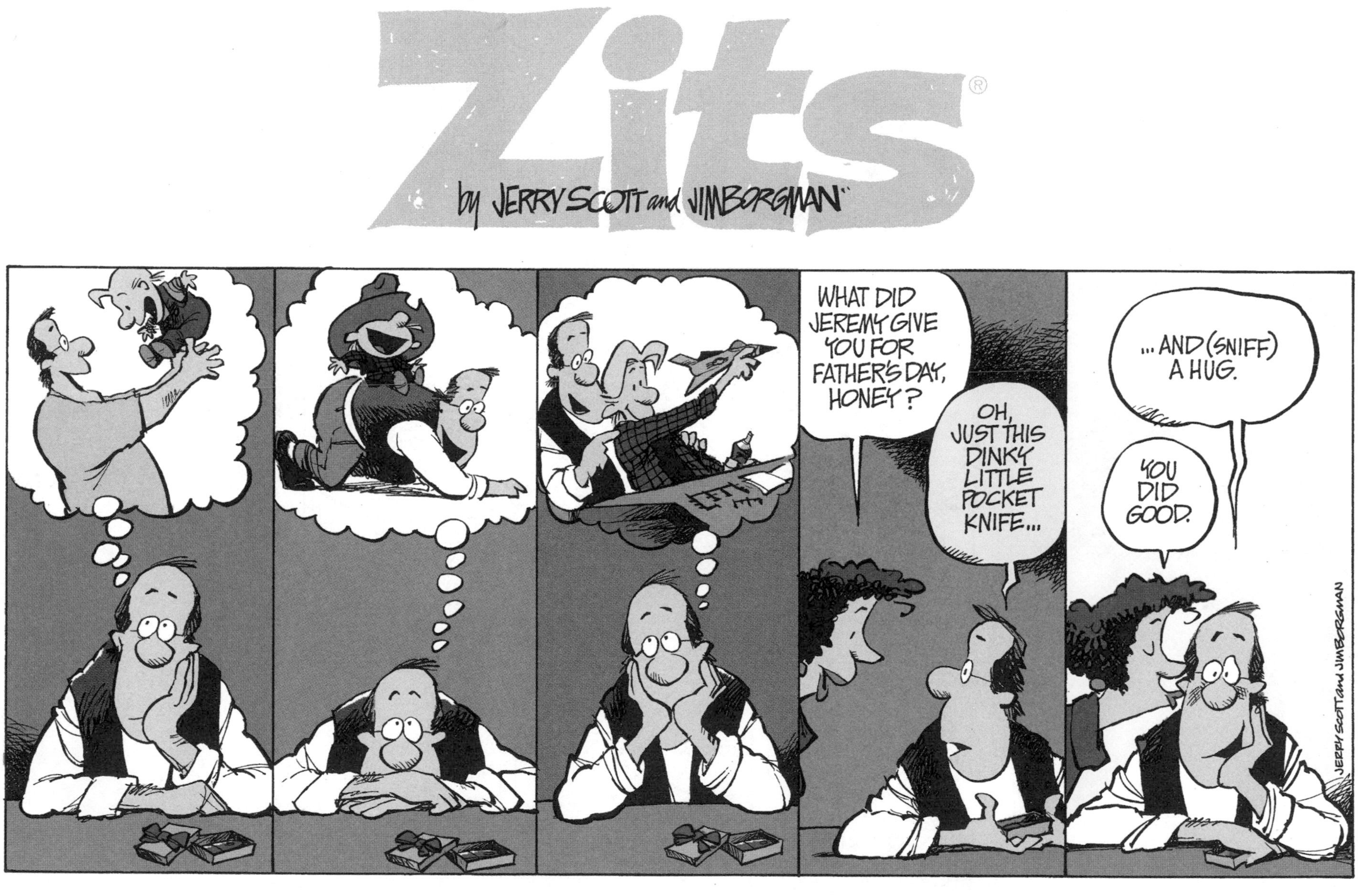
Zits®
by JERRY SCOTT and JIM BORGMAN
WHAT DID JEREMY GIVE YOU FOR FATHER'S DAY, HONEY?
OH, JUST THIS DINKY LITTLE POCKET KNIFE...
...AND (SNIFF) A HUG.
YOU DID GOOD.
JERRY SCOTT and JIM BORGMAN

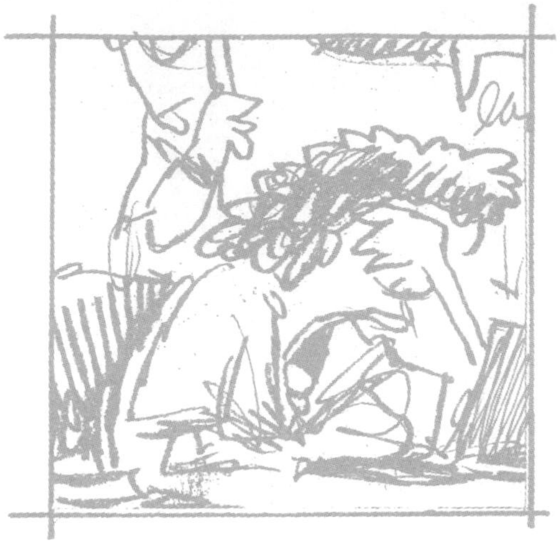

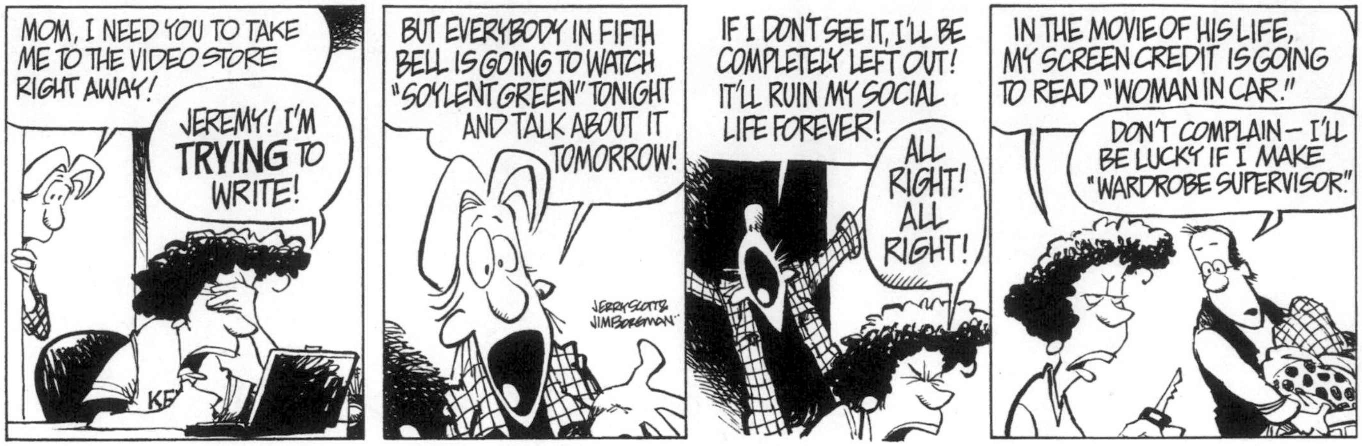
MOM, I NEED YOU TO TAKE ME TO THE VIDEO STORE RIGHT AWAY!
JEREMY! I'M **TRYING** TO WRITE!
BUT EVERYBODY IN FIFTH BELL IS GOING TO WATCH "SOYLENT GREEN" TONIGHT AND TALK ABOUT IT TOMORROW!
JERRY SCOTT & JIMBORGMAN
IF I DON'T SEE IT, I'LL BE COMPLETELY LEFT OUT! IT'LL RUIN MY SOCIAL LIFE FOREVER!
ALL RIGHT! ALL RIGHT! ALL RIGHT!
IN THE MOVIE OF HIS LIFE, MY SCREEN CREDIT IS GOING TO READ "WOMAN IN CAR."
DON'T COMPLAIN – I'LL BE LUCKY IF I MAKE "WARDROBE SUPERVISOR."

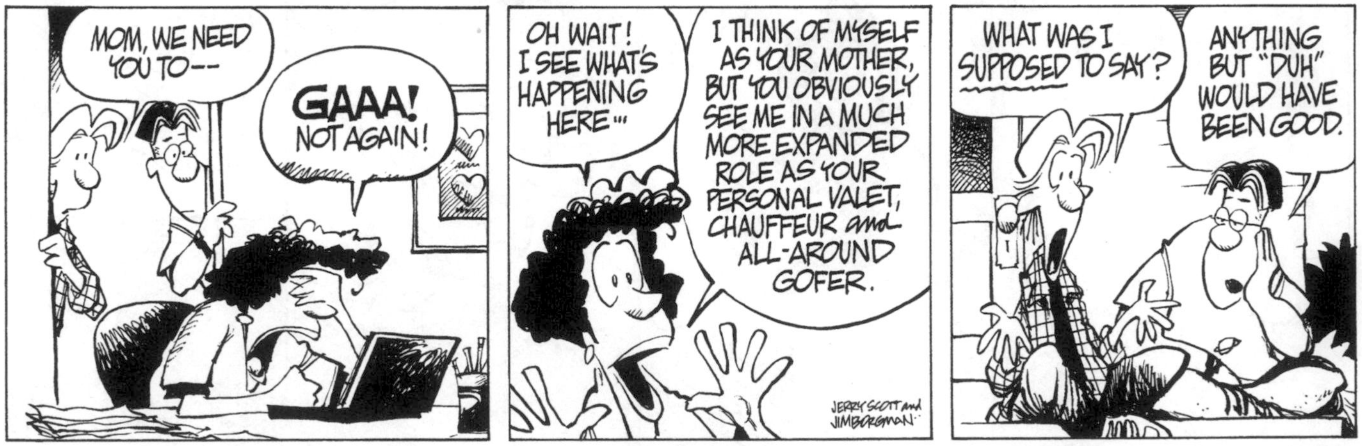
MOM, WE NEED YOU TO--
GAAA! NOT AGAIN!
OH WAIT! I SEE WHAT'S HAPPENING HERE...
I THINK OF MYSELF AS YOUR MOTHER, BUT YOU OBVIOUSLY SEE ME IN A MUCH MORE EXPANDED ROLE AS YOUR PERSONAL VALET, CHAUFFEUR and ALL-AROUND GOFER.
JERRY SCOTT and JIMBORGMAN
WHAT WAS I SUPPOSED TO SAY?
ANYTHING BUT "DUH" WOULD HAVE BEEN GOOD.

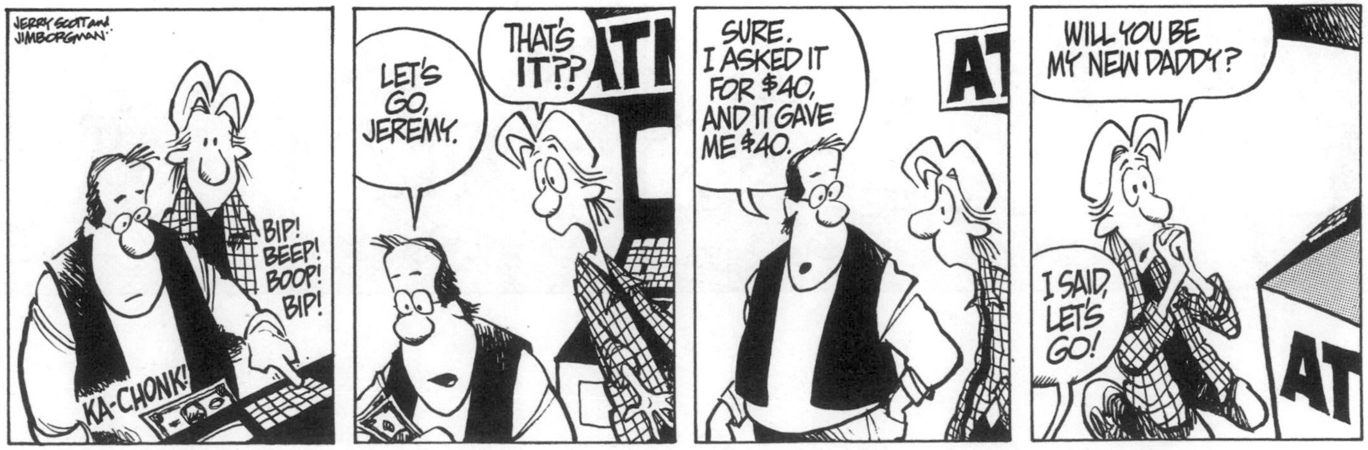
JERRY SCOTT and JIMBORGMAN
BIP! BEEP! BOOP! BIP!
KA-CHONK!
LET'S GO, JEREMY.
THAT'S **IT**??
SURE. I ASKED IT FOR $40, AND IT GAVE ME $40.
WILL YOU BE MY NEW DADDY?
I SAID, LET'S GO!

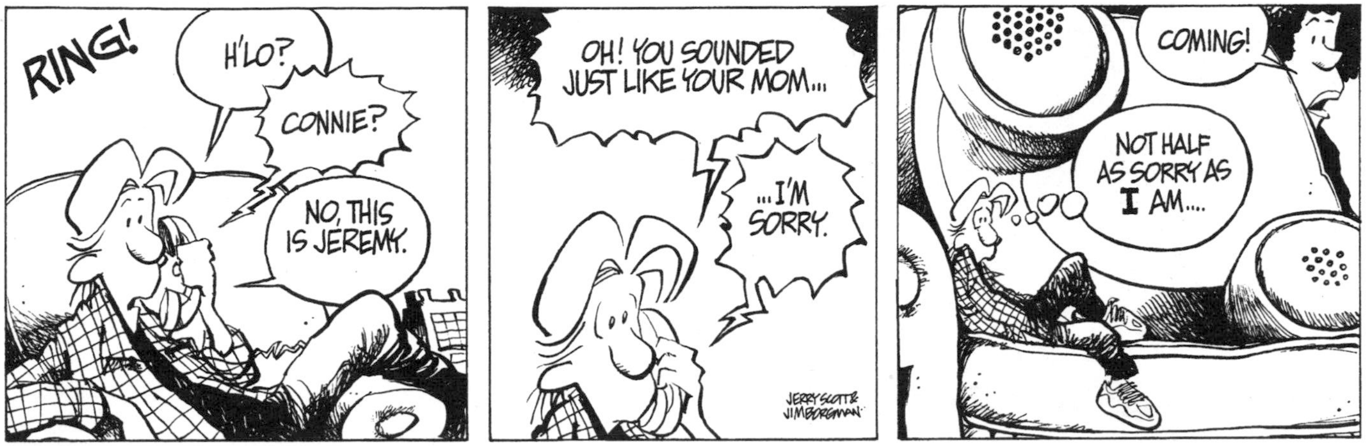
RING!
H'LO?
CONNIE?
NO, THIS IS JEREMY.
OH! YOU SOUNDED JUST LIKE YOUR MOM...
...I'M SORRY.
JERRY SCOTT & JIM BORGMAN
COMING!
NOT HALF AS SORRY AS I AM....

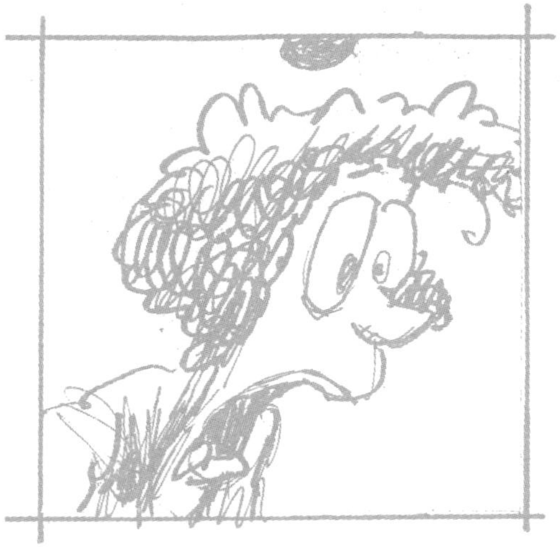

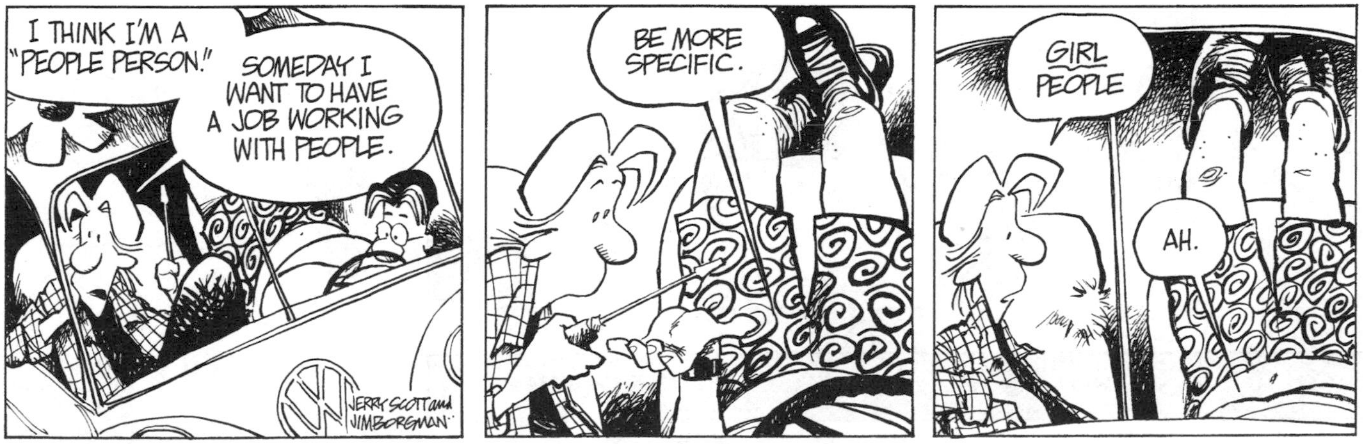
I THINK I'M A "PEOPLE PERSON."
SOMEDAY I WANT TO HAVE A JOB WORKING WITH PEOPLE.
JERRY SCOTT and JIM BORGMAN
BE MORE SPECIFIC.
GIRL PEOPLE
AH.

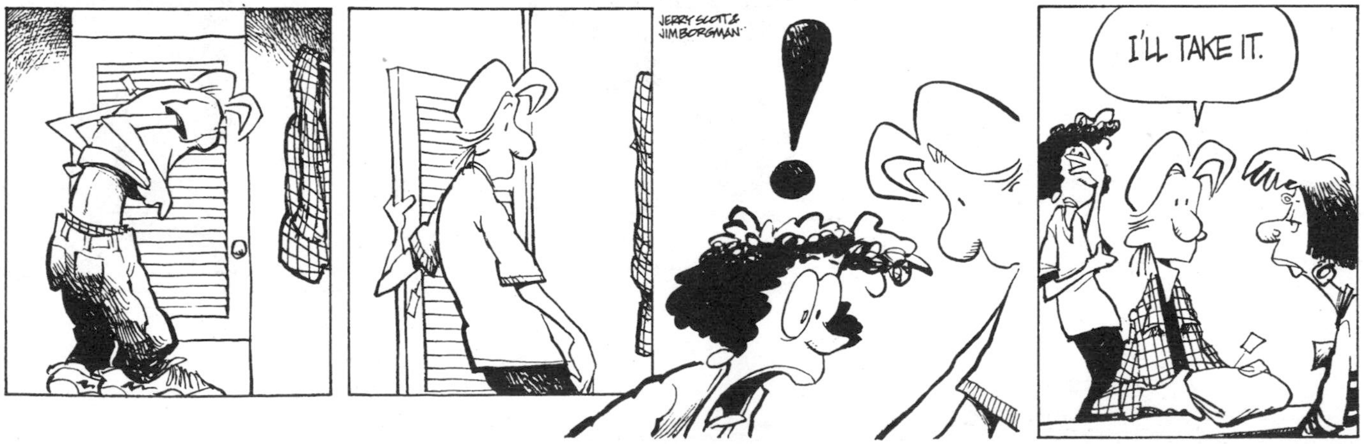
JERRY SCOTT & JIM BORGMAN
!
I'LL TAKE IT.

Zits®

by JERRY SCOTT and JIM BORGMAN

YAWN!
5:30 AM
6:00 AM
6:30 AM
7:00 AM
7:30 AM
Z
Z
Z
Z
NO MATTER HOW HARD I TRY, I CAN NEVER SEEM TO GET OUT OF THE HOUSE BEFORE 7:30!
YOU NEED A SYSTEM.
JERRY SCOTT and JIM BORGMAN

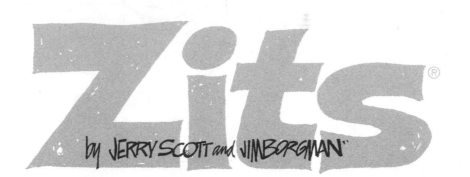

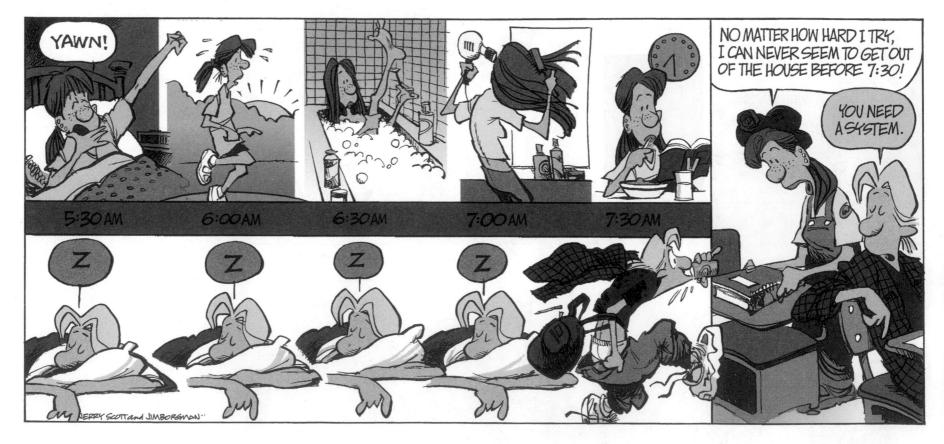

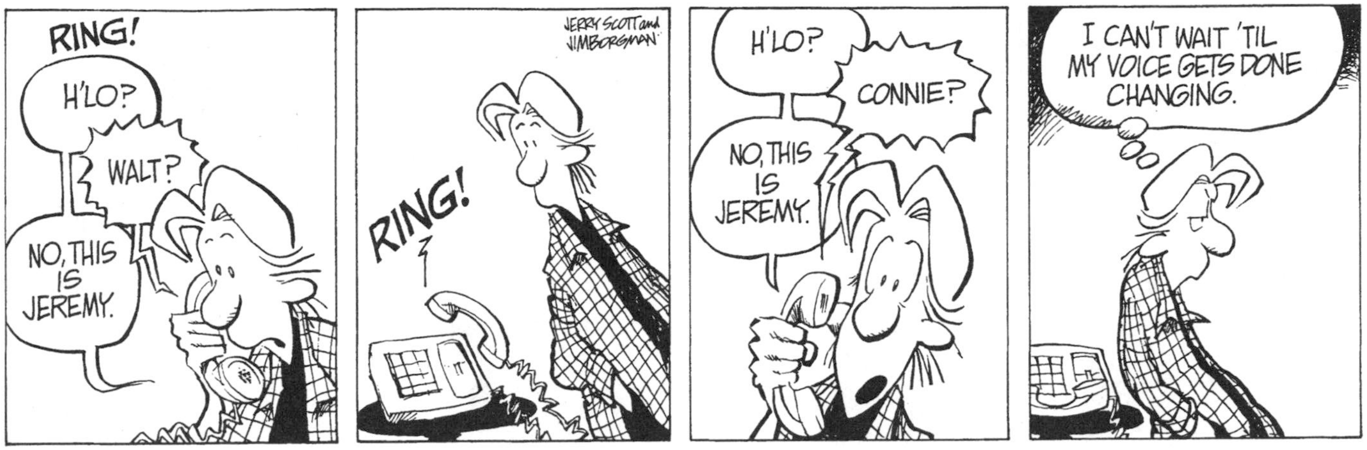
RING!
H'LO?
WALT?
NO, THIS IS JEREMY.
JERRY SCOTT and JIM BORGMAN
RING!
H'LO?
CONNIE?
NO, THIS IS JEREMY.
I CAN'T WAIT 'TIL MY VOICE GETS DONE CHANGING.

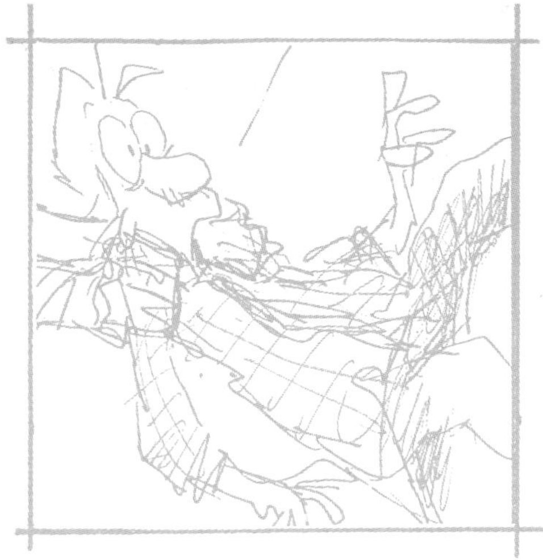

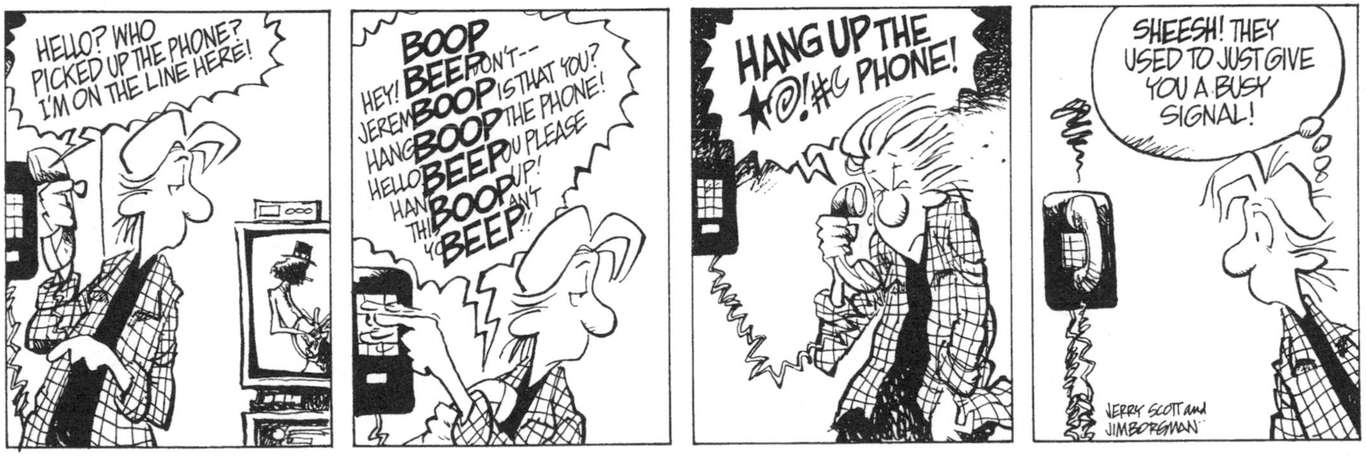
HELLO? WHO PICKED UP THE PHONE? I'M ON THE LINE HERE!
BOOP
BEEP
BOOP
BOOP
BOOP
BEEP
BOOP
BEEP
HANG UP THE ★@!#☾ PHONE!
SHEESH! THEY USED TO JUST GIVE YOU A BUSY SIGNAL!
JERRY SCOTT and JIM BORGMAN

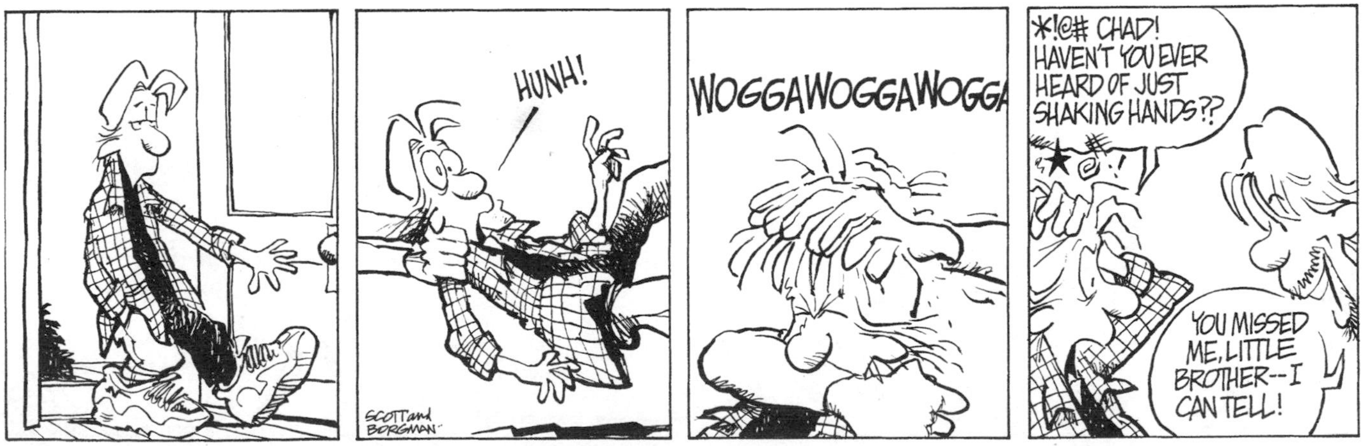
HUNH!
SCOTT and BORGMAN
WOGGAWOGGAWOGGA
*!@# CHAD! HAVEN'T YOU EVER HEARD OF JUST SHAKING HANDS??
YOU MISSED ME, LITTLE BROTHER--I CAN TELL!

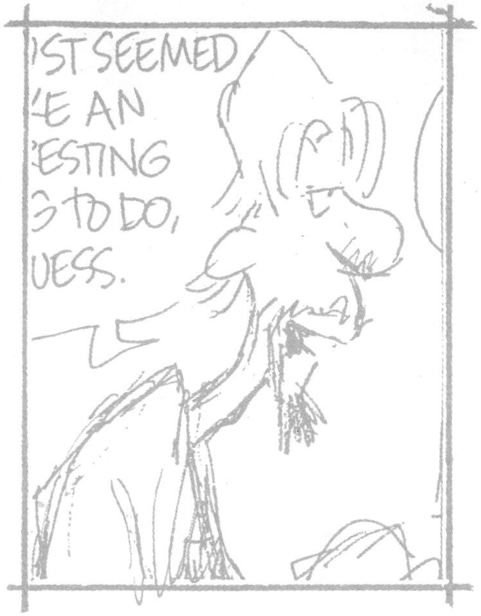

IST SEEMED
'E AN
'ESTING
G TO DO,
UESS.

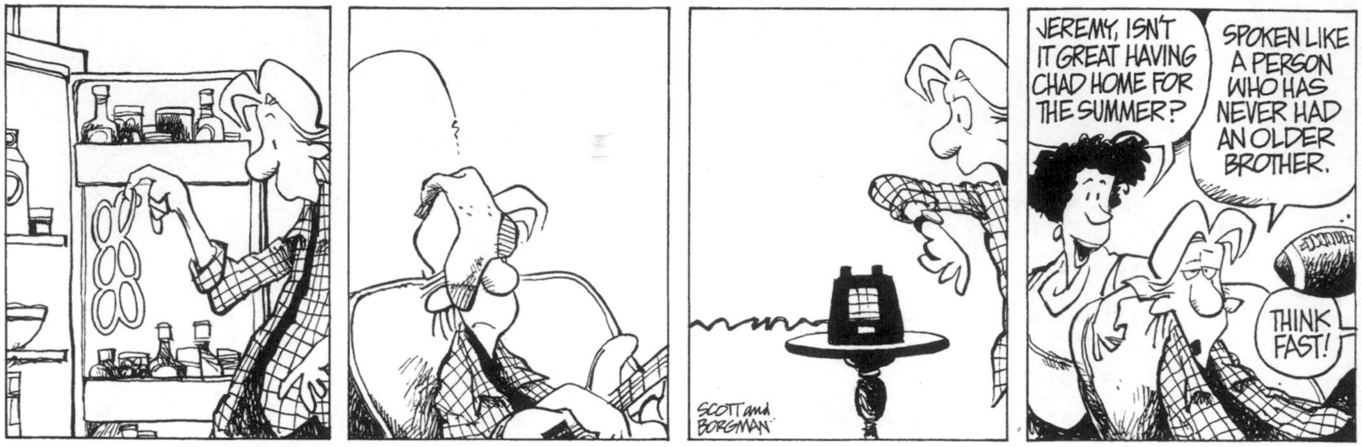

SCOTT and BORGMAN
JEREMY, ISN'T IT GREAT HAVING CHAD HOME FOR THE SUMMER?
SPOKEN LIKE A PERSON WHO HAS NEVER HAD AN OLDER BROTHER.
THINK FAST!

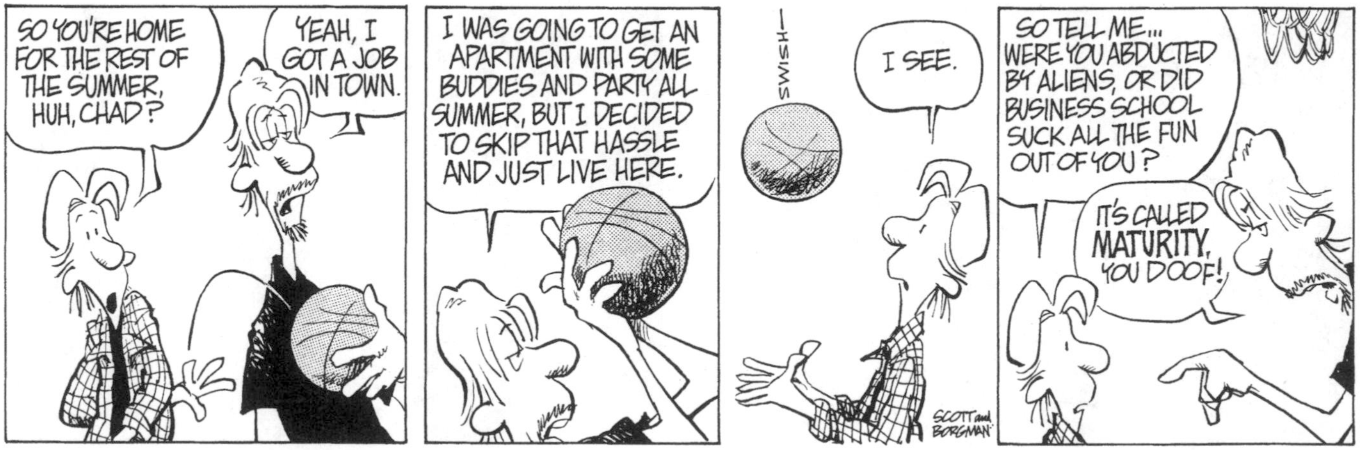

SO YOU'RE HOME FOR THE REST OF THE SUMMER, HUH, CHAD?
YEAH, I GOT A JOB IN TOWN.
I WAS GOING TO GET AN APARTMENT WITH SOME BUDDIES AND PARTY ALL SUMMER, BUT I DECIDED TO SKIP THAT HASSLE AND JUST LIVE HERE.
SWISH
I SEE.
SCOTT and BORGMAN
SO TELL ME... WERE YOU ABDUCTED BY ALIENS, OR DID BUSINESS SCHOOL SUCK ALL THE FUN OUT OF YOU?
IT'S CALLED **MATURITY**, YOU DOOF!

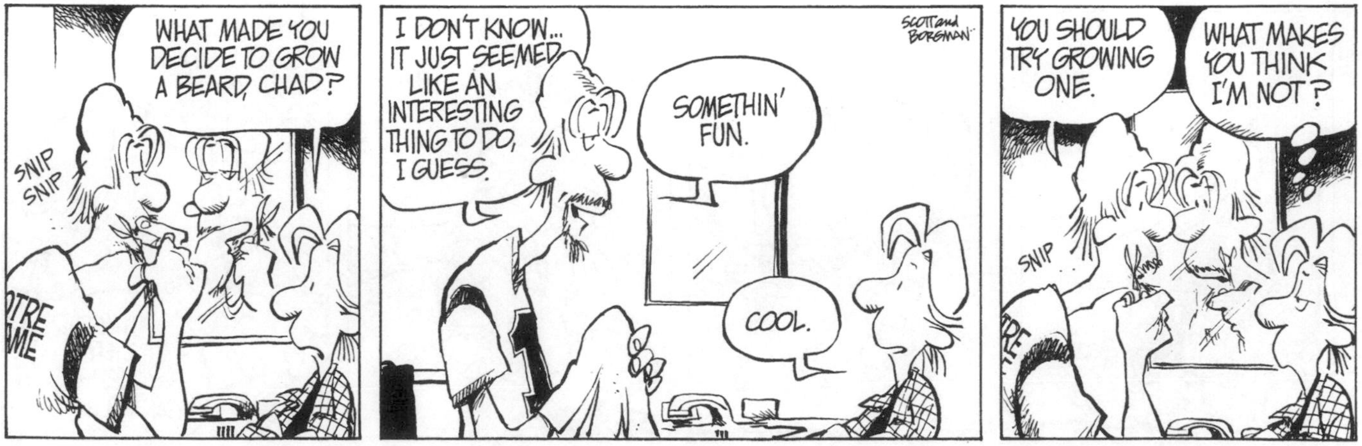

WHAT MADE YOU DECIDE TO GROW A BEARD, CHAD?
SNIP SNIP
NOTRE DAME
SCOTT and BORGMAN
I DON'T KNOW... IT JUST SEEMED LIKE AN INTERESTING THING TO DO, I GUESS.
SOMETHIN' FUN.
COOL.
YOU SHOULD TRY GROWING ONE.
WHAT MAKES YOU THINK I'M NOT?
SNIP

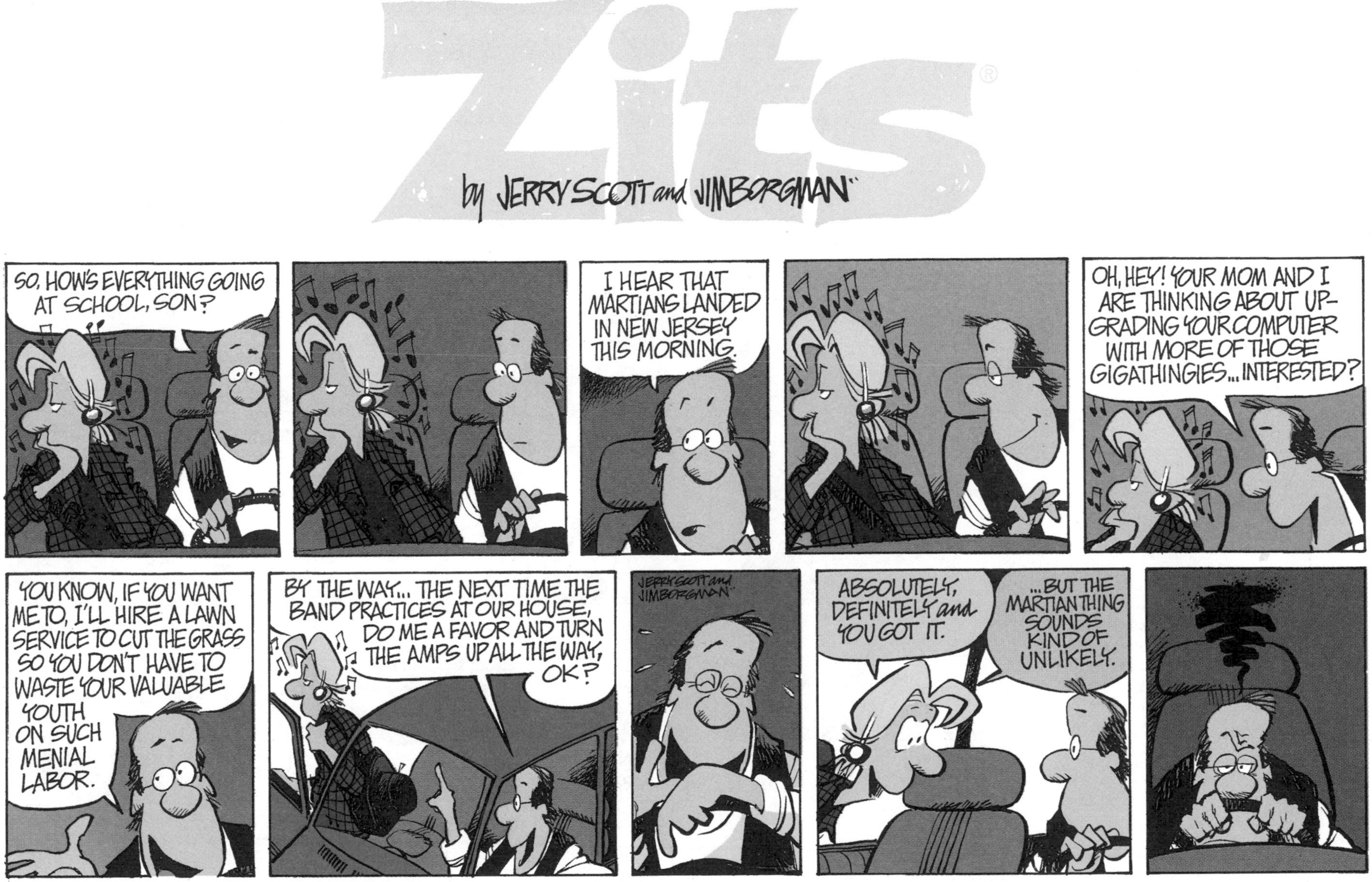
Zits
by JERRY SCOTT and JIM BORGMAN
SO, HOW'S EVERYTHING GOING AT SCHOOL, SON?
I HEAR THAT MARTIANS LANDED IN NEW JERSEY THIS MORNING.
OH, HEY! YOUR MOM AND I ARE THINKING ABOUT UP-GRADING YOUR COMPUTER WITH MORE OF THOSE GIGATHINGIES... INTERESTED?
YOU KNOW, IF YOU WANT ME TO, I'LL HIRE A LAWN SERVICE TO CUT THE GRASS SO YOU DON'T HAVE TO WASTE YOUR VALUABLE YOUTH ON SUCH MENIAL LABOR.
BY THE WAY... THE NEXT TIME THE BAND PRACTICES AT OUR HOUSE, DO ME A FAVOR AND TURN THE AMPS UP ALL THE WAY, OK?
JERRY SCOTT and JIM BORGMAN
ABSOLUTELY, DEFINITELY and YOU GOT IT.
...BUT THE MARTIAN THING SOUNDS KIND OF UNLIKELY.

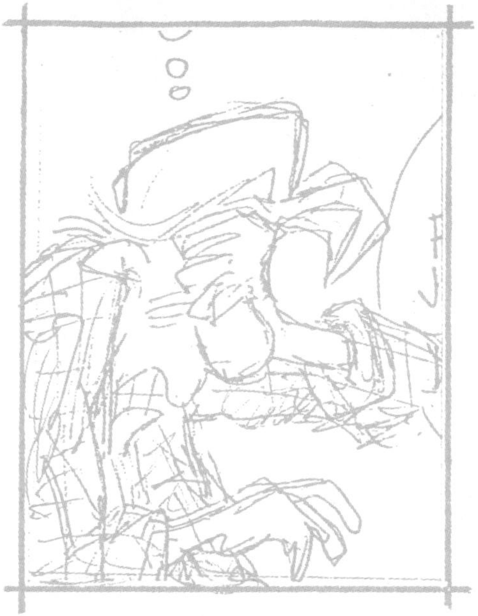

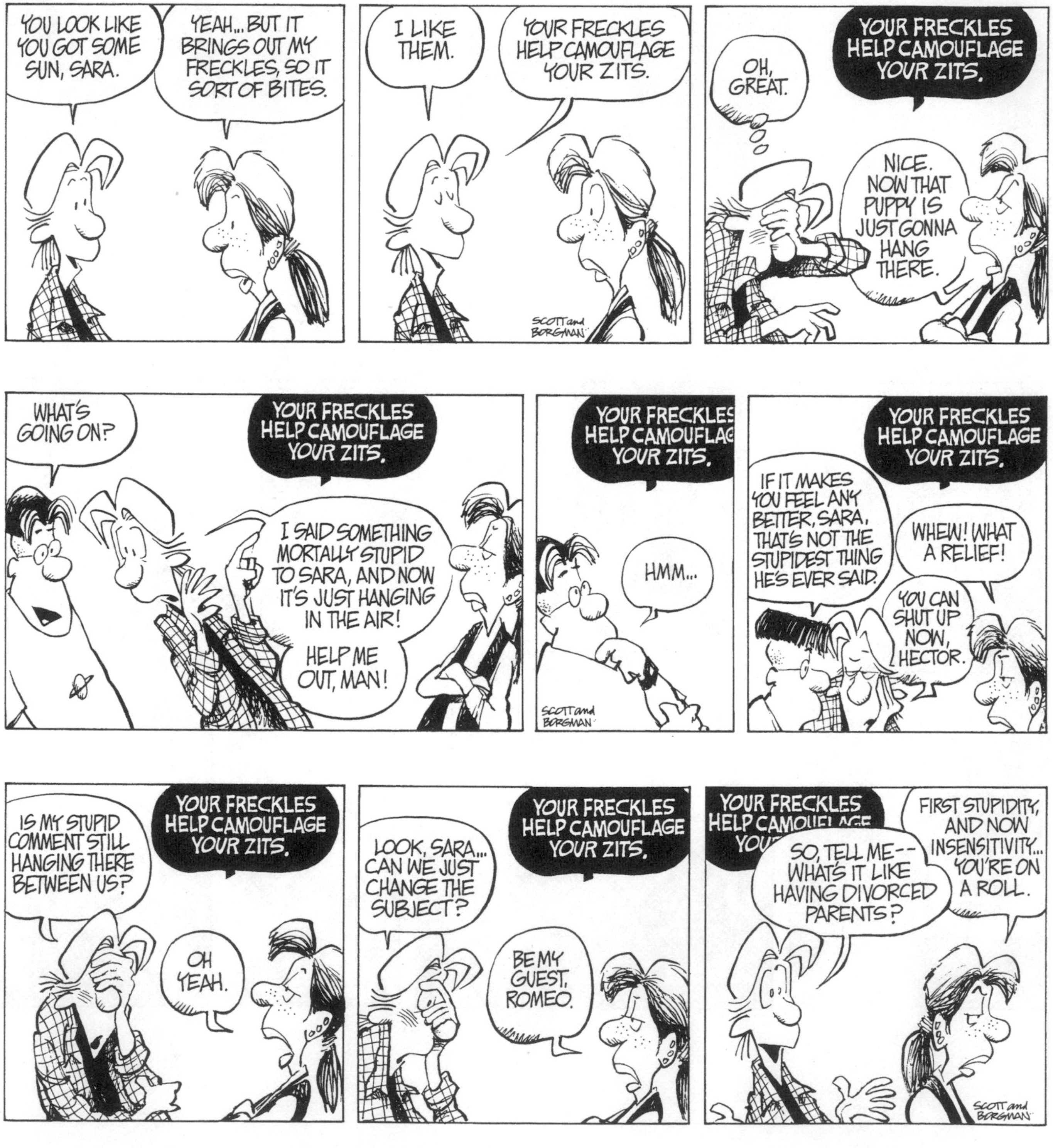

YOU LOOK LIKE YOU GOT SOME SUN, SARA.
YEAH... BUT IT BRINGS OUT MY FRECKLES, SO IT SORT OF BITES.
I LIKE THEM.
YOUR FRECKLES HELP CAMOUFLAGE YOUR ZITS.
SCOTT and BORGMAN
OH, GREAT.
YOUR FRECKLES HELP CAMOUFLAGE YOUR ZITS.
NICE. NOW THAT PUPPY IS JUST GONNA HANG THERE.
WHAT'S GOING ON?
YOUR FRECKLES HELP CAMOUFLAGE YOUR ZITS.
I SAID SOMETHING MORTALLY STUPID TO SARA, AND NOW IT'S JUST HANGING IN THE AIR!
HELP ME OUT, MAN!
YOUR FRECKLES HELP CAMOUFLAGE YOUR ZITS.
HMM...
SCOTT and BORGMAN
YOUR FRECKLES HELP CAMOUFLAGE YOUR ZITS.
IF IT MAKES YOU FEEL ANY BETTER, SARA, THAT'S NOT THE STUPIDEST THING HE'S EVER SAID.
WHEW! WHAT A RELIEF!
YOU CAN SHUT UP NOW, HECTOR.
IS MY STUPID COMMENT STILL HANGING THERE BETWEEN US?
YOUR FRECKLES HELP CAMOUFLAGE YOUR ZITS.
OH YEAH.
LOOK, SARA... CAN WE JUST CHANGE THE SUBJECT?
YOUR FRECKLES HELP CAMOUFLAGE YOUR ZITS.
BE MY GUEST, ROMEO.
SO, TELL ME-- WHAT'S IT LIKE HAVING DIVORCED PARENTS?
FIRST STUPIDITY, AND NOW INSENSITIVITY... YOU'RE ON A ROLL.
SCOTT and BORGMAN

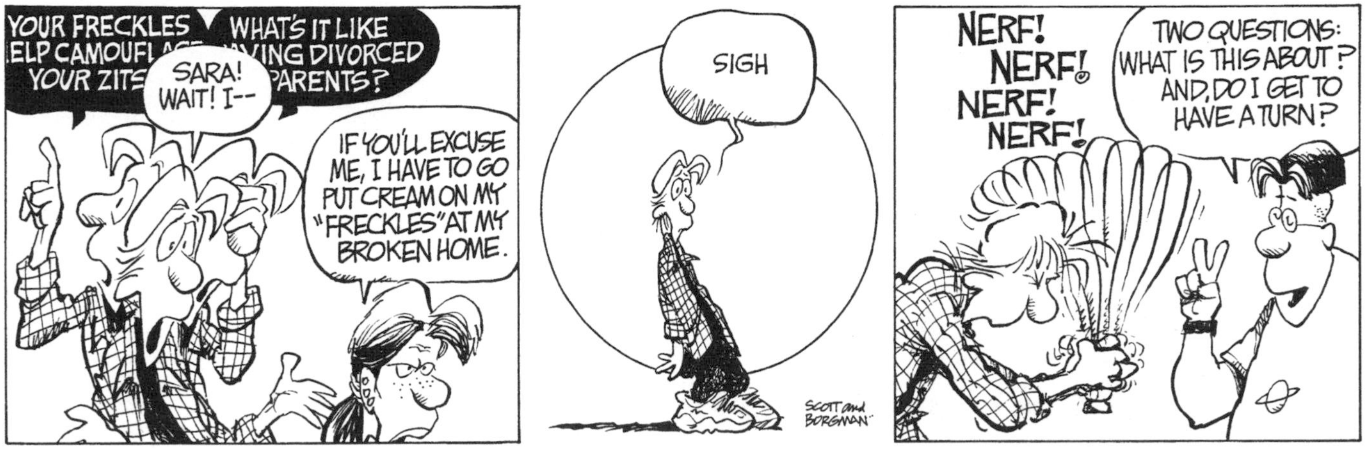
YOUR FRECKLES
ELP CAMOUFLA
YOUR ZITS
WHAT'S IT LIKE
VING DIVORCED
PARENTS?
SARA! WAIT! I--
IF YOU'LL EXCUSE ME, I HAVE TO GO PUT CREAM ON MY "FRECKLES" AT MY BROKEN HOME.
SIGH
SCOTT and BORGMAN
NERF! NERF! NERF! NERF!
TWO QUESTIONS: WHAT IS THIS ABOUT? AND, DO I GET TO HAVE A TURN?

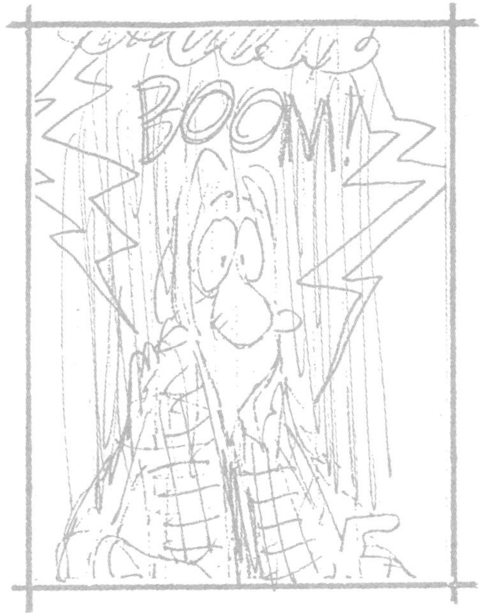
BOOM!

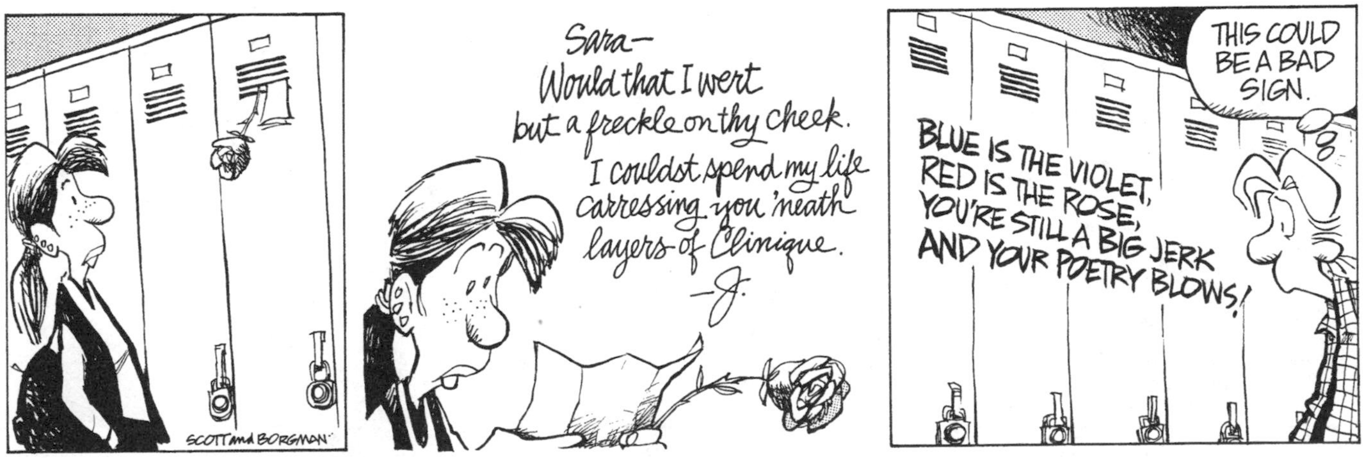
SCOTT and BORGMAN
Sara—
Would that I wert but a freckle on thy cheek.
I couldst spend my life carressing you 'neath layers of Clinique.
—J.
THIS COULD BE A BAD SIGN.
BLUE IS THE VIOLET, RED IS THE ROSE, YOU'RE STILL A BIG JERK AND YOUR POETRY BLOWS!

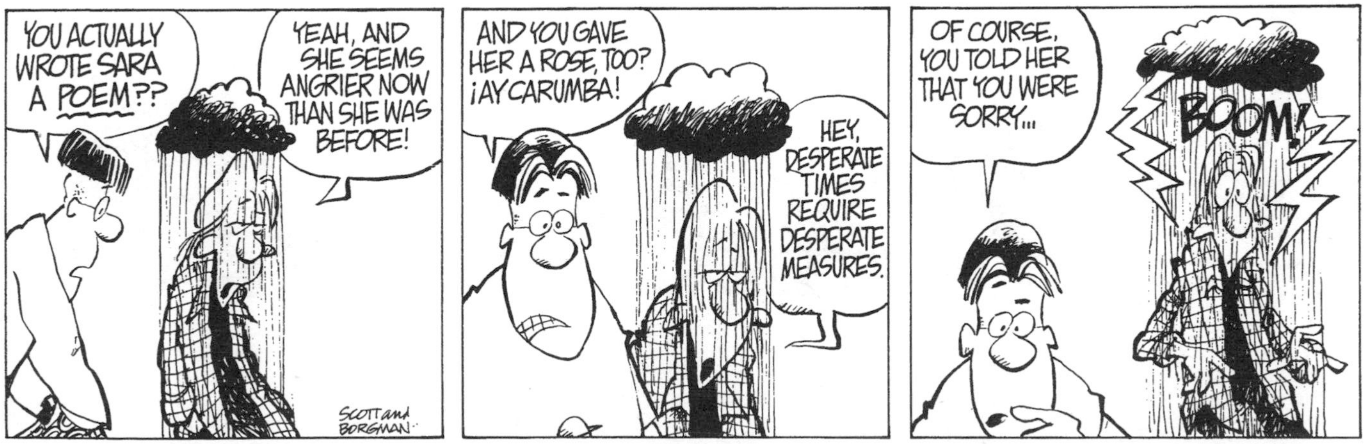
YOU ACTUALLY WROTE SARA A POEM??
YEAH, AND SHE SEEMS ANGRIER NOW THAN SHE WAS BEFORE!
SCOTT and BORGMAN
AND YOU GAVE HER A ROSE, TOO? ¡AY CARUMBA!
HEY, DESPERATE TIMES REQUIRE DESPERATE MEASURES.
OF COURSE, YOU TOLD HER THAT YOU WERE SORRY...
BOOM!

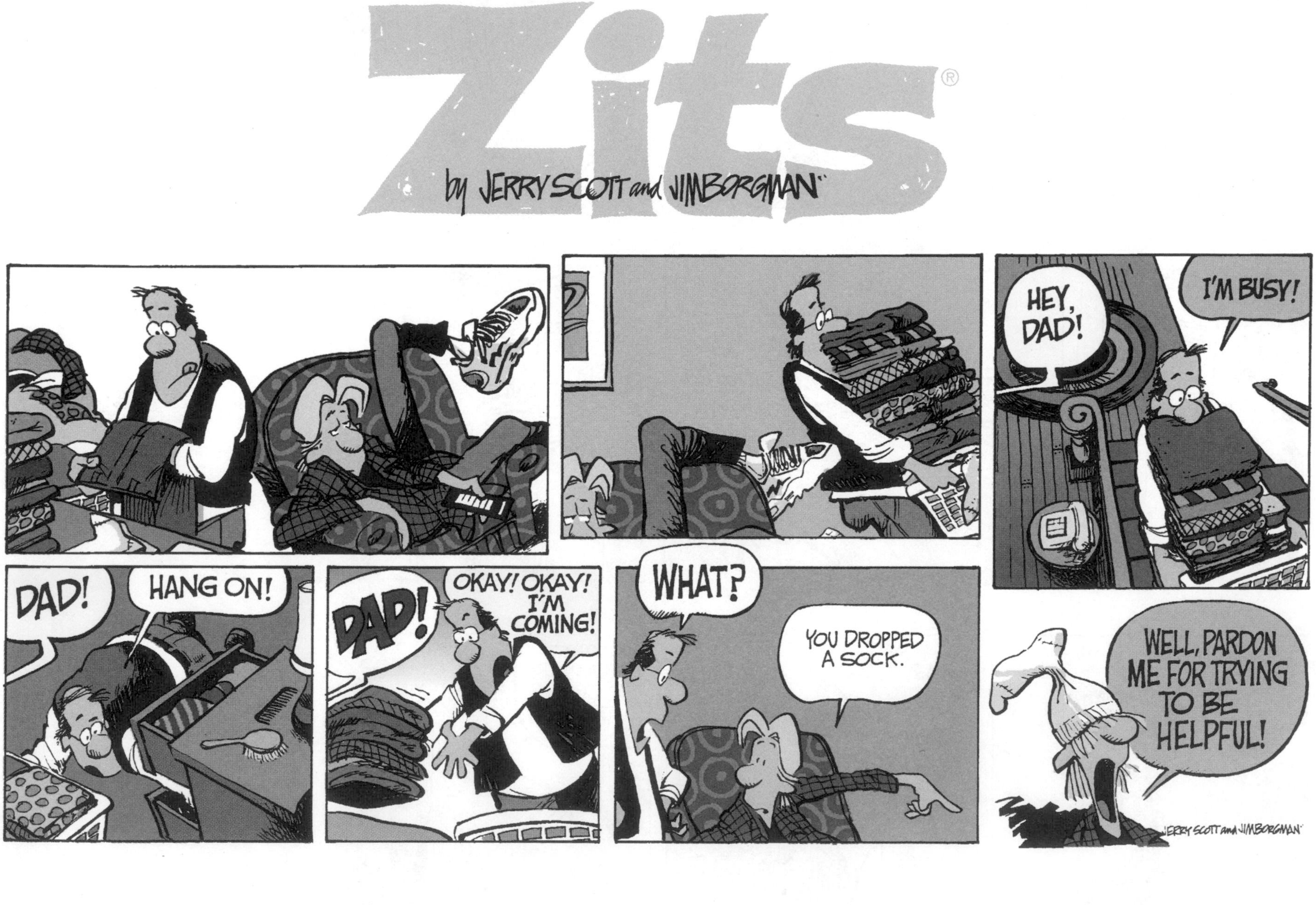
Zits®
by JERRY SCOTT and JIM BORGMAN
HEY, DAD!
I'M BUSY!
DAD!
HANG ON!
DAD!
OKAY! OKAY! I'M COMING!
WHAT?
YOU DROPPED A SOCK.
WELL, PARDON ME FOR TRYING TO BE HELPFUL!
JERRY SCOTT and JIM BORGMAN

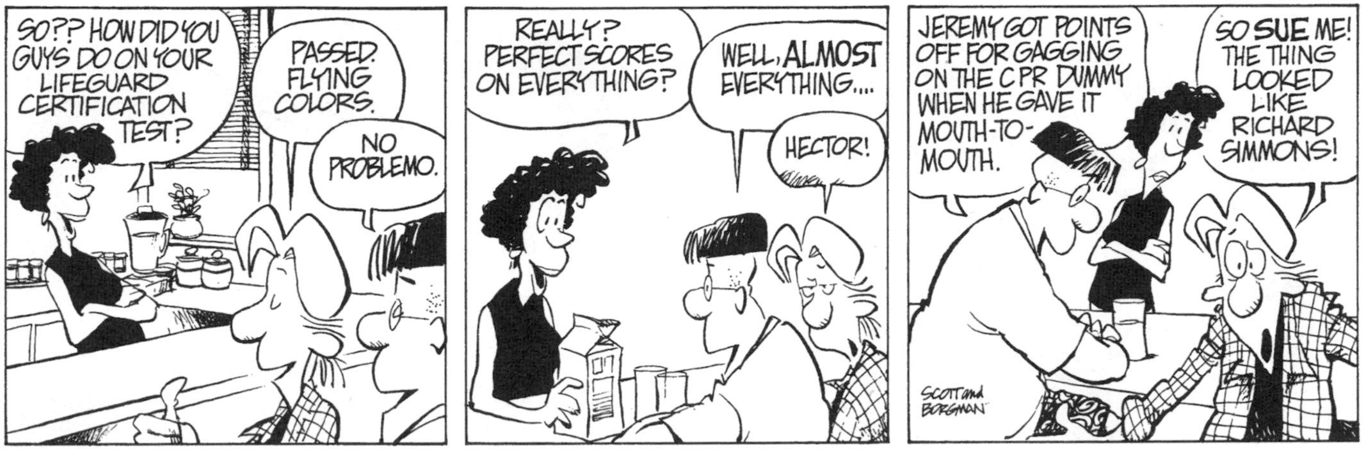
SO?? HOW DID YOU GUYS DO ON YOUR LIFEGUARD CERTIFICATION TEST?
PASSED. FLYING COLORS.
NO PROBLEMO.
REALLY? PERFECT SCORES ON EVERYTHING?
WELL, ALMOST EVERYTHING....
HECTOR!
JEREMY GOT POINTS OFF FOR GAGGING ON THE CPR DUMMY WHEN HE GAVE IT MOUTH-TO-MOUTH.
SO SUE ME! THE THING LOOKED LIKE RICHARD SIMMONS!
SCOTT and BORGMAN

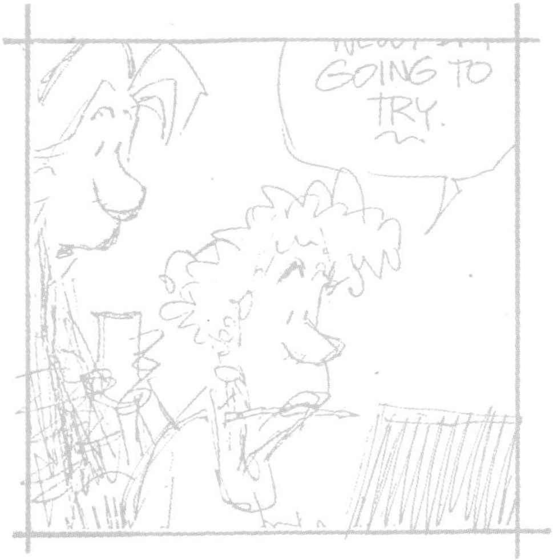
GOING TO
TRY.

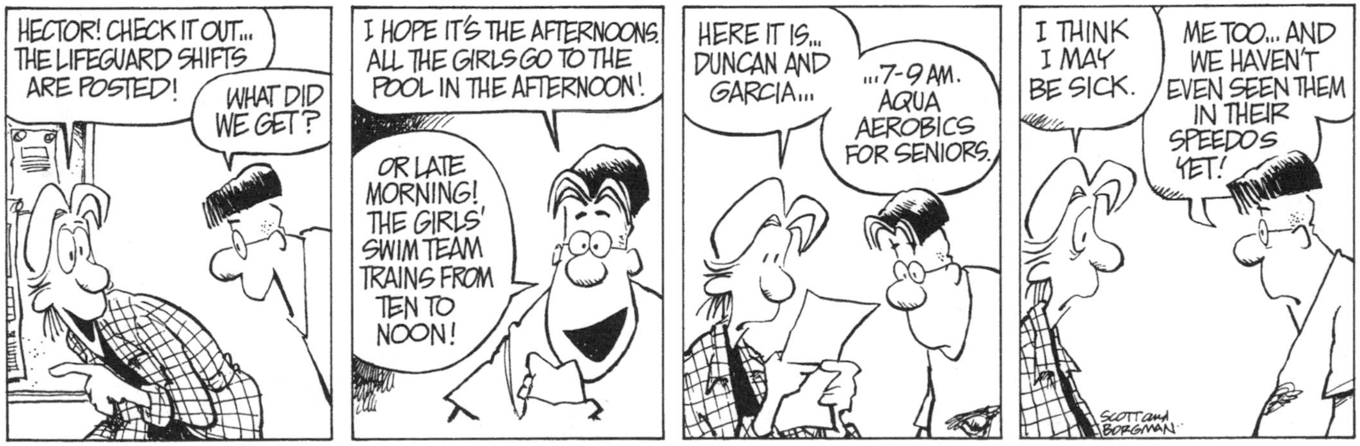
HECTOR! CHECK IT OUT... THE LIFEGUARD SHIFTS ARE POSTED!
WHAT DID WE GET?
I HOPE IT'S THE AFTERNOONS. ALL THE GIRLS GO TO THE POOL IN THE AFTERNOON!
OR LATE MORNING! THE GIRLS' SWIM TEAM TRAINS FROM TEN TO NOON!
HERE IT IS... DUNCAN AND GARCIA...
...7-9 AM. AQUA AEROBICS FOR SENIORS.
I THINK I MAY BE SICK.
ME TOO... AND WE HAVEN'T EVEN SEEN THEM IN THEIR SPEEDOS YET!
SCOTT and BORGMAN

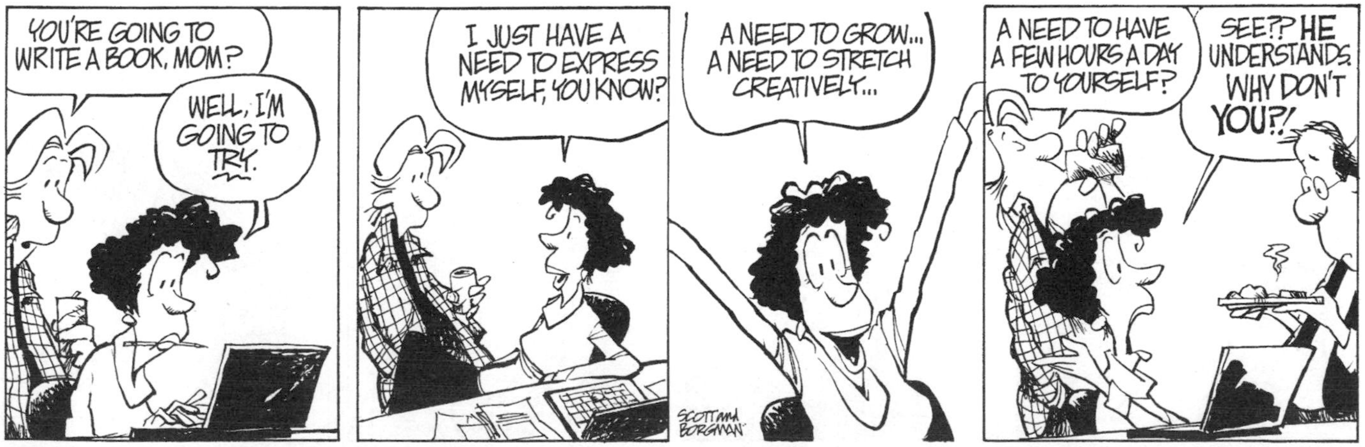
YOU'RE GOING TO WRITE A BOOK, MOM?
WELL, I'M GOING TO TRY.
I JUST HAVE A NEED TO EXPRESS MYSELF, YOU KNOW?
A NEED TO GROW... A NEED TO STRETCH CREATIVELY...
SCOTT and BORGMAN
A NEED TO HAVE A FEW HOURS A DAY TO YOURSELF?
SEE?? HE UNDERSTANDS. WHY DON'T YOU?!

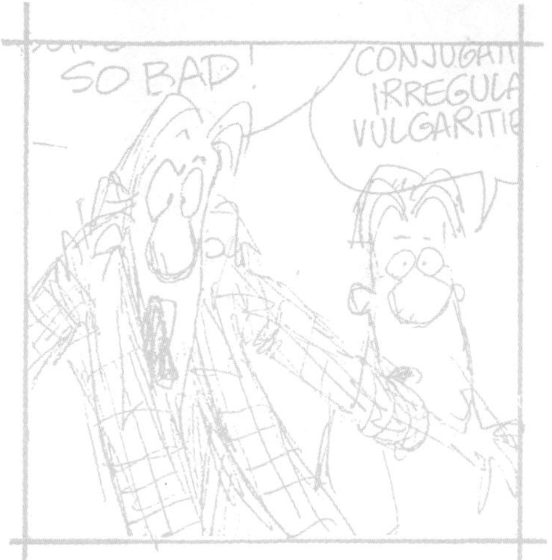
SO BAD!
CONJUGATI
IRREGULA
VULGARITIE

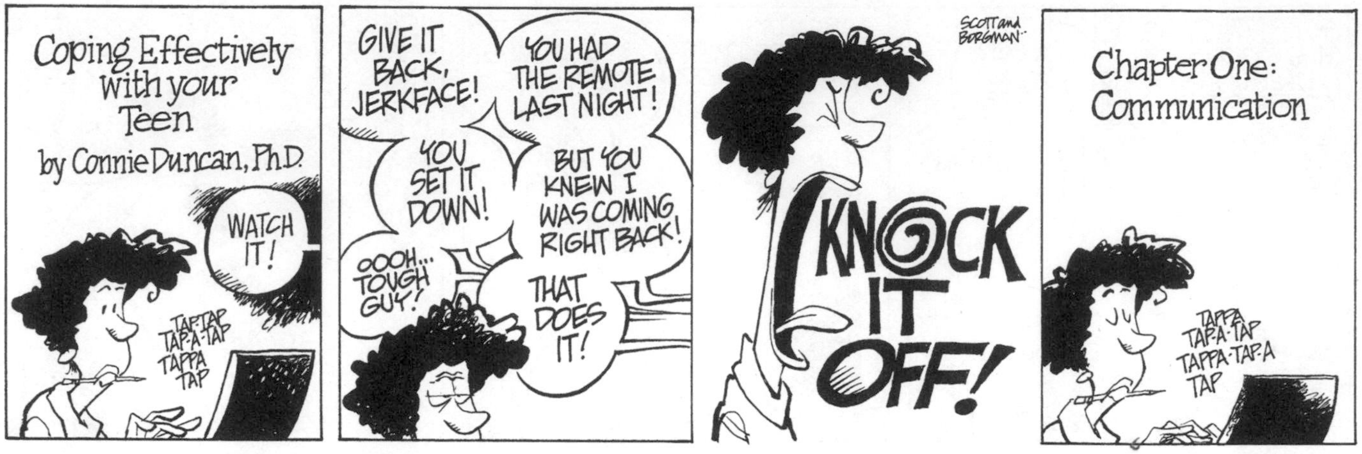
Coping Effectively with your Teen
by Connie Duncan, Ph.D.
WATCH IT!
TAPTAP TAP-A-TAP TAPPA TAP
GIVE IT BACK, JERKFACE!
YOU HAD THE REMOTE LAST NIGHT!
YOU SET IT DOWN!
BUT YOU KNEW I WAS COMING RIGHT BACK!
OOOH... TOUGH GUY!
THAT DOES IT!
SCOTT AND BORGMAN
KNOCK IT OFF!
Chapter One: Communication
TAPPA TAP-A-TAP TAPPA-TAP-A TAP

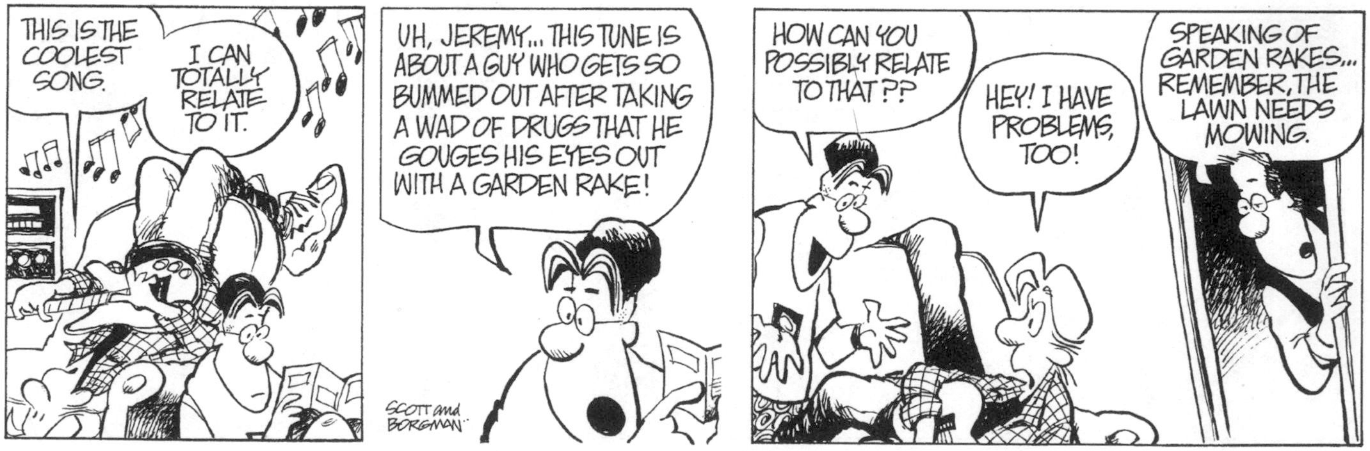
THIS IS THE COOLEST SONG.
I CAN TOTALLY RELATE TO IT.
UH, JEREMY... THIS TUNE IS ABOUT A GUY WHO GETS SO BUMMED OUT AFTER TAKING A WAD OF DRUGS THAT HE GOUGES HIS EYES OUT WITH A GARDEN RAKE!
SCOTT AND BORGMAN
HOW CAN YOU POSSIBLY RELATE TO THAT??
HEY! I HAVE PROBLEMS, TOO!
SPEAKING OF GARDEN RAKES... REMEMBER, THE LAWN NEEDS MOWING.

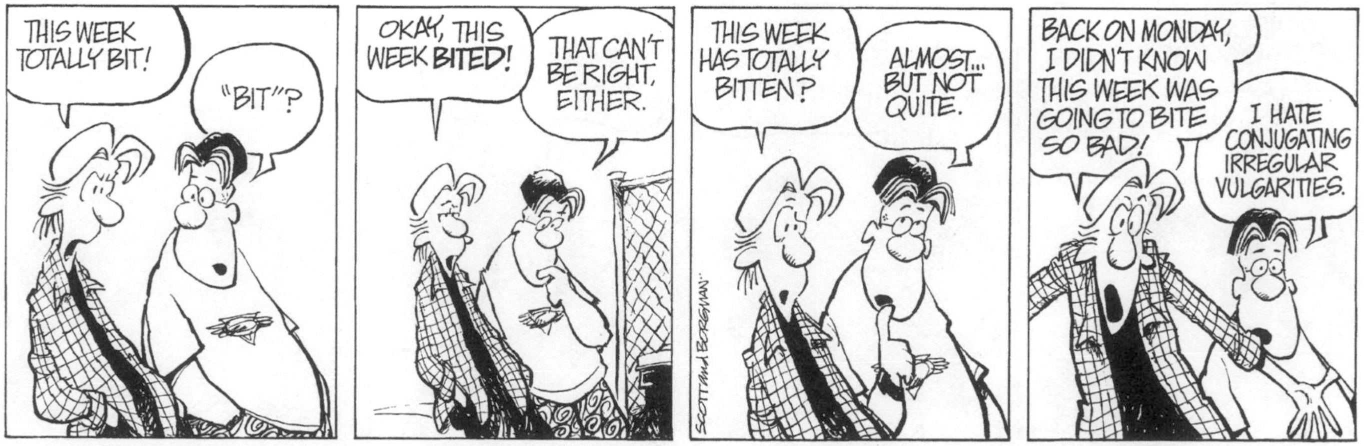
THIS WEEK TOTALLY BIT!
"BIT"?
OKAY, THIS WEEK BITED!
THAT CAN'T BE RIGHT, EITHER.
THIS WEEK HAS TOTALLY BITTEN?
ALMOST... BUT NOT QUITE.
SCOTT AND BORGMAN
BACK ON MONDAY, I DIDN'T KNOW THIS WEEK WAS GOING TO BITE SO BAD!
I HATE CONJUGATING IRREGULAR VULGARITIES.

Zits®

by JERRY SCOTT and JIM BORGMAN™

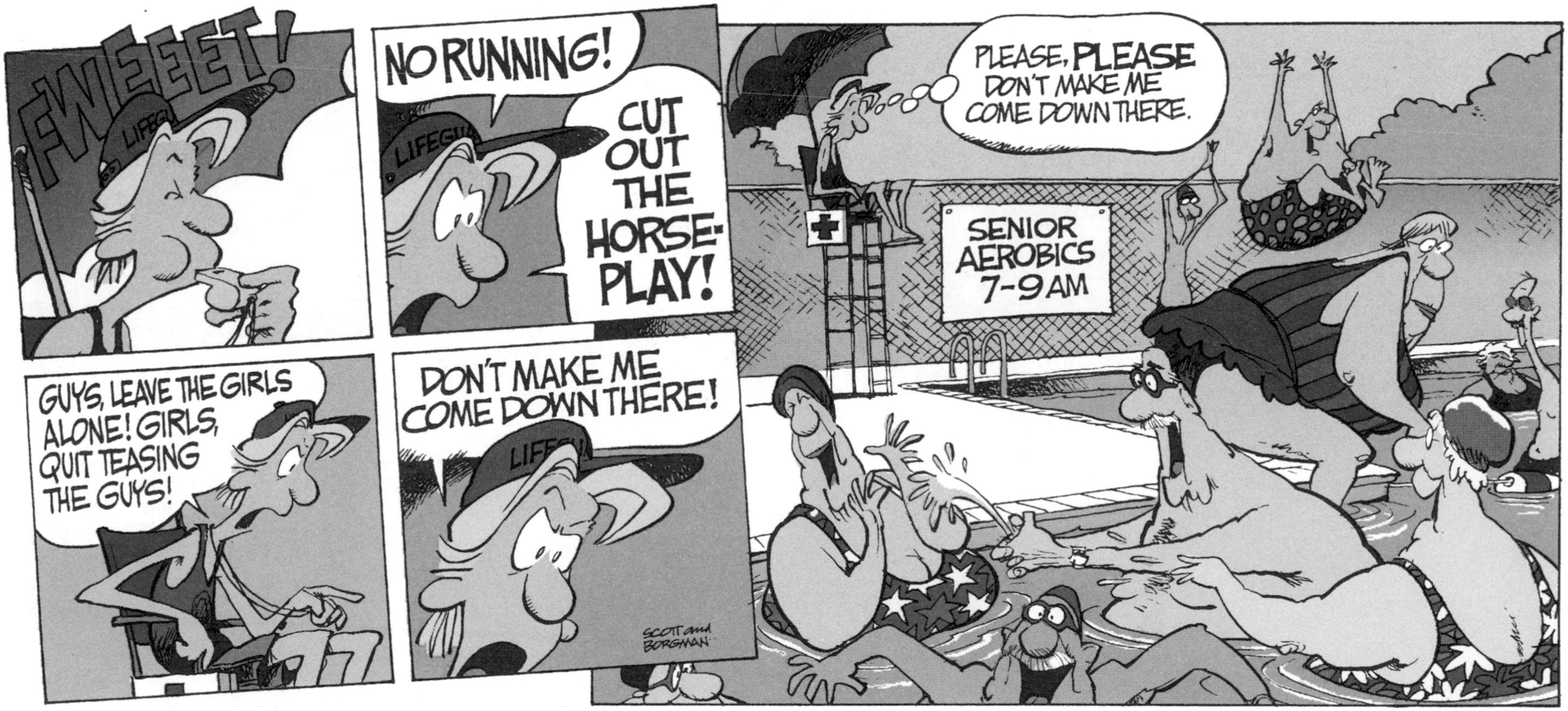
FWEEEET!
NO RUNNING!
CUT OUT THE HORSE-PLAY!
GUYS, LEAVE THE GIRLS ALONE! GIRLS, QUIT TEASING THE GUYS!
DON'T MAKE ME COME DOWN THERE!
SCOTT and BORGMAN
PLEASE, PLEASE DON'T MAKE ME COME DOWN THERE.
SENIOR AEROBICS 7-9 AM

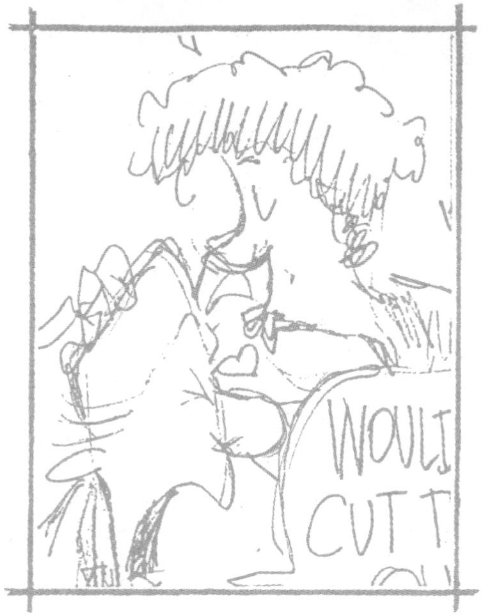

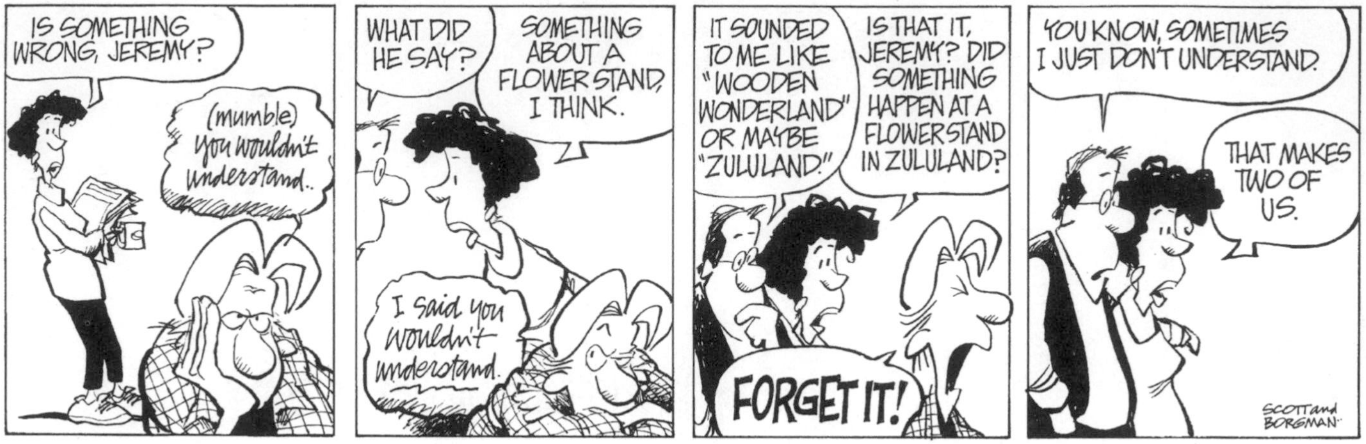

IS SOMETHING WRONG, JEREMY?
(mumble) You wouldn't understand..
WHAT DID HE SAY?
SOMETHING ABOUT A FLOWER STAND, I THINK.
I said you wouldn't understand.
IT SOUNDED TO ME LIKE "WOODEN WONDERLAND" OR MAYBE "ZULULAND."
IS THAT IT, JEREMY? DID SOMETHING HAPPEN AT A FLOWER STAND IN ZULULAND?
FORGET IT!
YOU KNOW, SOMETIMES I JUST DON'T UNDERSTAND.
THAT MAKES TWO OF US.
SCOTT and BORGMAN

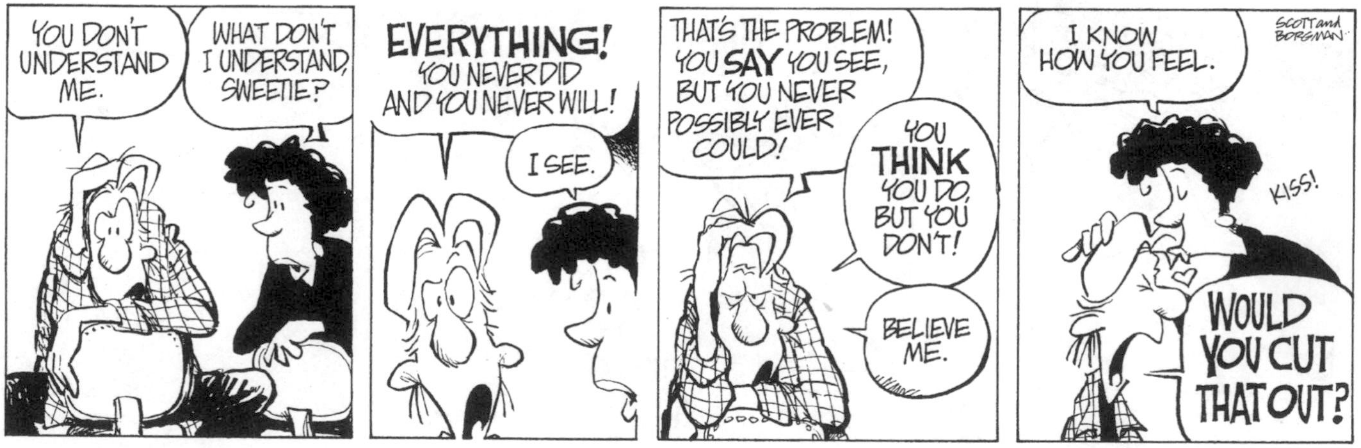

YOU DON'T UNDERSTAND ME.
WHAT DON'T I UNDERSTAND, SWEETIE?
EVERYTHING! YOU NEVER DID AND YOU NEVER WILL!
I SEE.
THAT'S THE PROBLEM! YOU SAY YOU SEE, BUT YOU NEVER POSSIBLY EVER COULD!
YOU THINK YOU DO, BUT YOU DON'T!
BELIEVE ME.
I KNOW HOW YOU FEEL.
SCOTT and BORGMAN
KISS!
WOULD YOU CUT THAT OUT?

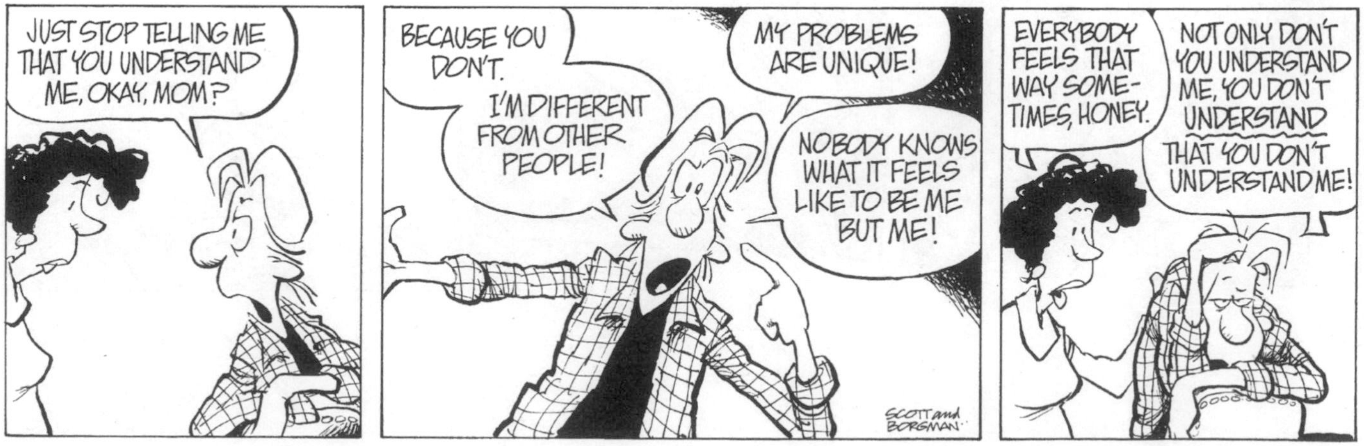

JUST STOP TELLING ME THAT YOU UNDERSTAND ME, OKAY, MOM?
BECAUSE YOU DON'T.
I'M DIFFERENT FROM OTHER PEOPLE!
MY PROBLEMS ARE UNIQUE!
NOBODY KNOWS WHAT IT FEELS LIKE TO BE ME BUT ME!
SCOTT and BORGMAN
EVERYBODY FEELS THAT WAY SOMETIMES, HONEY.
NOT ONLY DON'T YOU UNDERSTAND ME, YOU DON'T UNDERSTAND THAT YOU DON'T UNDERSTAND ME!

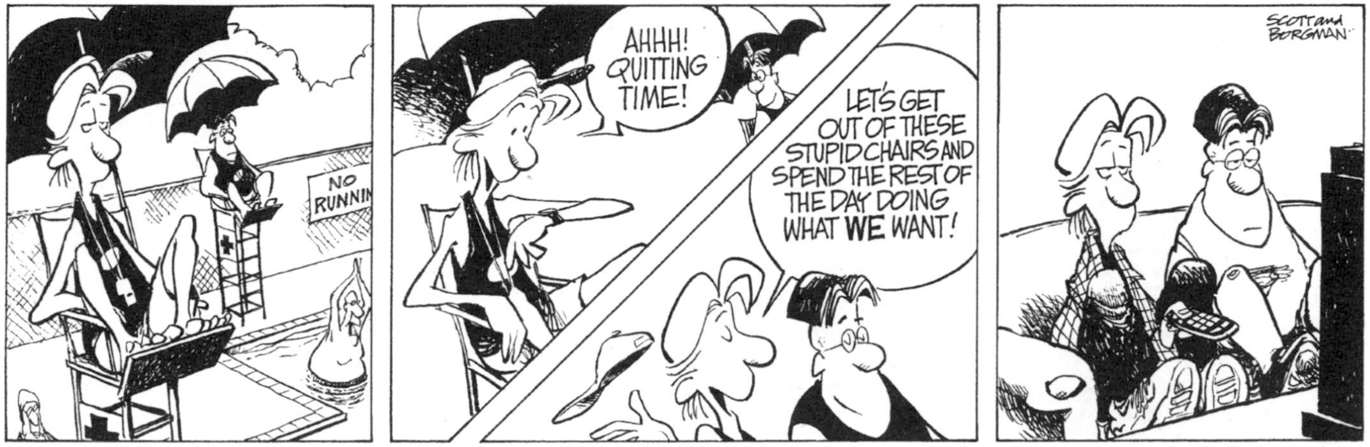
SCOTT and BORGMAN
NO RUNNIN
AHHH! QUITTING TIME!
LET'S GET OUT OF THESE STUPID CHAIRS AND SPEND THE REST OF THE DAY DOING WHAT **WE** WANT!

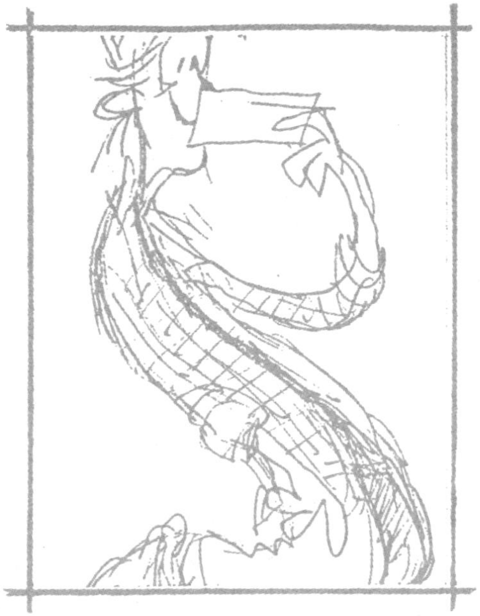

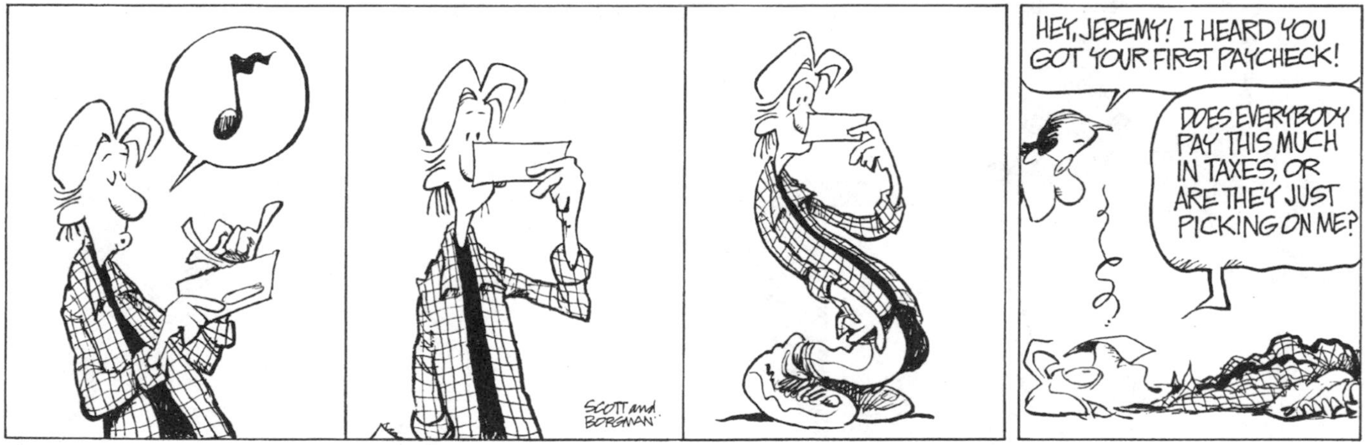
SCOTT and BORGMAN
HEY, JEREMY! I HEARD YOU GOT YOUR FIRST PAYCHECK!
DOES EVERYBODY PAY THIS MUCH IN TAXES, OR ARE THEY JUST PICKING ON ME?

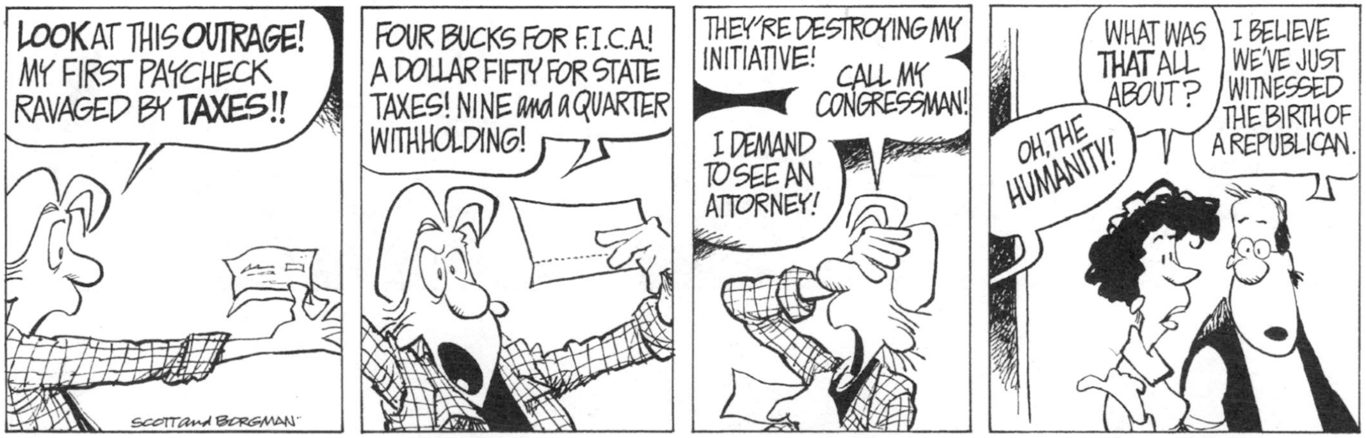
LOOK AT THIS **OUTRAGE!** MY FIRST PAYCHECK RAVAGED BY **TAXES!!**
SCOTT and BORGMAN
FOUR BUCKS FOR F.I.C.A.! A DOLLAR FIFTY FOR STATE TAXES! NINE *and a* QUARTER WITHHOLDING!
THEY'RE DESTROYING MY INITIATIVE!
CALL MY CONGRESSMAN!
I DEMAND TO SEE AN ATTORNEY!
WHAT WAS **THAT** ALL ABOUT?
I BELIEVE WE'VE JUST WITNESSED THE BIRTH OF A REPUBLICAN.
OH, THE HUMANITY!

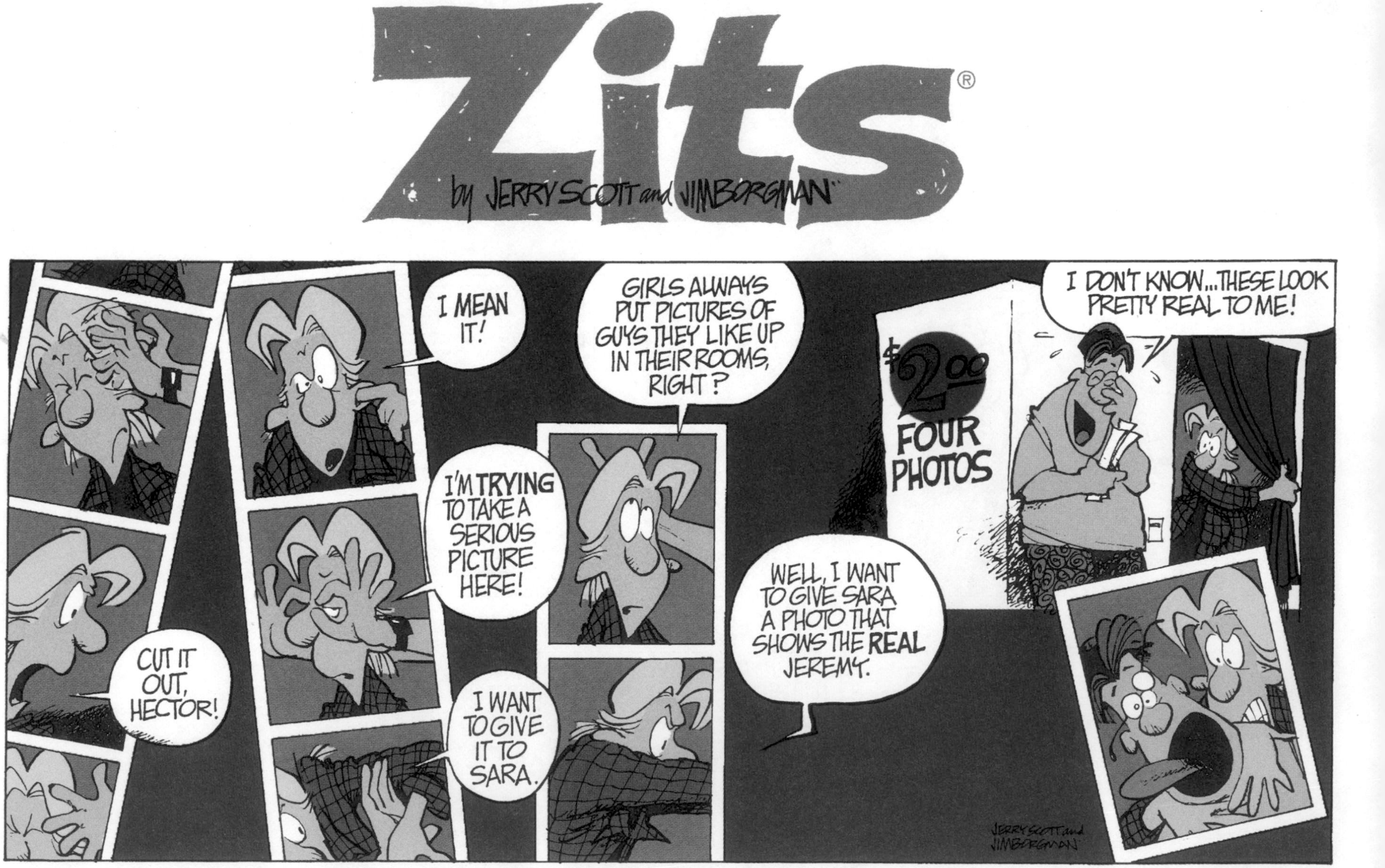
Zits®
by JERRY SCOTT and JIM BORGMAN
I MEAN IT!
CUT IT OUT, HECTOR!
I'M **TRYING** TO TAKE A SERIOUS PICTURE HERE!
I WANT TO GIVE IT TO SARA.
GIRLS ALWAYS PUT PICTURES OF GUYS THEY LIKE UP IN THEIR ROOMS, RIGHT?
WELL, I WANT TO GIVE SARA A PHOTO THAT SHOWS THE **REAL** JEREMY.
$2.00
FOUR PHOTOS
I DON'T KNOW...THESE LOOK PRETTY REAL TO ME!
JERRY SCOTT and JIM BORGMAN

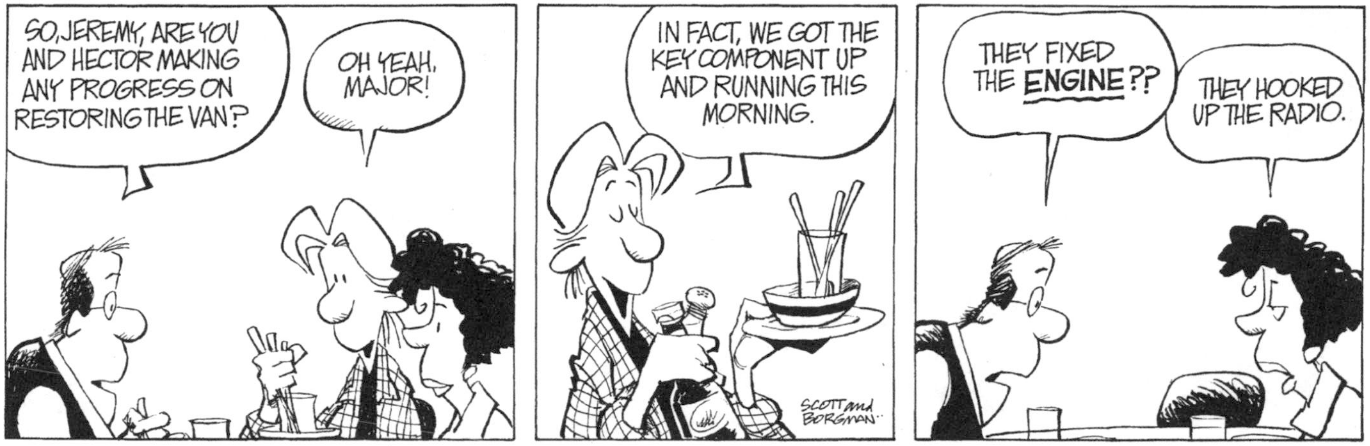
SO, JEREMY, ARE YOU AND HECTOR MAKING ANY PROGRESS ON RESTORING THE VAN?
OH YEAH, MAJOR!
IN FACT, WE GOT THE KEY COMPONENT UP AND RUNNING THIS MORNING.
SCOTT and BORGMAN
THEY FIXED THE ENGINE??
THEY HOOKED UP THE RADIO.

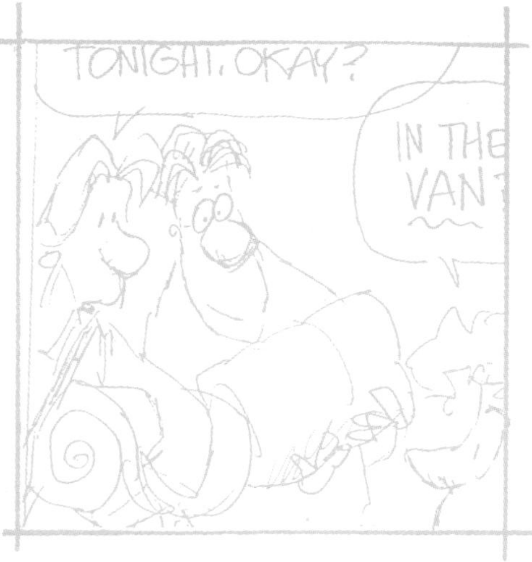
TONIGHT, OKAY?

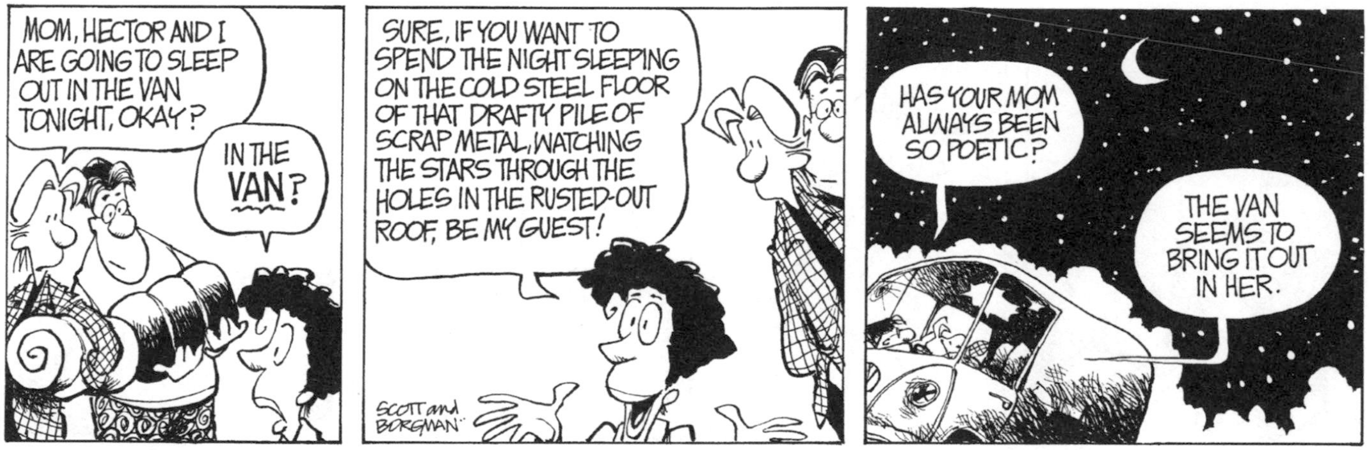
MOM, HECTOR AND I ARE GOING TO SLEEP OUT IN THE VAN TONIGHT, OKAY?
IN THE VAN?
SURE, IF YOU WANT TO SPEND THE NIGHT SLEEPING ON THE COLD STEEL FLOOR OF THAT DRAFTY PILE OF SCRAP METAL, WATCHING THE STARS THROUGH THE HOLES IN THE RUSTED-OUT ROOF, BE MY GUEST!
SCOTT and BORGMAN
HAS YOUR MOM ALWAYS BEEN SO POETIC?
THE VAN SEEMS TO BRING IT OUT IN HER.

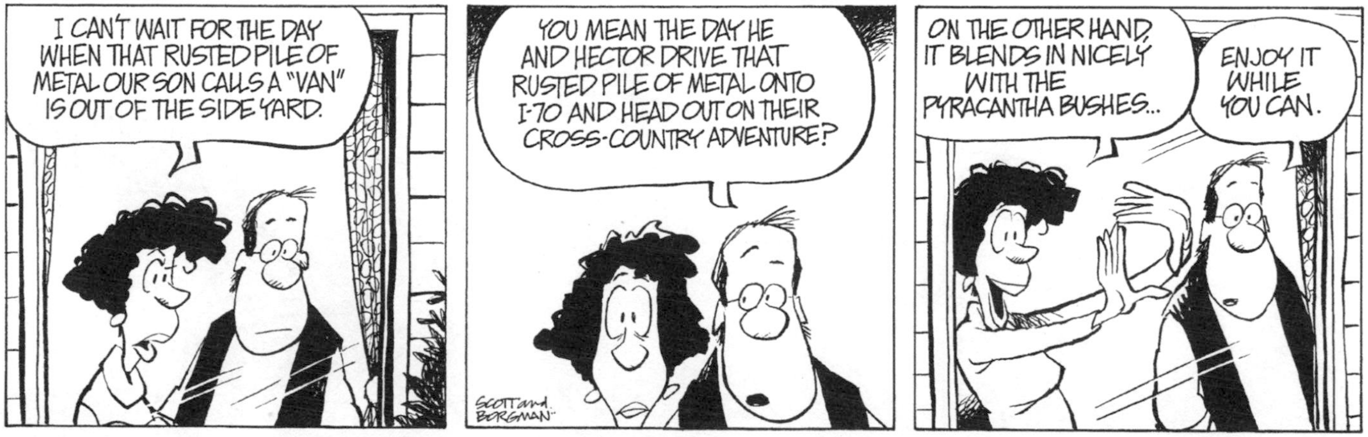
I CAN'T WAIT FOR THE DAY WHEN THAT RUSTED PILE OF METAL OUR SON CALLS A "VAN" IS OUT OF THE SIDE YARD.
YOU MEAN THE DAY HE AND HECTOR DRIVE THAT RUSTED PILE OF METAL ONTO I-70 AND HEAD OUT ON THEIR CROSS-COUNTRY ADVENTURE?
SCOTT and BORGMAN
ON THE OTHER HAND, IT BLENDS IN NICELY WITH THE PYRACANTHA BUSHES...
ENJOY IT WHILE YOU CAN.

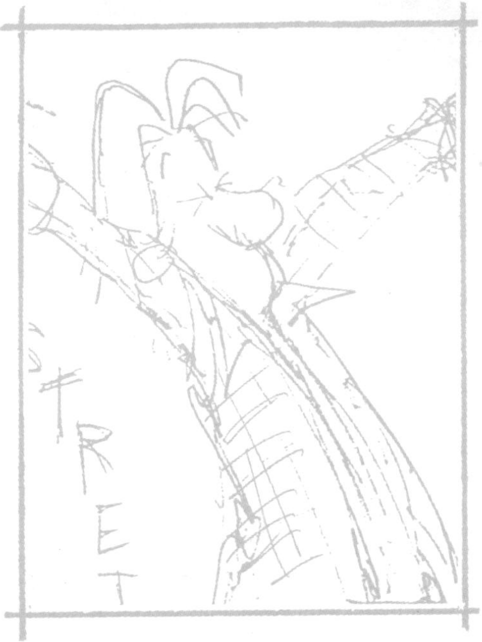
STRET

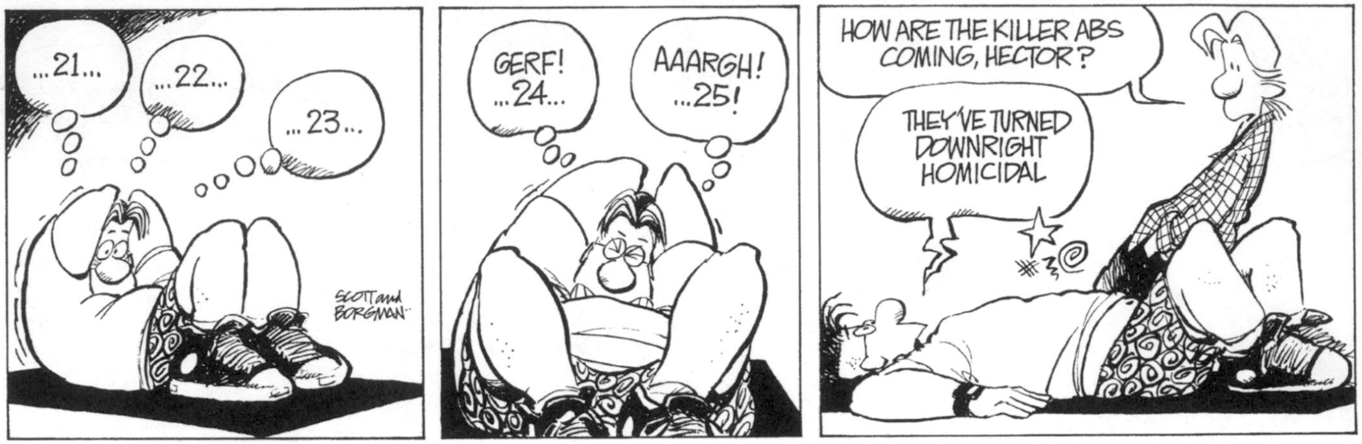
...21...
...22...
...23...
SCOTT and BORGMAN
GERF! ...24...
AAARGH! ...25!
HOW ARE THE KILLER ABS COMING, HECTOR?
THEY'VE TURNED DOWNRIGHT HOMICIDAL

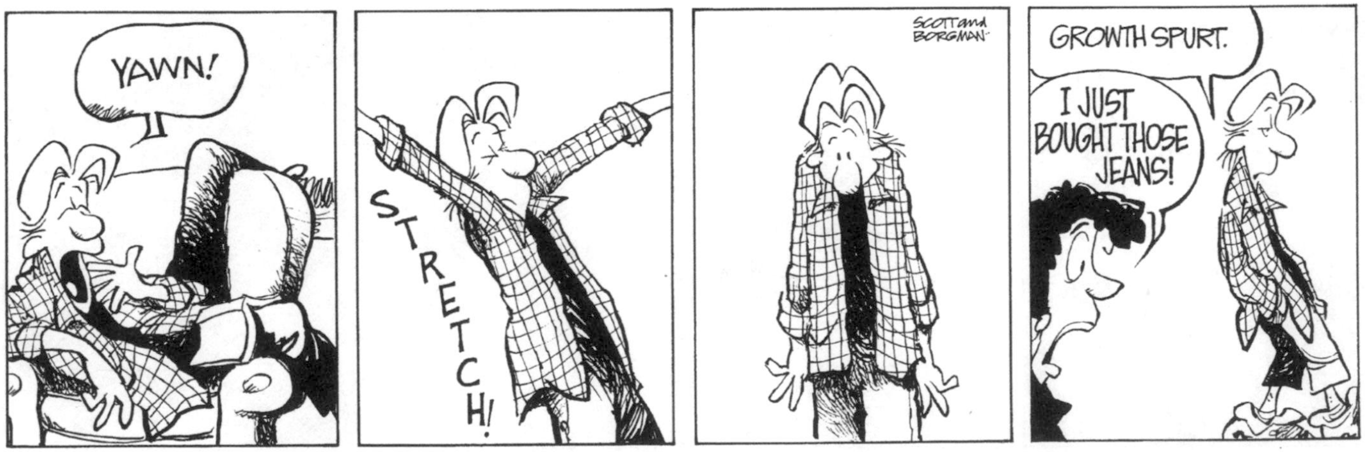
YAWN!
STRETCH!
SCOTT and BORGMAN
GROWTH SPURT.
I JUST BOUGHT THOSE JEANS!

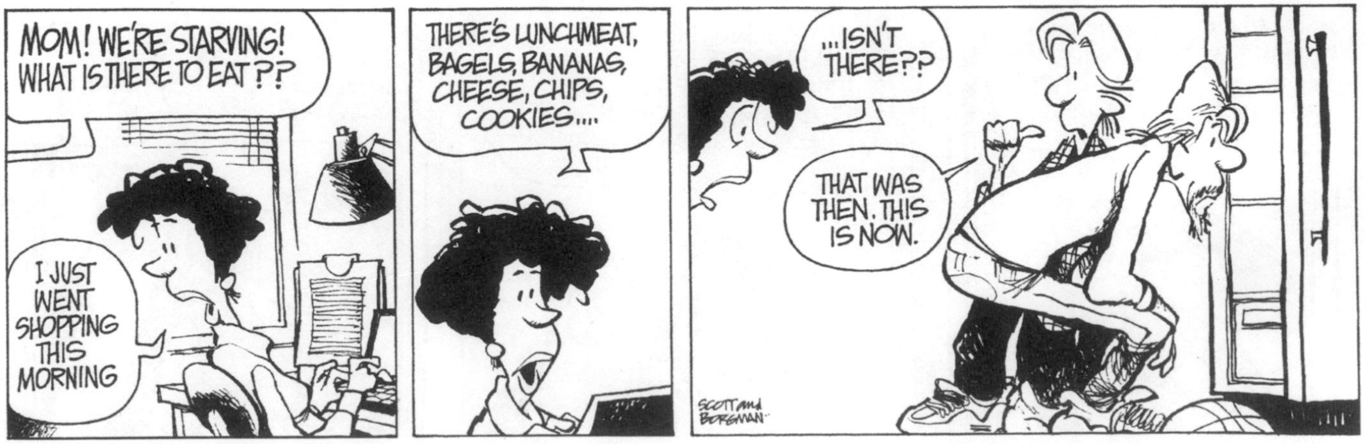
MOM! WE'RE STARVING! WHAT IS THERE TO EAT??
I JUST WENT SHOPPING THIS MORNING
THERE'S LUNCHMEAT, BAGELS, BANANAS, CHEESE, CHIPS, COOKIES....
...ISN'T THERE??
THAT WAS THEN. THIS IS NOW.
SCOTT and BORGMAN

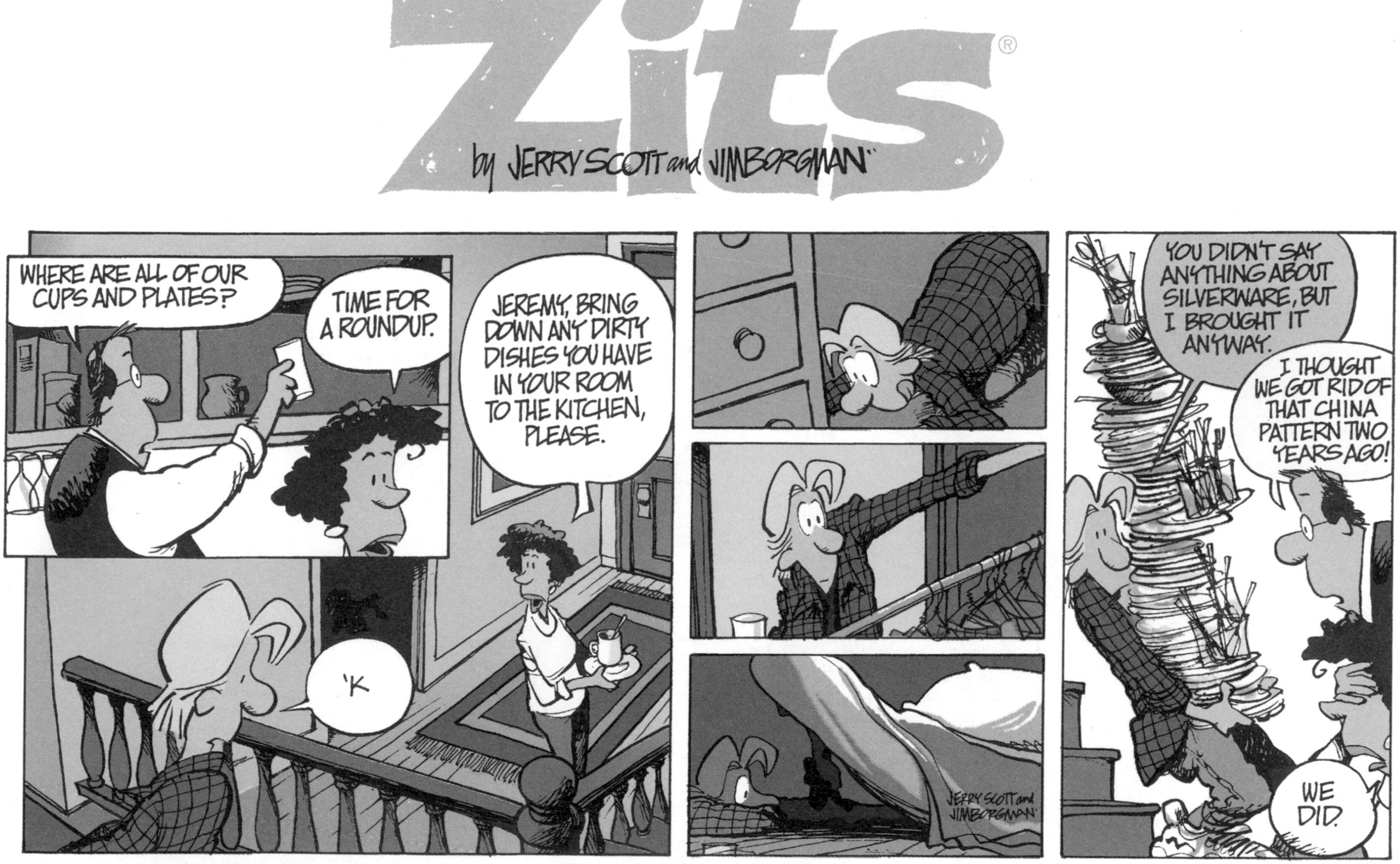
Zits®
by JERRY SCOTT and JIM BORGMAN
WHERE ARE ALL OF OUR CUPS AND PLATES?
TIME FOR A ROUNDUP.
JEREMY, BRING DOWN ANY DIRTY DISHES YOU HAVE IN YOUR ROOM TO THE KITCHEN, PLEASE.
'K
JERRY SCOTT and JIM BORGMAN
YOU DIDN'T SAY ANYTHING ABOUT SILVERWARE, BUT I BROUGHT IT ANYWAY.
I THOUGHT WE GOT RID OF THAT CHINA PATTERN TWO YEARS AGO!
WE DID.

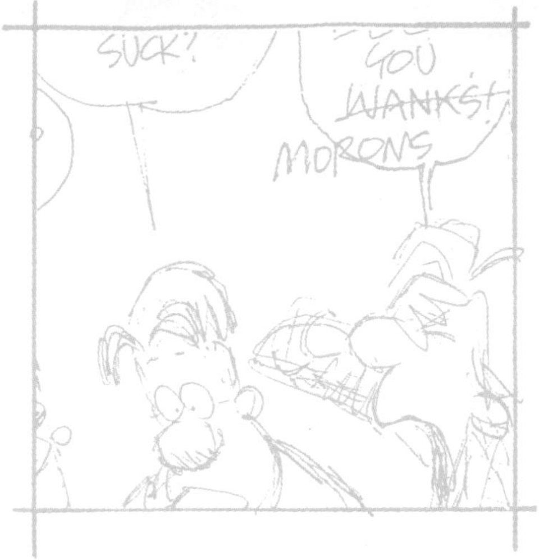
SUCK?
YOU ~~WANKS!~~ MORONS

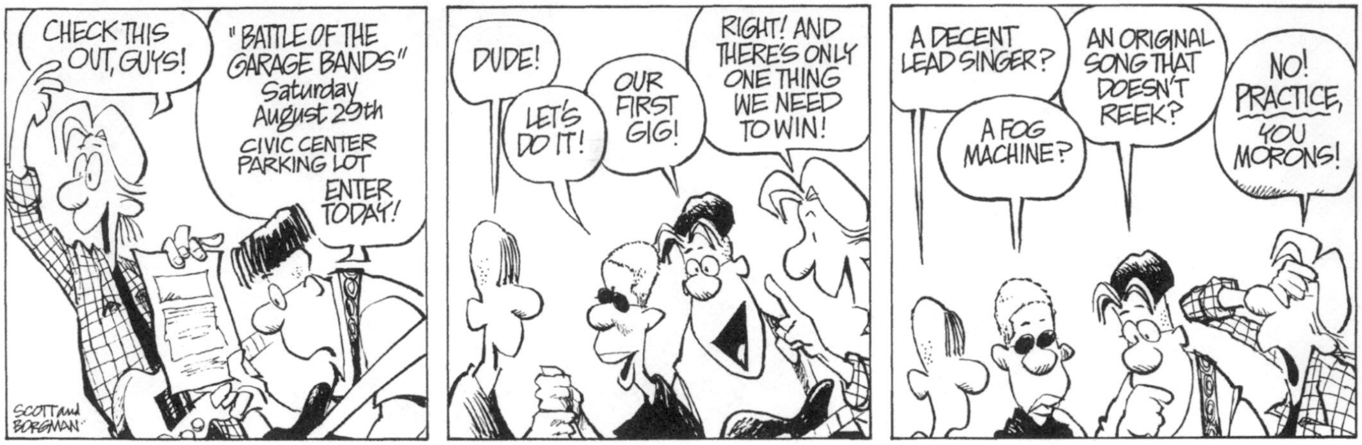
CHECK THIS OUT, GUYS!
"BATTLE OF THE GARAGE BANDS" Saturday August 29th CIVIC CENTER PARKING LOT ENTER TODAY!
SCOTT and BORGMAN
DUDE!
LET'S DO IT!
OUR FIRST GIG!
RIGHT! AND THERE'S ONLY ONE THING WE NEED TO WIN!
A DECENT LEAD SINGER?
A FOG MACHINE?
AN ORIGINAL SONG THAT DOESN'T REEK?
NO! PRACTICE, YOU MORONS!

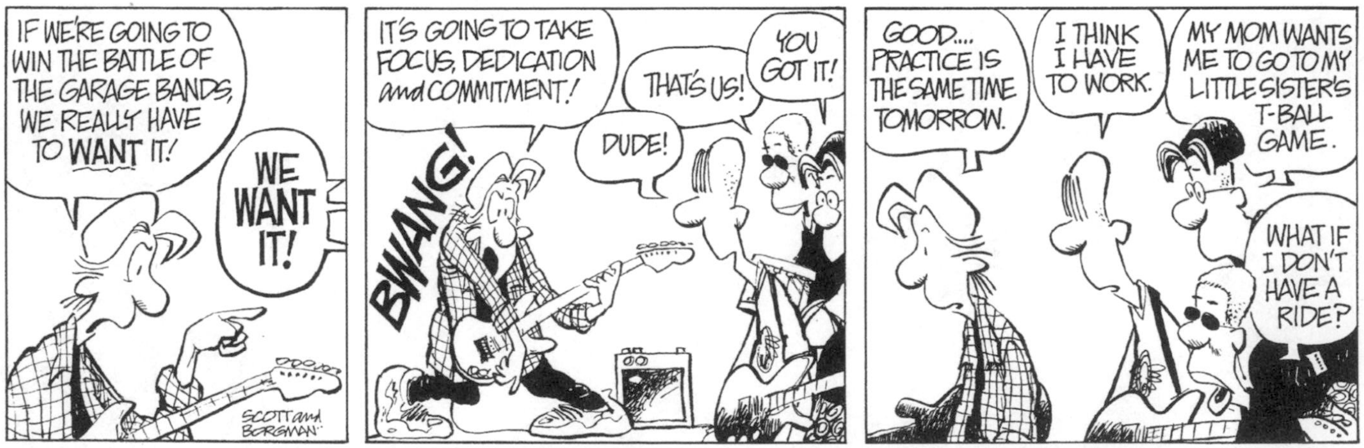
IF WE'RE GOING TO WIN THE BATTLE OF THE GARAGE BANDS, WE REALLY HAVE TO WANT IT!
WE WANT IT!
SCOTT and BORGMAN
IT'S GOING TO TAKE FOCUS, DEDICATION and COMMITMENT!
BWANG!
DUDE!
THAT'S US!
YOU GOT IT!
GOOD.... PRACTICE IS THE SAME TIME TOMORROW.
I THINK I HAVE TO WORK.
MY MOM WANTS ME TO GO TO MY LITTLE SISTER'S T-BALL GAME.
WHAT IF I DON'T HAVE A RIDE?

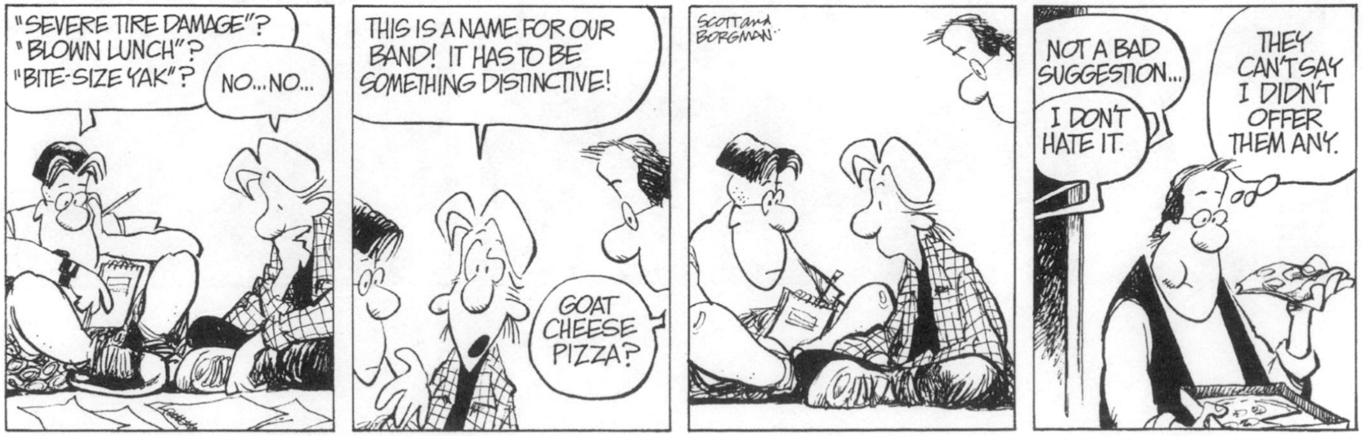
"SEVERE TIRE DAMAGE"? "BLOWN LUNCH"? "BITE-SIZE YAK"?
NO... NO...
THIS IS A NAME FOR OUR BAND! IT HAS TO BE SOMETHING DISTINCTIVE!
GOAT CHEESE PIZZA?
SCOTT and BORGMAN
NOT A BAD SUGGESTION...
I DON'T HATE IT.
THEY CAN'T SAY I DIDN'T OFFER THEM ANY.

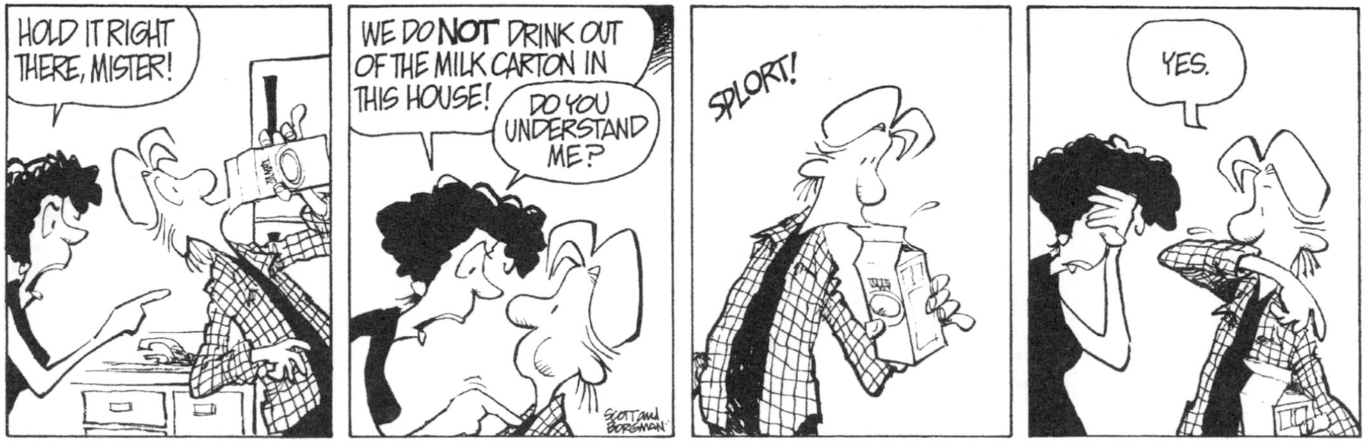
HOLD IT RIGHT THERE, MISTER!
WE DO NOT DRINK OUT OF THE MILK CARTON IN THIS HOUSE!
DO YOU UNDERSTAND ME?
SPLORT!
YES.
SCOTT and BORGMAN

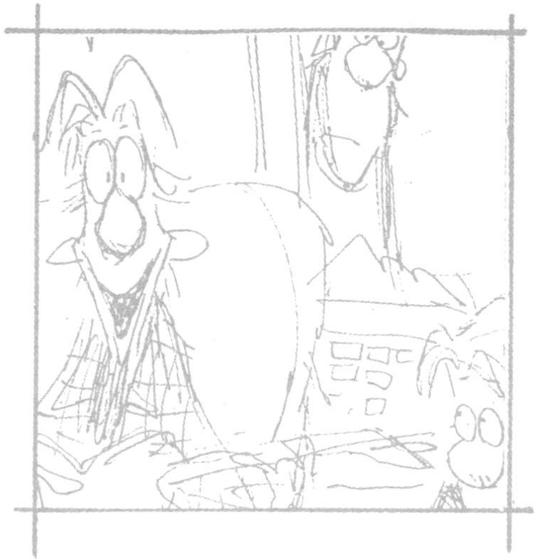

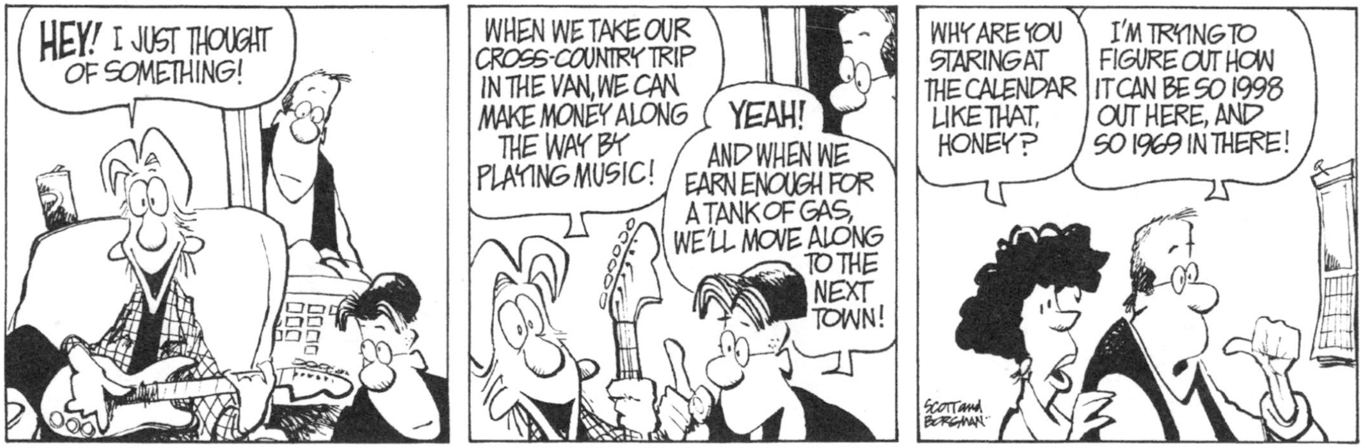
HEY! I JUST THOUGHT OF SOMETHING!
WHEN WE TAKE OUR CROSS-COUNTRY TRIP IN THE VAN, WE CAN MAKE MONEY ALONG THE WAY BY PLAYING MUSIC!
YEAH!
AND WHEN WE EARN ENOUGH FOR A TANK OF GAS, WE'LL MOVE ALONG TO THE NEXT TOWN!
WHY ARE YOU STARING AT THE CALENDAR LIKE THAT, HONEY?
I'M TRYING TO FIGURE OUT HOW IT CAN BE SO 1998 OUT HERE, AND SO 1969 IN THERE!
SCOTT and BORGMAN

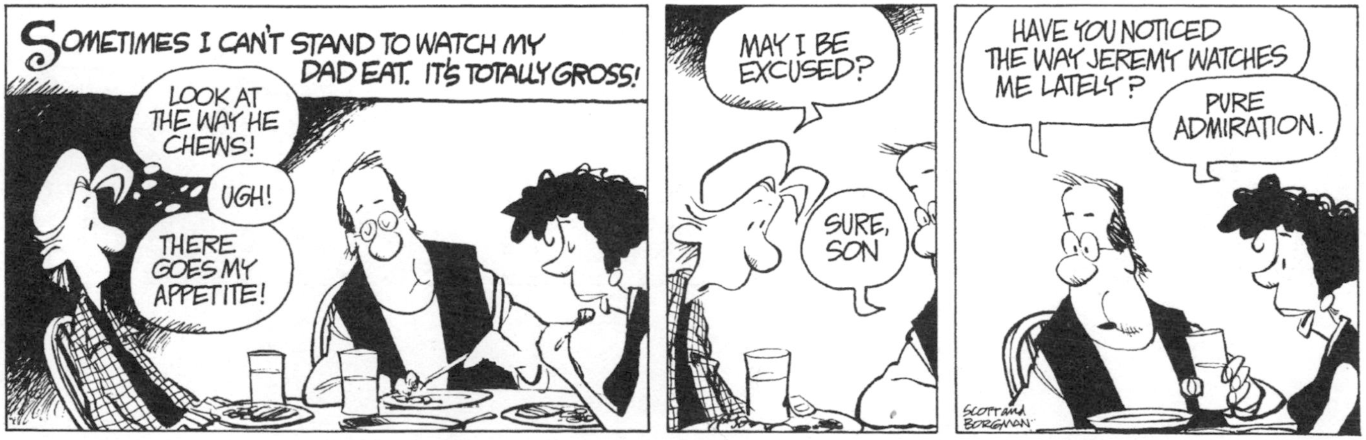
SOMETIMES I CAN'T STAND TO WATCH MY DAD EAT. IT'S TOTALLY GROSS!
LOOK AT THE WAY HE CHEWS!
UGH!
THERE GOES MY APPETITE!
MAY I BE EXCUSED?
SURE, SON
HAVE YOU NOTICED THE WAY JEREMY WATCHES ME LATELY?
PURE ADMIRATION.
SCOTT and BORGMAN

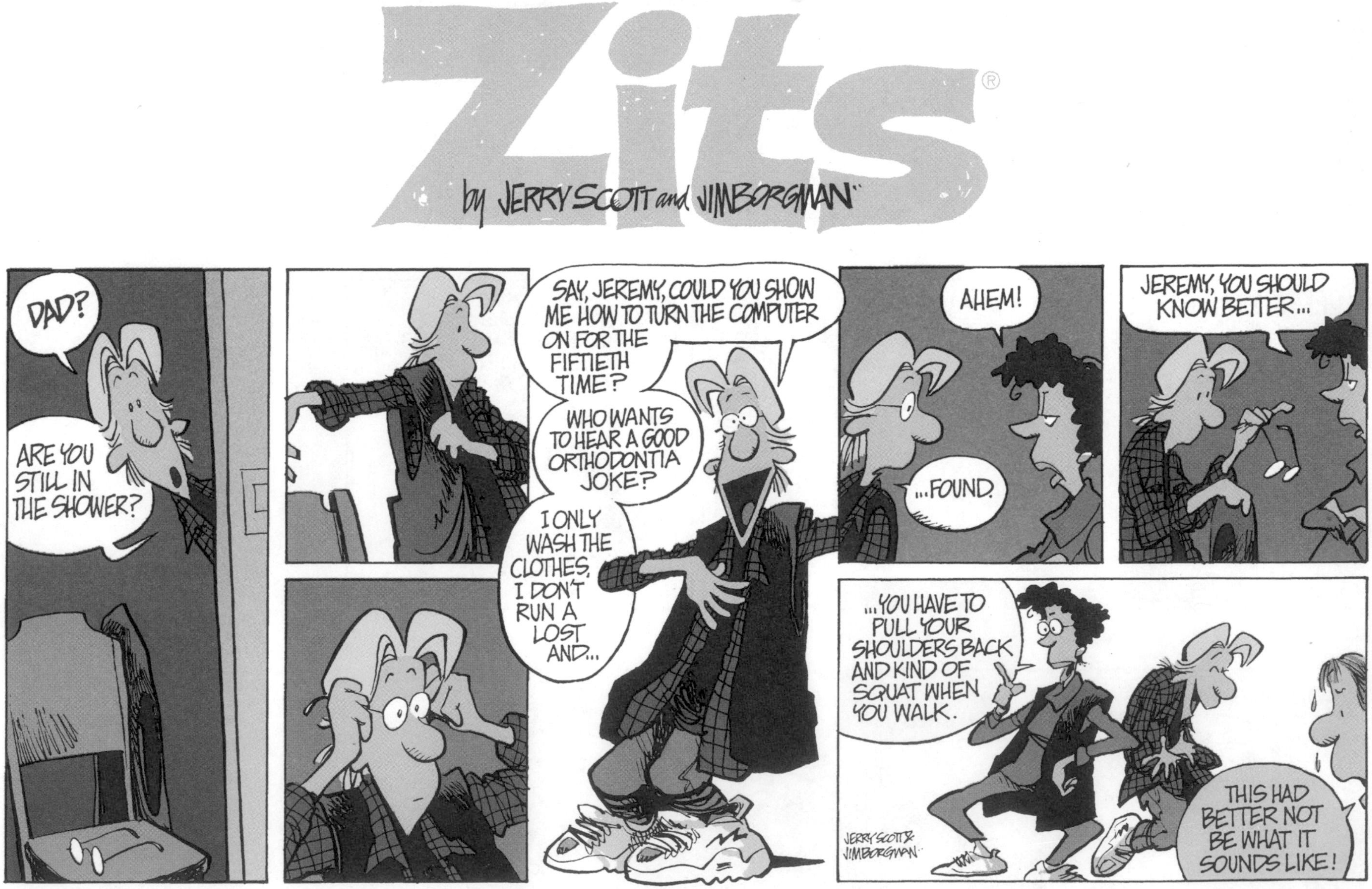
Zits®
by JERRY SCOTT and JIM BORGMAN
DAD?
ARE YOU STILL IN THE SHOWER?
SAY, JEREMY, COULD YOU SHOW ME HOW TO TURN THE COMPUTER ON FOR THE FIFTIETH TIME?
WHO WANTS TO HEAR A GOOD ORTHODONTIA JOKE?
I ONLY WASH THE CLOTHES, I DON'T RUN A LOST AND...
AHEM!
...FOUND.
JEREMY, YOU SHOULD KNOW BETTER...
...YOU HAVE TO PULL YOUR SHOULDERS BACK AND KIND OF SQUAT WHEN YOU WALK.
THIS HAD BETTER NOT BE WHAT IT SOUNDS LIKE!
JERRY SCOTT & JIM BORGMAN

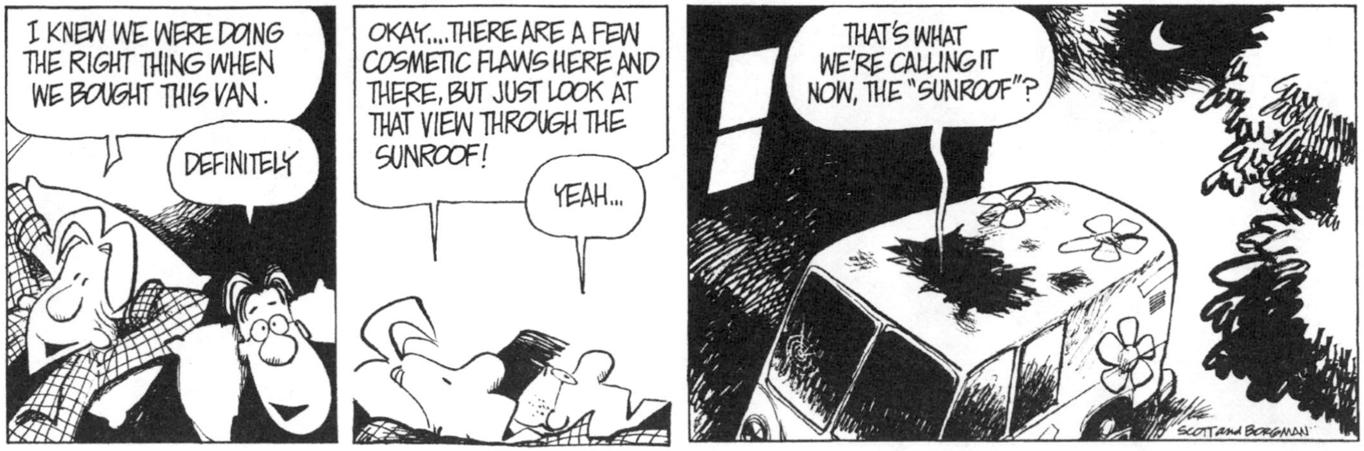
I KNEW WE WERE DOING THE RIGHT THING WHEN WE BOUGHT THIS VAN.
DEFINITELY
OKAY....THERE ARE A FEW COSMETIC FLAWS HERE AND THERE, BUT JUST LOOK AT THAT VIEW THROUGH THE SUNROOF!
YEAH...
THAT'S WHAT WE'RE CALLING IT NOW, THE "SUNROOF"?
SCOTT and BORGMAN

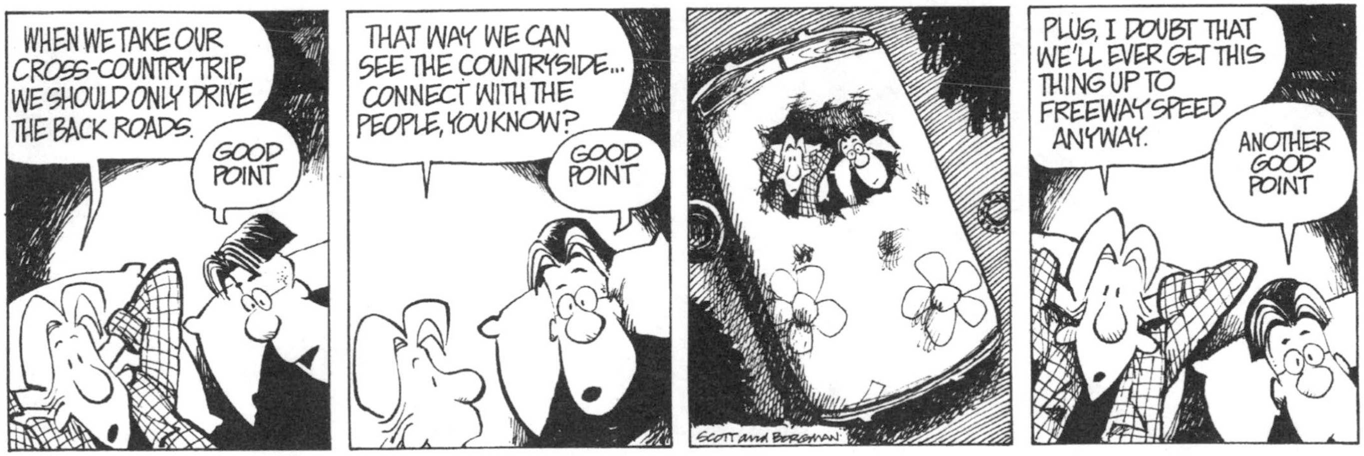
WHEN WE TAKE OUR CROSS-COUNTRY TRIP, WE SHOULD ONLY DRIVE THE BACK ROADS.
GOOD POINT
THAT WAY WE CAN SEE THE COUNTRYSIDE... CONNECT WITH THE PEOPLE, YOU KNOW?
GOOD POINT
SCOTT and BORGMAN
PLUS, I DOUBT THAT WE'LL EVER GET THIS THING UP TO FREEWAY SPEED ANYWAY.
ANOTHER GOOD POINT

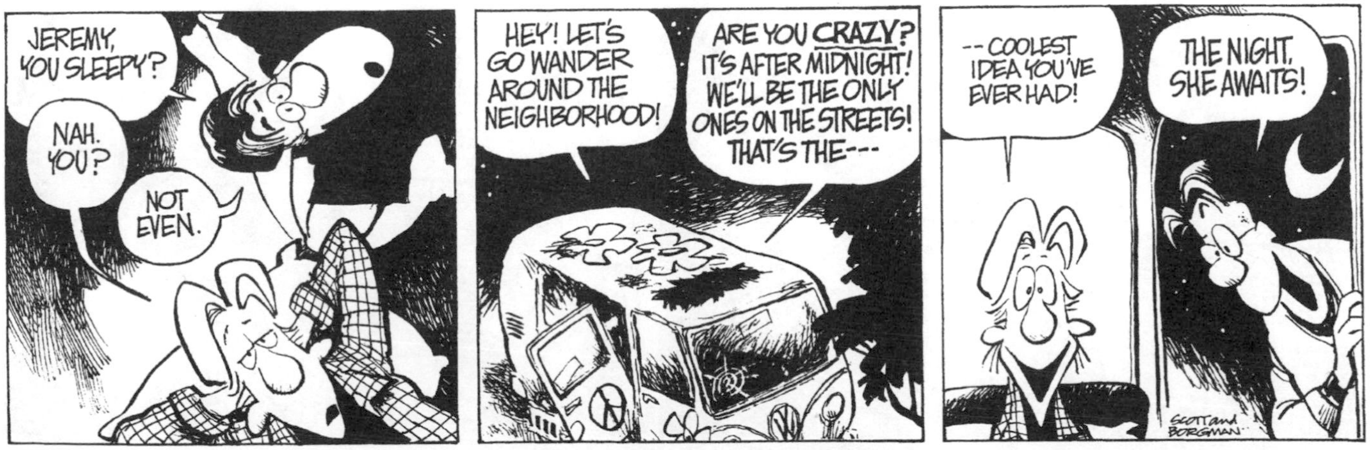
JEREMY, YOU SLEEPY?
NAH. YOU?
NOT EVEN.
HEY! LET'S GO WANDER AROUND THE NEIGHBORHOOD!
ARE YOU CRAZY? IT'S AFTER MIDNIGHT! WE'LL BE THE ONLY ONES ON THE STREETS! THAT'S THE---
--COOLEST IDEA YOU'VE EVER HAD!
THE NIGHT, SHE AWAITS!
SCOTT and BORGMAN

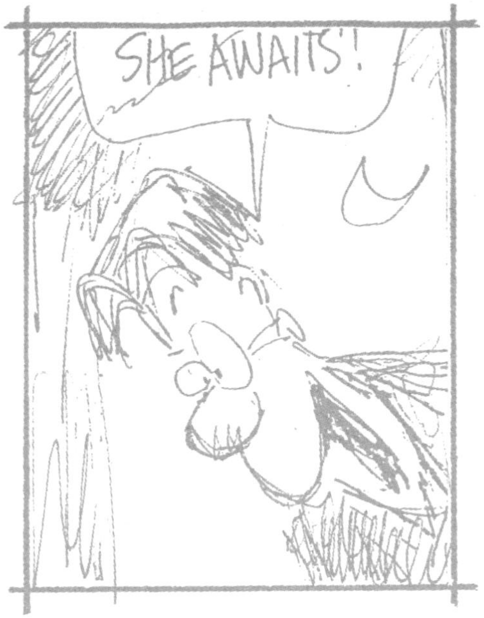
SHE AWAITS!

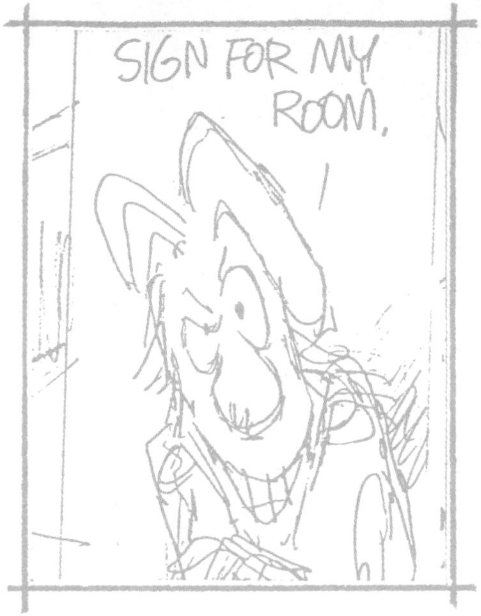
SIGN FOR MY ROOM.

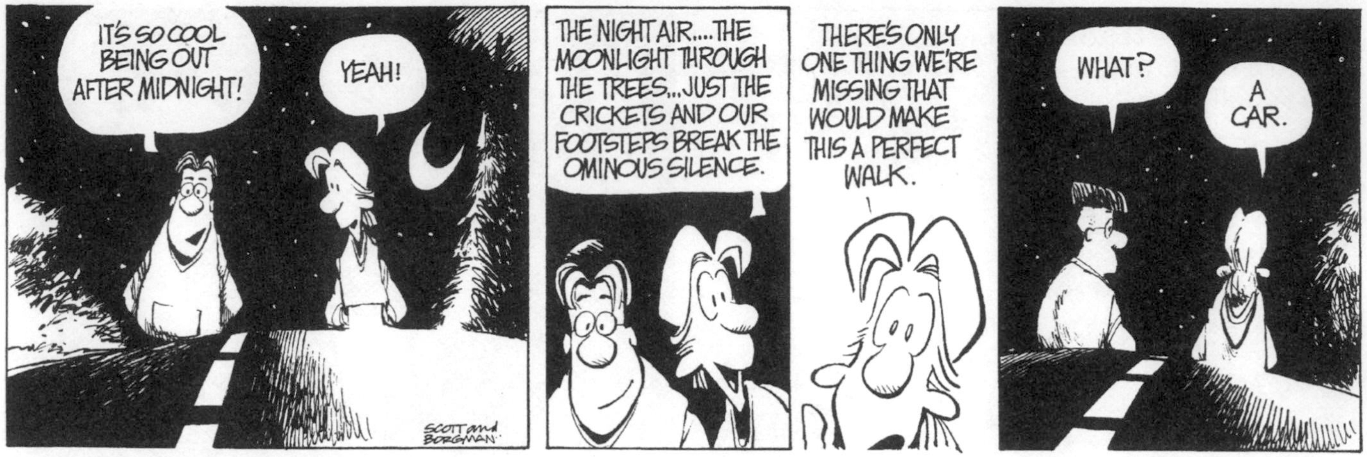
IT'S SO COOL BEING OUT AFTER MIDNIGHT!
YEAH!
SCOTT and BORGMAN
THE NIGHT AIR.... THE MOONLIGHT THROUGH THE TREES... JUST THE CRICKETS AND OUR FOOTSTEPS BREAK THE OMINOUS SILENCE.
THERE'S ONLY ONE THING WE'RE MISSING THAT WOULD MAKE THIS A PERFECT WALK.
WHAT?
A CAR.

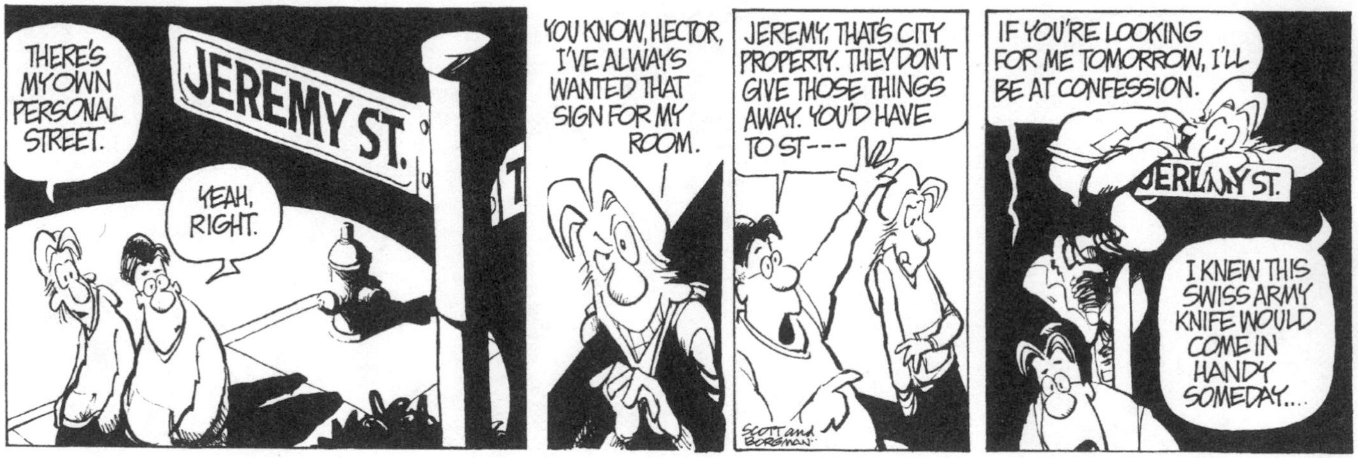
THERE'S MY OWN PERSONAL STREET.
JEREMY ST.
YEAH, RIGHT.
YOU KNOW, HECTOR, I'VE ALWAYS WANTED THAT SIGN FOR MY ROOM.
JEREMY, THAT'S CITY PROPERTY. THEY DON'T GIVE THOSE THINGS AWAY. YOU'D HAVE TO ST---
SCOTT and BORGMAN
IF YOU'RE LOOKING FOR ME TOMORROW, I'LL BE AT CONFESSION.
I KNEW THIS SWISS ARMY KNIFE WOULD COME IN HANDY SOMEDAY....

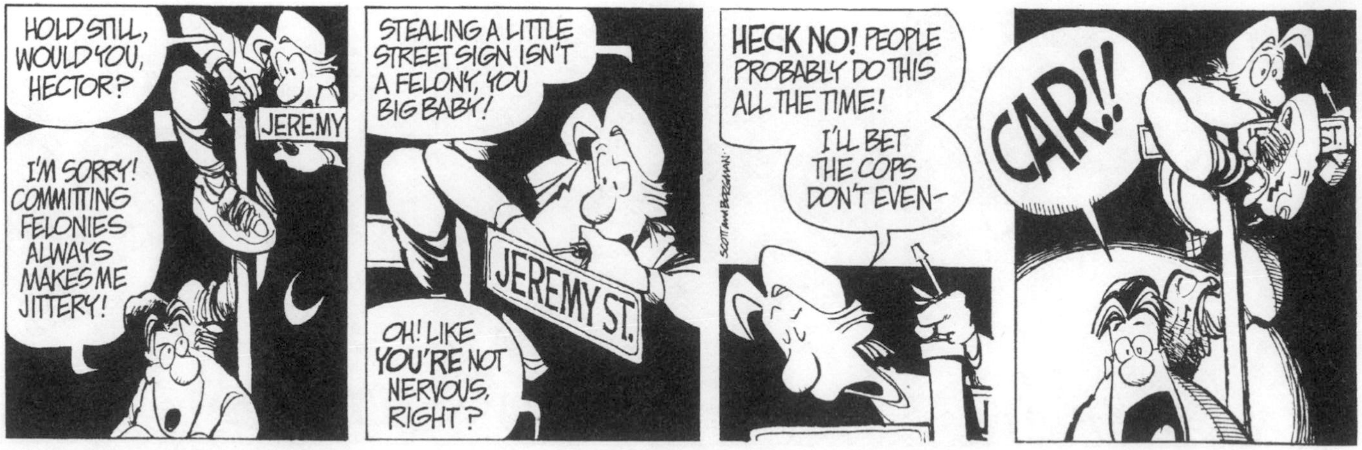
HOLD STILL, WOULD YOU, HECTOR?
JEREMY
I'M SORRY! COMMITTING FELONIES ALWAYS MAKES ME JITTERY!
STEALING A LITTLE STREET SIGN ISN'T A FELONY, YOU BIG BABY!
JEREMY ST.
OH! LIKE YOU'RE NOT NERVOUS, RIGHT?
SCOTT and BORGMAN
HECK NO! PEOPLE PROBABLY DO THIS ALL THE TIME!
I'LL BET THE COPS DON'T EVEN-
CAR!!

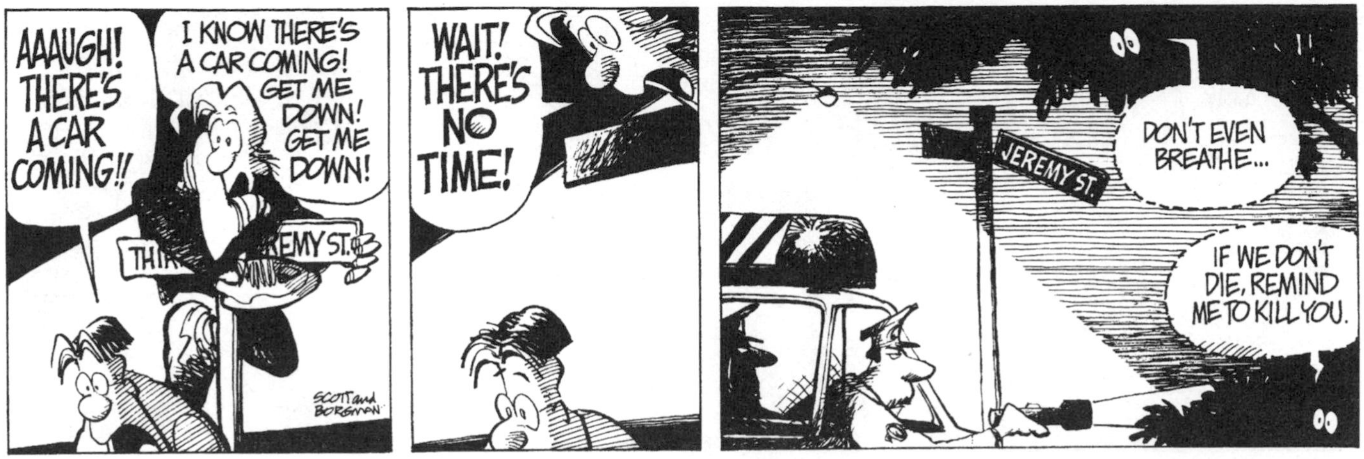
AAAUGH! THERE'S A CAR COMING!!
I KNOW THERE'S A CAR COMING! GET ME DOWN! GET ME DOWN!
SCOTT and BORGMAN
WAIT! THERE'S NO TIME!
JEREMY ST.
DON'T EVEN BREATHE...
IF WE DON'T DIE, REMIND ME TO KILL YOU.

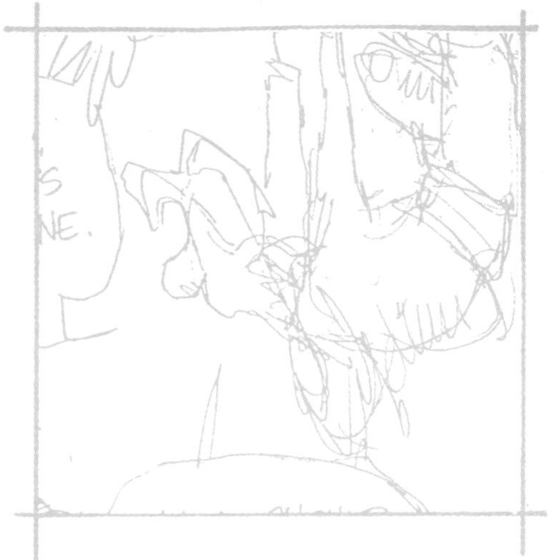

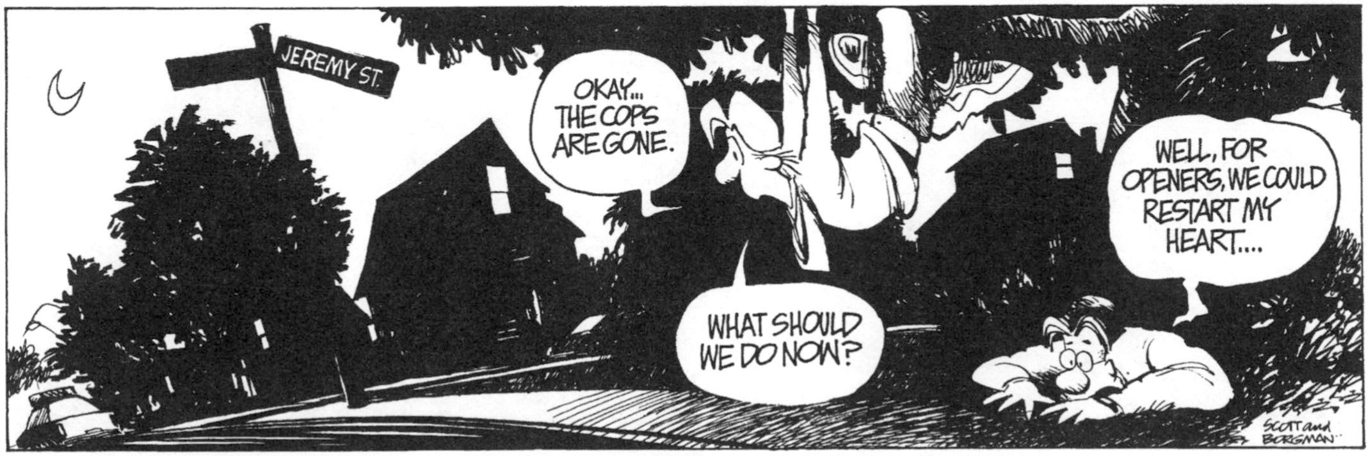
JEREMY ST.
OKAY... THE COPS ARE GONE.
WHAT SHOULD WE DO NOW?
WELL, FOR OPENERS, WE COULD RESTART MY HEART....
SCOTT and BORGMAN

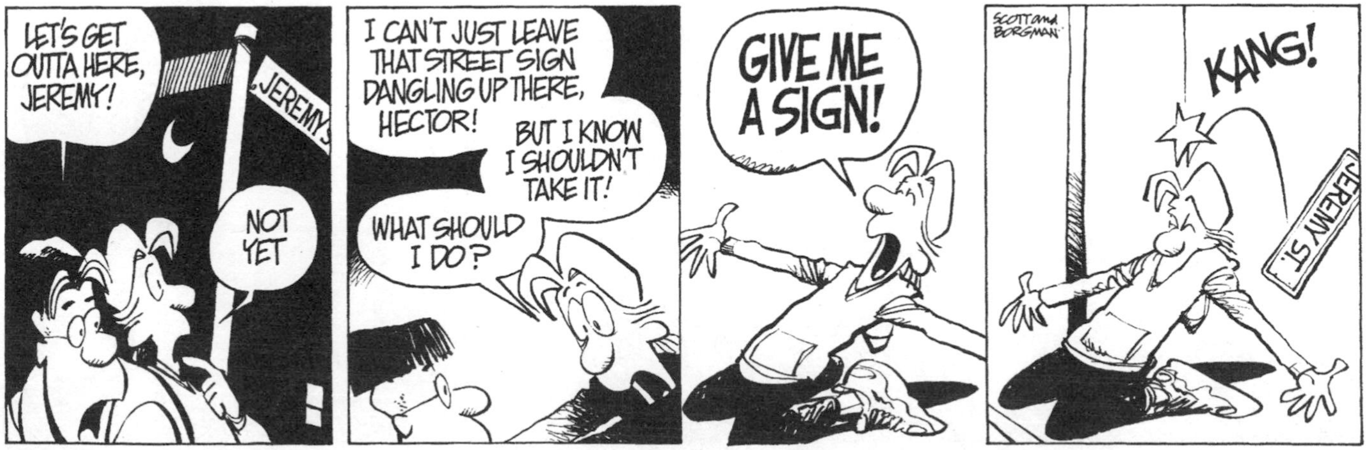
LET'S GET OUTTA HERE, JEREMY!
NOT YET
I CAN'T JUST LEAVE THAT STREET SIGN DANGLING UP THERE, HECTOR!
BUT I KNOW I SHOULDN'T TAKE IT!
WHAT SHOULD I DO?
GIVE ME A SIGN!
SCOTT and BORGMAN
KANG!
JEREMY ST.

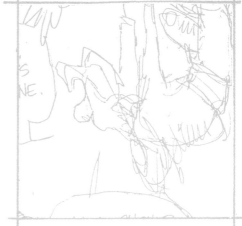

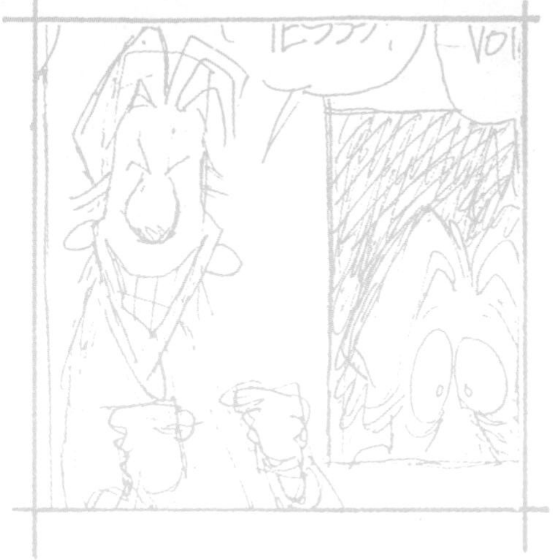

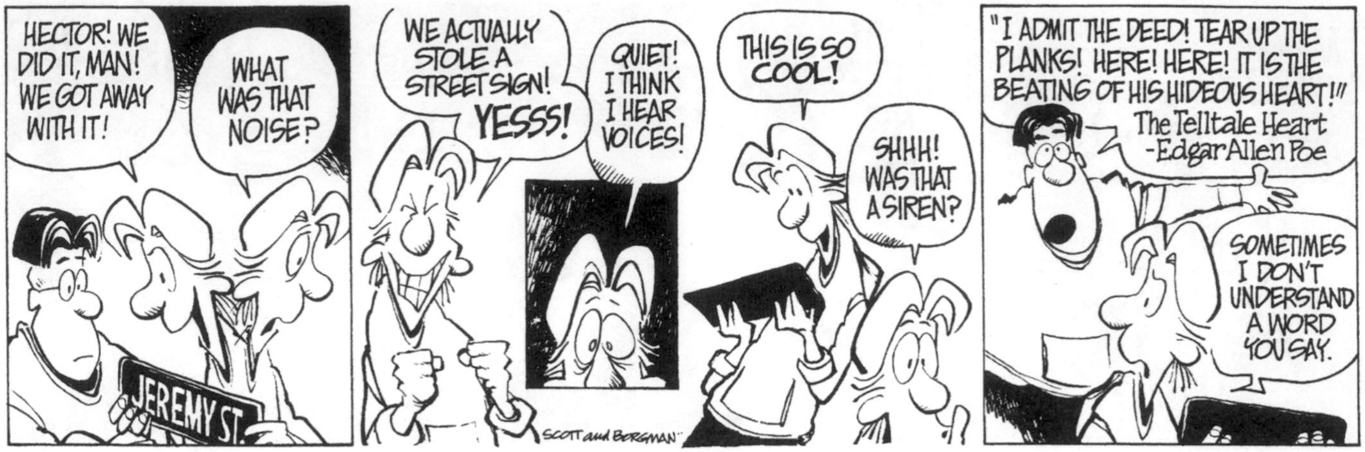
HECTOR! WE DID IT, MAN! WE GOT AWAY WITH IT!
WHAT WAS THAT NOISE?
JEREMY ST.
WE ACTUALLY STOLE A STREET SIGN! YESSS!
QUIET! I THINK I HEAR VOICES!
SCOTT and BORGMAN
THIS IS SO COOL!
SHHH! WAS THAT A SIREN?
"I ADMIT THE DEED! TEAR UP THE PLANKS! HERE! HERE! IT IS THE BEATING OF HIS HIDEOUS HEART!"
The Telltale Heart -Edgar Allen Poe
SOMETIMES I DON'T UNDERSTAND A WORD YOU SAY.

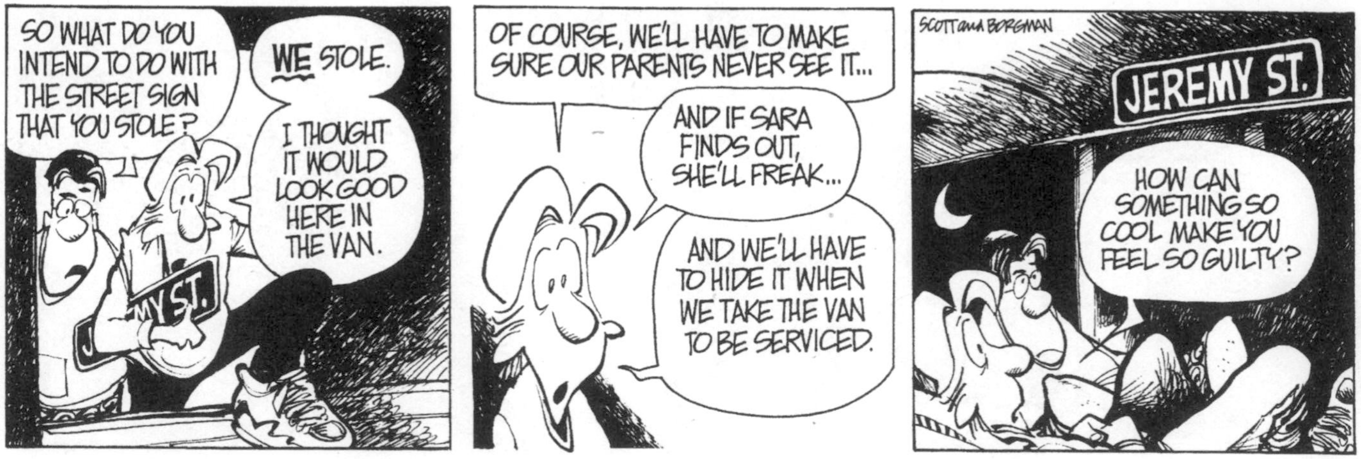
SO WHAT DO YOU INTEND TO DO WITH THE STREET SIGN THAT YOU STOLE?
WE STOLE.
I THOUGHT IT WOULD LOOK GOOD HERE IN THE VAN.
MY ST.
OF COURSE, WE'LL HAVE TO MAKE SURE OUR PARENTS NEVER SEE IT...
AND IF SARA FINDS OUT, SHE'LL FREAK...
AND WE'LL HAVE TO HIDE IT WHEN WE TAKE THE VAN TO BE SERVICED.
SCOTT and BORGMAN
JEREMY ST.
HOW CAN SOMETHING SO COOL MAKE YOU FEEL SO GUILTY?

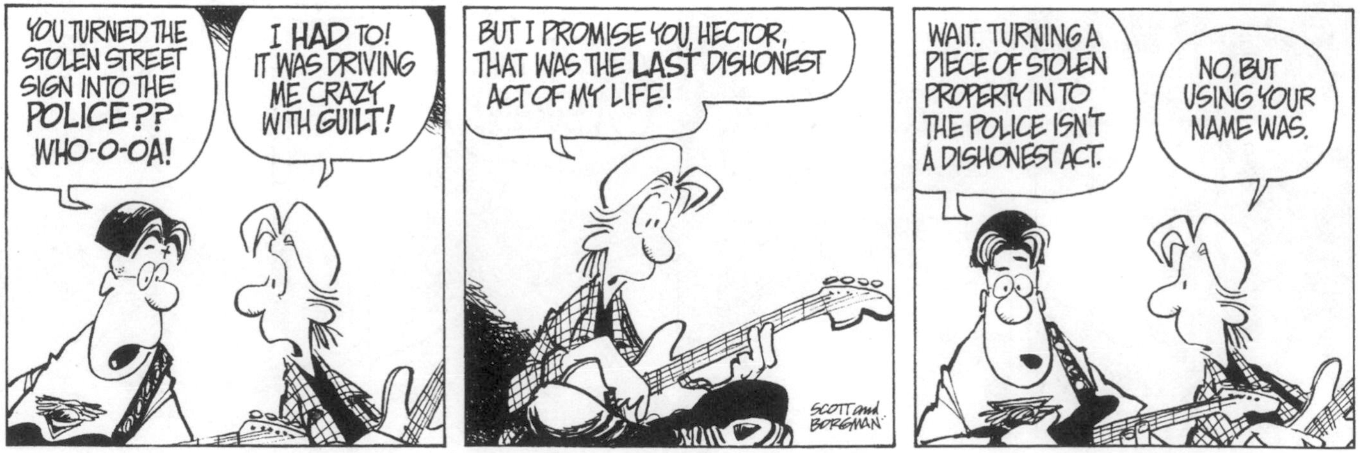
YOU TURNED THE STOLEN STREET SIGN INTO THE POLICE?? WHO-O-OA!
I HAD TO! IT WAS DRIVING ME CRAZY WITH GUILT!
BUT I PROMISE YOU, HECTOR, THAT WAS THE LAST DISHONEST ACT OF MY LIFE!
SCOTT and BORGMAN
WAIT. TURNING A PIECE OF STOLEN PROPERTY IN TO THE POLICE ISN'T A DISHONEST ACT.
NO, BUT USING YOUR NAME WAS.

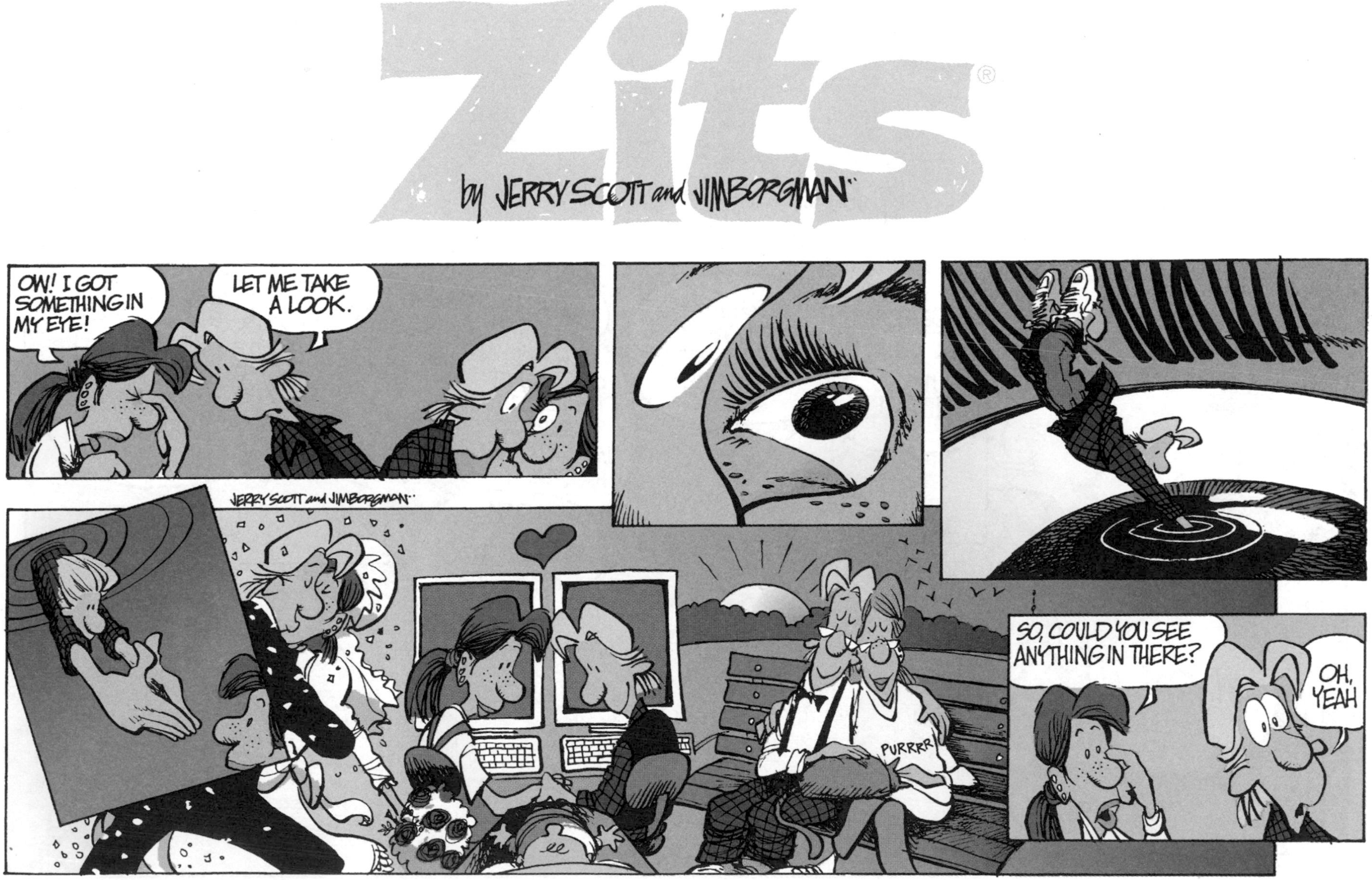
Zits®
by JERRY SCOTT and JIMBORGMAN
OW! I GOT SOMETHING IN MY EYE!
LET ME TAKE A LOOK.
JERRY SCOTT and JIMBORGMAN
PURRRR
SO, COULD YOU SEE ANYTHING IN THERE?
OH, YEAH

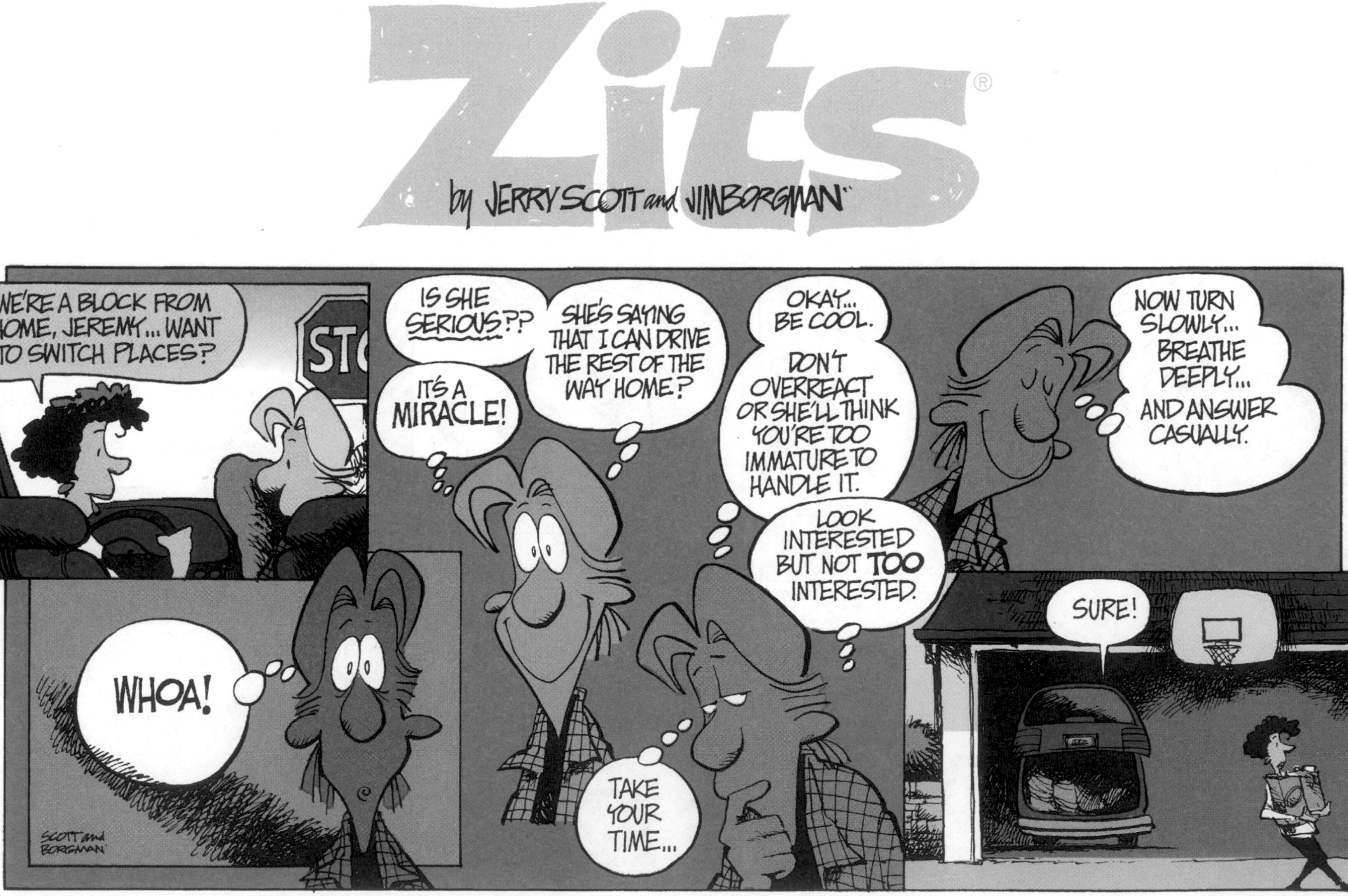

Zits®
by JERRY SCOTT and JIM BORGMAN
WE'RE A BLOCK FROM HOME, JEREMY... WANT TO SWITCH PLACES?
STO
WHOA!
IS SHE SERIOUS??
IT'S A MIRACLE!
SHE'S SAYING THAT I CAN DRIVE THE REST OF THE WAY HOME?
OKAY... BE COOL.
DON'T OVERREACT OR SHE'LL THINK YOU'RE TOO IMMATURE TO HANDLE IT.
LOOK INTERESTED BUT NOT TOO INTERESTED.
TAKE YOUR TIME...
NOW TURN SLOWLY... BREATHE DEEPLY... AND ANSWER CASUALLY.
SURE!
SCOTT and BORGMAN

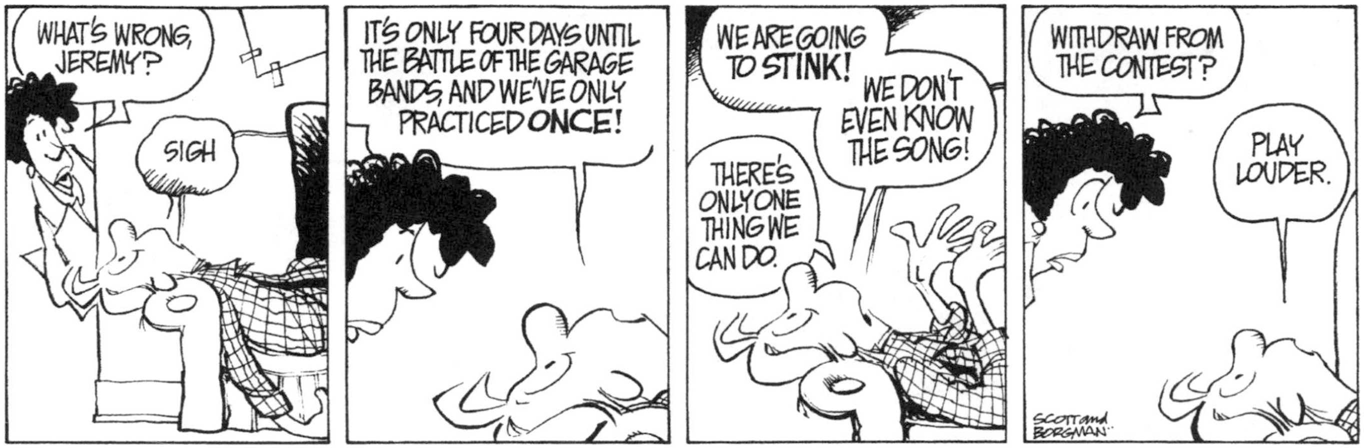
WHAT'S WRONG, JEREMY?
SIGH
IT'S ONLY FOUR DAYS UNTIL THE BATTLE OF THE GARAGE BANDS, AND WE'VE ONLY PRACTICED ONCE!
WE ARE GOING TO STINK!
WE DON'T EVEN KNOW THE SONG!
THERE'S ONLY ONE THING WE CAN DO.
WITHDRAW FROM THE CONTEST?
PLAY LOUDER.
SCOTT and BORGMAN

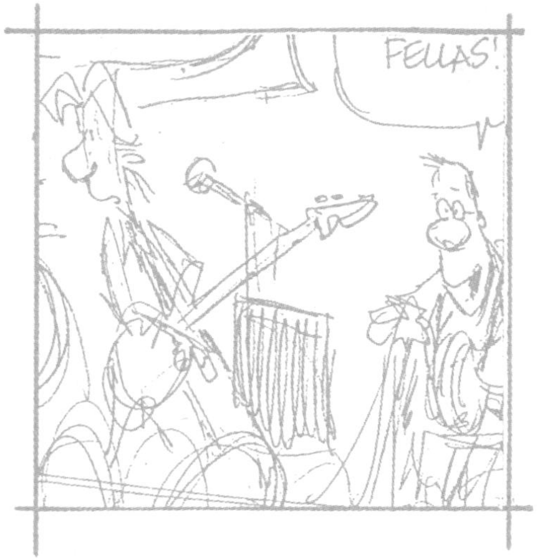
FELLAS!

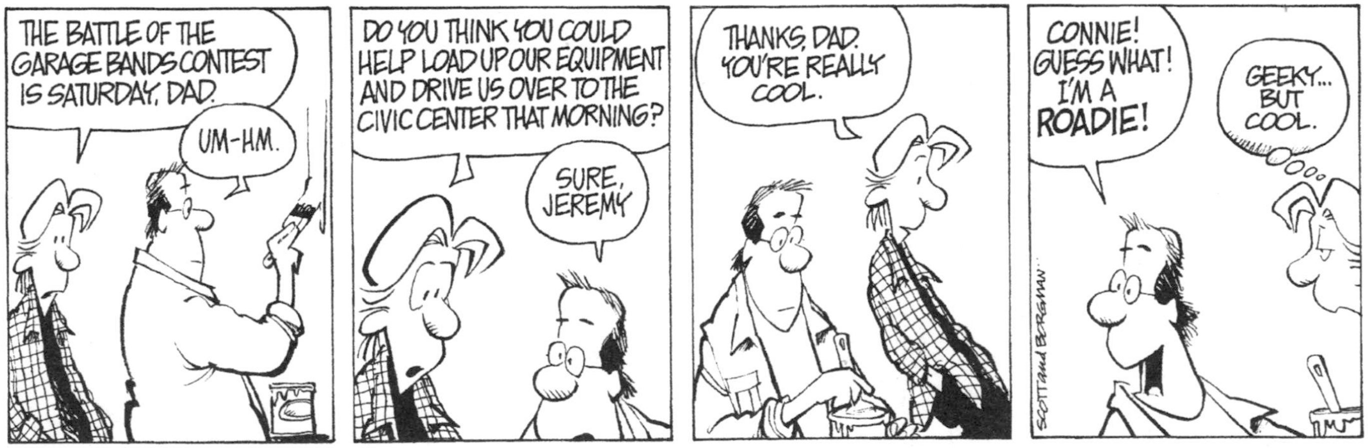
THE BATTLE OF THE GARAGE BANDS CONTEST IS SATURDAY, DAD.
UM-HM.
DO YOU THINK YOU COULD HELP LOAD UP OUR EQUIPMENT AND DRIVE US OVER TO THE CIVIC CENTER THAT MORNING?
SURE, JEREMY
THANKS, DAD. YOU'RE REALLY COOL.
SCOTT and BORGMAN
CONNIE! GUESS WHAT! I'M A ROADIE!
GEEKY... BUT COOL.

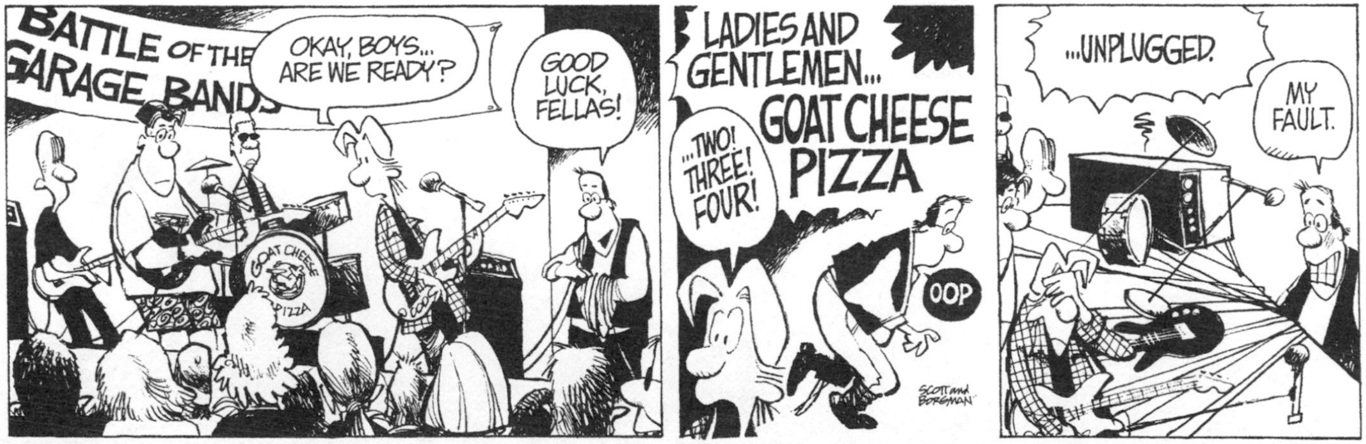
BATTLE OF THE GARAGE BANDS
OKAY, BOYS... ARE WE READY?
GOOD LUCK, FELLAS!
GOAT CHEESE PIZZA
LADIES AND GENTLEMEN... GOAT CHEESE PIZZA
...TWO! THREE! FOUR!
OOP
SCOTT and BORGMAN
...UNPLUGGED.
MY FAULT.

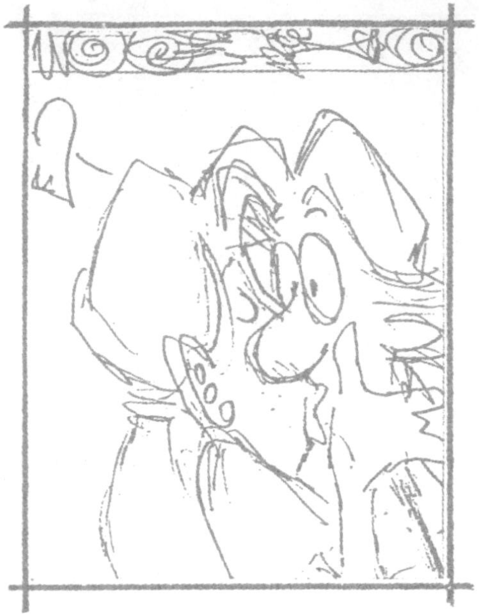

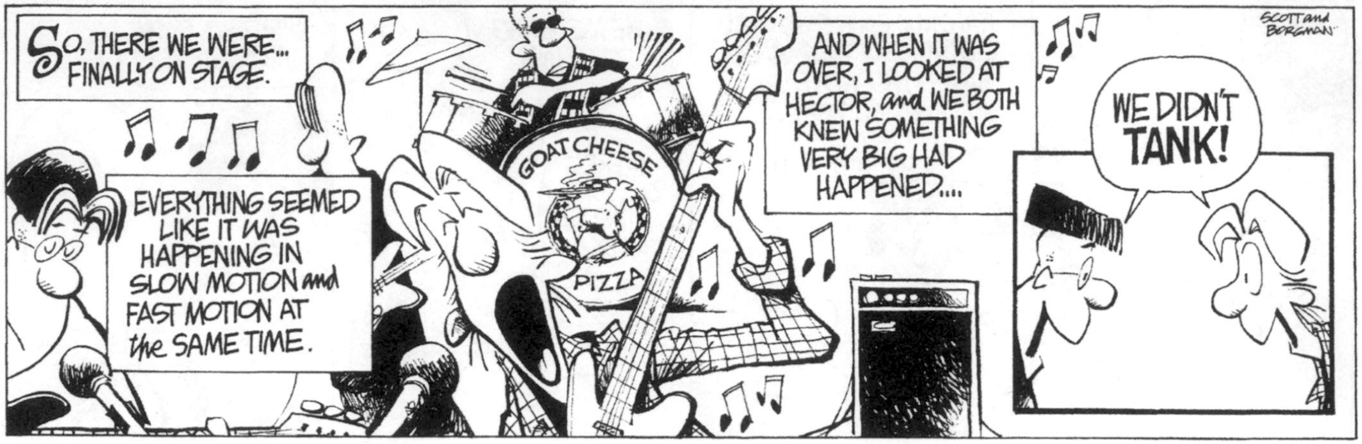
SO, THERE WE WERE... FINALLY ON STAGE.
EVERYTHING SEEMED LIKE IT WAS HAPPENING IN SLOW MOTION and FAST MOTION AT the SAME TIME.
GOAT CHEESE PIZZA
AND WHEN IT WAS OVER, I LOOKED AT HECTOR, and WE BOTH KNEW SOMETHING VERY BIG HAD HAPPENED....
WE DIDN'T TANK!
SCOTT and BORGMAN

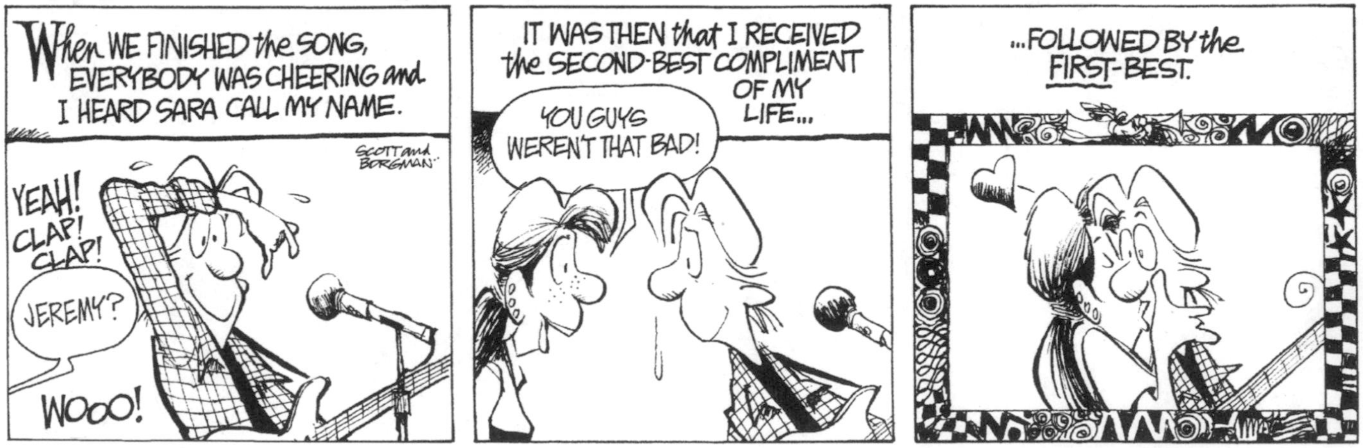
When WE FINISHED the SONG, EVERYBODY WAS CHEERING and I HEARD SARA CALL MY NAME.
SCOTT and BORGMAN
YEAH! CLAP! CLAP!
JEREMY?
WOOO!
IT WAS THEN that I RECEIVED the SECOND-BEST COMPLIMENT OF MY LIFE...
YOU GUYS WEREN'T THAT BAD!
...FOLLOWED BY the FIRST-BEST.

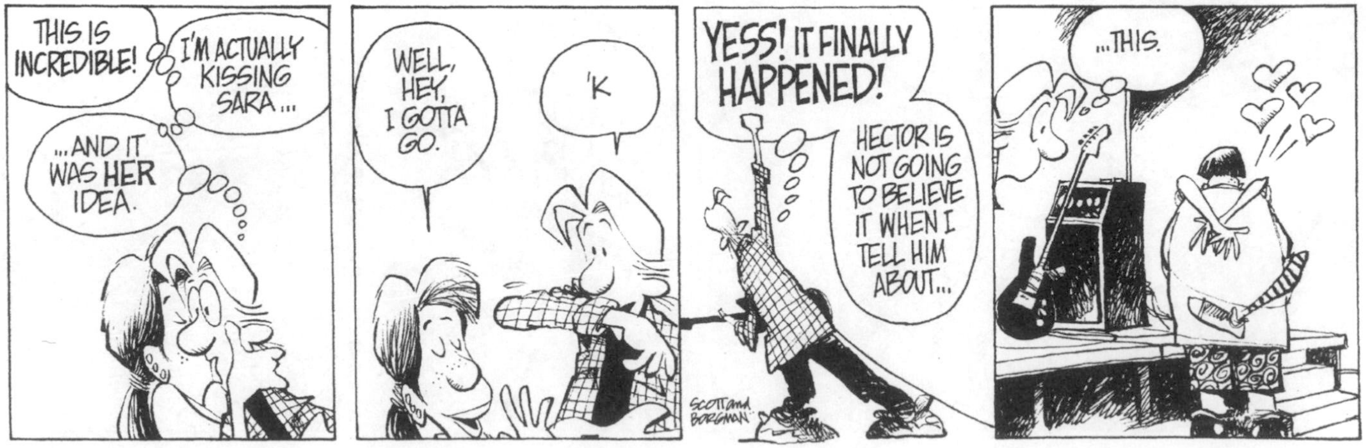
THIS IS INCREDIBLE!
I'M ACTUALLY KISSING SARA...
...AND IT WAS HER IDEA.
WELL, HEY, I GOTTA GO.
'K
YESS! IT FINALLY HAPPENED!
HECTOR IS NOT GOING TO BELIEVE IT WHEN I TELL HIM ABOUT...
SCOTT and BORGMAN
...THIS.

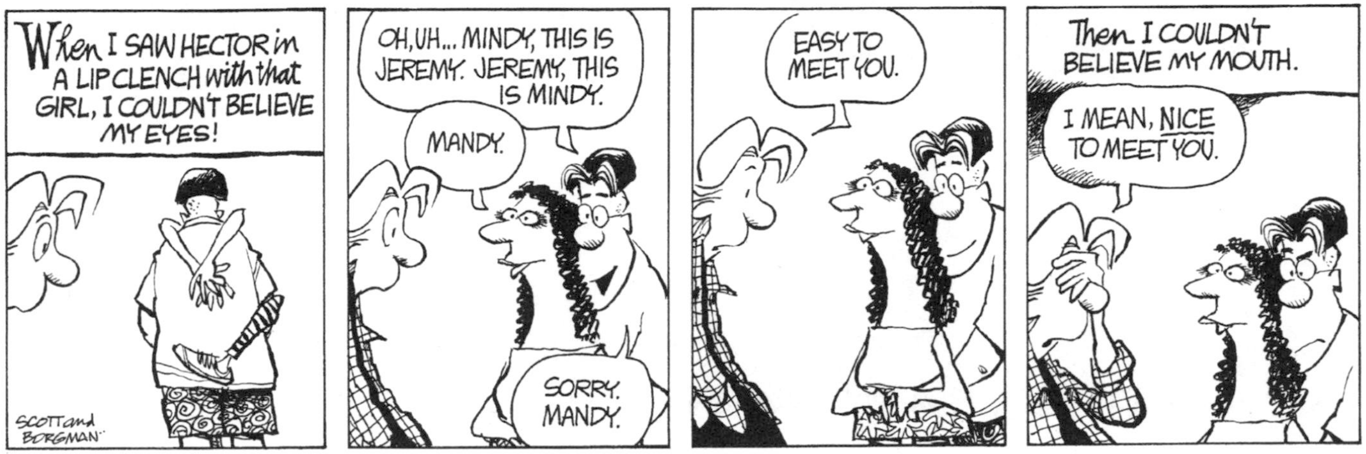
When I SAW HECTOR in A LIP CLENCH with that GIRL, I COULDN'T BELIEVE MY EYES!
SCOTT and BORGMAN
OH, UH... MINDY, THIS IS JEREMY. JEREMY, THIS IS MINDY.
MANDY.
SORRY. MANDY.
EASY TO MEET YOU.
Then I COULDN'T BELIEVE MY MOUTH.
I MEAN, NICE TO MEET YOU.

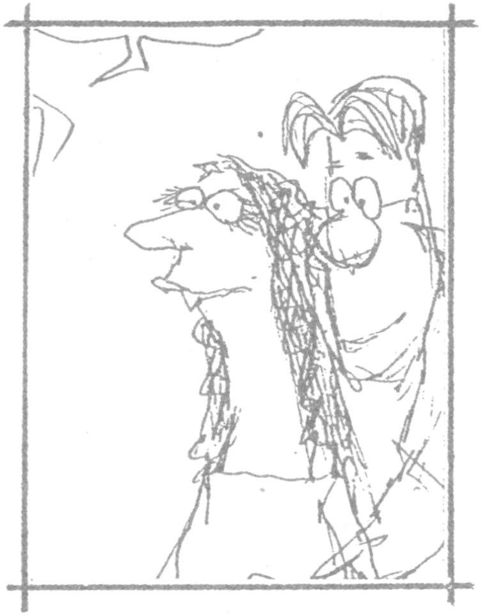

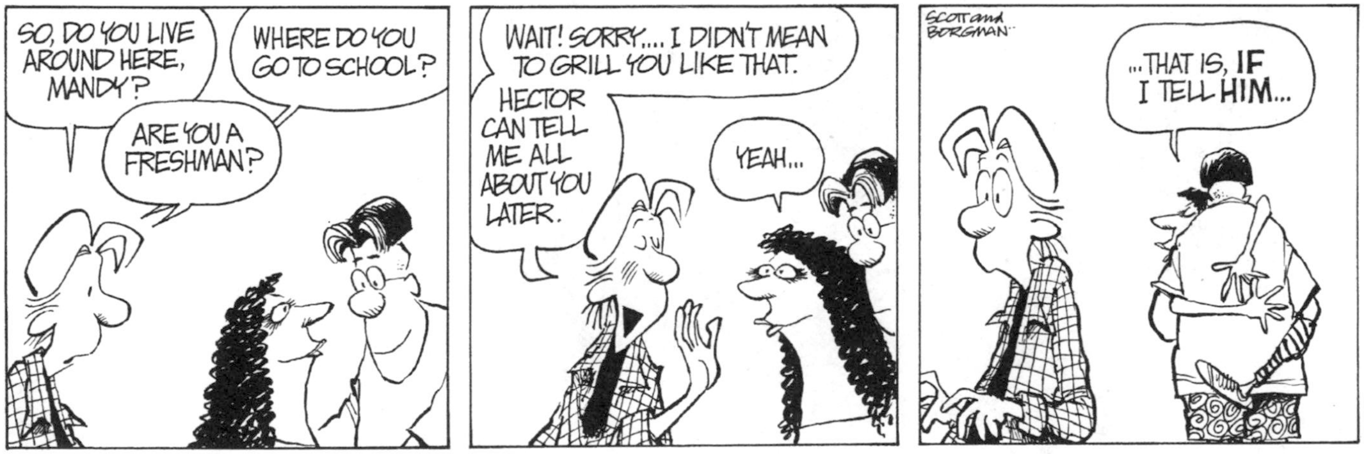
SO, DO YOU LIVE AROUND HERE, MANDY?
ARE YOU A FRESHMAN?
WHERE DO YOU GO TO SCHOOL?
WAIT! SORRY.... I DIDN'T MEAN TO GRILL YOU LIKE THAT.
HECTOR CAN TELL ME ALL ABOUT YOU LATER.
YEAH...
SCOTT and BORGMAN
...THAT IS, IF I TELL HIM...

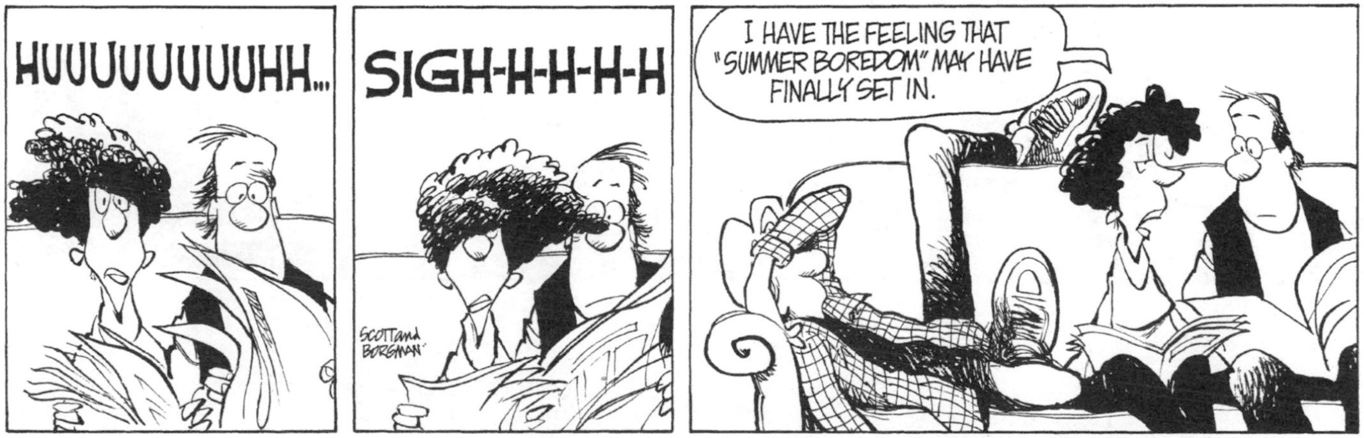
HUUUUUUUUHH...
SIGH-H-H-H-H
SCOTT and BORGMAN
I HAVE THE FEELING THAT "SUMMER BOREDOM" MAY HAVE FINALLY SET IN.

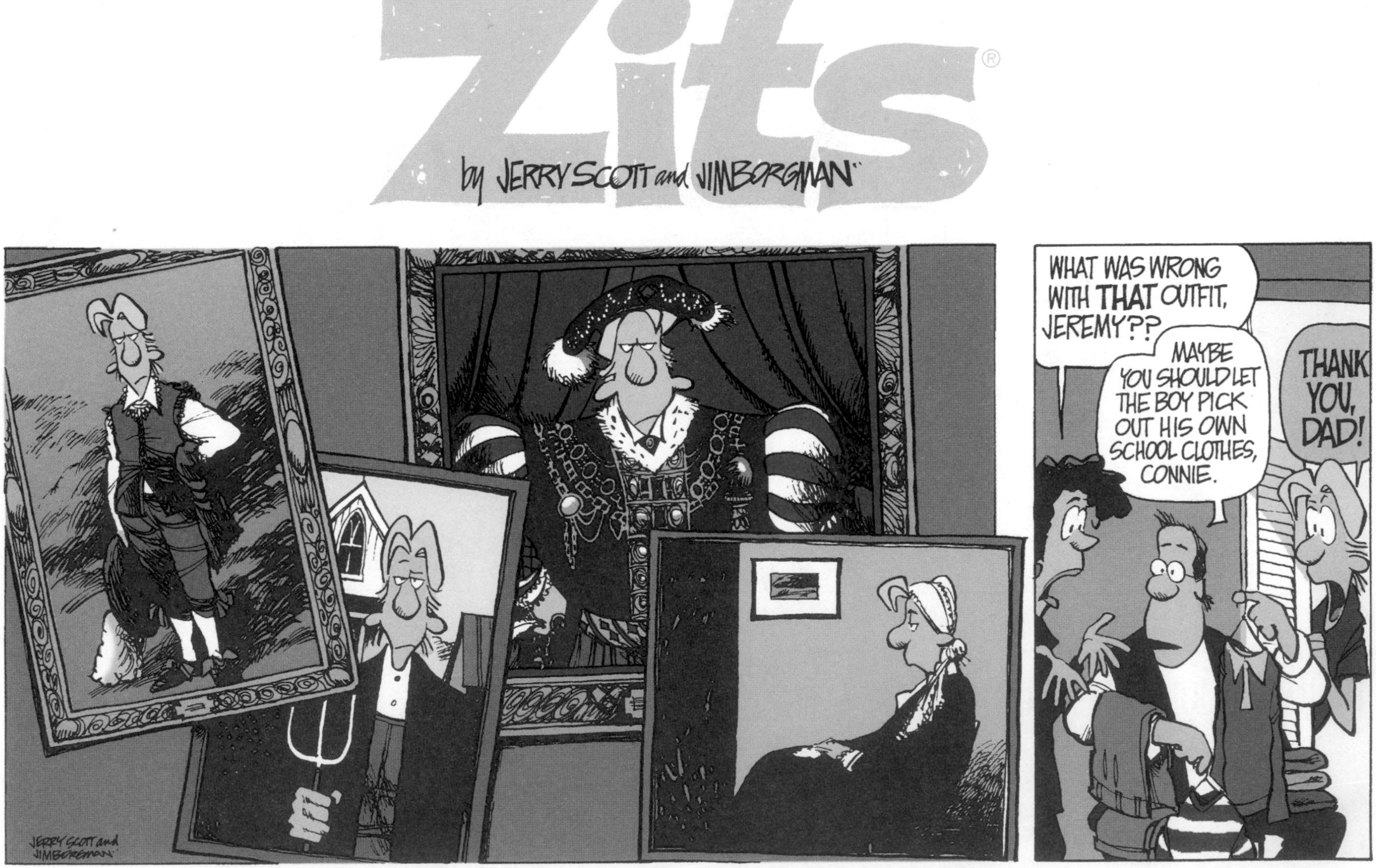
Zits®
by JERRY SCOTT and JIM BORGMAN
JERRY SCOTT and JIM BORGMAN
WHAT WAS WRONG WITH THAT OUTFIT, JEREMY??
MAYBE YOU SHOULD LET THE BOY PICK OUT HIS OWN SCHOOL CLOTHES, CONNIE.
THANK YOU, DAD!

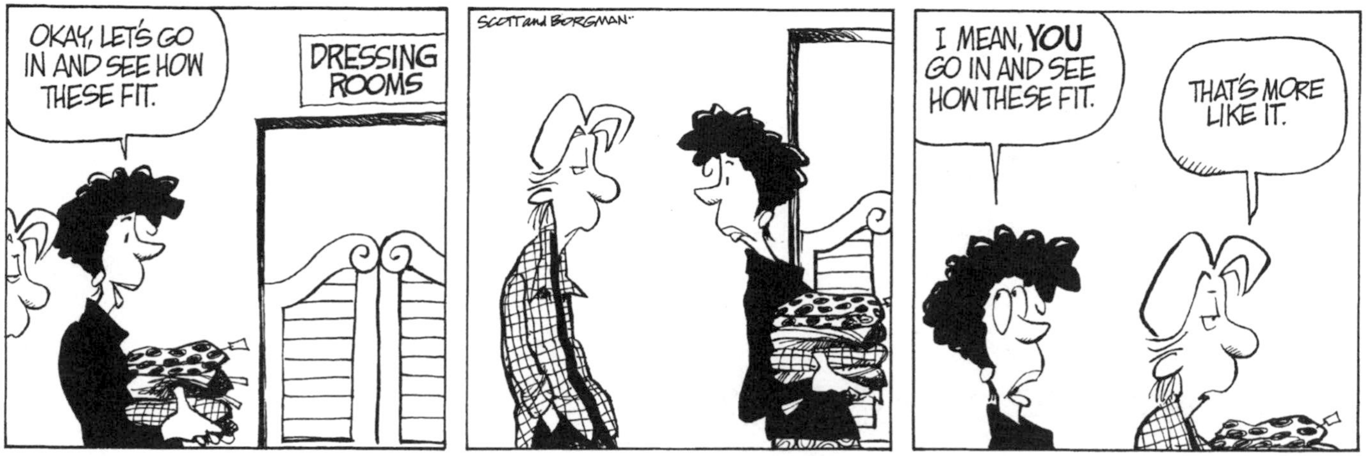
OKAY, LET'S GO IN AND SEE HOW THESE FIT.
DRESSING ROOMS
SCOTT and BORGMAN
I MEAN, **YOU** GO IN AND SEE HOW THESE FIT.
THAT'S MORE LIKE IT.

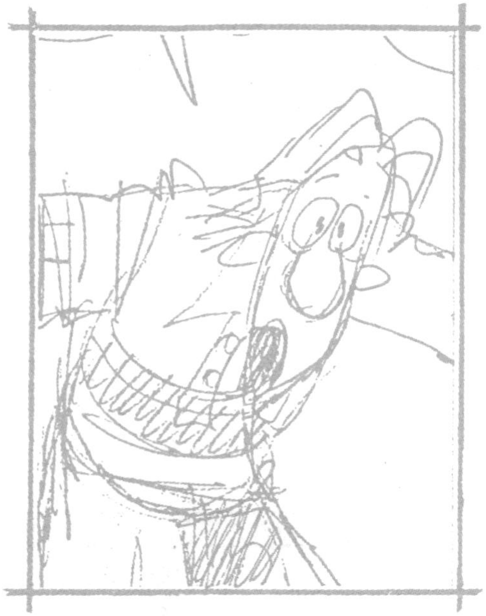

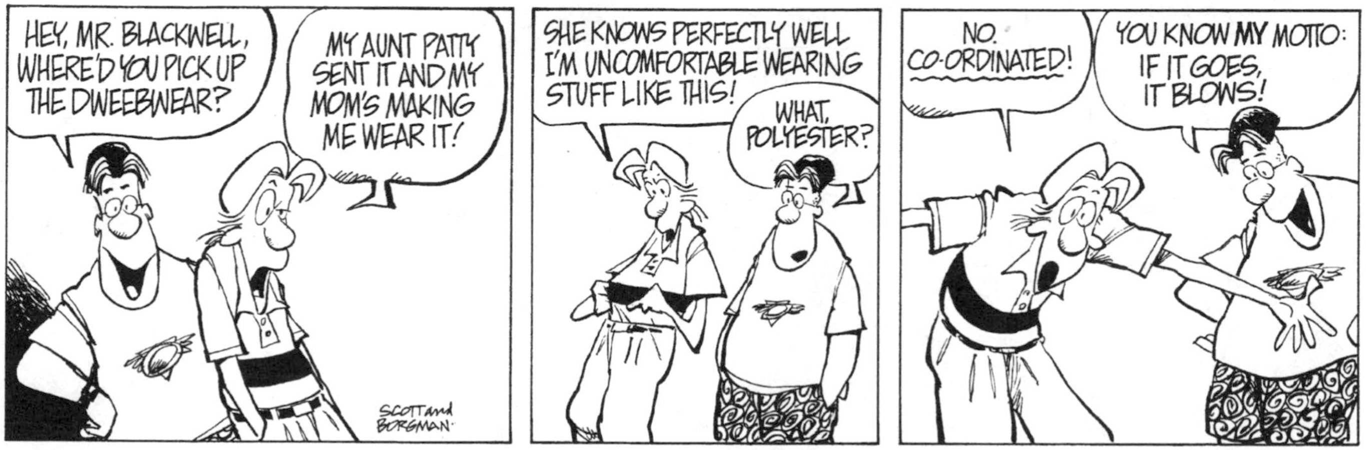
HEY, MR. BLACKWELL, WHERE'D YOU PICK UP THE DWEEBWEAR?
MY AUNT PATTY SENT IT AND MY MOM'S MAKING ME WEAR IT!
SCOTT and BORGMAN
SHE KNOWS PERFECTLY WELL I'M UNCOMFORTABLE WEARING STUFF LIKE THIS!
WHAT, POLYESTER?
NO. CO-ORDINATED!
YOU KNOW **MY** MOTTO: IF IT GOES, IT BLOWS!

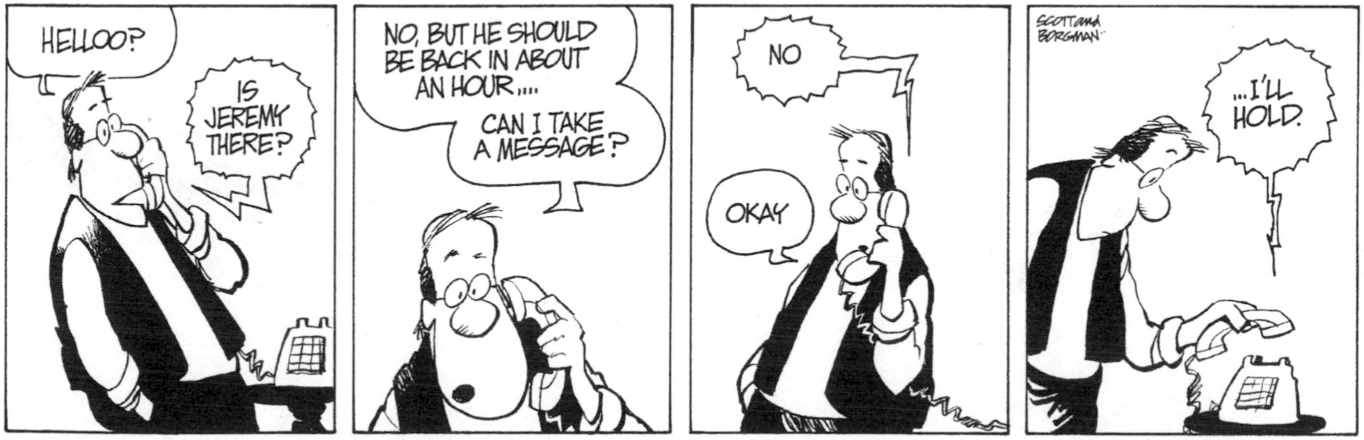
HELLOO?
IS JEREMY THERE?
NO, BUT HE SHOULD BE BACK IN ABOUT AN HOUR....
CAN I TAKE A MESSAGE?
NO
OKAY
SCOTT and BORGMAN
...I'LL HOLD.

Zits®

by JERRY SCOTT and JIM BORGMAN

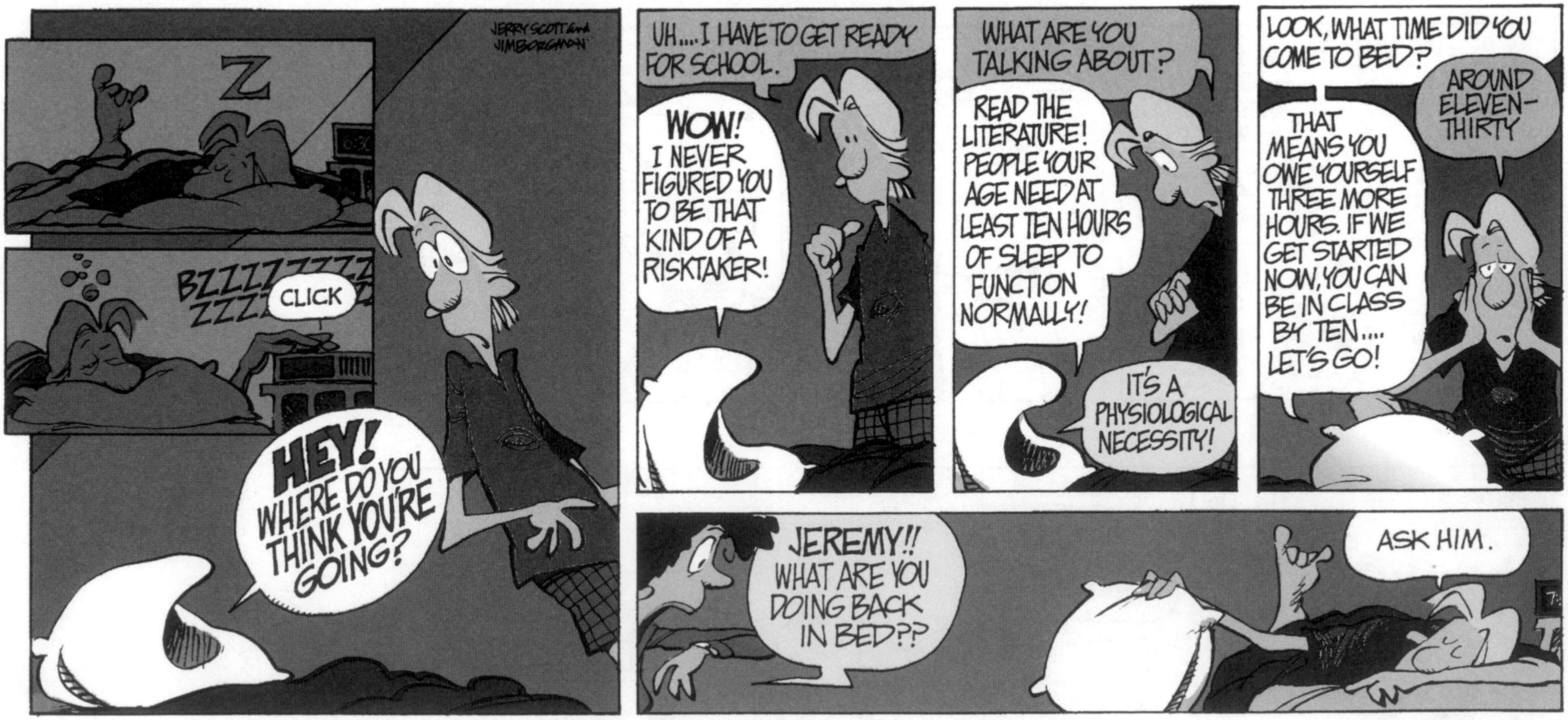
JERRY SCOTT and JIM BORGMAN
Z
BZZZZZZZZ ZZZZ
CLICK
HEY! WHERE DO YOU THINK YOU'RE GOING?
UH.... I HAVE TO GET READY FOR SCHOOL.
WOW! I NEVER FIGURED YOU TO BE THAT KIND OF A RISKTAKER!
WHAT ARE YOU TALKING ABOUT?
READ THE LITERATURE! PEOPLE YOUR AGE NEED AT LEAST TEN HOURS OF SLEEP TO FUNCTION NORMALLY!
IT'S A PHYSIOLOGICAL NECESSITY!
LOOK, WHAT TIME DID YOU COME TO BED?
AROUND ELEVEN-THIRTY
THAT MEANS YOU OWE YOURSELF THREE MORE HOURS. IF WE GET STARTED NOW, YOU CAN BE IN CLASS BY TEN.... LET'S GO!
JEREMY!! WHAT ARE YOU DOING BACK IN BED??
ASK HIM.

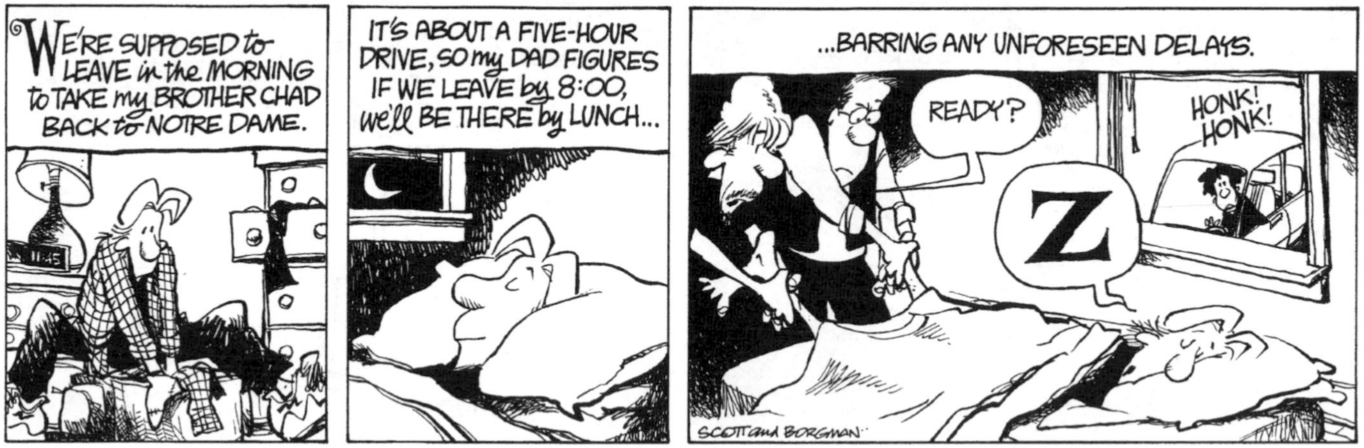
WE'RE SUPPOSED to LEAVE in the MORNING to TAKE my BROTHER CHAD BACK to NOTRE DAME.
IT'S ABOUT A FIVE-HOUR DRIVE, SO my DAD FIGURES IF WE LEAVE by 8:00, we'll BE THERE by LUNCH...
...BARRING ANY UNFORESEEN DELAYS.
READY?
Z
HONK! HONK!
SCOTT and BORGMAN

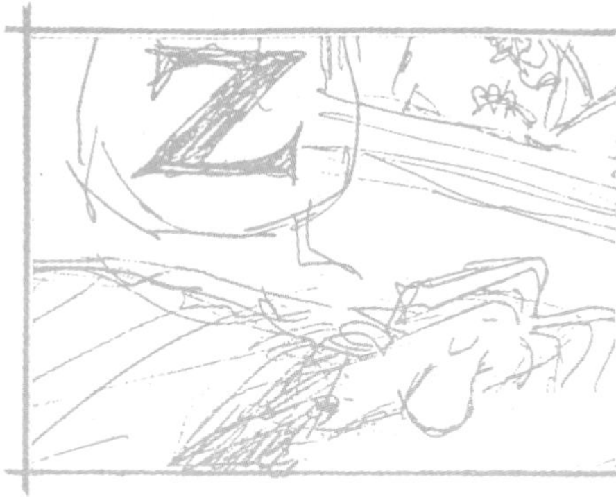
Z

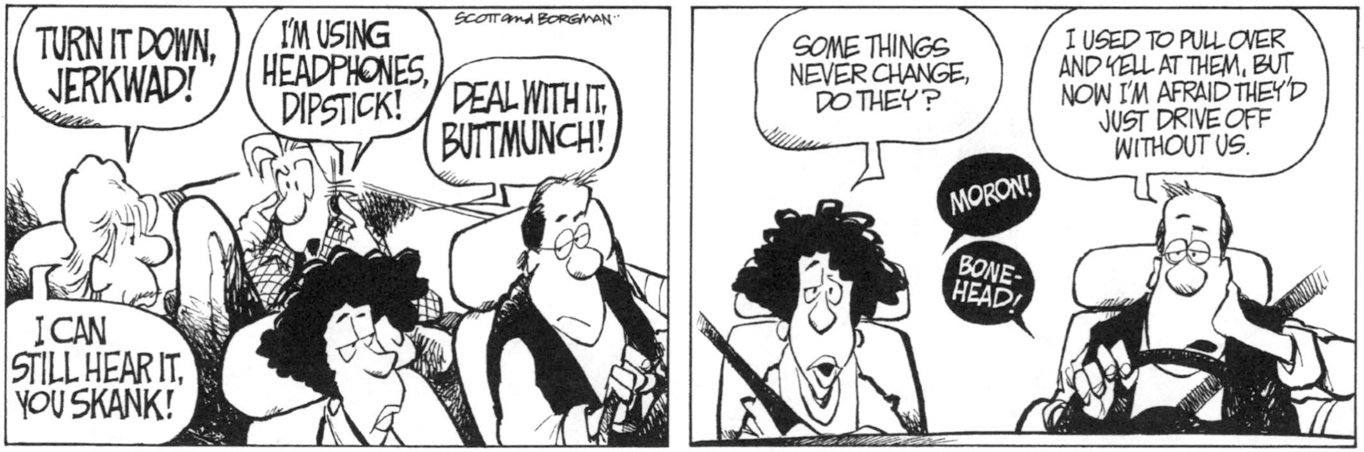
TURN IT DOWN, JERKWAD!
I'M USING HEADPHONES, DIPSTICK!
DEAL WITH IT, BUTTMUNCH!
I CAN STILL HEAR IT, YOU SKANK!
SCOTT and BORGMAN
SOME THINGS NEVER CHANGE, DO THEY?
MORON!
BONE-HEAD!
I USED TO PULL OVER AND YELL AT THEM, BUT NOW I'M AFRAID THEY'D JUST DRIVE OFF WITHOUT US.

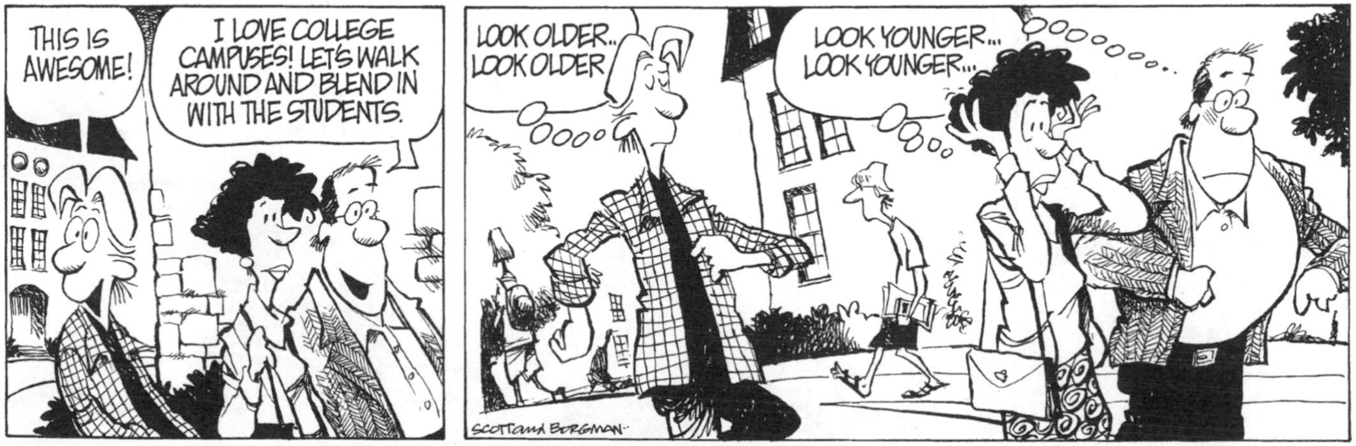
THIS IS AWESOME!
I LOVE COLLEGE CAMPUSES! LET'S WALK AROUND AND BLEND IN WITH THE STUDENTS.
LOOK OLDER.. LOOK OLDER
LOOK YOUNGER... LOOK YOUNGER...
SCOTT and BORGMAN

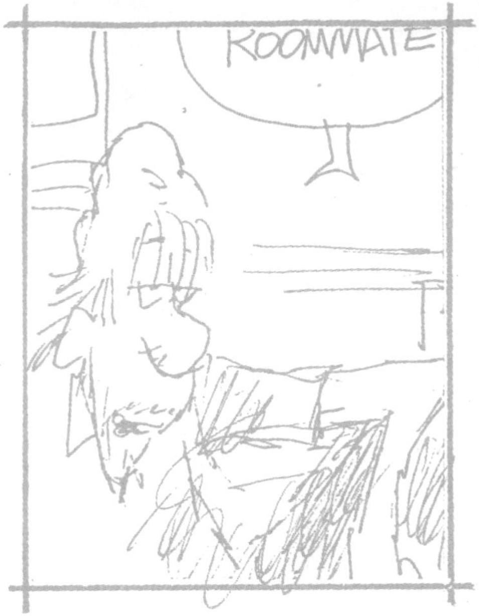
ROOMMATE

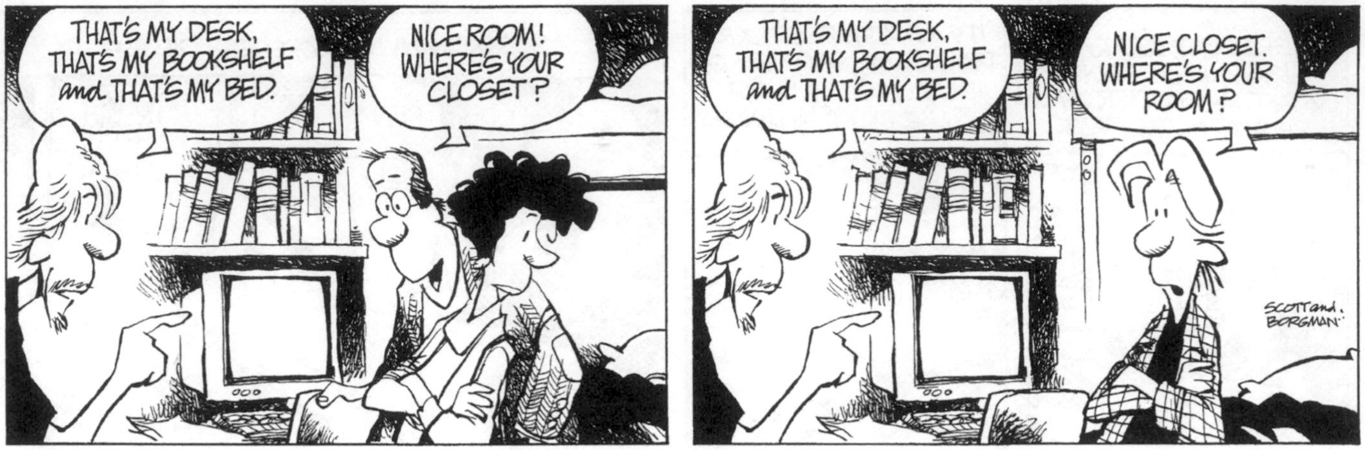
THAT'S MY DESK, THAT'S MY BOOKSHELF and THAT'S MY BED.
NICE ROOM! WHERE'S YOUR CLOSET?
THAT'S MY DESK, THAT'S MY BOOKSHELF and THAT'S MY BED.
NICE CLOSET. WHERE'S YOUR ROOM?
SCOTT and BORGMAN

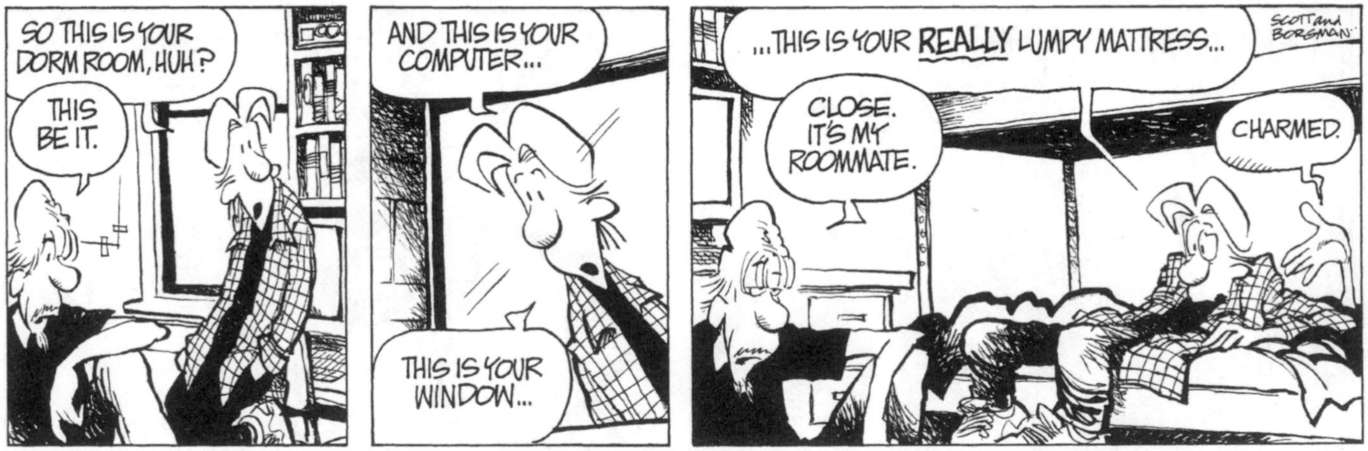
SO THIS IS YOUR DORM ROOM, HUH?
THIS BE IT.
AND THIS IS YOUR COMPUTER...
THIS IS YOUR WINDOW...
...THIS IS YOUR REALLY LUMPY MATTRESS...
CLOSE. IT'S MY ROOMMATE.
CHARMED.
SCOTT and BORGMAN

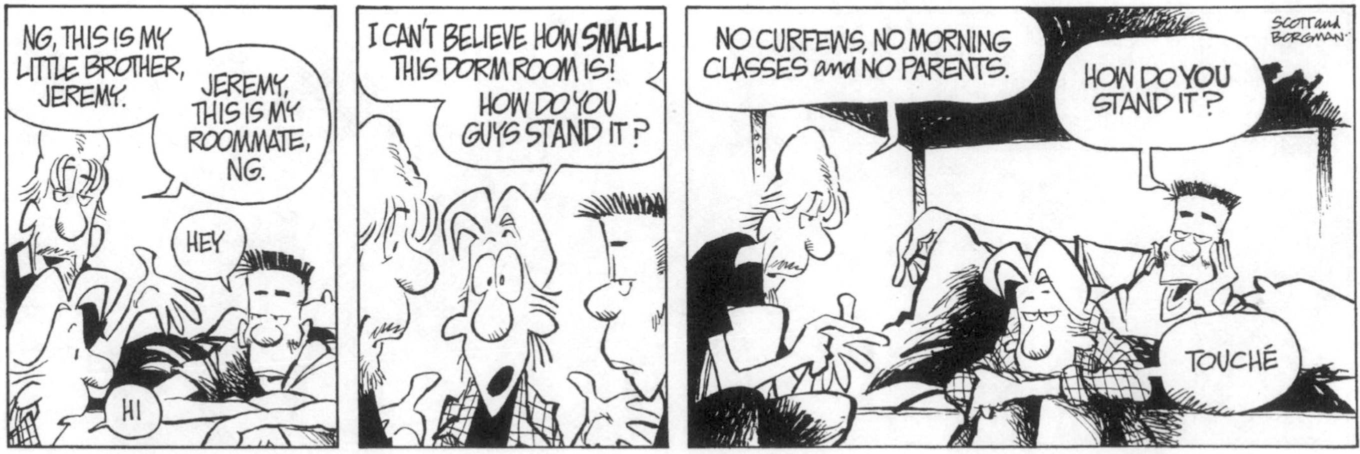
NG, THIS IS MY LITTLE BROTHER, JEREMY.
JEREMY, THIS IS MY ROOMMATE, NG.
HEY
HI
I CAN'T BELIEVE HOW SMALL THIS DORM ROOM IS!
HOW DO YOU GUYS STAND IT?
NO CURFEWS, NO MORNING CLASSES and NO PARENTS.
HOW DO YOU STAND IT?
TOUCHÉ
SCOTT and BORGMAN

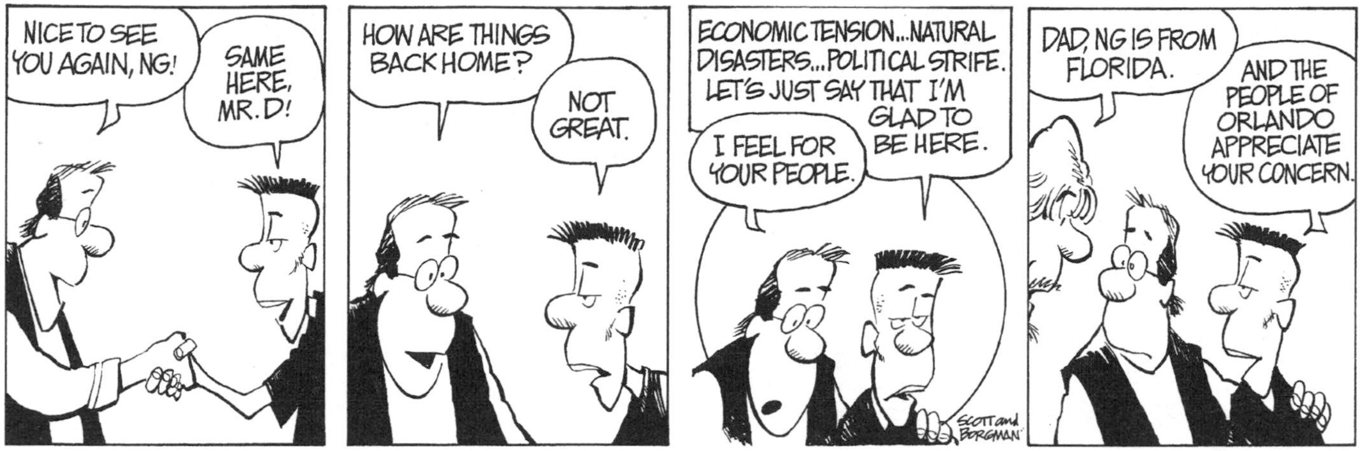
NICE TO SEE YOU AGAIN, NG!
SAME HERE, MR. D!
HOW ARE THINGS BACK HOME?
NOT GREAT.
ECONOMIC TENSION...NATURAL DISASTERS...POLITICAL STRIFE. LET'S JUST SAY THAT I'M GLAD TO BE HERE.
I FEEL FOR YOUR PEOPLE.
SCOTT and BORGMAN
DAD, NG IS FROM FLORIDA.
AND THE PEOPLE OF ORLANDO APPRECIATE YOUR CONCERN.

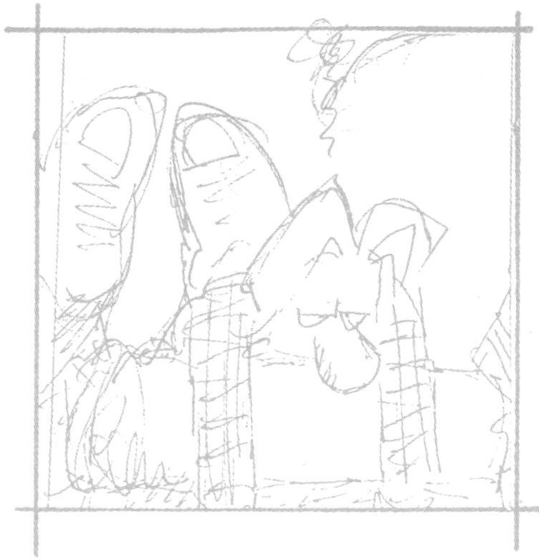

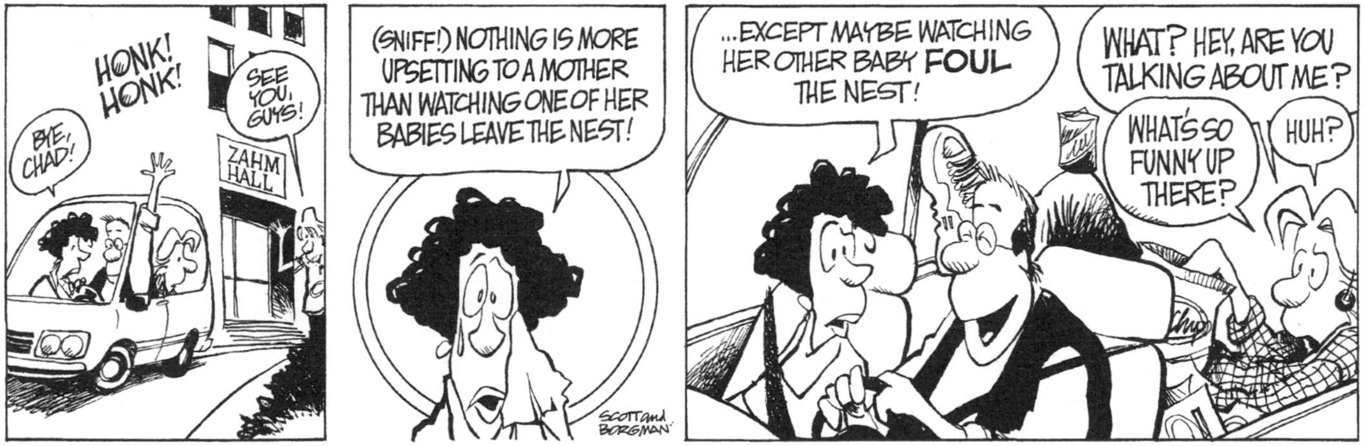
HONK! HONK!
BYE, CHAD!
SEE YOU, GUYS!
ZAHM HALL
(SNIFF!) NOTHING IS MORE UPSETTING TO A MOTHER THAN WATCHING ONE OF HER BABIES LEAVE THE NEST!
SCOTT and BORGMAN
...EXCEPT MAYBE WATCHING HER OTHER BABY FOUL THE NEST!
WHAT? HEY, ARE YOU TALKING ABOUT ME?
WHAT'S SO FUNNY UP THERE?
HUH?

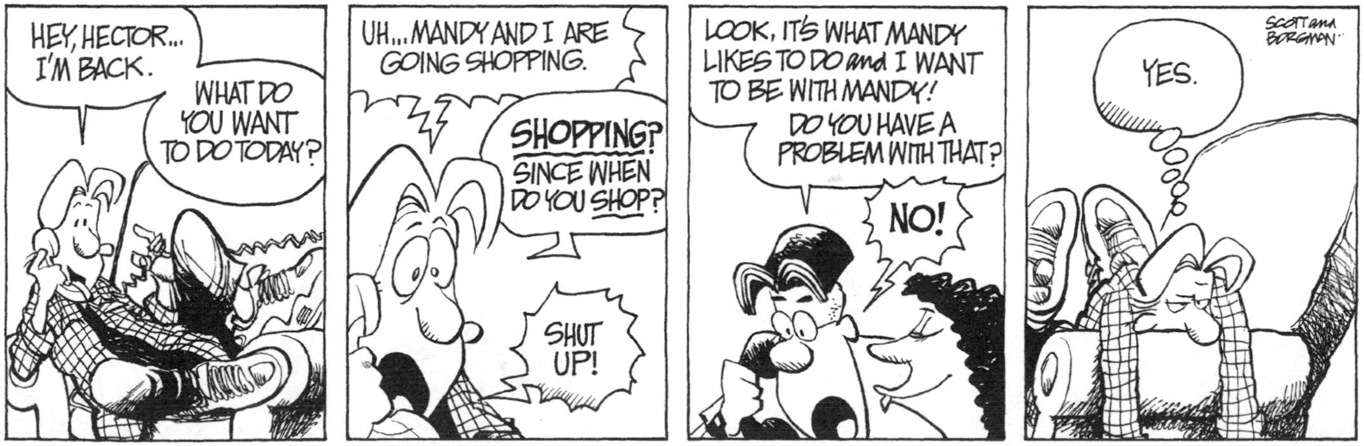
HEY, HECTOR... I'M BACK.
WHAT DO YOU WANT TO DO TODAY?
UH,...MANDY AND I ARE GOING SHOPPING.
SHOPPING? SINCE WHEN DO YOU SHOP?
SHUT UP!
LOOK, IT'S WHAT MANDY LIKES TO DO and I WANT TO BE WITH MANDY!
DO YOU HAVE A PROBLEM WITH THAT?
NO!
SCOTT and BORGMAN
YES.

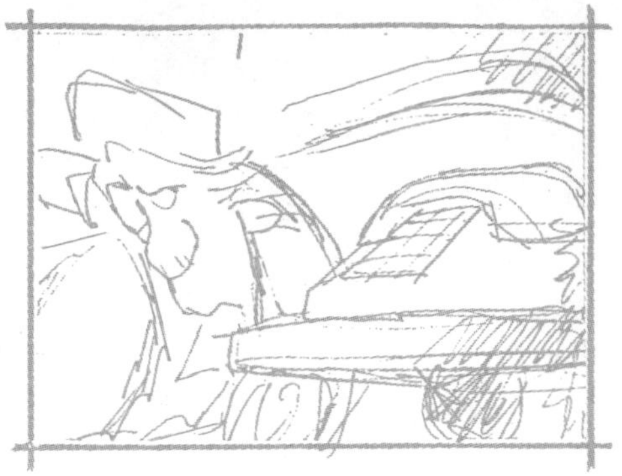

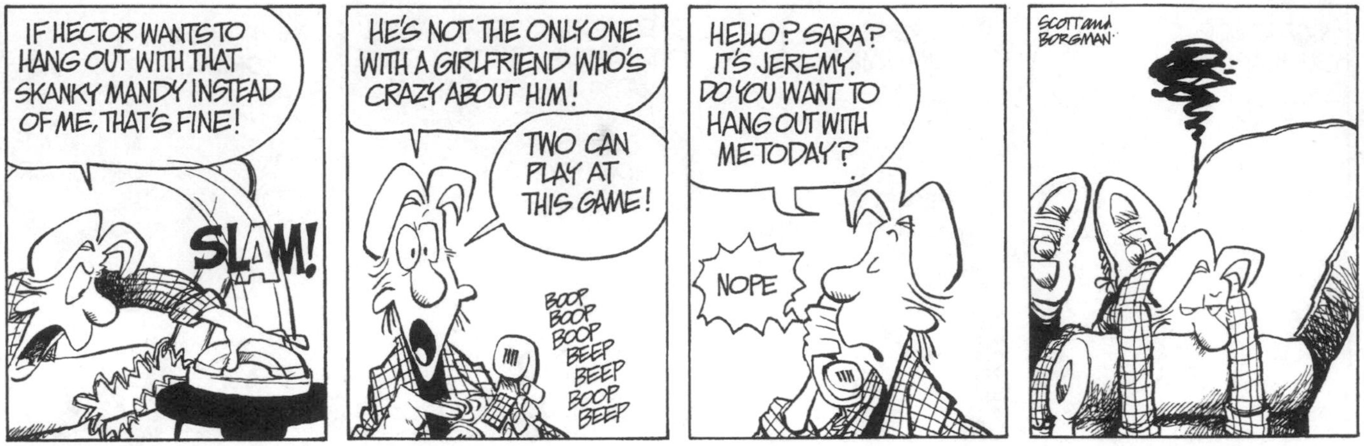
IF HECTOR WANTS TO HANG OUT WITH THAT SKANKY MANDY INSTEAD OF ME, THAT'S FINE!
SLAM!
HE'S NOT THE ONLY ONE WITH A GIRLFRIEND WHO'S CRAZY ABOUT HIM!
TWO CAN PLAY AT THIS GAME!
BOOP BOOP BOOP BEEP BEEP BOOP BEEP
HELLO? SARA? IT'S JEREMY. DO YOU WANT TO HANG OUT WITH ME TODAY?
NOPE
SCOTT and BORGMAN

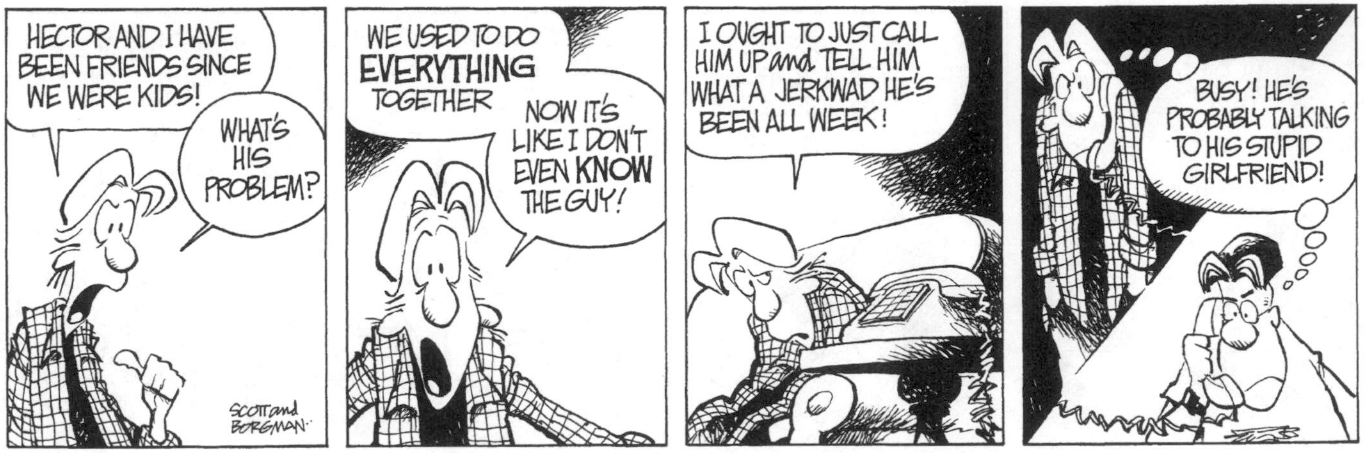
HECTOR AND I HAVE BEEN FRIENDS SINCE WE WERE KIDS!
WHAT'S HIS PROBLEM?
SCOTT and BORGMAN
WE USED TO DO EVERYTHING TOGETHER
NOW IT'S LIKE I DON'T EVEN KNOW THE GUY!
I OUGHT TO JUST CALL HIM UP and TELL HIM WHAT A JERKWAD HE'S BEEN ALL WEEK!
BUSY! HE'S PROBABLY TALKING TO HIS STUPID GIRLFRIEND!

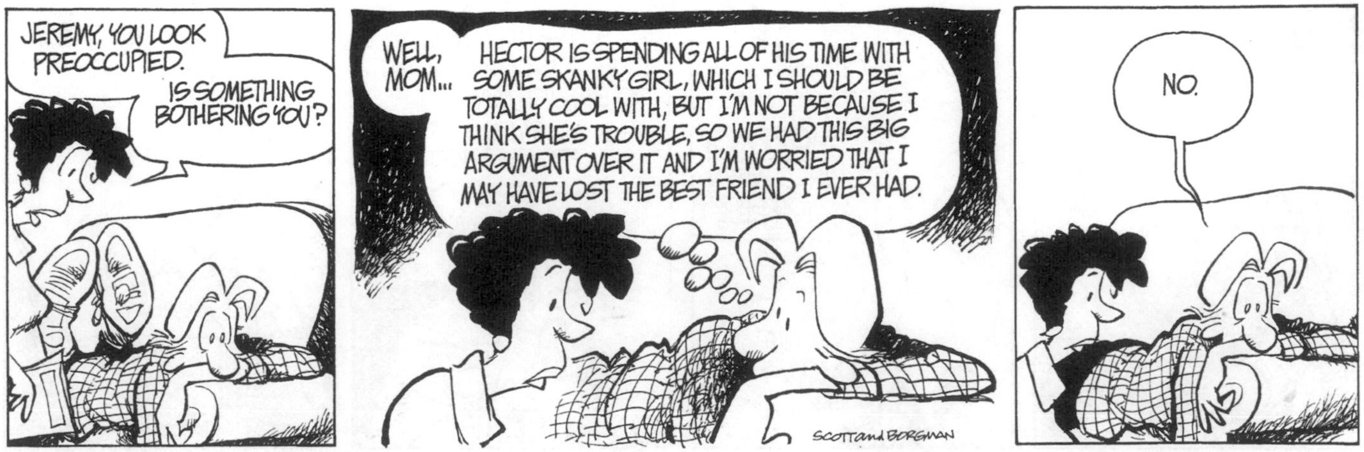
JEREMY, YOU LOOK PREOCCUPIED.
IS SOMETHING BOTHERING YOU?
WELL, MOM...
HECTOR IS SPENDING ALL OF HIS TIME WITH SOME SKANKY GIRL, WHICH I SHOULD BE TOTALLY COOL WITH, BUT I'M NOT BECAUSE I THINK SHE'S TROUBLE, SO WE HAD THIS BIG ARGUMENT OVER IT AND I'M WORRIED THAT I MAY HAVE LOST THE BEST FRIEND I EVER HAD.
SCOTT and BORGMAN
NO.

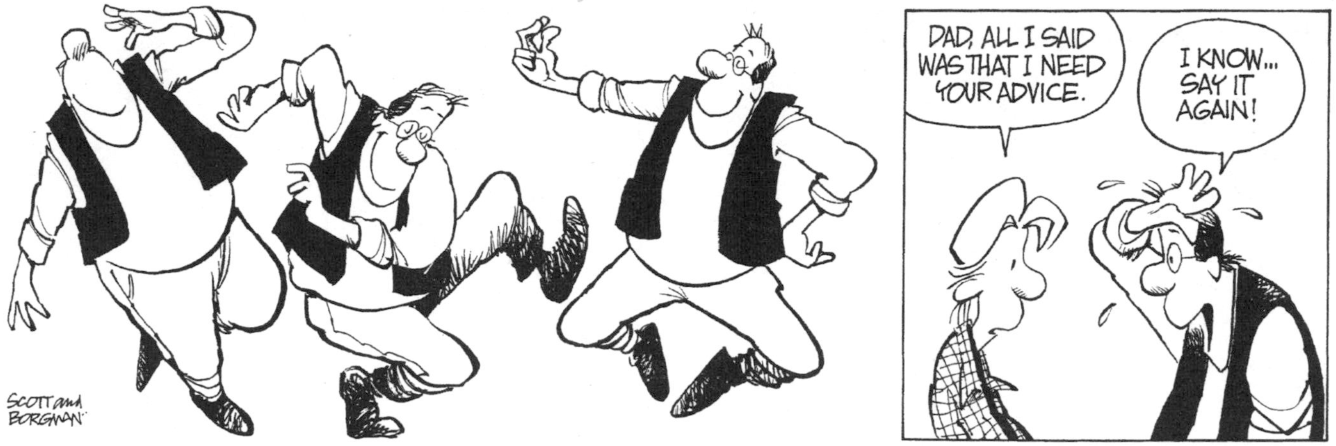
SCOTT and BORGMAN
DAD, ALL I SAID WAS THAT I NEED YOUR ADVICE.
I KNOW... SAY IT AGAIN!

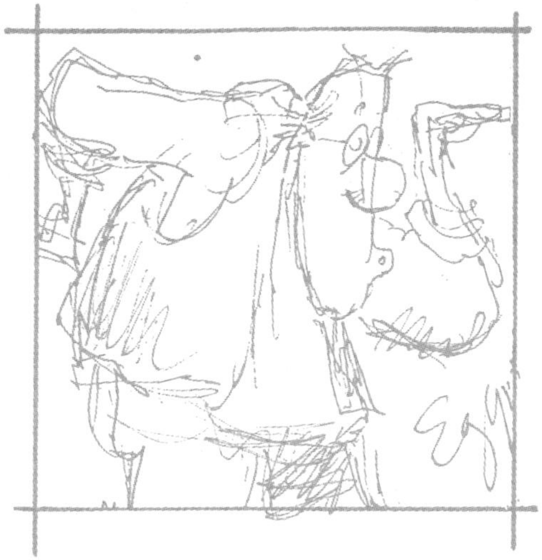

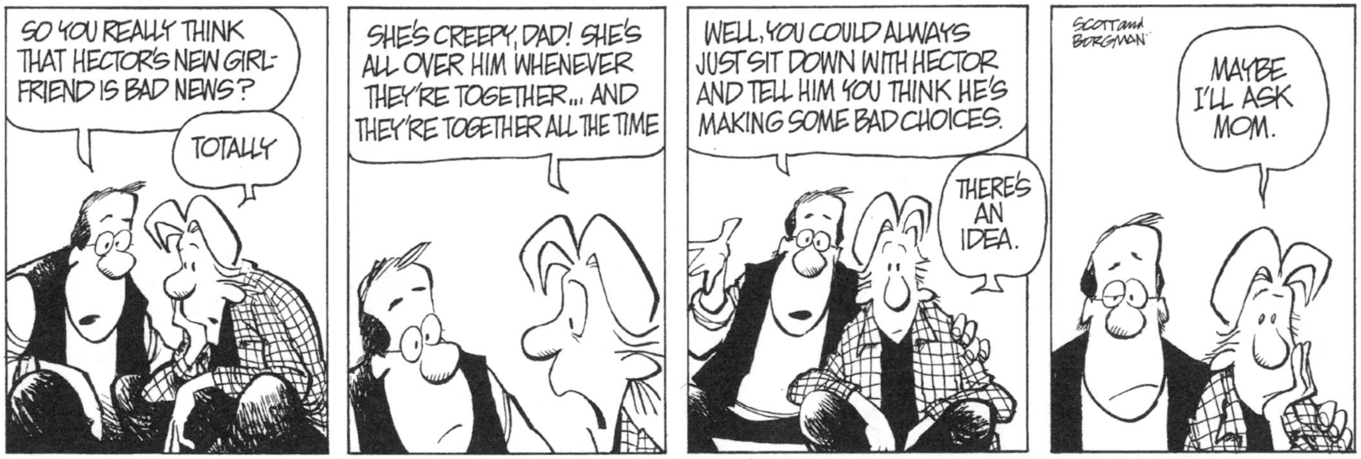
SO YOU REALLY THINK THAT HECTOR'S NEW GIRL-FRIEND IS BAD NEWS?
TOTALLY
SHE'S CREEPY, DAD! SHE'S ALL OVER HIM WHENEVER THEY'RE TOGETHER... AND THEY'RE TOGETHER ALL THE TIME
WELL, YOU COULD ALWAYS JUST SIT DOWN WITH HECTOR AND TELL HIM YOU THINK HE'S MAKING SOME BAD CHOICES.
THERE'S AN IDEA.
SCOTT and BORGMAN
MAYBE I'LL ASK MOM.

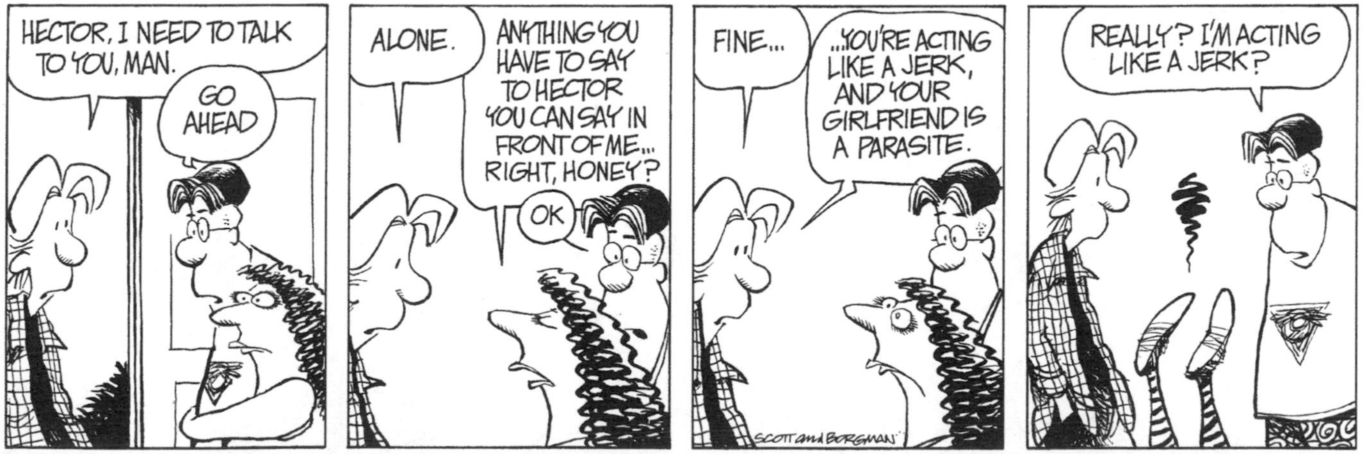
HECTOR, I NEED TO TALK TO YOU, MAN.
GO AHEAD
ALONE.
ANYTHING YOU HAVE TO SAY TO HECTOR YOU CAN SAY IN FRONT OF ME... RIGHT, HONEY?
OK
FINE...
...YOU'RE ACTING LIKE A JERK, AND YOUR GIRLFRIEND IS A PARASITE.
SCOTT and BORGMAN
REALLY? I'M ACTING LIKE A JERK?

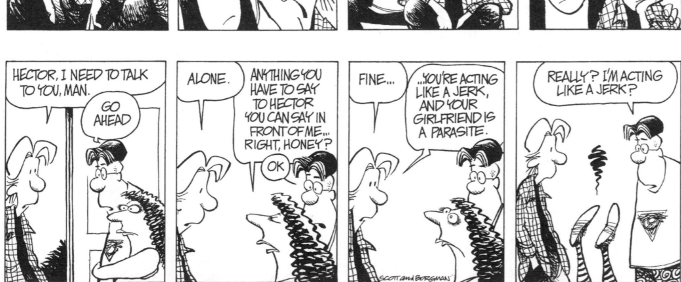

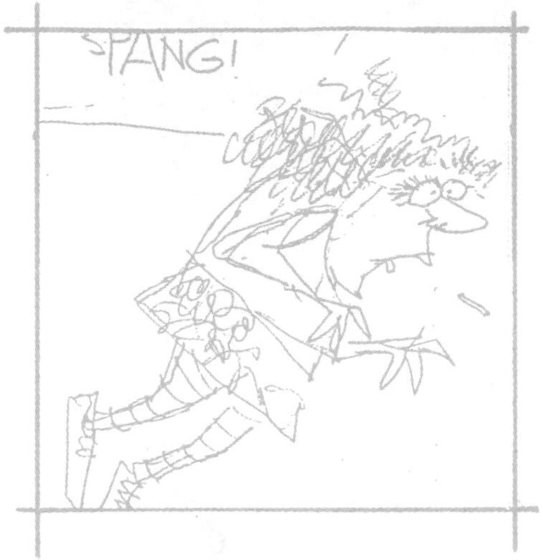

SPANG!

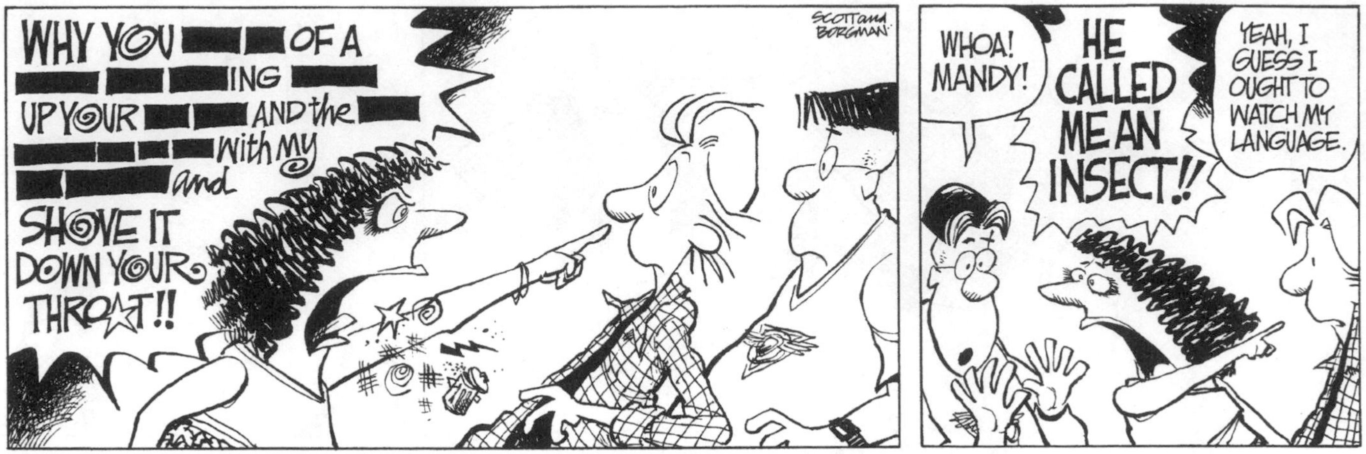

SCOTT and BORGMAN
WHY YOU [redacted] OF A [redacted] ING [redacted] UP YOUR [redacted] AND the [redacted] with my [redacted] and SHOVE IT DOWN YOUR THROAT!!
WHOA! MANDY!
HE CALLED ME AN INSECT!!
YEAH, I GUESS I OUGHT TO WATCH MY LANGUAGE.

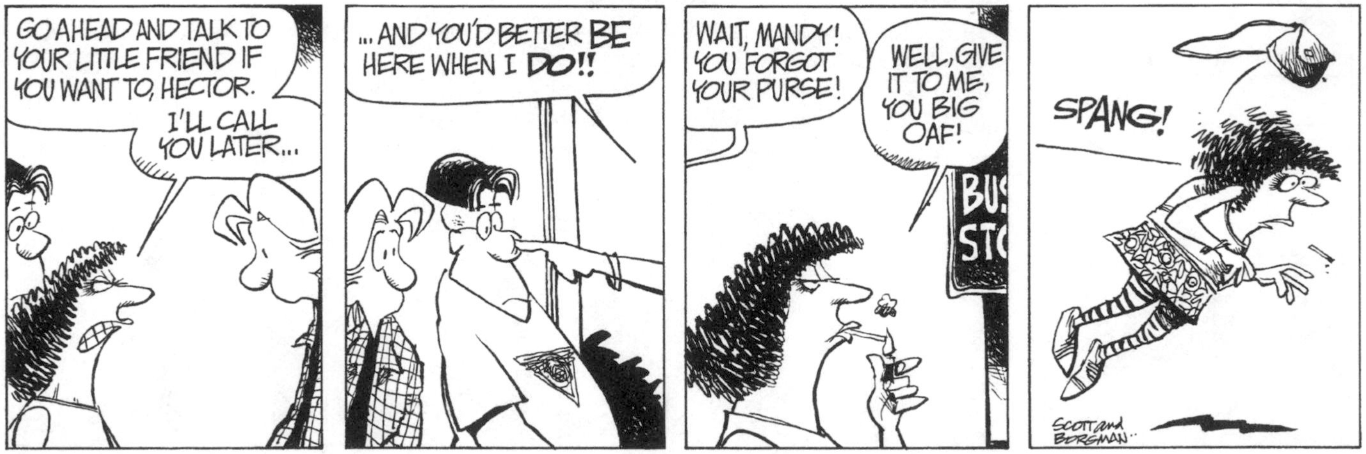

GO AHEAD AND TALK TO YOUR LITTLE FRIEND IF YOU WANT TO, HECTOR.
I'LL CALL YOU LATER...
... AND YOU'D BETTER BE HERE WHEN I DO!!
WAIT, MANDY! YOU FORGOT YOUR PURSE!
WELL, GIVE IT TO ME, YOU BIG OAF!
BUS STO
SPANG!
SCOTT and BORGMAN

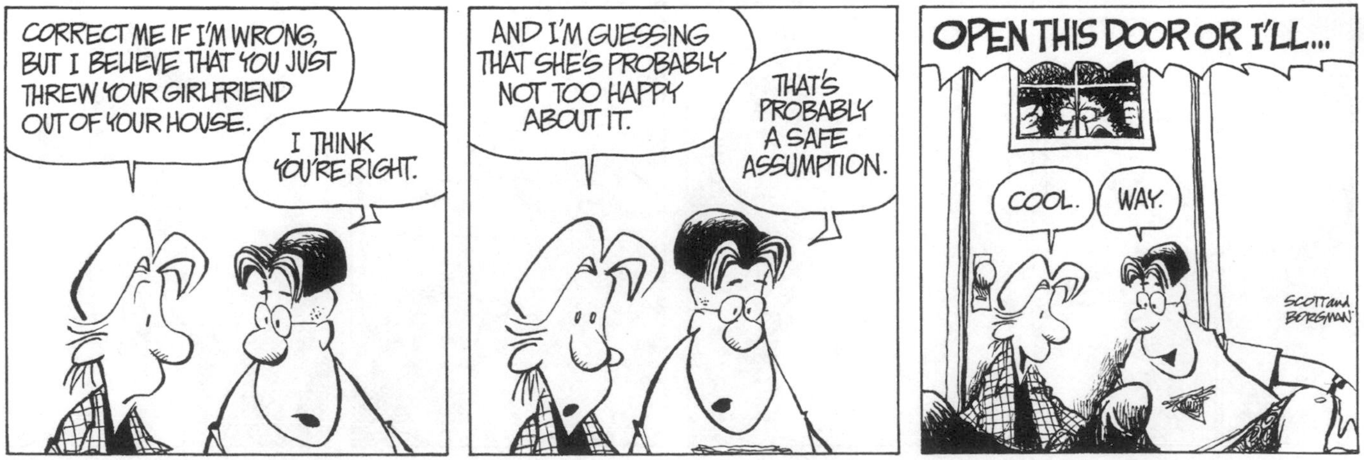

CORRECT ME IF I'M WRONG, BUT I BELIEVE THAT YOU JUST THREW YOUR GIRLFRIEND OUT OF YOUR HOUSE.
I THINK YOU'RE RIGHT.
AND I'M GUESSING THAT SHE'S PROBABLY NOT TOO HAPPY ABOUT IT.
THAT'S PROBABLY A SAFE ASSUMPTION.
OPEN THIS DOOR OR I'LL...
COOL.
WAY.
SCOTT and BORGMAN

Zits®

by JERRY SCOTT and JIM BORGMAN

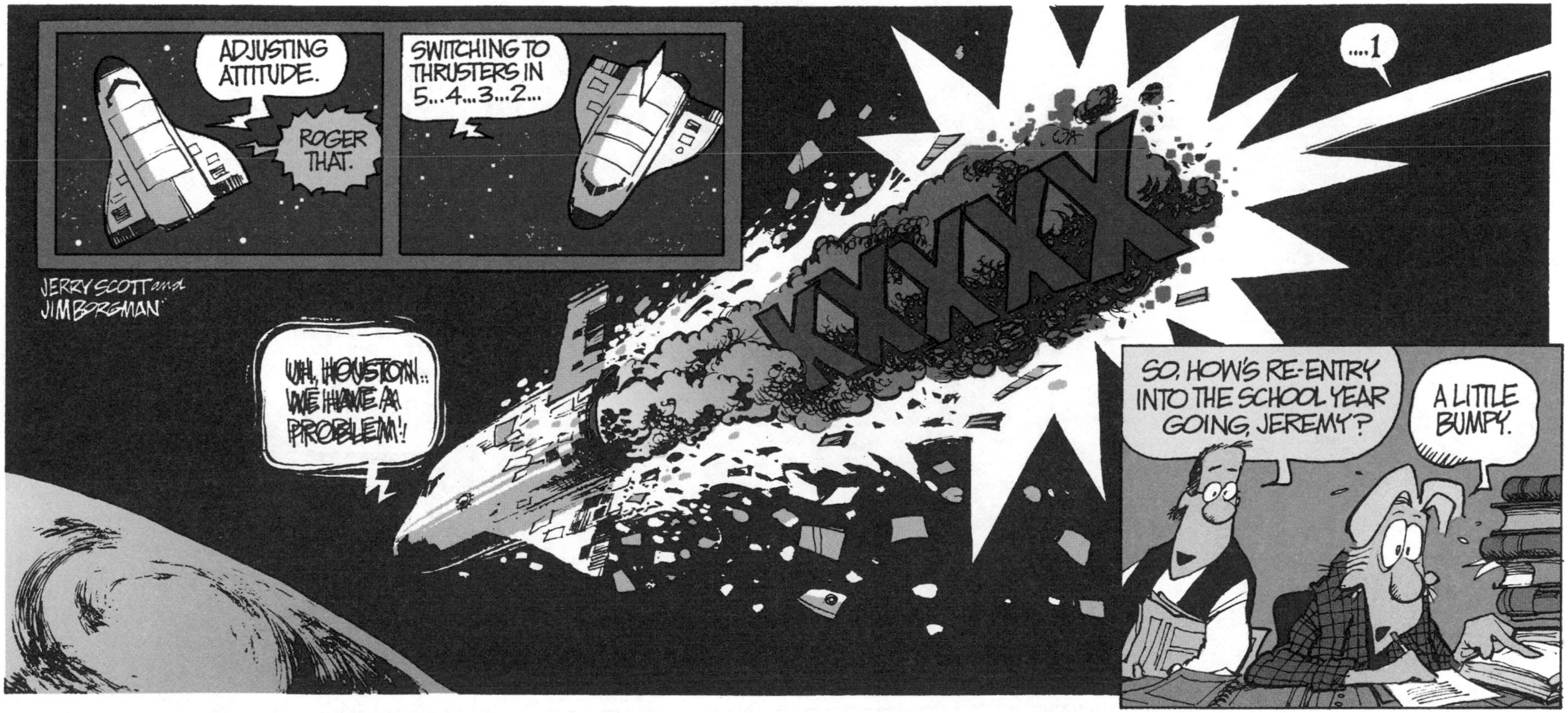
ADJUSTING ATTITUDE.
ROGER THAT.
SWITCHING TO THRUSTERS IN 5...4...3...2...
....1
JERRY SCOTT and JIM BORGMAN
UH, HOUSTON... WE HAVE A PROBLEM!!
SO, HOW'S RE-ENTRY INTO THE SCHOOL YEAR GOING, JEREMY?
A LITTLE BUMPY.

Zits®

by JERRY SCOTT and JIM BORGMAN

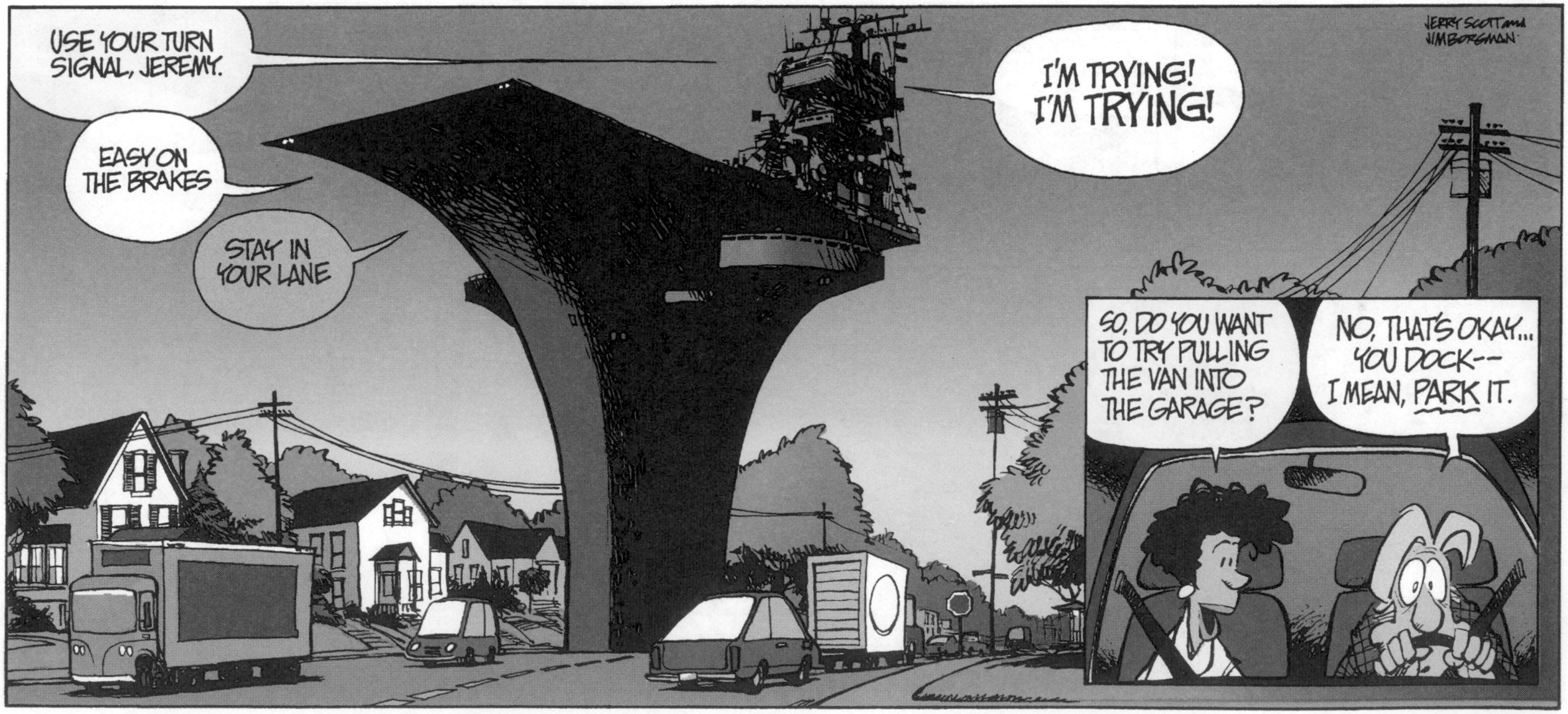
JERRY SCOTT and JIM BORGMAN
USE YOUR TURN SIGNAL, JEREMY.
EASY ON THE BRAKES
STAY IN YOUR LANE
I'M TRYING! I'M TRYING!
SO, DO YOU WANT TO TRY PULLING THE VAN INTO THE GARAGE?
NO, THAT'S OKAY... YOU DOCK-- I MEAN, PARK IT.

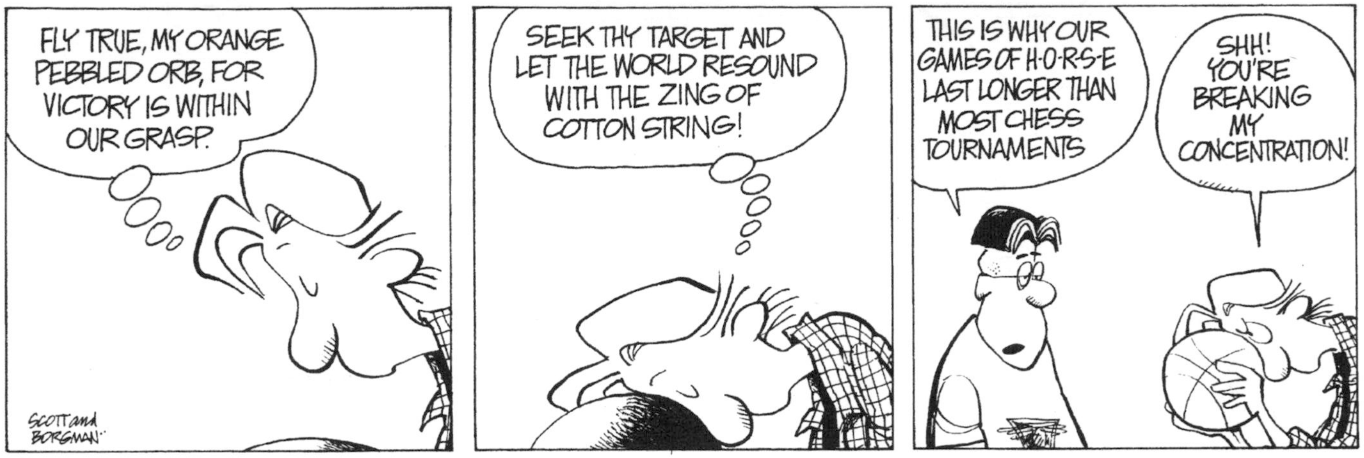
FLY TRUE, MY ORANGE PEBBLED ORB, FOR VICTORY IS WITHIN OUR GRASP.
SCOTT and BORGMAN
SEEK THY TARGET AND LET THE WORLD RESOUND WITH THE ZING OF COTTON STRING!
THIS IS WHY OUR GAMES OF H-O-R-S-E LAST LONGER THAN MOST CHESS TOURNAMENTS
SHH! YOU'RE BREAKING MY CONCENTRATION!

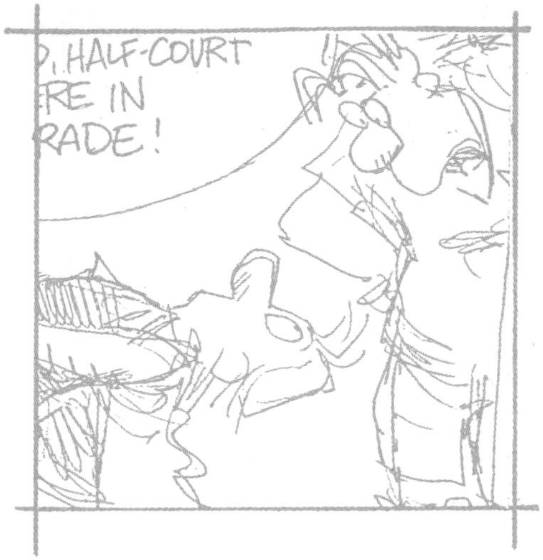
D, HALF-COURT
RE IN
RADE!

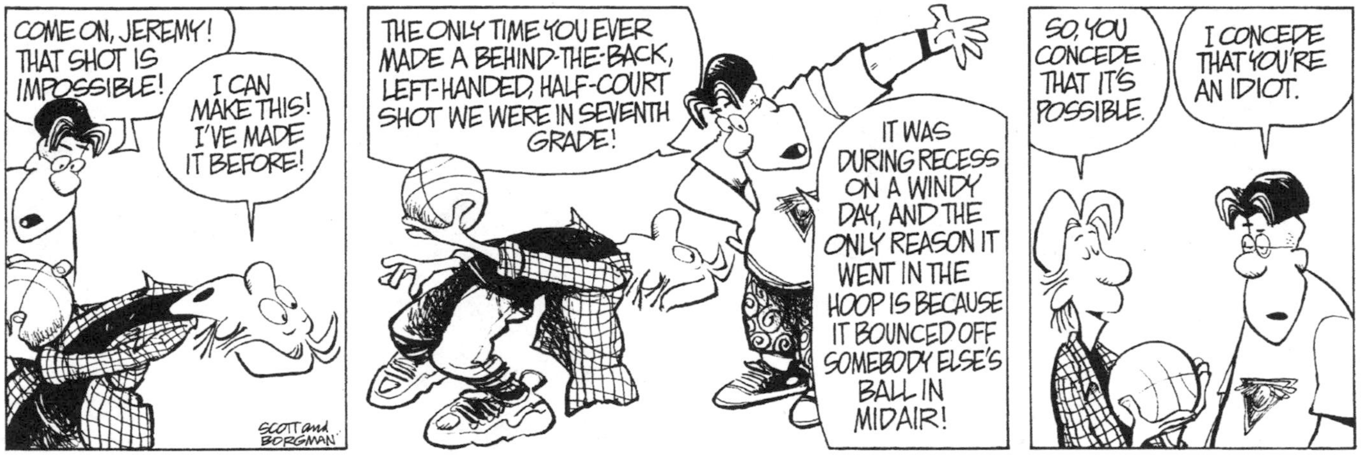
COME ON, JEREMY! THAT SHOT IS IMPOSSIBLE!
I CAN MAKE THIS! I'VE MADE IT BEFORE!
SCOTT and BORGMAN
THE ONLY TIME YOU EVER MADE A BEHIND-THE-BACK, LEFT-HANDED, HALF-COURT SHOT WE WERE IN SEVENTH GRADE!
IT WAS DURING RECESS ON A WINDY DAY, AND THE ONLY REASON IT WENT IN THE HOOP IS BECAUSE IT BOUNCED OFF SOMEBODY ELSE'S BALL IN MIDAIR!
SO, YOU CONCEDE THAT IT'S POSSIBLE.
I CONCEDE THAT YOU'RE AN IDIOT.

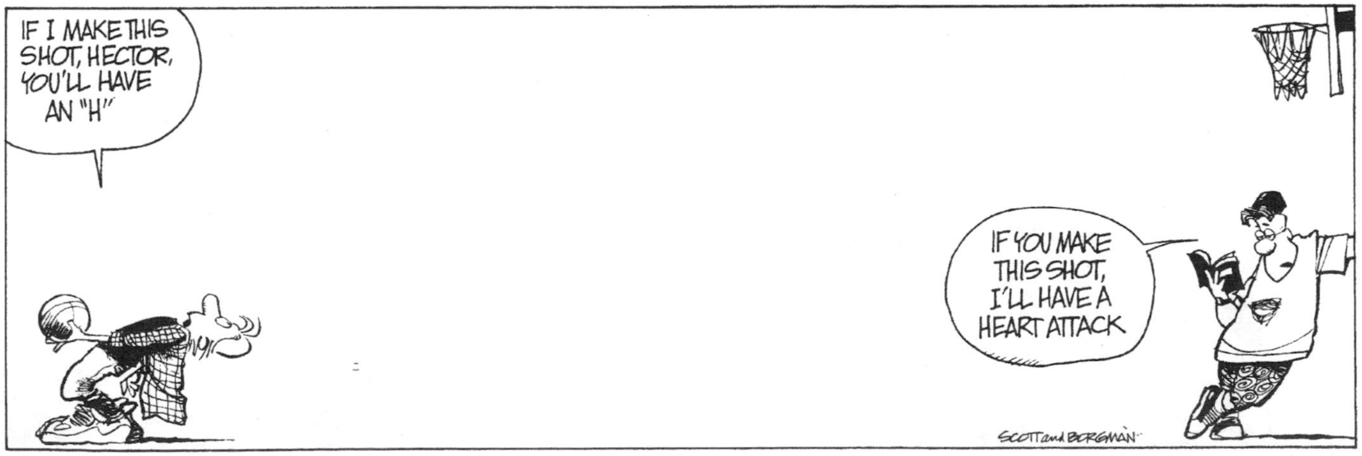
IF I MAKE THIS SHOT, HECTOR, YOU'LL HAVE AN "H"
IF YOU MAKE THIS SHOT, I'LL HAVE A HEART ATTACK
SCOTT and BORGMAN

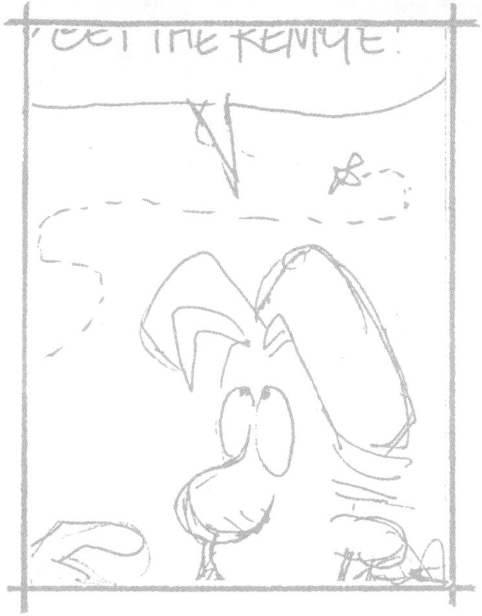

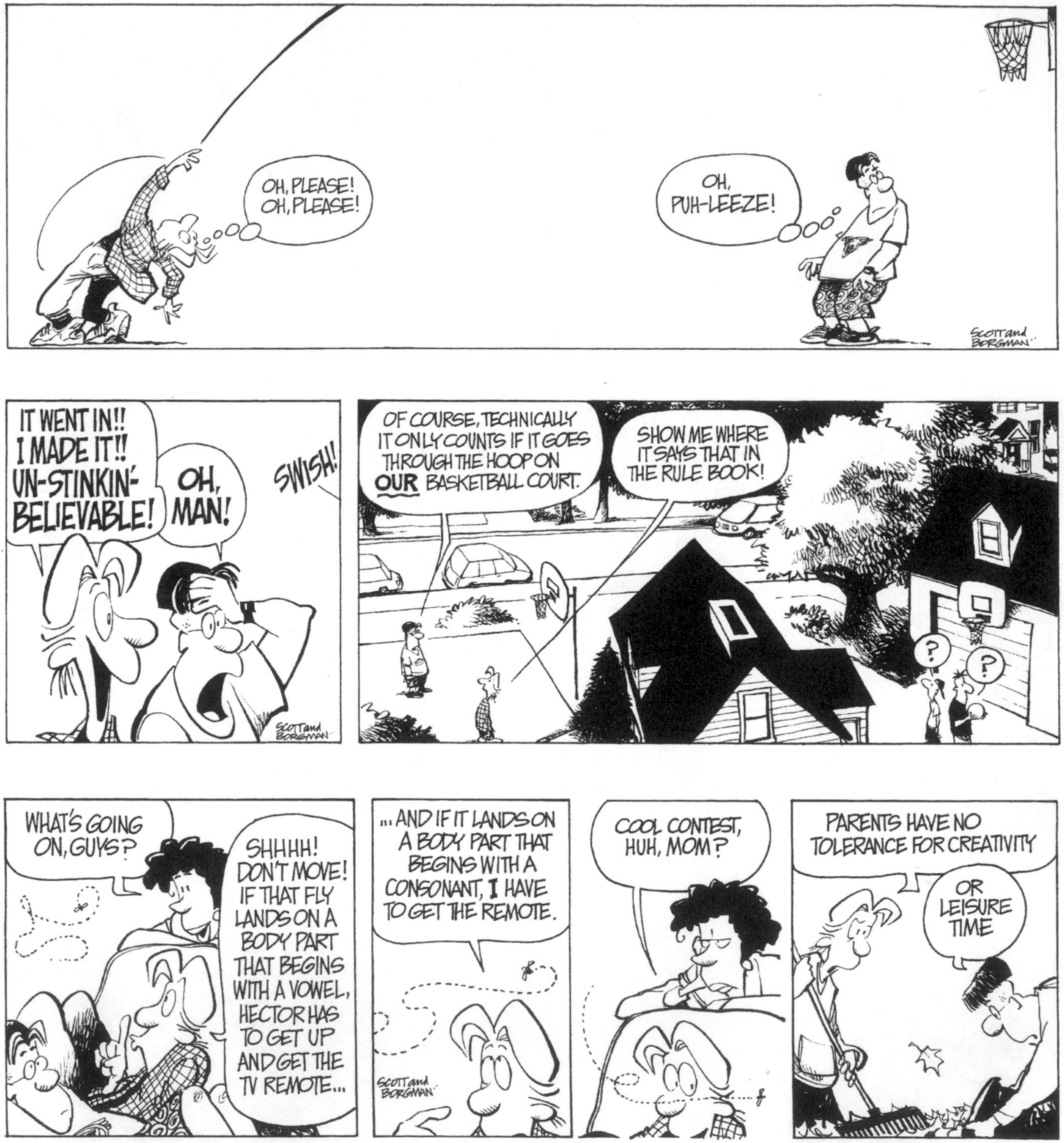
OH, PLEASE! OH, PLEASE!
OH, PUH-LEEZE!
SCOTT and BORGMAN
IT WENT IN!! I MADE IT!! UN-STINKIN'-BELIEVABLE!
OH, MAN!
SWISH!
SCOTT and BORGMAN
OF COURSE, TECHNICALLY IT ONLY COUNTS IF IT GOES THROUGH THE HOOP ON OUR BASKETBALL COURT.
SHOW ME WHERE IT SAYS THAT IN THE RULE BOOK!
?
?
WHAT'S GOING ON, GUYS?
SHHHH! DON'T MOVE! IF THAT FLY LANDS ON A BODY PART THAT BEGINS WITH A VOWEL, HECTOR HAS TO GET UP AND GET THE TV REMOTE...
...AND IF IT LANDS ON A BODY PART THAT BEGINS WITH A CONSONANT, I HAVE TO GET THE REMOTE.
SCOTT and BORGMAN
COOL CONTEST, HUH, MOM?
PARENTS HAVE NO TOLERANCE FOR CREATIVITY
OR LEISURE TIME

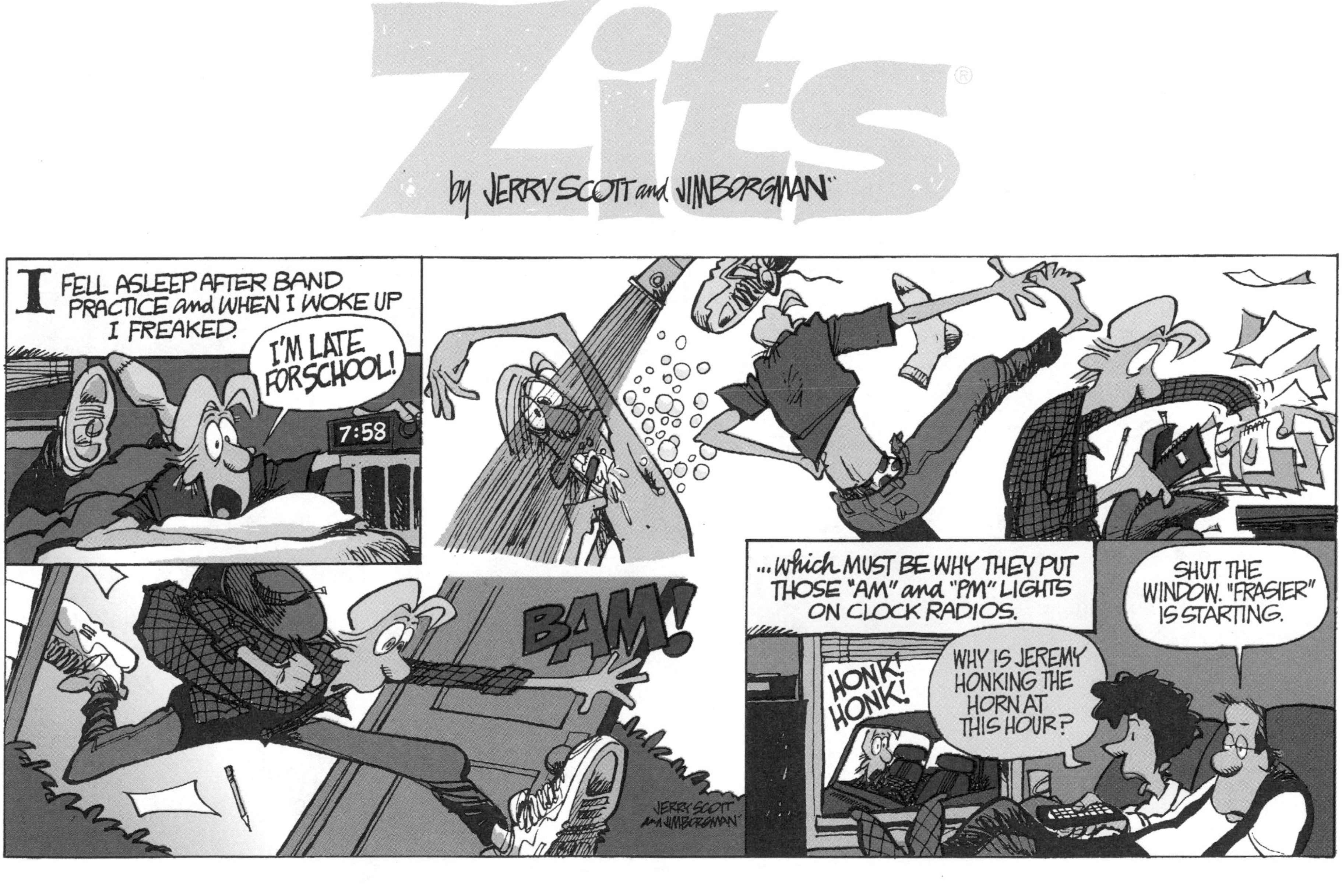
Zits®
by JERRY SCOTT and JIM BORGMAN
I FELL ASLEEP AFTER BAND PRACTICE and WHEN I WOKE UP I FREAKED.
I'M LATE FOR SCHOOL!
7:58
BAM!
JERRY SCOTT and JIM BORGMAN
...which MUST BE WHY THEY PUT THOSE "AM" and "PM" LIGHTS ON CLOCK RADIOS.
HONK! HONK!
WHY IS JEREMY HONKING THE HORN AT THIS HOUR?
SHUT THE WINDOW. "FRASIER" IS STARTING.

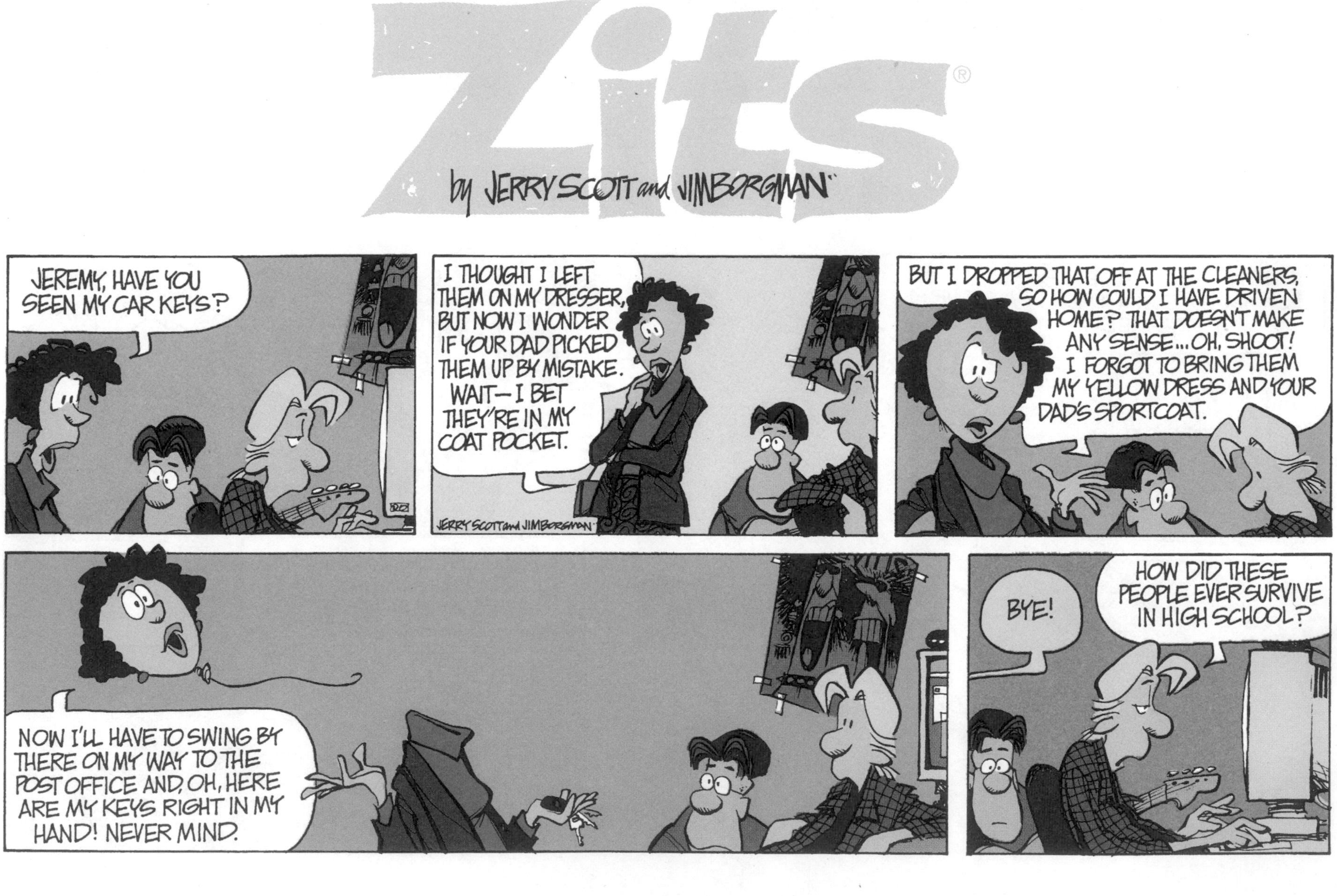
Zits®
by JERRY SCOTT and JIM BORGMAN
JEREMY, HAVE YOU SEEN MY CAR KEYS?
I THOUGHT I LEFT THEM ON MY DRESSER, BUT NOW I WONDER IF YOUR DAD PICKED THEM UP BY MISTAKE.
WAIT—I BET THEY'RE IN MY COAT POCKET.
JERRY SCOTT and JIM BORGMAN
BUT I DROPPED THAT OFF AT THE CLEANERS, SO HOW COULD I HAVE DRIVEN HOME? THAT DOESN'T MAKE ANY SENSE...OH, SHOOT! I FORGOT TO BRING THEM MY YELLOW DRESS AND YOUR DAD'S SPORTCOAT.
NOW I'LL HAVE TO SWING BY THERE ON MY WAY TO THE POST OFFICE AND, OH, HERE ARE MY KEYS RIGHT IN MY HAND! NEVER MIND.
BYE!
HOW DID THESE PEOPLE EVER SURVIVE IN HIGH SCHOOL?

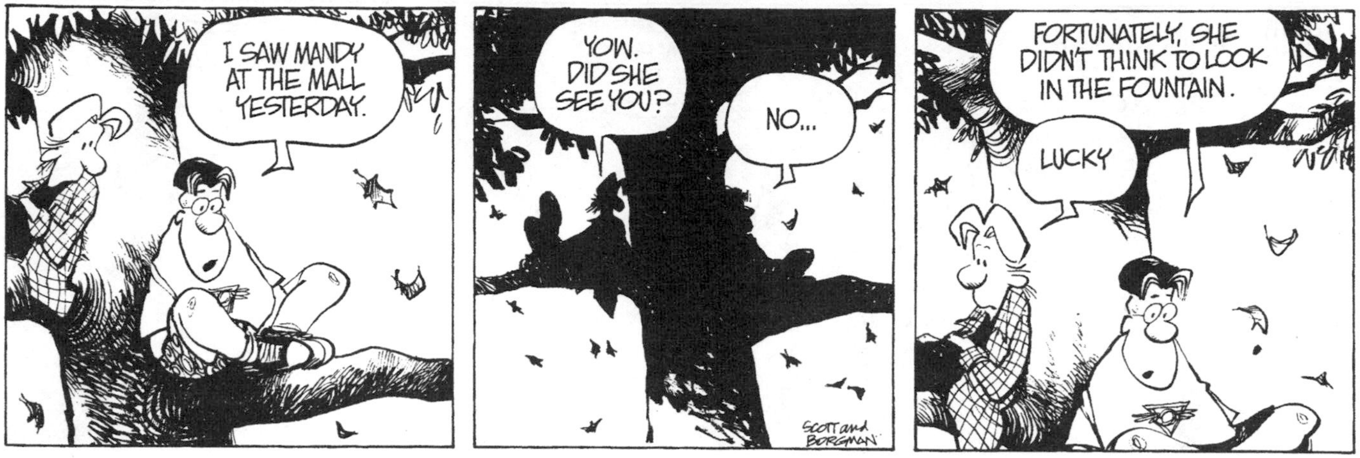
I SAW MANDY AT THE MALL YESTERDAY.
YOW. DID SHE SEE YOU?
NO...
FORTUNATELY, SHE DIDN'T THINK TO LOOK IN THE FOUNTAIN.
LUCKY
SCOTT and BORGMAN

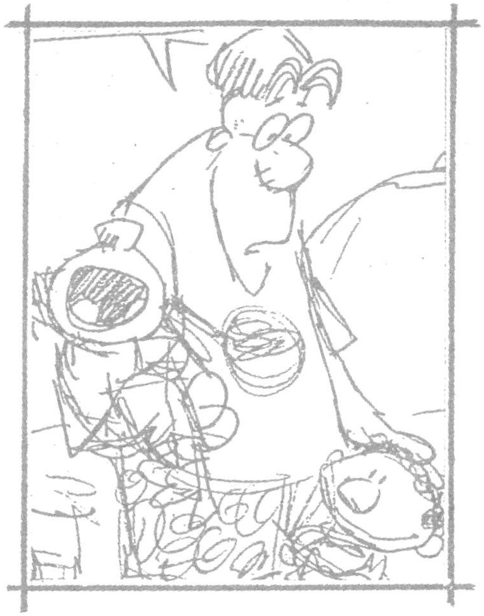

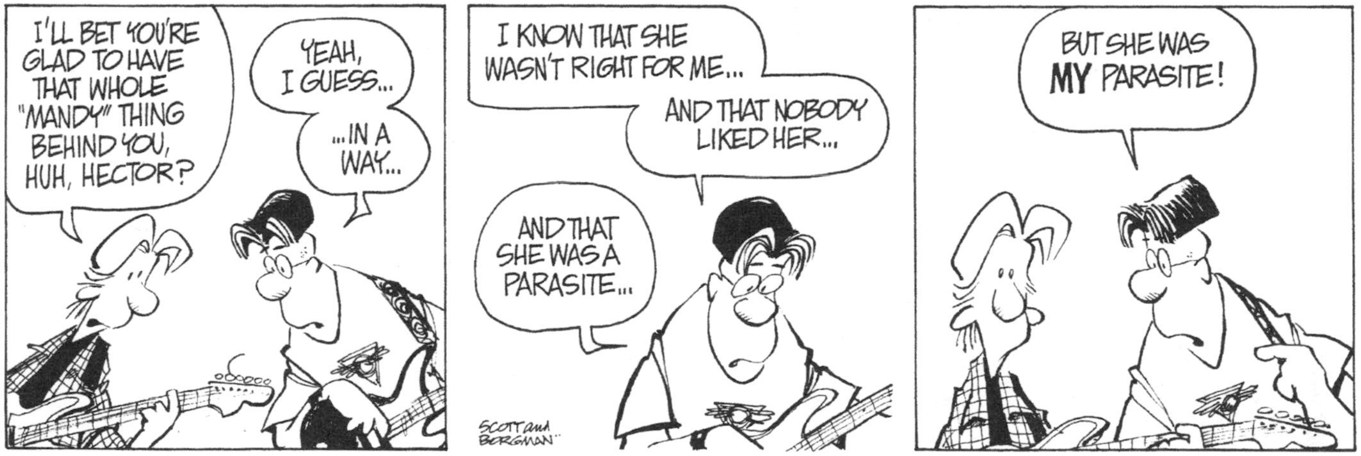
I'LL BET YOU'RE GLAD TO HAVE THAT WHOLE "MANDY" THING BEHIND YOU, HUH, HECTOR?
YEAH, I GUESS...
...IN A WAY...
I KNOW THAT SHE WASN'T RIGHT FOR ME...
AND THAT NOBODY LIKED HER...
AND THAT SHE WAS A PARASITE...
SCOTT and BORGMAN
BUT SHE WAS **MY** PARASITE!

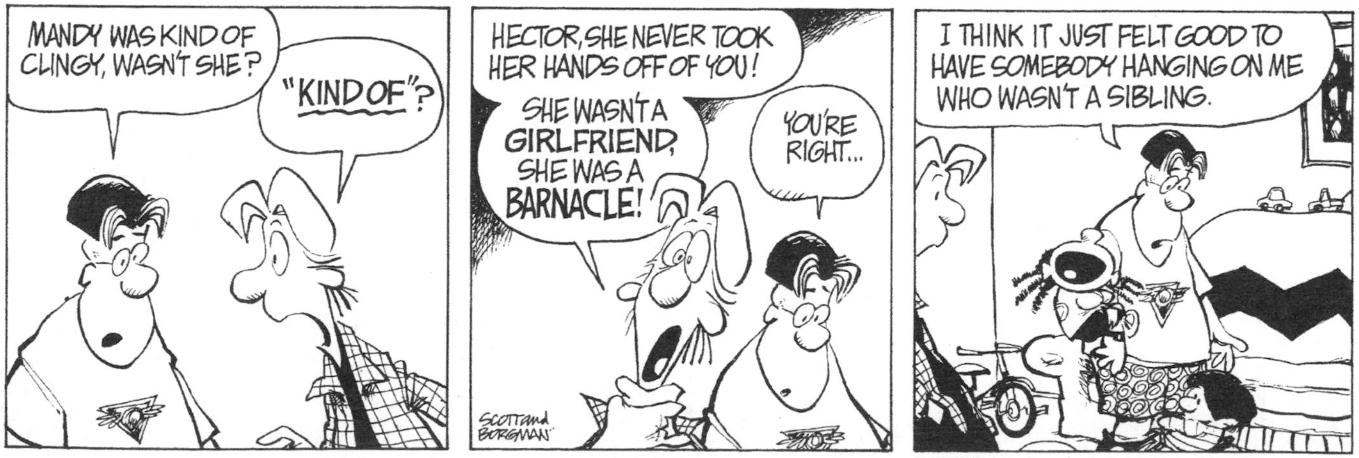
MANDY WAS KIND OF CLINGY, WASN'T SHE?
"KIND OF"?
HECTOR, SHE NEVER TOOK HER HANDS OFF OF YOU!
SHE WASN'T A **GIRLFRIEND**, SHE WAS A **BARNACLE**!
YOU'RE RIGHT...
SCOTT and BORGMAN
I THINK IT JUST FELT GOOD TO HAVE SOMEBODY HANGING ON ME WHO WASN'T A SIBLING.

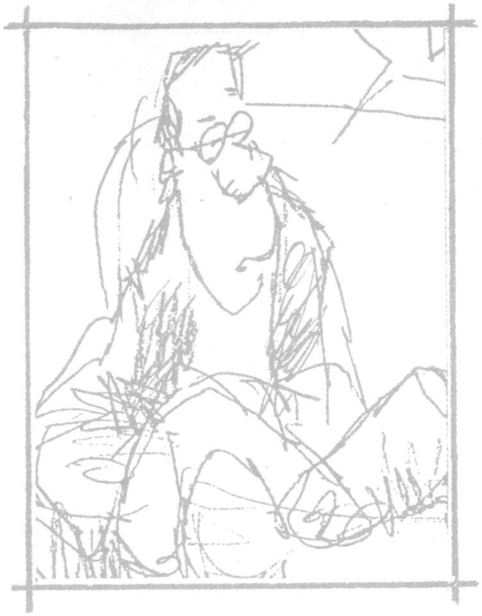

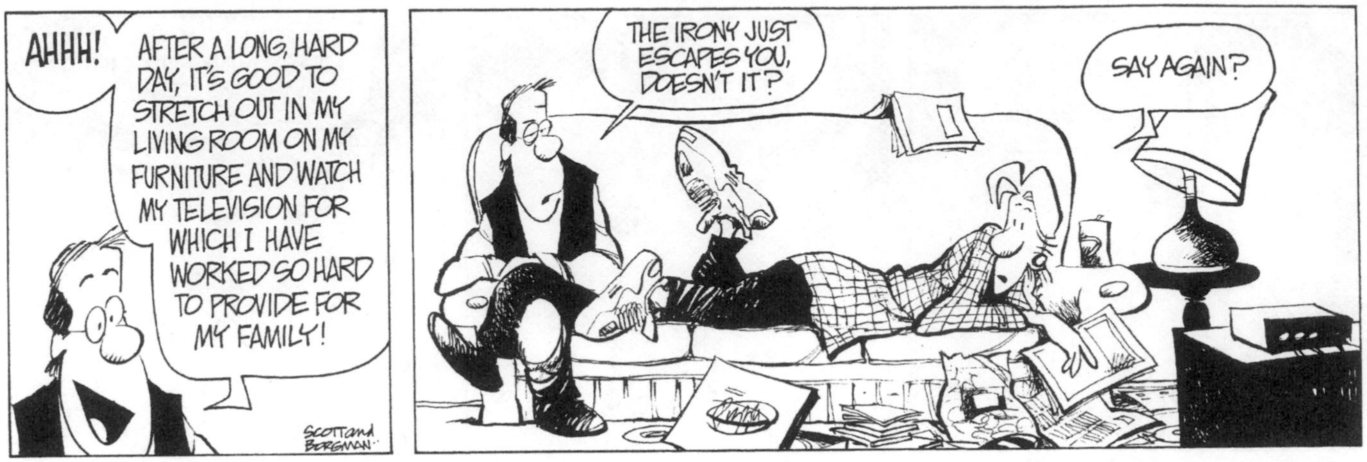
AHHH!
AFTER A LONG, HARD DAY, IT'S GOOD TO STRETCH OUT IN MY LIVING ROOM ON MY FURNITURE AND WATCH MY TELEVISION FOR WHICH I HAVE WORKED SO HARD TO PROVIDE FOR MY FAMILY!
SCOTT and BORGMAN
THE IRONY JUST ESCAPES YOU, DOESN'T IT?
SAY AGAIN?

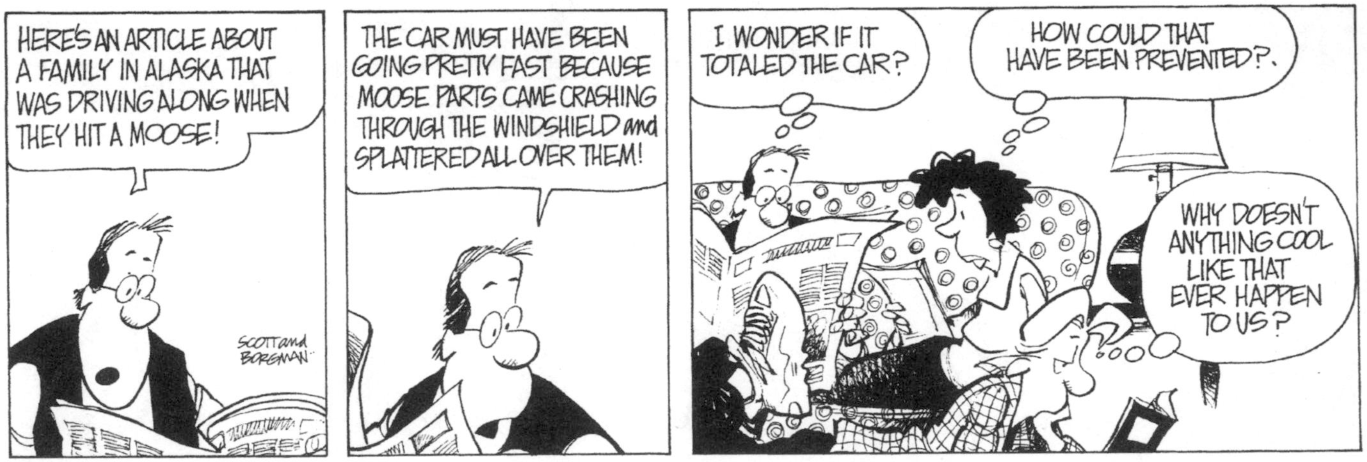
HERE'S AN ARTICLE ABOUT A FAMILY IN ALASKA THAT WAS DRIVING ALONG WHEN THEY HIT A MOOSE!
SCOTT and BORGMAN
THE CAR MUST HAVE BEEN GOING PRETTY FAST BECAUSE MOOSE PARTS CAME CRASHING THROUGH THE WINDSHIELD and SPLATTERED ALL OVER THEM!
I WONDER IF IT TOTALED THE CAR?
HOW COULD THAT HAVE BEEN PREVENTED?
WHY DOESN'T ANYTHING COOL LIKE THAT EVER HAPPEN TO US?

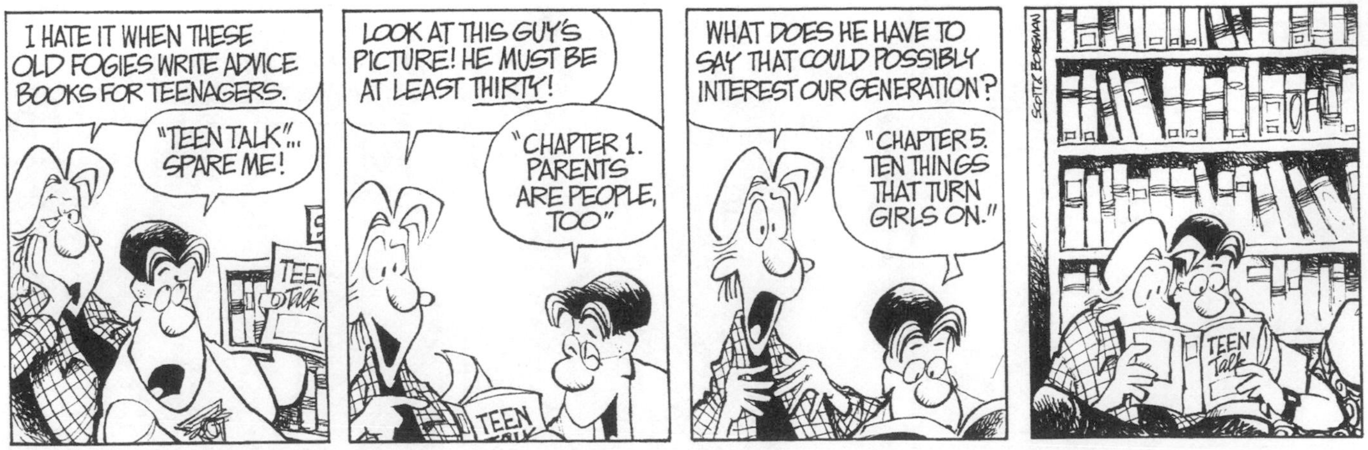
I HATE IT WHEN THESE OLD FOGIES WRITE ADVICE BOOKS FOR TEENAGERS.
"TEEN TALK"... SPARE ME!
TEEN Talk
LOOK AT THIS GUY'S PICTURE! HE MUST BE AT LEAST THIRTY!
"CHAPTER 1. PARENTS ARE PEOPLE, TOO"
TEEN
WHAT DOES HE HAVE TO SAY THAT COULD POSSIBLY INTEREST OUR GENERATION?
"CHAPTER 5. TEN THINGS THAT TURN GIRLS ON."
SCOTT & BORGMAN
TEEN Talk

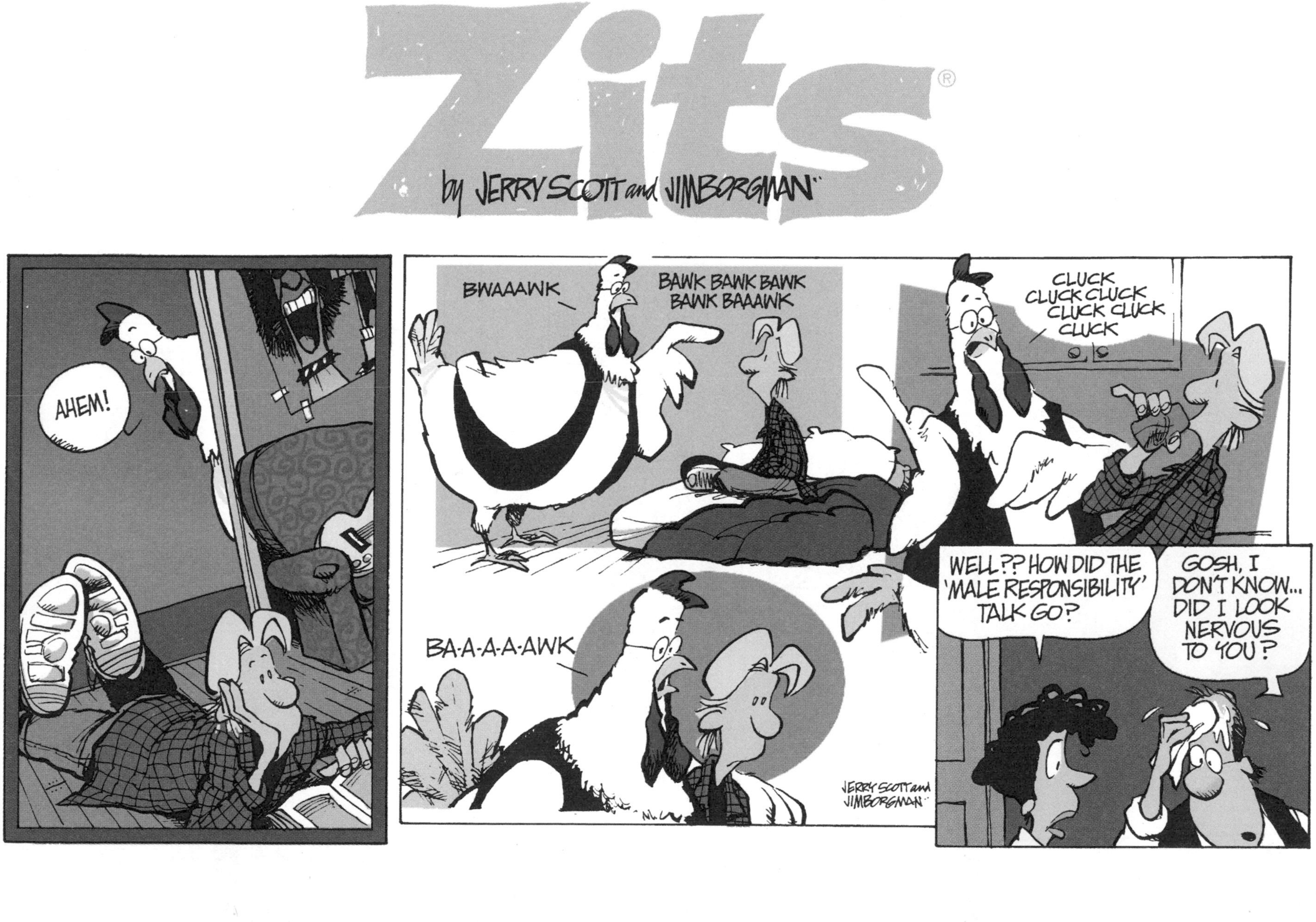
Zits®
by JERRY SCOTT and JIM BORGMAN
AHEM!
BWAAAWK
BAWK BAWK BAWK BAWK BAAAWK
CLUCK CLUCK CLUCK CLUCK CLUCK CLUCK
BA-A-A-A-AWK
JERRY SCOTT and JIM BORGMAN
WELL?? HOW DID THE 'MALE RESPONSIBILITY' TALK GO?
GOSH, I DON'T KNOW... DID I LOOK NERVOUS TO YOU?

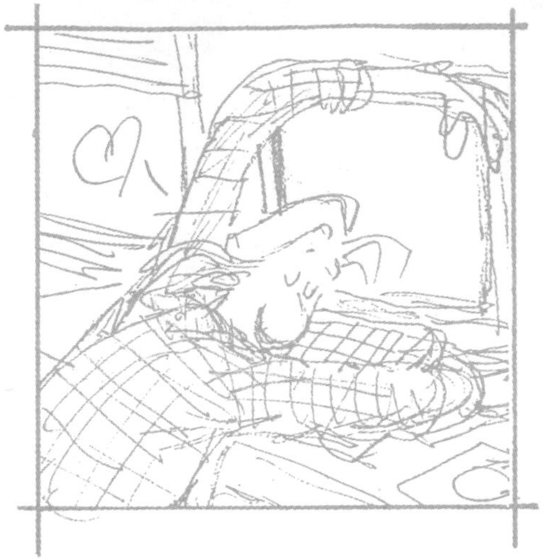

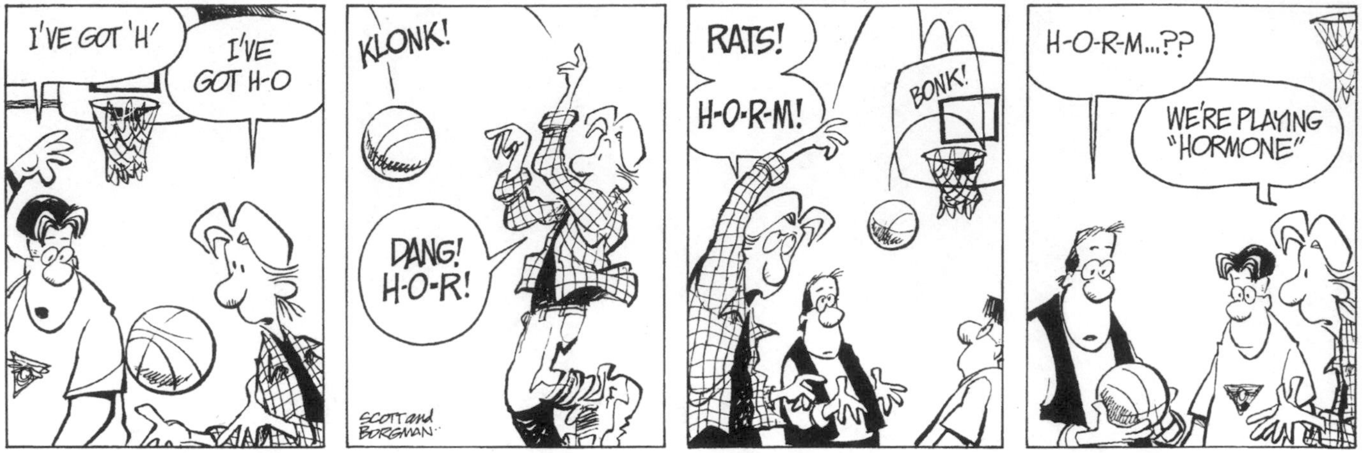
I'VE GOT 'H'
I'VE GOT H-O
KLONK!
DANG! H-O-R!
SCOTT and BORGMAN
RATS!
H-O-R-M!
BONK!
H-O-R-M...??
WE'RE PLAYING "HORMONE"

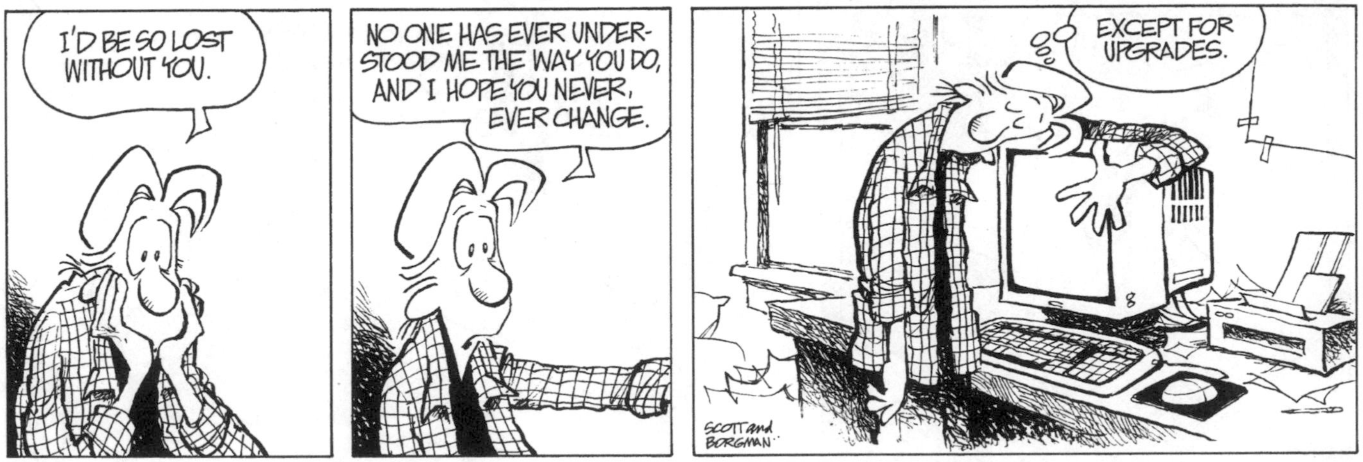
I'D BE SO LOST WITHOUT YOU.
NO ONE HAS EVER UNDERSTOOD ME THE WAY YOU DO, AND I HOPE YOU NEVER, EVER CHANGE.
EXCEPT FOR UPGRADES.
SCOTT and BORGMAN

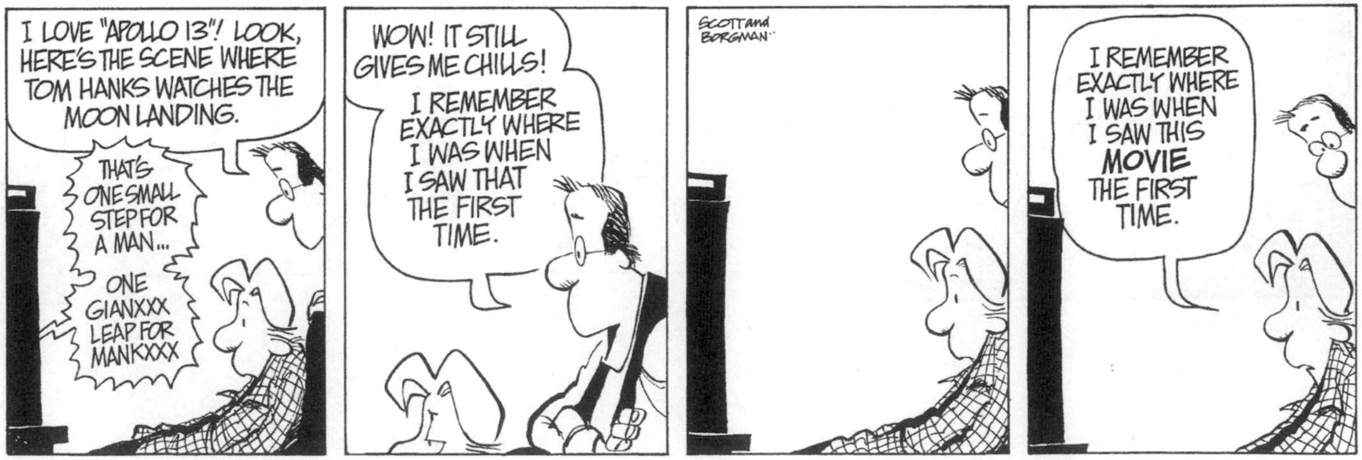
I LOVE "APOLLO 13"! LOOK, HERE'S THE SCENE WHERE TOM HANKS WATCHES THE MOON LANDING.
THAT'S ONE SMALL STEP FOR A MAN... ONE GIANXXX LEAP FOR MANKXXX
WOW! IT STILL GIVES ME CHILLS!
I REMEMBER EXACTLY WHERE I WAS WHEN I SAW THAT THE FIRST TIME.
SCOTT and BORGMAN
I REMEMBER EXACTLY WHERE I WAS WHEN I SAW THIS **MOVIE** THE FIRST TIME.

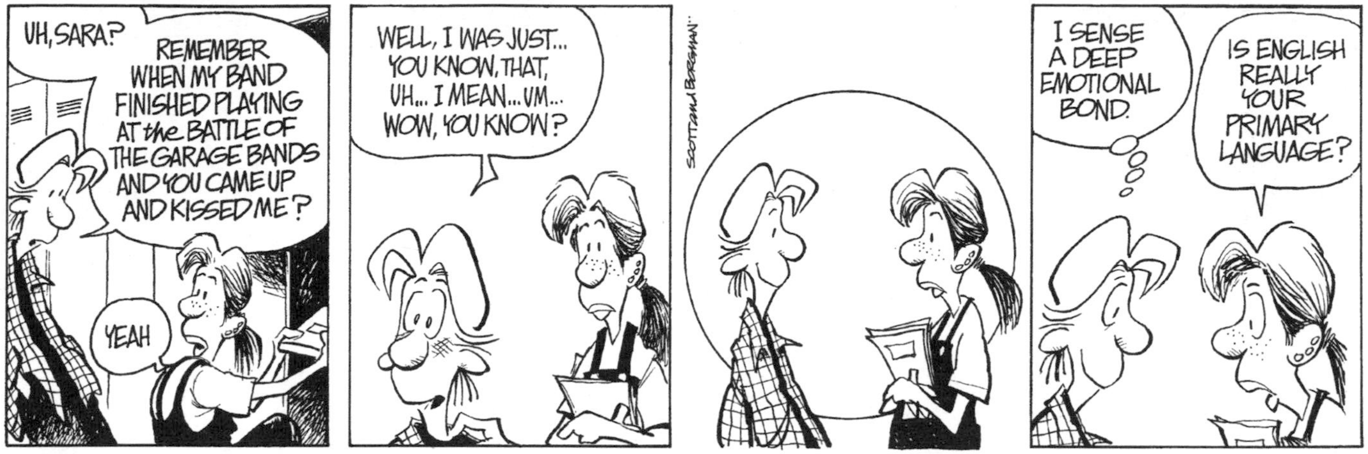
UH, SARA?
REMEMBER WHEN MY BAND FINISHED PLAYING AT the BATTLE OF THE GARAGE BANDS AND YOU CAME UP AND KISSED ME?
YEAH
WELL, I WAS JUST... YOU KNOW, THAT, UH... I MEAN... UM... WOW, YOU KNOW?
SCOTT and BORGMAN
I SENSE A DEEP EMOTIONAL BOND.
IS ENGLISH REALLY YOUR PRIMARY LANGUAGE?

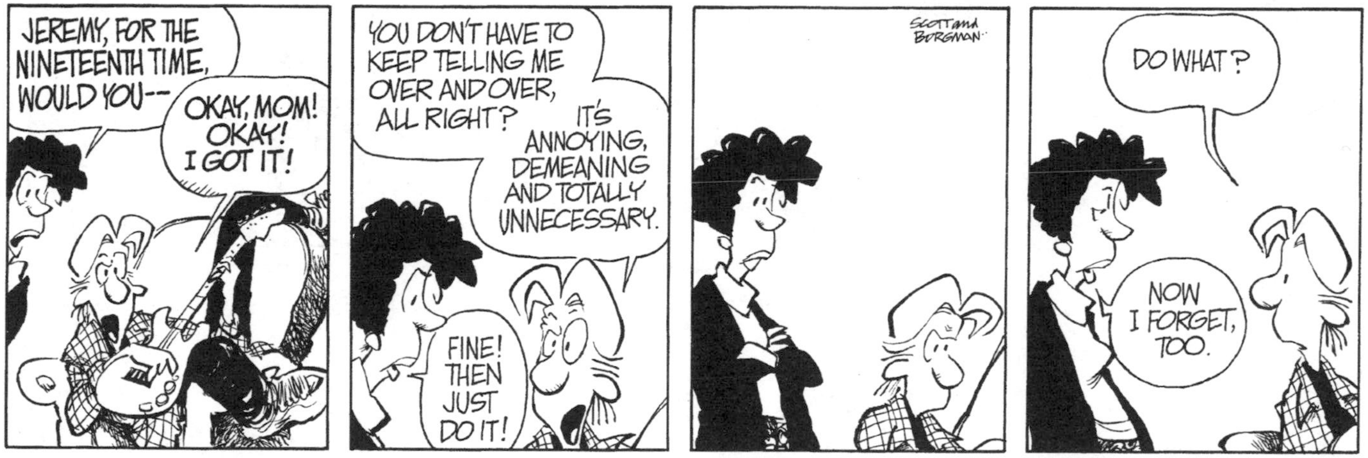
JEREMY, FOR THE NINETEENTH TIME, WOULD YOU--
OKAY, MOM! OKAY! I GOT IT!
YOU DON'T HAVE TO KEEP TELLING ME OVER AND OVER, ALL RIGHT?
IT'S ANNOYING, DEMEANING AND TOTALLY UNNECESSARY.
FINE! THEN JUST DO IT!
SCOTT and BORGMAN
DO WHAT?
NOW I FORGET, TOO.

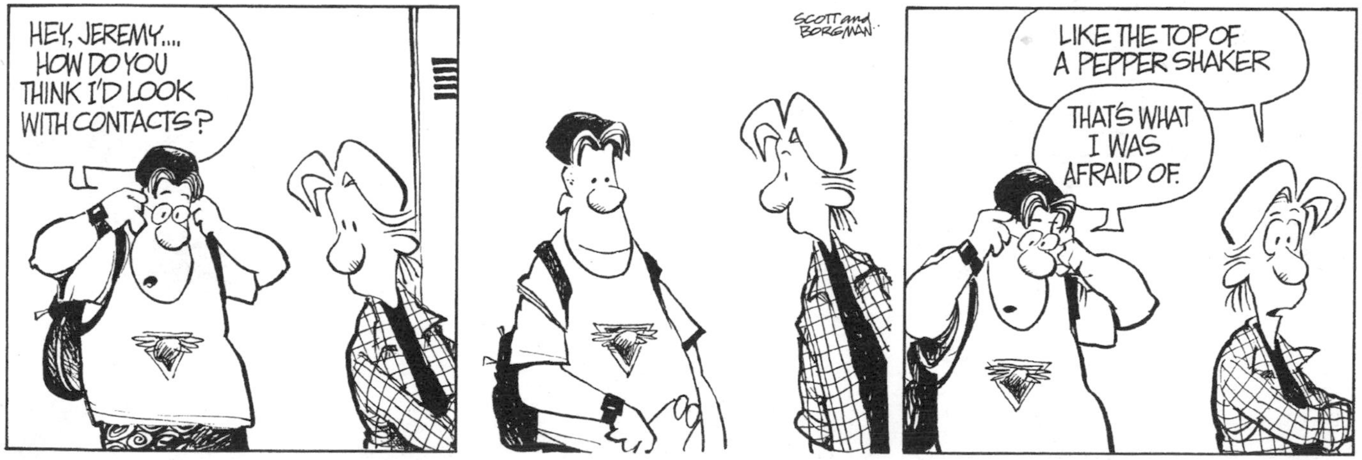
HEY, JEREMY.... HOW DO YOU THINK I'D LOOK WITH CONTACTS?
SCOTT and BORGMAN
LIKE THE TOP OF A PEPPER SHAKER
THAT'S WHAT I WAS AFRAID OF.

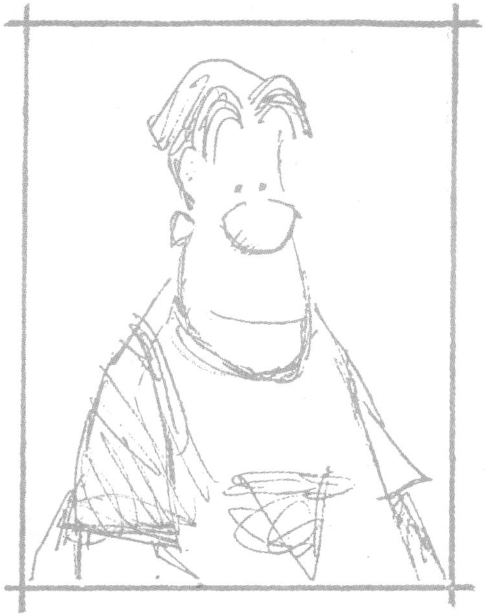

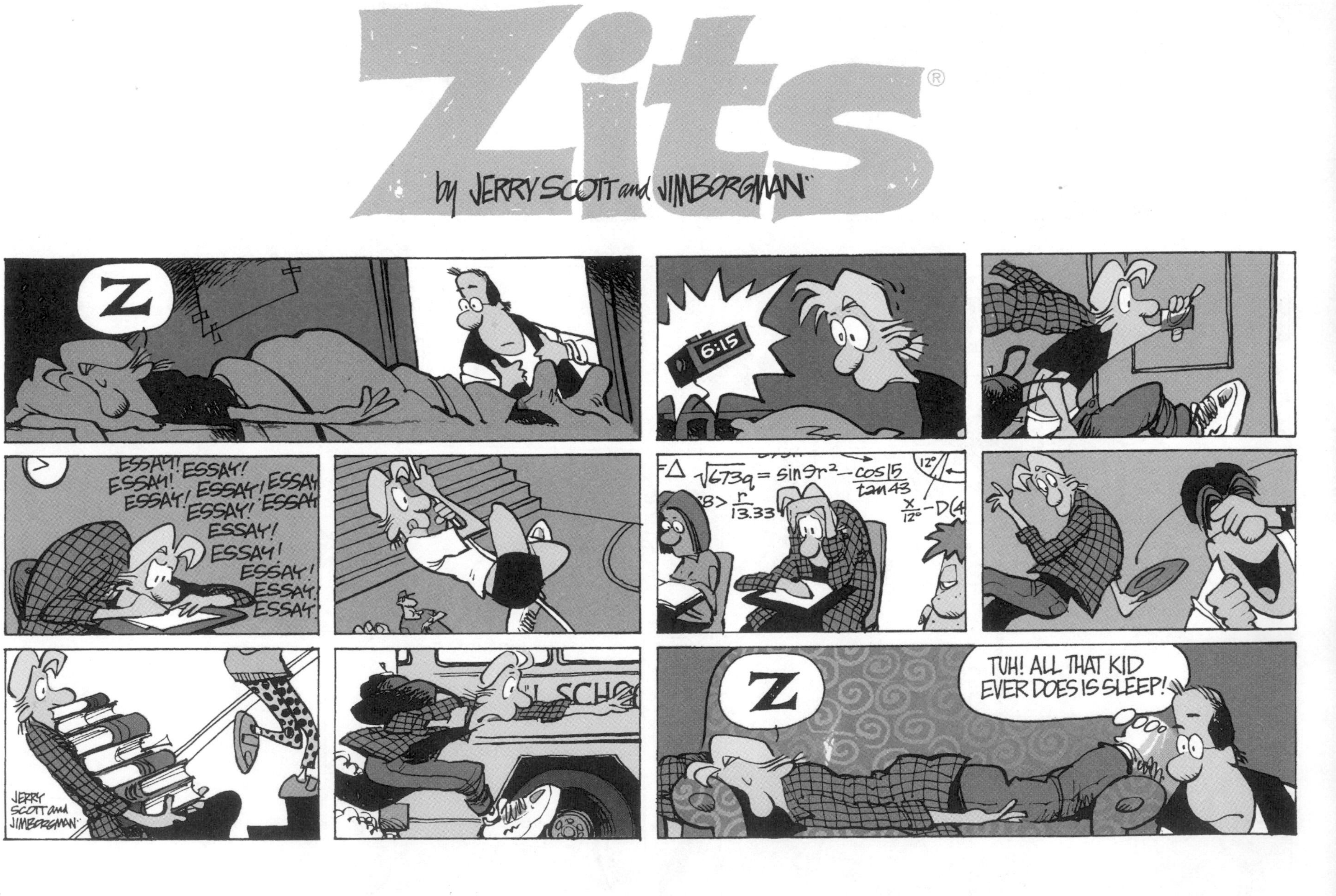
Zits®
by JERRY SCOTT and JIM BORGMAN
Z
6:15
ESSAY! ESSAY! ESSAY! ESSAY! ESSAY! ESSAY! ESSAY! ESSAY! ESSAY! ESSAY! ESSAY! ESSAY! ESSAY! ESSAY!
JERRY SCOTT and JIM BORGMAN
Z
TUH! ALL THAT KID EVER DOES IS SLEEP!

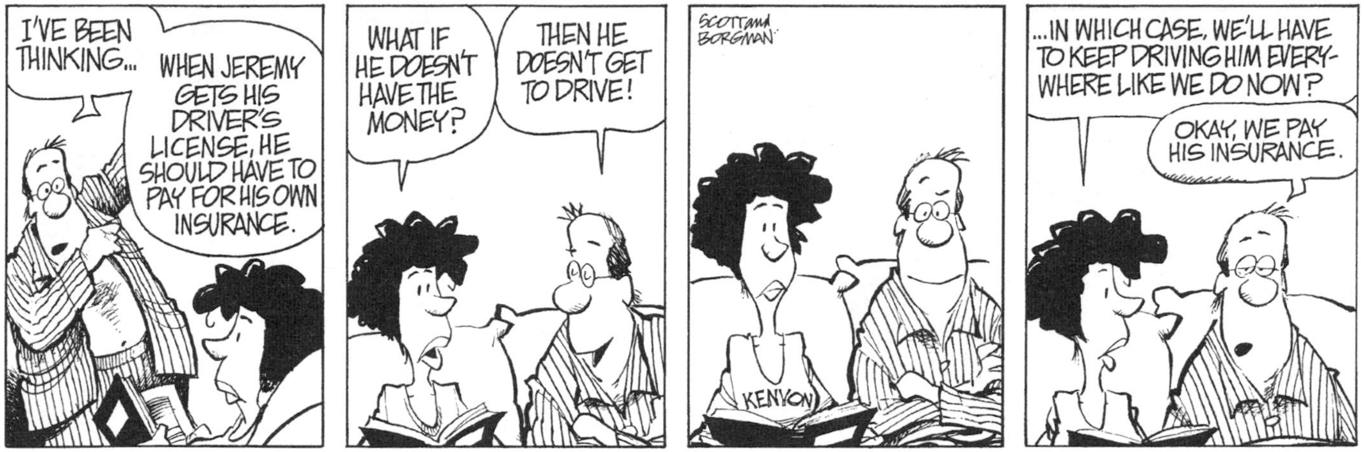
I'VE BEEN THINKING...
WHEN JEREMY GETS HIS DRIVER'S LICENSE, HE SHOULD HAVE TO PAY FOR HIS OWN INSURANCE.
WHAT IF HE DOESN'T HAVE THE MONEY?
THEN HE DOESN'T GET TO DRIVE!
SCOTT and BORGMAN
KENYON
...IN WHICH CASE, WE'LL HAVE TO KEEP DRIVING HIM EVERYWHERE LIKE WE DO NOW?
OKAY, WE PAY HIS INSURANCE.

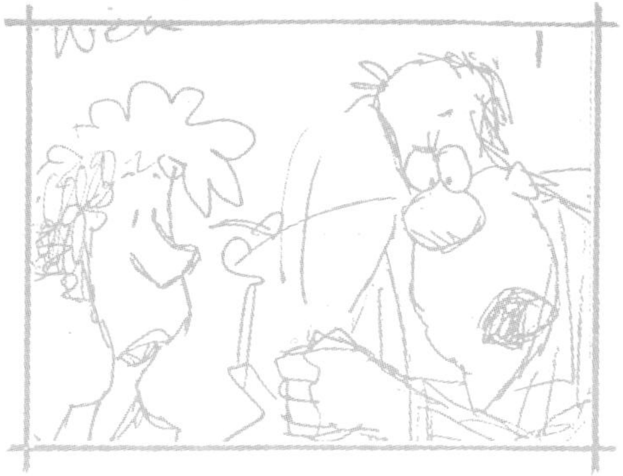

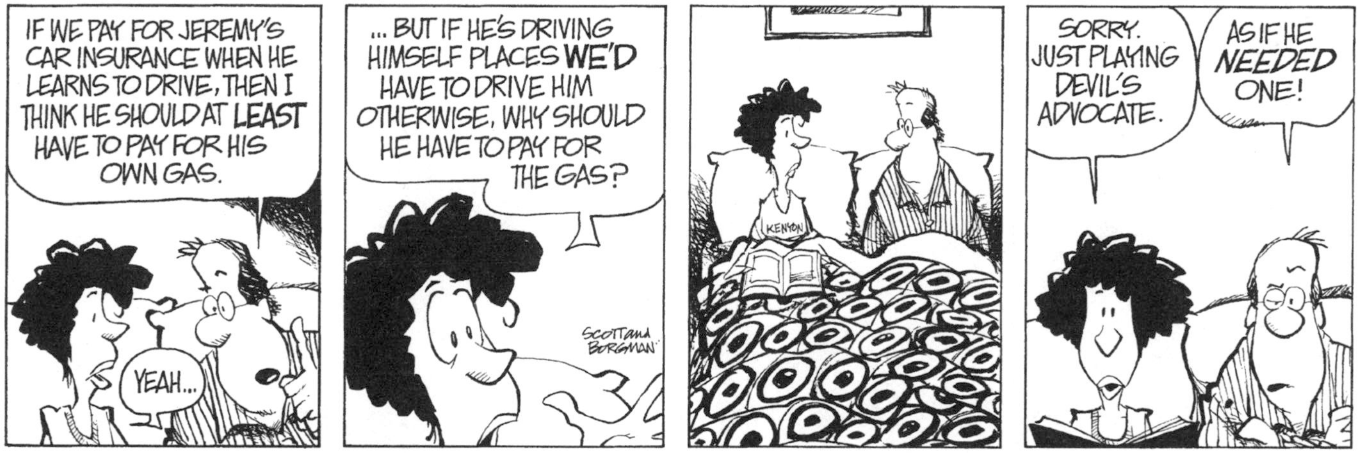
IF WE PAY FOR JEREMY'S CAR INSURANCE WHEN HE LEARNS TO DRIVE, THEN I THINK HE SHOULD AT LEAST HAVE TO PAY FOR HIS OWN GAS.
YEAH...
... BUT IF HE'S DRIVING HIMSELF PLACES WE'D HAVE TO DRIVE HIM OTHERWISE, WHY SHOULD HE HAVE TO PAY FOR THE GAS?
SCOTT and BORGMAN
KENYON
SORRY. JUST PLAYING DEVIL'S ADVOCATE.
AS IF HE NEEDED ONE!

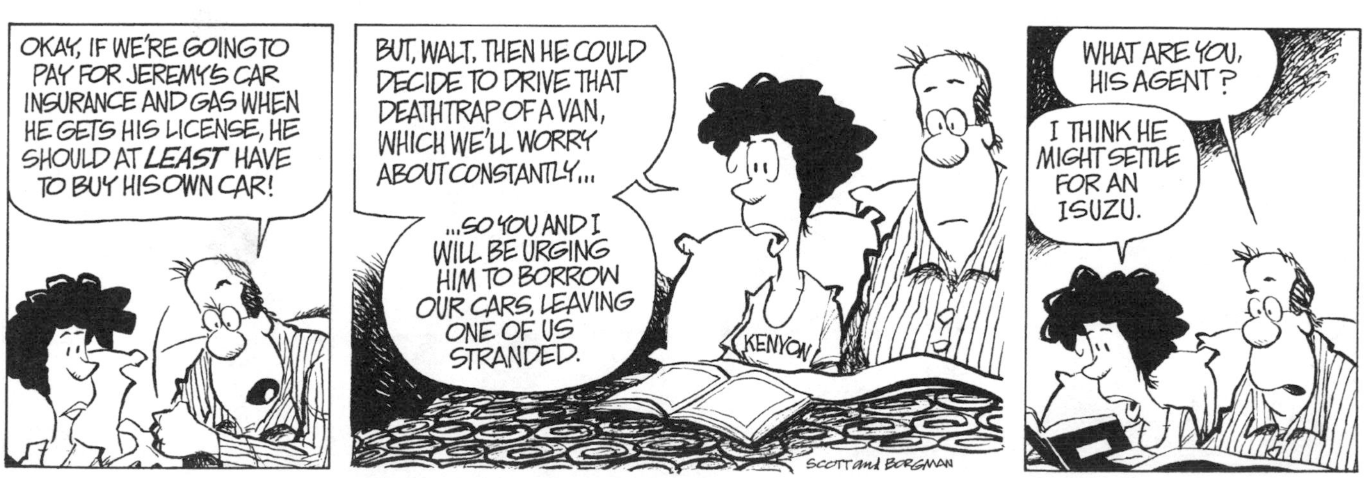
OKAY, IF WE'RE GOING TO PAY FOR JEREMY'S CAR INSURANCE AND GAS WHEN HE GETS HIS LICENSE, HE SHOULD AT LEAST HAVE TO BUY HIS OWN CAR!
BUT, WALT, THEN HE COULD DECIDE TO DRIVE THAT DEATHTRAP OF A VAN, WHICH WE'LL WORRY ABOUT CONSTANTLY...
...SO YOU AND I WILL BE URGING HIM TO BORROW OUR CARS, LEAVING ONE OF US STRANDED.
KENYON
SCOTT and BORGMAN
WHAT ARE YOU, HIS AGENT?
I THINK HE MIGHT SETTLE FOR AN ISUZU.

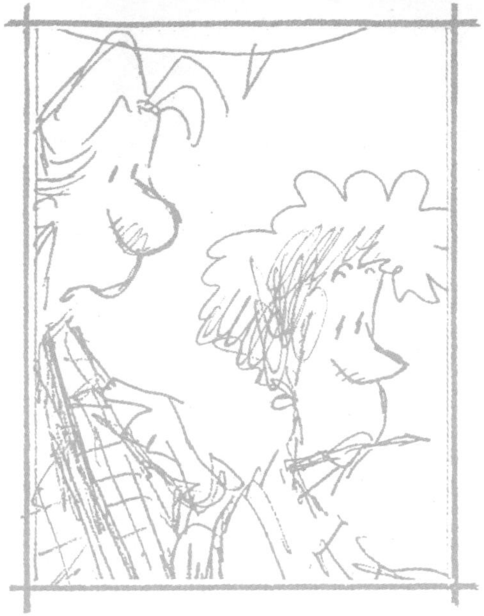

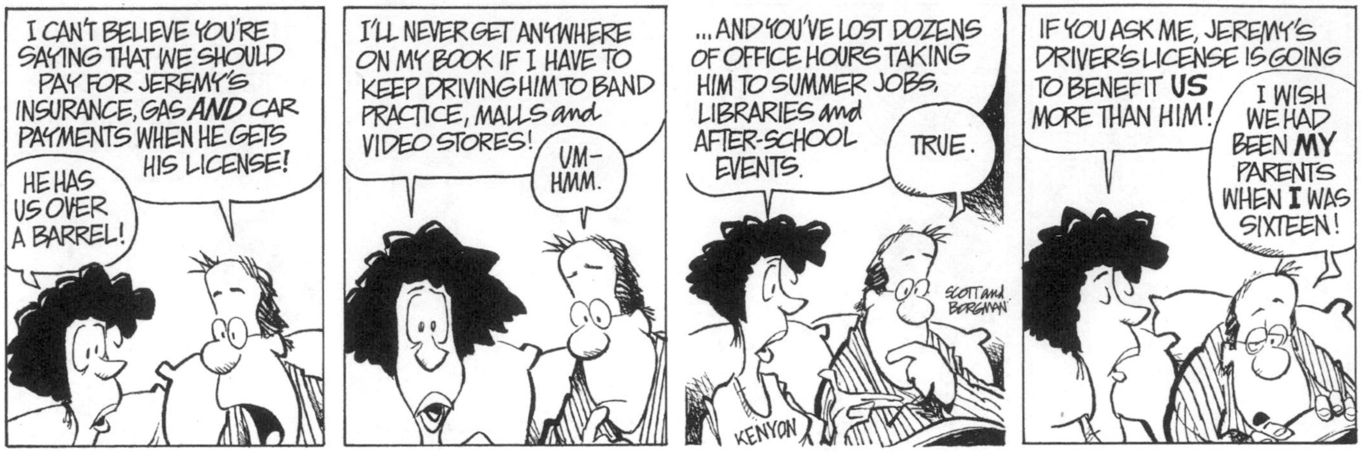

I CAN'T BELIEVE YOU'RE SAYING THAT WE SHOULD PAY FOR JEREMY'S INSURANCE, GAS AND CAR PAYMENTS WHEN HE GETS HIS LICENSE!
HE HAS US OVER A BARREL!
I'LL NEVER GET ANYWHERE ON MY BOOK IF I HAVE TO KEEP DRIVING HIM TO BAND PRACTICE, MALLS and VIDEO STORES!
UM-HMM.
...AND YOU'VE LOST DOZENS OF OFFICE HOURS TAKING HIM TO SUMMER JOBS, LIBRARIES and AFTER-SCHOOL EVENTS.
TRUE.
KENYON
SCOTT and BORGMAN
IF YOU ASK ME, JEREMY'S DRIVER'S LICENSE IS GOING TO BENEFIT US MORE THAN HIM!
I WISH WE HAD BEEN MY PARENTS WHEN I WAS SIXTEEN!

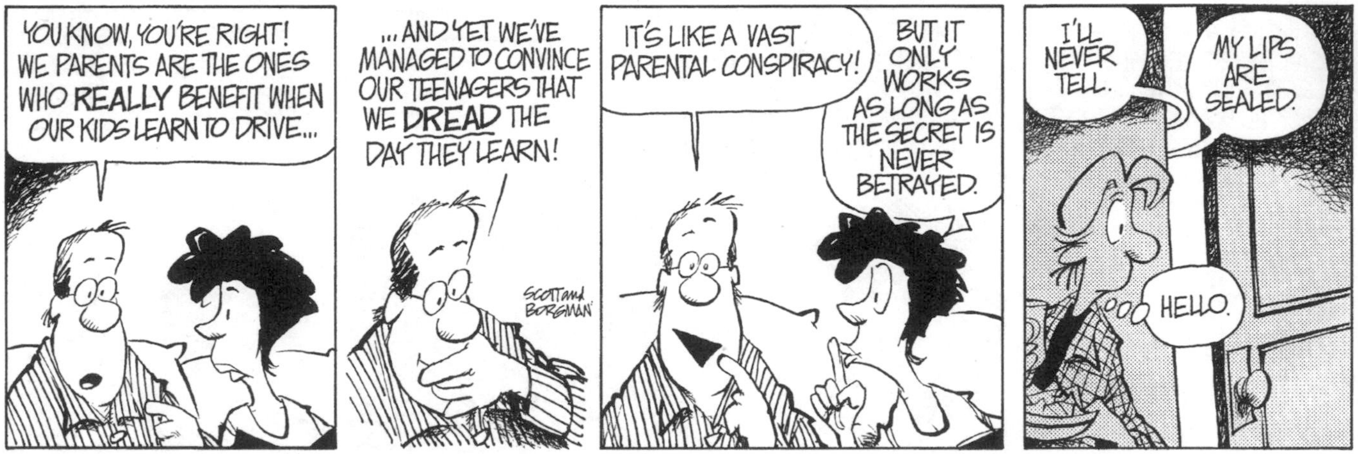

YOU KNOW, YOU'RE RIGHT! WE PARENTS ARE THE ONES WHO REALLY BENEFIT WHEN OUR KIDS LEARN TO DRIVE...
...AND YET WE'VE MANAGED TO CONVINCE OUR TEENAGERS THAT WE DREAD THE DAY THEY LEARN!
SCOTT and BORGMAN
IT'S LIKE A VAST PARENTAL CONSPIRACY!
BUT IT ONLY WORKS AS LONG AS THE SECRET IS NEVER BETRAYED.
I'LL NEVER TELL.
MY LIPS ARE SEALED.
HELLO.

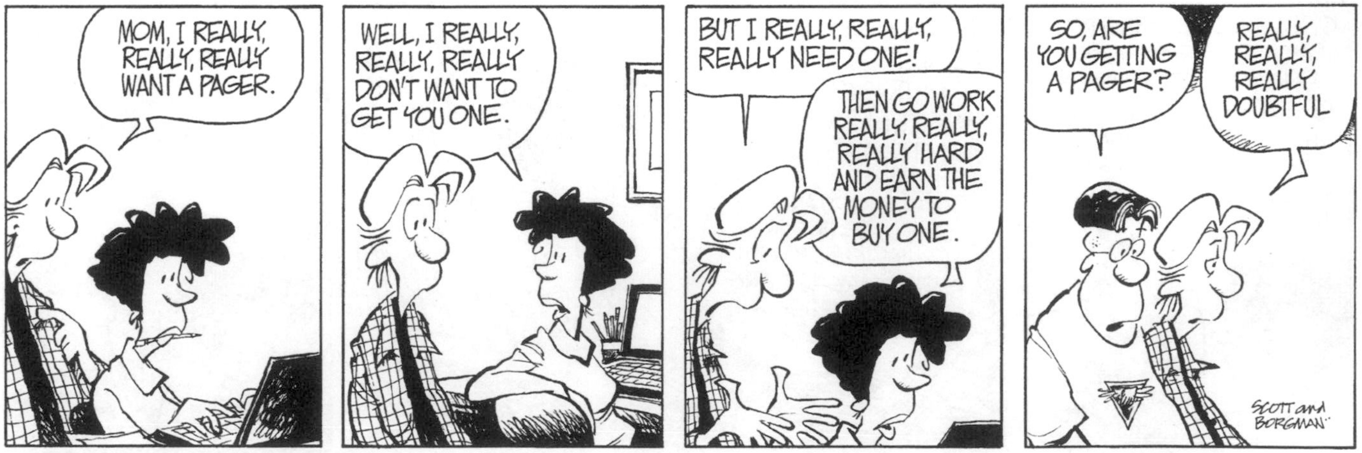

MOM, I REALLY, REALLY, REALLY WANT A PAGER.
WELL, I REALLY, REALLY, REALLY DON'T WANT TO GET YOU ONE.
BUT I REALLY, REALLY, REALLY NEED ONE!
THEN GO WORK REALLY, REALLY, REALLY HARD AND EARN THE MONEY TO BUY ONE.
SO, ARE YOU GETTING A PAGER?
REALLY, REALLY, REALLY DOUBTFUL
SCOTT and BORGMAN

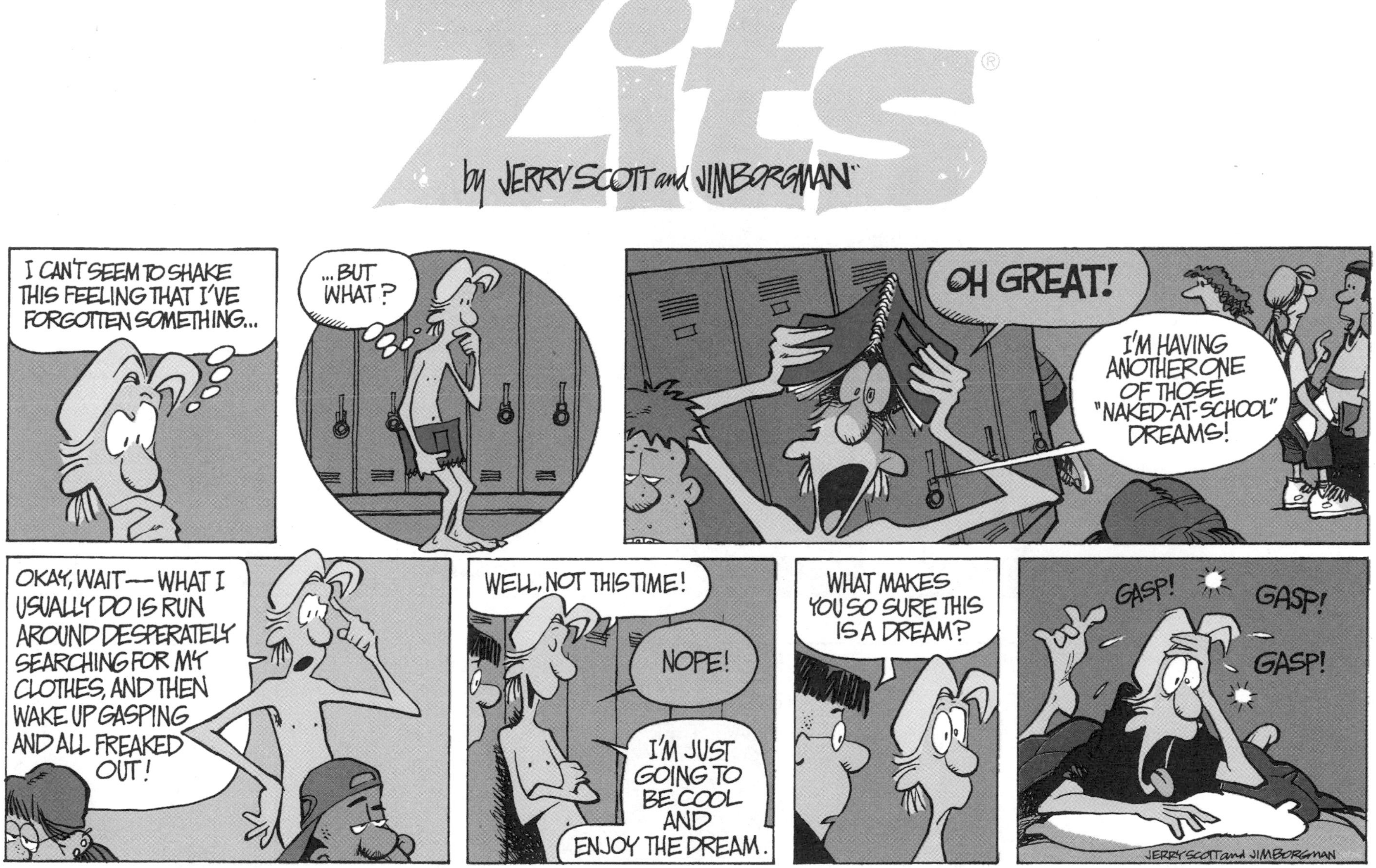
Zits®
by JERRY SCOTT and JIM BORGMAN
I CAN'T SEEM TO SHAKE THIS FEELING THAT I'VE FORGOTTEN SOMETHING...
...BUT WHAT?
OH GREAT!
I'M HAVING ANOTHER ONE OF THOSE "NAKED-AT-SCHOOL" DREAMS!
OKAY, WAIT— WHAT I USUALLY DO IS RUN AROUND DESPERATELY SEARCHING FOR MY CLOTHES, AND THEN WAKE UP GASPING AND ALL FREAKED OUT!
WELL, NOT THIS TIME!
NOPE!
I'M JUST GOING TO BE COOL AND ENJOY THE DREAM.
WHAT MAKES YOU SO SURE THIS IS A DREAM?
GASP!
GASP!
GASP!
JERRY SCOTT and JIM BORGMAN

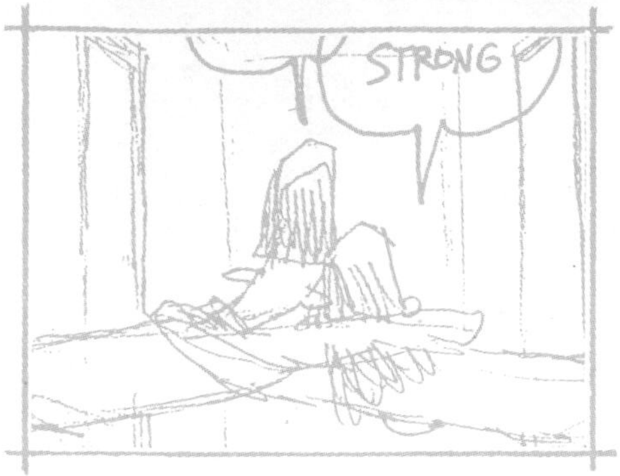
STRONG

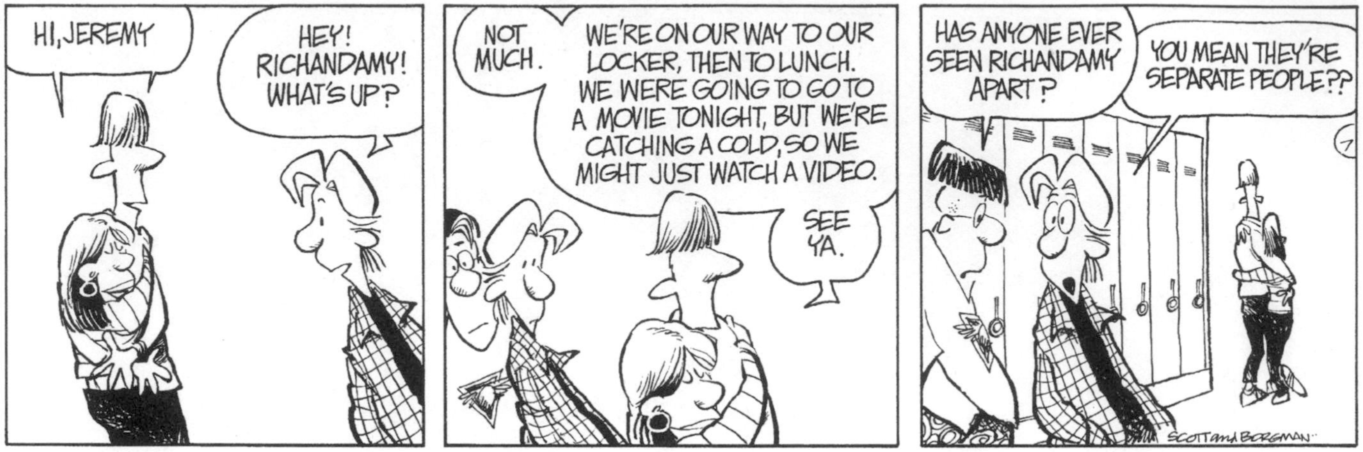
HI, JEREMY
HEY! RICHANDAMY! WHAT'S UP?
NOT MUCH.
WE'RE ON OUR WAY TO OUR LOCKER, THEN TO LUNCH. WE WERE GOING TO GO TO A MOVIE TONIGHT, BUT WE'RE CATCHING A COLD, SO WE MIGHT JUST WATCH A VIDEO.
SEE YA.
HAS ANYONE EVER SEEN RICHANDAMY APART?
YOU MEAN THEY'RE SEPARATE PEOPLE??
SCOTT and BORGMAN

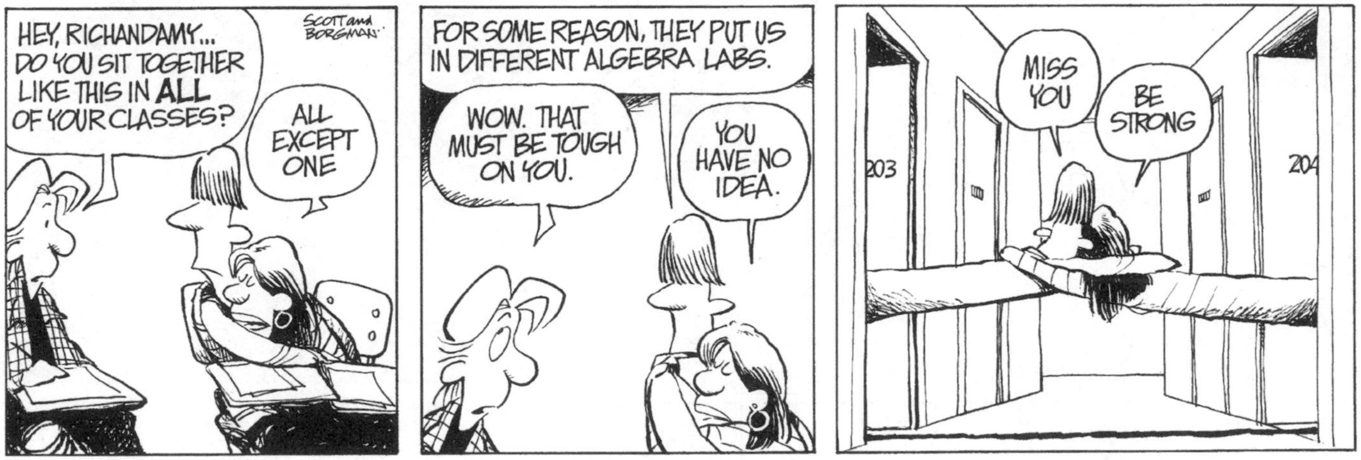
HEY, RICHANDAMY... DO YOU SIT TOGETHER LIKE THIS IN ALL OF YOUR CLASSES?
ALL EXCEPT ONE
SCOTT and BORGMAN
FOR SOME REASON, THEY PUT US IN DIFFERENT ALGEBRA LABS.
WOW. THAT MUST BE TOUGH ON YOU.
YOU HAVE NO IDEA.
MISS YOU
BE STRONG
203
204

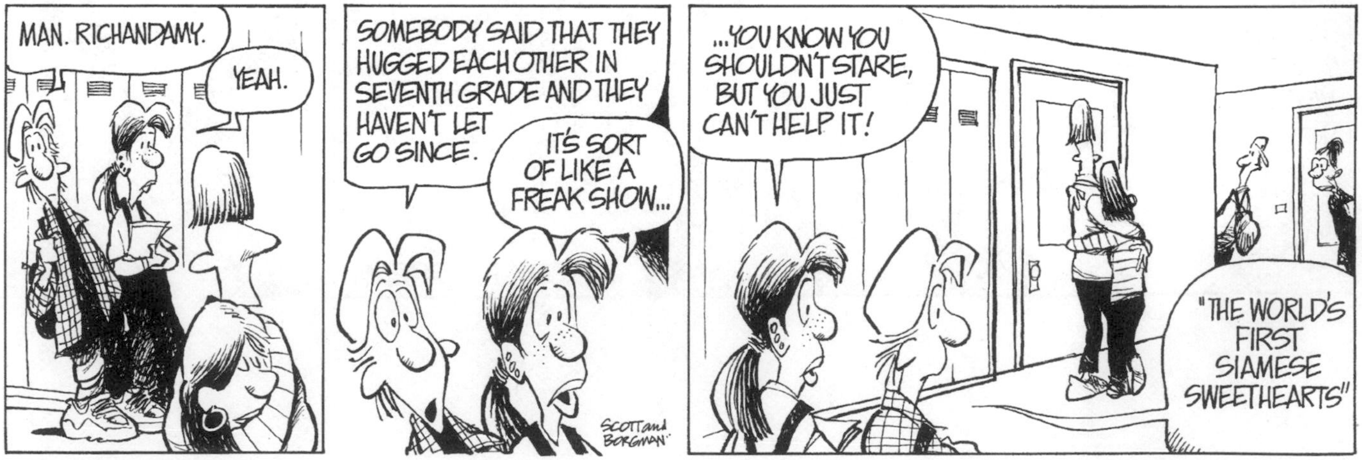
MAN. RICHANDAMY.
YEAH.
SOMEBODY SAID THAT THEY HUGGED EACH OTHER IN SEVENTH GRADE AND THEY HAVEN'T LET GO SINCE.
IT'S SORT OF LIKE A FREAK SHOW...
SCOTT and BORGMAN
...YOU KNOW YOU SHOULDN'T STARE, BUT YOU JUST CAN'T HELP IT!
"THE WORLD'S FIRST SIAMESE SWEETHEARTS"

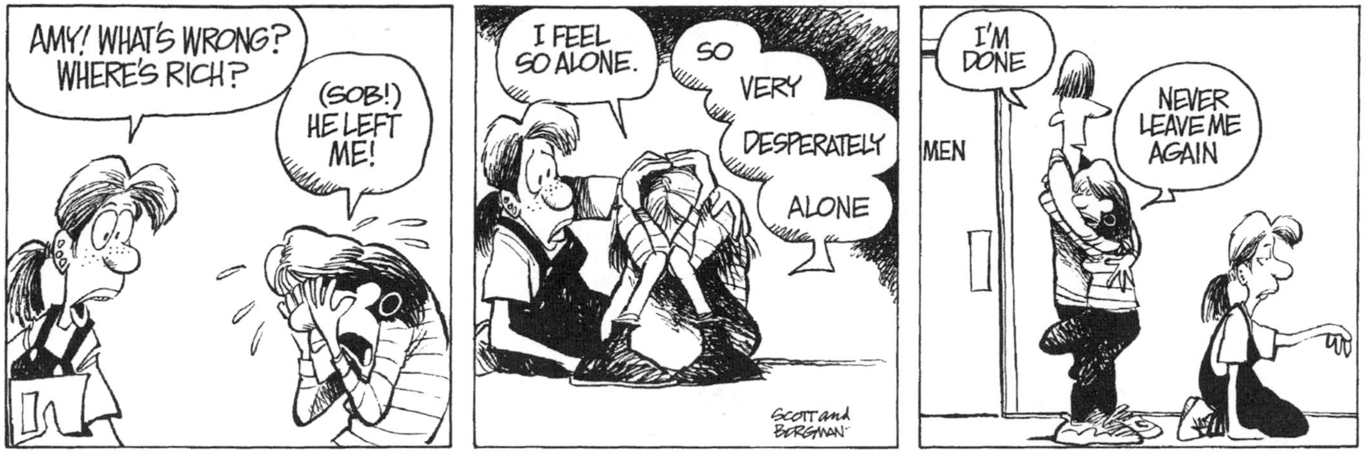
AMY! WHAT'S WRONG? WHERE'S RICH?
(SOB!) HE LEFT ME!
I FEEL SO ALONE.
SO
VERY
DESPERATELY
ALONE
SCOTT and BORGMAN
MEN
I'M DONE
NEVER LEAVE ME AGAIN

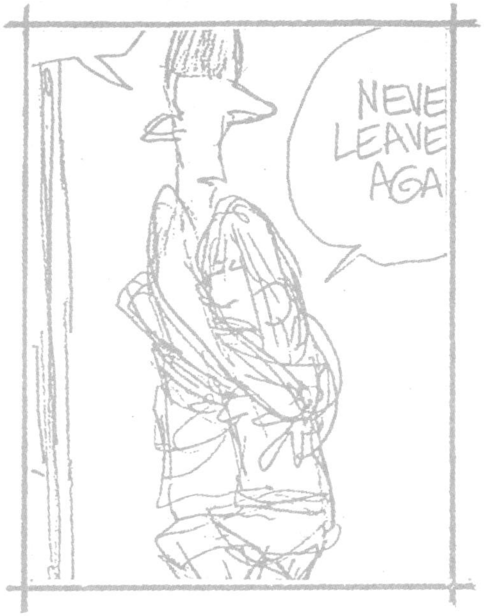
NEVE
LEAVE
AGA

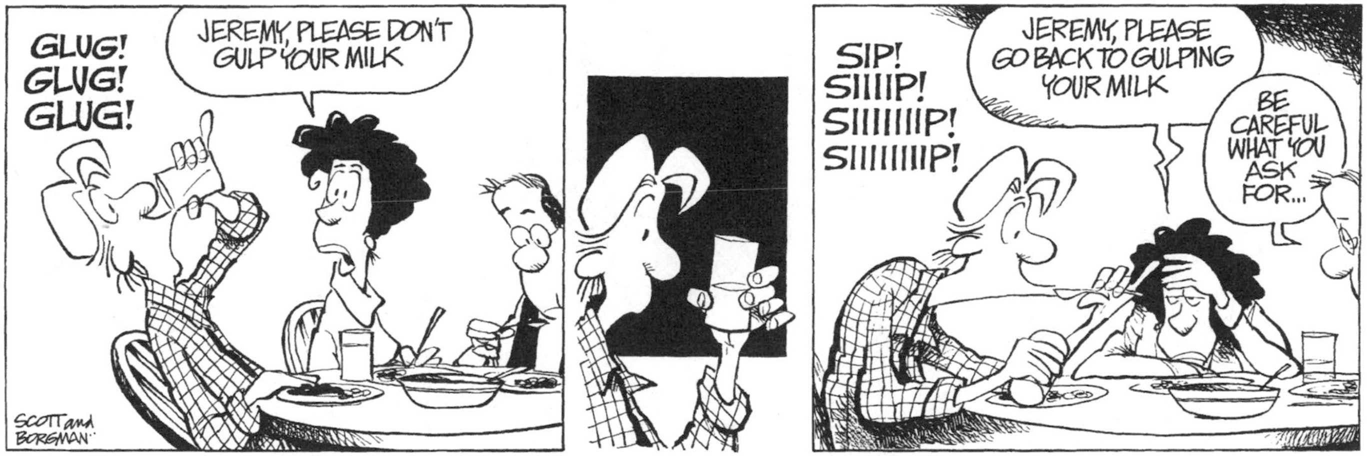
GLUG! GLUG! GLUG!
JEREMY, PLEASE DON'T GULP YOUR MILK
SCOTT and BORGMAN
SIP! SIIIIP! SIIIIIIIP! SIIIIIIIIP!
JEREMY, PLEASE GO BACK TO GULPING YOUR MILK
BE CAREFUL WHAT YOU ASK FOR...

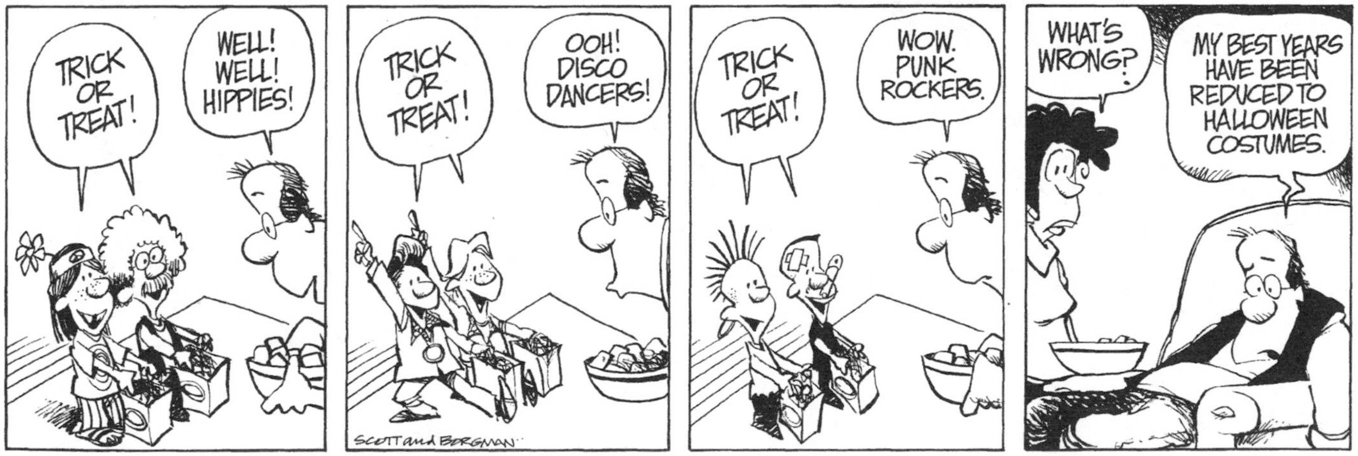
TRICK OR TREAT!
WELL! WELL! HIPPIES!
TRICK OR TREAT!
OOH! DISCO DANCERS!
SCOTT and BORGMAN
TRICK OR TREAT!
WOW. PUNK ROCKERS.
WHAT'S WRONG?
MY BEST YEARS HAVE BEEN REDUCED TO HALLOWEEN COSTUMES.

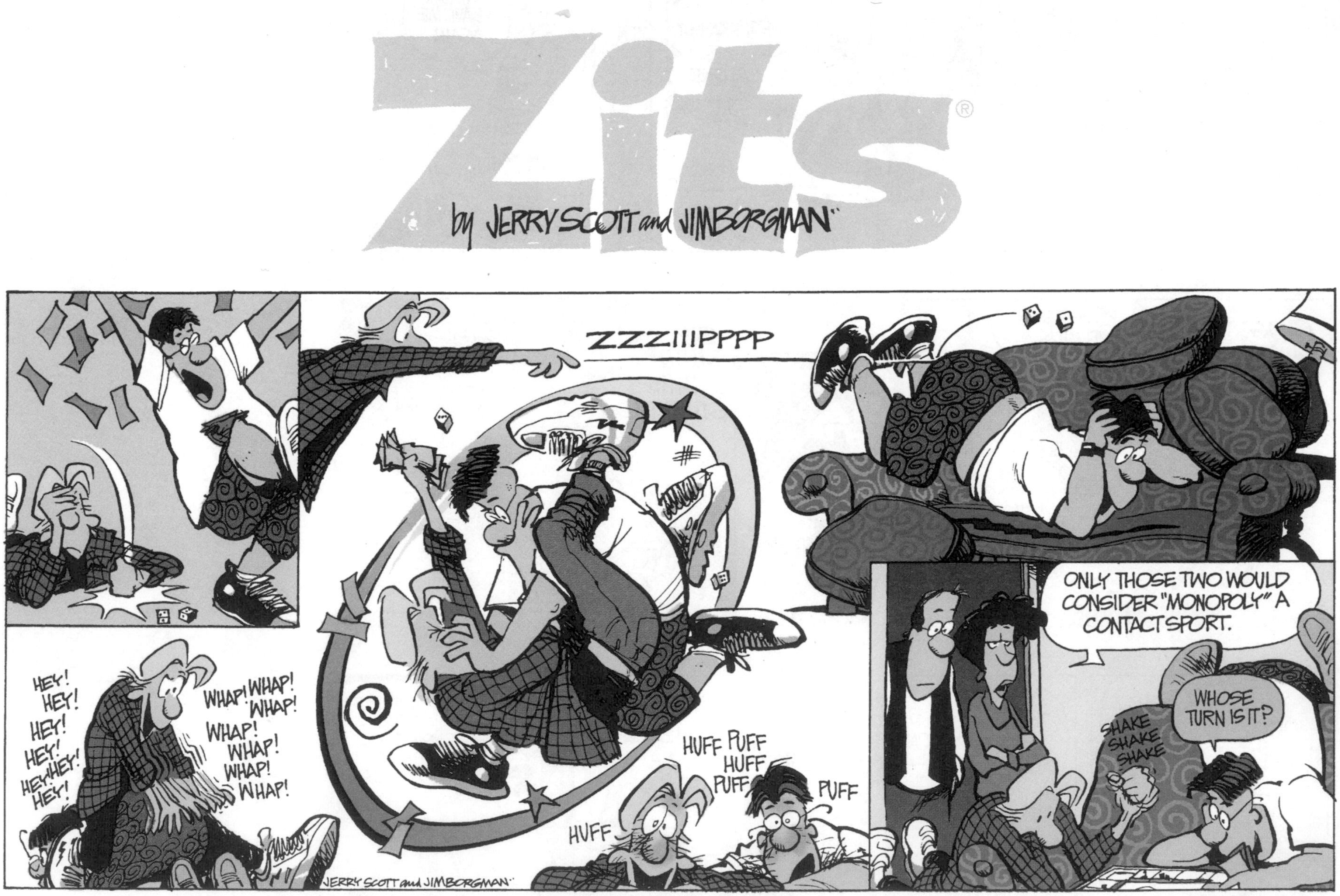
Zits
by JERRY SCOTT and JIM BORGMAN
ZZZIIIPPPP
HEY! HEY! HEY! HEY! HEY! HEY! HEY!
WHAP! WHAP! WHAP! WHAP! WHAP! WHAP! WHAP!
HUFF PUFF HUFF PUFF
PUFF
HUFF
ONLY THOSE TWO WOULD CONSIDER "MONOPOLY" A CONTACT SPORT.
SHAKE SHAKE SHAKE
WHOSE TURN IS IT?

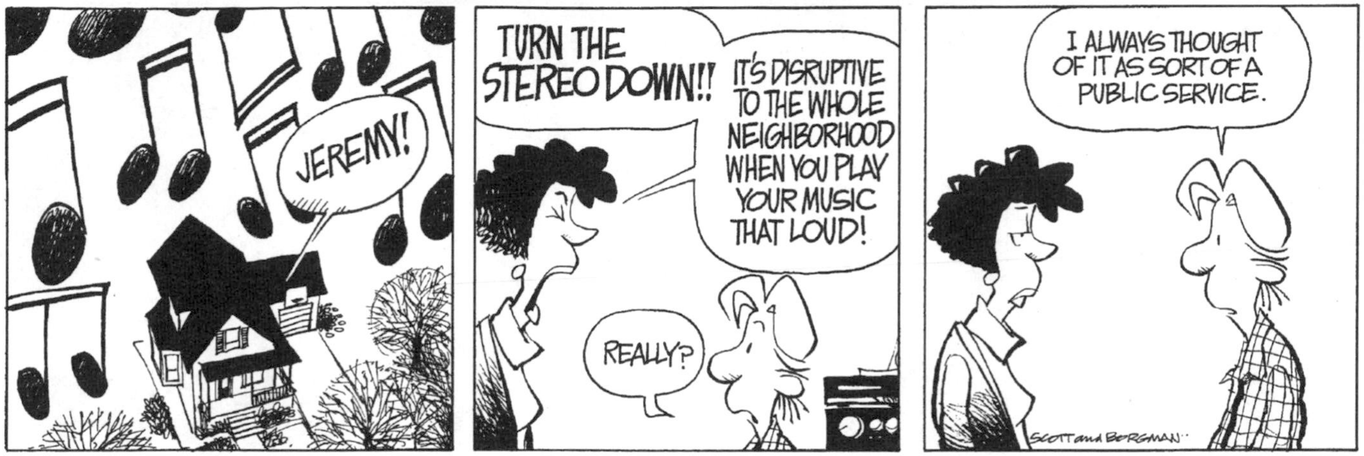
JEREMY!
TURN THE STEREO DOWN!!
IT'S DISRUPTIVE TO THE WHOLE NEIGHBORHOOD WHEN YOU PLAY YOUR MUSIC THAT LOUD!
REALLY?
I ALWAYS THOUGHT OF IT AS SORT OF A PUBLIC SERVICE.
SCOTT and BORGMAN

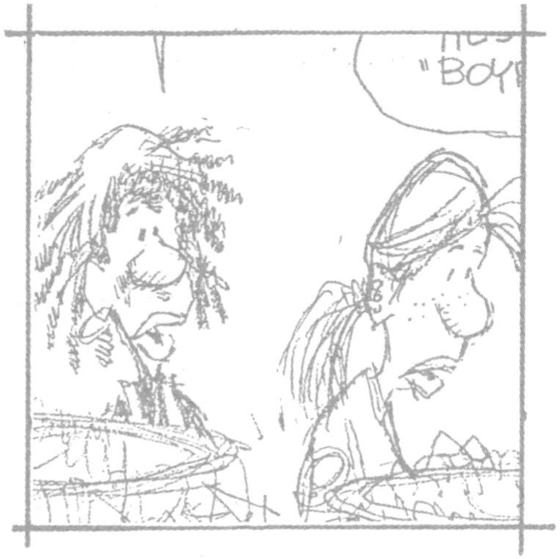

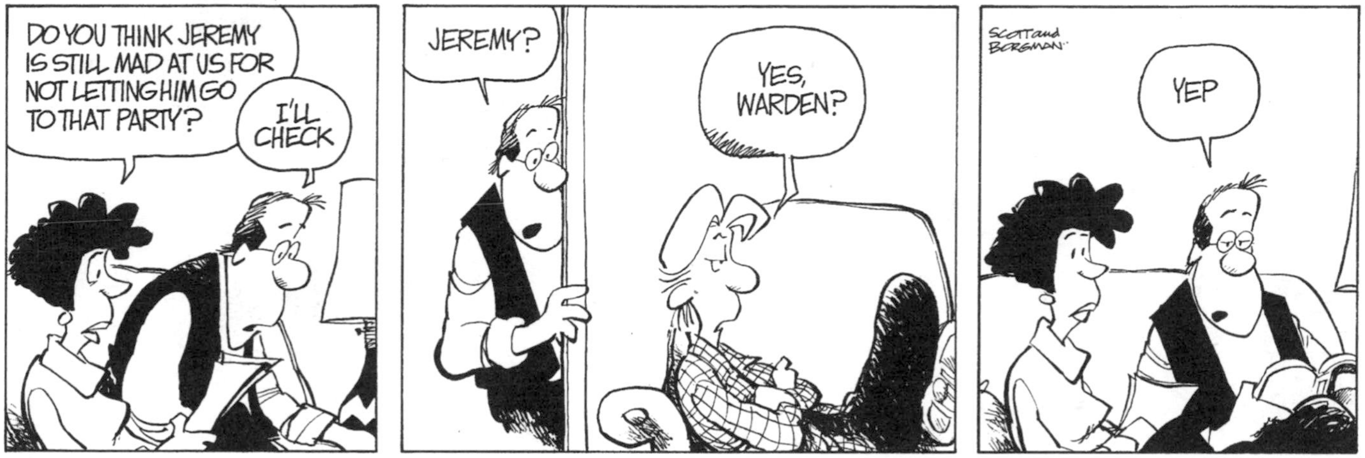
DO YOU THINK JEREMY IS STILL MAD AT US FOR NOT LETTING HIM GO TO THAT PARTY?
I'LL CHECK
JEREMY?
YES, WARDEN?
SCOTT and BORGMAN
YEP

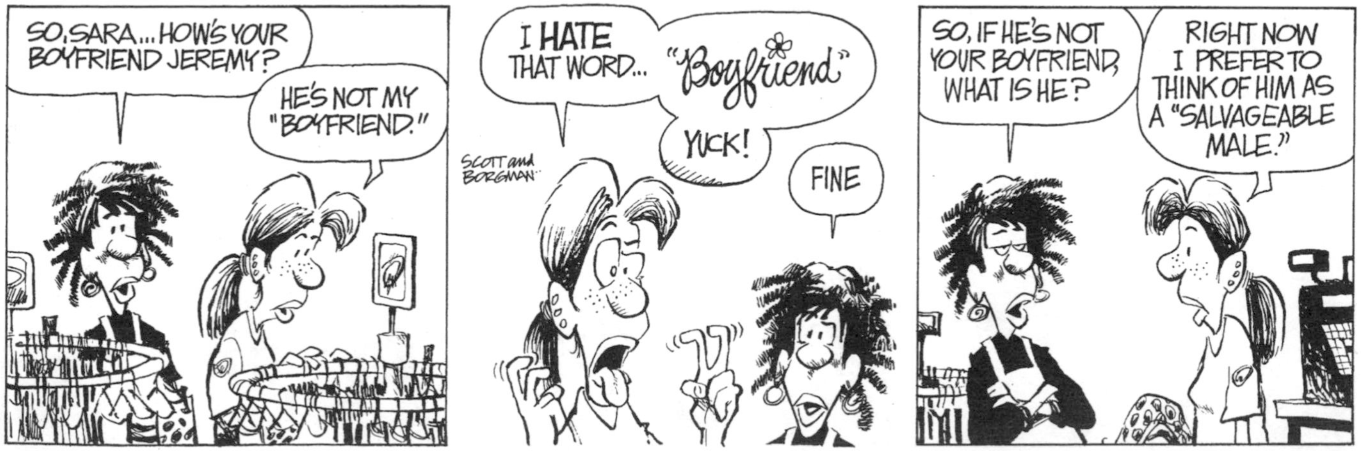
SO, SARA... HOW'S YOUR BOYFRIEND JEREMY?
HE'S NOT MY "BOYFRIEND."
SCOTT and BORGMAN
I **HATE** THAT WORD...
"Boyfriend"
YUCK!
FINE
SO, IF HE'S NOT YOUR BOYFRIEND, WHAT IS HE?
RIGHT NOW I PREFER TO THINK OF HIM AS A "SALVAGEABLE MALE."

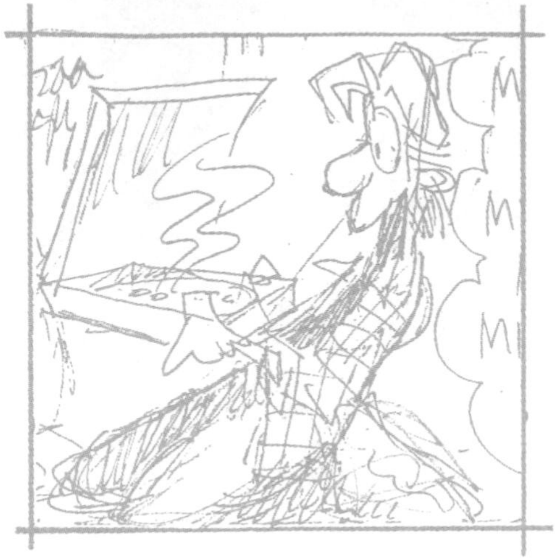

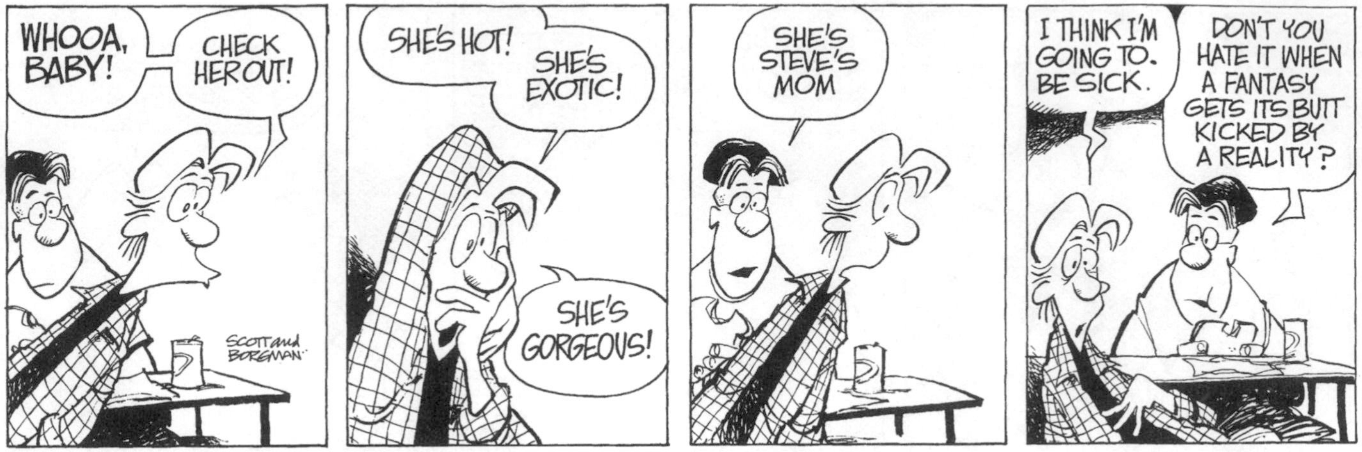

WHOOA, BABY!
CHECK HER OUT!
SCOTT and BORGMAN
SHE'S HOT!
SHE'S EXOTIC!
SHE'S GORGEOUS!
SHE'S STEVE'S MOM
I THINK I'M GOING TO BE SICK.
DON'T YOU HATE IT WHEN A FANTASY GETS ITS BUTT KICKED BY A REALITY?

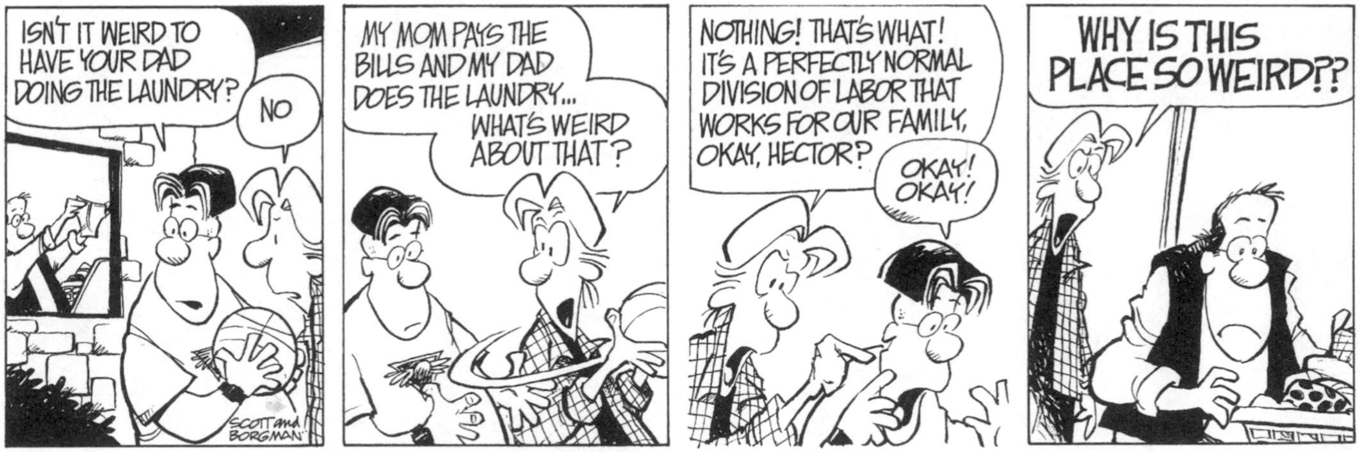

ISN'T IT WEIRD TO HAVE YOUR DAD DOING THE LAUNDRY?
NO
SCOTT and BORGMAN
MY MOM PAYS THE BILLS AND MY DAD DOES THE LAUNDRY...
WHAT'S WEIRD ABOUT THAT?
NOTHING! THAT'S WHAT! IT'S A PERFECTLY NORMAL DIVISION OF LABOR THAT WORKS FOR OUR FAMILY, OKAY, HECTOR?
OKAY! OKAY!
WHY IS THIS PLACE SO WEIRD??

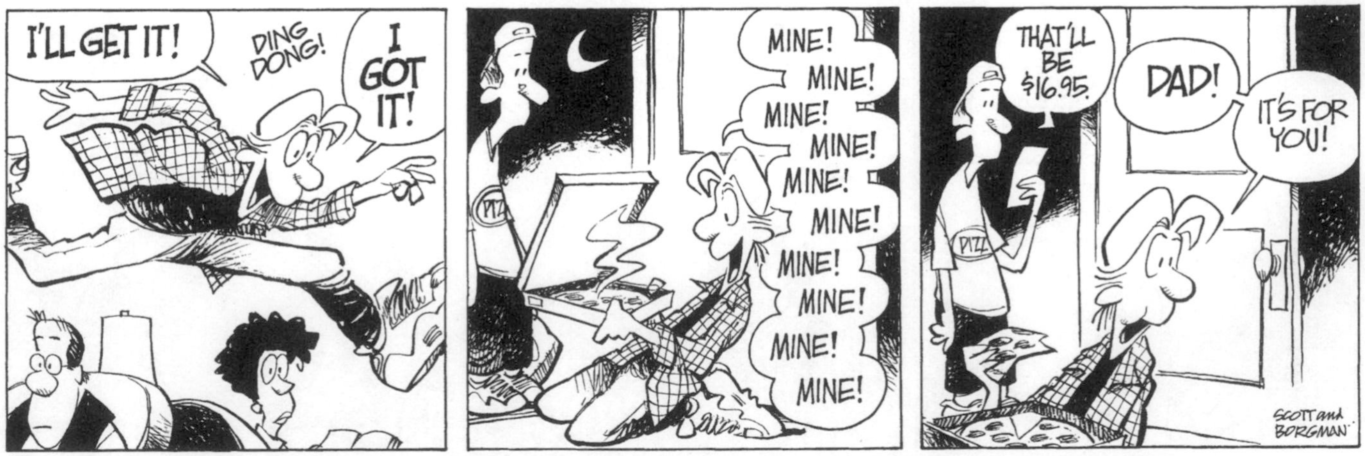

I'LL GET IT!
DING DONG!
I GOT IT!
MINE!
MINE!
MINE!
MINE!
MINE!
MINE!
MINE!
MINE!
MINE!
MINE!
THAT'LL BE $16.95.
DAD!
IT'S FOR YOU!
SCOTT and BORGMAN

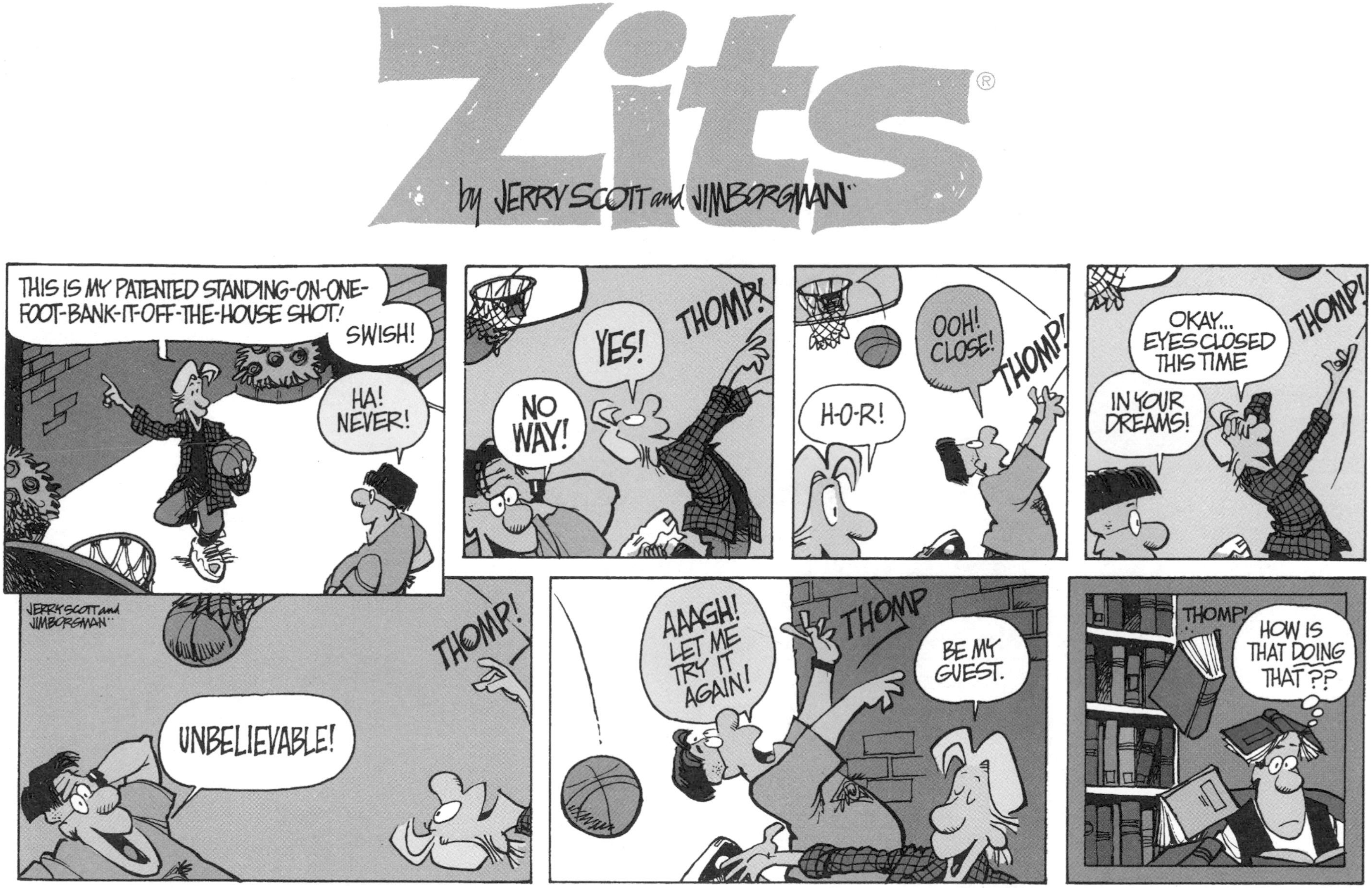
Zits®
by JERRY SCOTT and JIM BORGMAN
THIS IS MY PATENTED STANDING-ON-ONE-FOOT-BANK-IT-OFF-THE-HOUSE SHOT!
SWISH!
HA! NEVER!
THOMP!
YES!
NO WAY!
OOH! CLOSE!
THOMP!
H-O-R!
OKAY... EYES CLOSED THIS TIME
THOMP!
IN YOUR DREAMS!
JERRY SCOTT and JIM BORGMAN
THOMP!
UNBELIEVABLE!
AAAGH! LET ME TRY IT AGAIN!
THOMP
BE MY GUEST.
THOMP!
HOW IS THAT DOING THAT??

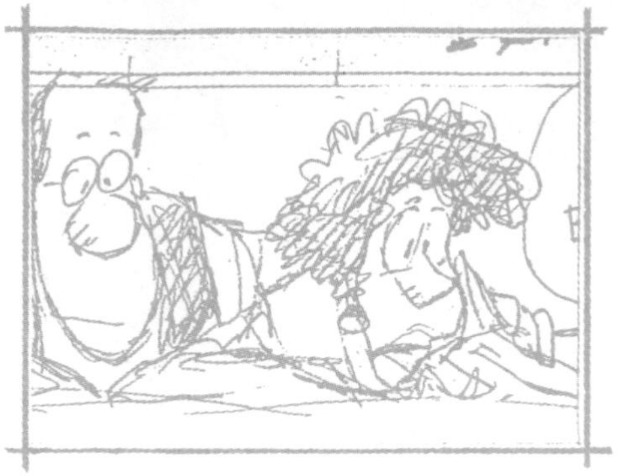

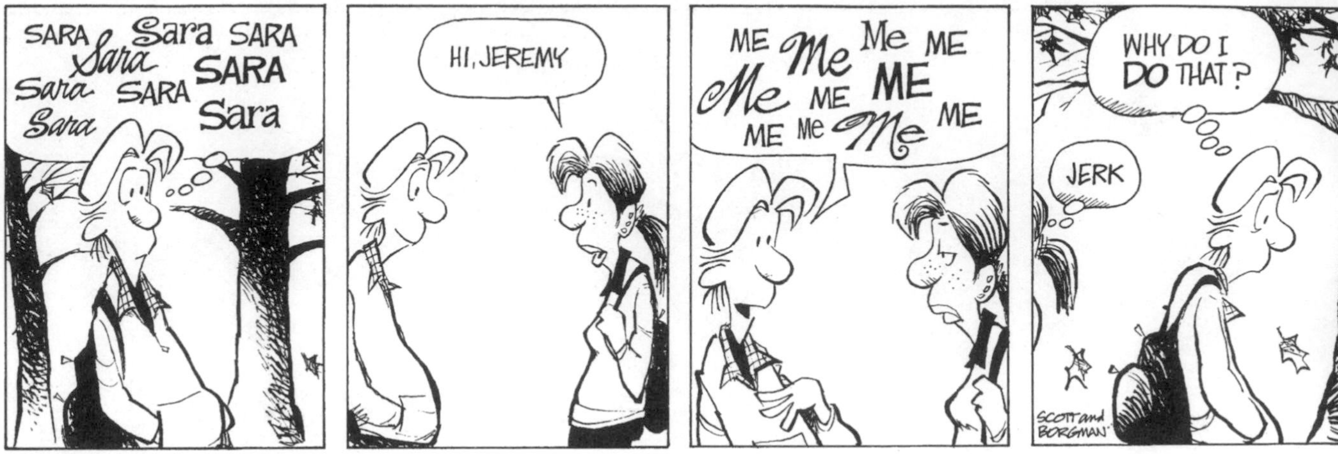
SARA Sara Sara SARA
Sara SARA
Sara SARA Sara
Sara
HI, JEREMY
ME Me Me ME
Me ME ME
ME Me Me ME
WHY DO I DO THAT?
JERK
SCOTT and BORGMAN

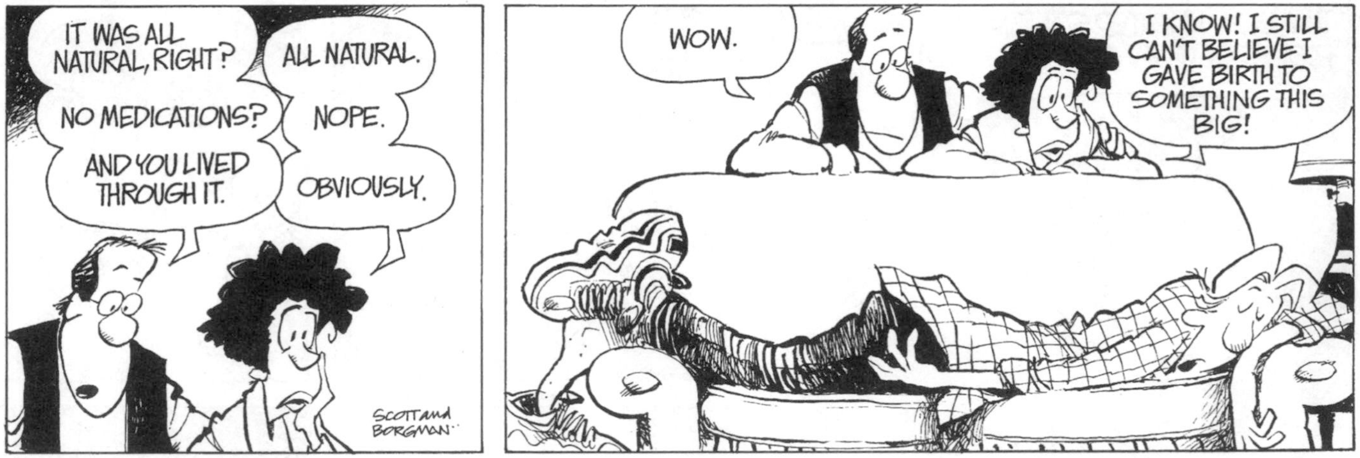
IT WAS ALL NATURAL, RIGHT?
ALL NATURAL.
NO MEDICATIONS?
NOPE.
AND YOU LIVED THROUGH IT.
OBVIOUSLY.
SCOTT and BORGMAN
WOW.
I KNOW! I STILL CAN'T BELIEVE I GAVE BIRTH TO SOMETHING THIS BIG!

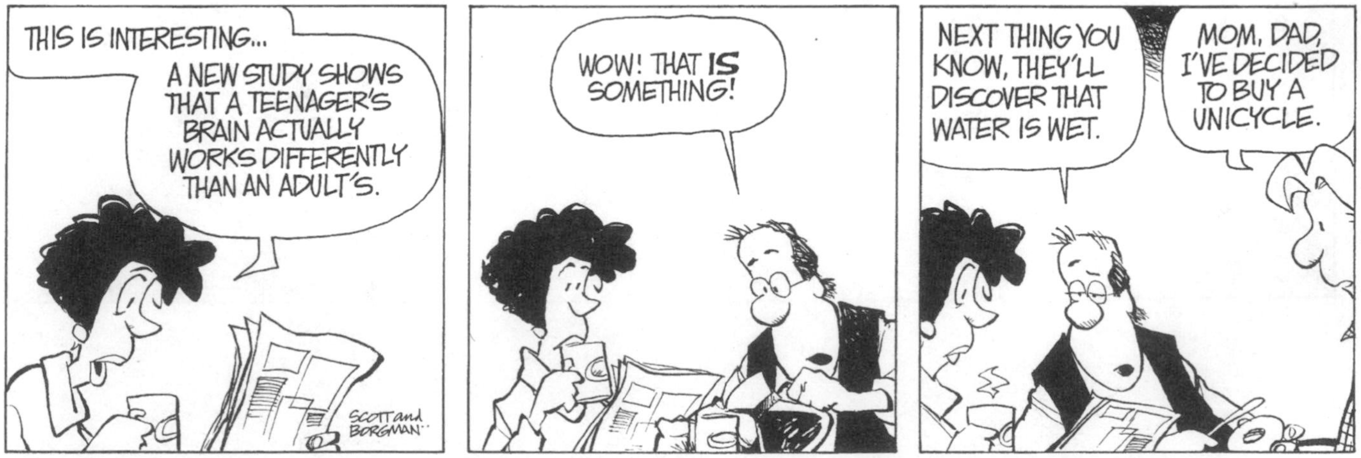
THIS IS INTERESTING...
A NEW STUDY SHOWS THAT A TEENAGER'S BRAIN ACTUALLY WORKS DIFFERENTLY THAN AN ADULT'S.
SCOTT and BORGMAN
WOW! THAT IS SOMETHING!
NEXT THING YOU KNOW, THEY'LL DISCOVER THAT WATER IS WET.
MOM, DAD, I'VE DECIDED TO BUY A UNICYCLE.

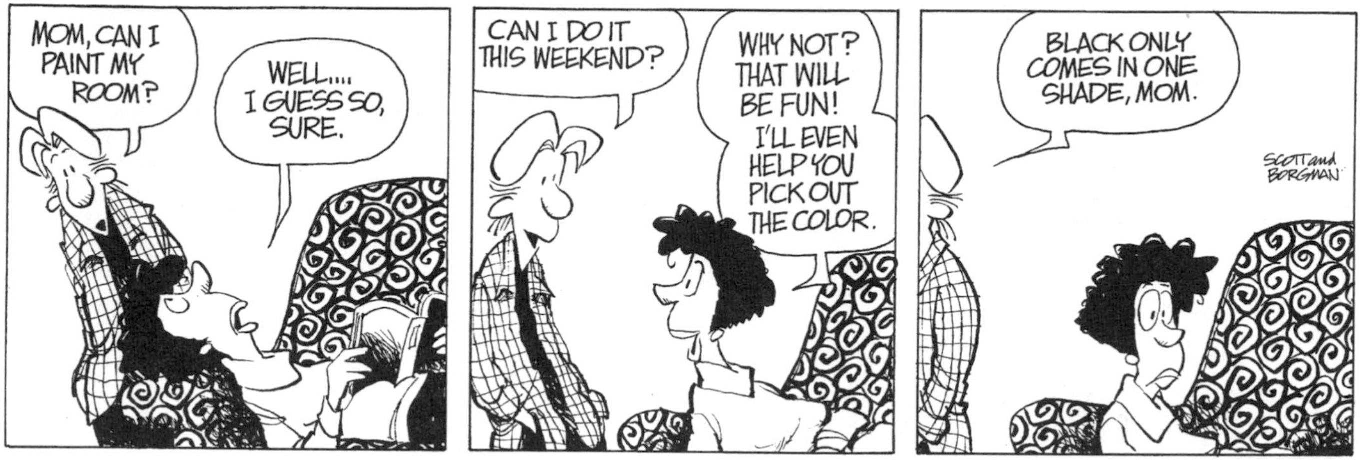
MOM, CAN I PAINT MY ROOM?
WELL.... I GUESS SO, SURE.
CAN I DO IT THIS WEEKEND?
WHY NOT? THAT WILL BE FUN!
I'LL EVEN HELP YOU PICK OUT THE COLOR.
BLACK ONLY COMES IN ONE SHADE, MOM.
SCOTT and BORGMAN

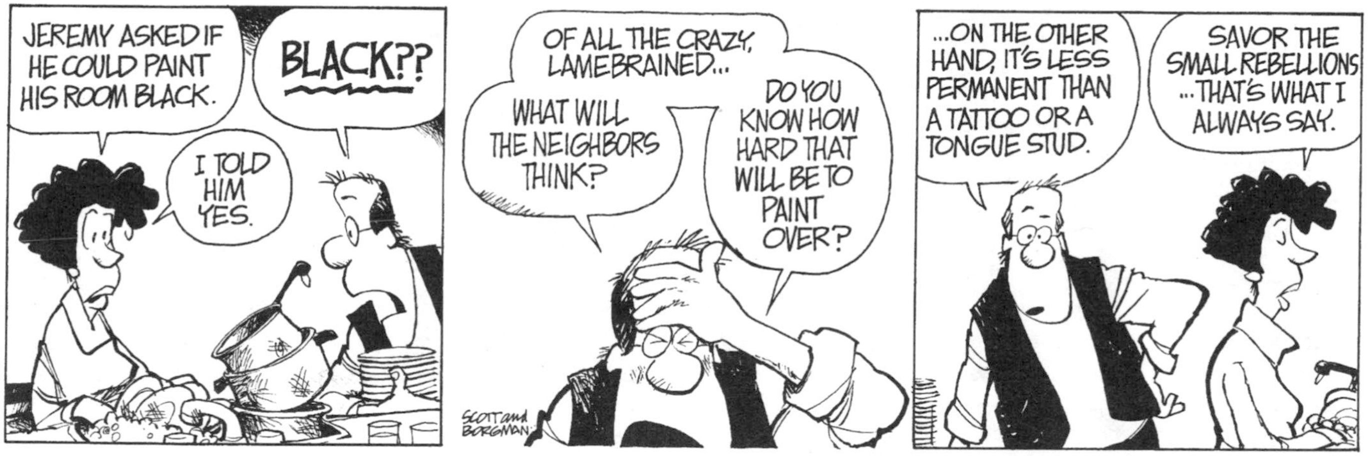
JEREMY ASKED IF HE COULD PAINT HIS ROOM BLACK.
BLACK??
I TOLD HIM YES.
OF ALL THE CRAZY, LAMEBRAINED...
WHAT WILL THE NEIGHBORS THINK?
DO YOU KNOW HOW HARD THAT WILL BE TO PAINT OVER?
SCOTT and BORGMAN
...ON THE OTHER HAND, IT'S LESS PERMANENT THAN A TATTOO OR A TONGUE STUD.
SAVOR THE SMALL REBELLIONS ...THAT'S WHAT I ALWAYS SAY.

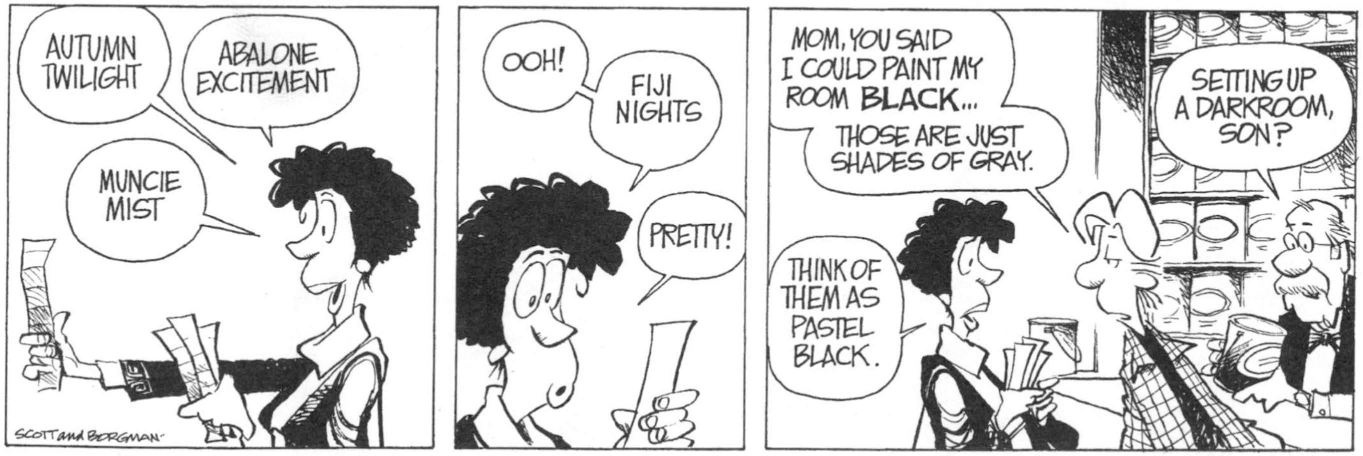
AUTUMN TWILIGHT
ABALONE EXCITEMENT
MUNCIE MIST
SCOTT and BORGMAN
OOH!
FIJI NIGHTS
PRETTY!
MOM, YOU SAID I COULD PAINT MY ROOM BLACK...
THOSE ARE JUST SHADES OF GRAY.
SETTING UP A DARKROOM, SON?
THINK OF THEM AS PASTEL BLACK.

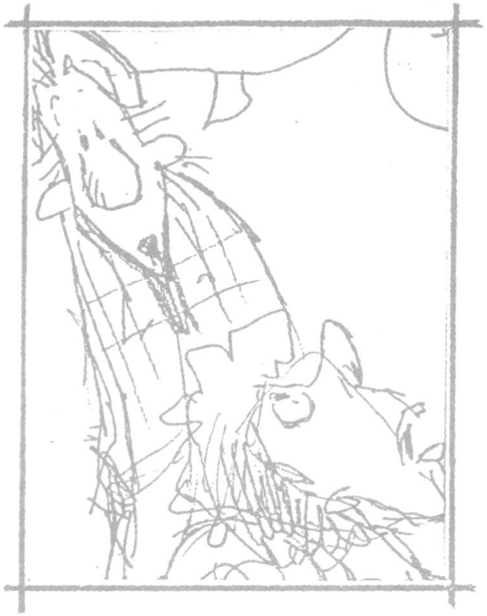

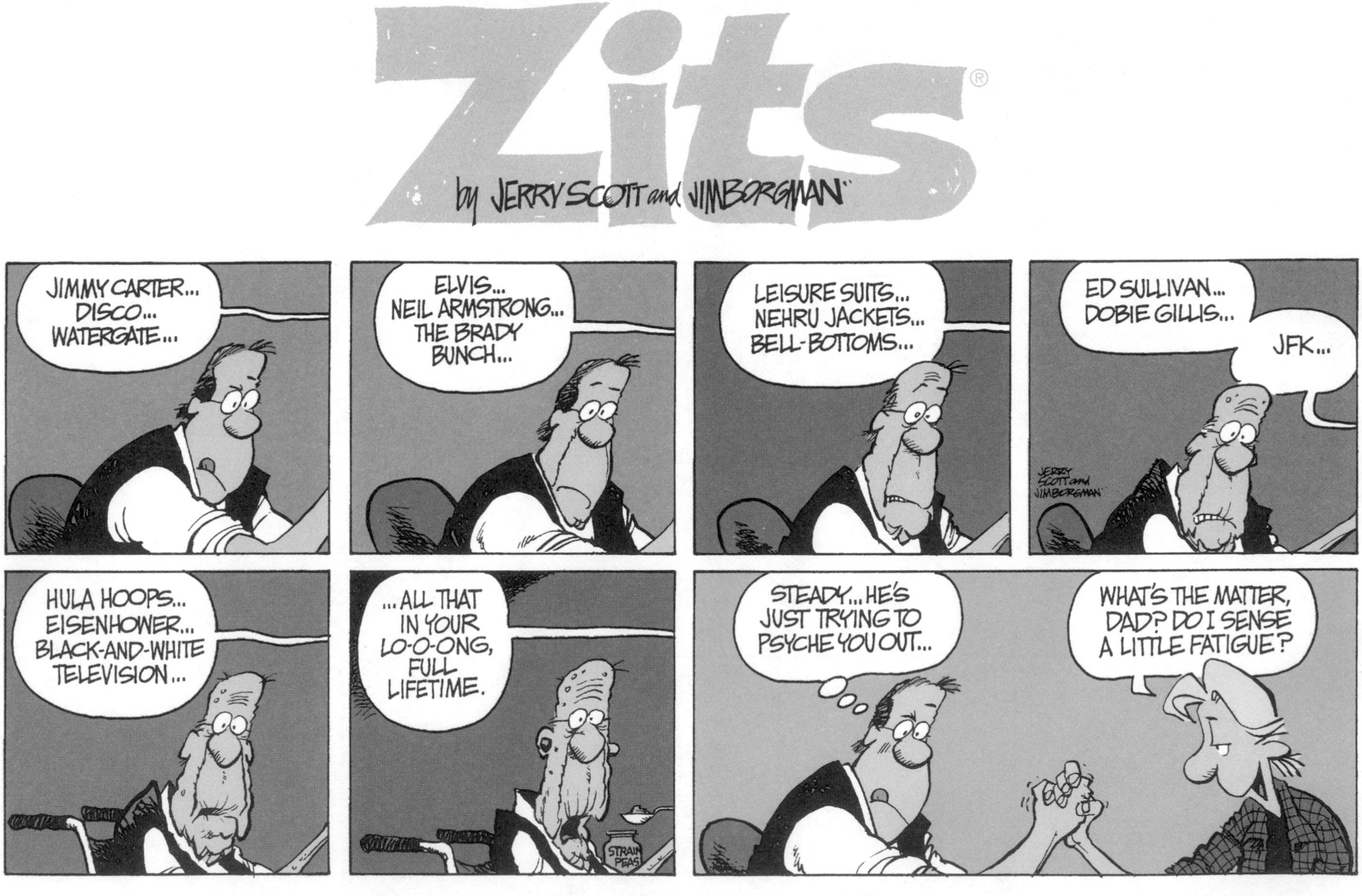
Zits®
by JERRY SCOTT and JIMBORGMAN
JIMMY CARTER... DISCO... WATERGATE...
ELVIS... NEIL ARMSTRONG... THE BRADY BUNCH...
LEISURE SUITS... NEHRU JACKETS... BELL-BOTTOMS...
ED SULLIVAN... DOBIE GILLIS...
JFK...
JERRY SCOTT and JIMBORGMAN
HULA HOOPS... EISENHOWER... BLACK-AND-WHITE TELEVISION...
...ALL THAT IN YOUR LO-O-ONG, FULL LIFETIME.
STRAIN PEAS
STEADY... HE'S JUST TRYING TO PSYCHE YOU OUT...
WHAT'S THE MATTER, DAD? DO I SENSE A LITTLE FATIGUE?

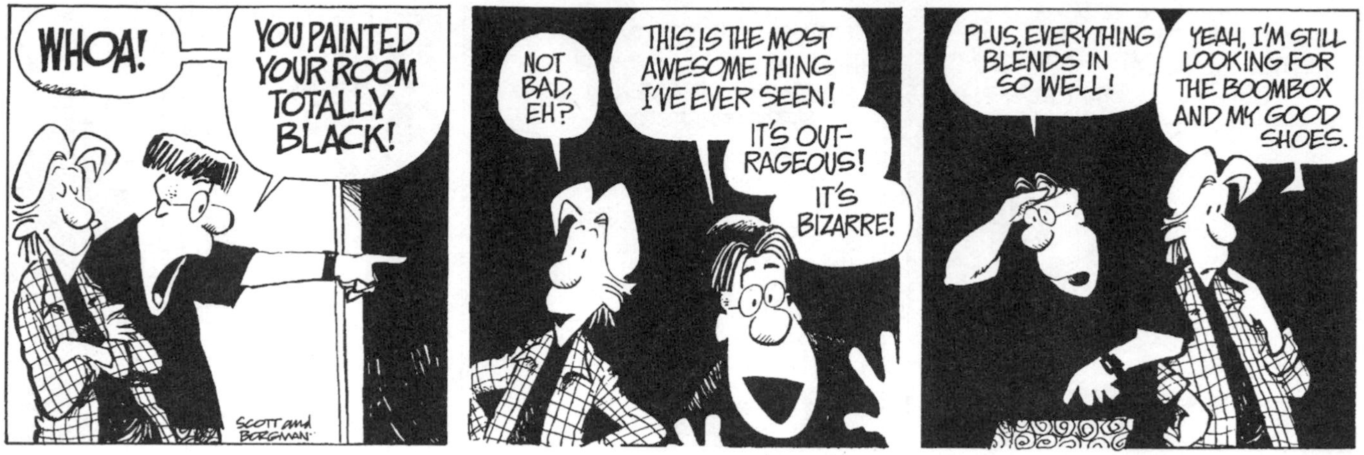
WHOA!
YOU PAINTED YOUR ROOM TOTALLY BLACK!
SCOTT and BORGMAN
NOT BAD, EH?
THIS IS THE MOST AWESOME THING I'VE EVER SEEN!
IT'S OUT-RAGEOUS!
IT'S BIZARRE!
PLUS, EVERYTHING BLENDS IN SO WELL!
YEAH, I'M STILL LOOKING FOR THE BOOMBOX AND MY GOOD SHOES.

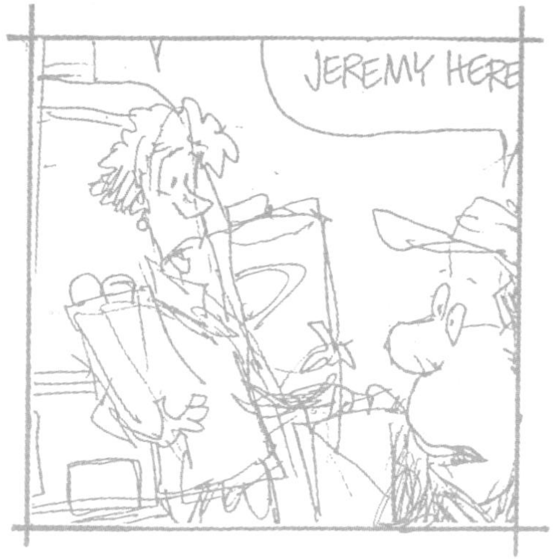
JEREMY HERE

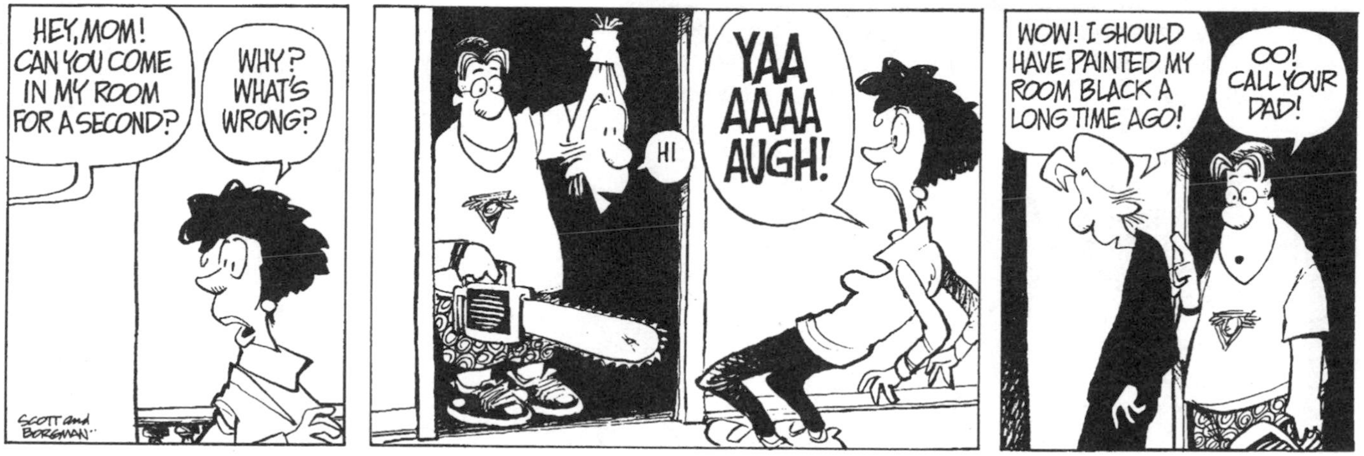
HEY, MOM! CAN YOU COME IN MY ROOM FOR A SECOND?
WHY? WHAT'S WRONG?
SCOTT and BORGMAN
HI
YAA AAAA AUGH!
WOW! I SHOULD HAVE PAINTED MY ROOM BLACK A LONG TIME AGO!
OO! CALL YOUR DAD!

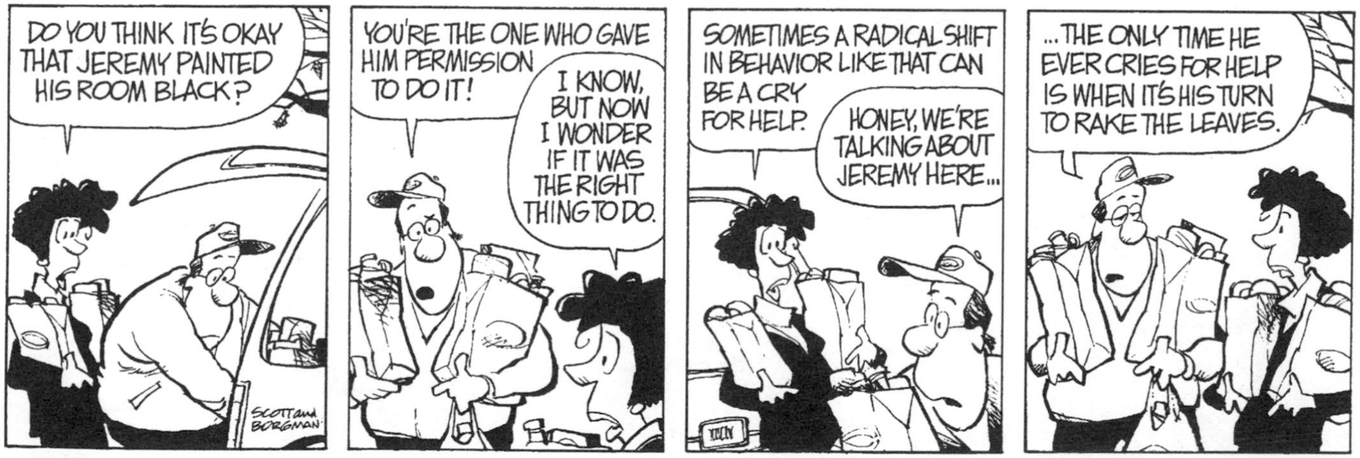
DO YOU THINK IT'S OKAY THAT JEREMY PAINTED HIS ROOM BLACK?
SCOTT and BORGMAN
YOU'RE THE ONE WHO GAVE HIM PERMISSION TO DO IT!
I KNOW, BUT NOW I WONDER IF IT WAS THE RIGHT THING TO DO.
SOMETIMES A RADICAL SHIFT IN BEHAVIOR LIKE THAT CAN BE A CRY FOR HELP.
HONEY, WE'RE TALKING ABOUT JEREMY HERE...
...THE ONLY TIME HE EVER CRIES FOR HELP IS WHEN IT'S HIS TURN TO RAKE THE LEAVES.

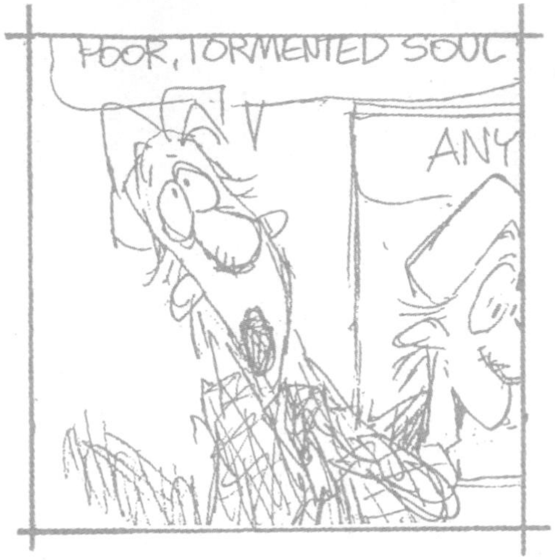
POOR, TORMENTED SOUL
ANY

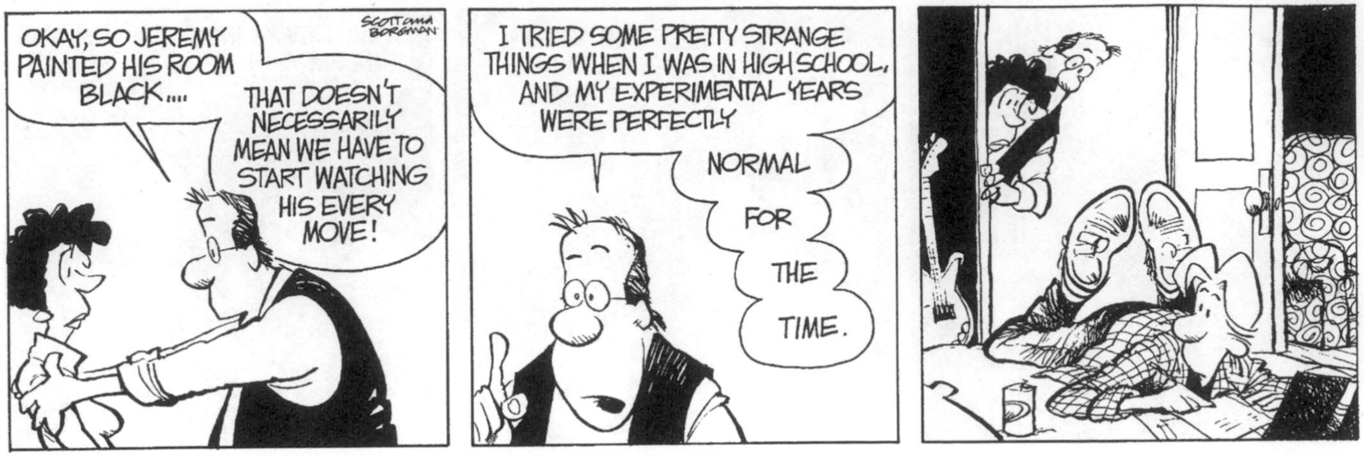
SCOTT and BORGMAN
OKAY, SO JEREMY PAINTED HIS ROOM BLACK....
THAT DOESN'T NECESSARILY MEAN WE HAVE TO START WATCHING HIS EVERY MOVE!
I TRIED SOME PRETTY STRANGE THINGS WHEN I WAS IN HIGH SCHOOL, AND MY EXPERIMENTAL YEARS WERE PERFECTLY
NORMAL FOR THE TIME.

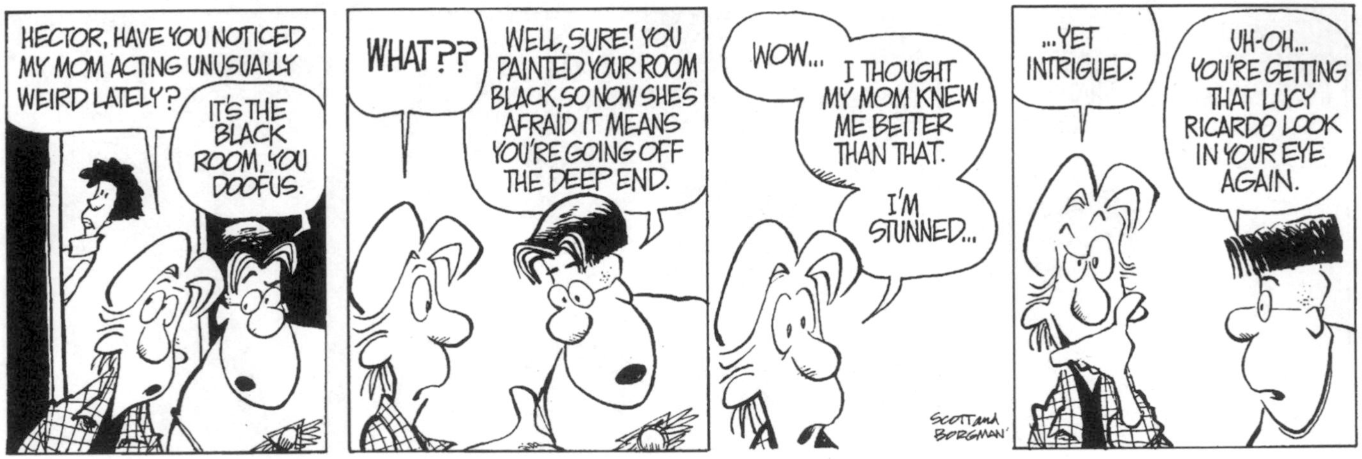
HECTOR, HAVE YOU NOTICED MY MOM ACTING UNUSUALLY WEIRD LATELY?
IT'S THE BLACK ROOM, YOU DOOFUS.
WHAT??
WELL, SURE! YOU PAINTED YOUR ROOM BLACK, SO NOW SHE'S AFRAID IT MEANS YOU'RE GOING OFF THE DEEP END.
WOW...
I THOUGHT MY MOM KNEW ME BETTER THAN THAT.
I'M STUNNED...
SCOTT and BORGMAN
...YET INTRIGUED.
UH-OH... YOU'RE GETTING THAT LUCY RICARDO LOOK IN YOUR EYE AGAIN.

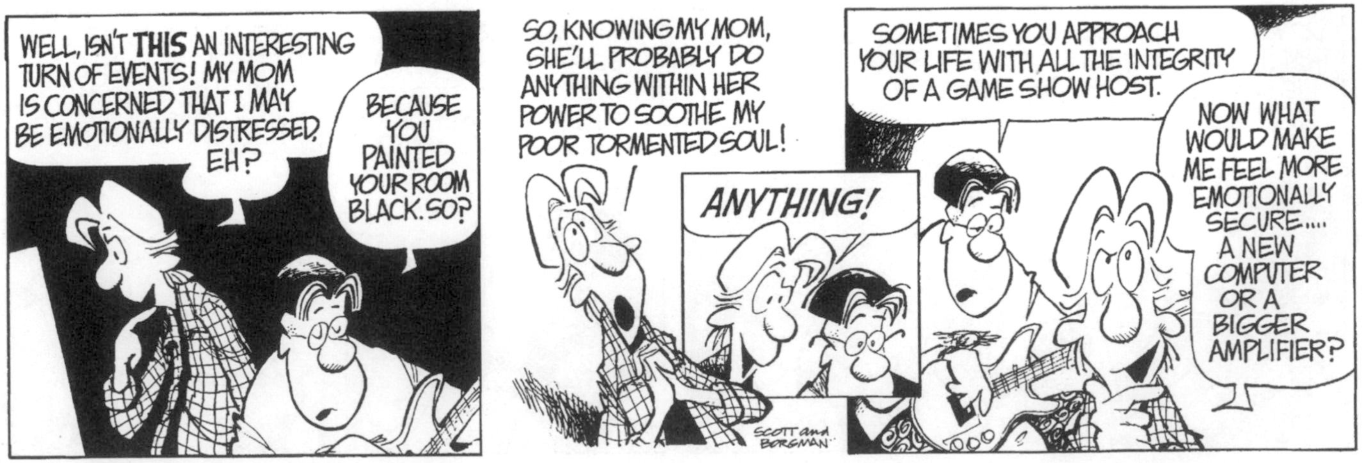
WELL, ISN'T THIS AN INTERESTING TURN OF EVENTS! MY MOM IS CONCERNED THAT I MAY BE EMOTIONALLY DISTRESSED, EH?
BECAUSE YOU PAINTED YOUR ROOM BLACK. SO?
SO, KNOWING MY MOM, SHE'LL PROBABLY DO ANYTHING WITHIN HER POWER TO SOOTHE MY POOR TORMENTED SOUL!
ANYTHING!
SCOTT and BORGMAN
SOMETIMES YOU APPROACH YOUR LIFE WITH ALL THE INTEGRITY OF A GAME SHOW HOST.
NOW WHAT WOULD MAKE ME FEEL MORE EMOTIONALLY SECURE.... A NEW COMPUTER OR A BIGGER AMPLIFIER?

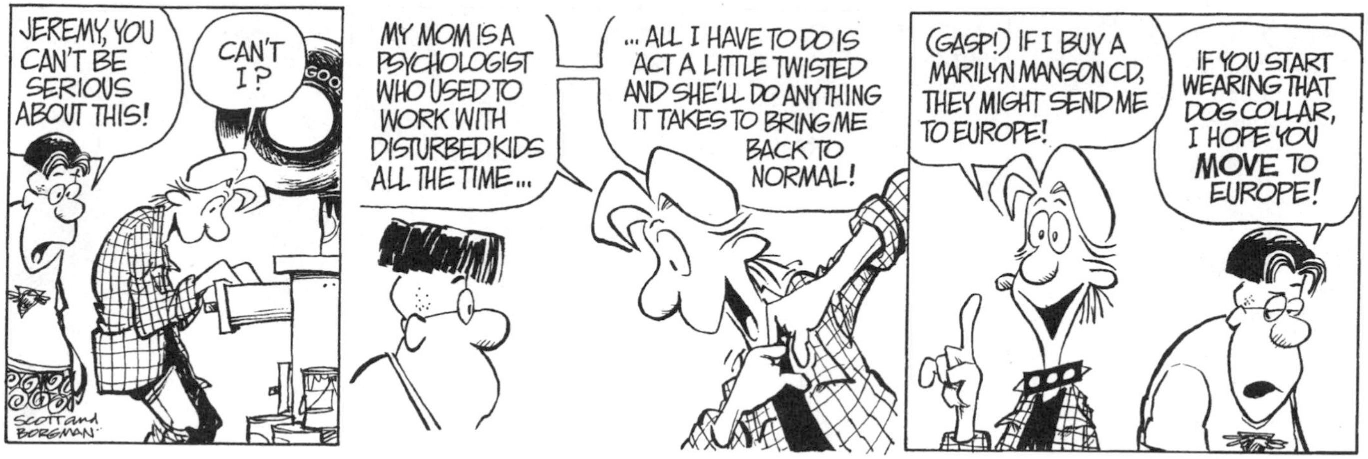
JEREMY, YOU CAN'T BE SERIOUS ABOUT THIS!
CAN'T I?
MY MOM IS A PSYCHOLOGIST WHO USED TO WORK WITH DISTURBED KIDS ALL THE TIME...
... ALL I HAVE TO DO IS ACT A LITTLE TWISTED AND SHE'LL DO ANYTHING IT TAKES TO BRING ME BACK TO NORMAL!
(GASP!) IF I BUY A MARILYN MANSON CD, THEY MIGHT SEND ME TO EUROPE!
IF YOU START WEARING THAT DOG COLLAR, I HOPE YOU MOVE TO EUROPE!
SCOTT and BORGMAN

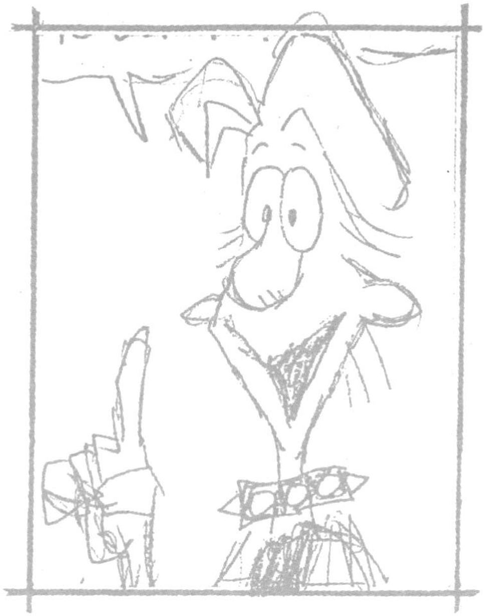

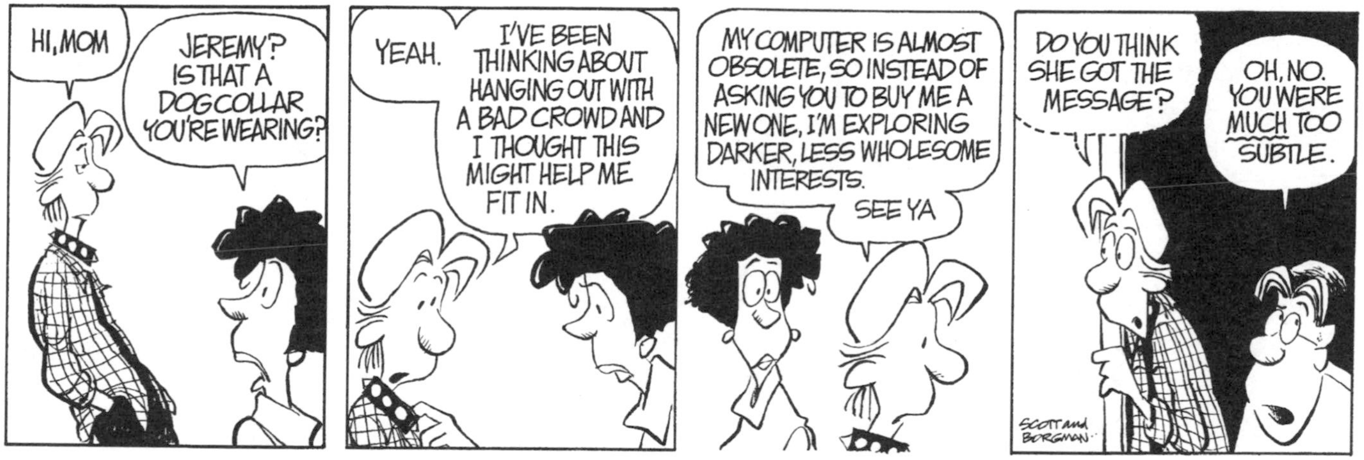
HI, MOM
JEREMY? IS THAT A DOG COLLAR YOU'RE WEARING?
YEAH.
I'VE BEEN THINKING ABOUT HANGING OUT WITH A BAD CROWD AND I THOUGHT THIS MIGHT HELP ME FIT IN.
MY COMPUTER IS ALMOST OBSOLETE, SO INSTEAD OF ASKING YOU TO BUY ME A NEW ONE, I'M EXPLORING DARKER, LESS WHOLESOME INTERESTS.
SEE YA
DO YOU THINK SHE GOT THE MESSAGE?
OH, NO. YOU WERE MUCH TOO SUBTLE.
SCOTT and BORGMAN

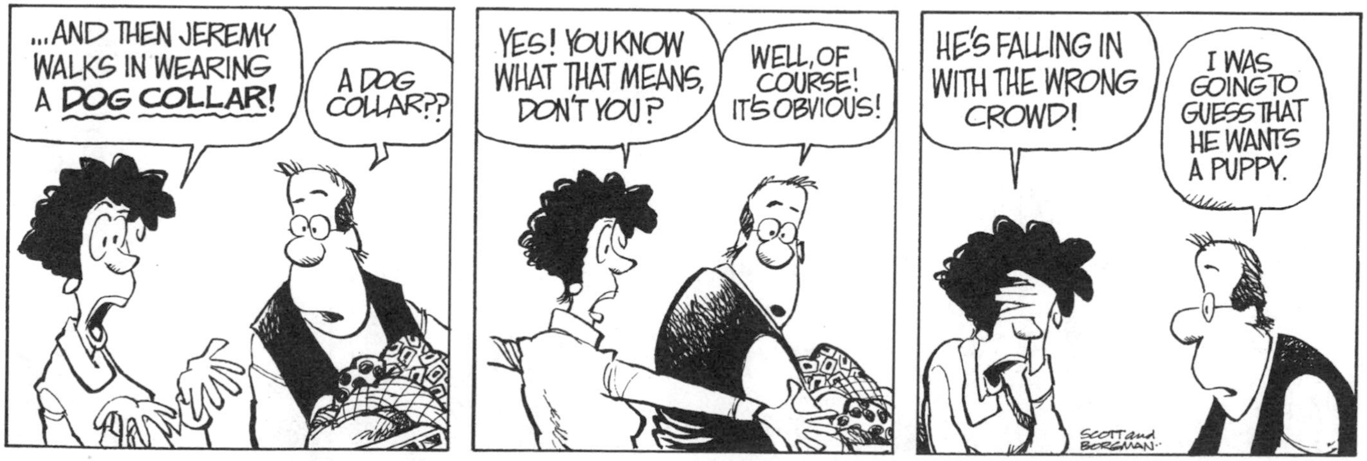
...AND THEN JEREMY WALKS IN WEARING A DOG COLLAR!
A DOG COLLAR??
YES! YOU KNOW WHAT THAT MEANS, DON'T YOU?
WELL, OF COURSE! IT'S OBVIOUS!
HE'S FALLING IN WITH THE WRONG CROWD!
I WAS GOING TO GUESS THAT HE WANTS A PUPPY.
SCOTT and BORGMAN

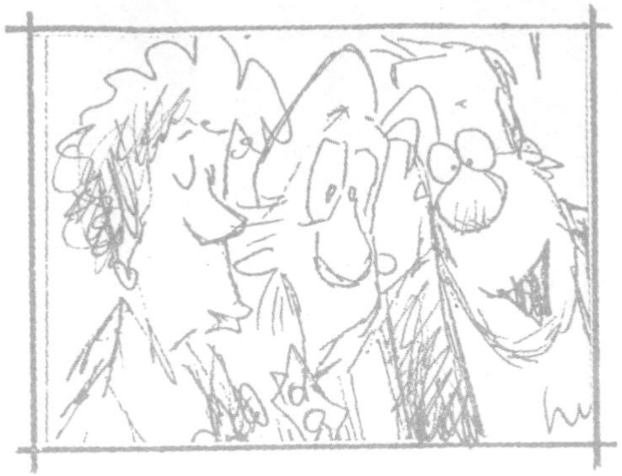

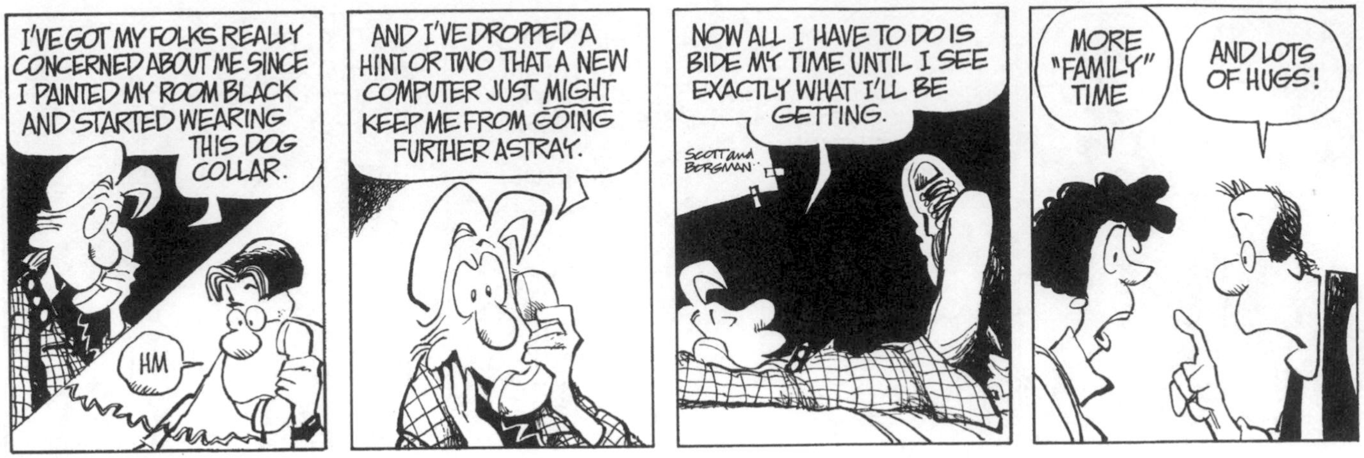
I'VE GOT MY FOLKS REALLY CONCERNED ABOUT ME SINCE I PAINTED MY ROOM BLACK AND STARTED WEARING THIS DOG COLLAR.
HM
AND I'VE DROPPED A HINT OR TWO THAT A NEW COMPUTER JUST MIGHT KEEP ME FROM GOING FURTHER ASTRAY.
NOW ALL I HAVE TO DO IS BIDE MY TIME UNTIL I SEE EXACTLY WHAT I'LL BE GETTING.
SCOTT and BORGMAN
MORE "FAMILY" TIME
AND LOTS OF HUGS!

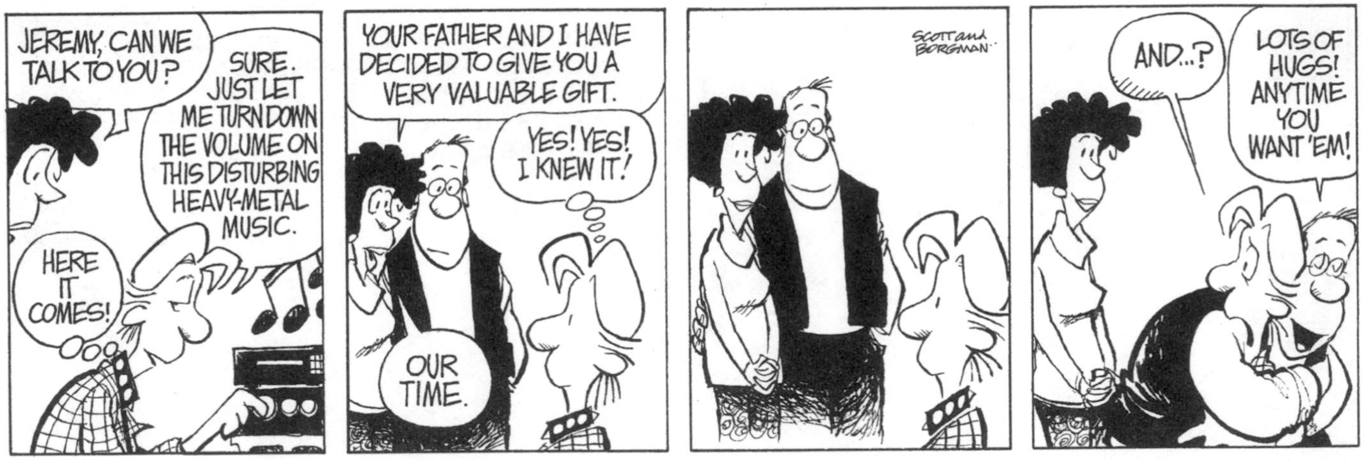
JEREMY, CAN WE TALK TO YOU?
SURE. JUST LET ME TURN DOWN THE VOLUME ON THIS DISTURBING HEAVY-METAL MUSIC.
HERE IT COMES!
YOUR FATHER AND I HAVE DECIDED TO GIVE YOU A VERY VALUABLE GIFT.
YES! YES! I KNEW IT!
OUR TIME.
SCOTT and BORGMAN
AND...?
LOTS OF HUGS! ANYTIME YOU WANT 'EM!

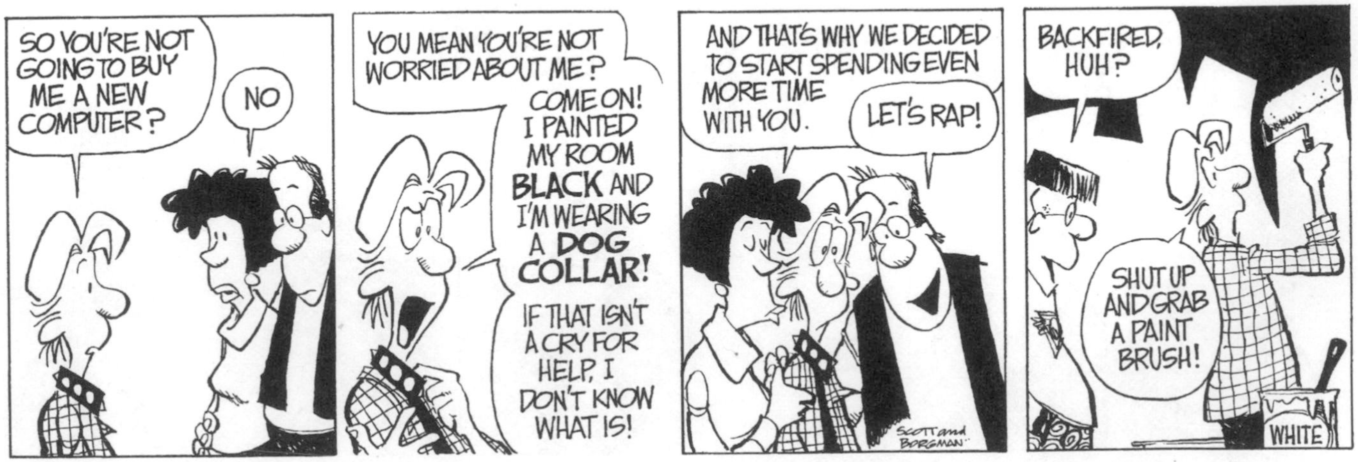
SO YOU'RE NOT GOING TO BUY ME A NEW COMPUTER?
NO
YOU MEAN YOU'RE NOT WORRIED ABOUT ME?
COME ON! I PAINTED MY ROOM BLACK AND I'M WEARING A DOG COLLAR!
IF THAT ISN'T A CRY FOR HELP, I DON'T KNOW WHAT IS!
AND THAT'S WHY WE DECIDED TO START SPENDING EVEN MORE TIME WITH YOU.
LET'S RAP!
SCOTT and BORGMAN
BACKFIRED, HUH?
SHUT UP AND GRAB A PAINT BRUSH!
WHITE

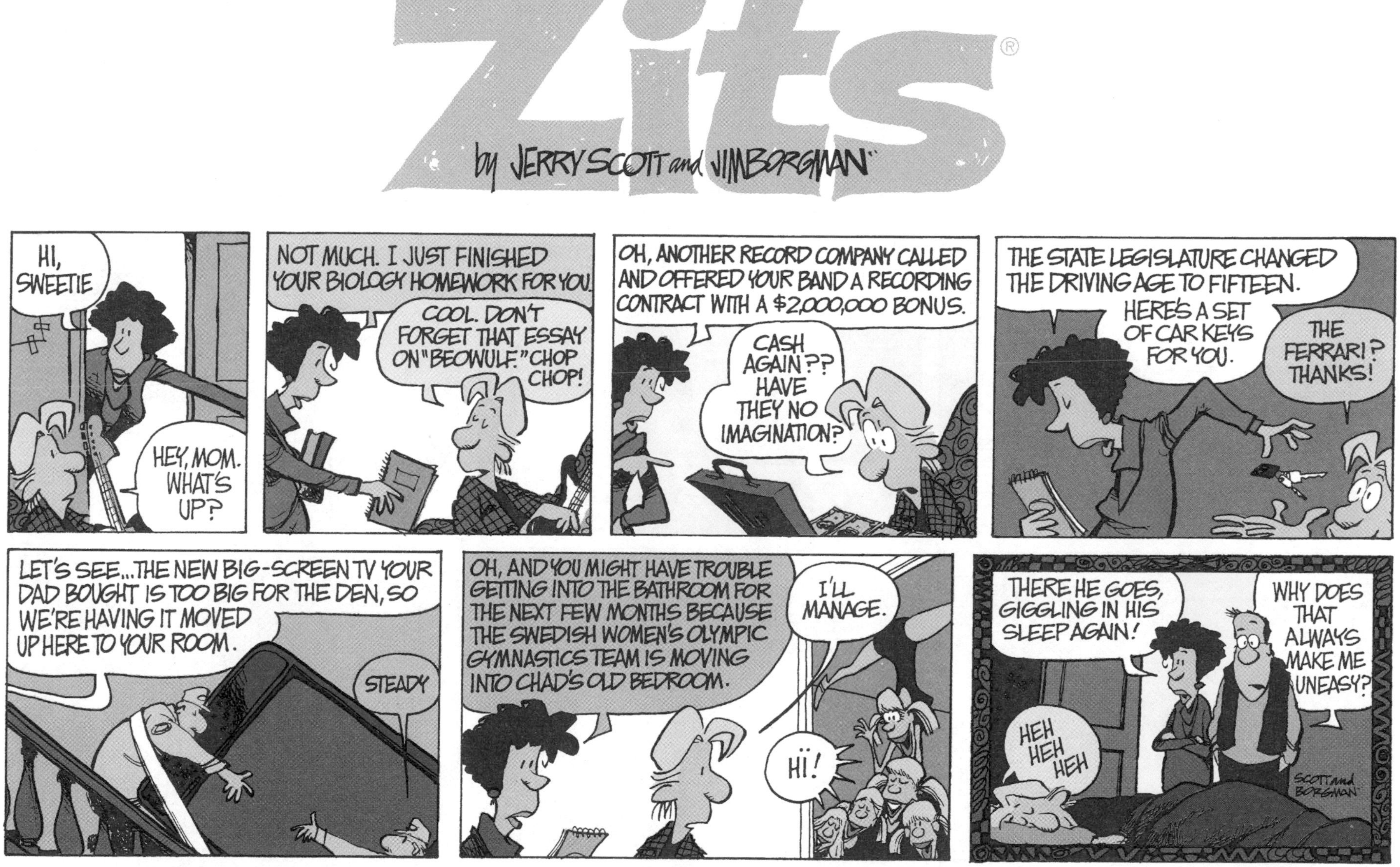
Zits®
by JERRY SCOTT and JIM BORGMAN
HI, SWEETIE
HEY, MOM. WHAT'S UP?
NOT MUCH. I JUST FINISHED YOUR BIOLOGY HOMEWORK FOR YOU.
COOL. DON'T FORGET THAT ESSAY ON "BEOWULF." CHOP CHOP!
OH, ANOTHER RECORD COMPANY CALLED AND OFFERED YOUR BAND A RECORDING CONTRACT WITH A $2,000,000 BONUS.
CASH AGAIN?? HAVE THEY NO IMAGINATION?
THE STATE LEGISLATURE CHANGED THE DRIVING AGE TO FIFTEEN.
HERE'S A SET OF CAR KEYS FOR YOU.
THE FERRARI? THANKS!
LET'S SEE... THE NEW BIG-SCREEN TV YOUR DAD BOUGHT IS TOO BIG FOR THE DEN, SO WE'RE HAVING IT MOVED UP HERE TO YOUR ROOM.
STEADY
OH, AND YOU MIGHT HAVE TROUBLE GETTING INTO THE BATHROOM FOR THE NEXT FEW MONTHS BECAUSE THE SWEDISH WOMEN'S OLYMPIC GYMNASTICS TEAM IS MOVING INTO CHAD'S OLD BEDROOM.
I'LL MANAGE.
HI!
THERE HE GOES, GIGGLING IN HIS SLEEP AGAIN!
WHY DOES THAT ALWAYS MAKE ME UNEASY?
HEH HEH HEH
SCOTT and BORGMAN

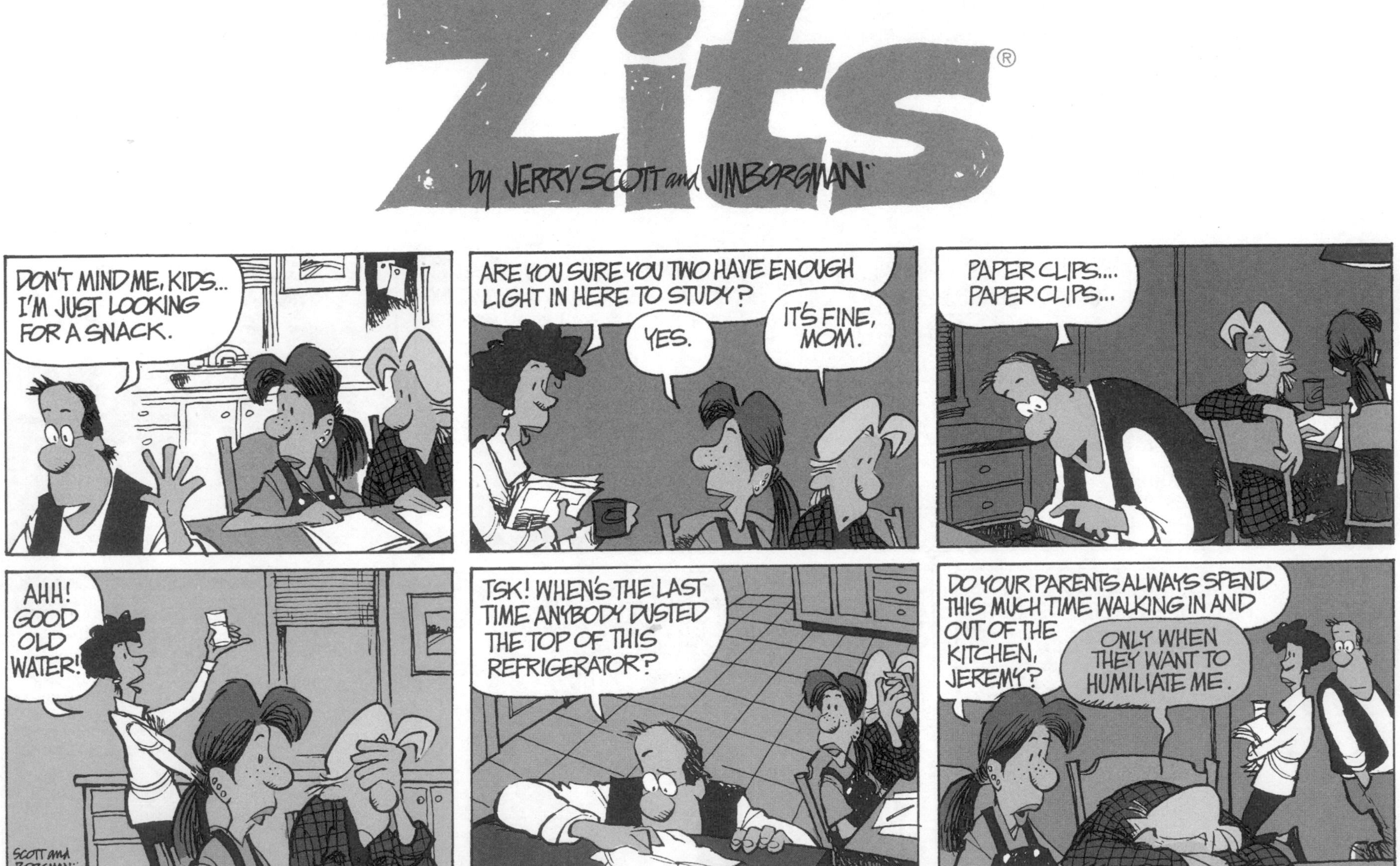

Zits®
by JERRY SCOTT and JIM BORGMAN
DON'T MIND ME, KIDS... I'M JUST LOOKING FOR A SNACK.
ARE YOU SURE YOU TWO HAVE ENOUGH LIGHT IN HERE TO STUDY?
YES.
IT'S FINE, MOM.
PAPER CLIPS.... PAPER CLIPS...
AHH! GOOD OLD WATER!
SCOTT and BORGMAN
TSK! WHEN'S THE LAST TIME ANYBODY DUSTED THE TOP OF THIS REFRIGERATOR?
DO YOUR PARENTS ALWAYS SPEND THIS MUCH TIME WALKING IN AND OUT OF THE KITCHEN, JEREMY?
ONLY WHEN THEY WANT TO HUMILIATE ME.

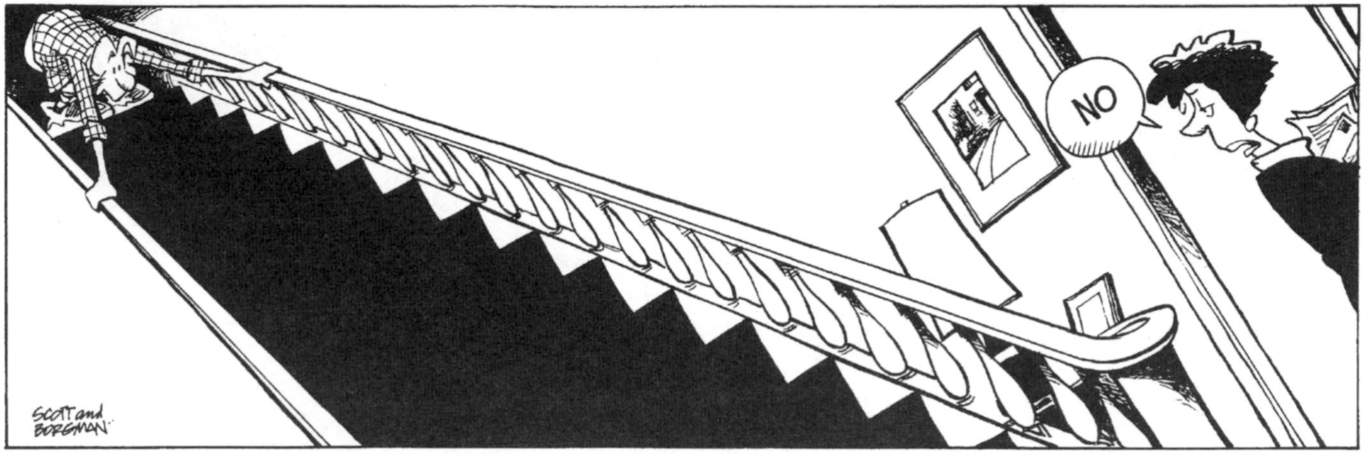
NO
SCOTT and BORGMAN

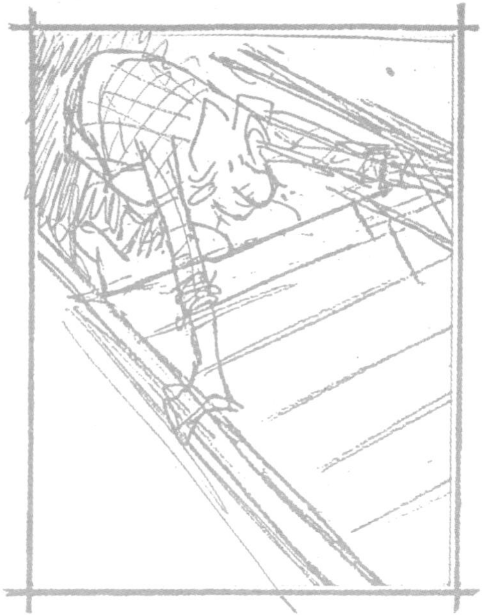

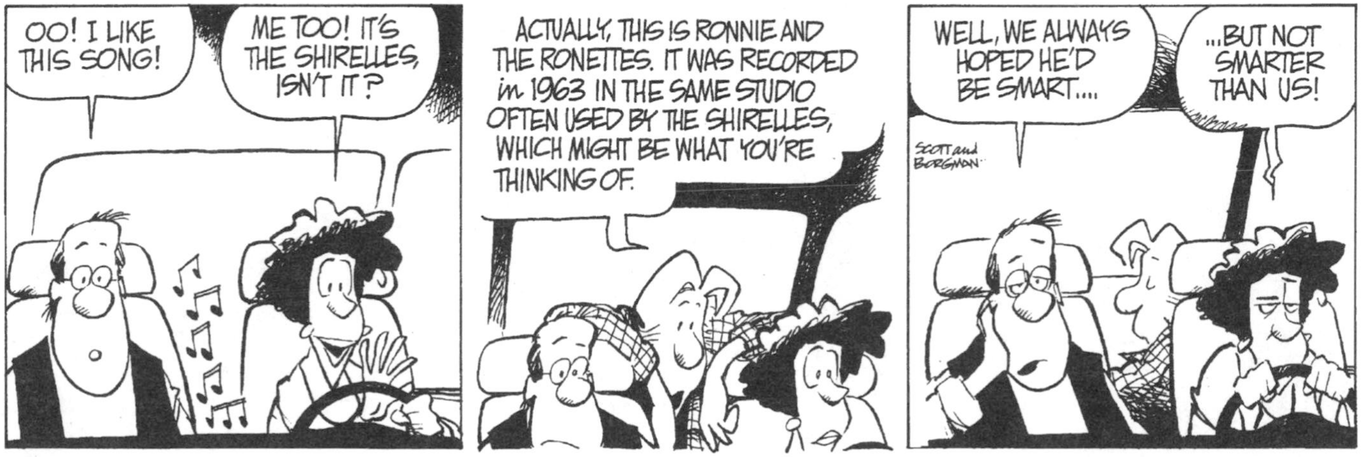
OO! I LIKE THIS SONG!
ME TOO! IT'S THE SHIRELLES, ISN'T IT?
ACTUALLY, THIS IS RONNIE AND THE RONETTES. IT WAS RECORDED in 1963 IN THE SAME STUDIO OFTEN USED BY THE SHIRELLES, WHICH MIGHT BE WHAT YOU'RE THINKING OF.
WELL, WE ALWAYS HOPED HE'D BE SMART....
...BUT NOT SMARTER THAN US!
SCOTT and BORGMAN

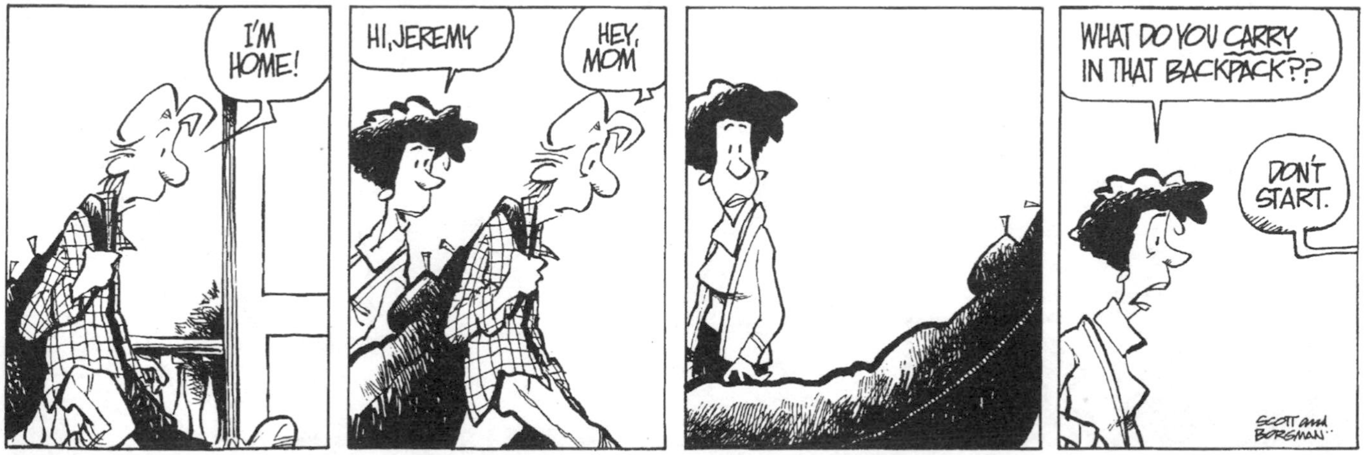
I'M HOME!
HI, JEREMY
HEY, MOM
WHAT DO YOU CARRY IN THAT BACKPACK??
DON'T START.
SCOTT and BORGMAN

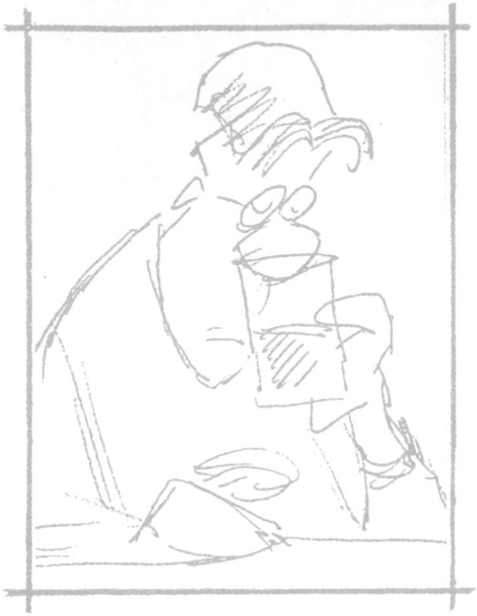

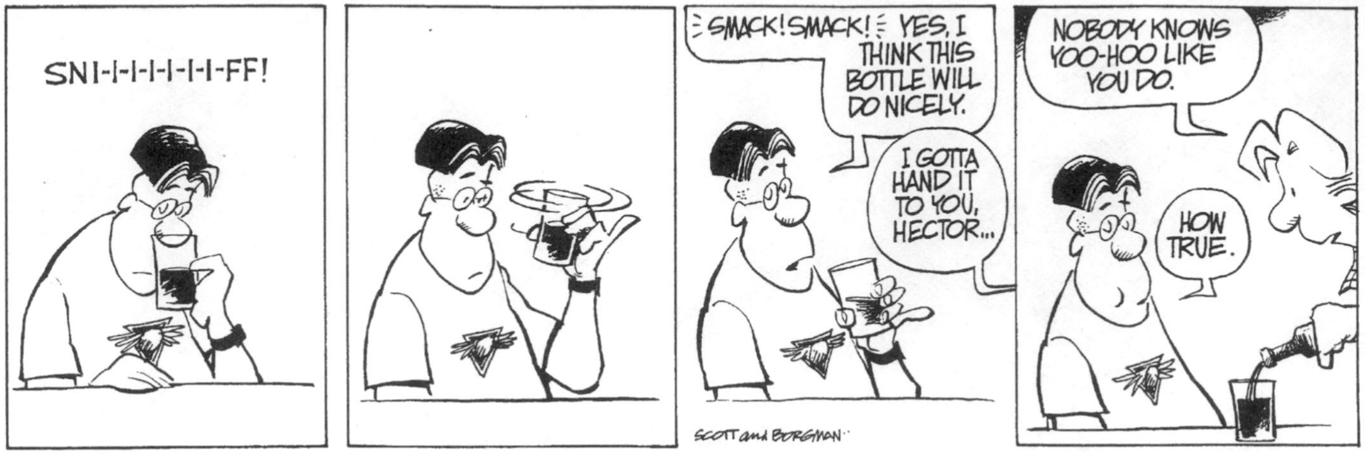
SNI-I-I-I-I-I-I-I-FF!
SMACK! SMACK! YES, I THINK THIS BOTTLE WILL DO NICELY.
I GOTTA HAND IT TO YOU, HECTOR...
SCOTT and BORGMAN
NOBODY KNOWS YOO-HOO LIKE YOU DO.
HOW TRUE.

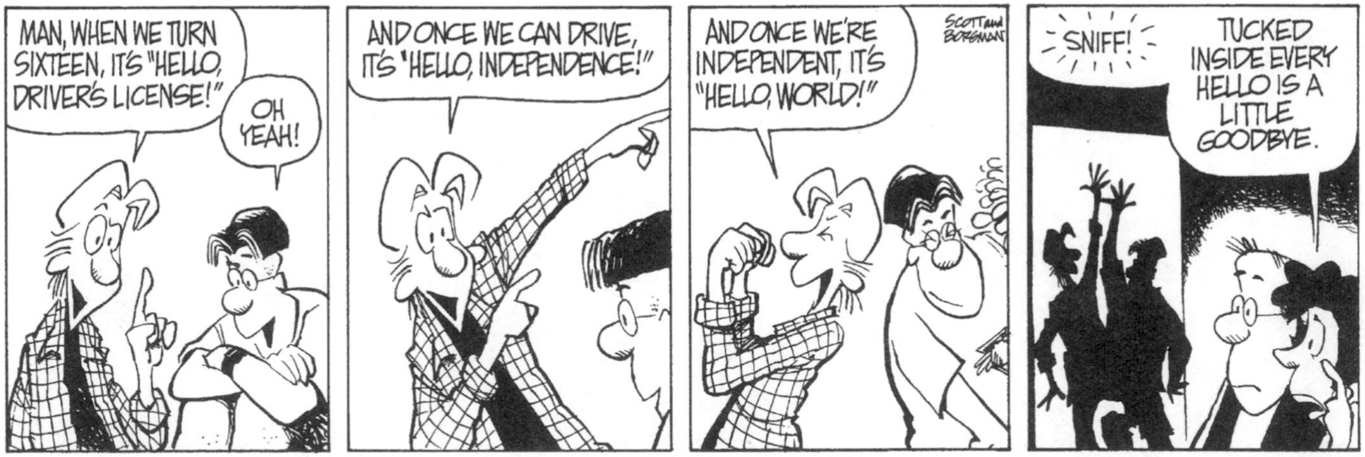
MAN, WHEN WE TURN SIXTEEN, IT'S "HELLO, DRIVER'S LICENSE!"
OH YEAH!
AND ONCE WE CAN DRIVE, IT'S "HELLO, INDEPENDENCE!"
AND ONCE WE'RE INDEPENDENT, IT'S "HELLO, WORLD!"
SCOTT and BORGMAN
SNIFF!
TUCKED INSIDE EVERY HELLO IS A LITTLE GOODBYE.

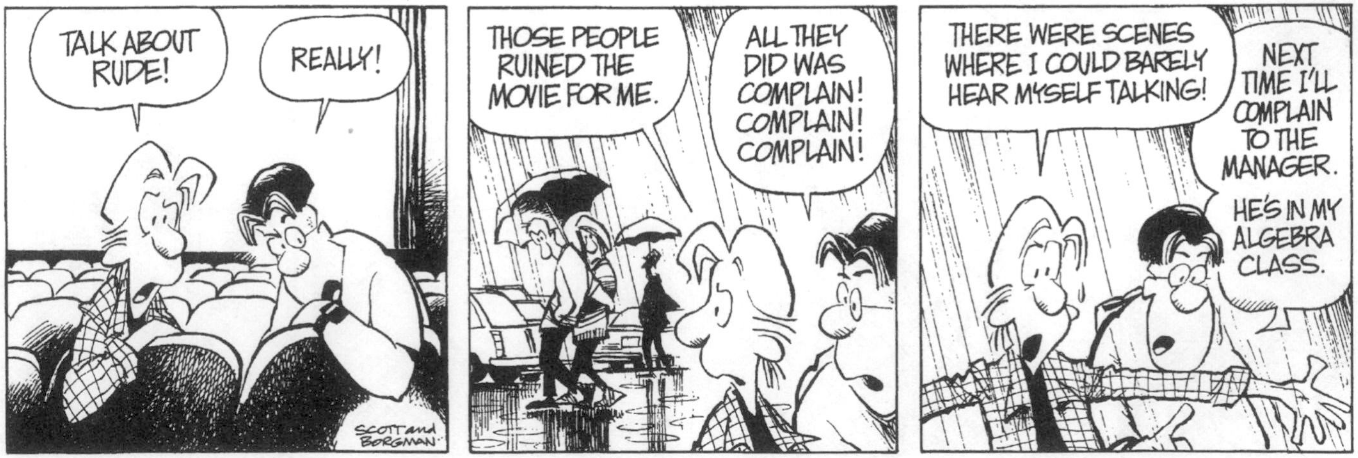
TALK ABOUT RUDE!
REALLY!
SCOTT and BORGMAN
THOSE PEOPLE RUINED THE MOVIE FOR ME.
ALL THEY DID WAS COMPLAIN! COMPLAIN! COMPLAIN!
THERE WERE SCENES WHERE I COULD BARELY HEAR MYSELF TALKING!
NEXT TIME I'LL COMPLAIN TO THE MANAGER.
HE'S IN MY ALGEBRA CLASS.

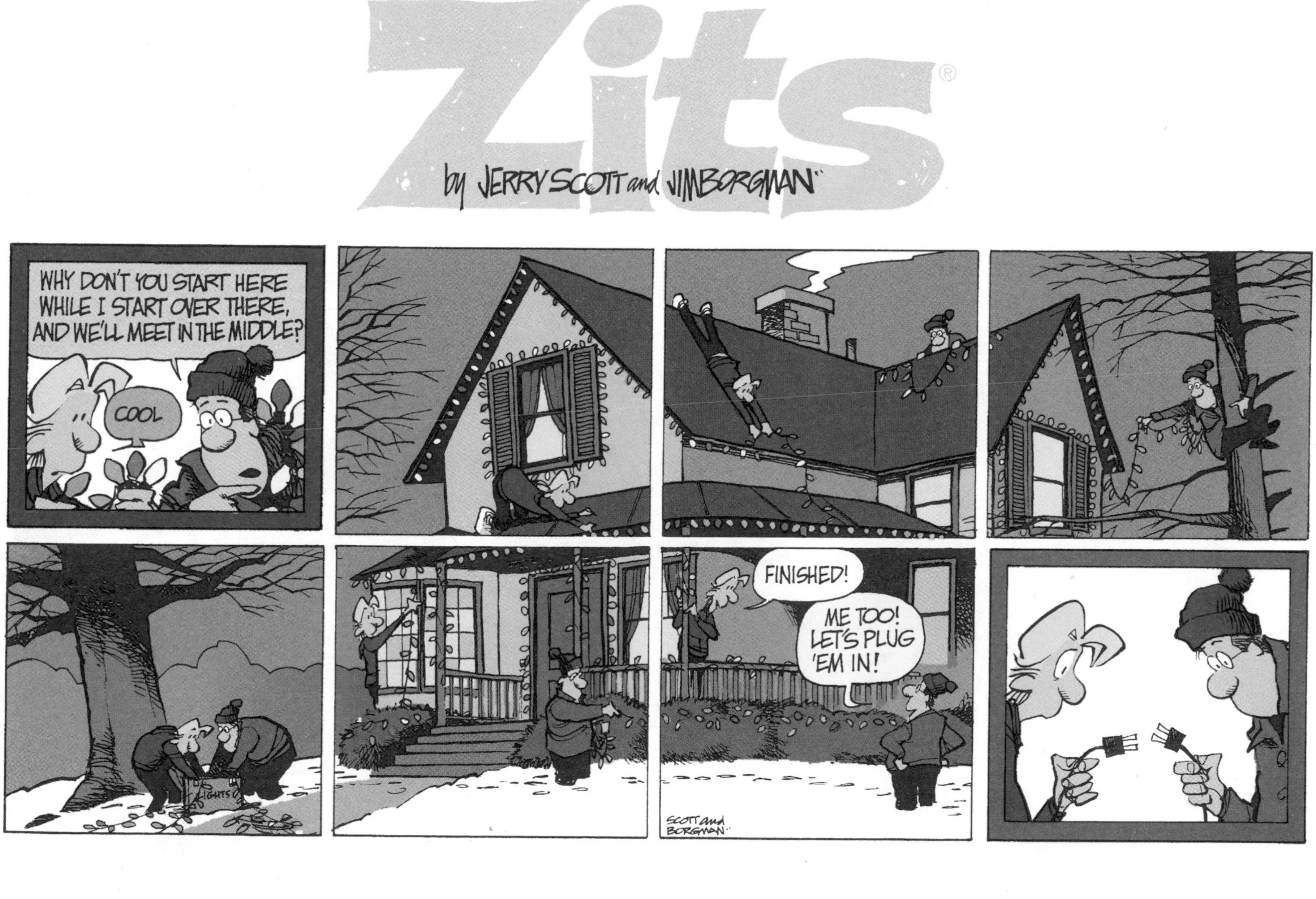
Zits®
by JERRY SCOTT and JIM BORGMAN
WHY DON'T YOU START HERE WHILE I START OVER THERE, AND WE'LL MEET IN THE MIDDLE?
COOL
LIGHTS
FINISHED!
ME TOO! LET'S PLUG 'EM IN!
SCOTT and BORGMAN

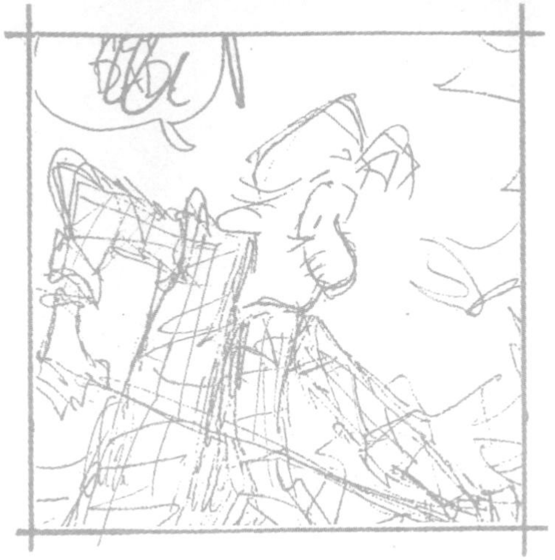

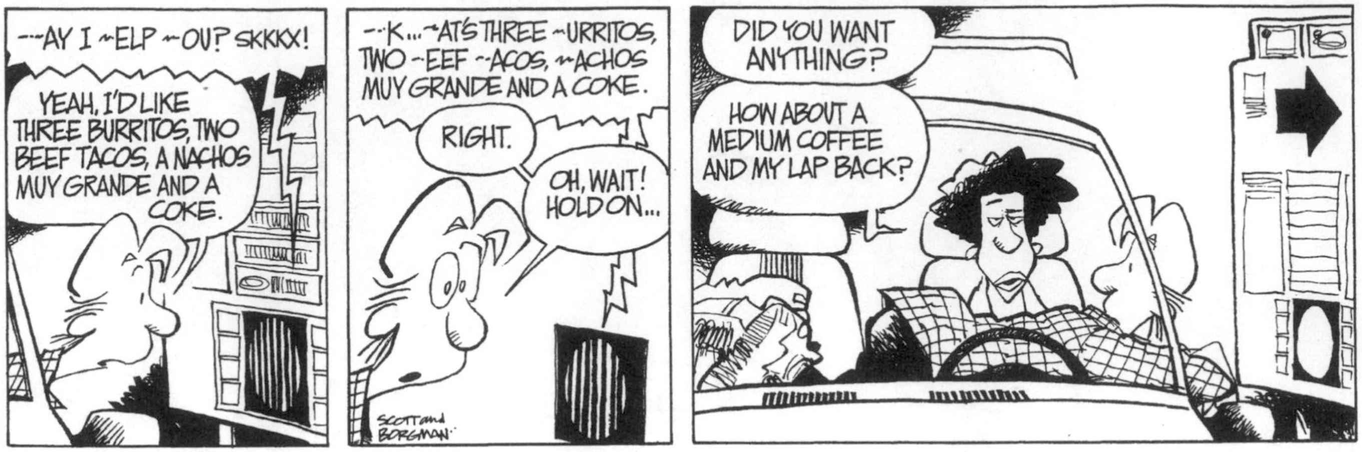
--AY I --ELP --OU? SKKKX!
YEAH, I'D LIKE THREE BURRITOS, TWO BEEF TACOS, A NACHOS MUY GRANDE AND A COKE.
--K... --AT'S THREE --URRITOS, TWO --EEF --ACOS, --ACHOS MUY GRANDE AND A COKE.
RIGHT.
OH, WAIT! HOLD ON...
SCOTT and BORGMAN
DID YOU WANT ANYTHING?
HOW ABOUT A MEDIUM COFFEE AND MY LAP BACK?

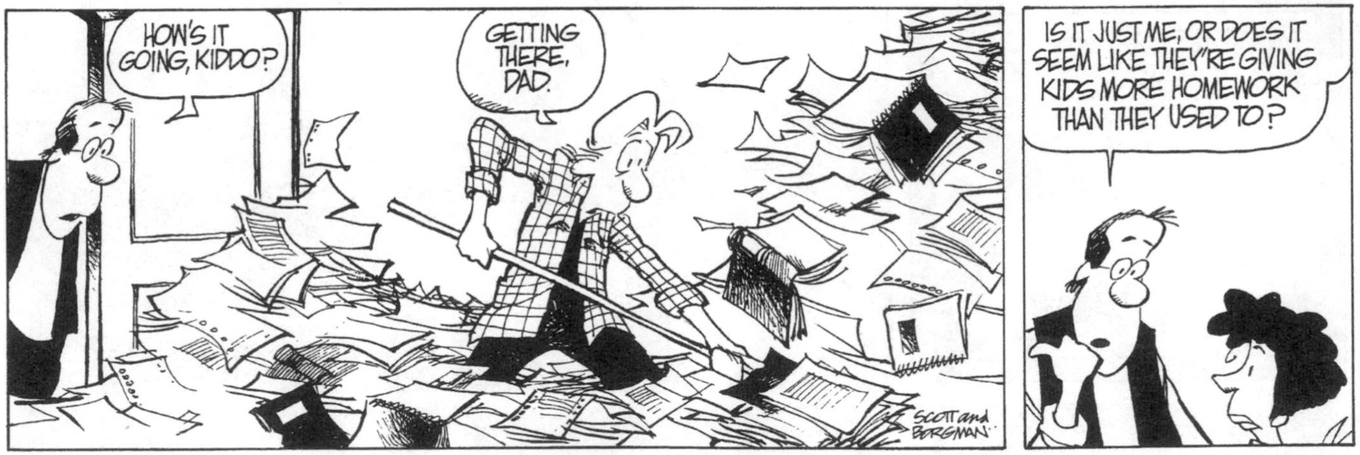
HOW'S IT GOING, KIDDO?
GETTING THERE, DAD.
SCOTT and BORGMAN
IS IT JUST ME, OR DOES IT SEEM LIKE THEY'RE GIVING KIDS MORE HOMEWORK THAN THEY USED TO?

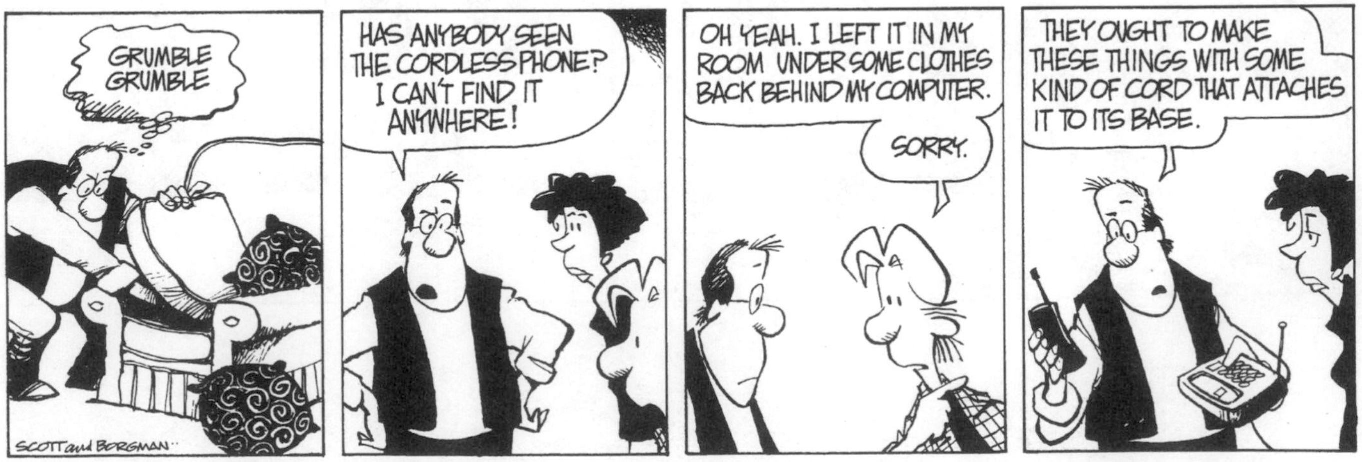
GRUMBLE GRUMBLE
SCOTT and BORGMAN
HAS ANYBODY SEEN THE CORDLESS PHONE? I CAN'T FIND IT ANYWHERE!
OH YEAH. I LEFT IT IN MY ROOM UNDER SOME CLOTHES BACK BEHIND MY COMPUTER.
SORRY.
THEY OUGHT TO MAKE THESE THINGS WITH SOME KIND OF CORD THAT ATTACHES IT TO ITS BASE.

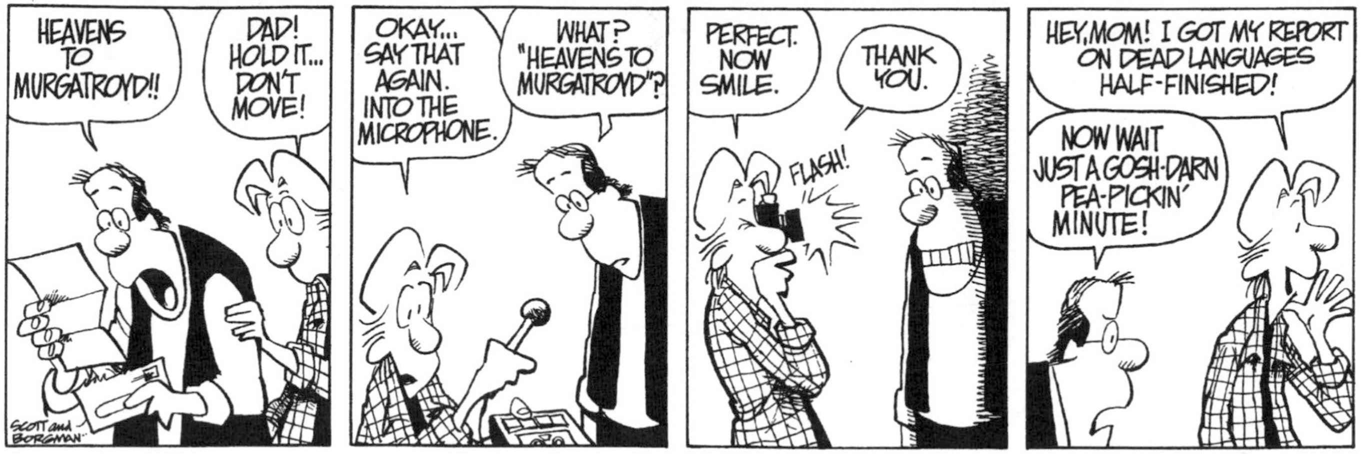
HEAVENS TO MURGATROYD!!
DAD! HOLD IT... DON'T MOVE!
SCOTT and BORGMAN
OKAY... SAY THAT AGAIN. INTO THE MICROPHONE.
WHAT? "HEAVENS TO MURGATROYD"?
PERFECT. NOW SMILE.
FLASH!
THANK YOU.
HEY, MOM! I GOT MY REPORT ON DEAD LANGUAGES HALF-FINISHED!
NOW WAIT JUST A GOSH-DARN PEA-PICKIN' MINUTE!

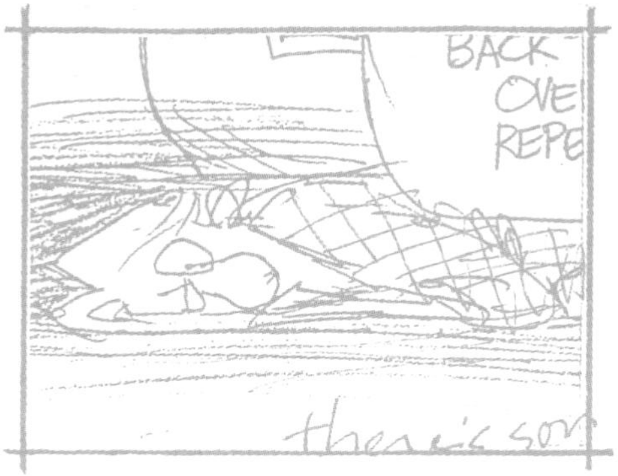
BACK

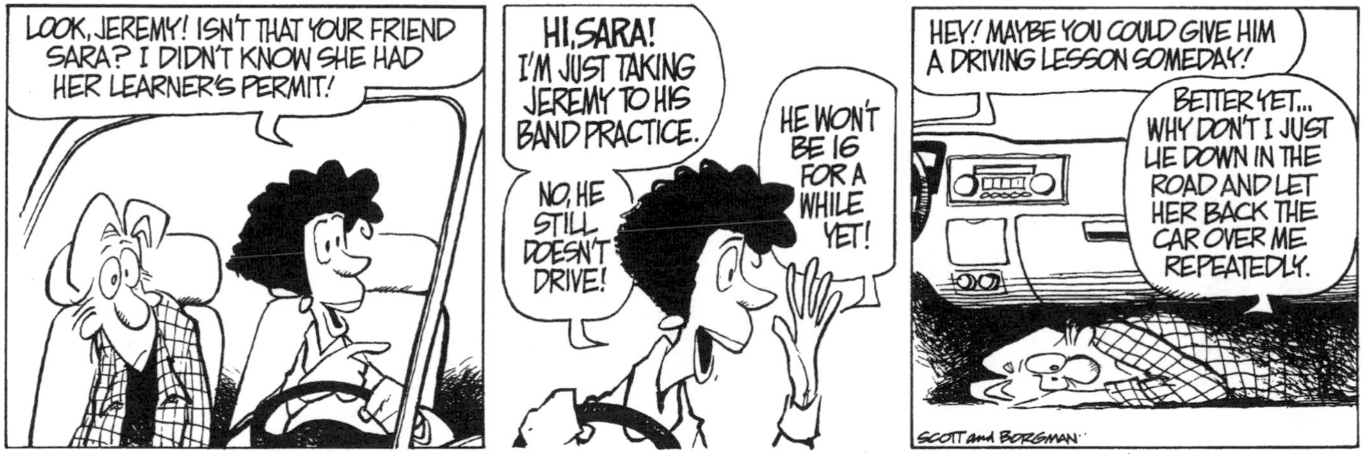
LOOK, JEREMY! ISN'T THAT YOUR FRIEND SARA? I DIDN'T KNOW SHE HAD HER LEARNER'S PERMIT!
HI, SARA! I'M JUST TAKING JEREMY TO HIS BAND PRACTICE.
NO, HE STILL DOESN'T DRIVE!
HE WON'T BE 16 FOR A WHILE YET!
HEY! MAYBE YOU COULD GIVE HIM A DRIVING LESSON SOMEDAY!
BETTER YET... WHY DON'T I JUST LIE DOWN IN THE ROAD AND LET HER BACK THE CAR OVER ME REPEATEDLY.
SCOTT and BORGMAN

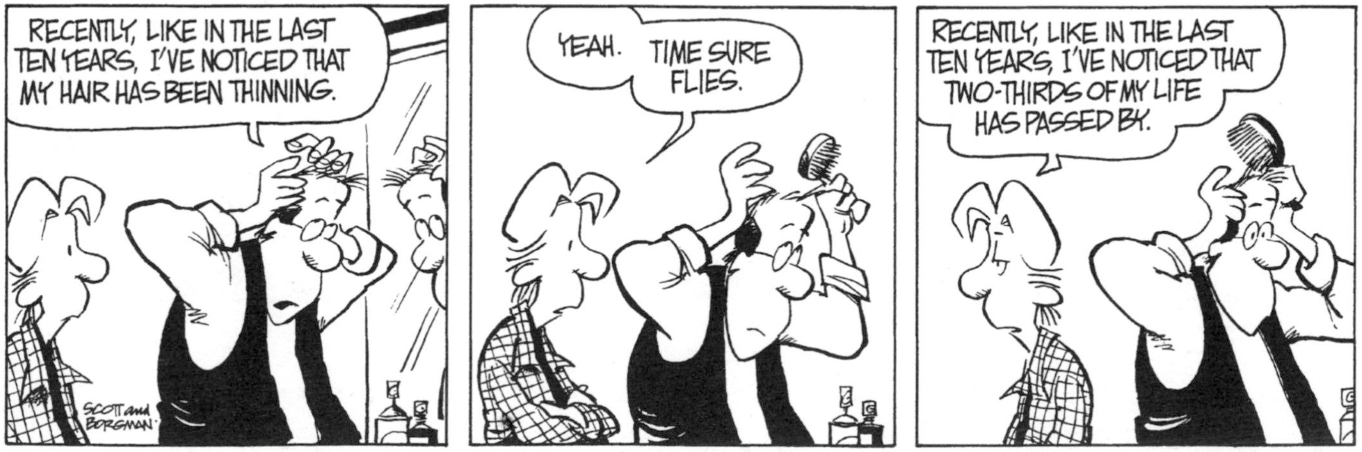
RECENTLY, LIKE IN THE LAST TEN YEARS, I'VE NOTICED THAT MY HAIR HAS BEEN THINNING.
SCOTT and BORGMAN
YEAH.
TIME SURE FLIES.
RECENTLY, LIKE IN THE LAST TEN YEARS, I'VE NOTICED THAT TWO-THIRDS OF MY LIFE HAS PASSED BY.

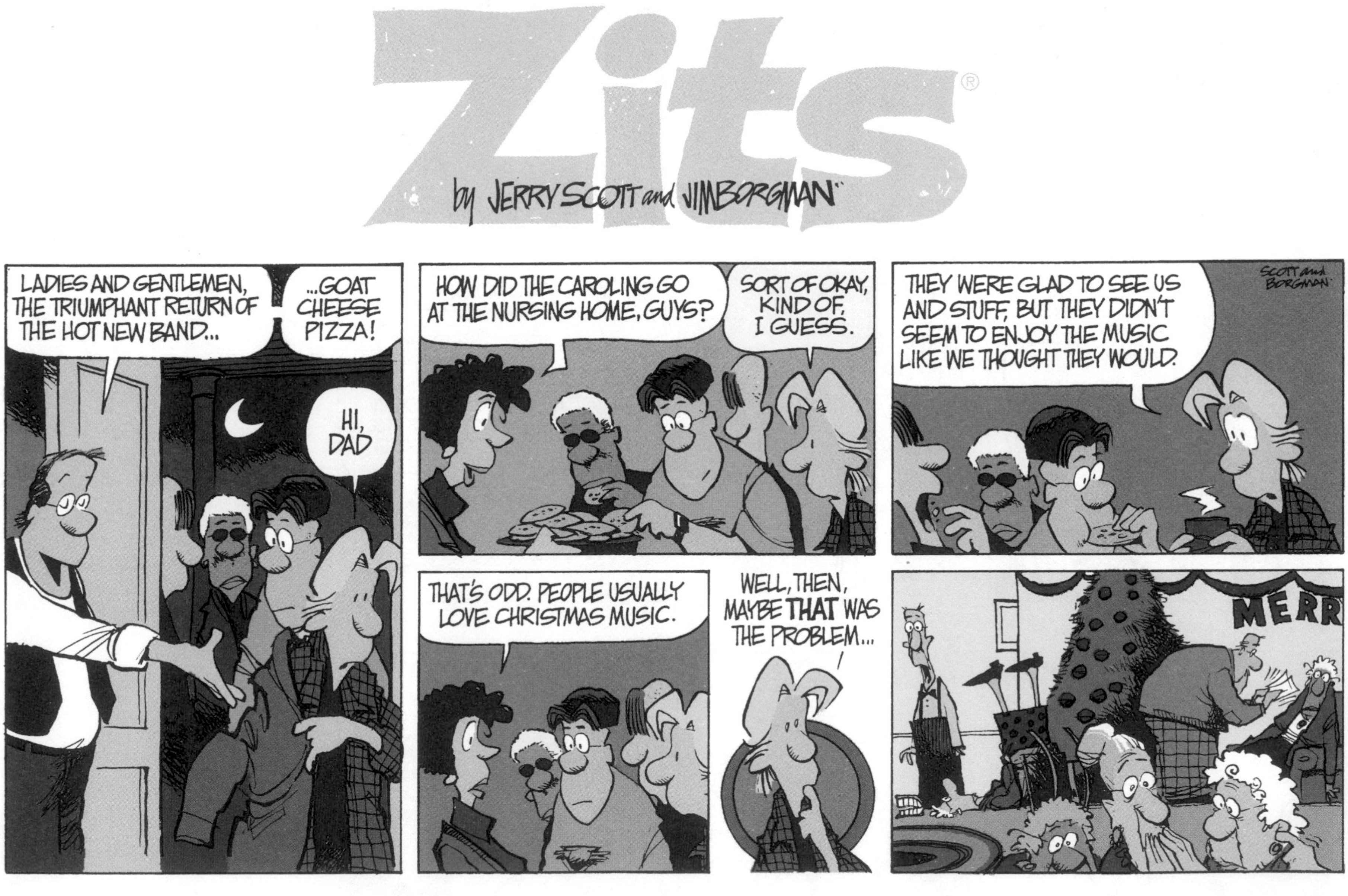
Zits
by JERRY SCOTT and JIM BORGMAN
LADIES AND GENTLEMEN, THE TRIUMPHANT RETURN OF THE HOT NEW BAND...
...GOAT CHEESE PIZZA!
HI, DAD
HOW DID THE CAROLING GO AT THE NURSING HOME, GUYS?
SORT OF OKAY, KIND OF, I GUESS.
THEY WERE GLAD TO SEE US AND STUFF, BUT THEY DIDN'T SEEM TO ENJOY THE MUSIC LIKE WE THOUGHT THEY WOULD.
SCOTT and BORGMAN
THAT'S ODD. PEOPLE USUALLY LOVE CHRISTMAS MUSIC.
WELL, THEN, MAYBE THAT WAS THE PROBLEM...
MERR

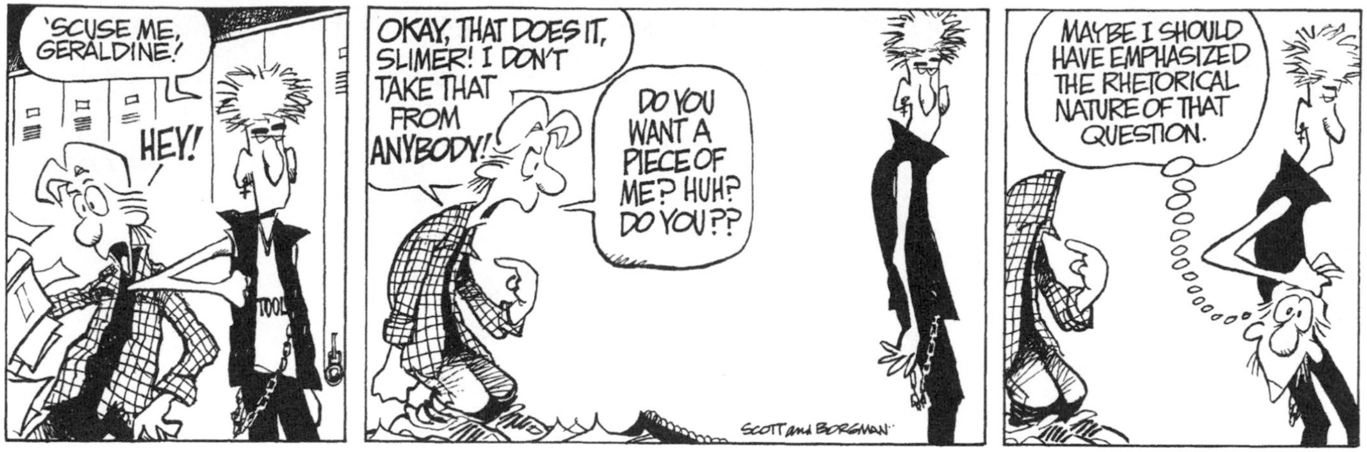
'SCUSE ME, GERALDINE!
HEY!
TOOL
OKAY, THAT DOES IT, SLIMER! I DON'T TAKE THAT FROM ANYBODY!
DO YOU WANT A PIECE OF ME? HUH? DO YOU??
SCOTT and BORGMAN
MAYBE I SHOULD HAVE EMPHASIZED THE RHETORICAL NATURE OF THAT QUESTION.

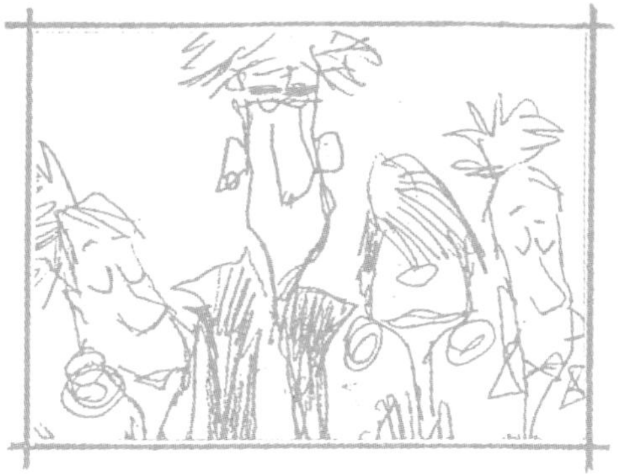

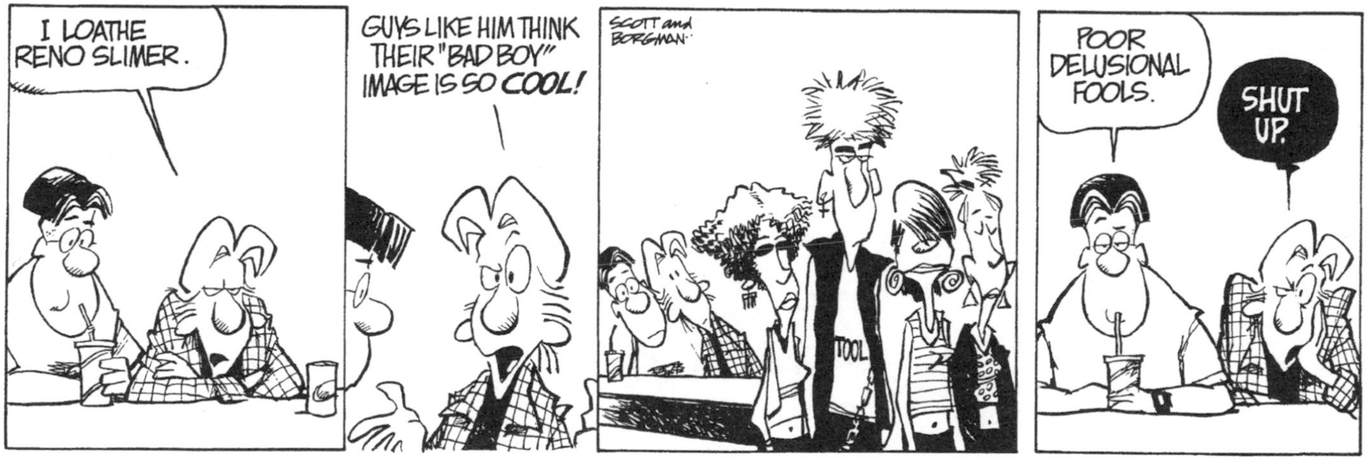
I LOATHE RENO SLIMER.
GUYS LIKE HIM THINK THEIR "BAD BOY" IMAGE IS SO COOL!
SCOTT and BORGMAN
TOOL
POOR DELUSIONAL FOOLS.
SHUT UP.

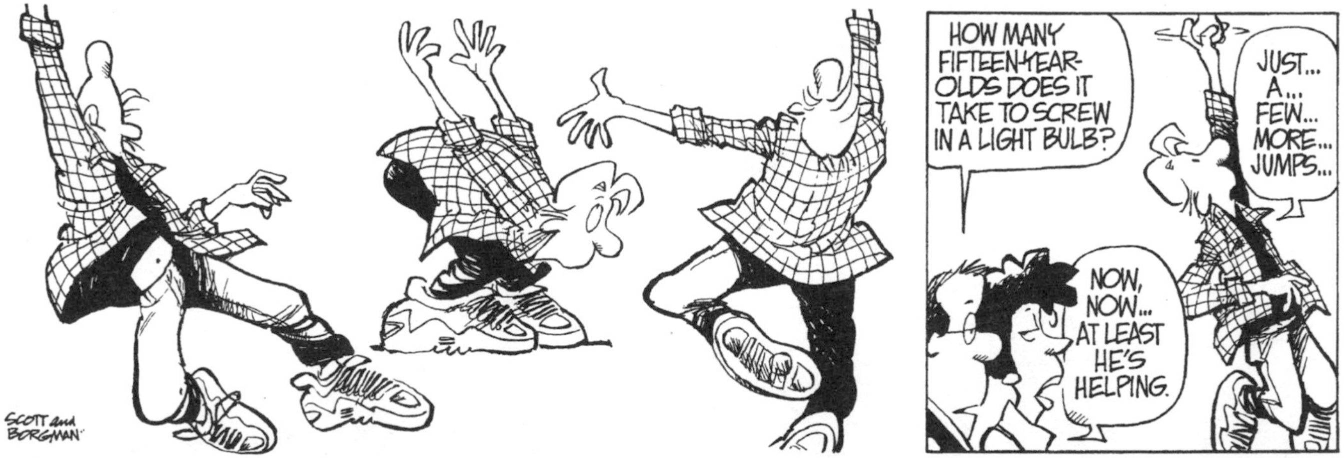
SCOTT and BORGMAN
HOW MANY FIFTEEN-YEAR-OLDS DOES IT TAKE TO SCREW IN A LIGHT BULB?
JUST... A... FEW... MORE... JUMPS...
NOW, NOW... AT LEAST HE'S HELPING.

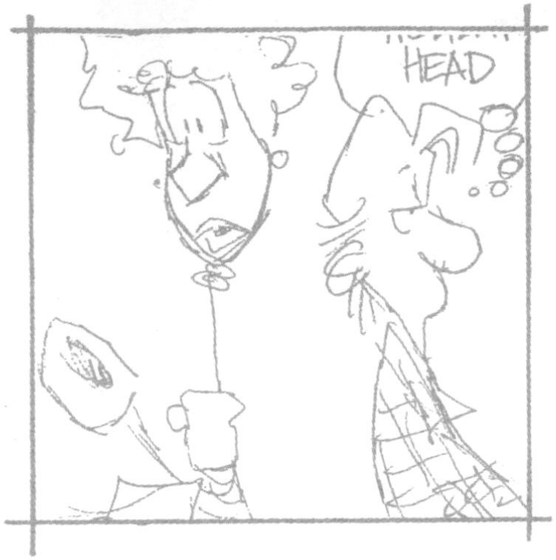
HEAD

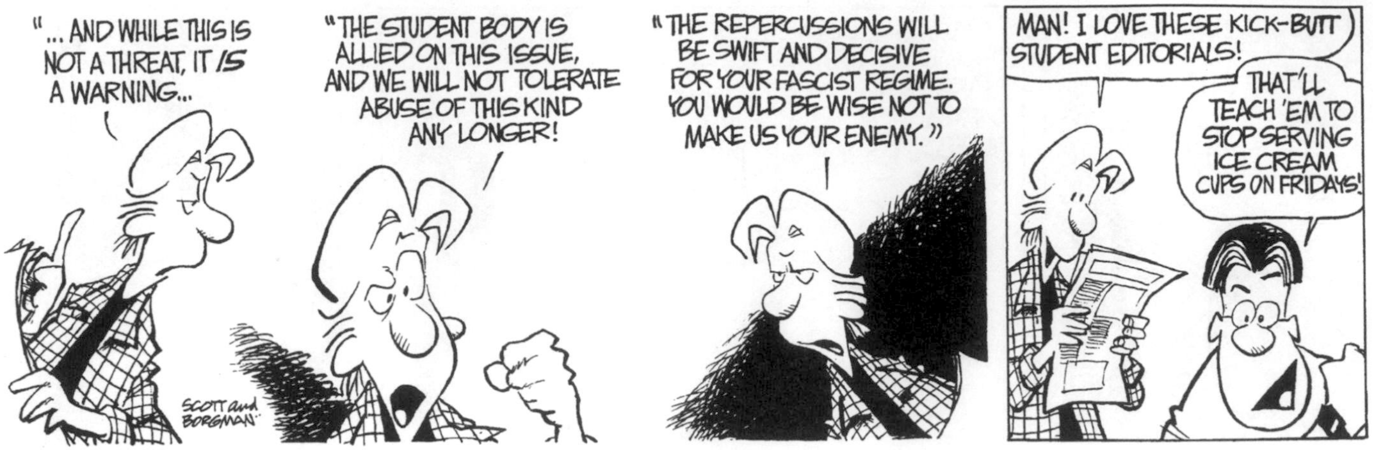
"... AND WHILE THIS IS NOT A THREAT, IT *IS* A WARNING...
"THE STUDENT BODY IS ALLIED ON THIS ISSUE, AND WE WILL NOT TOLERATE ABUSE OF THIS KIND ANY LONGER!
"THE REPERCUSSIONS WILL BE SWIFT AND DECISIVE FOR YOUR FASCIST REGIME. YOU WOULD BE WISE NOT TO MAKE US YOUR ENEMY."
MAN! I LOVE THESE KICK-BUTT STUDENT EDITORIALS!
THAT'LL TEACH 'EM TO STOP SERVING ICE CREAM CUPS ON FRIDAYS!
SCOTT and BORGMAN

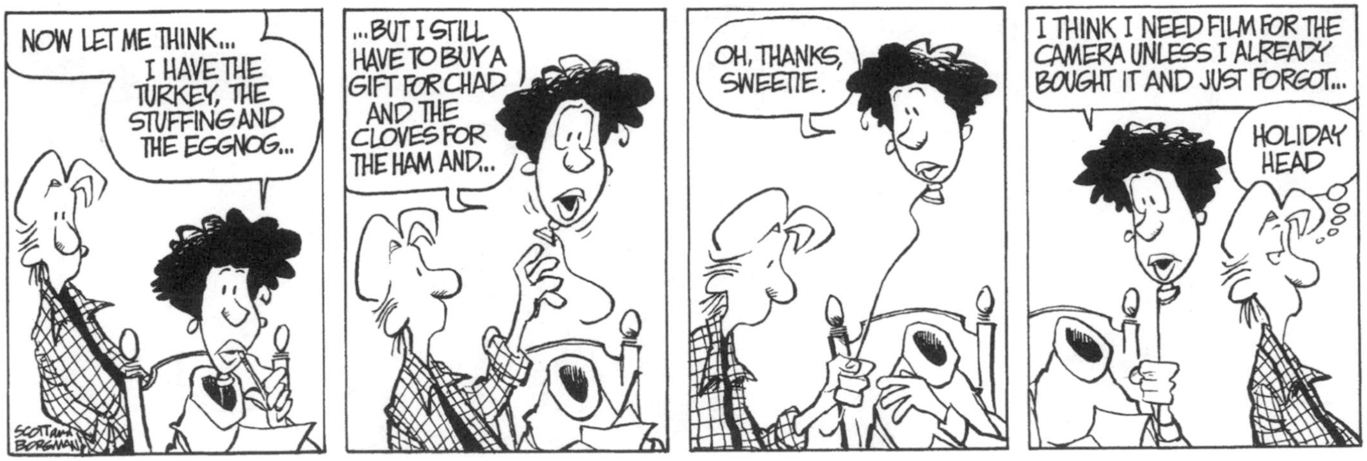
NOW LET ME THINK... I HAVE THE TURKEY, THE STUFFING AND THE EGGNOG...
...BUT I STILL HAVE TO BUY A GIFT FOR CHAD AND THE CLOVES FOR THE HAM AND...
OH, THANKS, SWEETIE.
I THINK I NEED FILM FOR THE CAMERA UNLESS I ALREADY BOUGHT IT AND JUST FORGOT...
HOLIDAY HEAD
SCOTT and BORGMAN

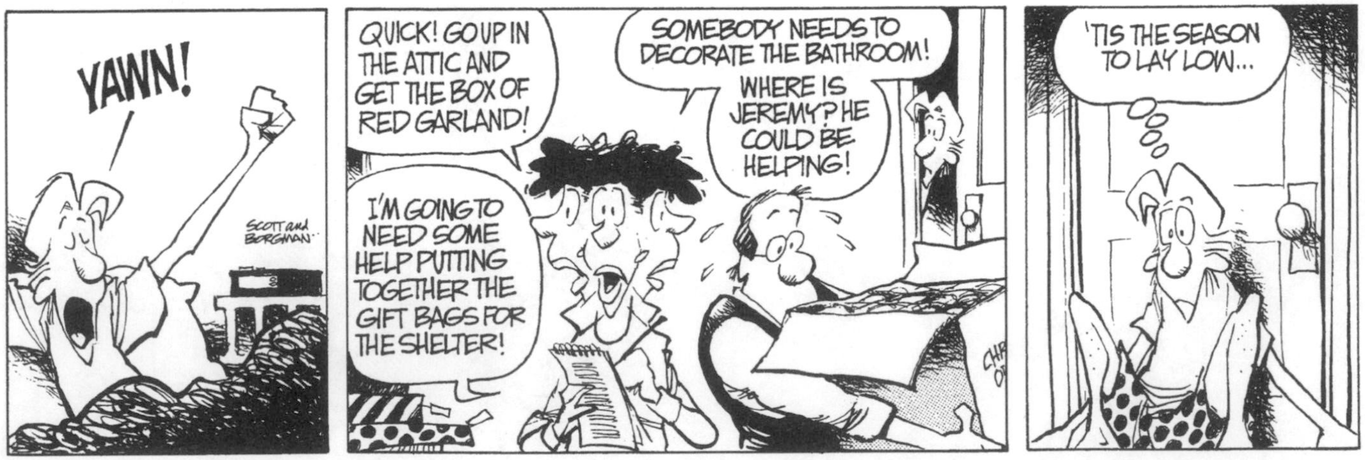
YAWN!
SCOTT and BORGMAN
QUICK! GO UP IN THE ATTIC AND GET THE BOX OF RED GARLAND!
I'M GOING TO NEED SOME HELP PUTTING TOGETHER THE GIFT BAGS FOR THE SHELTER!
SOMEBODY NEEDS TO DECORATE THE BATHROOM!
WHERE IS JEREMY? HE COULD BE HELPING!
'TIS THE SEASON TO LAY LOW...

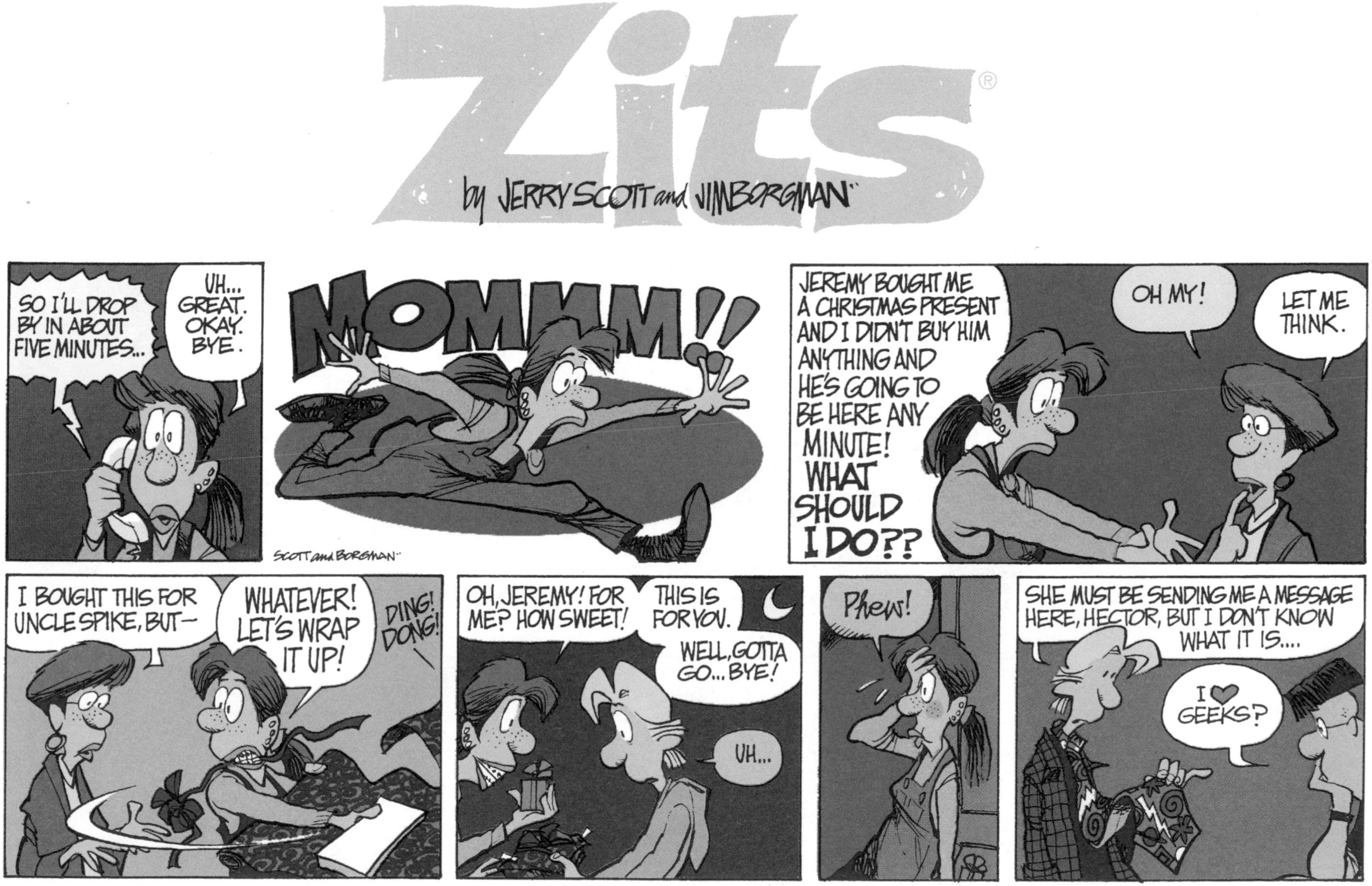
Zits
by JERRY SCOTT and JIM BORGMAN
SO I'LL DROP BY IN ABOUT FIVE MINUTES...
UH... GREAT. OKAY. BYE.
MOMMM!!
SCOTT and BORGMAN
JEREMY BOUGHT ME A CHRISTMAS PRESENT AND I DIDN'T BUY HIM ANYTHING AND HE'S GOING TO BE HERE ANY MINUTE! WHAT SHOULD I DO??
OH MY!
LET ME THINK.
I BOUGHT THIS FOR UNCLE SPIKE, BUT—
WHATEVER! LET'S WRAP IT UP!
DING! DONG!
OH, JEREMY! FOR ME? HOW SWEET!
THIS IS FOR YOU.
WELL, GOTTA GO... BYE!
UH...
Phew!
SHE MUST BE SENDING ME A MESSAGE HERE, HECTOR, BUT I DON'T KNOW WHAT IT IS....
I ♥ GEEKS?

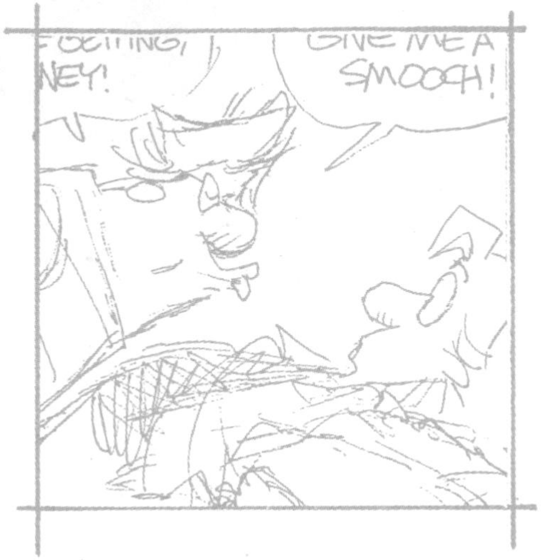
GIVE ME A SMOOCH!

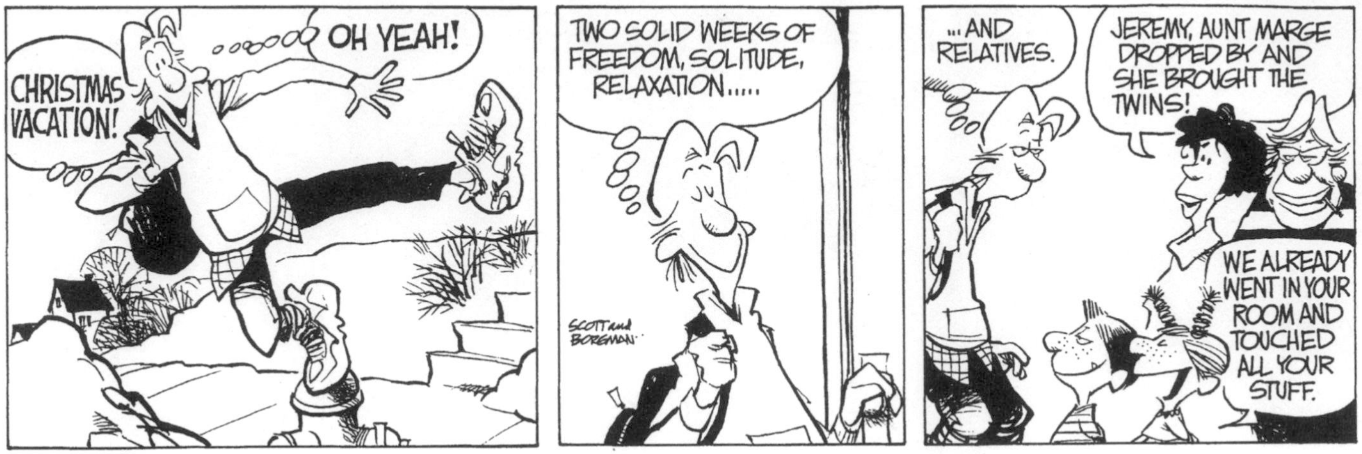
CHRISTMAS VACATION!
OH YEAH!
TWO SOLID WEEKS OF FREEDOM, SOLITUDE, RELAXATION.....
SCOTT and BORGMAN
...AND RELATIVES.
JEREMY, AUNT MARGE DROPPED BY AND SHE BROUGHT THE TWINS!
WE ALREADY WENT IN YOUR ROOM AND TOUCHED ALL YOUR STUFF.

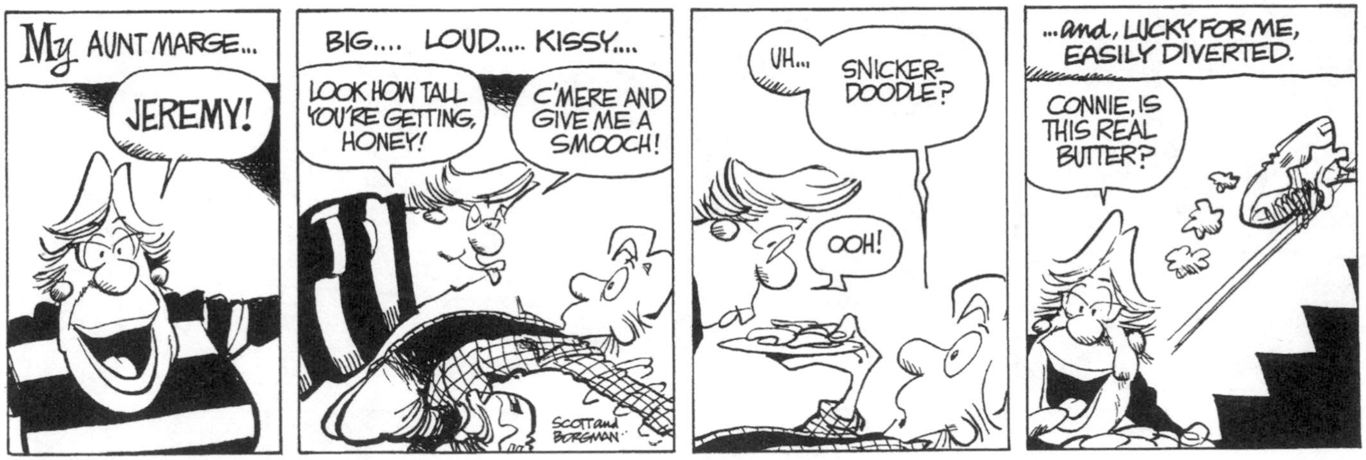
My AUNT MARGE...
JEREMY!
BIG.... LOUD..... KISSY....
LOOK HOW TALL YOU'RE GETTING, HONEY!
C'MERE AND GIVE ME A SMOOCH!
SCOTT and BORGMAN
UH...
SNICKER-DOODLE?
OOH!
...and, LUCKY FOR ME, EASILY DIVERTED.
CONNIE, IS THIS REAL BUTTER?

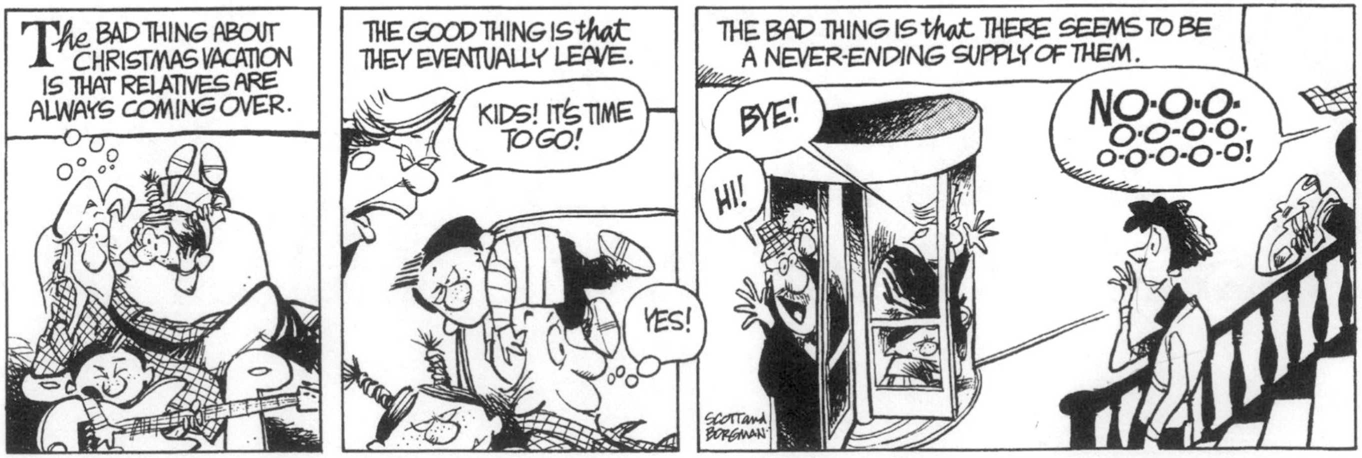
The BAD THING ABOUT CHRISTMAS VACATION IS THAT RELATIVES ARE ALWAYS COMING OVER.
THE GOOD THING IS that THEY EVENTUALLY LEAVE.
KIDS! IT'S TIME TO GO!
YES!
THE BAD THING IS that THERE SEEMS TO BE A NEVER-ENDING SUPPLY OF THEM.
BYE!
HI!
NO·O·O· O·O·O·O·O· O·O·O·O·O·O!
SCOTT and BORGMAN

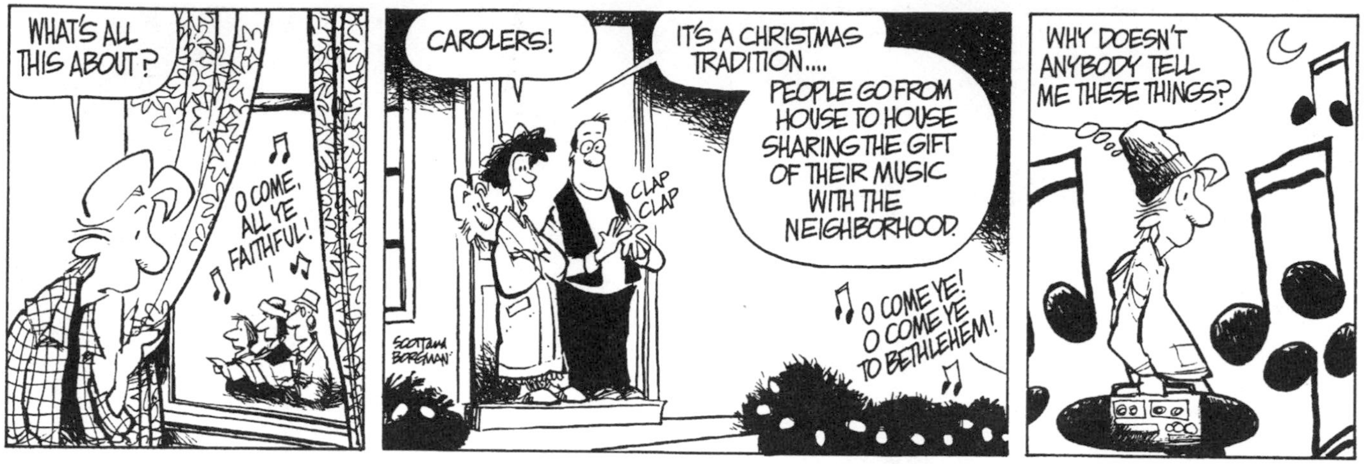
WHAT'S ALL THIS ABOUT?
O COME, ALL YE FAITHFUL!
CAROLERS!
IT'S A CHRISTMAS TRADITION....
PEOPLE GO FROM HOUSE TO HOUSE SHARING THE GIFT OF THEIR MUSIC WITH THE NEIGHBORHOOD.
CLAP CLAP
O COME YE! O COME YE TO BETHLEHEM!
SCOTT AND BORGMAN
WHY DOESN'T ANYBODY TELL ME THESE THINGS?

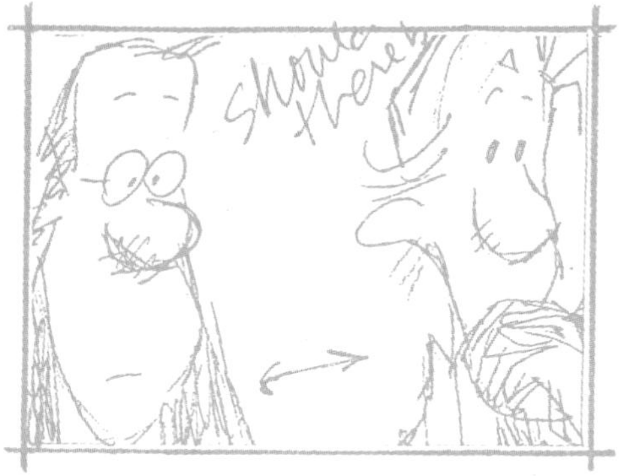

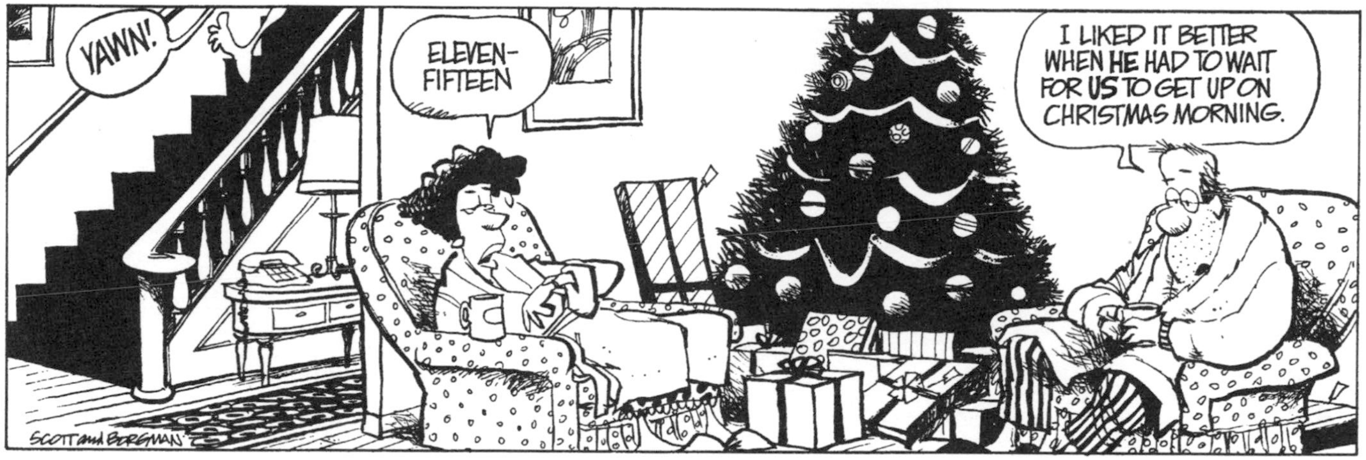
YAWN!
ELEVEN-FIFTEEN
I LIKED IT BETTER WHEN HE HAD TO WAIT FOR US TO GET UP ON CHRISTMAS MORNING.
SCOTT AND BORGMAN

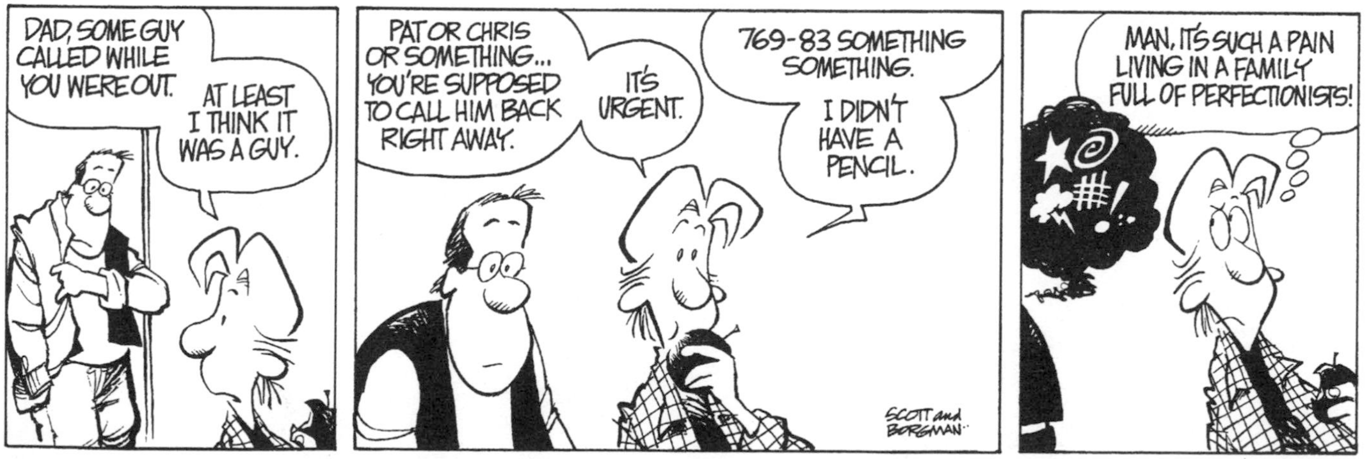
DAD, SOME GUY CALLED WHILE YOU WERE OUT.
AT LEAST I THINK IT WAS A GUY.
PAT OR CHRIS OR SOMETHING... YOU'RE SUPPOSED TO CALL HIM BACK RIGHT AWAY.
IT'S URGENT.
769-83 SOMETHING SOMETHING.
I DIDN'T HAVE A PENCIL.
SCOTT AND BORGMAN
MAN, IT'S SUCH A PAIN LIVING IN A FAMILY FULL OF PERFECTIONISTS!

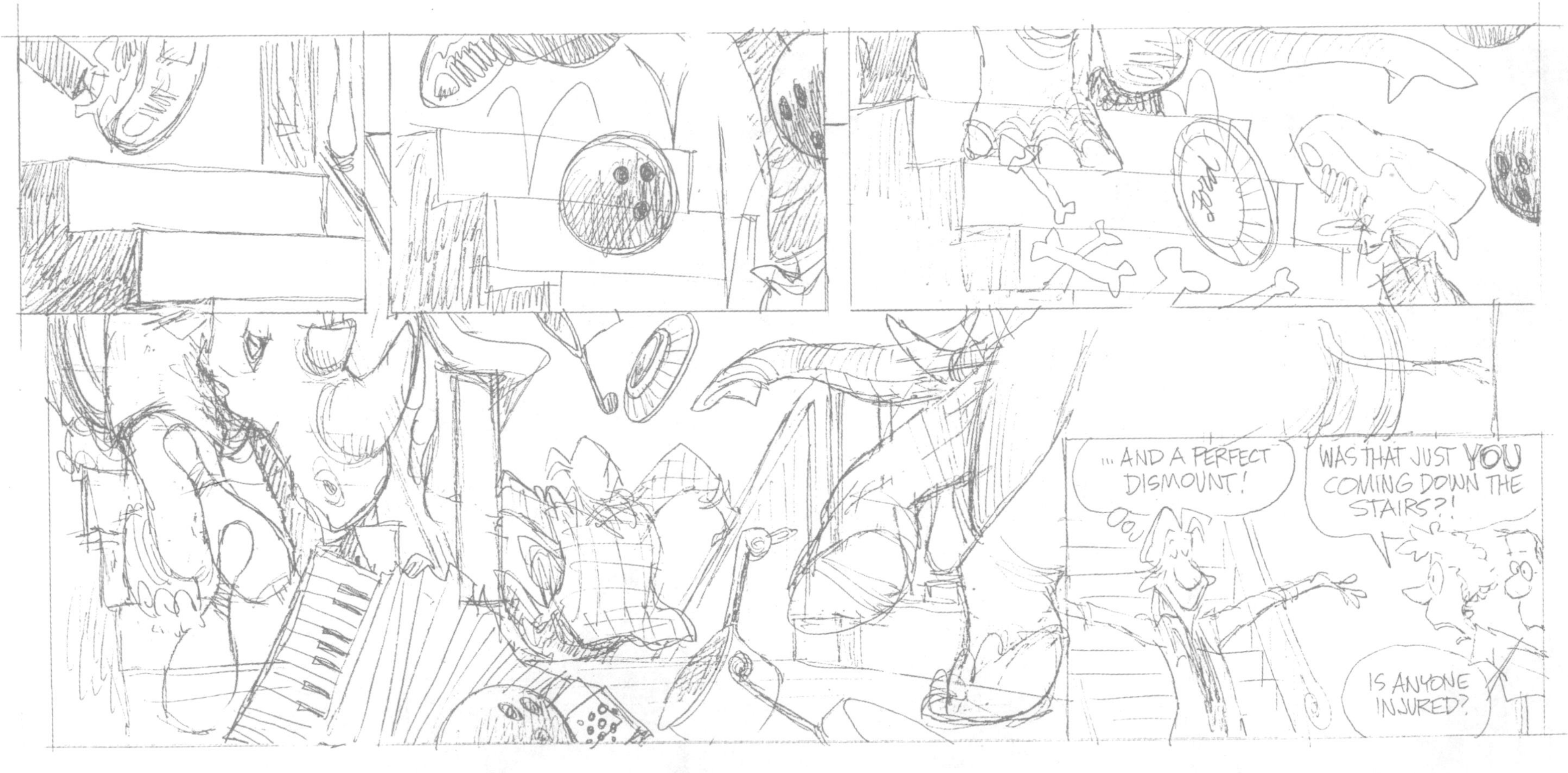
...AND A PERFECT DISMOUNT!
WAS THAT JUST YOU COMING DOWN THE STAIRS?!
IS ANYONE INJURED?

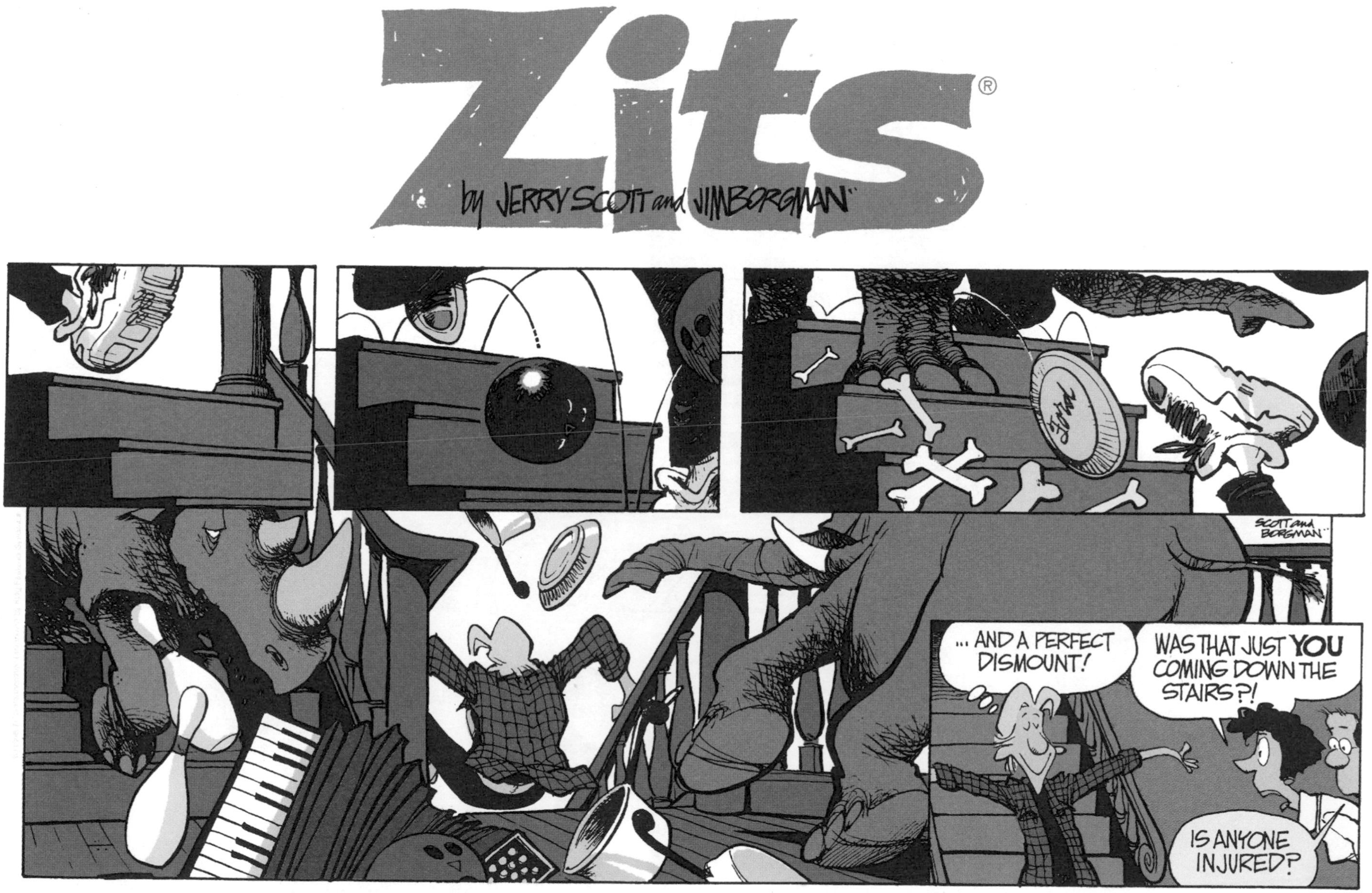
Zits®
by JERRY SCOTT and JIM BORGMAN
SCOTT and BORGMAN
... AND A PERFECT DISMOUNT!
WAS THAT JUST **YOU** COMING DOWN THE STAIRS?!
IS ANYONE INJURED?

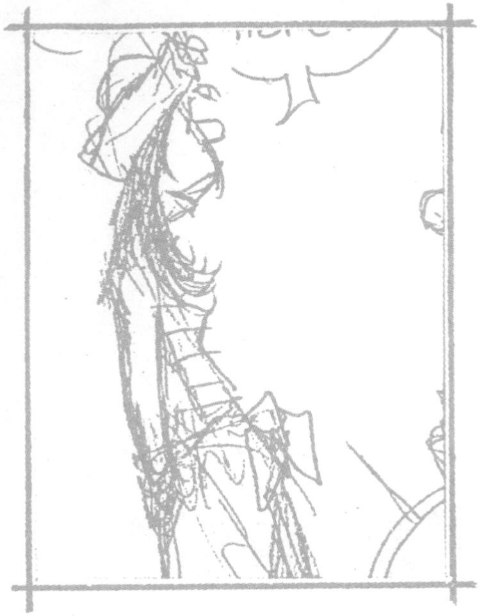

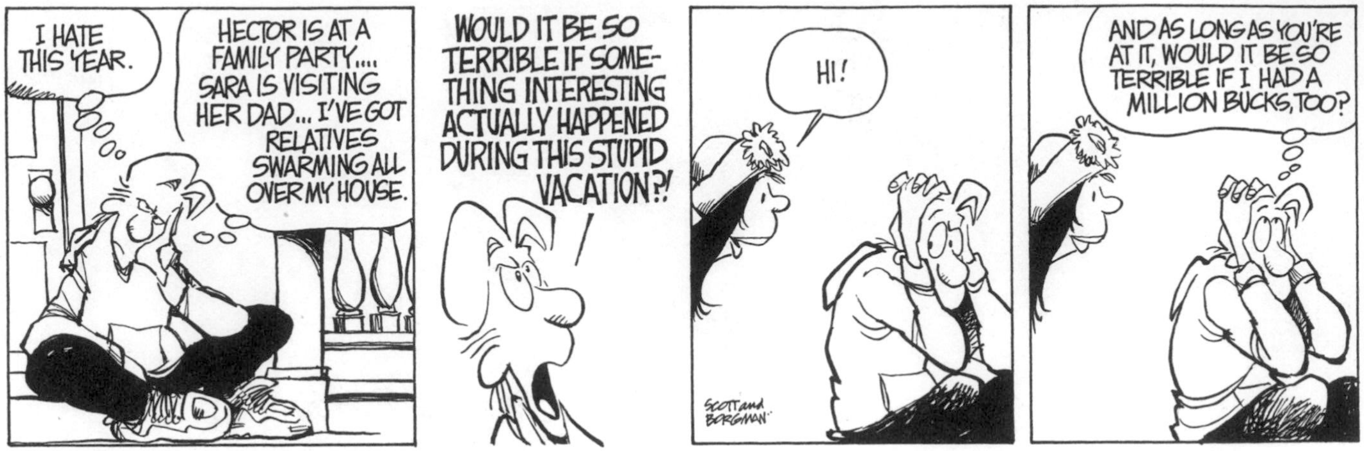
I HATE THIS YEAR.
HECTOR IS AT A FAMILY PARTY.... SARA IS VISITING HER DAD... I'VE GOT RELATIVES SWARMING ALL OVER MY HOUSE.
WOULD IT BE SO TERRIBLE IF SOMETHING INTERESTING ACTUALLY HAPPENED DURING THIS STUPID VACATION?!
HI!
SCOTT and BORGMAN
AND AS LONG AS YOU'RE AT IT, WOULD IT BE SO TERRIBLE IF I HAD A MILLION BUCKS, TOO?

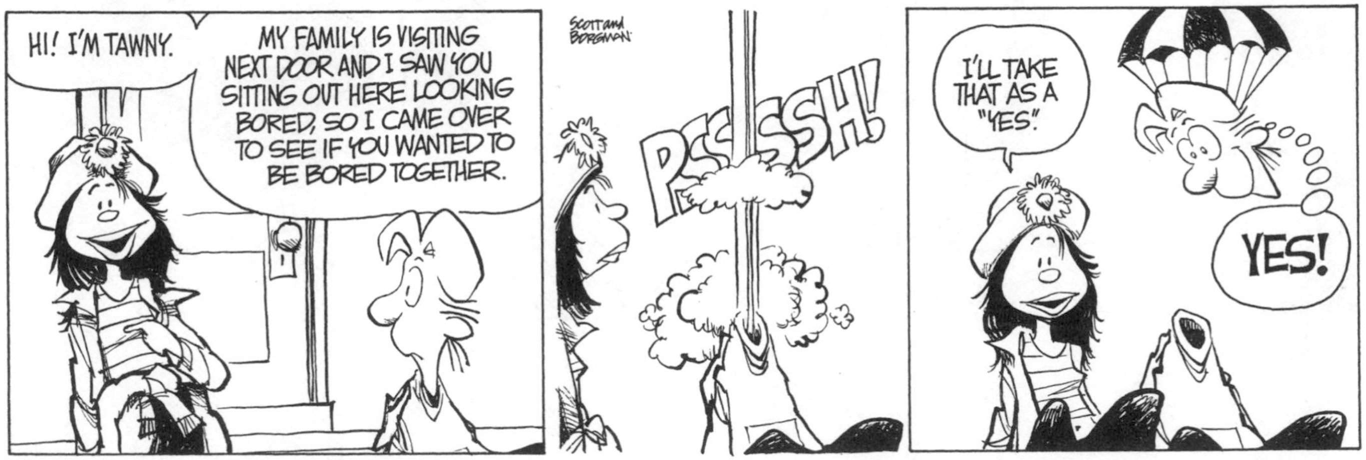
HI! I'M TAWNY.
MY FAMILY IS VISITING NEXT DOOR AND I SAW YOU SITTING OUT HERE LOOKING BORED, SO I CAME OVER TO SEE IF YOU WANTED TO BE BORED TOGETHER.
SCOTT and BORGMAN
PSSSSSH!
I'LL TAKE THAT AS A "YES."
YES!

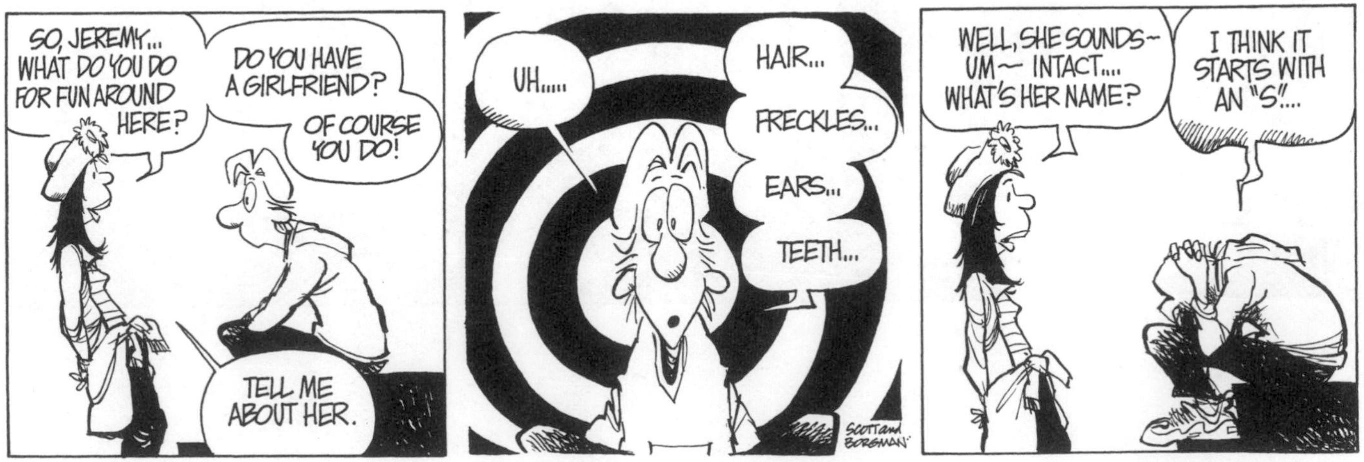
SO, JEREMY... WHAT DO YOU DO FOR FUN AROUND HERE?
DO YOU HAVE A GIRLFRIEND?
OF COURSE YOU DO!
TELL ME ABOUT HER.
UH.....
HAIR...
FRECKLES...
EARS...
TEETH...
SCOTT and BORGMAN
WELL, SHE SOUNDS~ UM~ INTACT.... WHAT'S HER NAME?
I THINK IT STARTS WITH AN "S"...

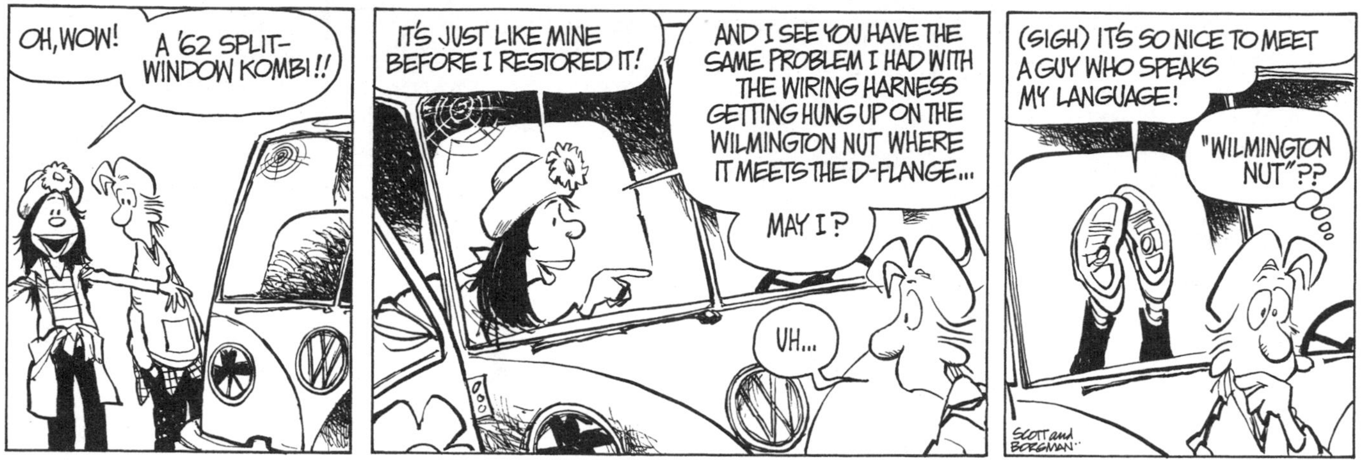
OH, WOW!
A '62 SPLIT-WINDOW KOMBI!!
IT'S JUST LIKE MINE BEFORE I RESTORED IT!
AND I SEE YOU HAVE THE SAME PROBLEM I HAD WITH THE WIRING HARNESS GETTING HUNG UP ON THE WILMINGTON NUT WHERE IT MEETS THE D-FLANGE...
MAY I?
UH...
(SIGH) IT'S SO NICE TO MEET A GUY WHO SPEAKS MY LANGUAGE!
"WILMINGTON NUT"??
SCOTT and BORGMAN

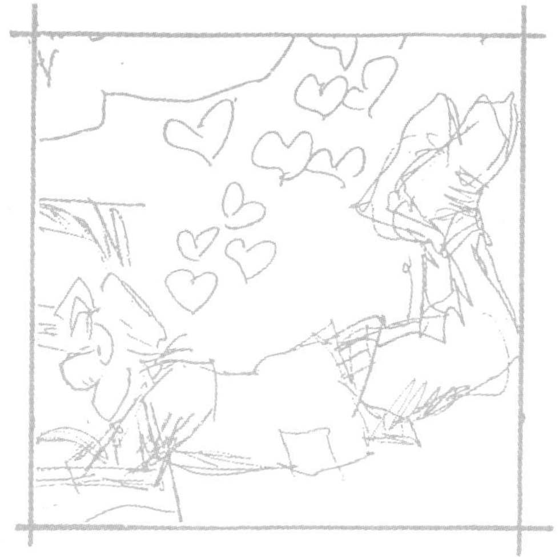

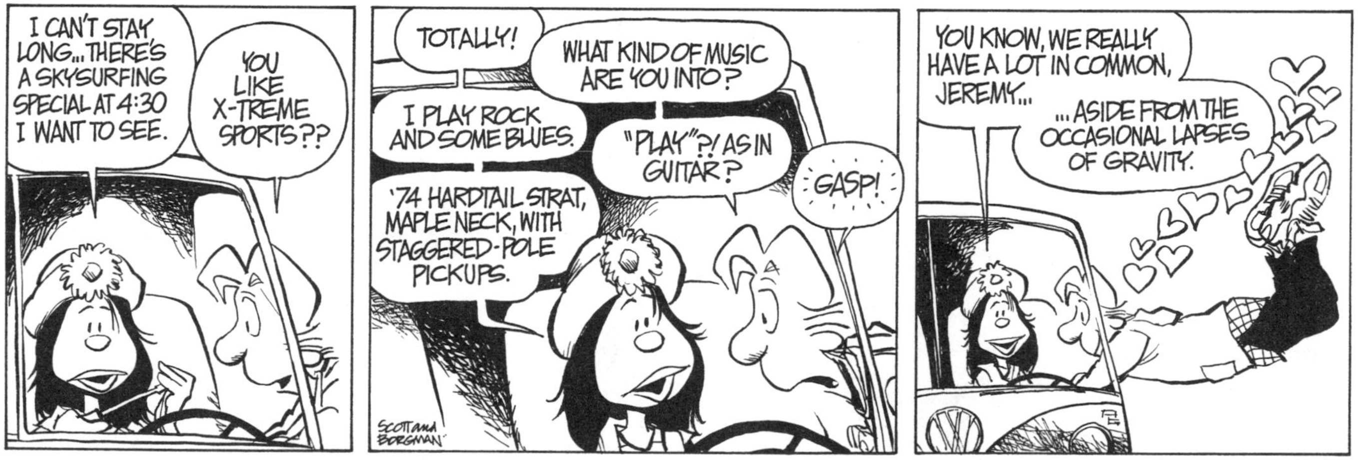
I CAN'T STAY LONG... THERE'S A SKYSURFING SPECIAL AT 4:30 I WANT TO SEE.
YOU LIKE X-TREME SPORTS??
TOTALLY!
WHAT KIND OF MUSIC ARE YOU INTO?
I PLAY ROCK AND SOME BLUES.
"PLAY"?! AS IN GUITAR?
GASP!
'74 HARDTAIL STRAT, MAPLE NECK, WITH STAGGERED-POLE PICKUPS.
SCOTT and BORGMAN
YOU KNOW, WE REALLY HAVE A LOT IN COMMON, JEREMY...
...ASIDE FROM THE OCCASIONAL LAPSES OF GRAVITY.

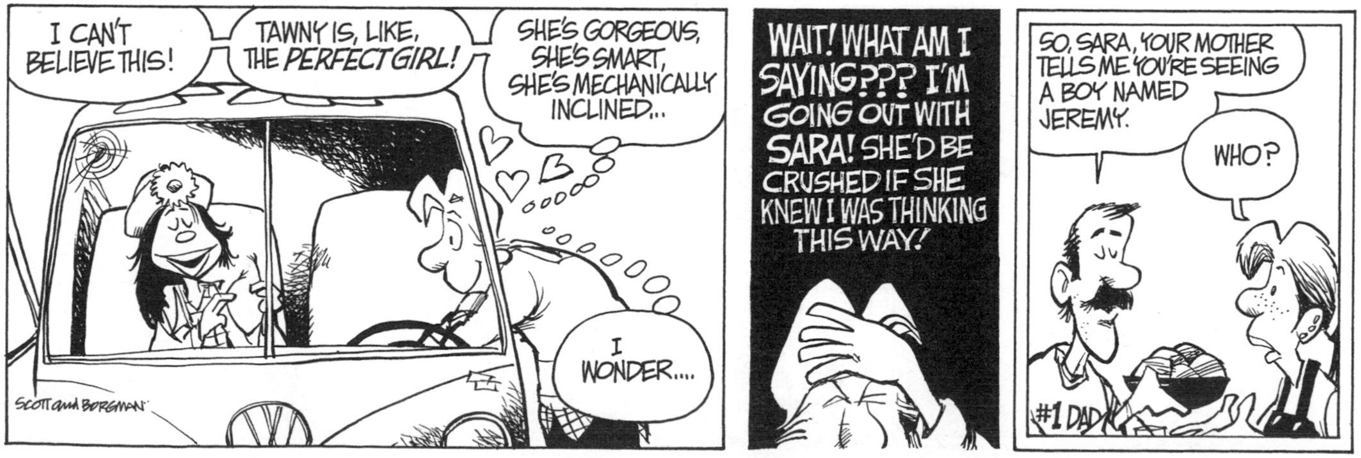
I CAN'T BELIEVE THIS!
TAWNY IS, LIKE, THE *PERFECT GIRL!*
SHE'S GORGEOUS, SHE'S SMART, SHE'S MECHANICALLY INCLINED...
I WONDER....
SCOTT and BORGMAN
WAIT! WHAT AM I SAYING??? I'M GOING OUT WITH SARA! SHE'D BE CRUSHED IF SHE KNEW I WAS THINKING THIS WAY!
SO, SARA, YOUR MOTHER TELLS ME YOU'RE SEEING A BOY NAMED JEREMY.
WHO?
#1 DAD

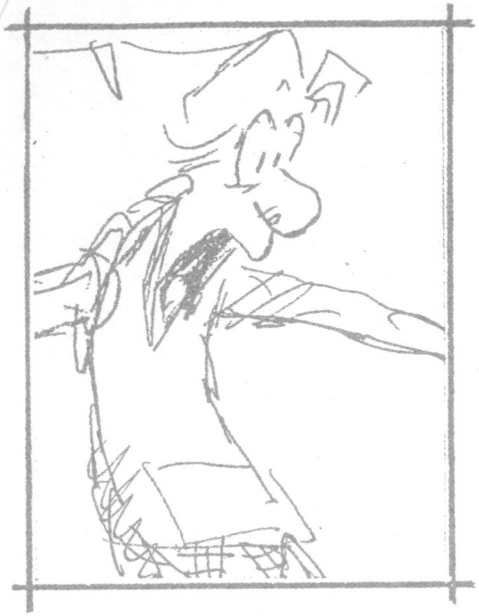

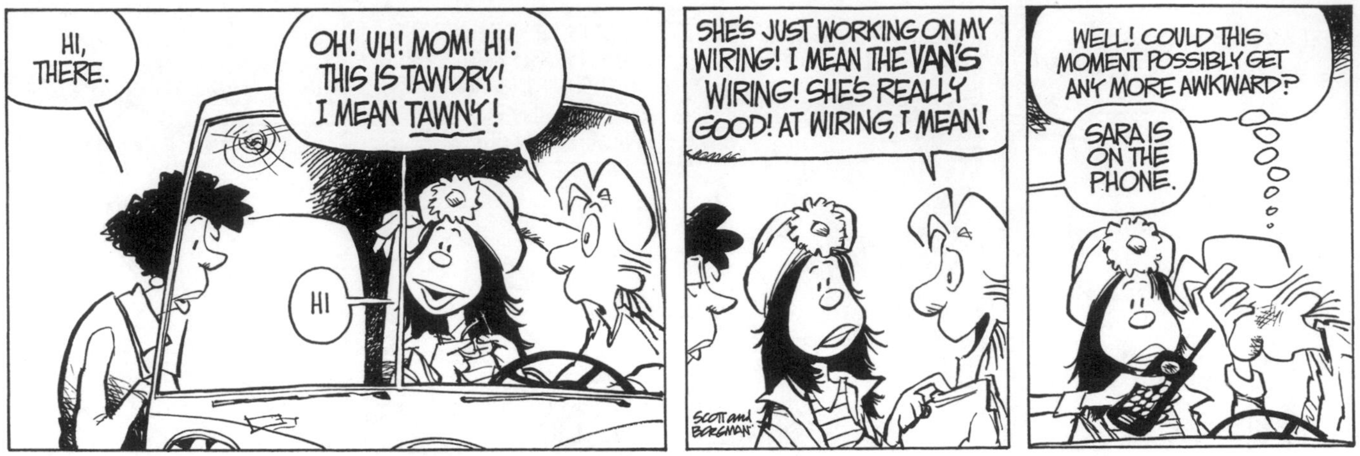

HI, THERE.
OH! UH! MOM! HI! THIS IS TAWDRY! I MEAN TAWNY!
HI
SHE'S JUST WORKING ON MY WIRING! I MEAN THE VAN'S WIRING! SHE'S REALLY GOOD! AT WIRING, I MEAN!
SCOTT and BORGMAN
WELL! COULD THIS MOMENT POSSIBLY GET ANY MORE AWKWARD?
SARA IS ON THE PHONE.

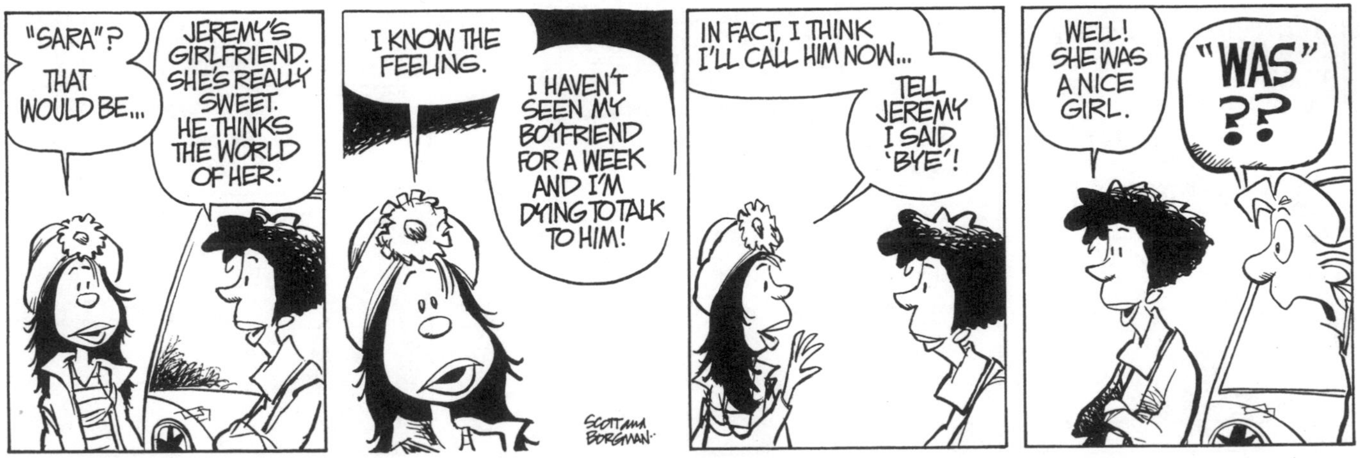

"SARA"? THAT WOULD BE...
JEREMY'S GIRLFRIEND. SHE'S REALLY SWEET. HE THINKS THE WORLD OF HER.
I KNOW THE FEELING.
I HAVEN'T SEEN MY BOYFRIEND FOR A WEEK AND I'M DYING TO TALK TO HIM!
SCOTT and BORGMAN
IN FACT, I THINK I'LL CALL HIM NOW...
TELL JEREMY I SAID 'BYE'!
WELL! SHE WAS A NICE GIRL.
"WAS" ??

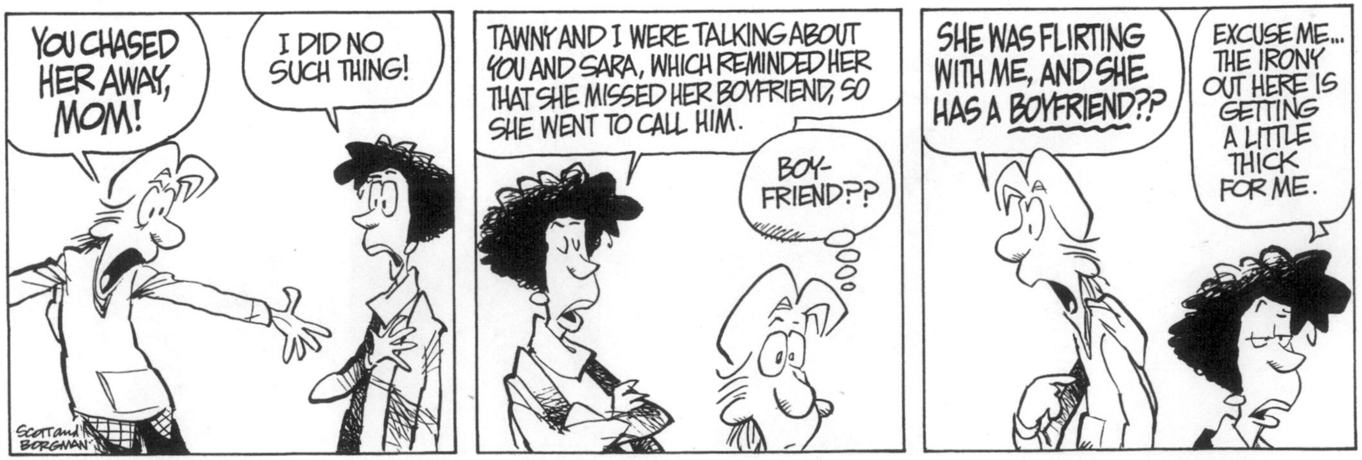

YOU CHASED HER AWAY, MOM!
I DID NO SUCH THING!
SCOTT and BORGMAN
TAWNY AND I WERE TALKING ABOUT YOU AND SARA, WHICH REMINDED HER THAT SHE MISSED HER BOYFRIEND, SO SHE WENT TO CALL HIM.
BOY-FRIEND??
SHE WAS FLIRTING WITH ME, AND SHE HAS A BOYFRIEND??
EXCUSE ME... THE IRONY OUT HERE IS GETTING A LITTLE THICK FOR ME.

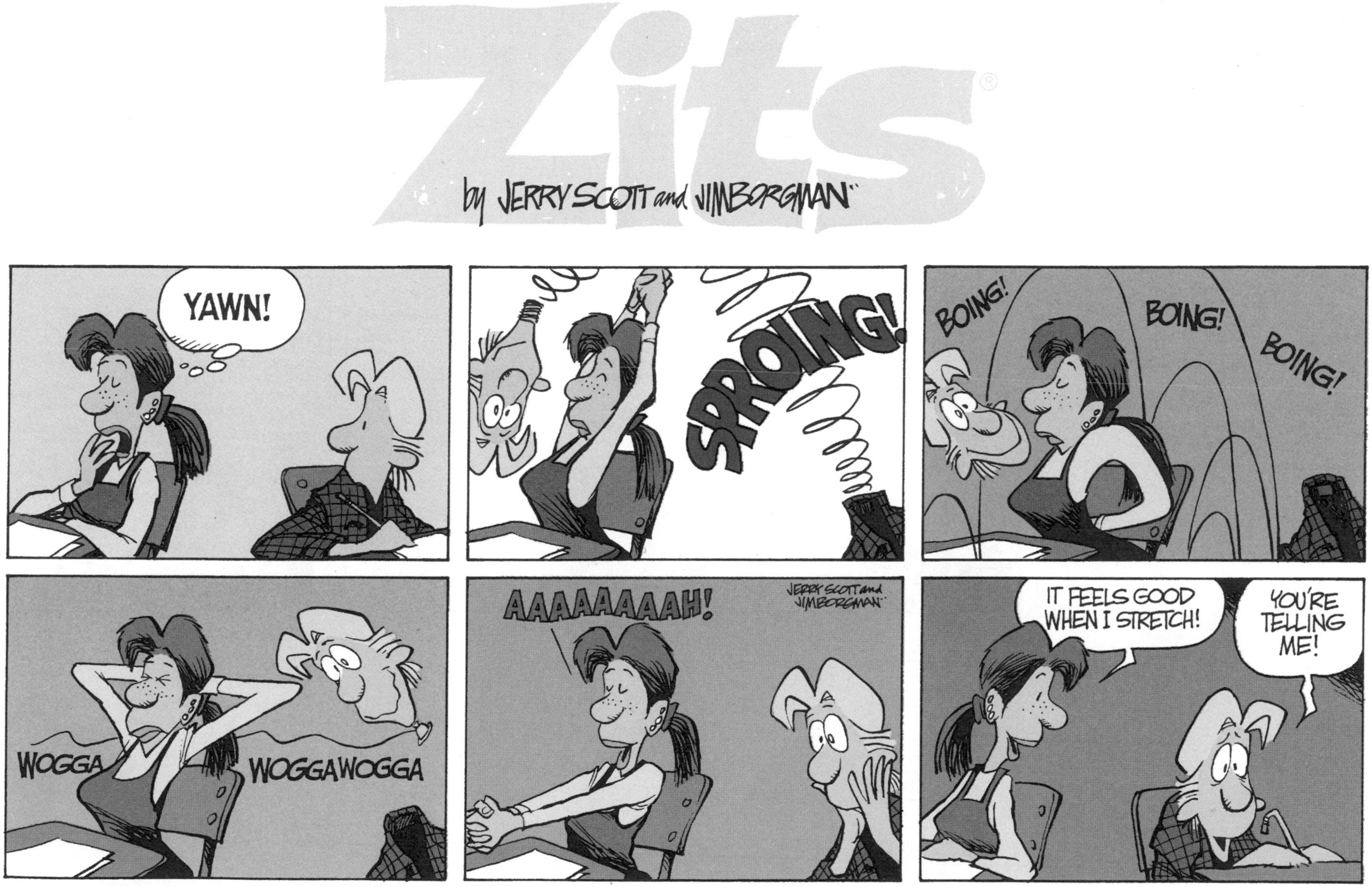
Zits®
by JERRY SCOTT and JIM BORGMAN
YAWN!
SPROING!
BOING!
BOING!
BOING!
WOGGA
WOGGAWOGGA
AAAAAAAAH!
JERRY SCOTT and JIM BORGMAN
IT FEELS GOOD WHEN I STRETCH!
YOU'RE TELLING ME!

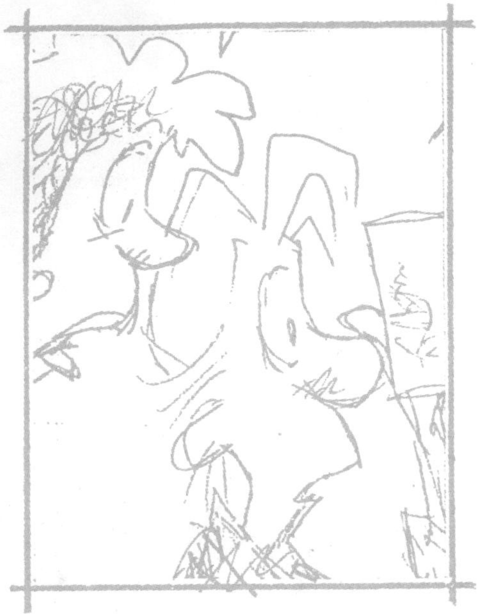

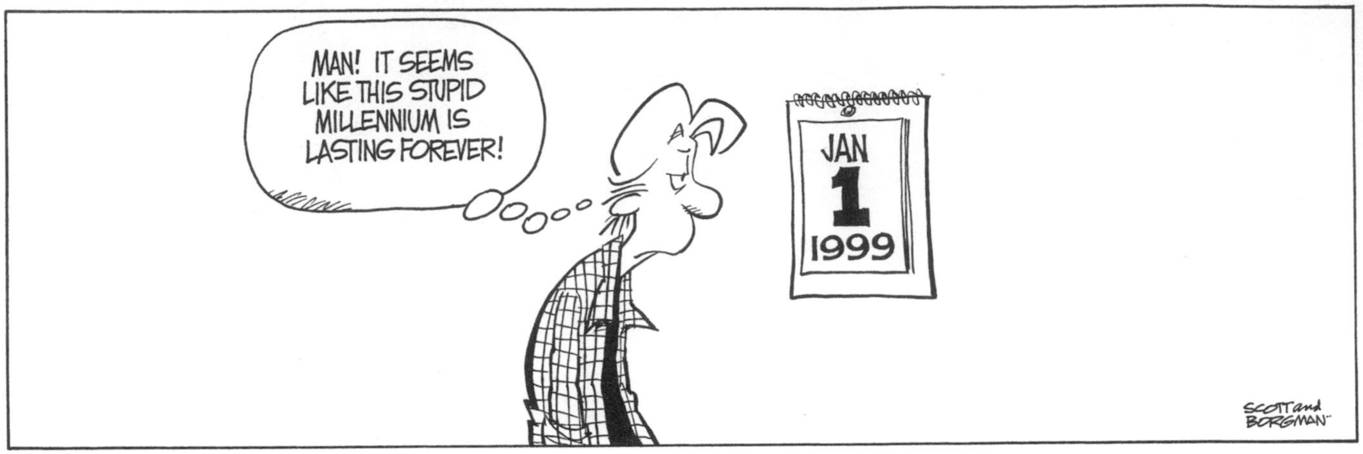

MAN! IT SEEMS LIKE THIS STUPID MILLENNIUM IS LASTING FOREVER!
JAN 1 1999
SCOTT and BORGMAN

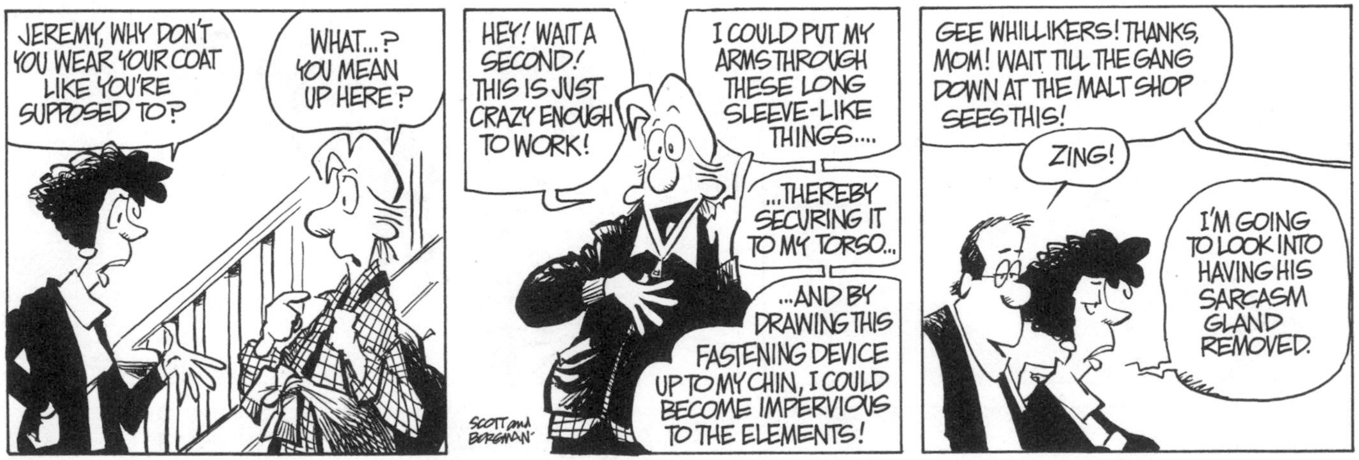

JEREMY, WHY DON'T YOU WEAR YOUR COAT LIKE YOU'RE SUPPOSED TO?
WHAT...? YOU MEAN UP HERE?
HEY! WAIT A SECOND! THIS IS JUST CRAZY ENOUGH TO WORK!
I COULD PUT MY ARMS THROUGH THESE LONG SLEEVE-LIKE THINGS....
...THEREBY SECURING IT TO MY TORSO...
...AND BY DRAWING THIS FASTENING DEVICE UP TO MY CHIN, I COULD BECOME IMPERVIOUS TO THE ELEMENTS!
SCOTT and BORGMAN
GEE WHILLIKERS! THANKS, MOM! WAIT TILL THE GANG DOWN AT THE MALT SHOP SEES THIS!
ZING!
I'M GOING TO LOOK INTO HAVING HIS SARCASM GLAND REMOVED.

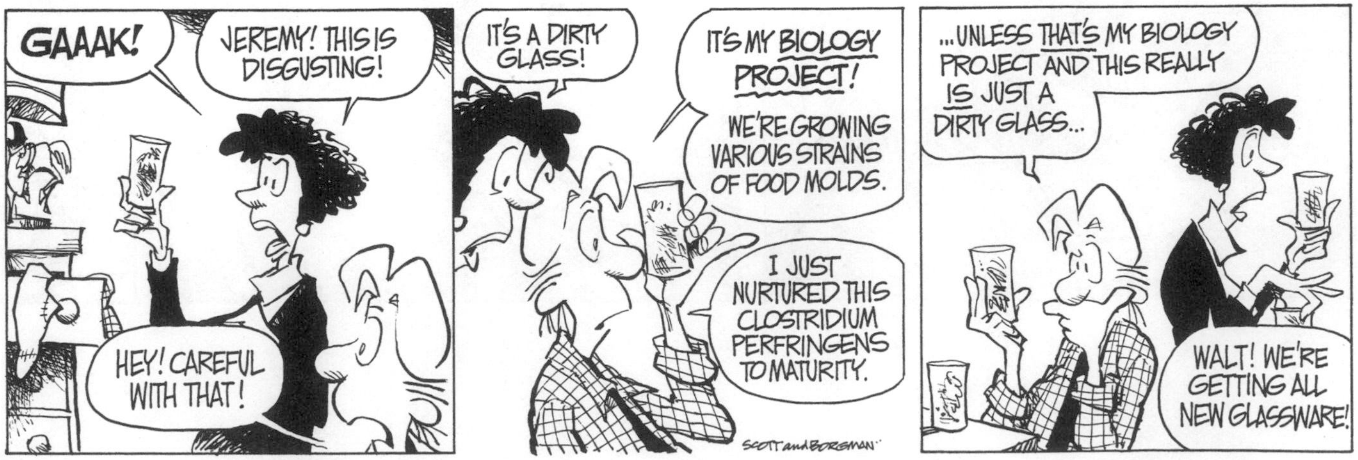

GAAAK!
JEREMY! THIS IS DISGUSTING!
HEY! CAREFUL WITH THAT!
IT'S A DIRTY GLASS!
IT'S MY BIOLOGY PROJECT!
WE'RE GROWING VARIOUS STRAINS OF FOOD MOLDS.
I JUST NURTURED THIS CLOSTRIDIUM PERFRINGENS TO MATURITY.
SCOTT and BORGMAN
...UNLESS THAT'S MY BIOLOGY PROJECT AND THIS REALLY IS JUST A DIRTY GLASS...
WALT! WE'RE GETTING ALL NEW GLASSWARE!

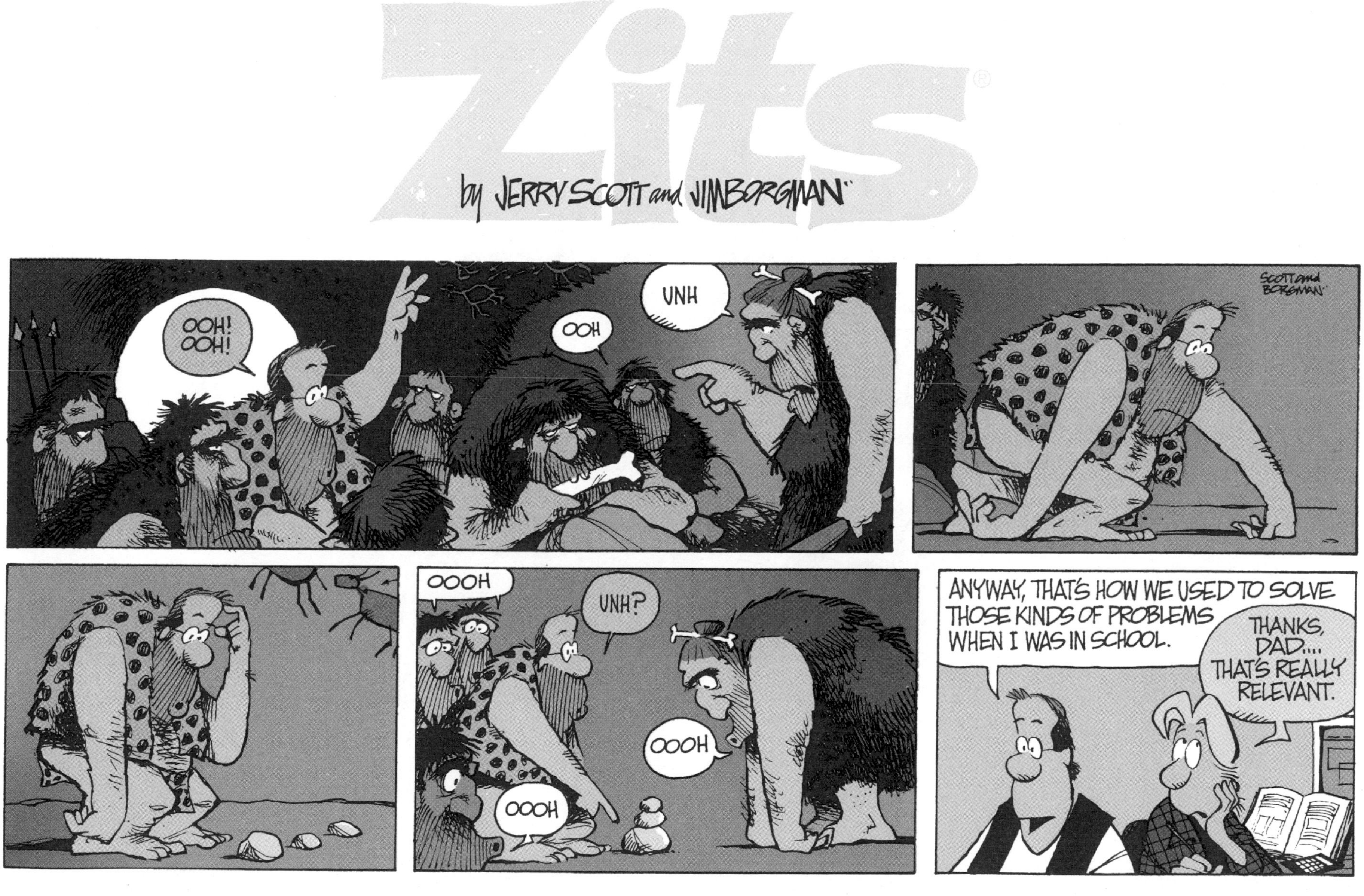
Zits
by JERRY SCOTT and JIM BORGMAN
OOH! OOH!
OOH
UNH
SCOTT and BORGMAN
OOOH
UNH?
OOOH
OOOH
ANYWAY, THAT'S HOW WE USED TO SOLVE THOSE KINDS OF PROBLEMS WHEN I WAS IN SCHOOL.
THANKS, DAD.... THAT'S REALLY RELEVANT.